European Politics

European Politics
A Reader

Edited by **MATTEI DOGAN** and **RICHARD ROSE**
Centre National   *University of Strathclyde*
de la Recherche Scientifique, Paris   *Glasgow*

Little, Brown and Company   Boston

JN
94
.A3
1971

COPYRIGHT © 1971 BY LITTLE, BROWN AND COMPANY (INC.)

ALL RIGHTS RESERVED. NO PART OF THIS BOOK MAY BE REPRODUCED IN ANY FORM OR BY ANY ELECTRONIC OR MECHANICAL MEANS INCLUDING INFORMATION STORAGE AND RETRIEVAL SYSTEMS WITHOUT PERMISSION IN WRITING FROM THE PUBLISHER, EXCEPT BY A REVIEWER WHO MAY QUOTE BRIEF PASSAGES IN A REVIEW.

LIBRARY OF CONGRESS CATALOG CARD NO. 73-134535

FIRST PRINTING

*Printed simultaneously in Canada by
Little, Brown & Company (Canada) Limited*

PRINTED IN THE UNITED STATES OF AMERICA

Contents

Introduction　　xi

CHAPTER ONE
Historical Roots　　1

HANS DAALDER
Parties, Elites and Political Developments in Western Europe　　4

REINHARD BENDIX AND STEIN ROKKAN
The Extension of Citizenship to the Lower Classes　　12

VAL R. LORWIN
*Working-Class Politics and
Economic Development in Western Europe*　　23

CHAPTER TWO
Political Cultures and Sub-Cultures　　37

STANLEY HOFFMANN
Tensions of Growth in Postwar France　　41

ERIC A. NORDLINGER
Democratic Stability in England　　51

SIDNEY VERBA
The Remaking of the German Political Culture   63

EDWARD C. BANFIELD
Amoral Familism in Southern Italy   78

ALESSANDRO PIZZORNO
Amoral Familism and Historical Marginality   87

CHAPTER THREE
Political Socialization   99

ROBERT E. LANE
Political Maturation in Germany and America   101

PHILIP E. CONVERSE AND GEORGES DUPEUX
Socialization into Apathy: France and America Compared   114

RONALD INGLEHART
Generational Change in Europe   120

FRANK A. PINNER
Students in the Postwar World   130

CHAPTER FOUR
Social Structure and Voting Alignments   143

S. M. LIPSET
The Changing Class Structure and Contemporary European Politics   146

RICHARD ROSE
Class and Party Divisions: Britain as a Test Case   159

KLAUS LIEPELT
The Infra-Structure of Party Support in Germany and Austria   183

JOSEPH LOPREATO
Social Mobility and Political Outlooks in Italy   202

CHAPTER FIVE
Political Parties 213

RICHARD ROSE AND DEREK URWIN
Social Cohesion, Political Parties and Strains in Regimes 217

MAURICE DUVERGER
The Eternal Morass: French Centrism 237

ROBERT T. MC KENZIE
Parties and the British Constitution 246

GERHARD LOEWENBERG
The Remaking of the German Party System 259

OTTO KIRCHHEIMER
The Waning of Opposition in Parliamentary Regimes 280

ERWIN K. SCHEUCH AND RUDOLF WILDENMANN
The Professionalization of Party Campaigning 296

GEORGES LAVAU
Parties of Interests or of Abstractions? 300

CHAPTER SIX
Pressure Groups 307

ROY MACRIDIS
Interest Groups in Comparative Analysis 310

HARRY ECKSTEIN
The Determinants of Pressure Group Politics 314

HENRY W. EHRMANN
Interest Groups and the Bureaucracy in Western Democracies 333

GIORGIO GALLI AND ALFONSO PRANDI
The Catholic Hierarchy and Christian Democracy in Italy 353

PETER MERKL
The Structure of Interests and Adenauer's Survival as Chancellor 360

CHAPTER SEVEN
Political Leaders 375

RALF DAHRENDORF
The Evolution of Ruling Groups in Europe 378

LEWIS J. EDINGER
AND DONALD D. SEARING
Social Background in Elite Analysis 390

GIOVANNI SARTORI
The Professionalization of Italian MP's 408

MATTEI DOGAN
Charisma and the Breakdown of Traditional Alignments 413

SAMUEL BRITTAN
An Elite Within an Elite 426

CHAPTER EIGHT
Centers of Power 441

ALFRED GROSSER
The Evolution of European Parliaments 445

A. H. BROWN
Prime Ministerial Power 459

KENNETH N. WALTZ
Executive Government in Britain: A Structural Analysis 482

MICHEL CROZIER
French Bureaucracy as a Cultural Phenomenon 489

BERNARD GOURNAY
Higher Civil Servants in France 501

JOSEPH LA PALOMBARA
Parentela Relationships in Italian Government 513

ROBERT C. FRIED
The Italian Prefectoral System 527

KARL W. DEUTSCH AND LEWIS J. EDINGER
Who Prevailed in the German Foreign Policy Process? 539

GERHARD LEHMBRUCH
The Ambiguous Coalition in West Germany 549

EDGAR MORIN
The Faceless Revolution 563

APPENDIX A
Bibliography 579

APPENDIX B
Basic Statistics 581

Contributors 589

Introduction

The aim of this book is to provide a sophisticated introduction to the politics of the four major societies of Europe: Britain, France, Germany, and Italy. Although these four countries do not constitute the whole of the continent, singly or collectively, they dominate European politics because of their intrinsic importance as nations and by influencing their neighbors. All have in common governments chosen by free elections, an advanced standard of socio-economic development, and a cultural heritage reaching back through feudalism to early Christian and Roman civilizations. Moreover, things held in common also distinguish these lands from old and important countries outside Europe, such as China, Japan, and India, as well as from the two most powerful neighbors of Europe today, Russia and the United States.

To compare all is not to confound all. A European, whether a social scientist, a factory worker, or a peasant, would hardly think Britain, France, Germany, and Italy identical in every major respect. The weight of different national histories, institutionalized in many ways, remains great. The purpose of comparatively analyzing these four countries is to see to what extent and under what circumstances they differ, as well as to identify ways in which countries similar in a number of social characteristics are also similar in their political systems.

Surprisingly, there is no commonly agreed meaning for the word "Europe." Dictionaries offer vague definitions or none at all. Europe is a term of convenience, rather than a precise social science concept. It can refer to people, to places, or to ways of doing things. The context tells more than the etymology what the word is meant to indicate. Its origin in Greek mythology emphasizes the antiquity of the term, and also its imprecision.

Geographically, Europe is familiar in its central physical features, but the outer boundaries are not all equally clear. The Arctic provides a clear boundary on the north, and the Mediterranean a southern limit.

To the west, the Atlantic provides another line of demarcation. The islands of Great Britain, Ireland, and Iceland are assigned to Europe, even though their insular position differentiates them from such lands as Germany and France. To the east, there is no clear geographical boundary, as centuries of invading armies have demonstrated. At some point east of Berlin, the Eurasian land mass ceases being European and becomes Asiatic. At some point south-east of Venice, the Western world shades into the Middle East. The point at which the line is drawn depends upon what one is trying to classify by differentiation.

While the physical contours of the land are relatively fixed, their political significance is not a constant. Reference to any historical atlas will show how fluid have been the boundaries of Europe and of the states within it. At the time of the discovery of America, the boundaries of France and England approximated their present-day territories, but neither Germany nor Italy was a meaningful political entity. In the age of exploration, European nations planted settlements in the Americas, Australia, and Asia, creating societies that were in origin, at least, European, even though thousands of miles away. Simultaneously, the Ottoman Empire brought the faith of Islam within a few hundred miles of Vienna and Venice, and even today Moslems can be found scattered in old Balkan domains. Germany and Italy were created as states in the second half of the nineteenth century. The westward advance of Russian troops to the German Elbe and to Prague at the end of World War II has most recently imposed major boundary changes upon the area conventionally described as Europe. The decisive importance of American military power in the two major European wars of this century illustrates the growing interpenetration of continents in the crudest of strategic terms.

In recent years many of the important questions that arise in the attempt to define Europe have been set aside by social scientists because of their interest in the underdeveloped countries of Africa and Asia. Studies in that field usually stress contrasts between Afro-Asian political systems and those alternatively termed "Western," "modern," "developed," or "stable and democratic." While each of these terms differs in meaning,[1] all group together such Western European nations as Britain and France with the United States and Canada. Some also include societies such as Russia and Japan, countries with many modern socioeconomic characteristics, but with very different political traditions from those of Western Europe and America. The preeminence of American scholars in the study of modernization means that the characteristics defining a "modern" society are more likely to approximate those of the United States than Italy or France. The contents of this volume will quickly bring home to American readers the extent to which configurations of political cultures and systems differ on the two sides of the Atlantic, notwithstanding the possession of a growing

[1] See Lucian W. Pye, *Aspects of Political Development* (Boston: Little, Brown, 1966), Ch. 2; and Stein Rokkan, editor, *Comparative Research across Cultures and Nations*.

INTRODUCTION

number of material things in common. Material resources affect politics, but a country's politics cannot be altered as fast as its economic system can change.

A useful social science definition of a region should try to maximize the differences between regions and to minimize differences within them.[2] Countries can be grouped in terms of characteristics found within each, such as language, religion, and economic strength, or by the relations between them. The importance attached to physical proximity in defining regions has history as well as habit for a justification. Peoples who live near each other in different countries today may have been under the same crown in the recent past, or exposed to the threat of the same advancing army. Yet internal variations inevitably remain. Germany provides an extreme example, for one part is currently under a Communist regime antithetical to the Federal West German Republic, the "Germany" of this volume. Even Britain owes its famed homogeneity to the preponderance of the industrial, urban English, and not to an identity of cultural outlooks. In parts of Wales, people still speak an ancient Celtic language, and in Northern Ireland religious tensions make the area no more typical of Britain than Mississippi is typical of the United States.

The choice of four countries to represent a continent rests upon practical considerations. If a country is to be understood in terms of a variety of political processes and through the eyes of many different authors, articles about one country could suffice to fill a book. Multiplying the materials by four results in this volume of substantial bulk. A greater range of countries could have been included here only by sacrificing depth. Fortunately, collective studies are already in print dealing with the Scandinavian nations of Europe, and also with the smaller European democracies.[3] Hopefully, this volume will eventually be complemented by collections which focus in some detail upon Eastern Europe, and upon regions outside Europe, too.

The structure of the book is intended to emphasize comparative analysis. Materials are grouped by topic rather than by country so that parts of each political system, whether socialization processes, pressure

---

[2] For discussions of regionalism, see, e.g., Bruce Russett, *International Regions and the International System* (Chicago: Rand, McNally, 1969), and Kevin R. Cox, "On the Utility and Definition of Regions in Comparative Political Sociology," *Comparative Political Studies* II: 1 (1969).

[3] See, e.g., *Scandinavian Political Studies* (New York: Columbia University Press, Vol. 1, 1966, and annually thereafter); A. Lijphart, *The Politics of Accommodation: Pluralism and Democracy in the Netherlands* (Berkeley: University of California Press, 1968); Val Lorwin, "Belgium: Religion, Class and Language in National Politics," and F. C. Engelmann, "Austria: The Pooling of Opposition," in Robert A. Dahl, editor, *Political Oppositions in Western Democracies* (New Haven: Yale, 1966); G. A. Codding, *The Federal Government of Switzerland* (Boston: Houghton Mifflin, 1961); and for theoretical analysis, Arend Lijphart, "Typologies of Democratic Systems," *Comparative Political Studies* I: 1 (1968), and Stein Rokkan, "The Structuring of Mass Politics in the Smaller European Democracies," *Comparative Studies in Society and History* X: 2 (1968).

groups, or centers of power, can be conveniently considered cross-nationally. Each chapter is introduced by at least one article discussing a political science concept in the light of empirical evidence drawn from two or more Western societies. In all, more than one-third of the articles involve explicit cross-national analysis, among European societies or between European countries and America. Transatlantic comparisons give insights concerning the extent to which these two major branches of the Western world are contrasting or similar. In some instances, no comparisons are possible, because articles of an acceptable standard are not always written at the same time in every country. At times, however, this is because the problems do not exist in comparable form cross-nationally. For example, the Catholic Church takes very different roles in the political systems of the four nations. An important part of the education of a comparative social scientist is learning whether there are, in fact as well as theory, cross-cultural equivalents for everything that students of politics want to write about.

No single point of view can dominate a collection of articles drawn from authors scattered among seven different countries and almost as many academic disciplines. Variations in perspectives have intellectual justification, too. It is a moot point whether the political system of a country differs more in the eyes of two people, one of whom lives there and the other does not, than it does in the eyes of two men, one of whom is a student of political history and the other of political sociology. In order to provide context and continuity for these selections, each chapter contains an introduction to the subject, and there are individual headnotes to introduce each article. Bibliographies provide references to additional sources of knowledge. Because the book is published in English, the bibliographical notes concentrate upon English-language sources. This is not to deny the importance of understanding the language of a land, if one is to appreciate the nuances of its culture and follow contemporary political discussions and ideological controversies.

In choosing individual articles, the chief criteria have been quality, relevance, permanence, and difficulty of access. While a concern with excellence is self-justifying, it is worth emphasizing that merit may take many different forms. For example, the character of an article discussing the French revolution of May 1968, written while events were not resolved, will be very different from that of an article summarizing a lengthy and complex statistical analysis of data about a much simpler problem. Relevance involves two things: the relationship of articles in this collection to each other, and their relationship to ideas important in understanding politics. While each article was written and can be read on its own, the selection and juxtaposition of articles is intended to enhance the cross-national aspects of national studies. The relatively recent growth of social-scientific interest in European politics means that the bulk of materials reviewed for inclusion here was published during the 1960's; the great majority of selections reprinted here was also published during this decade. Insofar as the writers have succeeded in making general statements about underlying phenomena in their societies, what they say should be durable since the basic character and problems of political systems change only slowly through time. Access to materials on European politics is difficult, for scholars as well as for students. Language constitutes one barrier, for important studies appear in at least four different languages. Distance presents another obstacle, for these articles are scattered over journals published in more than half-a-dozen countries on two continents. Disciplinary specializations further increase problems of access. For example, one major study of working-class politics in Europe was initially published in the *American Historical Review!* In making selections, at the margin the editors have tried to include articles that would be difficult for readers to know about otherwise. Ten articles printed here appear in English for the first time.

In emphasizing one approach to political studies, we necessarily have had to exclude others that students of European politics should know. We did this in the knowledge that no single book about Europe can stand alone. The classics of European social science, such as Tocqueville, Marx, Bagehot, and Pareto, have been omitted because their works are easily available elsewhere. We have also omitted selections from well-known and widely available contemporary books, such as Almond and Verba's *The Civic Culture* and Maurice Duverger's *Political Parties*. It would require separate volumes to treat properly such important phenomena of the recent past as the transition to industrialization in early twentieth-century Europe and the rise and fall of Fascism between 1918 and 1945. We have therefore concentrated upon selections concerning Europe since 1945. Ideas and ideologies important in the political controversies of Europe from the time of the Reformation to the present are also outside our terms of reference. More than one volume is required to do justice to the conflicts of basic values that have been so much a part of European intellectual life. Because social circumstances affect politics in many ways, a number of articles discuss enduring and changing features of European society; nonetheless, a reader primarily about politics cannot touch upon all aspects of life in modern societies. The data in the appendices and in the bibliographies provide guidance to further information and ideas. Writings of considerable methodological significance that only incidentally make reference to substantive European phenomena are not prominent here; such scholarly work is best studied in other contexts. Occasionally, we have had to omit articles on subjects of general interest for lack of acceptable analyses. Reciprocally, where a subject has attracted much scholarly attention pressures of space have compelled the omission of articles of high merit. No book can hope to be up to date in its references to contemporary events. For this purpose, leading European newspapers, such as *Le Monde* and the *Neue Zürcher Zeitung*, can be used to follow politics as Europeans do themselves.

Even a comparison of two English-language papers, the *New York Times* and the *Times* of London, will illustrate how different are the day-to-day concerns of informed people on opposite sides of the Atlantic.

Many social scientists, including both editors, have lived in several countries. Of the forty-eight contributors of articles, twenty-two were born and now work in Europe and thirteen were born in America; the remaining thirteen were born on one side of the Atlantic and work on the other. Nearly all the American-born authors have spent substantial periods of study or teaching in one or more European societies. Reciprocally, most of the European-born authors have studied or taught in American universities. All students of comparative politics must move from country to country to gain knowledge of and empathy with different cultures. This is true whether one travels by jet plane or by those flights of the mind that contribute the concepts and theories that make possible meaningful comparisons among nations.

European Politics

Europe, *daughter of Agenor, king of Phoenicia, was abducted by Jupiter who took her to Crete, where she gave birth to a son, Minos.*
Years later, she gave birth to a daughter, called America. . . .

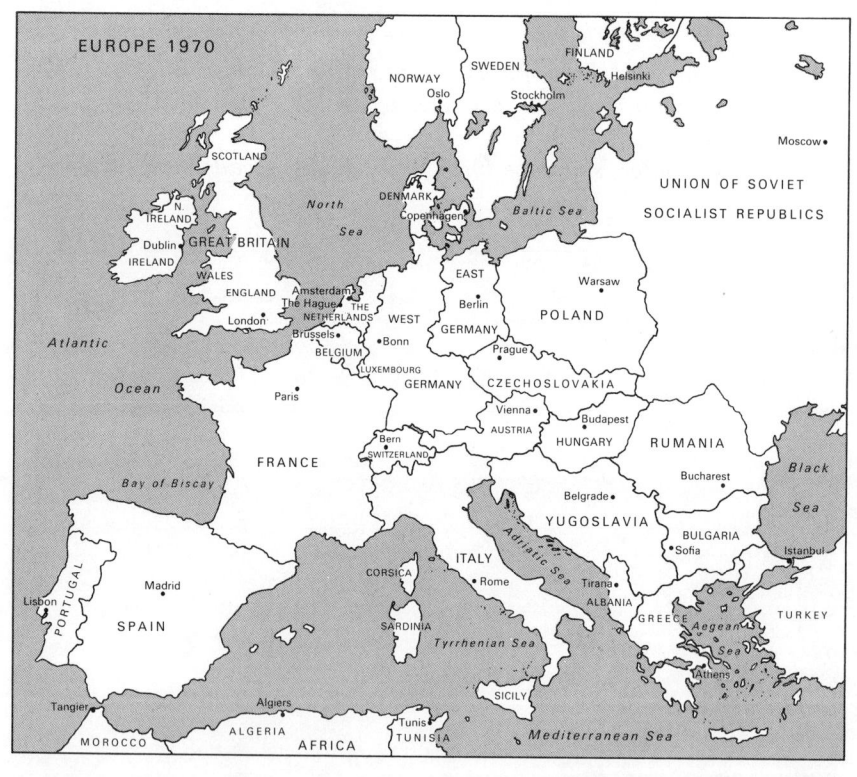

CHAPTER
ONE

Historical Roots

Europe is an old society. This fact is evident in the landscape, in the architecture, and, not least, in the political institutions and values of the people who live there. Most Continental countries follow Roman law, a legal system with origins two thousand years ago; England has a common law tradition a thousand years old. The religious differences that separate Protestant and Catholic Europe are four centuries old. Even variations in economic enterprise and growth can, as Max Weber and R. H. Tawney have shown, be traced back four centuries for their origins. While antiquity is a common attribute among European states, it is often a divisive force. The things that distinguish Europeans from each other also have their origins far back in time, and have often led them into conflict.

The importance of the past in Europe may seem strange to an American. Yet all Europeans are not tradition-bound, nor are all Americans emancipated from the influence of events that occurred before they were born. Recent sociological studies of American history, such as S. M. Lipset's *America — The First New Nation,* have shown that there are ways in which Americans are as tradition-minded as Europeans, or as people who live on any continent. The strangeness of much of Europe arises from the fact that many events of the American past which remain influential even today are alien to the historical circumstances of Europe. This is true of the 17th century development of the slave trade, the 18th century American revolution, and the 19th century settlement of the virgin lands of the Western frontier. Such unusual or unique events, commingled with the presence in America of phenomena also common to Europe, such as industrialization and universal suffrage, result in a mix of traditions very different from those of England, France, Italy, and Germany.

The differences between Europe and America, as well as differences among European societies, have not arisen from random events in the past, or from anything so simple as good kings and bad kings. One of the most important problems in contemporary social science is to account for variations in contemporary European societies by reference to their past. These efforts are not mere antiquarianism. Research in political socialization and culture has shown time and again that the political outlook of adults of all ages reflects the influence of events that happened much earlier in their lives, or in the lives of generations of ancestors. S. M. Lipset and Stein Rokkan have distinguished four crises of the past still relevant to such things as the number and character of the parties competing at elections today.[1] The first crisis is that of the 16th century Reformation and the 17th century Counter-Reformation. The second is that of the early 19th century upsurge of nationalism, following the great upheavals of the French Revolution and the Napoleonic wars. The third is 19th century industrialization, involving conflicts between urban and landed sections of society, and then conflicts between urbanized manual workers and middle classes. The final crisis that they describe is the conflict between international Communism and nationally oriented Socialism, arising from the events of the Russian revolution in 1917. In post-1945 Europe, the major event has been the emergence of an integrationist outlook, expressed in such institutions as the European Common Market. This may be considered the start of a new tradition, or, alternatively, the revival of a more cosmopolitan European tradition, that gave little heed to nationalistic considerations in pre-19th century dynastic Europe. Even the insular English in 1714 imported and installed as King George I, a German nobleman who spoke no English.

Ironically, the great attention given to Afro-Asian nations in recent years has stimulated renewed interest in the causes and consequences of the development of European states. Immediately, this arises from the fact that the peoples of ex-colonial countries were exposed to and assimilated many European influences from imperial powers, most notably from Britain and France. At another level, this interest arises from the fact that our models of social and political change have all been developed from European experience. This is true of liberal democrats and of Marxists alike. Such an intellectual bias is entirely reasonable, for only European societies offer an empirical basis for formulating and testing generalizations; only these societies, or their offshoots in the New World, have yet undergone full industrialization. Whether the experiences of European societies are capable of generalization to Afro-Asian countries is a moot point. It is, prima facie, reasonable to assume that models drawn from this continent are as relevant to the non-Western world as those based on American experience; the largest of the non-Western societies — China and India — much more nearly resemble Europe than America in their antiquity.

---

[1] See S. M. Lipset and Stein Rokkan, "Cleavage Structures, Party Systems and Voter Alignments," in *Party Systems and Voter Alignments* (New York: Free Press, 1967).

Bibliography

The point of departure for many analyses of social and political change in modern Europe is, implicitly or explicitly, the writings of one of the founders of modern social science, Karl Marx. *The Communist Manifesto* (1848) was an attempt to understand newly industrializing European societies, as well as an attempt to change their course. Much modern social science challenges Marx's hypotheses. The best known re-analysis is contained in studies by Max Weber, *The Protestant Ethic and the Spirit of Capitalism,* and in R. H. Tawney, *Religion and the Rise of Capitalism.* A recent re-interpretation of this literature, in the light of events in the post–World War II world, is Raymond Aron's *Eighteen Lectures on Industrial Society* (London: Weidenfeld and Nicolson, 1967). Dissatisfaction with the relatively deterministic framework of Marx has also led to a new interest in other 19th century writers who analyzed the changes that were part of their lives. Particularly relevant are Alexis de Tocqueville's *The Ancient Regime and the French Revolution,* and his *Democracy in America* (1835). Walter Bagehot's writings, particularly *The English Constitution* (1867), provide a complementary point of view. For two different efforts to link the study of European and non-European societies, see, e.g., Gabriel Almond, "Introduction," in G. Almond and J. S. Coleman, *The Politics of the Developing Areas* (Princeton University Press, 1960) and S. P. Huntington, *Political Order in Changing Societies* (New Haven: Yale University Press, 1968). A particularly stimulating attempt to place the "new" societies of America, Canada, Australia, South Africa, and Latin America in their proper European context is contained in Louis Hartz, editor, *The Founding of New Societies* (New York: Harcourt, 1964); and in Karl W. Deutsch and William J. Foltz, editors, *Nation-Building* (New York: Atherton Press, 1963).

A most penetrating analysis of nationalism in its historical dimension is Karl W. Deutsch, *Nationalism and Social Communication: An Inquiry into the Foundations of Nationality* (Cambridge, Mass.: M.I.T. Press, 2nd edition, 1966). The first two parts of Stein Rokkan, *Citizens Elections Parties: Approaches to the Comparative Study of the Processes of Development* (Oslo: Universitetsforlaget, 1970), are devoted to the development of nations in terms of mass politics. Reinhard Bendix, editor, *State and Society* (Boston: Little, Brown, 1968), contains a selection of articles on various historical aspects of the Western European societies. On the rebuilding of German democracy, see Peter H. Merkl, *The Origins of the West German Republic* (New York: Oxford University Press, 1965).

In the same vein as Tocqueville is Raymond Aron's book, *Industrial Society* (New York: Praeger, 1967). See also by the same author, *France: Steadfast and Changing* (Cambridge, Mass.: Harvard University Press, 1960), among his many publications in French and in English.

HANS DAALDER

Parties, Elites and Political Developments in Western Europe

The diffusion of liberal democratic institutions in Europe did not lead inevitably to the establishment of stable political regimes. Though England has had stable representative government since the conclusion of its 17th century Civil War, France has experienced, from the Revolution of 1789 until today, recurring and often successful challenges to its regimes. In Italy and Germany the delay of national unification until the late 19th century and the late introduction of democratic institutions in the 20th century has produced an irregular history of fascism and democratic government. In this selection, Hans Daalder shows how variations in 20th century European experience relate to historical differences in elite attitudes toward the masses in pre-democratic Europe, and to differences in political institutions established long before universal suffrage was ever considered practical politics in Europe.

The starting point of this paper is the proposition that European states fall prima facie into at least three distinct groups: (1) countries which developed slowly from oligarchies into consistently stable democracies: e.g. Britain, the Scandinavian countries, The Netherlands, Belgium, and Switzerland; (2) countries which have undergone serious reversals in political regime, whereby democratic constitutions have given way to autocratic or even totalitarian systems of government: e.g. France, Germany, Austria, and Italy; and (3) countries which continue to have authoritarian regimes of a somewhat traditional nature,

From Joseph LaPalombara and Myron Weiner, eds., *Political Parties and Political Development*, pp. 44–52 (Copyright © 1966 Princeton University Press: Princeton Paperback, 1969). Reprinted by permission of Princeton University Press.

and in which democratic groups tend to form at most an underground or exiled opposition: i.e. Spain and Portugal.[1]

It is much easier to say what factors are *not* responsible for these differences in political development than to indicate their actual causes. Obviously there is no immediate relationship to differences in stages of economic development. In the group of stable democracies there are countries that underwent the industrial revolution relatively early (Britain, Belgium) and countries which entered the modern industrial era late (e.g. Norway and The Netherlands). Similarly, German industrial development came relatively early and in full force; yet here the lapse into totalitarian dictatorship was the most gruesome ever. Moreover rapid economic development did not save the French Fourth Republic, nor does it stabilize political conditions in Italy.

Consequently it will be necessary to probe deeper and to seek for other factors that are often of an historical nature. The main variables on which this paper will center are: (1) the importance of the earlier elite setting; (2) the degree of coincidence or disparity between political and economic developments; (3) the "reach" or "permeation" of (democratic) parties as against other power holders in various European societies; and (4) the cleavage lines of the party system itself.

It is not suggested that these factors are sufficient to give a satisfactory explanation of the very complex and diverse processes of development which European countries underwent, whether generally or individually. They have been selected primarily because of their interest for comparative purposes in accordance with the terms of reference set for the papers in this volume.

DIFFERENCES IN POLITICAL DEVELOPMENT BEFORE THE NINETEENTH CENTURY

The great complexity of the relationships among various social classes and status groups in European society, as that between state and society generally, has tended to be confused by the cliché assumption (found typically in college textbooks as well as the *Communist Manifesto*) that there was a "natural" evolution in Europe from feudalism through absolutism and bourgeois revolution toward modern democracy. This view is an egregious simplification for a variety of reasons.

First, it pays far too little attention to the fact that the term "feudalism" is used to describe fundamentally different structures in medieval Europe. The political relationships among king, aristocracy, clergy, cities, and peasantry as well as the economic relationships among landowners, burghers, artisans, peasants, and serfs showed great variation. If the starting point differs how can one expect linear or even parallel developments afterwards?

Second, present-day European states originated in very different

---

[1] As the main focus of this paper is on problems of political development, I shall not deal further with the latter group in the pages that follow.

ways. Roughly speaking, one can divide these states, according to the manner in which political unification came about, into four groups: (1) those in which effective centralization came early and with relatively little tension (e.g. Britain, Sweden); (2) those in which centralization came early but against considerable resistance (e.g. France); (3) those in which centralization came late but fairly gradually (e.g. The Netherlands, Switzerland); and finally (4) those in which central political power was established only as a consequence of considerable political violence in the nineteenth century (Germany, Italy).

Of these four groups, (1) and (3) had eventually rather similar characteristics. There was at no time a violent clash between political and social realities. Central power enmeshed itself gradually into the social system, and both regional and social groupings in turn achieved a growing influence on the center, thus making for a society which was both truly integrated and fairly pluralistic in nature. Things were different in France, Germany, and Italy. There central control tended to be imposed by military and bureaucratic power. Hence the state came to some degree to hover above the society; the ruled came to feel themselves subjects rather than citizens, and to regard authority with a mixture of deference and distrust rather than as a responsive and responsible agency in which they had a share.[2]

Third, differences in the manner of social and economic development, even before the nineteenth century, tended to strengthen this contrast. In Britain and The Netherlands economic development ever since the middle ages was relatively free from state intervention. Autonomous economic development tended to make the newly rising bourgeoisie a much more powerful challenger of the powers that were than equivalent groupings could be in, say, Colbertist France or Cameralist Prussia. In the latter countries the state took a much more active hand in economic development, and in the process bureaucrats tended to become more managerial while the bourgeoisie tended to become more officialized than was true in Britain or the Low Countries. In the latter case, civil freedoms and a measure of responsible government preceded the establishment of a powerful central bureaucracy; in France the new social forces were eventually powerful enough to revolt, but in the process they succeeded only in building up safeguards against the bureaucracy rather than absorbing it or making it fully accountable; in the German Reich, finally, liberal groups failed to seize power and fell prey to the stronger hold of the *Polizei-* or *Beamtenstaat*.

Finally, European societies experienced different effects from the religious wars and their aftermath. In some countries the religious composition of the population remained homogeneous (whether Roman

---

[2] In Germany most political forces submitted fairly rapidly to the existence of the new *Reich*, in contrast to the situation in Italy, where Church resistance and regional opposition continued for a much longer time. This made the existence of the new Italian state for a long time more precarious but may, on the other hand, have provided a safety valve that prevented nationalist unifiers from going to the extremes experienced in Germany.

Catholic or Lutheran). There the church often remained for long an appendage of the upper classes; if this assisted them in their bid for the support of more traditionally oriented lower-class elements, it also tended eventually to provoke both fundamentalist and anticlerical protest. In other countries (notably in Switzerland, The Netherlands, Britain, and parts of Germany) various religious groups contested with one another until they finally reached some measure of tolerance or accommodation. In this way religious pluralism[3] and religious dissent often provided the spearhead of political resistance against entrenched elites, ultimately forcing a recognition of the limits of state power and of the justice of individual and corporate rights.

THE TRANSITION TO MODERN DEMOCRATIC POLITICS

Through such factors (and others such as the incidents of geography and war)[4] some political systems in Europe had hardened along autocratic lines by the eighteenth century, while others had maintained or even strengthened a pluralist setting that, however oligarchical, allowed a measure of political influence to a variety of political and social groups. This vital difference was to affect the establishment of political parties during the nineteenth century in at least two respects: in the ease with which they became a recognized part of the political system, and in the role which they came to assume within it.

In Britain, the Low Countries, Switzerland, and Sweden, conciliar forms of government, whether in cities or in the center, had a long and honorable tradition. The style of politics tended to be one of careful adjustment, of shared responsibility, of due respect for ancient

---

[3] The fact of religious pluralism seems more important than the particular religion in question. Whereas the Catholic Church in the Latin countries identified closely with vested social interests and alienated large sections of the population in the process, Dutch Catholics turned into a distinct protest group that pleaded for a separation of church and state, represented a considerable challenge of the outs against the dominant Liberal bourgeoisie, and maintained an effective hold on lower-class groups. Similarly, Lutheranism tended to be much more an instrument of vested authority in Germany than in Switzerland, while in Scandinavia it played the dual role of both maintaining an official religion and inspiring fundamentalist protest against a too modernist sphere in the central cities. Calvinism too was in practice much more nonconformist in some societies than in others, depending on whether its hold was strongest on existing elites or on lower-class elements.

[4] Geographic factors made certain European societies more secure from foreign attack than others: the insular position of England, the mountains of Switzerland, the rivers and canals of The Netherlands made these countries to a large extent immune against invasion on land. Consequently there was no urgent need for them to develop large standing armies. This had profound consequences for domestic political and administrative structures. In Lord Esher's telling phrase, the Navy often proved "a constitutional force," while an army was more readily "a royal force" (*Journals and Letters of Reginald, Viscount Esher*, London, 1934, Vol. I, p. 269). Similarly, the early development of a citizen-militia in Switzerland was a great deal removed from the compulsory militarization of Prussian *Untertanen*.

privileges. Attempts at absolute kingship eventually broke on the concerted strength of particularist interests, whether corporative, regional, or social. As the political order was in a very real sense built upon parts, the idea that men could reasonably be partisans found ready recognition even before the age of formalized party politics. There never was a "monochromatic, unicentric world," in Sartori's sense, to form an obstacle to the formation of parties.[5]

In these countries the view that government was somehow a trust toward the governed had old roots, however elitist actual systems tended to be until late in the nineteenth century. Intra-elite competition, being a recognized and even institutionalized phenomenon, made it easier to weather what the editors* have called the crisis of participation. Conflicts between towns, between town and country, or among various religious groups created certain links between clashing oligarchies and sub-political groups below them. Competing elites sometimes sought lower-class support to strengthen their position, thus granting the lesser orders a political title and whetting their political appetites. Conversely, new claimants could exercise some influence on an oligarchical system simply by the threat of potential support to one or other side within it. Once some social groups were granted a measure of influence, this tended to provoke further demands from those yet further down until, finally, the burden of proof in the suffrage debate came to rest on those who defended restriction rather than on those who advocated extension of suffrage. Some upper-class groups came to doubt their own title, while most came to realize that fighting democracy might be more dangerous to their social position than democracy itself. Thus both pressures from competing elites downward and concomitant pressures from sub-elites upward made for a competitive gradual extension of democratic rights.

This process was facilitated by the circumstance that it came about in slow, evolutionary ways. Neither in political theory nor in actual behavior was there an abrupt transition from elite politics to mass politicization. Political newcomers were slowly accommodated. At any one time they tended to be given at most only part-power — enough to give them a sense of involvement and political efficacy but not enough to completely overthrow the evolving society. Older political styles that had been developed to guarantee the rights of aristocrats or *hauts bourgeois* were thus more easily transferred. The "political domain," to use Neumann's term,[6] expanded only slowly. Since at any one time the political stakes were relatively modest, the upper classes were less afraid and the lower classes less threatening. Older and newer

[5] Giovanni Sartori, *Parties and Party Systems*, New York: Harper and Row, forthcoming.
* [That is, Joseph LaPalombara and Myron Weiner; see their editorial introduction to *Political Parties and Political Development*. — Editors' note.]
[6] Sigmund Neumann, *Modern Political Parties*, Chicago: University of Chicago Press, 1956, p. 404.

elites were thus held more easily within the bounds of one constitutional, if changing, political system that neither alienated the one into reactionary nor the other into revolutionary onslaughts on it. In time, however, the over-all political order could thus become more truly responsive to the demands of a wide variety of political groups within it. In 1867 Bagehot thought "dignified parts of government" necessary to keep the masses from interfering with the "efficient government" of the few; a century later the many were efficiently using those very same "dignified parts of government" to secure substantial concessions to themselves.[7]

Developments were very different in those societies where power was heavily concentrated by the end of the eighteenth century. In France royal absolutism provoked truly revolutionary resistance of a much more drastic and upsetting character than appeared in the English Civil War of the seventeenth century, let alone in the Glorious Revolution of 1688. If the king called on the *droit divin* to claim absolute power, so did liberal thinkers of the Enlightenment on the basis of the nation or the people. From the outset a leading strand of French democratic thought became therefore "totalitarian" in Talmon's sense,[8] becoming highly suspicious, for instance, of *corps intermédiaires* between the individual and the state. If in the countries described earlier pluralism seemed the natural corollary of liberty, in the latter it was often regarded as the prolongation of inequality and privilege. The traumas of the French Revolution created lasting and bitter divisions in French society. Articulate political groups continued to harbor fears and suspicions of one another, doubting one another's intentions and having different views of the legitimacy of past regimes and present institutions. Paradoxically, in that European country where popular sovereignty was proclaimed first and most explicitly no governmental system ever rested on a universal basis of popular support and respect. Traditionalist groups continued to be politically strong, and the newer bourgeoisie and the rising working classes came to be divided in their respective allegiances. Democratic regimes met with a continuous threat from the right. Democratic groups suspected the state even when they were nominally in control of it. This in turn made it more difficult for successive regimes to achieve their goals or to capitalize on their positive achievements and to gain legitimacy and lasting adherence throughout the nation.

In Prussia, and later in the German Reich, the bureaucratization and militarization of the society had gone much further than in France before the existing power division was challenged. In France democ-

[7] Walter Bagehot, *The English Constitution*, London, 1867, World's Classics ed., Oxford, 1952, pp. 4ff. The fact that most of the countries here treated have remained monarchies would seem to have been a consequence more than a cause of these developments.

[8] J. L. Talmon, *The Origins of Totalitarian Democracy*, London, 1952, *passim*.

ratizing forces generally triumphed, however precariously. In Germany the Kaiser-*Junker*-Army-Bureaucracy[9] complex was for a long time strong enough to manipulate the new social forces rather than to have to adjust to them. From the outset large sections of the new industrial capitalist classes were drawn into the existing power cluster; this left the fate of German liberalism to the faltering hands of mainly professional and intellectual groups rather than to a strongly unified economic class. In most European countries bourgeois elements had triumphed sufficiently to occupy key positions in the political system before the real onslaught of the working classes was felt. In Germany, on the other hand, the existing power groups were powerful enough to maintain themselves against both, even offsetting bourgeois demands for responsible parliamentary government with a careful weaning and manipulation of the new working classes. Typically, a democratic breakthrough came not of its own strength but only in the aftermath of lost wars. The explicit democratic articles of the Weimar Constitution were to become the hallmark of success of democratic forms on paper at the expense of social substance.

THE DIFFERENT ROLE OF PARTIES

The role of parties in European countries varied considerably with such substantial differences in actual political development.

In countries where modern mass democracy evolved slowly from a preexisting pluralist society various regional, social and ideological groupings tended to form what might be called "proto-parties" at a rather early stage. Consisting of informal groupings seeking to obtain preferential treatment for themselves and the definite interests which they represented, they tended to fill certain functions of the modern political party (such as interest aggregation and to a lesser extent political recruitment), but not others (such as political socialization and political mobilization). As the increasing power of parliamentary assemblies tended to bring such groupings nearer to the effective decision-making centers, organization came to be at a premium. Similarly, when new social claimants came to exert pressure for representation, organization outside the parliament became not only profitable but essential for political survival. The process of party formation tended to spread therefore from existing competing elites downwards, but this very process also facilitated a reciprocal movement. Party organization itself created many new elite-posts even if only at sub-parliamentary levels. Second-rung leaders who provided an essential link with important elements in the expanding electorate had to be accommodated, and some in time fought their way to the top. Party competition for various groups

---

[9] For a sophisticated analysis of the way in which the Prussian *Junkers* maintained their social position and lost their political independence by their submission to the "new social factor . . . the state power" see Joseph Schumpeter, "Social Classes in an Ethnically Homogeneous Environment," in *Imperialism and Social Classes*, Meridian Books ed., 1960, pp. 144ff.

in the electorate made some existing parties more responsive to new demands, while new social groupings came to imitate and expand existing forms of party organization.

In countries where autocratic regimes prevailed longer the development of parties showed different characteristics.

Autocracy in its more explicit forms was incompatible with free party organization. Instead factionalism and a limited measure of interest representation tended to predominate. Democratic stirrings could take form only in intellectual protest movements or outright conspiratorial activity. Thus even some of the earlier democratizing movements, both on the liberal and on the socialist side, showed strong influences of secret societies.[10]

In the more limited autocracies that the constitutional lawyers of another day used to call constitutional monarchies (as distinct from parliamentary monarchies) a measure of party organization could come about more easily. Even traditionalist political forces had eventually to resort to at least nominal electoral processes; but in their case parties were not so much the cause as a symptom of effective political power. Certain bourgeois and professional groups sought to use the parliamentary benches for a measure of oppositional politics that was often ineffective for lack of courage and organization. Further to the left, certain *Weltanschauungsparteien* showed tighter organizational forms and ideological programs; their verbal fervor tended to be symptomatic, however, of their weak position in the present. They made up for their lack of current influence with the vista of an utopian future, and could be "wholistic" in their ideological claims precisely because they had little chance ever to be confronted with the compromises that partial power entails; only a more basic political and social revolution could change their role in a fundamental fashion.

Finally, under conditions of more democratic rule the political role of parties became more important. But often past divorce from active political power continued to hinder them in the exercise of their nominal functions, while at the same time their somewhat timid hold on governmental power was endangered by the hidden sabotage or open competition from anti-democratic groups.

[10] Note, for example, the role of the Free Masons in building up early Liberal and Radical parties, and the influence throughout Europe of Mazzini's *La Giovane Italia*. See Guglielmo Negri, *Three Essays on Comparative Politics*, Milan, 1964, pp. 50ff.

REINHARD BENDIX
and STEIN ROKKAN

The Extension of Citizenship to the Lower Classes

Unlike the United States, European governments were not based on the sovereignty of the people, with the implied right of each individual to influence "his" government. Instead, they derived their powers from older claims to centralized authority, reaching as far back as medieval theories of monarchy. Establishing the right of subjects to influence the state by means of the right to vote thus meant a major change in conceptions of the state and its subjects. As Bendix and Rokkan show, the distinction gradually disappeared between those with the right to influence government and the voteless mass, who had the duties of citizenship without its rights. Ironically, the major contemporary struggle to abolish this distinction does not occur in Europe, but in the actions of the American federal government seeking to enfranchise Negroes in the United States South, and in the farthest corner of the United Kingdom of Great Britain and Northern Ireland.

In the nation-state each citizen stands in a direct relation to the sovereign authority of the country in contrast with the medieval polity in which that direct relation is enjoyed only by the great men of the realm. Therefore, a core element of nation-building is the codification of the rights and duties of all adults who are classified as citizens. The question is how exclusively or inclusively citizenship is defined. Some notable exceptions aside, citizenship at first excludes all socially and economically dependent persons. In the course of the nineteenth century this massive restriction is gradually reduced until eventually

From Reinhard Bendix, *Nation-Building and Citizenship*, pp. 74–79, 93–101 (New York: John Wiley and Sons, 1964), with footnotes abridged. Reprinted by permission. This is a revised version by Bendix of a paper originally presented to the World Congress of the International Sociological Association, Washington, D.C., 1962.

all adults are classified as citizens. In Western Europe this extension of national citizenship is set apart from the rest of the world by the common traditions of the *Ständestaat*. The gradual integration of the national community since the French Revolution reflects these traditions wherever the extension of citizenship is discussed in terms of the "fourth estate," that is, in terms of extending the principle of *functional representation* to those previously excluded from citizenship. On the other hand, the French Revolution also advanced the *plebiscitarian principle*. According to this principle all powers intervening between the individual and the state must be destroyed (such as estates, corporations, etc.), so that all citizens as individuals possess equal rights before the sovereign, national authority.

A word should be added concerning the two adjectives "functional" and "plebiscitarian." The phrase "functional representation" derives from the medieval political structure in which it is deemed proper, for example, that the elders or grand master of a guild represent it in a municipal assembly. Here function refers generically to any kind of activity considered appropriate for an estate. Used more broadly, the term "function" designates *group-specific activities or rights and duties*. As such it encompasses both observations of behavior and ethical mandates of what is thought proper. The latter imply very different theories of society, however. In medieval society the rank and proper functions of the constituent groups are fixed in a hierarchical order. In modern Western societies this older view has been superseded by concepts of group function which presuppose the ideal of equality, except where medieval connotations linger on. The term "plebiscite" refers to the *direct vote on an important public issue by all qualified electors* of a community. The broader the community, the more minimal the qualifications stipulated for the electors, and hence the larger the number of persons standing in a direct relationship to public authority, the more will the plebiscitarian principle conflict with the functional. The specific meaning of both principles varies naturally with the definitions of group-specific activities and the extent and qualifications of community membership.

Various accommodations between the functional and plebiscitarian principle have characterized the sequence of enactments and codifications through which citizenship became national in many countries of Western Europe. To examine this development comparatively the several rights of citizenship must be distinguished and analyzed. In his study of *Citizenship and Social Class*, T. H. Marshall formulates a threefold typology of rights:

— *civil* rights such as "liberty of person, freedom of speech, thought and faith, the right to own property and to conclude valid contracts, and the right to justice";
— *political* rights such as the franchise and the right of access to public office;
— *social* rights ranging from "the right to a modicum of economic welfare and security to the right to share to the full in the social heritage

and to live the life of a civilized being according to the standards prevailing in the society."[1]

Four sets of public institutions correspond to these three types of rights:

> the *courts,* for the safeguarding of civil rights and, specifically, for the protection of all rights extended to the less articulate members of the national community;
>
> the local and national *representative bodies* as avenues of access to participation in public decision-making and legislation;
>
> the *social services,* to ensure some minimum of protection against poverty, sickness, and other misfortunes, and the *schools,* to make it possible for all members of the community to receive at least the basic elements of an education.

Initially, these rights of citizenship emerge with the establishment of equal rights under the law. The individual is free to conclude valid contracts, to acquire, and dispose of, property. Legal equality advances at the expense of legal protection of inherited privileges. Each man now possesses the right to act as an independent unit; however, the law only defines his legal capacity, but is silent on his ability to use it. In addition, civil rights are extended to illegitimate children, foreigners, and Jews; the principle of legal equality helps to eliminate hereditary servitude, equalize the status of husband and wife, circumscribe the extent of parental power, facilitate divorce, and legalize civil marriage. Accordingly, the extension of civil rights benefits the inarticulate sections of the population, giving a positive libertarian meaning to the legal recognition of individuality.

Still, this gain of legal equality stands side by side with the fact of social and economic inequality. Tocqueville and others point out that in medieval society many dependent persons were protected in some measure against the harshness of life by custom and paternal benevolence, albeit at the price of personal subservience. The new freedom of the wage contract quickly destroyed whatever protection of that kind had existed.[2] For a time at least, no new protections are instituted in place of the old; hence class prejudice and economic inequalities readily exclude the vast majority of the lower class from the enjoyment of their legal rights. The right of the individual to assert and defend his basic civil freedoms on terms of equality with others and by due process of law is *formal* in the sense that legal powers are guaranteed in the absence of any attempt to assist the individual in his use of these powers. As Anton Menger observed in 1899: "Our codes of private law do not contain a single clause which assigns to the in-

---

[1] The essay referred to has been reprinted in T. H. Marshall, *Class, Citizenship and Social Development* (Garden City, New York: Doubleday & Co., Inc., 1964), pp. 71–72. The following discussion is greatly indebted to Professor Marshall's analysis.

[2] Alexis de Tocqueville, *Democracy in America* (New York: Vintage Books, 1954), II, pp. 187–190.

dividual even such goods and services as are indispensable to the maintenance of his existence."[3] In this sense the equality of citizenship and the inequalities of social class develop together.

The juxtaposition of legal equality and social and economic inequalities inspired the great political debates which accompany the nation-building of nineteenth-century Europe. These debates turn on the types and degrees of inequality or insecurity that should be considered intolerable and the methods that should be used to alleviate them. The spokesmen of a consistent laissez-faire position seek to answer this question within the framework of formal civil rights. Having won legal recognition for the exercise of individual rights, they insist that to remain legitimate the government must abide by the rule of law. It is consistent with this position that in most European countries the first Factory Acts seek to protect women and children, who at the time are not considered citizens in the sense of legal equality.[4] By the same criterion all adult males are citizens because they have the power to engage in the economic struggle and take care of themselves. Accordingly, they are excluded from any legitimate claim to protection. In this way formally guaranteed rights benefit the fortunate and more fitfully those who are legally defined as unequal, while the whole burden of rapid economic change falls upon the "laboring poor" and thus provides a basis for agitation at an early time.

This agitation is political from the beginning. One of the earliest results of the legislative protection of freedom of contract is the legislative prohibition of trade unions. But where legislative means are used both to protect the individual's freedom of contract and deny the lower classes the rights needed to avail themselves of the same freedom (i.e., the right of association), the attacks upon inequality necessarily broaden. Equality is no longer sought through freedom of contract alone, but through the establishment of social and political rights as well. The nation-states of Western Europe can look back on longer or shorter histories of legislative actions and administrative decisions which have increased the equality of subjects from the different strata of the population in terms of their legal capacity and their legal status.[5] For each nation-state and for each set of institutions we can pinpoint

[3] Anton Menger, *The Right to the Whole Product of Labor* (London: Macmillan and Co., 1899), pp. 3-4.

[4] Ideological equalitarianism as well as an interest in breaking down familial restrictions upon the freedom of economic action were presumably the reason why protection was first extended to these most inarticulate sections of the "lower class." . . .

[5] When all adult citizens are equal before the law and free to cast their vote, the exercise of these rights depends upon a person's ability and willingness to use the legal powers to which he is entitled. On the other hand, the legal status of the citizens involves rights and duties which cannot be voluntarily changed without intervention by the State. A discussion of the conceptual distinction between capacity as "the legal power of doing" and status as "the legal state of being" is contained in R. H. Graveson, *Status in the Common Law* (London: Athlone Press, 1953), pp. 55-57.

chronologies of the public measures taken and trace the sequences of pressures and counterpressures, bargains and maneuvers, behind each extension of rights beyond the strata of the traditionally privileged. The extension of various rights to the lower classes constitutes a development characteristic of each country. A detailed consideration of each such development would note the considerable degree to which legal enactments are denied or violated in practice. It would thus emphasize how the issue of the civic position of the lower classes was faced or evaded in each country, what policy alternatives were under consideration, and by what successive steps the rights of citizenship were extended eventually. A full analysis could illuminate each step along the way, but it would also obscure the over-all process of nation-building.

For taken together, the developments of the several European countries also constitute the transformation from the estate societies of the eighteenth to the welfare state of the twentieth centuries. A comparative study of this transformation from the standpoint of national citizenship will inevitably appear abstract if juxtaposed with the specific chronology and detailed analysis of successive legislative enactments in each country. However, such a study will have the advantage of emphasizing the truth that, considered cumulatively and in the long run, legislative enactments have extended the rights of citizenship to the lower classes and thus represent a genuinely comparable process in nineteenth- and twentieth-century Europe.

The following discussion is limited to one aspect of Western European nation-building: *the entry of the lower classes into the arena of national politics*. Only those policies are considered which have immediate relevance for lower-class movements seeking to enter national politics.*. . .

The basic condition for the development toward universal rights of political participation was the *unification of the national system of representation*. In the late Middle Ages the principle of territorial representation had on the Continent increasingly given way to a system of representation by *estates:* each estate sent its separate representatives to deliberate at the center of territorial authority and each had its separate assembly. Only in England was the original system of territorial representation retained: the House of Commons was not an assembly of the burgher estates but a body of legislators representing the constituent localities of the realm, the counties and the boroughs. The greater openness of English society made it possible to keep up the territorial channels of representation, and this, in turn, set the stage for a much smoother transition to a unified regime of equalitarian democracy.[6]

---

* [The authors discuss the development of civil and social rights, before turning to the question of the extension of political rights. — Editors' note.]

[6] This question of territorial vs. functional representation is at the heart of the debate over the reasons for the survival of Parliament during the age of absolutism. . . .

Regardless of the principle of representation in these *anciens régimes,* only the economically independent heads of households could take part in public life. This participation was a right they derived not from their membership in any national community but from their ownership of territory and capital or from their status within legally defined functional corporations such as the nobility, the church, or the guilds of merchants or artisans. There was no representation of individuals: the members of the assemblies represented recognized stakes in the system, whether in the form of property holdings or in the form of professional privileges.

The French Revolution brought about a fundamental change in the conception of representation: the basic unit was no longer the household, the property, or the corporation, but the *individual citizen;* and representation was no longer channeled through separate functional bodies but through a *unified national assembly* of legislators. The law of August 11, 1792, went so far as to give the franchise to all French males over 21 who were not servants, paupers, or *vagabonds,* and the Constitution of 1793 did not even exclude paupers if they had resided more than six months in the *canton.* The Restoration did not bring back representation by estates: instead the *régime censitaire* introduced an abstract monetary criterion which cut decisively across the earlier criteria of ascribed status.

A new phase in this development opened up with the Revolution of 1848 and the rapid spread of movements for representative democracy through most of Europe. Napoleon III demonstrated the possibilities of plebiscitarian rule, and leaders of the established elites became increasingly torn between their fears of the consequences of rapid extensions of the suffrage to the lower classes and their fascination with the possibilities of strengthening the powers of the nation-state through the mobilization of the working class in its service.[7] These conflicts of strategy produced a great variety of transitional compromises in the different countries. The starting points for these developments were the provisions of the *Ständestaat* and the post-revolutionary *régime censitaire,* and the end points were the promulgations of universal adult suffrage. But the steps taken and the paths chosen from the one point to the other varied markedly from country to country and reflected basic differences in the dominant values and character of each social structure.[8]

We may conveniently distinguish five major sets of criteria used

[7] ... In a number of countries the demands for universal manhood suffrage became intimately tied in with the need for universal *conscription.* In Sweden the principal argument for the breakup of the four-estate *Riksdag* was the need for a strengthening of national defense. In the Swedish suffrage debates, the slogan "one man, one vote, one gun" reflects this tie up between franchise and military recruitment.

[8] The details of these developments have been set out in such compendia as Georg Meyer, *Das parlamentarische Wahlrecht* (Berlin: Haering, 1901), and Karl Braunias, *Das parlamentarische Wahlrecht* (Berlin: de Gruyter, 1932), Vol. 2.

in limiting the franchise during this transitional period: (1) traditional *estate* criteria: restriction of franchise to heads of households within each of the established status groups as defined by law; (2) *régime censitaire:* restrictions based on the value of land or capital or on the amounts of yearly taxes on property and/or income; (3) *régime capacitaire:* restrictions by literacy, formal education, or appointment to public office; (4) *household responsibility* criteria: restrictions to heads of households occupying own dwellings of a minimum given volume or lodged in premises for a given minimum rent; (5) *residence* criteria: restrictions to citizens registered as residents either in the local community, the constituency, or the national territory for a given minimum of months or years.

The Norwegian Constitution of 1814 provides a good example of an early compromise between estate criteria, the *régime censitaire* and the *principe capacitaire.* The franchise was given to four categories of citizens: two of these, the *burghers* of incorporated cities and the *peasants* (freeholders and leaseholders), corresponded to the old estates; a third, applicable only in cities and towns, was defined by ownership of real estate of a given minimum value; and the fourth was simply made up of all officials of the national government. This system gave a clear numerical majority to the farmers, but as a political precaution the interests of the burghers and officials were protected through inequalities in the distribution of mandates between urban and rural constituencies.[9] The simplicity of the social structure made the Norwegian compromise a straightforward one: the age-old division between peasant and burgher estates corresponded to an established administrative division into rural districts and chartered towns, and the only class of voters explicitly placed above this territorial-functional division was the king's officials, the effective rulers of the nation for several decades to come.

Much more complex compromises had to be devised in multinational polities such as Austria. In the old Habsburg territories the typical *Landtag* had consisted of four *curiae:* the nobles, the knights, the prelates, and the representatives of cities and markets. The *Februarpatent* of 1861 kept the division into four *curiae,* but transformed the estate criteria into criteria of *interest representation.* The nobles and the knights were succeeded by a *curia* of the largest landowners. The ecclesiastical estate was broadened into a *curia* of *Virilstimmen* representing universities as well as dioceses. The burgher estate was no longer exclusively represented by spokesmen for cities and markets, but also through the *chambers of commerce and the professions:* this was the first recognition of a corporatist principle which was to become of central importance in the ideological debates in Austria in the twentieth century. To these three was added a *peasant* division: this was new in the na-

---

[9] See Stein Rokkan, "Geography, Region and Social Class: Cross-Cutting Cleavages in Norwegian Politics," in S. M. Lipset and Stein Rokkan, eds., *Party Systems and Voter Alignments* (New York: The Free Press of Glencoe, 1967).

tional system; direct peasant representation of the type so well known in the Nordic countries had only existed in Tyrol and Vorarlberg. The most interesting feature of the Austrian sequence of compromises was the handling of the lower classes so far excluded from participation in the politics of the nation. True to their tradition of functional representation, the Austrian statesmen did not admit these new citizens *on a par* with the already enfranchised, but placed them in a new, a fifth curia, *die allgemeine Wählerklasse*. This, however, was only a transitional measure: eleven years later even the Austrian *Abgeordnetenhaus* fell in with the trend toward equalitarian mass democracy and was transformed into a unified national assembly based on universal manhood suffrage.

The rise of commercial and industrial capitalism favored the spread of the *régime censitaire*. The ideological basis was Benjamin Constant's argument that the affairs of the national community must be left to those with "real stakes" in it through the possession of land or through investments in business. The *principe capacitaire* was essentially an extension of this criterion: the franchise was accorded not only to those who own land or have invested in business but also to those who have acquired a direct interest in the maintenance of the polity through their investments in professional skills and their appointment to positions of public trust. The implicit notion is that only such citizens can form rational judgments of the policies to be pursued by the government. A Norwegian authority on constitutional law links the two elements together in his statement: "Suffrage . . . should be reserved to the citizens who have *judgment* enough to understand who would prove the best representatives, and *independence* enough to stick to their conviction in this matter."[10]

This question of criteria of intellectual independence was at the heart of the struggles between liberals and conservatives over the organization of the suffrage. Liberals favored the *régime censitaire* and feared the possibilities of electoral manipulation inherent in the extension of the suffrage to the economically dependent. Conservatives, once they recognized the importance of the vote as a basis of local power, tended to favor the enfranchisement of the "lower orders": they had good reason to expect that, at least on the patriarchal estates in the countryside, those in positions of dependence would naturally vote for the local notables. This conflict reached a climax in the discussions at the German National Assembly in Frankfurt in 1848–49. The Constitutional Commission had recommended that the franchise should be restricted to all *independent* citizens, and this term was at first interpreted to exclude all servants and all wage earners. This interpretation met with violent protests in the Assembly. There was general agreement that subjects who received public assistance or were in bankruptcy were not independent and should be excluded from the franchise, but there was

[10] T. H. Aschehoug, *Norges nuvaerende Statsforfatning* (Christiania: Aschehoug, 1875), Vol. I, p. 280.

extensive disagreement on the rights of servants and workers. The left claimed full rights for the lower classes and was only moderately opposed by the conservatives. The result was the promulgation of universal manhood suffrage. As it happened, this law could not be enforced at the time: it took another 17 years until Bismarck was able to make it the basis for the organization of the *Reichstag* of the North German Federation. The Prussian Chancellor had already had the experience of a system of universal suffrage, but a markedly unequal one — the Prussian system of three-class suffrage introduced by royal decree in 1849. Under that system the "lower orders" had been given the right to vote, but the weight of their votes was infinitesimal in comparison with those of the middle classes and the landowners. This system had obviously served to bolster the power of the *Gutsbesitzer*, particularly east of the Elbe: the law had simply multiplied by n the number of votes at their disposal, since they counted on being able to control without much difficulty the behavior of their dependents and their workers at the polls.[11] Bismarck detested the three-class system for its emphasis on abstract monetary criteria and its many injustices, but he was convinced that a change to equal suffrage for all men would not affect the power structure in the countryside: on the contrary it would strengthen even further the landed interests against the financial. Generally, in the countryside the extensions of the suffrage tended to strengthen the conservative forces.[12]

There was much more uncertainty about the consequences of an extended suffrage for the politics of the urban areas. The emergence and growth of a class of *wage earners outside the immediate household* of the employer raised new problems for the definition of political citizenship. In the established socio-economic terminology their status was one of dependence, but it was not evident that they would inevitably follow their employers politically. The crucial battles in the development toward universal suffrage concerned the status of these emerging strata within the political community. A great variety of transitional compromises were debated and several were actually tried out. The basic strategy was to underscore the structural differentiations within the wage-earning strata. Some varieties of *régime censitaire* in fact admitted the better paid wage workers, particularly if they had houses of their own.[13] The householder and lodger franchise in Britain similarly served to integrate the better-off working class within the system and to

---

[11] For a recent detailed account see Th. Nipperdey, *Die Organisation der deutschen Parteien vor 1918* (Düsseldorf: Droste, 1961), Chap. V. . . .

[12] See D. C. Moore, "The Other Face of Reform," *Victorian Studies*, V (September 1961), pp. 7–34 and G. Kitson Clark, *The Making of Victorian England* (London: Methuen, 1962), especially Chap. VII.

[13] A special tax census taken in Norway in 1876 indicates that more than one-quarter of the urban workers who were on the tax rolls were enfranchised under the system adopted in 1814: by contrast only 3 per cent of the workers in the rural areas had been given the vote. See Statistisk Centralbureau ser. C. No. 14, 1877, pp. 340–341.

keep out only the "real proletariat," migrants and marginal workers without established local ties. The retention of residence requirements has served similar functions even after the disappearance of all economic qualifications for suffrage: these restrictions are adhered to most stubbornly in the provisions for local elections.

Another set of strategies in this battle to control the onrush of mass democracy comprises the institutions of *weighted* suffrage and *plural votes*. The crudest examples are no doubt the Austrian *Kurien* and the Prussian three-class system: universal suffrage is granted, but the weights of the votes given to the lower classes are infinitesimal in comparison with those of the established landed or financial elite. The most innocuous system of plural voting is perhaps the British provision for extra votes for university graduates and for owners of business premises in different constituencies. Sociologically the most interesting is the Belgian system of plural voting devised in 1893: universal manhood suffrage is introduced, but extra votes are given not only on *capacitaire* criteria but also to *pères de famille* upon reaching the respectable age of 35. The basic motive is clearly to underscore structural differentiations within the lower strata and to exclude from the system the elements least committed to the established social order.

Closely related to these strategies is the stubborn resistance to changes in the delimitation of constituencies. Rapid urbanization produces glaring inequalities even under conditions of formally equal universal suffrage. The injustices of the Prussian districting provisions were the object of acrimonious debate for decades. The extreme solution adopted in the Weimar Republic — the establishment of a unitary system of proportional representation for the entire Reich — no doubt gives every voter the same abstract chance to influence the distribution of seats, but at the same time brings to the fore the inherent difficulties of such standardization across localities of very different structure. The continued overrepresentation of rural areas in the United States is another example.

The entry of the lower classes into the political arena also raises a series of problems for the *administration of elections*. Sociologically the most interesting issue is the safeguarding of the *independence of the individual electoral decision*. The defenders of estate traditions and the *régime censitaire* argue that economically dependent subjects cannot be expected to form independent political judgments and would, if enfranchised, corrupt the system through the sale of votes and through violent intimidation. Corrupt practices were, of course, widespread in many countries long before the extension of the suffrage, but the enfranchisement of large sections of the lower classes generally provides added incentive to reforms in the administration and control of elections. The secrecy of the ballot is a central problem in this debate.[14]

---

[14] A recent one-nation account of the development of standards for the control of elections is Cornelius O'Leary, *The Elimination of Corrupt Practices in British Elections, 1868–1911* (Oxford: Clarendon Press, 1962).

The traditional notion was that the vote was a public act and only to be entrusted to men who could openly stand by their opinions. The Prussian system of oral voting was defended in these terms, but was maintained for so long largely because it proved an easy way of controlling the votes of farm laborers.

The secret ballot essentially appeals to the liberal urban mentality: it fits as another element into the anonymous, privatized culture of the city, described by Georg Simmel. The decisive factor, however, is the emergence of the lower-class vote as a factor in national politics and the need to neutralize the threatening working-class organizations: the provisions for secrecy isolate the dependent worker not only from his superiors but also from his peers. Given the state of electoral statistics, it is very difficult to determine with any exactitude the effects of secrecy on the actual behavior of workers at the polls. But it seems inherently likely, given a minimum amount of cross-class communications, that secrecy helps to reduce the likelihood of a polarization of political life on the basis of social class.

In this respect the secret ballot represents the national and plebiscitarian principle of civic integration, in contrast to working-class organizations which exemplify the principle of functional representation. That is, the claims of trade unions and labor parties which seek recognition for the rights of the *fourth estate* are counterbalanced by the claims of the *national* community and its spokesmen. The provision for secret voting puts the individual before a personal choice and makes him at least temporarily independent of his immediate environment: in the voting booth he can be a national citizen. The provisions for secret voting make it possible for the inarticulate rank and file to escape the pressure for political partisanship and at the same time put the onus of political visibility on the activists within the working-class movement. In sociological terms we can say, therefore, that the national electoral system opens up channels for the expression of secret loyalties while the political struggle makes it necessary for the party activist to publicize his views and expose himself to censure where he deviates from the "establishment."[15]

The extension of citizenship to the lower classes of Western Europe can thus be viewed from several complementary points of view. In terms of the comparison between the medieval and the modern political structure the discussion exemplifies the simultaneous trends toward

---

[15] Some socialist parties try to counteract these effects of secret voting by establishing intimate ties with trade unions. Note in this respect the controversy over the political levy paid by members of British trade unions as discussed in Martin Harrison, *Trade Unions and the Labour Party since 1945* (London: Allen & Unwin, 1960), Chap. 1. Trade union members who wish to be excused from payment hand a "contracting-out" form to their branch secretary, but although the payment is nominal and the procedure simple, controversy has been intense, in part because "contracting-out" is a public act which indirectly jeopardizes the secrecy of the ballot.

equality and a nationwide, governmental authority. The constitution of a modern nation-state is typically the fountainhead of the rights of citizenship, and these rights are a token of nationwide equality. Politics itself has become nationwide, and the "lower classes" now have the opportunity of active participation.

VAL R. LORWIN

Working-Class Politics and Economic Development in Western Europe

Studies of the relationship between social and political change have concentrated much attention upon the presumed increase in political conflict arising from the creation of a large industrial working class in European societies. In Germany, Italy, and France, the "left" parties have not held power on their own since 1945. The British Labour Party has done respectably in postwar elections, but at times its leadership has notably disengaged from traditional Socialist principles. The failure of working-class parties to seize power — either by force or by the ballot — can be interpreted as a series of exceptions to generalizations about working-class political action, or as a stimulus to rethink assumptions positing the victory of Socialist parties as a necessary concomitant of industrialization and universal suffrage. Val Lorwin tests these clear-cut and simple assumptions against the complex, often imprecise, but nonetheless ineluctable record of the European working-class movements. He shows that the social institutions actually found among working classes are less readily capable of gaining and holding political power than is conventionally assumed.

How far has economic development conditioned working-class politics in Western Europe in the last century and a half? Are there stages of economic development in which protest is always sharp and others in which it is dull? To what extent are the differences in protest among the nations due to differences in economic growth, to what extent to different patterns of general historical development caused by other factors? What types of studies may promote our understanding of these questions? These are questions I propose to raise or to discuss here.

The study of economic development has had a tremendous revival in the last decade. This revival springs largely from considerations of public policy, an honorable stimulus to scholars' quickened interest. One source is the pressure of the economically underdeveloped countries, those we used to call "backward" countries but which are often extremely "forward" these days. Another is the threat of economic stagnation in older industrial nations. A third is the concern of the democracies for their very survival in the face of the vast economic growth of the Soviet Union and, in the offing, of Communist China.

"Economic development," the economist James S. Duesenberry says, "seems to be one of those peculiar phrases whose meaning everyone knows without the aid of any formal definition. Onward and upward expresses the term's meaning as well as anything else."[1] Here I should like to consider the effects of long-range economic change, which includes some regression as well as the "onward and upward" which generally marks our period. Not only are changes in total national product and product per head important, but so are the types of industry, the size of enterprise, the structure of ownership and quality of management, the sources of the labor force, the patterns of occupations, the distribution of income, and the nature of the industrial and urban communities.[2]

From *American Historical Review,* LXIII, 1958, pp. 338–351. Reprinted by permission.

An earlier version of this paper was read at a session of the annual meeting of the American Historical Association, St. Louis, December 30, 1956. I thank the Inter-University Study of Labor Problems in Economic Development for making possible much of the research on which this paper is based.

[1] *Papers and Proceedings of the American Economic Association, 1951,* p. 558, a discussion of papers on economic growth in the United States. Economists, as M. M. Postan remarks, "have now moved into regions which historians have always regarded as their own. Yet, so far, the growing proximity has not done much to bring historical and theoretical study together." See his "Economic Growth" ("Essays in Bibliography and Criticism," XXIII), reviewing W. W. Rostow, *The Process of Economic Growth,* in *Economic History Review,* 2d ser., VI (1953), no. 1, 78–83.

[2] For recent discussion of some of the relevant considerations, chiefly by economists, see Simon Kuznets, "Toward a Theory of Economic Growth," in Robert Lekachman, ed., *National Policy for Economic Welfare at Home and Abroad* (Garden City, 1955), pp. 12–103; Kuznets, Wilbert E. Moore, and Joseph J. Spengler, eds., *Economic Growth: Brazil, India, Japan* (Durham, N.C., 1955), which includes general essays; Universities-National Bureau

The other side of the problem is the politics of labor, particularly the politics of protest. I shall include in political protest primarily fundamental protest against the social and political order (what Otto Kirchheimer has called "the opposition of principle"), but also the loyal opposition within the framework of the existing regime, and even some pressure group politics.[3] The distinctions have not always been clear to those who protest; often they have been even less clear to those to whom petition or clamor has been addressed — government, bourgeoisie, or fellow workers.

Working-class protest, like economic development, has been a matter of some agitated public concern since the Second World War. But people have been proclaiming it a chief problem of modern times since Carlyle wrote of the "bitter discontent gone fierce and mad, the wrong conditions therefore or the wrong disposition of the Working Classes of England"[4] and Harriet Martineau warned that "this great question of the rights of labor . . . cannot be neglected under a lighter penalty than ruin to all."[5]

A few hardy souls have sought to identify historical truth on these matters by quantitative methods, shrinking neither from the paucity of data nor the conceptual difficulties of the task. For all but very recent periods the data are sketchy, and "guesstimates" are difficult and shaky. Comparisons in time multiply the difficulties, as the composition of what is being compared changes — but the efforts are worth making. Economic growth may be measured in figures of national income

---

Committee for Economic Research, *Capital Formation and Economic Growth* (Princeton, 1955); Norman S. Buchanan and Howard S. Ellis, *Approaches to Economic Development* (New York, 1955); S. Herbert Frankel, *The Economic Impact on Under-developed Societies* (Oxford, 1953); W. W. Rostow, *The Process of Economic Growth* (New York, 1952); Colin Clark, *The Conditions of Economic Progress* (2d ed., London, 1951); Bert F. Hoselitz, ed., *The Progress of Underdeveloped Areas* (Chicago, 1953); Léon H. Dupriez, ed., *Economic Progress*, Conference of International Economic Association (Louvain, 1955); and W. Arthur Lewis, *The Theory of Economic Growth* (London, 1955). Specifically discussing labor, see Wilbert E. Moore, *Industrialization and Labor* (Ithaca, N.Y., 1951), with descriptive material from Mexico; Clark Kerr and Abraham Siegel, "The Structuring of the Labor Force in Industrial Society: New Dimensions and New Questions," *Industrial and Labor Relations Review*, VIII (Jan., 1955), 151–68; Clark Kerr, Frederick H. Harbison, John T. Dunlop, and Charles A. Myers, "The Labor Problem in Economic Development," *International Labour Review*, LXXI (March, 1955), 223–35; Reinhard Bendix, *Work and Authority in Industry, Ideologies of Management in the Course of Industrialization* (New York, 1956); and R. L. Aronson and J. P. Windmuller, eds., *Labor, Management and Economic Growth* (Ithaca, N. Y., 1954).

[3] For a distinction between labor "pressure group" and "political" action, see Adolf Sturmthal, *The Tragedy of European Labor, 1918–1939* (New York, 1943).

[4] Thomas Carlyle, "Chartism," *Critical and Miscellaneous Essays,* in *Works* (30 vols., New York, 1900), XXIX, 119.

[5] *A History of the Peace: Being a History of England from 1816 to 1854* (4 vols., Boston, 1866), IV, 622.

or industrial production, in national totals and per head. We may try to measure not only the community's income but — still more difficult — the workers' shares of the community's income. People do not revolt against averages, however. We must try to separate groups of workers whose special grievances may set off widespread protest when the economy as a whole is moving forward. We must recognize the lags in political responses to objective conditions. Attitudes generated by economic regression may not manifest themselves in behavior until after economic recovery.

W. W. Rostow, in his valuable book on the nineteenth-century British economy, has a "social tension chart" for the years 1790–1850.[6] The chart records quantitatively factors that produce, or might produce, social tensions (wheat prices and the trade cycle, for unemployment), but not the tensions or manifestations of tension themselves. We are here, morever, in the short-run ups and downs of business cycles, rather than in stages of economic growth.

On the axis of protest, too, measurement is difficult. It is easy to overestimate the evidence that is quantifiable. In recent decades many nations have recorded the man-days lost by strikes, but these numbers represent no uniform quantities; there are great differences in the intensity of protest, and political content, from one strike to another.

Political protest can be measured in some of its more orderly forms: party membership, election results, and — for the most recent years, in many nations — whatever it is people tell to those who take public opinion polls. For periods before the working class attained full suffrage, however, the test of votes is only partially applicable, and complete and equal manhood suffrage was not attained until the First World War in most of the advanced European nations. We do not know how workers voted, moreover, or who voted for the parties claiming to represent the working class, except in some one-industry areas like the miners' constituencies. Nor have all Socialist votes or all Communist votes been of equal intensity as protests. Some votes have implied rejection of the social order; others, merely hopes of immediate economic self-interest; still others, vague and diffuse frustrations.[7]

On the eve of the Industrial Revolution, Henry Fielding remarked: "The sufferings of the poor are less observed than their misdeeds. . . . They starve, and freeze, and rot among themselves, but they beg, and steal, and rob among their betters."[8] Soon the laboring poor were able to do more, when they were thrown out of work or their wages were cut, than "beg and steal and rob among their betters." Modern economic

---

[6] *British Economy of the Nineteenth Century* (Oxford, 1948), pp. 123–25. Cf. E. J. Hobsbawm, "Economic Fluctuations and Some Social Movements since 1800," *Economic History Review*, 2d ser., V, no. 1 (1952), 1–25.

[7] For criticism of an attempt at quantitative analysis of protest in earlier periods, see Crane Brinton, *The Anatomy of Revolution* (rev. ed., New York, 1952), p. 28.

[8] *A Proposal for Making an Effectual Provision for the Poor, 1753*, in *Works* (16 vols., New York, 1902), XIII, 141.

development created a new sort of political protest by generating the industrial, essentially urban, wage-earning groups in such numbers and force that they were, for all their medieval and early modern predecessors, in most ways a new class — as yet only "camped in society . . . not established there."[9] This was, said the ex-worker Denis Poulot, "the terrible sphinx which is called the people . . . this great mass of workers which does not know what it is, except that it suffers."[10] Huddled in the wretched new factory towns or in the slums of renowned old cities, oppressed by long hours of work, arbitrary shop rules, and monotony, sorely tried by recurrent unemployment, unlettered, this mass inspired more fear than solicitude. Lord Liverpool, congratulated by Chateaubriand on the solidity of British institutions, pointed to the capital outside his windows and replied: "What can be stable with these enormous cities? One insurrection in London and all is lost."[11]

Hunger will turn political. In the hard year of 1819 the banners of the crowd at Peterloo, before the Yeomen rode them down, typified the mixture of the economic and the political: "A Fair Day's Wage for a Fair Day's Work," "No Corn Laws," and "Equal Representation or Death."[12]

It was not hunger alone. "The poor have hearts as well as stomachs," said Cooke Taylor but deemed it a fact not known to many who passed for wise men.[13] Carlyle knew it: "It is not what a man outwardly has or wants that constitutes the happiness or misery of him. Nakedness, hunger, distress of all kinds, death itself have been cheerfully suffered, when the heart was right. It is the feeling of injustice that is insupportable to all men. . . . No man can bear it or ought to bear it."[14]

Michel Chevalier looked at manufacturing and said: "Fixed points are totally lacking. There is no bond between superior and inferior, no rapprochement between equals. . . . Nothing holds, nothing lasts."[15] Slowly, "fixed points" were established; the working classes gained in education, self-discipline, and political experience. In the course of industrialization in every Western country, despite crises and wars, workers' levels of living improved vastly. Did this resolve working-class protest?

Continuing economic development would resolve the very protest it brought into being, Marx argued, but only by the inevitable substitution of a new order for the capitalist society, which would prove incapable of continuing the triumphant progress of economic growth.

[9] Michel Chevalier, *De l'industrie manufacturière en France* (Paris, 1841), p. 37.
[10] *Le Sublime* (3d ed., Paris, 1887; first pub. in 1870), p. 27.
[11] Chateaubriand, *Mémoires d'outre-tombe* (Brussels, 1849), IV, 210.
[12] F. A. Bruton, ed., *Three Accounts of Peterloo by Eyewitnesses* (Manchester, 1921); William Page, ed., *Commerce and Industry* (2 vols., London, 1919), II, 47.
[13] *Notes of a Tour in the Manufacturing Districts of Lancashire* . . . (London, 1842), p. 157.
[14] "Chartism," pp. 144–45.
[15] *Op. cit.*, p. 38.

Until the coming of the new order, declared the *Communist Manifesto*, "the development of class antagonism keeps even pace with the development of industry," and in *Capital* Marx affirmed that "there is a steady intensification of the wrath of the working class." (I use a few of Marx's significant statements as beginning points for discussion, not attempting an analysis of Marx or Marxism.)

These predictions have been contradicted by the experience (thus far) of all the Western nations except France and Italy — nor do France and Italy actually support the prophecy. Here is one of the ironies of the history of Marxist prediction.[16] Only in the two countries where, among all the great industrial nations of the free world, capitalism has shown the least sustained dynamism has the "wrath of the working class" permitted the Communist party to take and hold a preponderant position among workers.[17] These two countries require a closer look.

In France and Italy, economic growth alone could not resolve the noneconomic problems created by wars, religious tensions, social distance, and the relations between the individual and the state. We cannot go into the noneconomic factors here. But the sense of injustice in these countries also grew, in part, out of the qualities of economic growth: the character of entrepreneurship, the distribution of income, and — even more — the nature of employer authority. The bourgeoisie of France and of Italy were insistent in their demands for protection against labor as well as protection against competition. Niggardly and tardy in concessions to their workers, they flaunted inequalities by their style of living. Their class consciousness helped shape the class consciousness of workers.

Workers, moreover, doubted the ability of their superiors to fulfill their economic functions as an entrepreneurial class. The slowness of economic growth evoked protest, particularly in France. Before the First World War, labor leaders shared with many orthodox economists and publicists the impression that their country was stagnating,[18] although it was progressing in the two decades before the war. The gloomy view arose in part from comparisons with the industrial growth of the United States and with the industrial and military growth of Germany. That view also reflected the state of labor organization, greater in the stagnant old industries such as building and in the thousands of small workshops of Paris than in the newer industries such as the booming

---

[16] Cf. D. W. Brogan (in a different connection): "It is one of history's favorite jokes to invert Marxian prophecy." Introduction to Alexander Werth, *The Twilight of France* (New York, 1942), p. vii.

[17] Nor, clearly, has the experience in the Soviet orbit borne out the Marxian prophecy any better, since revolution won in countries in early stages of industrial capitalism and had to be imposed from without on more advanced countries.

[18] For one excellent example of such writing, see Henri Truchy, "Essai sur le commerce extérieur de la France de 1881 à 1902," *Revue d'économie politique*, XVIII (1904), 543–87.

steel mills of Lorraine. Later, in the interwar period, the labor movement was strong in the civil administration and public service industries rather than in the new and technically progressive branches of private industry — chemicals, synthetic fibers, automobiles.

French employers groaned constantly about their high costs, especially of labor, and their inability to compete with foreign producers.[19] Labor leaders argued, however, that the employers' difficulties really came from their sterility; "their very slow progress, from their timidity; their uncertainty, from their lack of initiative. We ask the French employers to resemble the American employer class. . . . We want a busy, active, humming country, a veritable beehive always awake. In that way our own force will be increased."[20] But the unions' own force remained weak. Their weakness, along with pessimism about the country's economic growth, gave to French labor that curious combination of low immediate hopes and utopian dreams which has characterized it during most of this century.

Management's own leaders praised smallness of scale and slowness to mechanize. In 1930 the president of the General Confederation of French Manufacturers congratulated his members on "the spirit of prudence in the management of firms, which is the surest guarantee against the dangers of a fearful crisis," and on "the French mentality of counting on regular and steady dividends, rather than on the sawtoothed variation of dividends fashionable in some great industrial nations."[21] The year of this speech marked the beginning of a decade of economic decline and stagnation in France.

The dramatic inequalities between the poorer, agricultural areas and the industrialized regions of both Italy and France created further tensions in each nation. Finally, the bourgeoisie showed a fear of the people and a political bankruptcy at history's critical hours. Workers in Italy and France tended to merge judgments of the political and the economic performance of the powers that were. Their doubts as to the competence and courage of the bourgeoisie deepened their feelings of both the injustice and the fragility of the social and political order. Here let us leave France and Italy to return to the general question.

Some would turn the Marxian assertion upside down and argue that there is a "hump of radicalism" early in a nation's industrial development and that once the economy, by a big "initial push," surmounts its early difficulties, protest inevitably falls off. The history of a number of countries gives support to this analysis. But, despite Marx and many anti-Marxists, in the history of social relationships the several factors never long "keep even pace" with each other. In England the working class has not seriously threatened the political order since Chartist

---

[19] American protectionists groaned too, but they paid relatively high wages while groaning.

[20] Victor Griffuelhes, "L'Infériorité des capitalistes français," *Mouvement socialiste*, no. 226, Dec., 1910, pp. 329–32.

[21] René-P. Duchemin, *Organisation syndicale patronale en France* (Paris, 1940), pp. 64, 68.

times, to be sure; but the syndicalists of the immediate pre-1914 period and the Socialists of the post-1918 period were far more critical of the social and economic order than the New Model unionists and the "Lib-Labs" of the 1850's, 1860's, and 1870's. France and Italy show a series of humps of radicalism.

Economic development has attenuated early protest by changes in the structure of the working classes. "Within the ranks of the proletariat," announced the *Communist Manifesto*, "the various interests and conditions of life are more and more equalized, in proportion as machinery obliterates all distinction of labor, and nearly everywhere reduces wages to the same low level. . . . The modern laborer, instead of rising with the progress of industry, sinks deeper and deeper below the conditions of existence of his own class."[22] Marx was observing a period of development in which the machine was breaking down old skills, especially in the textile trades. The historian was being unhistorical in assuming that the trend must continue.

By the turn of the century it was already clear to a good observer like Eduard Bernstein (who was aided by residence in England) that economic growth and social reforms were blurring the sharpness of class among wage and salaried workers.[23] This is the now familiar phenomenon of the rise of the "new middle class." (Let us accent the word "new," for we use the old, imprecise words "middle class" for lack of a more descriptive phrase.) George Orwell spoke of the "upward and downward extension of the middle class" and of the growing importance of the people of "indeterminate social class."[24] This is the result of the swelling of the so-called tertiary sector of the economy — of public administration, commerce, services, and, within the industrial sector itself, the expansion of professional, technical, and administrative jobs.[25] Even among those in traditional forms of wage employment, middle-class attitudes have flourished, made possible not only by higher real wages and greater leisure but also by enhanced security, housing in socially mixed communities, longer schooling, and an increasingly classless culture wafted on mass communications.

The people of the new middle class have most often sought individual

[22] Lack of space prevents discussion of the obviously related theme of the proletarianization of middle-class strata and the polarization of classes.

[23] *Evolutionary Socialism: A Criticism and Affirmation*, trans. by E. C. Harvey (London, 1909), esp. pp. 103–106, 206–207, 219. See also Peter Gay, *The Dilemma of Democratic Socialism: Eduard Bernstein's Challenge to Marx* (New York, 1952).

[24] *The Lion and the Unicorn* (London, 1941), pp. 53–54.

[25] Michel Collinet, *Essai sur la condition ouvrière, 1900–1950* (Paris, 1951); Hans Speier, *Social Order and the Risks of War* (New York, 1952), a collection of earlier essays, esp. pp. 19–26, 53–67; Reinhard Bendix and S. M. Lipset, eds., *Class, Status and Power: A Reader in Social Stratification* (Glencoe, Ill., 1953); G. D. H. Cole, *Studies in Class Structure* (London, 1955); Raymond Aron, "Social Structure and the Ruling Class," *British Journal of Sociology*, I, nos. 1–2, 1–16, 126–43; Georges Friedmann, ed., *Villes et Campagnes: Deuxième Semaine Sociologique* . . . (Paris, 1953); Michel Crozier, "Les Tertiaires et le Socialisme," *Esprit*, XXIV, no. 238, 706–15; E. F. M. Durbin, *The Politics of Democratic Socialism* (London, 1940), Pt. II, sec. 4.

rather than collective solutions. Their political preferences have been divided — although unevenly — among almost all the parties. On the Continent in crisis times, fearful of being dragged down to proletarian status, many have hearkened to authoritarian voices. The new middle class called into question many of the traditional appeals of working-class politics. The parties of labor were obliged to appeal to other classes and to more complex attitudes than, rightly or wrongly, they formerly took for granted among workers.

Another change which came with economic growth was the differentiation between the economic and the political organizations of the working classes. Early forms of action had confused the economic and political. Then there generally came a separation between unions and political parties and, albeit with interlocking directorates and memberships, a cooperative division of function. France, Italy, and Spain, however, did not achieve this division of labor; while England was developing "Sidney Webbicalism,"[26] they developed syndicalism. This was the confounding of politics and economics in the name of "a-political" action. Anarcho-syndicalism, with its refusal to recognize the reality of politics and its disdain for parliamentary democracy, had fateful consequences. It prevented an effective working relationship of the unions with the socialist parties, to the great mischief of both, and helped leave workers poorly prepared later to distinguish between democratic political protest and communist politics.

Politics could not be denied, however much some workers' leaders might plead the sufficiency of economic action. No movement came to be more dependent on political action for economic gains than the "a-political" French unions. Even the robust British workers' consumer cooperatives, founded on the Rochdale principle of political neutrality, formed a Cooperative party (which became a small tail to the Labour party kite). When British labor attempted in the 1926 general strike to solve by industrial action a problem too big for industrial action alone, the result was catastrophe. Even there, moreover, the Trades Union Congress used its economic power in only a halfhearted way for fear of damaging the nation's political foundations.

The once lively anarchist and syndicalist movements practically disappeared under the hammer of economic development. The libertarian movements could not survive in the climate of assembly line production, modern industrial organization, or the modern welfare state. It was the communists, opposed though they were to the deepest libertarian impulses, who by their militant rejection of bourgeois society claimed most of the anarchists' and syndicalists' following. To the completely power-centered movement fell the heritage of those who had refused to come to any terms with political power.

Among the socialists, the bearded prophets gave way to the smooth-chinned organizers, parliamentarians, and planners. Socialist militancy

---

[26] The term is *Punch's,* quoted by G. D. H. Cole, *The World of Labour* (4th ed., London, 1920), p. 3. In Italy syndicalism was important but not the dominant current.

was a victim of socialist success, itself made possible by economic growth. Economic growth produced a margin of well-being and facilitated the compromises and generosity which reconciled groups to each other in most of the liberal democracies.

Along with socialist militancy, socialist certitudes faded. The motto of "Socialism in our time" was amended, at least sotto voce, to "Socialism . . . but not in our time." Socialism became less than ever a doctrine and more a political temper. Despite an addiction to worn-out slogans, it was mellowed and strengthened, particularly after the First World War, by its identification with the noneconomic values of national life against threats from extreme left and extreme right.

Where it was most doctrinal, socialism was least effective — and often least true to its own doctrine. It proved most effective where it was most pragmatic, in the lands where the habits of civic responsibility and political compromise were strong; these were all (except Switzerland) constitutional monarchies. In France and in Italy, however, the Communist party rushed into the gap between socialist reasonableness and workers' old resentments, between socialist uncertainties and workers' pent-up hopes. Spain and Portugal were limiting cases; their hours of democracy were of the briefest, in part because of long economic stagnation.

"Modern industrial labor, modern subjugation to capital, the same in England as in France, in America as in Germany, has stripped [the proletarian] of every trace of national character. . . . National differences, and antagonisms between people, are daily more and more vanishing," said the *Communist Manifesto*. Instead, the working-class movements have all followed different national patterns. For many years it could be said that the only thing the socialists had nationalized was socialism.

Britain developed a labor movement of class solidarity and class organization without class hatred; France and Italy, class hatred but ineffectual class organization. Scandinavia developed on the British pattern, overcoming class conflict and moving on to an even higher degree of class restraint and responsibility than Britain's. The Belgian, Dutch, and Swiss working classes have shown a remarkable degree of responsibility, although their highly developed class organizations have followed the religious and political cleavages in each nation. The Communist Internationals have exercised central controls, but over parties which have differed not only from continent to continent but also from nation to contiguous Western European nation.

"A number of things govern men," said Montesquieu, "climate, religion, laws, maxims of government, the examples of things past, customs, manners; from all this there is formed a general spirit."[27]

---

[27] The year 1956 reminded us again, in hope and tragedy, of the "general spirit" of peoples. Upsurge against Soviet rule came, where if anywhere among the satellites one might have expected it, from the "brave" and "romantic" Poles and Hungarians.

Economic development was only one of the factors that influenced social structures, cultural patterns, political habits and institutions, and what for short we call national character.

National character is often a bundle of contradictions, however, and it changes in time. The form and temper of working-class action also change. In Norway, for example, the tremendous onrush of industrialization early in this century evoked a radical protest which gave the union movement a syndicalist turn and took the Labor party into the Communist International.[28] But the party soon broke with the Comintern, and party and unions developed into one of the most solid — yet independent and imaginative — labor movements in the world.

In Belgium, about 1891, social conflict seemed so irreconcilable that Paul Vinogradoff thought revolution must break out in this "overcrowded country, where the extremes of socialist and Catholic opinion were at that time most in evidence,"[29] and that such a revolution would touch off a general European war. But before the First World War, Belgian workers had somehow assimilated their conflicts in a structure of compromise and appeared as among the most moderate in Europe.

The study of differences and similarities between the nations, as well as change within the nations, sheds light on our problems. One may, for example, compare France and Belgium, separated by a rather artificial frontier but by many historical differences. The reconciliation of the Belgian working class to the political and social order, divided though the workers are by language and religion and the Flemish-Walloon question, makes a vivid contrast with the experience of France. The differences did not arise from the material fruits of economic growth, for both long were rather low-wage countries, and Belgian wages were the lower. In some ways the two countries had similar economic development. But Belgium's industrialization began earlier; it was more dependent on international commerce, both for markets and for its transit trade; it had a faster growing population; and it became much more urbanized than France. The small new nation, "the cockpit of Europe," could not permit itself social and political conflict to the breaking point. Perhaps France could not either, but it was harder for the bigger nation to realize it.

Comparisons of different groups within nations and among nations are of the essence too. Some occupations seem prone to long phases of radicalism.[30] Dangerous trades, unsteady employment, and isolation from the larger community are some of the factors which make for radicalism among dockers, seamen, lumbermen, and miners in many

---

[28] Walter Galenson, *Labor in Norway* (Cambridge, Mass., 1949) and "Scandinavia," in Galenson, ed., *Comparative Labor Movements* (New York, 1952).

[29] H. A. L. Fisher, "Memoir," in *The Collected Papers of Paul Vinogradoff* (2 vols., Oxford, 1928), I, 19.

[30] See for example Clark Kerr and Abraham Siegel, "The Interindustry Propensity to Strike," in A. Kornhauser, *et al.*, eds., *Industrial Conflict* (New York, 1954), pp. 189–212; K. G. J. C. Knowles, *Strikes* (Oxford, 1952).

— though not all — countries. Yet radicalism has had successes among the more stable occupations too.

It is not generally those who are in the greatest economic distress who are the leaders in protest. First, one may recognize the element of chance in the occupational selection of leaders of protest (as in all selections of leadership). It is happenstance that the lifelong leader of the French unions, Léon Jouhaux, came out of a match factory and that the great leader of Danish Social Democracy, Thorvald Stauning, came out of the cigar maker's trade. Beyond the chance elements, however, there is a process of selection for leadership of protest from strength rather than misery, by the capacity of the group rather than its economic distress. First those in the skilled artisan trades (notably the printers and building craftsmen), then the metal workers, miners, and railroad men have been in the vanguard in many lands. In relation to economic development, some of the leaders have come from the groups of skilled operatives menaced by technological change, others from skilled or semi-skilled workers in positions of continuing opportunity or in stable, strategic locations in the industrial process.

Urban and regional social history and political history for the industrial age mostly remain to be written.[31] Description may be aided and informed by comparison. Birmingham may be compared with Manchester and Leeds, Birmingham with Lyons; Asa Briggs has done both for the early nineteenth century.[32] Comparisons within nations may point up the importance of factors quite different from those which emerge from comparisons between nations. In France and Italy, syndicalism seems related to comparative national economic retardation. In Spain, syndicalism was strong in the economically most advanced region of a country as a whole terribly retarded; the reasons were in the Catalans' political autonomism as well as in their economic advance.[33]

Apparently similar economic trends may give rise to, or at least be accompanied by, different consequences of protest. British miners' protest mounted bitterly as the coal industry sank into the doldrums of the 1920's. On the other hand, the porcelain workers of Limoges, vigorous socialists at the turn of the century, became torpid as their industry declined into torpor.

---

[31] On the need for regional and local studies, see Carl E. Schorske, *German Social Democracy, 1905–1917* (Cambridge, Mass., 1955), pp. 341–42; Georges Duveau, "Comment étudier la vie ouvrière," in *Revue d'histoire économique et sociale*, XXVI, no. 1 (1940–1947), 11–21; J.-D. Reynaud and Alain Touraine, "Les ouvriers," in Maurice Duverger, ed., *Partis politiques et classes sociales en France* (Paris, 1955), pp. 34–35, 41–42; Gabriel Le Bras, *Études de Sociologie religieuse* (2 vols., Paris, 1956), esp. II, 546–57.

[32] "The Background of the Parliamentary Reform Movement in Three English Cities, 1830–2," *Cambridge Historical Journal*, X (1952), 293–317 and "Social Structure and Politics in Birmingham and Lyons (1825–1848)," *British Journal of Sociology*, I, no. 1 (1950), 67–80.

[33] Gerald Brenan, *The Spanish Labyrinth: An Account of the Social and Political Background of the Civil War* (Cambridge, Eng., 1944).

If only in passing and by inference, I hope to have recalled some examples of the particular subjects which invite the historian and some of the values of comparative studies.[34] We need to study many more individuals, in biographies, and many more occupations and industries, in their settings of period and place, as, with fond intensity and imaginative erudition, Georges Duveau has studied the workers of the Second Empire,[35] before we can safely generalize. But men will, as men should, generalize long before they can safely generalize.

Here I have thought that modest ground-clearing considerations would be most useful. To assume my share of responsibility, however, I offer a few working hypotheses. For some of them, the nature of the evidence has been hinted at in the preceding pages; for others, not even that. They are not meant to be "laws" or "universal" but merely to sum up a few aspects of the experience of the past 150 years in one area of the world, an area full of intriguing differences yet with enough homogeneity in culture and industrial development to make generalization valid and comparison significant.

> Economic development is process, environment, and goal; it provides a framework, and sets problems, for man's capacities for political and social action.
>
> Rapid growth in the early stages of industrialization generates protest by reason of the bewildering dislocations and (for many) the sacrifices out of current consumption which it imposes. Continued economic growth permits the satisfaction of much of this protest. But some attitudes of protest persist well beyond the economic conditions which aroused them.
>
> Sluggish economic growth may generate the deepest and longest lasting protest by reason of the society's inability to provide well-being and social justice to match social aspirations and by reason of the economic elite's failure to inspire confidence. Slow growth of cities and slow recruitment of the industrial work force facilitate the carry-over of traditions of protest from generation to generation.

[34] Cf. the report of the Social Science Research Council Seminar on Research in Comparative Politics, *American Political Science Review*, XLVII (Sept., 1953), 641–75; Roy Macridis, *The Study of Comparative Government* (Garden City, 1955). On comparative labor history, see Selig Perlman, *A Theory of the Labor Movement* (New York, 1928); Adolf Sturmthal, *Unity and Diversity in European Labor* (Glencoe, Ill., 1953); Walter Galenson, ed., *Comparative Labor Movements* (New York, 1952), pp. ix–xiv; Lewis L. Lorwin, *Labor and Internationalism* (New York, 1929), esp. chap. xxiv. In "Recent Research on Western European Labor Movements," *Proceedings of the Seventh Annual Meeting of the Industrial Relations Research Association* (Madison, 1955), pp. 69–80, I have summarized a few of the main lines of labor history in publications since 1946.

[35] *La Vie ouvrière en France sous le Second Empire* (Paris, 1946) and *La Pensée ouvrière sur l'éducation pendant la Seconde République et le Second Empire* (Paris, 1948).

The gradual delineation of the separate (but overlapping) spheres and organizations of political and industrial protest makes for reconciliation and absorption of protest in each sphere.

The labor movements most dependent on the state may show the greatest hostility to the state. The working classes best integrated with their national communities are those which have built labor movements that are more or less autonomous centers of power.

The successive phases of a nation's economic development are not inevitably reflected in corresponding attitudes and behavior of labor protest. Moreover, different phases of development exist side by side in the same regions and industries. Different forms of working-class politics also exist side by side.

National differences shape the response of workers and labor movements to economic change. These differences are only in part due to the differences in patterns of economic development. In large part they are due to noneconomic factors — politics and religion, cultural patterns and class feeling — and to historical accident and personalities. ("Everything is dependent on everything," however, and most of the noneconomic factors are themselves conditioned by economic change.)

These are a few of the problems on which we need further descriptive findings and further comparative analysis. Comparative studies may remind those of us who wear monographic spectacles to look up to the horizon from time to time and may remind those who strain at the horizon to put on the spectacles occasionally for closer observation.

It is to the more modest forms of comparative historical work that I refer, not to the abused "grand manner" of universal history. Yet even modest comparative studies will help put our problems in their broader settings of the history of man's relation to his work and his fellows, of the history of social organization and political striving, of the endless searches for justice, order, and freedom.

CHAPTER
TWO

Political Cultures and Sub-Cultures

The concept of political culture is a convenient shorthand way of referring to the values, beliefs, and emotions that give meaning to political life. In analyzing the political culture, one can conveniently distinguish outlooks toward the national community (e.g., "the German *Volk*"); toward specific political institutions and offices (e.g., the *Fifth* French Republic); toward particular incumbents of such offices (e.g., President *de Gaulle*); and toward the policy outputs of the system of government (e.g., the British *Welfare* state). The sum of individual beliefs, values, and emotions constitutes the political culture of a country. While analytically separate from the total culture, which includes attitudes toward such things as family relations and economic activity, the political culture tends to be affected by general social norms.

Logically and historically, the political culture antedates the birth of any individual, for it consists of outlooks that have been formed gradually through the centuries. This continuity is as noticeable in the persisting divisions of France as in the stable society of England. As an individual matures, he acquires an awareness of the culture through a lengthy process of political socialization. (See Chapter Three.) The political predispositions that a person has at the beginning of his adult life are affected by his exposure to pre-existing and persisting cultural attitudes. It does not follow from this, however, that the political culture ultimately "causes" individuals to think as they do. Culture is a social-psychological variable providing an immediate and succinct description of how individuals acquire orientations that are shared with millions of fellow citizens. But it also poses fundamental sociological and political questions. We need to know too what makes political cultures take the very different forms that they have within an area as relatively compact as Western Europe.

The unity that social scientists necessarily impose upon a political culture for purposes of analysis should not lead readers to assume that there is complete harmony within a society. The histories of 20th century France, Germany, and Italy provide ample reminders that this is not the case. When value differences within a society are substantial, one can analytically differentiate political sub-cultures, such as that of Italian Communists or Italian Christian Democrats. When differences in outlooks are linked to specific political positions, such as that of party propagandist or civil servant, one can also distinguish role cultures. In addition to marked differences between sub-cultures within a nation, across national boundaries men with the same political roles, such as civil servants or soldiers, can have a common role culture.

In their pioneering study, *The Civic Culture,* Gabriel Almond and Sidney Verba distinguish three broad types of political culture. A parochial political culture is one in which people being governed have very little awareness of the central political features of their state. Today, such outlooks are found in significant but decreasing frequency in the Afro-Asian world. In Europe, the consequences of massive 20th century land warfare, followed by the development of the mass media, have made even the rural peasantry well aware of the powers of regimes. A subject political culture is one in which people are aware of the general character of government and of the demands that it makes upon them, e.g., taxation and military service. In a participant political culture, people are also conscious of opportunities to influence government through such institutions as parties and pressure groups; a number see themselves able to influence government. A "civic" political culture is one in which the readiness of individuals to influence government is benignly fused with a willingness to submit to its regulations; simultaneously, the governors of a society are prepared to recognize some parts of life as private and free from government intervention.

In comparative analysis, it is as difficult as it is necessary to abstract a few features of a national culture and let these stand for the whole. The Almond-Verba study concentrated especially upon the extent to which citizens felt competent to influence government. On survey data measures of subjective competence, Britain and America were classified as most nearly approximating the ideal civic culture, with Germany some distance from this ideal-type goal, and Italy more remote. If the authors had studied France, Frenchmen might have shown themselves feeling all-powerful yet very constrained. To rank each of these countries according to one important aspect of the political culture should not be taken to imply that the cultures are similar in the total configuration of values, beliefs, and emotions. There are more than linguistic differences in the ways that Englishmen, Frenchmen, Germans, and Italians think and talk about politics.

In each European national culture, there is a variety of sub-cultures. But very few studies are to be found in European literature utilizing explicitly the concept of political sub-culture. On the contrary, a large number of authors utilize neighboring concepts, some of them very old: alienation, of Marxist inspiration; anomia, suggested by the French sociologist Durkheim; *Gemeinschaft* (closed community), proposed by the German sociologist Tönnies; *malcostume* and *sottogoverno* currently used in the Italian literature; *Weltanschauung*, which is internationally adopted in its German expression; and concepts such as incivism, social trauma, social segregation, and social deviation. In cultural anthropology, A. Kroeber and C. K. Kluckhohn, in their *Culture: a Critical Review of Concepts and Definitions* (Cambridge, Mass.: Harvard University Press, 1952), have catalogued 160 definitions and 7 categories of the word "culture." In cross-national comparisons it is important to be more aware of the functional equivalence of the concepts than the words. The following selections are intended to emphasize aspects of political cultures and sub-cultures that are especially distinctive in each society.

Bibliography

The most important work in the field is *The Civic Culture* (Princeton University Press, 1963) by Gabriel Almond and Sidney Verba. Some themes in this study were originally outlined, with special reference to Europe, in Almond's article, "Comparative Political Systems," *Journal of Politics* XVIII: 3 (1956). They are further explored in Lucian W. Pye and Sidney Verba, editors, *Political Culture and Political Development* (Princeton University Press, 1965). In addition to general theoretical statements, this volume contains chapters on England, Germany, and Italy by Richard Rose, Sidney Verba, and Joseph LaPalombara respectively. Many of the major concepts used in the analysis of political cultures are also treated at length in David Easton's *A Systems Analysis of Political Life* (New York: Wiley, 1965).

The presence or absence of major cultural cleavages within European societies is discussed at length by contributors to Robert A. Dahl's volume, *Political Oppositions in Western Democracies* (New Haven: Yale University Press, 1966). It includes chapters on Britain by Allen Potter, France by Alfred Grosser, Germany by Otto Kirchheimer, and Italy by Samuel Barnes. Especially relevant for a modern-day understanding of the "deferential" side of English culture are R. T. McKenzie and Allen Silver, *Angels in Marble* (London: Heinemann, 1968) and Eric Nordlinger, *The Working Class Tories* (London: MacGibbon & Kee, 1967). Cultural divisions in France today are analyzed by a range of experts in a book edited by Stanley Hoffmann, *In Search of France* (Cambridge, Mass.: Harvard University Press, 1963). For post-war Germany, the best book-length introduction is Lewis J. Edinger, *Politics in Germany* (Boston: Little, Brown, 1968). Guenther Roth's *The Social Democrats of Imperial Germany* (Totowa, N.J.: Bedminster Press, 1963) provides useful historical background to the working class subculture. Village life in Southern France is studied in Laurence Wylie, *Village in the Vaucluse* (New York: Harper Colophon edition, 1964).

The intellectuals have a more important role in European society than in American national culture. An excellent selection of writings on the political involvement of intellectuals and the part they play is

George B. de Huszar, editor, *The Intellectuals: a Controversial Portrait* (New York: Free Press, 1960). Of the seventy articles contained, more than two-thirds are written by European scholars or essayists. The book is highly recommended for an understanding of European national cultures at the elite level.

Raymond Aron's *The Opium of the Intellectuals* (New York: Norton, 1962), first published in French in 1955, is one of the best portrayals of certain types of communist intellectuals, and is, at the same time, an excellent analysis of the alienation of some intellectuals. See, by the same author, *Introduction to the Philosophy of History* (Boston: Beacon Press, 1961).

STANLEY HOFFMANN

Tensions of Growth in Postwar France

For generations, France paradoxically combined governments that often changed their labels if not their policies, and a population that showed great conservatism in its socio-economic system, and in its cultural values. Some Frenchmen even conserved revolutionary political outlooks and pre-industrial or anti-industrial economic views. Since the 1950's, French society has undergone a rapid process of economic development by industrialization, the modernization of agriculture, and urbanization. This has changed France from an example of a stagnant society to an exemplar of economic growth. The actions of government have been considered particularly significant, as a stimulus to growth through economic planning. Stanley Hoffmann addresses himself to a review of the problems of changing structures of power in his review of France in the Fifth Republic.

France's society in the early 1960's is a mixture of the old and the new. The changes which are taking place are the most far-reaching since the French Revolution; the stalemate society is dead. But these changes are too recent to have destroyed completely the old pattern and too sweeping to take place without tensions. . . .

CHANGES IN THE SOCIO-ECONOMIC SYSTEM

The transformation of the old balance of French society, begun in the war years, has been drastic.

Reprinted by permission of the publishers from Stanley Hoffmann, *et al.*, *In Search of France* (Cambridge, Mass.: Harvard University Press), pp. 60–74, 90, 108–9. Copyright, 1963, by the President and Fellows of Harvard College.

INNOVATIONS. If we take an over-all look we find that the combination of "new men and new attitudes" inherited from the war period has made French society much less different from the societies of other industrial nations. Insofar as the stalemate society still had the marks of France's old feudal order, one may say that the final elimination of feudalism is in progress. Let us not decide at this point whether the old values have been eliminated with it; what we can observe is a thoroughly new set of attitudes, which may correspond either to new values or to the need to adjust to a new situation created from the outside even though the old values themselves have not disappeared. It is certain that should such attitudes persist, the new behavior will ultimately affect the values as well. But we are dealing here with a "revolution" which is both recent and incomplete, and values can be assessed only over a much longer time.

What has happened in France has been happening almost all over Western Europe, particularly in Northern Italy and in West Germany. Everywhere, as in France, the percentage of the population employed in agriculture goes down and the percentage of managers, executives, and employees goes up. In the civil service, in business, in professional organizations, even in the military forces, new groups of "technocrats" appear — men who specialize in the management of a highly industrialized and bureaucratic society, men who earn high incomes without necessarily owning much capital.

A hierarchy based on skills and performance is beginning to emerge in France. Expansion has at last attracted public attention to economic matters. Within the business world, a kind of managerial revolution has led to a new conception of profits, in which management and ownership are less tightly fused and in which the firm's power counts more than the owner's fortune. Increasing concern for forecasting has led to internal reorganization of management. The productivity of labor has increased by around five percent a year since the war. Outside business, a revolution in the way of life has begun. An increasing proportion of the Frenchman's income goes for health, housing, and transportation; a decreasing one is lavished on food. The village is less important as an economic unit. The family is less tightly closed: there is growing cooperation between families in order to share the comforts and gadgets of industrial society, and the spectacular "car rush," which has given to France the highest ratio of cars per population in Western Europe, has increased the circle of acquaintances of family members far beyond the village or small town. The spread of television has lifted their horizons. The attitudes toward credit and savings have been reversed. There is less distance than before between ranks and statuses, although there may be even more distance between incomes. . . .

Although these developments are not characteristic of France alone, the way in which they have taken place in France is unique and fascinating. Given the classical style of authority and France's resulting centralization, the change could occur only if the initiative came from the top. The state took over the direction of the economy in 1944–1946 and thus gave the decisive impulse — a major revolution indeed by comparison with the Third Republic's limited state, whose interventions were merely those of a watchdog of the stalemate society. The role of the state has been double.

On the one hand, it has taken direct responsibility for an important public sector, modernizing it and increasing its production; also the rate of public investments and expenditures for family allowances, housing, professional training, school construction, and other "economic and social action" has been kept high enough to encourage and speed up France's economic conversion (the provisions of the Fourth Economic Plan and the budget for 1962 are particularly impressive in this respect).

On the other hand, the state has put pressure on the private sector of the economy to force that sector out of past habits. Here, the Planning Commission has been of special importance, since its role consists of connecting the state with the leaders of French business, and thus transmitting the state's impulse. The state has promoted change by exploiting that very craving for security which had previously slowed down change. That is, the state has done its best to lower the risks of change. . . . Thus, the old practices of state aid continued — but such aid was now serving as a crutch instead of a wheelchair. The incentives include depreciation allowances which encourage businessmen to increase their investments; other tax measures which favor industrial mergers; financial aid to incite businessmen to move out of Paris; priority access to credit; subsidies for research projects; special agreements to facilitate the start of new manufactures; and equipment subsidies in depressed areas. Also, the state has put its own statistical and forecasting services at the disposal of businessmen. Many of the decisions on agriculture . . . were designed to orient the farmers toward production for which demand is likely to increase (such as meat, milk, fruits, and vegetables) and help them to organize a better distribution of their products.

The leaders of French business (and, to a much lesser extent, those of French agriculture) have in turn transmitted this impulse downward. What has convinced them of the need for expansion was, first, the fact that in 1945 the choice was no longer between the risks of expansion and the comforts of stability, but between modernization and extinction; secondly, the push and the incentives from the state's credit and investment policies; and thirdly, the compelling momentum of the state's decision to create a common Western European market. In this last area French business did not give in without a battle; the opposition of the steel industry to the Schuman plan for a coal and steel community was quite spectacular. But the failure of this opposition helped convince the leaders of French business that adaptation was the best part of wisdom. Here again, the way in which the European Communities have gently reduced risks . . . has complemented the lessons of the failure to prevent the birth of those Communities;

for the European "technocrats" have been extremely lenient toward cartel agreements, at least in the decisive first years of the Communities' existence. As a result, the old "static equilibrium" has been replaced with a forward-rolling "bicycle equilibrium," as someone has called it. Planning and forecasting had to be adopted both by the state and by business. In a nation with a rising population and with a growing desire to improve its way of life after many years of stagnation and deprivation and with new outlets opening in Europe, it was no longer possible either to treat demand as static or to consider only the local or regional market. Businessmen have kept the rate of investment high, and a number of industries have pushed their exports considerably. The compelling logic of economic rationality began to win out, not because of myriads of individual decisions of independent entrepreneurs, but because of the machinery set up from above. The impulse was transmitted downward (especially in the steel and electronics industries) by the large firms, on which the state relied; the movement has led in turn to further concentration, in industry and now also in commerce. It has also led to a further weakening of the prewar solidarity between big and small business, for in most industries (with the significant exception of textiles) the bigger firms have been the most productive and the most eager to get out of past routines. Thus, even determined or nostalgic defenders of the old restrictive order have had to give in or give way. Businessmen, shopkeepers, and peasants alike are more dependent now on the national economy than on a mere segment of it; it is striking to hear the peasants' organizations today demand what amounts to long-term national planning of agricultural production, even at the expense of private property.

Another important aspect of the change can be seen in the industrial workers — both their way of life and their conduct. Their way of life has moved noticeably toward that of the bourgeois, thanks to the rise in the standard of living, to gradual improvements in housing, to paid holidays and household appliances, and to the ownership of cars in which to escape from the suburbs on weekends and to experience the "glorious uncertainty" and equality of this national sport, driving. The increasing specialization of industrial tasks fragments the workers as a class and diversifies their reactions to other groups or to the state. The proportion of factory workers among wage-earners is going down. The nature of much industrial labor today integrates the worker's life into the plant; his wages depend on the prosperity of the business much more than on his own individual efficiency; his job security has become a matter of joint interest for management and labor. Willingness to buy on the installment plan integrates many workers into the rest of society. As a consequence, their enthusiasm for strikes and their militancy in unions or parties have considerably decreased; the unions have compromised with employers in numerous collective agreements, including the famous "Renault contract." The social activities of the *comités d'entreprises* have been impressive. There is also evidence of an increasing willingness to change jobs or residence, at least among workers who are relatively well off and who want to preserve or improve their standard of living. Between bourgeois and workers there seems to be even a partial rapprochement in values — the bourgeois having left behind the ideal of thrift and the fear of industrialization or proletarianization, the workers having on the whole given up the apocalyptic dream of collective ascent out of the proletarian ghetto.

TENSIONS OF GROWTH. The changes so far in the old economic and social system have not been easy. Some of the difficulties stem from the very process of economic growth. Three kinds of problems have risen in that connection.

First, the process has inevitably created tensions between "ascending" and "descending" groups. The descenders include inefficient producers of industry, agriculture, and commerce who feel that they are losing the protection of the old society and of its state, and who are obliged to give up what they are doing; this may well mean becoming someone else's employee — a genuine "fall" within the value system of the old society to which they have remained faithful. The "new spirit" in the organizations which represent France's various economic activities has impelled the major ones sooner or later, with varying degrees of enthusiasm, to plead with their members against fruitless resistance to adaptation. Partly as a consequence, dissident associations or movements of protest have appeared — the poujadists, for example, among the shopkeepers and artisans (and among the peasants of various areas), and other groups among the underprivileged farmers of central France and Brittany. There was also the spectacular resisttance of Decazeville's miners to any reconversion which would not preserve the special rights they owed to being miners. The policy of regional development (*aménagement du territoire*) has so far been a failure; west of a line drawn from Marseilles to Le Havre, the average income is smaller by half than the income east of that line where eighty percent of France's industrial activities are concentrated (hence the vigor of Brittany's charge of neglect). It is ironical that the maldistribution of growth has brought signs of a new fragmentation based on geographical unevenness, in place of the fading fragmentation of the stalemate society.

Secondly, even among the ascending groups, tensions appear because of the differing rates of growth among the various prosperous sectors and regions. Thus, in addition to those peasants whose farms are too poor or too small to keep above subsistence level, many peasants are deep in debt because they bought tractors and chemical fertilizers, or switched production in order to improve both their output and their income. These too have found good reasons to rebel. They observe that the result of their efforts is an overproduction which brings prices down. They note that their products are less protected than others (such as wheat and beets) which constitute a far smaller share of total agricultural income but which are sponsored by wealthy representatives of big-farm areas. They find that the antiquated system of distribution penalizes producers and consumers alike for the benefit of a whole series of intermediaries. They realize that the increase of the peasant's income in the past twenty years has remained much below that of the rest of France — largely because this is the area in which state protection has remained far too long of the wheelchair variety. Similarly the employees of nationalized enterprises protest when they notice that wages go up faster in the private sector. Since the state has to watch constantly the danger of inflation, there has inevitably been unevenness between sectors, which has led to recurrent troubles.

Finally, there have been traces of a kind of contest between the young and the old, or rather signs of a push of the suddenly much increased population under thirty or thirty-five years old against a society ill-prepared for them. In the civil service, in politics, and at the head of the main private collective organizations, far younger men than before the war are in control, and this circumstance encourages such a push, rather than making the young men more patient. Thus, there is a movement of young peasants who advocate a scheme for the retirement of peasants over sixty-five and for a drastic regrouping of small farms. Students and professors have vociferously called for a much higher educational budget, for crash plans of school construction, and for state allowances to students at the university level.

Such tensions are not exceptional by themselves: any industrial society which is not ruled by a totalitarian regime is marked, as Raymond Aron puts it, by "querulous satisfaction." However, there are many reasons why in France the margin between satisfaction and general protest is so slim. Without even mentioning now the flaws of the political system which contribute to reducing the margin, one must note that France experiences at the same time the quarrels of an industrial society and those of industrialization.

RESIDUES OF THE PAST. In addition to these difficulties growing out of the process of growth, France is bothered by traditional forces and attitudes which are the residue of the old stalemate society. This is a second vast category of difficulties. Here again, several kinds of problems can be distinguished.

First, there are all the groups which resist change by exploiting privileges of old standing, which the state has been unwilling or unable to dismantle — usually for political reasons. For instance, France's fiscal legislation is remarkable not so much for the huge proportion of indirect to direct taxes (it has been argued that France's indirect taxes are far less regressive than other indirect tax systems) but for the way in which the income tax is levied on small businessmen, on farmers, on shopkeepers and artisans. The *forfait* method — the basing of taxes not on actual net income but on estimated net income, in an amount determined by agreement between the taxpayer and tax authorities — results in a considerable undervaluation of income. Designed to avoid "fiscal inquisition," it saves such taxpayers from the need to keep complicated accounts, but it also saves them from any fiscal pressure to modernize; justified by the underdevelopment of those sectors, it perpetuates their underdevelopment and thus preserves a surplus of inefficient enterprises. Similarly, a celebrated report has recently denounced the obstacles to expansion represented by "closed" professions (pharmacists, *notaires*, millers) or by past laws which give inexpugnable property or tenure rights to owners of commercial enterprises, to owners of real estate, or to farmers, and thus slow down mobility and modernization. Here again, no reform has taken place. As a result, what an official publication politely calls the "spontaneous protectionism" of France's domestic commerce has been kept intact.

Secondly, another residue of the past has been a persistence of social fragmentation. Thus, France's social security consists of a maze of special systems which try to adapt to the peculiar needs of various elements of the population, but also tend to preserve traditional distinctions of questionable usefulness, and increase the profits of intermediaries. The school system suffers heavily from being fragmented into too many compartments; despite recent reforms, the barrier between primary and secondary education has not been removed. Another example is the sharp distinction between various categories of housing — between high-rent modern apartments and low-rent housing, and, within the low-rent category, between postwar housing projects and old houses still benefiting from interwar rent-control measures.

The examples of the school and housing systems point to a third residue: factors which slow down social mobility and perpetuate a social hierarchy definitely not based on technical skills alone. The range of social inequality remains excessively high. Studies of expenditures for health and holidays are revealing. . . . The social security program has not been used as an instrument of income redistribution, both because of the fragmentation I have mentioned and because of the fact that the contributions to the program are not proportional to income. Even housing projects created in order to help the poorer citizens have often been "diverted" toward the middle classes. The most effective and resilient barrage on the road toward greater mobility and equality remains the school system: the percentage of sons of workers and farmers gets smaller and smaller as one looks successively at the higher grades in secondary schools and at the university. This discrepancy is due not merely to inequality in income and the insufficiency of the state's scholarship program, but also to structural obstacles (such as too scanty transportation of school children to secondary schools in rural areas) and to traditional attitudes. The son of a small white-collar employee is more likely to get to secondary school than the son of a worker with the same income, because of the past ideology, among the "consensus groups," of individual social ascent through education. As a result, even though the effects of change are beginning to be felt — the social origins of the new technical executives are far from limited to the middle classes — an industrial worker's son has only one chance out of five of becoming anything but a wage-earner, and two chances out of five of being anything but an industrial worker.

A final residue, resulting in large part from such persistent inequality, is the disaffection and distrust which the industrial workers continue to feel, and with which they keep talking about the rest of society. Though their behavior expresses far less opposition than before, surveys, interviews, and more importantly, votes in political and union elections show that the old resentments are not dead. Grudging resignation and a willingness to accept individual escape into middle-class status may have replaced the former impulse toward "collective organized resistance," but far from erasing a sense of frustration, they are the contemporary expressions of such a feeling. To realize that no regime will ever abolish hierarchical work and consequently to want to escape from it by one's own means is very different from accepting one's present status as a fair one and endorsing a society whose system of education does not appear to create real equality of opportunity. The failure of the *comités d'entreprises* in their economic tasks has kept alive the unions' dream of "management supervision" by the workers but has also shown its infeasibility at present. The fiasco of Gaullist-sponsored schemes of "labor-capital association" also points to continuing refusal on the workers' part to accept the legitimacy of capitalist enterprise — at least on the local level. . . .

THE STYLE OF AUTHORITY CHALLENGED

The traditional style of authority has recently — and almost for the first time since Tocqueville — come under scrutiny and attack. This is an indication both of change and of continuity.

There is no question that the familiar pattern is beginning to show signs of wear and tear. The authority of the parents in the family is weaker, and the other members become more self-reliant. Centralization, though not reversed, has been affected by the creation of regional expansion committees, by the state-supported policy of industrial decentralization, by the procedures of consultation and cooperation which the Planning Commission follows, and by the revival of some provincial universities. As a result of such developments, and also of the economic changes and the growth of the new associations, the role of groups in French society has tended to be less negative and defensive; a switch from mere protectionism to adaptation, from mere resistance to cooperation with public authorities, has been noticeable. The decline of fragmentation has corresponded to the rise of an *économie concertée* which simply does not allow for the kind of semiclandestine independence and separatism that groups enjoyed before. The principal associations realize that their special interests cannot be isolated from those of the other groups. . . . As for leaders, including civil servants in the planning committees and heads of the various economic associations, their role has far exceeded the previous limits of "noninterventionist" authority, but it has not been purely and simply authoritarian either, for they have sought the cooperation of their associates and subordinates.

The system of education, which was so decisive in shaping the traditional style, is being less reformed than submerged by the tremendous increase in enrollment in secondary education, so that several new curricula are now surrounding the old system of essentially nontechnical and bourgeois *lycée* education. In those new programs, there is less emphasis on abstract principles, competition, and individualism, more on sports, teamwork, and "concrete methods." The secondary school teacher is less frequently an *agrégé,* member of the intellectual elite. . . .

On the other hand, the traditional style of authority has proved to be singularly resilient. Although the role of the state has changed from "noninterventionist" to "active leadership," this change has come about in the time-honored way — from the top — and not in response to initiatives from below. Such initiatives have been uneven; they have come mainly in economic affairs, where the pressure from the top was strongest, and have been rarest in social affairs, where the state left little room for them. Survival of the traditional style in society is illustrated by the continued "apoplexy at the center," that is, the apparently irreversible and alarming growth of the Paris area. The old pattern of authority is apparent even in the new planning machinery, since the directives are drafted by a relatively small number of men, composed primarily of representatives of the top civil service and of the business associations; the final say remains with the civil servants, and the participation of labor delegates is often minimal or nominal. France's traditional style is not one which makes cooperation between "leaders" and "public" easy; observers have noted that the associating of family organizations to social security programs has, so to speak, sterilized their representative function. The unions are reluctant to switch from grievances to cooperation. Even in business, the conspiratorial air of French associations has not vanished entirely; businessmen, when making agreements, continue to prefer secrecy to candor. Thus there is a lag of social behavior behind economic structures. Precisely because the traditional style was the product of a social hierarchy inherited from the feudal order, the fact that this hierarchy has not yet entirely disappeared delays the change in authority relations.

But it is in the system of education, despite the changes I have mentioned, that the old style can still be found to reign supreme. Here is the root of the lag. There is still too much emphasis on individual perfection rather than on the common good, too much competition and too little teamwork, too much *culture de la différence* and not enough study of the world around the individual. The traditional secondary education, that of the *lycées,* may be submerged but it is not defeated. It remains privileged as long as the *baccalauréat* is not abolished; and the *baccalauréat* is still the prerequisite to university education and thus to the top functions of society. Therefore this system continues to recruit France's future leaders from a rather narrow section of the population, just as it did under the stalemate society which, however, needed smaller elites than the industrial society of today with its extensive division of labor. Characteristically, it is the fear of arbitrary decisions by the students' own school teachers which contributes to preserve the *baccalauréat* examinations, where cramming is "redeemed" by the fact that examining board and candidate are anonymous and unknown to each other. In higher education, the *agrégation,* necessary for obtaining the top teaching jobs, recruits fewer and fewer people precisely because the boards refuse to lower their standards; consequently, more and more teachers are not *agrégés* — a sign of change — but the *agrégation* remains the most coveted goal and the old hierarchy is jealously preserved, even at the cost of increasing irrelevance. Only a drastic reform of secondary and higher education will be able to affect decisively, though gradually, France's traditional style of authority.

Thus, all the residues and tensions of the new French society point in the same direction: the need for state measures to break resistance and to preserve the momentum of change. Hence the importance of the political system. . . .

. . . Various theories which have flourished in the early 1960's, and which have in common the belief that the age of political peace and quiet could easily be reached because of those developments, are wide of the mark. Nothing remains further from the truth than the notion that economic modernization produces political rationalization and that it would be easy to devise stable institutions adapted to the new society. The story of recent years in France shows just the opposite. . . .

. . . What France needs most is what she has always been least able to breed, and what she must discard is what has been most resilient. What is wanted is a new democratic style of authority, allowing for extended and powerful leadership and at the same time for participation.

In the past, France's fear of authority has severely curtailed the scope of authority and, in the political system, except during emergencies, the intensity of authority as well. These limits she cannot afford any more. None of those residues of the stalemate society which slow down economic growth and social mobility can be eliminated without strong authority. The bureaucracy cannot do it alone, so long as pressure groups — whether an alcohol lobby or a teachers' union — find through the parties a permanent access to veto power. Nor can the tensions of growth be managed by the bureaucracy alone. Nor can weak governments define a foreign policy and defend France's claims. One understands then why the need for powerful institutions, even though they are not the panacea which Gaullism once saw in them, nevertheless remains compelling. It is tempting to contrast *"le calme raisonné de la profondeur française"* with the superficial agitation of politics. It is possible to point out that people's lives are only marginally affected by the political system, that in so far as people depend on the state the bureaucracy serves their needs. It is easy to show that just behind the distorting mirror of politics, old issues are being swept away and France is readjusting to the world. But the fact is that the mirror is what the people see, and the mirror itself becomes a major issue — far more real in people's minds, and just as real for the social scientist, as the growing consensus on substantive issues.

ERIC A. NORDLINGER

Democratic Stability in England

The gradual evolution of government in England from a feudal monarchy to a stable representative government, without the revolutionary upheavals of French or German society, has allowed traditional deferential and acquiescent attitudes toward authority to become fused with democratic values. The respect for social and political authority shown in modern England contrasts markedly with the egalitarian and independent ethos of the American political culture as well as with the rebellious attitudes of French workers. Drawing upon data from a specially constructed survey of manual workers, Eric A. Nordlinger shows how their attitudes toward political authority contribute to the stability, decisional effectiveness and representativeness of British democracy. He suggests that the non-elite's attitudes toward authority are perhaps the most important dimension of political culture ensuring democratic viability.

How can the performance of democratic systems be explained? Are there perhaps certain general conditions that help explain the striking differences in performance between British government on the one hand and the French, Italian, and Weimar Republics on the other? One approach to the development of a theory of stable democracy is to begin with the critical attributes of democratic government, relying upon a deductive strategy at the outset, rather than attempting to evaluate the validity of the numerous factors that have been said to account for democratic performance.

The crucial characteristic of government is its possession of authority, which has been defined by Weber and by most social scientists since him, as the ability to engender an extensive level of voluntary submission.[1] As the repository for this authority, democratic governments are charged with two responsibilities: to govern and to represent the citizens. As a government, it must be able to lead; as a democratic government, it must respond to the wishes of the electorate. All governments need a sufficiently wide scope of authority if they are to govern in an independent fashion when conditions and events demand it. Governments must maintain a broad enough plain of authority in order to be able to make decisions without first having to consider public opinion polls, and even to take actions that are distinctly unpopular among the voters. Without this leeway there is a high probability that the government's effectiveness will be impaired, in turn leading to governmental instability. At the same time, a democratic government must be attuned to public opinion, remaining responsive to the wishes of the non-elite. Otherwise the democratic system would be no more than a façade. Even though a democratic government may have some difficulty in concurrently leading and mirroring public opinion, it must nevertheless incorporate these frequently incompatible activities into its behavioral equation. If the two are not balanced, there will either be governmental ineffectiveness and instability, or inauthentic democracy in which the political elite is able to disregard the non-elite's demands.[2]

The problem is now posed somewhat more clearly. Instead of asking under what conditions democratic governments are stable, we can start by logically inferring the conditions under which these two imperative

---

Abridged from Eric A. Nordlinger, *The Working Class Tories*, pp. 226–247 (London: MacGibbon and Kee, 1967), with amendments by the author. Published in the United States by the University of California Press. Reprinted by permission of the author, MacGibbon and Kee, and the Regents of the University of California.

[1] Max Weber, *The Theory of Social and Economic Organization*, 1947, p. 324.

[2] Eckstein has placed the appropriate label of "balanced disparities" upon these two necessary activities of democratic governments. See *A Theory of Stable Democray*, p. 29. A similar point is made in Bernard Berelson et al., *Voting*, 1954, Chapter XIV. The point that contradictory demands are placed upon a democratic government — the balance between "power and responsiveness" as Almond and Verba call it — also serves as the starting point of these two writers' theory of stable democracy. *The Civic Culture*, 1963, pp. 476–479. By implication, Aristotle makes a closely related argument in Books IV, V and VI of *The Politics*.

activities of democratic systems are fulfilled. The position taken here is that these conditions are to be found primarily within the non-elite rather than the political elite; that when the non-elite acts in a certain manner, the political elite will respond in such a fashion so as to produce a stable democratic system — at least with respect to the developed "western" democracies. Specifically, stable democracy is thought to require a non-elite political culture characterized by a dualistic orientation towards political authority. The political culture must contain a mixture of different sets of attitudes towards political authority: an acquiescent set accepting political authority, recognizing that it is the function of government to govern, and thereby leading to the acceptance of independent governmental authority; and secondly, a set of directive attitudes towards political authority based upon the normative belief that it is the function of higher authorities to be attuned to the self-interested claims and views of reality put forward by the non-elite, thereby setting up powerful incentives and penalties for keeping the political elite responsive to the electorate. . . .

England ranks exceptionally high in the three criteria of democratic performance — stability, decisional effectiveness, and democratic authenticity. In terms of stability, less than half a dozen twentieth-century governments have been forced to go to the country before the expiration of their constitutionally prescribed four- to five-year term of office. In those few instances in which governments were restructured without the calling of a General Election — when, for example, a Lloyd George replaced a Herbert Asquith or a Harold Macmillan supplanted an Anthony Eden — the changes were carried out quickly with imperceptible disruptions to the Government's activities. The constitutional framework has only suffered from two frontal attacks, revolving around the powers of the House of Lords and the position of Ireland, and although they occurred almost simultaneously, even this additional difficulty did not cause any lasting damage to the constitution. For the most part, constitutional changes have occurred in an orderly and piecemeal fashion, without detracting from the extensive legitimacy accorded the constitution. The government's decisional efficiency — its ability to take decisive and independent action when it believes such action to be called for — has not been impaired by a fragmentation of the party system, structural impediments, or constitutional roadblocks. In terms of authenticity (or the *degree* to which the regime is democratic), electoral majorities have with but one exception been automatically translated into governmental majorities, while the decisive decision-making power has remained in the hands of constitutionally responsible cabinet ministers rather than civil servants.[3] It is this exceptional stability of the system that may be accounted for by the non-elite's orientation towards political authority.

In the previous discussion of the political culture approach, it was

---

[3] Herbert Spiro has written of the constitution's stability, the absence of violence, and the efficiency and "resoluteness" of British Governments. *Government by Constitution* 1959, pp. 123–125.

stated that attitudes could be differentiated according to the types of political objects and relationships towards which the actors are orienting their behaviour. The cultural dimension which we have conceptualized as attitudes towards political authority can then be broken down and operationalized according to the four types of political objects and relationships which have been employed in this study: the sphere of independent action allowed the government; the acceptance or rejection of the party leaders' definition of the "correct" position on substantive policy issues; the non-elite's normatively proper influence upon governmental decisions; and the role of the individual as a political activist. By drawing together the relevant strands of Chapters 3, 4 and 5, it will be seen that the English working-class manifests the postulated mixture of acquiescent and directive attitudes towards each of these political objects and relationships.

The scope of independent action allowed the Government is closely bound up with the hypothesized requirement for stable democracy; without such leeway governments would not be able to act quickly or effectively since it would first be necessary to secure the electorate's consent — and that consent may not be forthcoming despite the Government's firm conviction that a decision must be taken. The workers' attitudes towards the Government's procedural authority were operationally defined by placing them in a hypothetical situation in which a Government staffed by the party to which the respondent is opposed believes one policy to be called for, whereas a majority in the electorate prefers another. It was found that approximately half of the workers interviewed (44 per cent of the Tories and 51 per cent of the Labour voters) would allow an "opposition" Government the independent authority to act as it sees fit despite the unpopularity of its policy. On the other hand, slightly less than half the workers (49 per cent of the Conservative and 40 per cent of the Labour voters) would disapprove of the Government acting contrary to the wishes of the majority. In this respect there thus appears to be a nearly equal balance between acquiescent and directive attitudes towards independent government action.

When we examine the workers' beliefs regarding the influence of the non-elite upon governmental decisions, it is eminently clear that the workers perceive the political system as hierarchically structured, in which their role is an "essentially passive" one. Only slightly more than 10 per cent of the workers believe the non-elite to have "a good deal" of influence upon governmental decisions. The vast majority believe the non-elite either to have "a little" influence upon governmental decisions or "none at all." More significant than the workers' perceptions are their normative reactions to their largely passive role, in which the Government initiates and makes policy while the non-elite is only able to hold them responsible in a tenuous fashion. In order to elicit their representational norms, the workers were asked whether the political system "ought" to be structured hierarchically. Among those respondents who perceive the non-elite to have "a little influence" upon government approximately two-thirds (79 per cent of the Conservative and 60 per cent of the Labour voters) replied that the non-elite ought only to have this modicum of political influence. In contrast, about one-third of these workers who believe themselves to have only "a little influence" upon government are dissatisfied with the situation as they perceive it. Amongst those workers believing themselves to have no influence whatsoever, slightly less than a third are normatively content with their political impotence, with some 60 per cent recording their dissatisfaction. Taking these data together, there appears to be an approximate balance between those workers with directive attitudes towards political authority who are dissatisfied with their modicum of influence upon governmental decisions, believing that they should have a larger role in directing the government, and those workers with acquiescent attitudes towards authority whose representational norms dictate a satisfaction with their minimal political role.

Not only do the workers manifest a dualistic orientation towards the Government's sphere of independent authority and the extent to which the non-elite is to be an integral part of the governmental decision-making process, this orientation is also directed towards the leaders of the political parties. Party leaders have been included here even though they are not always the incumbents of governmental positions of authority. For at a minimum they are potential occupants of executive and legislative positions. As such, it is necessary that they are both independent of and dependent upon the non-elite in their role of party leader, for many of the decisions made in that capacity are implemented in their executive and legislative roles. The workers were asked about their probable reactions to a situation in which their own views on a particular policy matter were in conflict with those of their party leaders. It then turns out that slightly more than half of both the Conservative and Labour supporters replied that they would alter their own positions in conformity with those of their party leaders. The reasons given by this group for their acquiescent predispositions did not always refer to the confidence that they have in the abilities of the party leadership. But leaving aside the different evaluational and normative bases of acquiescence towards political authority — a vast subject that would require a separate study — the relevant point regarding the relationship between the operation of the political system and the non-elite's attitudes is that these workers are apparently willing to forgo their own views when these do not accord with those of their party leaders. They are ready and willing to accept political leadership. In contrast to this group of workers making up somewhat more than half the sample, there are those workers making up one-third of the sample who replied that they would maintain their own views in the face of their party's position.[4] These workers cannot be said to be taking up a directive stance vis-à-vis their party leaders since they are not replying that they would attempt to influence the leaders' positions. All that can be said about them is that they are unwilling to adopt an acquiescent posture.

[4] See earlier chapters of *The Working Class Tories*.

The fourth dimension of political authority treated here is the conception of the self as a political activist or inactivist, what has sometimes been termed participation or non-participation. Although not conceived as such in other studies, participation and non-participation may be interpreted as one type of attitude towards political authority. Almond and Verba's use of the term political participation is very similar to the way in which the directive attitude is employed here, both referring to a predisposition to view government in instrumental terms and to act in such a way so as to influence governmental decisions. In fact, the question used in the present study to get at potential activism is taken almost directly from *The Civic Culture*. But as was already noted, political passivity, or non-participation, is not always equivalent to the assumption of an acquiescent stance towards governmental authority, necessarily entailing a respect for that authority. For non-participation may be found together with a thorough-going political cynicism, political alienation or a refusal to accord the governmental system legitimacy. And as Kornhauser has argued, mass apathy may be highly unstable, transforming itself into extremist attacks against the regime during crisis periods.[5] Yet in the case of the English manual workers, it is possible to interpret non-participatory attitudes as nearly equivalent to acquiescent ones given the minimal extent to which the workers are politically alienated and the widespread (if not complete) acceptance of the regime's legitimacy. When we then examine the data on political participation and non-participation, the former being taken as an indicator of a directive and the latter as an indicator of an acquiescent attitude towards political authority, we find the English working class conforming to another dimension of the dualistic orientation. On the basis of their responses to the question asking them how likely it is that they would make an attempt to influence the Government if it were considering a regulation that they thought was "very unjust or harmful," the respondents were classified as potential activists or inactivists. It then turns out that over half the workers (61 per cent among the Tories and 56 per cent amongst the Labour voters) are potential activists; they are predisposed towards participation in the decision-making process under stress conditions, although it is realized that not all of these workers would actually make the effort were such a situation to arise. In comparison, somewhat more than a third of the workers (34 per cent and 43 per cent of the Conservative and Labour voters respectively) replied that they would not bestir themselves in an effort to influence the Government; that they would, in effect, acquiesce in the exercise of authority by the Government even when it is thought that the Government is not acting in their best interests.

Up to this point it has only been shown that directive and acquiescent attitudes are both present in the working-class political culture. But they must not only be present or balanced one against the other, they must also be distributed according to a certain pattern. Stated nega-

---

[5] See William Kornhauser, *The Politics of Mass Society,* 1959.

tively, it is necessary that there should not be a congruence between a society's fundamental lines of political conflict and the two opposing attitudes, for such a balance could easily entail a dysfunctional segmentalization in which opposing attitudes towards governmental authority, and thus conflicting procedural norms, are superimposed upon substantive, ideological and cultural divisions. Not only would political conflicts then be particularly difficult to settle without agreement upon conflict-resolving procedures, they would possibly escalate until even the constitutional framework was called into question. There can either be a *mixture* of acquiescent and directive attitudes within individuals or within the major groupings around which political conflict centres. From the preceding data, it is clear that the two sets of attitudes are distributed in such a way as to satisfy the second condition. One of this study's most significant conclusions is that acquiescent attitudes are found almost as frequently amongst the working-class Labour voters as amongst the Tories, and this despite the Labour Party's "democratic" and egalitarian ideology. Thus at least with respect to the working class, acquiescent and directive attitudes are found on both sides of the country's main line of political cleavage. We have here not a case in which the two attitudes are only balanced within the working class, with the Tories primarily subscribing to an acquiescent set of attitudes and the Labour voters mainly adhering to a directive set, but in which the two attitudes are found mixed together in both political camps.

It can also be shown that the first pattern by which the two sets of attitudes can be mixed is also fulfilled by our working-class respondents; that acquiescent and directive attitudes are found mixed together within individuals. For example, among those Tories who are potential activists and who perceive the non-elite to have little or no influence upon governmental decisions, only 41 per cent are normatively dissatisfied with this situation. That is to say, amongst those workers with directive predispositions on the activist dimension of attitudes towards political authority, only 41 per cent maintain representational norms that are also of a directive nature, while another 54 per cent of the Tory group manifests a mixture of acquiescent and directive attitudes on these two dimensions. Similarly, amongst those Conservatives whose representational norms are not satisfied (who thereby manifest a directive attitude towards political authority), 33 per cent take up an acquiescent position on another dimension by allowing a Government constituted by the party which they oppose to act contrary to the wishes of the majority. In both instances the data indicate that many individual workers do not adhere solely to either a directive or acquiescent attitude, but that a directive attitude with respect to one dimension of political authority is commonly found together with an acquiescent predisposition on another dimension. Although only two examples have been offered, the statement is true of both Conservative and Labour voters with regard to every set of inter-relations between the four dimensions of attitudes towards political authority that were used in this study.

* * *

Having shown how the English working class conforms to the requirements of the dualistic orientation, we now run up against a major problem in attempting to apply the theory of democratic stability to England. The theory utilizes the attitudes towards authority of a country's entire non-elite as the explanatory variable, not just the attitudes of the working class. Yet the present study's concentration upon the working class unfortunately leaves it denuded of any data regarding middle-class attitudes towards authority. There is no satisfactory way to get around this difficulty, and in reading the balance of this section this *caveat* ought to be kept in mind.

However, notwithstanding this gap in the study, there is reason to think that the middle class' attitudes toward political authority do not significantly differ from those of the working class. In the first place, no writer has suggested that such a difference exists; that the middle class is more prone to question and limit governmental authority, for example. If there were such a difference, it is reasonable to assume that at least one or two students of English politics would have recognized it. In fact, those writers who have analysed the English political culture — Bagehot, Beer, Eckstein, and Rose — have all pointed to the procedural consensus found throughout the society; and the consensus that they have in mind is very much the one that is characteristic of the workers' attitudes that have been spelled out in the present study. And in concluding an historical survey of authority and paternalism in Britain, A. P. Thornton wrote that contemporary Britain does "not distrust the presence of strong central government, since the entire evolution of the country — its laws, its liberties, and its assumptions about both — was dependent on that government's efficiency at any given time. It was still habituated to authority, and still — despite the satire from the flanks of the middle-class — inclined to that deference to it that Bagehot had commented on a century before, although more perceptive as to its nature."[6] While this historian remains aware of the many class differences — one could easily say "two cultures" — found throughout British history, for present purposes it is significant that he does not point to a contrast between working- and middle-class attitudes towards governmental authority. Secondly, looking at the political behaviour of working-class and middle-class people there does not appear to be any significant difference in their political style. For example, in comparing working-class and middle-class dominated pressure groups it is difficult to detect any differences in the degree to which they make unacceptable demands upon the Government. Thirdly, given the fact that the great majority of middle-class voters are Conservative supporters, and considering that it is the Tories' hierarchical traditions that form the core of the country's political culture, it is reasonable to presume that these middle-class Conservatives are securely wedded to an acquiescent set of attitudes towards political authority, while Tory

---

[6] A. P. Thornton, *The Habit of Authority: Paternalism in British History*: 1966, p. 386.

notions of constitutionalism and consent would suggest the presence of directive attitudes.

Thus in attempting to suggest that the middle class' attitudes towards authority do not significantly differ from the working class', it can at least be said that no writer has noted such a difference, and that this "negative" conclusion is supported by a few impressions and inferences. But to repeat, this by no means ought to be taken to imply that the point has been established. . . .

A number of arguments have been offered for thinking that a mixture of acquiescent and directive attitudes to authority helps account for the performance of democratic governments in general, and for the viability of British democracy in particular. The importance of the dualistic orientation may be further established by indicating how it is related to three other attitudinal conditions set out by Almond and Verba in their theory of stable democracy. . . . First, it may be that when acquiescent and directive attitudes are present those attitudes identified by Almond and Verba as necessary for democratic viability are also present; knowing that the former is characteristic of the non-elite political culture, we would also expect the latter to be present. Secondly, the dualistic orientation may be functionally equivalent to other political attitudes. . . . That is to say, Almond and Verba maintain that their three attitudinal conditions perform certain functions (or contribute certain benefits) in the realization of democratic stability, yet these *same* functions are performed when a mixture of acquiescent and directive attitudes are present.

Almond and Verba are most convincing in maintaining that stable democracy requires a balance between an emotional (or affective) and an unemotional (or affectively neutral) orientation to politics. "Politics must not be so instrumental and pragmatic that participants lose all emotional involvement in it. On the other hand, the level of affective orientation towards politics ought not to become too intense."[7] If there is only a modicum of "system affect" the attachments to the political system will not be lasting ones, especially during times of adversity and crisis, while a purely pragmatic politics without meaningful emotional attachments may also lead to a dysfunctional cynicism. In contrast, there are the dysfunctional consequences following from an overabundance of emotional attachments: it endangers the balance between participation and passivity; it would "raise the stakes" of politics and lead to the formation of mass movements; such intense attachments to subgroups can lead to fragmentation of the political system; and excessive emotional loyalty towards the elite would lead its members to become less responsive to the non-elites given the latter's unquestioning attachments.

With regard to the relationship between this emotional balance and attitudes toward authority, it could be argued that when the latter is present the former will also be present, thereby underlining the im-

[7] *Op. cit.*, p. 488.

portance of the dualistic orientation in accounting for democratic performance. Given the presence of this dualistic orientation, the emotional balance that Almond and Verba call for logically (and presumably empirically) follows from it. Given the presence of this orientation towards political authority, it is difficult to see how there can be either an overabundance of emotional attachments or affective neutrality. Acquiescent attitudes towards governmental authority are explicitly founded upon a respect for and an emotional attachment to the government. Acquiescent attitudes are then psychologically dissonant with a purely instrumental attitude towards the government; for a person who is willing to accept the government's wide-ranging authority is sure to have some affective attachments to that government. At the same time, directive attitudes towards authority are unlikely to be held in conjunction with overly pervasive, intensive, and unquestioning attachments to the political system and the elite. How is it possible for an individual holding to the normative belief that he ought to be able to direct the manner in which the government's authority is exercised — that the government ought to be even minimally responsive to his demands — simultaneously offer the government and its incumbents his unquestioning loyalty, irrespective of whether or not they are responsive to his interests? It therefore seems warranted to suggest that if the dualistic orientation is present, the balance between emotional and purely instrumental or pragmatic attachments will also be present, for the presence of acquiescent attitudes eliminates the possibility of purely instrumental attitudes while the presence of directive attitudes obviates the possibility of an excessive emotionalism.[8]

This hypothesis is apparently valid in the case of the English non-elite insofar as it is characterized by both the dualistic orientation and a balanced affective set of attitudes, the former ensuring the presence of the latter. Acquiescent attitudes are intimately associated with an emotional commitment to the system's procedural and symbolic elements, while the directive attitudes guarantee the absence of an excessively emotion-laden politics, concomitantly introducing a set of pragmatic attachments to individual political leaders and substantive issues. Eckstein's generalizations about the British political culture emphasize the presence of a balanced affective orientation: "the British invest with very high effect the procedural aspects of their government and with very low effect its substantive aspects; they behave like ideologists with regard to rules and like pragmatists in regard to policies."[9] Elsewhere, Eckstein has arrived at a similar statement by a different path. According to him, the British have a "profound emotional attachment to persons and institutions that are, from a superficial practical standpoint, mere glitter and gloss . . . (and) although they

---

[8] The proposition cannot, however, be stated in the reverse manner; the dualistic orientation is not necessarily present when the affective neutrality balance is present.
[9] *A Theory of Stable Democracy,* op. cit., pp. 30–31.

probably have as much need for emotional behaviour as any other people, (they) can act with sober pragmatism in parliamentary politics because their political passions are channelled towards and satisfied by other aspects of the political system: their ceremonial institutions — above all, of course, the monarchy."[10] Here then is an emotional balance, and a highly functional one at that: affective predispositions are directed towards the systems's symbols of legitimacy and its procedural rules, whereas affectively neutral attitudes are manifested towards substantive issues and political sub-groups, the one ensuring acquiescence towards governmental authority even under adverse conditions, the other allowing for the settlement of conflicts at a low emotional plateau.

Emotional orientations towards politics are particularly difficult to isolate in a survey study. However, at least one aspect of our data directly indicates the presence of an emotional balance amongst the manual workers. The measured affective content of partisan attitudes is seen in the limited extent to which both Tory and Labour voters adhere to a set of negative beliefs about the party which they oppose. Negative attitudes towards the "opposition" party are not transformed into excessively hostile ones based upon strong emotional dislikes. For the data show that negative attitudes towards the "opposition" party are tempered by a respect for these party leaders and a partial agreement with their policies.

Almond and Verba's second condition for stable democracy is a balance between consensus and cleavage. Cleavage serves as the basis for the political competition which is a defining characteristic of democratic systems. If there were not any cleavage, politics would lack any meaning for the non-elite leading to a disaffection from the system, with the elite consequently becoming unresponsive to the non-elite. Yet, if there were excessive cleavage — if there were little or no consensus — the polity would be pulled asunder by the intensity of political, social and economic conflict; and without a procedural consensus there would not be any conflict-resolving norms to which political differences could be referred and settled. In short, a necessary condition for stable democracy is what Talcott Parsons once called a "limited polarization" of society.

What Almond and Verba fear in this connection is that with the existence of deep cleavages the over-arching consensus necessary for the orderly settling of disputes will not exist, and that even if the conflicts are only of a substantive, as opposed to a procedural type, governmental stability would be adversely affected. However, it is highly improbable that we would be able to locate a political system that is rendered asunder by such deep cleavages when the non-elite's attitudes towards political authority conform to the postulates of the dualistic orientation. If there is a *mixture* of acquiescent and directive attitudes, this in itself is evidence of a procedural consensus. In particular, acquiescence towards political authority, combining the belief that the

---

[10] Harry Eckstein, "The British Political System," in Beer and Ulam, *Patterns of Goverment,* 1958, p. 71.

government is there to govern and that it is the government's responsibility to settle outstanding conflicts, is as good an indication as any that there is a procedural consensus. Moreover, this particular type of consensus is especially functional for the orderly resolution of conflicts. The belief that it is the government's responsibility to govern will temper even the deepest substantive cleavages and thereby facilitate their resolution. Thus what we are suggesting here is the functional equivalence of tempered cleavages and a mixture of acquiescent and directive attitudes. Indeed, the latter may be of even greater importance insofar as a practically unchallenged consensus regarding procedural values grows out of it — something which we have already seen to be true of England.

The third variable analyzed by Almond and Verba is the need for diffuse social trustfulness. These feelings of mutual trust characterizing the non-elites' social and economic relations "temper the extent to which emotional commitment to a particular subgroup leads to political fragmentation. This general set of social attitudes, this sense of community over and above political differences, keeps the affective attachments to political groups from challenging the stability of the system."[11] This point certainly makes good sense. However, as was already suggested, acquiescent attitudes also have the effect of dampening those centrifugal forces flowing from especially emotional attachments to political subgroups. Acquiescent attitudes not only presuppose a primary emotional attachment to the political system rather than to any of its subgroups, but they are also intrinsically connected with the belief that it is the function of government to govern, thereby mitigating any exclusive subgroup attachments which threaten to cripple the regime.

Moreover social trust significantly affects the extent to which the political elite is trusted and respected, or seen as deceitful and corrupt. If one's neighbours, acquaintances, and business associates are seen in a suspicious light, how much more so would we expect politicians to be eyed in this fashion, residing at a marked social and geographic distance from their constituents, who are thus more easily able to place uncomplimentary interpretations upon their actions. For the non-elite to maintain acquiescent attitudes toward authority figures, respecting and deferring to their actions and offices, the non-elite must believe in the basically good intentions of the political elites. And these beliefs tend to be rooted in a diffuse sense of social trust.

According to this line of reasoning, there is a close connection between acquiescence and social trust, the former being largely dependent upon the latter. In comparative perspective there is some evidence to indicate that the two are found together in Britain. In order to get at these attitudes of social trust, Almond and Verba employed the set of five questions constituting a "faith in people" scale as developed by

---

[11] *Op. cit.*, p. 490.

Morris Rosenberg.[12] When the respondents were asked whether or not most people can be trusted, an especially striking difference comes to light; whereas 49 per cent of the British respondents said that "most people can be trusted," only 7 per cent of the Italians replied in the affirmative. Or to take another question indicating relative frequency of attitudes of social trust amongst the British — one which asks the respondents whether they agree with the statement that "most people are more inclined to help others than to think of themselves first" — it was found that 28 per cent of the British sample believed others to be altruistic compared to 5 per cent of the Italian sample.[13]

[12] "Misanthropy and Political Ideology," *American Sociological Review,* Vol. XXI, pp. 690–695.
[13] Almond and Verba, *op. cit.,* p. 267.

SIDNEY VERBA

The Remaking of the German Political Culture

The ability of the German people to accommodate themselves to life under political regimes as different as the Nazi Reich and the federal government of West Germany today raises basic questions about societies. The quickness with which the Germans adopted democratic institutions following their defeat in World War II may be interpreted as evidence of the malleability of cultural outlooks. The traumatic experience of defeat certainly provided a strong incentive for Germans to adopt new outlooks. Yet it might reflect nothing more than the persistence of the form of democratic institutions, while the substance of earlier, illiberal German values persists. Sidney Verba's study is notable for the author's ability to consider simultaneously both the practical and theoretical issues of German de-nazification.

For those interested in the problem of the creation of a political culture a study of postwar German political attitudes is a valuable exercise. In the past decade and a half Germany has been faced with the problem of the remaking of a political culture. If there is uncertainty about the future of German democracy, it is not so much uncertainty about the constitutional structure of the Bonn Republic as about the political attitudes that lie behind the Constitution. The government institutions of a stable democracy exist, as do the non-government political institutions. But have German political ways of thinking been reshaped to provide a basis for a democratic political system?

There are several reasons why the analysis of German political attitudes since 1945 ought to be rewarding to the student of political culture and political change. In the first place, Germany is a highly modern, industrialized nation. It has a relatively high standard of living, an expanding economy, a highly developed system of mass media, widespread literacy, and a good school system. If, as some recent students have argued, stable democracy and high levels of economic development are closely related, Germany becomes an interesting deviant case.[1] Second, a study of German democracy in the Bonn Republic can be easily put in a comparative framework, for we have the previous attempt to create democracy in Germany with which to compare it. We may ask, as many others have, "Is Bonn Weimar?" But perhaps the most important reason why the question of German political culture is so interesting has to do with the intellectual history of attempts to understand Germany. To a large extent the psycho-cultural study of politics has its origin in German experience. Many of the classic works on the non-political roots of political attitudes — works that delved into psychological and social variables — were written by men trying to answer questions raised by German National Socialism. One thinks immediately of Adorno, Horkheimer, Lewin, and Fromm, as well as of the postwar studies of German political character.[2] While more traditional explanations of politics in terms of constitutions, issues, and institutions might have been satisfactory as an explanation of the failure

---

Abridged from Sidney Verba, "Germany: the Remaking of Political Culture," in Lucian Pye and Sidney Verba, eds., *Political Culture and Political Development*, pp. 131–154 (Copyright © 1965 by Princeton University Press). Reprinted by permission of Princeton University Press.

Note: The author is grateful to the Center of International Studies of Princeton University and to the Center for Advanced Study in the Behavioral Sciences for providing the opportunity to prepare this paper.

[1] See Seymour M. Lipset, *Political Man,* Garden City, Doubleday, 1960, Chap. 2.

[2] See among others Bertram Schaffner, *Fatherland: A Study of Authoritarianism in the German Family,* New York, Columbia University Press, 1948; Henry V. Dicks, "Some Psychological Studies of German Character," in T. H. Pear, ed., *Psychological Factors of Peace and War,* New York, Philosophical Library, 1950; and David Rodnick, *Post-War Germans,* New Haven, Yale University Press, 1948.

of German democracy in the early 1930's, they appeared quite inadequate to explain the particular type of political system and ideology which replaced it. The explanation of Nazism required deeper social and psychological probing. In studying German political attitudes, therefore, we shall be studying an interesting part of the history of political analysis as well.

It may be, furthermore, that the experience of Germany with the problem of political culture change is more relevant to the problems of the new nations than is the experience of many other Western nations — though whether the experience of any Western nation is particularly relevant remains an open question. In some respects the position of Germany in 1945 resembles that of the new nations. Not only was Germany faced with the problem of the creation of new basic political attitudes; it was also faced with the more pressing problems of rebuilding an economy and a nation. The Germans had not merely to create new citizens but to create a new political and constitutional structure and find a position in world society at the same time. There was not only the problem of changing the schools but of rebuilding the schools. And within the realm of attitude change itself the number of crucial new attitudes that were needed was large. The legitimacy of the old political system was shattered with no new one to take its place, and the fundamental problem of national identity was unsolved. Of course the parallel should not be pushed too far. Germany in 1945 was by no means an underdeveloped new nation. But it was faced with a cumulation of problems in many ways similar to those confronting new nations.

The study of German political culture since World War II ought to be instructive for another purpose. Rarely has a nation undergone so self-conscious an attempt to change and remold politics and political attitudes in a democratic direction. Much of this change began under the auspices of the occupying powers, but it has been the continuing explicit concern of many Germans — particularly German educators — ever since. The study of Germany thus becomes a case study of the possibilities of the conscious manipulative change of fundamental political attitudes, in particular of change in the direction of more democratic attitudes. . . .

Those who deal with the question of the future of German democracy may be concerned with one or more of three different questions. One question has to do with the level of democracy Germany has attained or will attain in the future, the extent to which there are diffusion of political power and guarantees of basic freedoms. Another question deals with the stability of German democracy, the extent to which the current pattern of German democratic government has a potentiality for survival. Thus, in connection with the first question, we ask how good a democracy Germany is; in connection with the second we ask how likely it is to last. There is a third question that also deserves separate consideration: if German democracy does not survive, what is the likelihood that it will be replaced by the extreme form of government created in the 1930's rather than by some more conservative and limited authoritarian system? . . .

Postwar prognostications of the future of Germany were gloomy. However difficult it had been to create a viable democracy in Germany after World War I, the situation after World War II was worse. Destruction and disillusionment were much greater. Furthermore students of Germany had come to the conclusion that the roots of Nazism and German authoritarianism were more than political; that they lay within German character and social structure.[3] In particular the German inability to achieve democracy was traced to the family. Within the family the German child was brought up to expect relationships of domination from authority figures. The father-dominated family (one writer wrote of the mother-dominated family,[4] but the impact on the child was the same) created submissive and dependent individuals. The expectations for the future of Germany were particularly gloomy with respect to youth. They had been raised under the Nazis and knew no other value system; yet this value system and the society based on it collapsed in 1945. And with the collapse came physical destruction and disruption of family life. The prediction for the future was a German youth made up of Nazi fanatics and aimless anomic youth bands.[5]

One was faced then with a picture of a Germany in which a vicious ideology either lived on to create havoc for the society or had disappeared, leaving a vacuum in its place; in which the basic formative institutions of society, family, and school produced citizens who yearned for domination; and in which the physical destruction was so great as to suggest that little energy would be available for political reconstruction. Yet the gloomy predictions about the future of Germany have not been fulfilled. In this paper we shall examine some data on postwar German attitudes in order to describe how those attitudes have developed since the war, to suggest some reasons why they did not develop as predicted, and to assess the relationship of these attitudes to the potentiality for democracy in Germany. . . .

THE GERMAN CITIZEN VIEWS THE POLITICAL SYSTEM

The most obvious characteristic of contemporary German political attitudes — especially in the light of the postwar predictions — is their conservative nature. The electorate has supported the moderate and broad-based parties of the middle, while the more radical right-wing and narrowly oriented refugee parties that appeared to be gaining strength at the beginning of the Bonn Republic have dropped in

---

[3] See Schaffner, *op. cit.*, and David Abrahamson, *Men, Mind and Power,* New York, Columbia University Press, 1945.

[4] Rodnick, *op cit.*

[5] See Howard Becker, *German Youth: Bond or Free,* Gary, Ind., Norman Paul Press, 1950.

strength. The political attitude of "no experimentation" is reflected in a general security-consciousness and conservatism of German youth, the group from which one might have expected the greatest degree of volatility. In a 1956 study of German youth 79 per cent of the respondents reported that they would prefer a secure and low-paying job to a less secure but higher-paying one;[6] and in a similar survey 68 per cent of German youth said they would prefer a job with a lower salary and a pension plan to a higher salary and no pension plan.[7]

This conservatism is reflected in the lack of intensity of German attitudes toward politics. Consider for instance the attitudes toward the particular regime in power. A series of polls taken over a decade indicates a striking stability in the public's evaluation of Adenauer's performance as Chancellor. Both the proportion that considered his work "very good" and the proportion considering his work "bad" have hovered around 10 per cent going neither much higher nor much lower, while the bulk of the population fell in between.[8] These results do not indicate overwhelming support for Dr. Adenauer but neither do they indicate strong opposition. And what is most important — given the history of intense partisan rivalry in pre-Nazi Germany — is the fact that expressions of support are often found among supporters of parties other than Adenauer's own CDU. Perhaps this attitude of neither strong support nor strong opposition toward Adenauer is the same as the German attitude toward the Bonn Republic and to democracy in general.

Since the formation of the Bonn Republic the numbers favoring a democratic form of government or a multi-party system over a single-party system have steadily increased. The proportion saying that democracy was the best form of government for Germany increased from 57 per cent in 1953 to 74 per cent in 1960, though a fairly steady 20 per cent replied that they do not know what government is best for Germany; and the proportion thinking it is better to have more than one political party rose steadily from 61 per cent in 1951 to 76 per cent in 1956.[9] And the proportion perceiving the Bonn political system as

---

[6] *Basic Orientation and Political Thinking of West German Youth and Their Leaders,* Frankfurt am Main, DIVO Institut, 1926, p. 31 (hereafter referred to as *DIVO Youth Study*).

[7] Elisabeth Noelle Neumann and Erich Peter Neumann, *Jahrbuch der Öffentlichen Meinung, 1957,* Allensbach am Bodensee, Verlag für Demoskopie, 1957, p. 135 (hereafter referred to as *Jahrbuch, 1957*). Karl Deutsch and Lewis Edinger report a similar caution and conservatism in relation to attitudes on foreign policy. See their *Germany Rejoins The Powers,* Stanford, Stanford University Press, 1959, Chap. 2.

[8] *EMNID Information,* October 1958, No. 42. If one looks at less intensely phrased responses than the responses that Adenauer's policies were "very good" or "bad," one finds a larger proportion supporting him. Thus, during his tenure of office, the proportion saying they "generally agree" with his policies stayed around 40 to 50 per cent with only a few fluctuations above or below. See Erich P. Neumann and Elisabeth Noelle, *Statistics on Adenauer,* Allensbach, 1962, pp. 40–44.

[9] *EMNID Information,* May, July, September and October (Nos. 19, 28, 35, and 40) 1960, and *Jahrbuch, 1957,* p. 259.

democratic — for instance, the proportion believing that one can speak his mind freely in Germany — also consistently goes up.[10] Figures of this sort are hard to interpret. Which is the significant finding — that "as many as" 70 per cent of the German respondents say that democracy is the best form of government, or that "as many as" 30 per cent say they think some other form is better or they do not know? Information of this sort tells us little about the state of German political opinions.[11] Perhaps more important than the reaction to the word "democracy" is the nature of democracy Germans believe they have or would like to have.

In one of the first postwar sociological studies of German youth by a German, Gerhard Baumert wrote that "when the American army brought great quantities of the basic necessities that the Europeans needed for survival, the notion 'democracy' became closely connected in the minds of German youth with the notions 'food, clothing, abundance.' "[12] This quotation suggests that "democracy" and what has come to be called the "economic miracle" are closely interconnected in German attitudes, and the evidence supports this proposition. It is not so much an intellectual connection between the terms democracy and economic progress. When asked to name the most important characteristics of democracy, less than 2 per cent of respondents in each of five different polls conducted from 1953 to 1959 mentioned economic advancement, and most respondents mentioned various freedoms or rule of the people.[13] The connection between democracy and the economic miracle lies in the fact that a good deal of the orientation of the individual to the state in Germany is a rather pragmatic orientation in which the economic services the state can provide are considered important. In 1947 Germans were asked, "Which of these two forms of government would you personally choose as better: a government which offers people economic security and a chance to make a good living, or a government which guarantees freedom of speech, suffrage, press, and religion?" Sixty-two per cent replied that they favored a government which provided economic security, while 26 per cent preferred a government which guaranteed freedom. (The rest had no opinion.)[14] It is probable that the dichotomy is a false one and that there is hope one would not have to choose, but it is instructive to note that, forced to choose, Ger-

---

[10] *Jahrbuch, 1957,* p. 165.

[11] Less structured questions may be more useful. The more unstructured the question, the less chance there is for individuals to answer with slogans. On unstructured questions the proportion favoring democracy tends to be quite a bit lower. In an analysis of a large series of systematic group discussions, for instance, it was found that about 10 per cent of the statements were prodemocratic; about 67 per cent were mixed, and about 27 per cent antidemocratic. See Friedrich Pollock, *Gruppenexperiment: Ein Studienbericht,* Frankfurt am Main, Europäische Verlagsanstalt, 1955, pp. 139–140.

[12] Gerhard Baumert, *Jugend der Nachkriegszeit,* Darmstadt, Edward Roether Verlag, 1952, p. 198.

[13] *EMNID Information,* January 1959, No. 5.

[14] *OMGUS* Report 74, October 27, 1947.

man respondents chose economic security. When an identical question was asked at the same time in the United States, 83 per cent chose freedom, while 12 per cent chose economic security.[15] Given the state of the German economy in 1947, one would expect answers of this sort, but three years later an almost identical percentage answered the same question the same way.[16] However, this still may reflect more a positive need for economic progress than a negative reaction to democratic government. In 1950, for instance, 58 per cent of the employed respondents wanted a government that stressed economic security, whereas 74 per cent of those unemployed considered this most important. (There is a less clear relationship with income level.)

The fact that Germans tended at the time of the founding of the Federal Republic to view the government as an economic and social service agency rather than as a guarantor of freedom and democracy has led to concern about the future of democracy in Germany. An attachment to a particular form of government based upon the economic performance of that government is too fragile. If the economic level falls, so may the government. Long-run political stability probably depends upon a more general commitment to the political system as legitimate over and above its day-to-day performance. But the fact that at the time of its founding the Bonn government was looked on as a system with mainly an economic task is not in itself cause for despair. Such a political orientation is to be expected in a situation in which economic needs are great. Furthermore it may be that through experience with the political system as an effectively functioning unit — one under which the economic demands of individuals are satisfied — a more general, positive attachment to the political system can be created. . . .

The kind of commitment to the political system that one finds has two characteristics: (1) it involves a certain pragmatic — perhaps even cynical — view of politics, combined with (2) the absence of the kind of intense rejection of politics that this pragmatic detachment might engender. In 1953 a sample of Germans was asked if they believed that the representatives in Bonn considered first the interests of the people or whether they considered first other interests. Thirty-nine per cent replied that Bonn considered the interests of the people first, 41 per cent mentioned other interests (personal interests, party interests, or specific interest groups), and 24 per cent said they did not know. It is hard to say how high a level of cynicism toward the Bonn government this represents, but what is significant is that in surveys carried on in the three succeeding years the results remained remarkably stable. By 1956, 38 per cent of the respondents said that the representatives in Bonn are interested primarily in the welfare

[15] National Opinion Research Center, *Opinion News*, August 1, 1948.
[16] Office of the High Commissioner for Germany, Office of Public Affairs, Reactions Analysis Staff, Report No. 50, Ser. 2, November 30, 1950 (hereafter referred to as *HICOG Reports*).

of the people, 36 per cent said they have other prime interests, and 28 per cent "do not know."[17] Unlike the responses about the desirability of democracy, which did change noticeably even within that short period, the responses that indicate respect for the actual operation of the government in Bonn do not change appreciably. Furthermore the answers about the prime interests of the representatives in Bonn appear to reflect closely the German citizen's own view of what is of prime importance. When asked how they would vote if they had to choose between a vote that would benefit themselves but not Germany, or Germany but not themselves, 37 per cent said they would vote so as to benefit themselves, 33 per cent so as to benefit Germany, and 30 per cent did not know.[18]

The pragmatic and perhaps cynical view of the political system reflected in the above data can best be appreciated in a comparative context. In our study of political attitudes in five nations Almond and I dealt with two types of attachment to the political system, what we call "output affect" and "system affect." The former refers to the level of satisfaction the individual expresses with the specific performance of the government; the latter, to his more general and diffuse attachment to the political system as a whole without reference to any particular aspect. In Germany one finds an expression of satisfaction with specific governmental performance more frequently than an expression of attachment to the system as a whole. This fact is highlighted by the comparable data from the other nations studied. In terms of output satisfaction the German data roughly resemble those in the United States and Britain; in terms of system affect the differences are sharp.[19] The absolute levels of system affect are, however, not what is of greatest interest here. Considering recent German history, it is to be expected that a much smaller proportion of individuals would report that they take pride in the political system of their nation (to take the specific measure of system affect used) than would so report in Britain and the United States. Nor is it unexpected that the nations would be more alike in the frequency with which satisfaction with specific governmental performance is expressed; the latter form of satisfaction can obviously develop more rapidly.

---

[17] *Jahrbuch, 1957,* p. 177. In 1950 a sample of 3,000 Germans in the American Zone were asked: "Do you find that the West Germany Government keeps the welfare of the West German people in view or do you believe that they primarily follow the aims of their parties?" At that earlier date a higher proportion answered that it kept the views of the West German people in view (52 per cent), but the different phrasing of the question makes the comparison over time a bit difficult (see *HICOG* Report, No. 28, Ser. 2, July 1950).

[18] Elisabeth Noelle and Erich Peter Neumann, *Jahrbuch der Öffentlichen Meinung 1947–1955,* Allensbach am Bodensee: Verlag für Demoskopie, 1956, p. 123 (hereafter referred to as *Jahrbuch, 1947–1955*).

[19] For the specific measures used and the data see G. A. Almond and S. Verba, *The Civic Culture,* Princeton: Princeton University Press, 1963, Chaps. 3 and 4.

What is of greatest interest is whether the level of system affect — of stable and diffuse attachment to the political system not based upon performance — is developing out of contact with the specific activities of the German government. Are contact with the government and participation within the political system leading to greater system affect? If so, one can predict that over time the stable functioning of the Bonn government will lead to the development of citizens committed to it over and above its specific performance at any particular time — a form of "rain or shine" commitment that may be necessary for long-run stability. Data collected by Almond and me are relevant here. We divided our respondents into three groups depending upon the extent of their subjective sense of ability to participate in and influence the government. This was done on the basis of scores on a scale of "subjective competence." Those who score high on the scale consider themselves capable of influencing the course of government action; those who score low consider themselves incapable.[20] The question we raise is: does a citizen's satisfaction with the government increase, the more he considers himself able to participate in the government? In our data we find that those who consider themselves competent to influence the government are more likely to express satisfaction with the specific output of the government in the United States, in Britain, and in Germany as well. For instance, 75 per cent of the respondents who scored high on the subjective competence scale in Germany (n:244) reported satisfaction with governmental output, in contrast with 62 per cent (n:233) of those who scored low.[21] Thus the individual who believes he can participate in decisions is more likely to express satisfaction with the output of the governmental decision-making process. The relationship between sense of ability to participate and more general system affect produces a sharp contrast to the above pattern. In the United States and Britain general system affect (as measured by the frequency with which individuals express pride in their political system) increases with the level of sense of ability to participate. Those high in sense of competence are more likely to express pride in the political system and less likely to say they are proud of "nothing" as citizens of their nations. In Germany, on the other hand, the pattern is quite different. There is apparently little relationship between an individual's sense of political competence and the likelihood that he will express pride in the political system. High scorers on the subjective competence scale are not more likely to say that they are proud of a political aspect of their nation than are low scorers. Furthermore, although those respondents high in subjective political competence are less likely to say that they do not know what they are proud of as Germans than are those low on subjective competence, they are just as likely to give a rather alienated response that they are proud of "nothing." In Germany the

[20] For a description of the scale used for these purposes see *ibid.*, Chap. 9.
[21] See *ibid.*, Chap. 9, Table 4.

sense of political competence does not appear to be related to a more general sense of system affect.[22] . . .

In general the data for Germany suggest that whatever attachment there is to the political system is mainly a pragmatic one. The individual who believes himself capable of participating within the political system is more satisfied with the system, but his satisfaction tends to be with the specific outputs of the system. If the hypothesis about the greater significance of system affect for the long-run stability of a political system is correct, it would appear that the sense of ability to participate in governmental decision processes that has developed since the war in Germany will foster the stability of the system so long as the performance of the system remains at a high level. If the performance of the system lags, the fact that some individuals feel capable of participating may add little to its capacity for survival.

These data as to contemporary German political attitudes must be evaluated, however, in the light of recent German political history — and when seen in this light, the picture is quite a bit brighter. A purely pragmatic politics that involves no emotional or ideological commitment is not a firm basis for a stable democracy, but then neither is its polar opposite. What is needed is a combination of pragmatism and deep commitment. Given the history of Germany's first attempt at democracy during the Weimar Republic — a republic torn by politically intense and irreconcilable ideologies — the rather stolid pragmatism of politics under Bonn can only be welcomed. The crucial point may not be the fact that there is little deep attachment to the system, but that there is little deep rejection of it. That Germans have a detached and somewhat cynical view of what goes on in politics is important, but it is more important that they do not totally reject the political system because of this — as Weimar politics was often rejected as a rather dirty form of horse trading. One of the reasons Weimar was rejected may be that it was expected to be an ideal democracy, and when it did not live up to that ideal, the rejection was total.[23] If contemporary Germans can see the blemishes in the Bonn democracy and yet not totally reject it, they may have learned a significant political lesson indeed.

THE GERMAN CITIZEN AS POLITICAL ACTOR

. . . What about German political activity since the war? One can argue that, though the level of activity is in a number of areas quite high, it neither represents a challenge to democracy nor indicates an

---

[22] *Ibid.*, Chap. 9, Table 5.
[23] See the discussion of the critical view held by many intellectuals of the system of parties and interest groups under Weimar, in Karl D. Bracher, *Die Auflösung der Weimarer Republik,* Villingen-Schwarzwald, 1960, pp. 37–44. By setting up an ideal image of a democracy in which the selfish interests of political parties and special groups played no role these writers were able effectively to discredit the parliamentary system under Weimar.

effectively functioning democracy. Voting participation, for instance, has been quite high in Germany since the war. In 1957 it went up to 88 per cent of those eligible to vote, a very high figure compared with those of most nations and a figure even higher than the voting participation in the hectic elections in Germany in the last years of Weimar, when the sudden increase of the vote had serious unstabilizing effects on the political system.[24] But there is clear indication that the increase in voting turnout that has gone on since the war does not represent the unstabilizing radicalization that the voting turnout increase in the late Weimar republic represented. Instead of the increase in votes going largely to the radical left- and right-wing parties, the increase in voting in Bonn has been going to the moderate center parties.[25] The interesting characteristic of the German vote is that, though it is high in frequency, it tends to be relatively low in intensity. German elections are carried on in comparative peace compared with the elections of the early 1930's.[26] In the 1957 election more than half of the voters for each of the major parties thought that nothing would change if the SPD (Social Democratic Party) was elected to replace the CDU (Christian Democratic Party), and a similar pattern was discernible in 1961.[27]

On the other hand, the high level of voting in the Bonn Republic does not mean a high level of effective participation in the political process, nor is it necessarily a reflection of a decline in the political passivity of which Germans have so often been accused. The high frequency of voting, coupled with the low involvement in the results, is probably an indicator of the relatively passive view of the vote in Germany. Rather than a means of control by non-elites over elites, it is considered more often to be an obligation to be discharged. Thirty-one per cent of German respondents reported that voting is one of the obligations they owe to their nation — a figure higher than that in any of the other four nations Almond and I studied. Furthermore many respondents explicitly stated that their obligation to participate in politics is exhausted by the fulfillment of their voting obligation. For instance, a German worker said that one's responsibility to the local community was to "choose a mayor at election time. That's all you need to do. The mayor takes care of everything." Or as a German housewife put it: "The people in the council are cleverer after all. They'll do a good job. You just have to vote for the right ones." Similar

[24] On German election participation see Erwin Faul, *Wahlen und Wähler in Westdeutschland*, Villingen, Ring-Verlag, 1960.

[25] Thus in 1949 the two major parties received 60 per cent of the vote; in 1953, 74 per cent of the vote; and in 1957 and 1961, 82 per cent of the vote (see Dolf Sternberger, "Mutation des Parteisystems" in Faul, *op.cit.*).

[26] See Uwe Kitzinger, *German Electoral Politics*, Oxford, Clarendon Press, 1960, pp. 270–272.

[27] DIVO Institut, *Untersuchung der Wählerschaft und Wahlentscheidung*, Frankfurt am Main, DIVO, 1959. See also Klaus D. Eberlein, "Die Wahlentscheidung vom 17 September, 1961, Ihre Ursachen und Wirkung," *Zeitschrift für Politik*, Vol. 9, 1962, pp. 237–257.

results are reported in a recent study in Hamburg. Over half of the respondents reported that one ought to vote even if one were completely indifferent as to the outcome of the election; and among those who thought one ought to vote under these circumstances the major reason given for voting was that one had an obligation or duty to do so.[28]

The attitudes toward the vote thus reflect the paradox of German political culture and are evidence for the point made earlier that the problems of the survivability of the Bonn democracy and the level of democracy under Bonn are different problems. That German voters are not intensely involved in the outcome of elections and that they do not anticipate radical changes if the opposition party is elected suggest that there exists in Germany the limited commitment to political controversy and the willingness to turn power over to political opponents that are needed for the stability of a democratic political system.[29] On the other hand, the orientation to the vote as an obligation that one owes one's country rather than an instrument that might affect the way in which the nation is run does not suggest a high level of democratic performance. Whereas the notion that the vote may have a real effect on governmental policies or on the incumbents of governmental office is compatible only with a democratic form of government, the notion that one performs a duty to one's country by voting is a view of the vote quite compatible with authoritarian forms.

The combination of high frequencies of formal participation and a passive orientation to that participation is reflected in other data on German political activities. If one compares levels of activity in the United States and Britain with those in Germany, one finds that the more passive and formal the activity, the more similar the three nations are. The greater the degree of active intervention by the individual involved in the particular activity and the less the activity is clearly formally structured, the more Germany tends to differ. Thus, in terms of exposure to communications about politics, information

---

[28] Wolfgang Hartenstein and Günter Schubert, *Mitlaufen oder Mitbestimmen. Untersuchung zum demokratischen Bewusstsein und zur politischen Tradition,* Frankfurt am Main, Europäische Verlagsanstalt, 1961, pp. 36–37. Similar results are reported in a study of students at Frankfurt University. Habermas reports that even among the most unpolitical of the students studied — those who consider political affairs to be none of their business, who know nothing about politics, and who prefer not to be involved — most replied that one had an obligation to vote in elections. See Jürgen Habermas *et al., Student und Politik: Eine Soziologische Untersuchung zum Politischen Bewusstsein Frankfurter Studenten,* Neuwied, Hermann Luchterhand Verlag, 1961, pp. 85–86.

[29] Under Weimar voters probably also believed that the outcome of elections made little difference. But this was because, under Weimar, governmental coalitions were created within the closed confines of the *Reichstag* and were in fact little affected by electoral results. Under the Bonn regime, where the question posed refers to the possibility of a CDU dominated government being replaced by an SPD dominated one, the meaning of the belief that the outcome of the election would make no difference is clearly different.

about politics (particularly about the formal structure), and participation in elections, German respondents report such activities as frequently as, if not more frequently than, do respondents in Britain and the United States. But when it comes to more active and informal participation — such as engaging in political discussion — the differences between Germany on the one hand and the United States and Britain on the other increase. Similarly, when asked how they would go about attempting to influence the government, Germans more frequently mention working through a formal organization and much less frequently talk of the possibility of forming some informal group.[30] One of the sharpest indicators of the passive nature of participation in Germany can be found in data on membership in formal organizations in the three nations discussed above. German males, British males, and American males are almost equally likely to be members of some formal organization. (The figures are 68 per cent among American males, and 66 per cent among British and German males.) But if one considers the proportion of organization members who have ever taken some active part in the operation of their organizations, a sharp difference appears among the nations. In the United States 41 per cent of the males who belong to some organization have taken some active role in that organization; in Britain the corresponding figure is 32 per cent; in Germany it is only 18 per cent.[31]

The passivity of the German involvement in politics is reflected also in the nature of the obligations to participate felt by Germans. Thus fewer German respondents say that the individual ought to take some active part in the affairs of his community than say so in Britain and the United States. In the United States 51 per cent of the respondents said that the individual ought to be active in the affairs of his community — attend meetings, join organizations, and so forth — as did 39 per cent of the British respondents; but only 20 per cent of the German respondents agreed with that viewpoint. In contrast, more respondents in Germany than in the other two nations said that the individual ought only to take some more passive part in the affairs of his community — keep informed, or just take an interest, or vote — (39 per cent in Germany, 31 per cent in Britain, and 27 per cent in the United States).[32] And there is little evidence that this sense of obligation to take an active community role has increased from a lower level since the formation of the Bonn Republic. . . . Insofar as an individual attempts to take some active role in connection with the government, he acts not as a democratic citizen actively attempting to exert political influence on the government, but rather as the subject of a *Rechtsstaat* defending his rights under the law — rights in the

---

[30] For these data see Almond and Verba, *op.cit.*, Chaps. 4 and 7.

[31] *Ibid.*, Chap. 11. Furthermore the degree of participation in an organization has an effect on political activities. Those who are active members of their organizations are also more likely to be active politically than are those whose organizational role is more passive.

[32] *Ibid.*, Chap. 6.

establishing of which he did not participate as an influential citizen. Almond and I found, for instance, that of the five nations we studied, only in Germany were respondents more likely to manifest what we call "administrative competence" (a sense of ability to have one's voice heard in bureaucratic situations) than "political competence" (a sense of ability to influence the legislature and other rule-making bodies at the time rules and laws are made).[33]

In general one finds a heavier stress in German political attitudes upon the more formal aspects of politics. Participation tends to be formal, and knowledge of governmental activities tends to be more of the formal-legal structure of government than of the actual operation of politics.[34] Furthermore Germans appear to be more at ease and competent in administrative situations. Though they express cynicism about the operation of the legislature, they are more sanguine about the sort of treatment they will get in administrative offices.[35]

Otto Kirchheimer has written of the "juridification of human relations" in the German Republic, by which he means the tendency to formalize and depersonalize political relationships — in a sense, to depoliticize them.[36] This tendency toward a dependence on explicit formal-legal rules to regulate political relations rather than on practices that have evolved more flexibly over time — what Spiro has called the "legalistic political style"[37] — is reflected here in the orientation of the ordinary man to his political system.

The other most striking characteristic of postwar German political culture suggested by the data on the German citizen as political actor is the lack of deep ideological commitments and divisions in Germany. The bulk of the electorate votes for the two major parties. The lack of ideological commitment of these parties is also reflected in the campaign appeals. The emphasis in both the Christian Democratic and Social Democratic Parties is upon symbols and tactics that appeal to as wide a range of voters as possible and that de-emphasize social conflict along ideological lines — as the SPD campaign slogan in 1961 put it, "With each other, not against each other." Recent studies of German electoral behavior suggest that the great ideological currents

---

[33] *Ibid.,* Chap. 8.

[34] German university students are more likely, for instance, to have information about formal aspects of the government structure than they are to understand the workings of actual politics. See Habermas *et al., op.cit.,* pp. 54–57.

[35] Almond and Verba, *op.cit.,* Chap. 8.

[36] Kirchheimer, "German Democracy in the 1950's," *World Politics,* Vol. 13, 1961, pp. 254–266.

[37] Herbert Spiro, *Government by Constitution,* New York, Random House, 1959, p. 181. This orientation is reflected also in the attitudes one finds toward conflict resolution. The tendency in Germany is to seek expert and objective means of resolving conflict rather than allowing the solution to emerge from the confrontation of the competing parties — a tendency to find a non-political rather than a political solution. See the discussion of German legal procedure and the procedures for settling labor-management disputes in Ralf Dahrendorf, "Demokratie und Sozialstruktur in Deutschland," *Archives Européennes de Sociologie,* Vol. I, 1960, pp. 50–85.

which in the past divided Germans along religious or class lines play little role in elections. Compared with the politics of Weimar Germany, it is clear that German political culture has undergone a significant degree of *Entideologisierung*.

The patterns of attitudes that have been sketched out above are different from what was expected at the end of the war. There are no strong ideologies, no radicalism, no bands of werewolves, no violent anti-democratic forces attempting to overthrow the government. Rather, if the pattern of attitudes is not what the pessimists expected, neither is it what the optimists would have liked to create. The politics of Germany reflects a pragmatism and passivity to governmental authority. Not that these are not useful and in fact necessary traits for the maintenance of democracy, but unless they are balanced by some degree of political activity and involvement and by some more general commitment to the political system, the commitment to democracy may be fragile. But the development of commitment may have its dangers. It has been suggested that political commitment in Germany has gone through sharp fluctuations. It has at times been very strong and matched by high levels of activity and involvement; at other times, weak and matched by passivity and unconcern. As Laqueur has put it, "patriotism has usually been all or nothing — either ultra-nationalist or nihilist, without roots or loyalties.[38] If this cyclical image of German political commitment is an accurate one, it is clear that politics in the first decade and a half of the Bonn Republic represented a period of low commitment. The essential problem is whether a pattern of commitment and activity can be created to assure that the stability of the system is not threatened by too sharp conflicts or by too intense involvement in politics. . . .

A balanced involvement in politics may be possible. Indications that there may be a future trend in this direction are found in the comparison of the attitudes of young and old in Germany. Passivity and political indifference do characterize young and old alike, but young differ from older citizens in that they are more likely to support democratic values and are less likely to think of political participation as involving essentially the fulfillment of an obligation.[39] But the future level and form of German political involvement are unpredictable because the issues of German politics — issues connected with both the German past and the German future — are so important.

[38] Walter Z. Laqueur, *Young Germany, A History of the German Youth Movement*, New York, Basic Books, 1962, p. 221.

[39] See Hartenstein and Schubert, *op.cit.*, pp. 41, 57, and 63.

EDWARD C. BANFIELD

Amoral Familism in Southern Italy

All societies have a sub-culture of poverty, but the degree, quantity, and political consequences of poverty vary considerably from nation to nation. Of the four lands considered in this volume, Italy has the highest proportion of impoverished citizens, and the lowest per capita standard of living. Moreover, poverty in Italy is found in the pre-industrial sector of society among people living in the countryside or in villages from which men walk out to the fields. The political consequences of this sub-cultural milieu are analyzed by Edward Banfield after a year living in a small village, given the pseudonym of Montegrano, in Southern Italy.

A very simple hypothesis . . . will enable an observer to predict how the Montegranesi will act in concrete circumstances. The hypothesis is that the Montegranesi act as if they were following this rule:

> Maximize the material, short-run advantage of the nuclear family; assume that all others will do likewise.

One whose behavior is consistent with this rule will be called an "amoral familist." The term is awkward and somewhat imprecise (one who follows the rule is without morality only in relation to persons outside the family — in relation to family members, he applies standards of right and wrong; one who has no family is of course an "amoral individualist"), but no other term seems better.

In this chapter, some logical implications of the rule are set forth. It will be seen that these describe the facts of behavior in the Montegrano district. The coincidence of facts and theory does not "prove"

Reprinted with footnotes omitted and minor abridgements from Ch. 5, "A Predictive Hypothesis," of Edward C. Banfield, *The Moral Basis of a Backward Society,* pp. 83–101 (© by The Free Press of Glencoe, a division of The Macmillan Company, 1958). Reprinted by permission of The Macmillan Company.

the theory. However, it does show that the theory will explain (in the sense of making intelligible and predictable) much behavior without being contradicted by any of the facts at hand.

1. *In a society of amoral families, no one will further the interest of the group or community except as it is to his private advantage to do so.* In other words, the hope of material gain in the short-run will be the only motive for concern with public affairs.

This principle is of course consistent with the entire absence of civic improvement associations, organized charities, and leading citizens who take initiative in public service.

A teacher who is a member of a leading family explained,

> I have always kept myself aloof from public questions, especially political ones. I think that all the parties are identical and those who belong to them — whether Communist, Christian Democrat, or other — are men who seek their own welfare and well-being. And then too, if you want to belong to one party, you are certain to be on the outs with the people of the other party.

Giovanni Gola, a merchant of upper-class origins, has never been a member of a political party because "It isn't convenient for me — I might lose some business."

Gola does not think of running for office because:

> I have all I can do to look after my own affairs. I do enough struggling in my business not to want to add to it in any political struggling. Once in office there would be a constant demand for favors or attentions. I'd have to spend all my time looking after other people's affairs . . . my own would have to be neglected. I don't feel like working hard any more. I am no longer young. [He is in his late forties.]

Those who run for office, Gola says, do so for private advantage.

> They get the office, and then they look after themselves. Some take office so as to be able to say, "I am the mayor." But really there isn't much honor attaching to an office; people here don't even respect the President of the Republic. In F—, the mayor wants to be mayor so that he can keep the population down.

2. *In a society of amoral familists only officials will concern themselves with public affairs, for only they are paid to do so. For a private citizen to take a serious interest in a public problem will be regarded as abnormal and even improper.*

Cavalier Rossi, one of the largest landowners of Montegrano, and the mayor of the nearby town of Capa, sees the need for many local public improvements. If he went to the prefect in Potenza as mayor of Capa, they would listen to him, he says. But if he went as a private citizen of Montegrano, they would say, "Who are you?" As a private citizen he might help a worker get a pension, but as for schools, hospitals, and such things, those are for the authorities to dole out. A private citizen can do nothing.

The trouble is only partly that officials will not listen to private citizens. To a considerable extent it is also that private citizens will not take responsibility in public matters. As Rossi explains,

> There are no leaders in Montegrano. People's minds are too unstable; they aren't firm; they get excited and make a decision. Then the next day they have changed their minds and fallen away. It's more or less the same way in Capa. There is lots of talk, but no real personal interest. It always comes to this: the mayor has to do it. They expect the mayor to do everything and to get everything — to make a world.

Farmuso, the director of the school district and formerly the Communist mayor of a town in another province, is earnest, energetic, and intelligent. He listed several things which might be done to improve the situation in Montegrano, but when he was asked if he could bring influence to bear to get any of them done, he said that he could not. . . .

3. *In a society of amoral familists there will be few checks on officials, for checking on officials will be the business of other officials only.*

When Farmuso, the school director, was asked what he would do if it came to his attention that a public official took bribes, he said that if the bribery were in his own department he would expose it at once. However, if it occurred outside his department, he would say nothing, for in that case it would be none of his concern.

A young schoolteacher, answering the same question, said that even if he could prove the bribery he would do nothing. "You are likely to be made a martyr," he explained. "It takes courage to do it. There are so many more dishonest people than honest ones that they can gang up on you . . . twist the facts so that you appear to be the guilty one. Remember Christ and the Pharisees."

A leading merchant would not expose bribery, because "Sooner or later someone would come to me and tell me it would be good if I didn't."

4. *In a society of amoral familists, organization (i.e., deliberately concerted action) will be very difficult to achieve and maintain. The inducements which lead people to contribute their activity to organizations are to an important degree unselfish (e.g., identification with the purpose of the organization) and they are often non-material (e.g., the intrinsic interest of the activity as a "game"). Moreover, it is a condition of successful organization that members have some trust in each other and some loyalty to the organization. In an organization with high morale it is taken for granted that they will make small sacrifices, and perhaps even large ones, for the sake of the organization.*

The only formal organizations which exist in Montegrano — the church and the state — are of course provided from the outside; if they were not, they could not exist. Inability to create and maintain organization is clearly of the greatest importance in retarding economic development in the region.

Despite the moral and other resources it can draw upon from the outside, the church in Montegrano suffers from the general inability to maintain organization. There are two parishes, each with its priest. Rivalry between the priests is so keen that neither can do anything out of the ordinary without having obstacles placed in his way by the other, and cooperation between them is wholly out of the question. (On one occasion they nearly came to blows in the public square; on another the saint of one parish was refused admittance to the church of the other when the *festa*-day procession stopped there on its route.) When some young men tried to organize a chapter of Catholic Action, a lay association to carry Catholic principles into secular life, they encountered so much sabotage from the feuding priests, neither of whom was willing to tolerate an activity for which the other might receive some credit, that the project was soon abandoned.

The Montegranesi might be expected not to make good soldiers. However brave he may be, the amoral familist does not win battles. Soldiers fight from loyalty to an organization, especially the primary groups of "buddies," not from self-interest narrowly conceived.

Lack of attachment even to kindred has impeded emigration and indirectly economic development. In the half century prior to 1922, there was heavy emigration from Montegrano to the United States and later to Argentina. In general, however, ties between the emigrants and those who remained at home were not strong enough to support "chains" of emigration. Hundreds of Montegranesi live in the hope that a brother or uncle in America will send a "call," but such calls rarely come. People are perplexed when their relatives in America do not answer their letters. The reason is, probably, that the letters from Montegrano always ask for something, and the emigrant, whose advantage now lies elsewhere, loses patience with them. The relative absence of emigration, as well as of gifts from persons who have emigrated, is a significant impediment to economic development. Some Italian towns, whose ethos is different, have benefited enormously from continuing close ties with emigrants who have prospered in the New World.

5. *In a society of amoral familists, office-holders, feeling no identification with the purposes of the organization, will not work harder than is necessary to keep their places or (if such is within the realm of possibility) to earn promotion. Similarly, professional people and educated people generally will lack a sense of mission or calling. Indeed, official position and special training will be regarded by their possessors as weapons to be used against others for private advantage.*

In southern Italy, the indifference of the bureaucracy is notorious. "A zealous official is as rare as a white fly," a man who had retired after 49 years in the public service remarked. "From the President of the Republic down to the last little Italian," a landowner said, "there is a complete lack of any sense of duty — especially of the sense of duty to do productive work." . . . For example, the pharmacist, a left-wing socialist who enjoys a government monopoly and is one of the richest men in town, feels himself under no obligation to stock the antibiotics and other new medicines which the doctor prescribes or to extend credit to those desperately in need. . . .

6. *In a society of amoral familists, the law will be disregarded when there is no reason to fear punishment. Therefore individuals will not enter into agreements which depend upon legal processes for their enforcement unless it is likely that the law will be enforced and unless the cost of securing enforcement will not be so great as to make the undertaking unprofitable.*

This, of course, is another impediment to organization and to economic and other development.

It is taken for granted that all those who can cheat on taxes will do so. Minimum wage laws and laws which require the employer to make social security payments on the wages of domestic servants are universally ignored.

An employer who can get away with it is almost sure to cheat his employees. If the employer is a local man, the worker can get justice by appealing to the Marshal, whose informal powers are great. Otherwise the worker is usually cheated. The new municipal building was built by contractors from Matera who paid Montegrano laborers less than the legal minimum and left town owing several of them wages for their last month's work. Since the employer was not a local man, the Marshal could no nothing. In principle the workers could appeal to a labor commission in Potenza. In practice they had to reconcile themselves to the fact that they had been cheated. . . .

Mutual distrust between landlords and tenants accounts in part for the number of tiny, owner-operated farms in Montegrano. Rather than work a larger unit on shares, an arrangement which would be more profitable but which would necessitate getting along with a landlord, the peasant prefers to go it alone on his uneconomic holding. Twenty-one peasants were asked which they would prefer, to own eight hectares of land or to sharecrop 40. One said he would prefer to sharecrop the larger holding "because even if I had to be under another and to work a little harder, the gain would be much more." None of the others thought the gain from the larger holding would offset the burden of having to get along with a landlord. Their explanations showed how anxiety, suspicion, and hate make cooperation burdensome. . . .

> I would prefer a little land of my own to renting 40 hectares because, as I have already said, I hate the rich who sit in the breeze all year and come around only when it is time to divide the produce which I have worked hard with so many sacrifices to grow.

7. *The amoral familist who is an office-holder will take bribes when he can get away with it. But whether he takes bribes or not, it will be assumed by the society of amoral familists that he does.*

There is no way of knowing to what extent bribery actually exists in Montegrano. There is abundant evidence, however, that it is widely believed to be common. The peasants are sure that the employment officer gives preference to those who bring him presents. They believe, too, that Mayor Spomo made a fortune by selling the communal forest without competitive bids. Better informed people say that it is highly unlikely that there is graft in the administration of the commune: its affairs are too closely supervised from Potenza. However, many upper class people agree that bribery and favoritism are widespread in southern Italy at large. A teacher said,

> Today one gets ahead only by bribes and recommendations. All of the examinations are infected with this disease and those who get ahead are the ones with the most drag. To me this is odious. I would do anything not to have to see it.

The principal merchant is building a cinema. Before it goes into operation he must have a permit from the proper authority. After months of waiting, his request for a permit had not been acted upon. "If I took an envelope with $160 and slipped it into the right pocket, I would have my permission right away," he told an interviewer. "It's the little yellow envelope that gets things done. Big and small, they all take bribes."

"Why don't you do it, then?"

"Because I don't have $160 to spare."

8. *In a society of amoral familists the weak will favor a regime which will maintain order with a strong hand.*

Until it involved them in war, Fascism appealed to many peasants — at least so they now say — because by enforcing the laws rigorously, it protected them. Here are some answers given by peasants to the question, "What did the Fascists claim to stand for?" . . .

> The Fascists wanted the peasants to have a better life. There was an eight-hour day and a standard rate of pay. It was a published rate. If a proprietor made you work ten hours you went to the employment office and they would force him to pay the right wage. Now it is everyone for himself, and everyone tries to get the most work for the least pay out of the peasant.

> I don't know what they wanted, but they did make severe laws. There was order and you had rights and duties. You had the right to be paid when you worked and it was a duty to pay workers for work done. They looked after the children too. There were subsidies for large families and help when a new baby was born. Nowadays there is supposed to be help, but it is not enforced.

> I do not remember what it was the Fascists wanted. I only remember that in those days one made out better than today. In those days the worker was well off and not unhappy. Also there were many more aids. Instead, today, nobody cares. If it were during the days of Fascism, the things that happen now would not happen. Today a worker must wait to be paid . . . must wait for the convenience of his employer. Many times months pass without his being paid. During Fascism, this would never have happened.

A landowner made a similar explanation:

> During Fascism, parents were really forced to send their children to school. There could be no excuses, like lack of clothes or books, because the government really provided those where necessary. There was an official who stood outside the school building each morning at 8:30. He gave the children bread and cheese or marmalade and the children would go into the school to eat. School would begin at nine. Now if ten suits are sent to the commune for the children, we are lucky if a cuff of one suit really gets here . . . it just melts by the wayside. The laws are all there, but no one enforces them.

A merchant argued that the consumer was better off under Fascist regulation than under present-day competition. "Cloth was grade-labelled and marked with a fixed price along the selvedge. Everything was controlled. . . ."

9. *In a society of amoral familists, the claim of any person or institution to be inspired by zeal for public rather than private advantage will be regarded as fraud.*

A young man said,

> If I decided that I wanted to do something for Montegrano, I would enter my name on the list at election time, and everyone would ask, "Why does he want to be mayor?" If ever anyone wants to do anything, the question always is: what is he after?

Anti-clericalism is widespread in Montegrano, and the usual objection to priests is that they are "money grubbers" and "hypocrites." In fact, the priests seem to be no more concerned with gain than are other professionals, and their level of living is no higher than that of the others. They are peculiarly liable to attack, however, because the church professes to be unselfish.

Socialists and Communists, like priests, are liable to be regarded as pious frauds. "There are socialists of the mouth and socialists of the heart," a peasant woman explained.

The extraordinary bitterness and, as it seems to an outsider, unfairness with which so many peasants accuse others of hypocrisy is to be understood, in part, perhaps, as an expression of guilt feelings. . . . The peasant is not unaware that charity is a virtue. Not practicing it himself, he feels some guilt therefore, and he projects this as hostility against those institutions, especially the church, which preach the virtue of charity and through which, perhaps, he would like to be vicariously virtuous.

10. *In the society of amoral familists there will be no connection between abstract political principle (i.e., ideology) and concrete behavior in the ordinary relationships of every day life.*

In Montegrano, the principal left-wing socialists are the doctor and the pharmacist, two of the town's most prosperous gentlemen. The doctor, although he has called upon the government to provide a hospital, has not arranged an emergency room or even equipped his own office. The pharmacist, a government-licensed monopolist, gives an absolute minimum of service at extremely high prices . . . and is wholly unconcerned with local affairs, i.e., those which would have implications for action by him.

The discrepancy between ideology and behavior in practical affairs tends to discredit ideology in the eyes of the peasants. . . .

11. *In a society of amoral familists there will be no leaders and no followers. No one will take the initiative in outlining a course of action and persuading others to embark upon it (except as it may be to his private advantage to do so) and, if one did offer leadership, the group would refuse it out of distrust.*

Apparently there has never been in Montegrano a peasant leader to other peasants. Objectively, there is a basis for such leadership to develop: the workers on road gangs, for example, share grievances and one would expect them to develop feelings of solidarity. . . .

The nearest approximation to leadership is the patron-client relationship. By doing small favors (e.g., by lending a few bushels of grain during the winter, by giving cast-off clothing, or by taking a child from a large family as a housemaid), a well-to-do person may accumulate a clientele of persons who owe him return favors and, of course, deference. Such clients constitute a "following," perhaps, but the patron is not a "leader" in any significant sense. In Montegrano, moreover, none of the well-to-do has troubled to develop much of a clientele. One reason is, perhaps, that the leading families are not engaged in factionable squabbles, and so the advantage to be had from a clientele does not outweigh the expense and inconvenience of maintaining it.

12. *The amoral familist will use his ballot to secure the greatest material gain in the short run. Although he may have decided views as to his long-run interest, his class interest, or the public interest, these will not affect his vote if the family's short-run, material advantage is in any way involved.*

Prato, for example, is a monarchist as a matter of principle: he was born and brought up one and he believes that monarchy is best because Italy is too poor to afford frequent elections. These principles do not affect his vote, however. "Before elections," he explains, "all the parties send people around who say, 'Vote for our party.' We always say 'Yes,' but when we go to vote, we vote for the party we think has given us the most." The Christian Democratic Party has given Prato a few days work on the roads each year. Therefore he votes for it. If it ceased to give him work and if there were no advantage to be had from voting for another party, he would be a monarchist again. If Mayor Spomo has influence with the Minister of Agriculture, he should be kept despite his haughtiness and his stealing. But if Councilmen Viva and Lasso can get a larger project than the mayor can get, or if they can get one quicker, then down with him.

13. *The amoral familist will value gains accruing to the community only insofar as he and his are likely to share them. In fact, he will vote against measures which will help the community without helping him because, even though his position is unchanged in absolute terms, he considers himself worse off if his neighbors' position changes for the better. Thus it may happen that measures which are of decided general*

benefit will provoke a protest vote from those who feel that they have not shared in them or have not shared in them sufficiently.

In 1954, the Christian Democratic Party showed the voters of Basso that vast sums had been spent on local public works. Nevertheless the vote went to the Communists. There are other reasons which help to account for the vote (the Christian Democratic candidate was a merchant who would not give credit and was cordially disliked and distrusted), but it seems likely that the very effectiveness of the Christian Democratic propaganda may have helped to cause its defeat. Seeing what vast sums had been expended, the voters asked themselves: Who got it all? Why didn't they give me my fair share?

No amoral familist ever gets what he regards as his fair share.

14. *In a society of amoral familists the voter will place little confidence in the promises of the parties. He will be apt to use his ballot to pay for favors already received (assuming, of course, that more are in prospect) rather than for favors which are merely promised.* ...

The principle of paying for favors received rather than for ones merely promised gives a great advantage to the party in power, of course. Its effect, however, is often more than offset by another principle, as follows:

15. *In a society of amoral familists it will be assumed that whatever group is in power is self-serving and corrupt. Hardly will an election be over before the voters will conclude that the new officials are enriching themselves at their expense and that they have no intention of keeping the promises they have made. Consequently, the self-serving voter will use his ballot to pay the incumbents not for benefits but for injuries, i.e., he will use it to administer punishment.*

Even though he has more to gain from it than from any other, the voter may punish a party if he is confident that it will be elected despite his vote. The ballot being secret, he can indulge his taste for revenge (or justice) without incurring losses. (Of course there is some danger that too many will calculate in this way, and that the election will therefore be lost by error.) ...

16. *Despite the willingness of voters to sell their votes, there will be no strong or stable political machines in a society of amoral familists. This will be true for at least three reasons: (a) the ballot being secret, the amoral voter cannot be depended upon to vote as he has been paid to vote; (b) there will not be enough short-run material gain from a machine to attract investment in it; and (c) for reasons explained above, it will be difficult to maintain formal organization of any kind whatever.*

Prato says "Yes" to all who ask for his vote. Since they cannot trust him to vote as he promises, none of the parties will offer to buy his vote. The pasta and sugar that are distributed by the parties are goodwill offerings rather than bribes. The amounts given are, of course, trivial in comparison to what would be paid if there were some way of enforcing the contract.

17. *In a society of amoral familists, party workers will sell their*

services to the highest bidders. Their tendency to change sides will make for sudden shifts in strength of the parties at the polls.

The sudden conversion of the secretary of the Montegrano branch of the Monarchist Party to Communist occurred because Monarchist headquarters in Naples was slow in paying him for his services. When he turned Communist, the Monarchists made a settlement. He then returned to his duties as if nothing had happened.

ALESSANDRO PIZZORNO

Amoral Familism and Historical Marginality

The outside observer — whether an American in Europe or a European in America — often has special insights to contribute to the understanding of political culture. What a native scholar regards as normal, because he himself learned to think in this manner, may strike a visiting scholar as puzzling or unique. This advantage, even when supplemented by lengthy periods of time spent as a participant-observer in a foreign society, inevitably involves limitations too. The following discussion of Edward Banfield's reactions to Italy, by the Italian sociologist Alessandro Pizzorno, illustrates how differences in cultural backgrounds will themselves affect the interpretations of social scientists.

Understandably enough, the model of amoral familism has not been too successful in Italy and has, instead, been received either with severe criticism, such as that of Gilberto Marselli,[1] or with silence and

Reprinted by permission of the author from *International Review of Community Development* XV: (1966), pp. 55–66.

[1] Gilberto A. Marselli, "American Sociologists and Italian Peasant Society: With Reference to the Book of Banfield," *Sociologia Ruralis*, III, 4, 1965.

indifference. Silence and indifference have been the attitude of most of the intellectuals interested in the *"Mezzogiorno."* This attitude cannot be explained so much by the severe judgment implicit in Banfield's interpretations as in the ambiguity of the scientific genus propounded in *The Moral Basis of a Backward Society.*

The book is in fact two things: the description of a concrete case and the presentation of a theoretical model. The first aspect is of most interest in Italy, and it has been criticized by Marselli, for example, for certain inexact statements or for lack of familiarity with the overall picture of southern culture, and especially with its historical precedents. An indifferent attitude has been taken by others, because the description of Montegrano has contributed little to the stream of hypotheses which have arisen around the southern question.

But the other aspect, the presentation of a theoretical model, was a more ambitious attempt, and more worthy of reply. The presentation of the model has been damaged by a contaminating mixture of theory and description, and by the lack of a satisfactory analysis that would unite and justify the various elements of the model. But this is secondary. The important point is that this idea of amoral familism continues to be discussed,[2] and there is no doubt that it has points of reference in reality. So can we make this a correct and useful working tool? Is it capable of explaining a set of facts in a satisfactory way? That is what I propose to analyze in this article.

The central point of Banfield's model can be expressed in this way: the Montegranians act as though they were following this rule, "Maximize the material, short-run advantage of the nuclear family; assume that all others will do likewise."[3] In other words, they do not have altruistic motivations, and they do not suppose that others have them either. I imagine Banfield would agree with us if we deduce, by implication, that a Montegranian would not make an appeal to the humanity of the butcher, the wine merchant or the baker, but would appeal to their egoism and the sheer advantage these would derive from supplying him with meat (on the rare occasions that he is able to buy it), wine or bread. If Banfield thinks this is really the case of the Montegranians, that they place no confidence in the generosity and humanity of others, but only in their egoism, we would say that — since these words are taken from Adam Smith (*The Wealth of Nations*, Cannan ed., New York, 1937, p. 14), and Adam Smith uses them to describe

---

[2] A recent case of an attempt to apply the concept of amoral familism to the study of a rural community is that of J. Galtung: "The Structure of Traditionalism: A Case Study from Western Sicily," *Journal of International Affairs,* XIX, 2, 1965. But Galtung confines himself to drawing an index from Banfield's conception of familism, of which he then measures the degree in various social groups within the community studied: and, rightly, he discards the interpretative model entirely.

[3] Edward Banfield, *The Moral Basis of a Backward Society* (Glencoe: The Free Press, 1958), p. 85. In successive citations, the page of this edition will be directly indicated in the text of the article.

the English society of his time — the Montegranian seems to be quite similar to a member of the British middle-class of the 18th century, when capitalism was flourishing.

Is this being a bit malicious? Polemically speaking, I would be tempted to say no, and gather other citations from Banfield that would reinforce this argument, which, as we shall see, is not as absurd as it might seem. Rather, it can be by-passed with the aid of two almost undetected phrases that enter into Banfield's definition, when he speaks of *material* advanges and of *short-run* advantages. We must therefore deduce that the man from Montegrano is different from Smith's "economic man," because of the fact that the advantages pursued by him are material and short-run. Banfield is probably not aware of the discriminatory value of these two adjectives, since he does not bother to define them; he assumes that they will be intuitively understood. My intuition, assisted by examples from Banfield's book, tells me that by *material* is quite probably meant *relative to consumption:* therefore, material advantages would be those that allow an increase in consumption. That explains why the nuclear family appears as the social unit of reference, that is, of *identification* of the individual, inasmuch as it is the seat at which consumption is carried out. On the other hand, one can depend less on intuition when it comes to evaluating whether the advantage is short-run or not. However, from the rest of the analysis, it seems clear that it is not a question of a temporal short-run, but a logical short-run, if such a term can be used. One who thinks only of his own short-run advantages is not so much incapable of deferring short-run consumption in order to have a larger amount of future consumption (incapable of saving, for example; or, paradoxically, incapable of waiting for the fruits of his labors from one agricultural season to another, etc.) as he is incapable of foreseeing the favorable effects of such action on his part, which can arise from a complex mechanism due to a certain chain of repercussions. I believe that Banfield would have to accept these definitions for the two terms used by him, and which I emphasize as being crucial for distinguishing the amoral familist from the normal, middle-class economic man.

However, if this be the case, a large part of the actions carried out by the Montegranians which he describes, and which, according to him, his model should completely account for, *cannot* be included in the category of a search for material advantages, that is, relative to an increase in material for consumption. Then, almost none of the actions described by him — or, to express it in a better way, the entire situation in Montegrano as he sees it — fits into the category of incapacity to foresee future effects of a given short-run action.

With regard to the first statement, we need only remember that every family in Montegrano is afraid of being cursed and of being the object of other families' hostility. It is clear that, at least in the short-run, curses heaped upon a family cannot in any way diminish its consumption of material goods. And if such an action could diminish it in the future (something that would not be easy to prove), the ability to calculate the long-run effects of a certain action on one's material interests would be developed in a very refined way in the Montegranians, in comparison to the known ability of a normal middle-class resident of a large modern city.

With regard to the second statement, no subtle reasoning is necessary; one only needs to read the author. In the first chapter, he indicates the problem which gives rise, according to him, to the need for suggesting a new interpretative model. This is the problem: the Montegranians do not do what they could in order to improve living conditions. And precisely: "No newspaper is published in Montegrano"; "none of the members [of the local 'circle'] has ever suggested that it concern itself with community affairs or that it undertake a 'project'"; "there are no organized voluntary charities in Montegrano"; "none of the many half-employed stone masons has ever given a day's work" to repairing the girls' orphanage maintained by the nuns; in addition, the Montegranians do not exert an organized pressure on the authorities for the scope of obtaining measures in their favor, such as road and school improvements, and the like.

We cannot say that this is an impressive list of things that the Montegranians could do and do not do, but we shall take it into consideration just the same. Let us pose two questions: Could the Montegranians do these things? If they did them, would they be useful to them?

The first question refers mostly to the matter of pressures that the Montegranians should bring to bear on the authorities for the purpose of obtaining measures favorable to their community. Here, it is worthwhile to discuss this matter more generally and also with reference to other studies done in Italy by Americans. In Italy, as in Germany, France and other countries with a Roman juridical tradition in contrast to Anglo-Saxon countries, administrative law does not consider negotiations between private citizen and public administrator for the purpose of establishing reciprocal interests in a given measure. Administrative order in these countries is an equalitarian victory obtained by the centralized authorities against particularism and possible private privileges. This has naturally led to the affirmation of the concept of the common good in a version that is, let us say, authoritarian. Direct relations between citizen or group of citizens and administrator is not provided for, because of the consideration that if a measure more favorable to the interests of that single private citizen could arise from this relation, something could also result to injure other unrepresented private interests.

One could say that to consider the needs of private citizens, in Italy, as in other countries with an analogous legal system, is not regarded as a praiseworthy quality of the administrator, and, on the contrary, it could be regarded as the first step to corruption. Is it good or bad that this is so? I should say that the reply depends on the aims of a legal system, and, therefore, depends on the social conditions within which this system operates. It can be noted that the opposite ideal system (Anglo-Saxon) presumes that *all interests* are capable of representing themselves with the public administration more or less in the same way; and in any case, that the natural functioning of a civil society tends to increase the occasions for diminishing unequal representation between interested parties. On the other hand, the European-type system assumes that some interested parties are better able to represent themselves and others less able to. Consequently, public administration has the job of bringing equality to the maximum possible level where inequality naturally exists and where the natural functioning of a civilized society does *not* increase opportunities for the emergence of equality, but perhaps has the opposite effect. The weakness in the Anglo-Saxon administrative concept is probably that of presuming an ideal functioning of civil society (the very supposition that is implicit in the Tocquevillian hypothesis that Banfield brought with him across the Atlantic to Montegrano). The weakness in the European administrative concept is that of presuming interventional powers for the administration which, in two ways, one is tempted to call "Napoleonic." Actually, the spirit — in extreme cases, such as those probably of southern Italy — remains largely pre-Napoleonic, and the administration is often too willing to listen to and yield to interests of privileged groups and individuals.

However things may be, it is clear that the Montegranians have nothing to do with this, and neither does amoral familism. If the public officials listen to anyone, they do so because of his influence. Even if the Montegranians busied themselves with public improvements, the officials would not listen to them, and they would have every right not to do so. Well-founded arguments for this attitude are not lacking: the decision to rebuild a school or a road at Montegrano cannot be made solely because the Montegranians think they need this and because they form an organization to further this cause. During recent years, events of this nature are very numerous in Italy, and the chaos of public works projects in the south bear eloquent witness of this fact: schools have been built in villages that are rapidly being depopulated, roads built where they were not needed as badly as in other areas, numerous useless public works projects carried out solely to please a given zone. All this has happened precisely because the citizens of a certain town busied themselves *too* much; they had a local member of Parliament or a priest who was a friend of a minister's brother, or an official of the Farmers' Union paid a visit to the town, etc. If Montegrano had done none of this at the time Banfield knew it (but immediately afterward they succeeded in getting a hospital), it must be considered an anomalous case in the *clientela* (patronage) system of southern Italy. If Banfield had been in a village in which roads and hospitals had been constructed, due to the initiative of a local member of Parliament, would he have deduced that amoral familism did not exist there?

The discussion takes on an entirely different tone if one argues from the point of view that the Montegranians would have had to levy taxes on themselves and then decide autonomously how to spend the accumulated funds. Naturally, at this point, it would have been necessary to calculate exactly, with all the figures available, the possibility of fiscal operations of this nature. Banfield does not make any such calculations.

But the real answer is in the last chapter of the book, where the author draws his conclusions. Our second question was: if the Montegranians were to act, would this be to their advantage? Here is what Banfield says: "If all of the measures that have been suggested here were pursued actively and effectively, there would be no dramatic improvement in the economic position of the village. These measures would lighten somewhat the heavy burden of humiliation which the peasant bears and this might dissipate the grim melancholia — *la miséria* — which has been the fixed mood of the village for longer than anyone can remember. But even with humiliation gone, hunger, fatigue, and anxiety would remain." In another part, he writes: "The Montegrano economy would not develop dramatically even if the villagers cooperated like bees." And again: "At best, however, such developments would have little impact on the poverty of the village."

So what then? The problem arose from the observation that the Montegranians do not do certain things that could lead to an improvement in their collective conditions, and, therefore, a new theoretical model was needed to interpret this otherwise incomprehensible fact. Now we become aware of the fact that even if the Montegranians did everything suggested, and the prefects, the government, etc., did many others, even if everything humanly possible was done, the conditions in Montegrano would not improve. Consequently, the Montegranians are right in not doing anything, because no one is silly enough to do things that serve no purpose! Community action is lacking, not because the bacillus of amoral familism dwells in the Montegranians, which impedes them from understanding the advantages of such action, but simply because they have arrived at the same conclusions as the political scientist from Harvard and Chicago: "There is nothing that can be done in Montegrano." And they have reached this conclusion without elaborating any particular theoretical model, but solely by thinking rationally.

"Why can nothing be done in Montegrano?" is, then, the question we should ask ourselves, and not "Why don't the Montegranians form an association to improve conditions in their community?" as Banfield asks. The latter question is not difficult to answer: because it would serve no purpose. Instead, in trying to answer the former, we shall obviously discard the original — but wrong — answer: "Because the population is made up of amoral familists." However, our question is somewhat imprecise, and the imprecise term is *Montegrano* itself. Is the object *Montegrano* a significant limit (I do not say "representative") for study? Is Montegrano a *community*, as Banfield implies throughout the study and, paradoxically, tries to deny throughout the study? There are two cases, in fact: either (1) Montegrano is a community, in which case the entire matter of amoral familism goes up in smoke, together with the assumption that no link of solidarity and no social structure between the State and the nuclear family exist, since a *community*, by definition, is a structure wider than the family and more restricted than the State that inserts itself between them when it exists; or (2) Montegrano is not a community — but only an aggregate of families within the confines of an administrative division — and thus it is not clear, first of all, what the study unit is and what could be learned from within an administrative division, instead of analyzing a real social structure. In the second place, why should the Montegranians trouble themselves to act as members of a community to the advantage of an administrative division?

I am not in search of paradoxes or ironies here, either. We shall see later on that Montegrano is not a community (or it is in the process of losing this status); therefore, it is no longer a significant social structure. And the Montegranians have understood this better than Banfield. For this reason, also, they feel it is not worth the effort to do anything for Montegrano, as Montegrano, per se.

Then, the question we must ask ourselves becomes: "Why can nothing be done under similar conditions?" And we must particularly ask of the researcher what these conditions are.

Banfield gives us a list. Here it is: (a) frightful misery; (b) degrading humiliation of manual laborers within a given system of class relationships; (c) high mortality rate — at least up to a short time ago — and, therefore, an existence impregnated with the anxiety of premature death; (d) absence of the extended family and reduction in the relationships of solidarity to include only the nuclear family; (e) rearing of children founded essentially on alternating rewards and punishments that are not justified by coherent principles. As can be seen, these conditions are fairly heterogeneous, and Banfield's model does not supply us with any organizing principle. In addition, although Banfield recognizes the importance of the first two, he abandons them at a certain point in order to concentrate on the other three, which seem to be systematically connected, and which constitute, precisely, the syndrome of amoral familism. It is not clear whether he does this because he believes these are the independent variables, or simply because they seem to be the most original variables, and they allow him to present a novel interpretation. In some passages, the justification seems to lie in the fact that amoral familism can be the strategic variable. The strategic variable is that variable that lends itself to manipulation, the one that can be subjected to operative intervention, and the one that can be most easily modified in order to modify the system. But later on, this very point, which seemed obvious to many at the first glance, appears to be impossible: modification of the ethos of amoral familism is more difficult than changing any other. In fact, this seems to persist even after abolishing the two objective factors concerned: poverty and high mortality rate.

. . . The essential conditions that make things as they are, are not those indicated by Banfield, or not those alone. There is at least one more, one which can account for many of the phenomena seen in Montegrano. Not that the conditions indicated by Banfield are irrelevant. With regard to the high mortality rate, the anxiety of death that is reflected in the culture, for example, Banfield's observations are very penetrating. Also, the results of the TAT seem to be very fitting. The fact that apprehensiveness about death is stronger where an extended family does not exist is also a valid observation. But to conclude from this, even hypothetically, that the absence of the extended family is the factor that inhibits certain people from overcoming miserable conditions and traditional class subjection is too far-reaching. In any case, an explanation should be given as to why families are not somewhat more extended at Montegrano. If, as Banfield says: "the answer is perhaps to be found principally in the circumstances of land tenure," amoral familism is logically reduced to a variable dependent on class relationships. If, as Banfield seems to imply in other points, the institution of the extended family does not develop because of the Montegranians' small-family egoism, we find ourselves in a logically vicious circle.

The problem of the effect that the presence or absence of the extended-family tradition (patriarchal or otherwise) can have on the social development and organization should not be overlooked, however. Banfield does not treat this problem adequately, probably because he did not have enough material for comparison. In addition (but I am guessing now, because I do not know the specific situation analyzed), it seems to me that Banfield did not follow up all the clues, which come out every now and then in the book, that would have allowed him to trace wider forms of solidarity than those of the nuclear family. Those who are familiar with southern Italy know the importance even now of the bonds with godparents (and ten years ago they were even stronger). It is true that their function is that of maintaining a bridge between the upper and lower classes for the purpose of avoiding breaks and resentments that could become dangerous. But the fact remains that it is not an irrelevant circumstance to be someone's godfather in a town of peasants, and it can constitute the foundation for a type of solidarity which, in turn, leads to economic or political consequences. The same can be said for the ties of clientela. It seems that the clientela does not exist at Montegrano. Perhaps this is so. But is Banfield sure that certain facts of political solidarity, certain sudden fluctuations in votes gained by one party or another, cannot be explained on the basis of an underlying framework of kinship, and thus on the basis of an implicit solidarity that cannot be traced in everyday actions or declarations, but which operates in particular circumstances, such as those of political action? Moreover, it is not unrealistic to advance the hypothesis that extended-family ties in southern Italy, if they do not have an economic function (and this is the situation observed in Montegrano), do, however, have a certain political importance. Extended-family ties, comparatico (relationships with godparents), and paternalistic ties with landowners were the ingredients with which the first web of clientela was woven, that prepolitical one which served to isolate and control the peasant population, forcing them into contact with the State by the sole means of property owners and lawyers. It is a fact that kinship and comparatico are, in such situations, the only comprehensible categories of extra-individual action, making them raw material for elementary and pre-party political action. It is too bad that these questions have never been systematically studied in Italy.[4] In any case, in order to face them, it does not seem productive to begin with the hypothesis that conflicts between brothers, hostility of married children toward the paternal family, absence of economic cooperation, are enough to rule out consideration of the role that kinships, natural or acquired, can play in the social life of peasant populations. An analogous hypothesis was also developed, contemporaneously with and independent of Banfield, by Luca Pinna,[5] with suggestive references to the consequences that the principle of equality among brothers who leave the paternal home has on both the economy and culture in Sardinia. But here again, the theory that solidarity ties do not exist outside the nuclear family was expressed in extreme terms. Here, also, the empirical evidence is not sufficient. Besides, there is unanimous opinion that the political importance of kinship ties, especially in Sardinia, is still very strong.

. . . What does Banfield tell us about friendship ties? Twenty-three Montegranians, asked to choose between a friend that "is avaricious but loyal" and one that "is generous but not especially loyal," prefer the former, as compared to two who prefer the latter. This is a surprising result in a population of amoral familists. How can it be explained, unless we assume that ties of friendship exist in Montegrano that are more important than the egoistic benefits which can be derived from a generous but not especially loyal friend? This seems to be confirmed by another result of the questionnaire: between a friend that "is pleasant and amiable but not steadfast" and one that "is a steadfast friend but often irritable and unpleasant," why should not an amoral familist, who feels no solidarity outside the family, choose the former? Instead, only seven choose it, as compared to eighteen who choose the second.

All this permits us to conclude: (a) that the profile of this society, which presumably exists in a void of sociability between the natural and extremely restricted solidarity of the nuclear family and the order imposed by State and Church, could probably be corrected by working out tenuous forms of intermediate solidarity — friendship, comparatico

---

[4] A rough theoretical discussion of the problem, with a bibliography, can be found in Eric R. Wolf's: "Kinship, Friendship, and Patron-Client Relations in Complex Societies," collected in *The Social Anthropology of Complex Societies,* Michael Banton ed., London, 1966.

[5] Luca Pinna, "Un'ipotesi antropologica per la conoscenza della Sardegna," *Ichnusa,* IX, 1, 1961. (An Anthropological Hypothesis for Understanding Sardinia.)

extended kinship, clientela (or, in other regions, the Mafia); (b) that — although expressed in extreme terms — the cause should be sought in objective conditions which are independent of the present action of the Montegranians.

This leads us to the two conditions first described by Banfield, and subsequently neglected when he became attracted to the novelty of the syndrome "death — nuclear family — education without principles." These two conditions are those dealing with class relationships and poverty. Wichers[6] rightly observed that Banfield could have profited by making a more thorough study of them in the specific situation, by investigating in detail the possible consequences of feudal traditions on the ethos in Montegrano, as well as the feeling that the peasant's life depends on the caprices of nature or of the landlord. Wichers himself develops them very well; thus, there is no need to rediscuss it here.

But I shall discuss it implicity by adding a specific element that I feel is the one serving best to account for a large part of the situation in Montegrano. To speak of poverty and feudalism, in fact, is not enough, because poor countries with a feudal tradition have subsequently been protagonists of progressive developments in civilization. Wichers foresees this objection and says that a situation of abandonment, such as that of Montegrano, arises as a consequence of a tradition of especially severe feudal relationships. Perhaps this is true, but in order to verify it, scales of types and of severity of feudal relationships would have to be drawn up. (Wichers gives an example of the work needed.)

However, there is a dimension capable of synthesizing these situations, and it is the one that is found between the two poles of being in the center or at the margin of historical progress. Certainly, "historical progress" is a concept for which it is difficult to trace empirical indicators; nonetheless, no one doubts what it is and *where* it is. No one doubts, and least of all the Montegranians, that between America and Montegrano, between the industrial triangle of northern Italy and Montegrano, between Rome and Montegrano, Montegrano is on the fringe.[7] But let us try to be more precise: the seat of historical progress

---

[6] A. J. Wichers, "Amoral Familism Reconsidered," *Sociologia Ruralis*, IV, 2, 1964, p. 170 and following.

[7] This interpretation of the marginality of a peasant community, such as Montegrano, seems to me to be very analogous to that expressed by Frank Cancian when — commenting on Banfield's book — he writes: "It is of fundamental importance to consider the fact the whole world does not appear equally hopeless to the peasant. In fact, he applies this concept of inability solely to himself and *to the environment in which he is living at the moment*. ... He feels that he could improve his situation if he could find work in a northern factory or could emigrate to America." (My italics.) (F. Cancian, "Il contadino meridionale: comportamento politico e visione del mondo," *Bollettino delle ricerche sociali*, October 1961, p. 269.) The same author reminds us that Friederick G. Friedmann, in "The World of 'la Miseria,'" *Partisan Review*, 1953, spoke of how the peasant felt himself to be an object of and not a protagonist in history. It seems to me that these are all statements which enter into this dimension of "centrality-periphery."

(I know this is an unelegant expression, but let's use it temporarily) is where the values by which everyone is judged — also those who are on the fringes — are elaborated. That is where individual success, as measured by these values, is attained. Where new goods are manufactured to replace antiquated ones. Where the power is and where one is better off. Finally, where one attempts to go. This last indicator, which is perhaps the most empirically testable, suggests that two kinds of seats of historical progress can be distinguished: those where accepted values prevail, and those where new efforts are made to create new values. The latter is pioneer territory, where one chooses to go (or at least accepts of one's own free will to be sent there), as are America, St. George, Utah — the Mormon community that Banfield compares with Montegrano — the Israeli kibbutzim, etc. When a pioneering movement does not exist (and not even Banfield asks that the Montegranians become pioneers), or when a system of self-generated progress does not, historical marginality exists — and so does Montegrano. That is, a place where any productive localization is anti-economical, in the strict and technical sense of the word (Banfield does not even mention this very simple fact); a place where both the slick products of industrial society and the unctuous favors of political society arrive from "outside" and are paid for at a high price. And above all, a place where even an illiterate person knows what he is up against perfectly (and how could he lack such knowledge?), and this very knowledge makes his situation worse, because it means that he is aware of the "outside values" and, therefore, in some way accepts the evaluation of himself according to them, knowing that he can never really "measure up." A place then where even the greatest effort results only in keeping misery going, in equipping their hell. And this is what Banfield asks the Montegranians to do, and is astonished because they do not do it. He does not imagine that in hell even the smallest effort to improve matters is intolerable; if one has to stay there, one is better off doing nothing. This is a piece of wisdom that Banfield certainly knows in his own terms, since he apparently accepts to remain, without showing that he wants to change it, in a system that creates infernos with napalm.

Or else, one tries to run away from an inferno, and, in fact, it seems that Montegranians have been doing this for some time. Thus, they are bringing about Montegrano's extinction as a community, the same extinction that already existed in the people's consciousness.

Naturally, this view of Montegrano, Montegrano-inferno, Montegrano-on-the-historical-fringe, non-community-minded Montegrano, is only an ideal type that does not exist in reality. In more general terms, the historical process that creates real Montegranos could perhaps be explained schematically as follows: the formation of capitalistic society leaves certain populations on its margins which, although they remain connected in some way with the rest of the social system, cannot keep up with its progress. The formative process of nations, on the other hand, can be considered as a process that, in one way or another, tends to recuperate these economically marginal populations by offering them a new identification — that of the nation. For various reasons, these attempts can be unsuccessful, or partially successful, or be successful at first and fail later on. The territories that are excluded from the process of national identification, after losing their local traditional community identification because the organization of the capitalistic system renders their isolation and their self-sufficiency useless, can be called marginal territories. In these, it is no longer possible to reconstruct the fabric of community identities that allows a population to carry out local organization. On the other hand, identification with the new system can occur solely individual by individual, in a place where a new life makes sense, that is, in seats of historical progress.

To conceive of communities, of community action, of community identification in historically marginal zones, as long as they remain such, does not make sense. The way is in a new (and this time, pathological) nationalistic identification (and this could explain Banfield's observations on the incidence of Fascism in Montegrano), or in waiting to be involved in a process of economic development originating externally, because of a change in the conditions of territorial economy and because of spread effects of economic growth. Or else the problem can be solved by getting out completely, that is, in making an individual choice to take part in progress, and emigrate. Montegrano, if it were in the middle of an industrial triangle, would have no relation to the ideal type we are discussing. The same is true of the natives of Montegrano if they were in America or in Milan.

When these possibilities do not exist, we have the human aggregates that Banfield refers to. They are probably richer in sub-cultural traits, which allow them to tolerate intolerable situations. But above all, as human aggregates, they are neither communities nor societies, and they no longer believe in ascribed solidarity and have not yet achieved new types of solidarity. These are situations that many novelists (Verga for one) and common sense have recognized. It is time that sociologists faced them systematically.

Banfield must be given credit for doing this, and for this reason his book is worth reconsidering. The principal point that led him astray was in having taken as the object of his study certain phenomena which he saw as being true in themselves and circumscribed, but which should have been defined and studied in relation to a wider system. Only then would he have made them what they really were.

CHAPTER
THREE

Political Socialization

Explaining political phenomena in terms of cultural influences is a deceptively easy task. At best, the outlooks embodied in a political culture can offer only short-range and approximate explanations of political behavior. Reference to cultural values in England and France can provide an immediate answer to the questions about why the English and the French act so differently toward their governments. Yet this in turn raises another question: Why do people in the two countries think about politics in such very different ways? Historical conditions provide one type of answer to this question: present outlooks are shaped by past circumstances.

The concept of political socialization provides an answer to the question: *how* do past differences influence people decades, generations, or centuries later? The French Revolution, for instance, is an event as remote in time as the American Revolution. Yet events from that era were re-enacted in Paris in 1968 by the great-great-great-great-great-grandchildren of the original revolutionaries. Patterns of behavior and states of mind are kept alive by a variety of socialization mechanisms, overtly or indirectly teaching the basic values, beliefs, and emotions that enable a person to understand his society. As French, German, and Italian societies illustrate, there is no certainty that the lessons learned will necessarily favor support for the existing regime.

Political socialization begins early in life, usually as a by-product of an individual's other social experience. From parents, children acquire their earliest knowledge about many things. Some ideas may be directly political, such as loyalty to the parents' political party, or a belief that it is dangerous to have a party loyalty. Many of the things that children learn from their parents, such as attitudes toward authority, have indirect political implications. A very considerable social science literature, for example, has stressed authoritarian family practices in Germany as a significant influence supporting anti-democratic political activity there. Educational institutions come next in point of time as potential molders of cultural outlooks. In most European societies, schools do not play as important a part in shaping the young as they do in American society. The average European child spends much less of his youth in school than does an American. In England, for instance, the majority of children today leave school at the age of 15. In addition, the schools have not been regarded by the state as a means of building national political loyalties, as has been the case in America, where the task of providing political socialization for immigrants' children was once a major political function of schools. Traditionally, the church was the agency providing elementary instruction in social values, and in political values too. In Protestant countries, the church was not likely to come into conflict with the state, because the latter usually controlled the former. In Catholic countries, however, conflicts between a supra-national church and national regimes for the loyalties of children have made education a source of important divisions within societies.

In England, the relative simplicity of the social structures makes it possible for attitudes to be transmitted between generations with few of the cross-pressures found in Continental societies. England also illustrates the fact that even when social structure is relatively simple, the process of socialization involves learning not only certain common values, but also processes of differentiation, in which young people learn how to adopt complementary roles, such as those of leader and led. The development of student rebellions everywhere in Europe in the late 1960's is a reminder that generational groups can also be joined in a relationship of mutual antagonism.

Bibliography

The most ambitious theoretical discussion of socialization experiences, drawing especially upon Britain and Germany, is in Harry Eckstein's "A Theory of Stable Democracy," a lengthy appendix of his Norwegian study, *Division and Cohesion in Democracy* (Princeton University Press, 1967). *The Civic Culture* by Gabriel Almond and Sidney Verba also emphasizes the significance of childhood experience, drawing evidence from the recollections that adult respondents have of their childhood. An especially noteworthy journal article is the comparative study of adolescents in Britain, Germany, Italy, and the United States by Jack Dennis, Leon Lindberg, Donald McCrone, and Rodney Stiefbold, "Political Socialization to Democratic Orientations in Four Western Systems," *Comparative Political Studies* 1: 1 (1968). British studies are reported in Chapter II and the bibliographical notes of Richard Rose, editor, *Studies in British Politics* (New York: St. Martin's, revised edition, 1969). The most convenient introductions to French and German studies can be found in Lewis J. Edinger, *Politics in Germany* (Boston: Little, Brown, 1968), Ch. 5, and Henry W. Ehrmann, *Politics in France* (Boston: Little, Brown, 1968), Ch. 3. See also, Fred Greenstein and Sidney Tarrow, "The Study of French Political Socialization," *World Politics*, XXII: 1 (1969); and L. Wylie, "Youth in France and the United States," *Daedalus*, XCI: 1 (1962). A wide-ranging comparative survey of the particular influences encouraging student political revolt can be found in a special issue of *Daedalus*, XCVII: 1 (Winter, 1968) from which the article by Frank A. Pinner is reprinted.

ROBERT E. LANE

Political Maturation in Germany and America

One of the major themes of The Civic Culture *by Gabriel Almond and Sidney Verba is the importance of parental influences in forming the political outlooks of individuals. The influence is not constant in importance or character from nation to nation. Germany and America, in popular stereotypes at least, present extreme contrasts between the traditional, paternalistic family, and the modern, permissive family. Robert Lane re-analyzes data from* The Civic Culture *study to examine the causes and political consequences of differences in family upbringing between and within these two cultures.*

The problem to which this paper is addressed is this: How does a sense of appropriate influence in adolescence, or the lack of such a sense, affect a person's political life in the United States and Germany? It would be pretentious to say that there is a developed theory to guide research along these lines; what is available is an arsenal of ideas, some of them very close to common sense (as this has itself been shaped by recent psychology), that have a bearing on character formation and political expression. But these ideas lead in different directions, with

Abridged from Robert E. Lane, "La Maturation politique de l'adolescent aux États-Unis et en Allemagne," *Revue française de sociologie* 7: Numéro Spécial, 1966, pp. 598–618. Reprinted by permission of the Éditions du Centre National de la Recherche Scientifique and of the author. The English version is by the author.

This paper is a revised version of a paper presented at the Sixth World Congress of the International Political Science Association, Geneva, 1964. I wish to acknowledge the help given me by Gerry Ruth Sack and Elizabeth Warren in making the statistical calculations presented below. Miss Warren programmed the data for computer calculation of chi squares. I am also grateful to John Helliwell, of Nuffield College, for consultation on various statistical matters, but hold him free of blame for any errors I may have committed in interpreting his advice.

respect to both participation and partisanship. Let us consider the probable political expression of three types of people, those who were influential as adolescents, those who were not and resented it, and those who were not and accepted this as appropriate to their youthful status. With respect to his participation in political life the adolescent who grows up feeling that he is appropriately influential in his family will:

1. adopt the political norms of his social groups, that is, he will participate in the same ways and to the same extent as the members of these groups do (this is the meaning of "adjustment"); or,
2. have the inner strength and self-confidence to seek leadership positions and be more than ordinarily active in the service of his political interests and ideals.

With respect to partisanship (left or right orientation), he will,

3. adopt group-modal positions, shun extremism and deviance, and work within the political tradition of his group membership; or
4. transcend the limits of his group tradition in either direction (left or right), thus pursuing his own convictions, rather than the group convictions.

If the central differentiating ingredient is self-esteem in the character of the adult who, more than others, believes he indeed did have influence as an adolescent, one would be hard put to it on theoretical grounds to say in which fashion this self-esteem would be expressed in political life.

Or consider the rebel, the person who felt he had little influence in adolescence and resented this, in this sense rebelling against the parental pattern of authority and dominance — how will he express this in political life? Theoretically we might expect any one of the following patterns, or perhaps a vacillation among them.

The adolescent who grows up feeling that he had little authority in his youth, and resents this, will follow one of the following participation patterns:

1. become hyper-active in politics to assuage his feelings of worthlessness and to demonstrate that he is after all an important and powerful person; or,
2. become politically inactive because he has never had the experience of influence, has not learned the necessary skills, has no sense that he can control events; or,
3. become modal and compulsively conformist in all things, following the cues of his social group, and participate exactly according to the social norms as he reads them.

And he will adopt one of the following partisanship (directional) patterns:

4. choose political positions deviant from those of his parental traditions, moving left, if they are rightist, or moving right, if they are leftist;

5. choose political positions which are nationally deviant, selecting national authorities as his targets rather than immediate group leaders and group conventions; this implies a more extremist and perhaps destructive style; or,
6. seek to restore his sense of worth and importance, damaged in adolescence, by adopting a modal, conformist pattern of partisanship within which he seeks recognition, power, and affection as outlined in pattern 1 above.

Or, finally, take the submissive person, one who feels he had little influence in adolescence and that this lack of influence was an appropriate state of affairs. Overtly at least he does not resent this situation. What of his political life?

The adolescent who grows up feeling that he had little authority in his youth and approves of this situation on the grounds that adolescents should not be influential will, first, adopt one of the following patterns of participation:

1. become conformist and participate modally, doing what is expected of him, no more and no less; or,
2. continue his pattern of submissiveness, let others take over the burden of voting, talking politics, following distant events, and so forth.

And one of the following patterns of partisanship:

1. become a conformist partisan of the political tradition of the parental social group; or
2. if his own adult social group differs from his parental group, adopt the political coloration of his own group, or some compromise between them; or,
3. because some resentment of one's inhibited youthful autonomy, although overtly denied, may yet "fester" and seek expression, become cynical, hostile, politically alienated.[1]

There are more or less substantial reasons for believing any one of these (hence, any finding will be liable to the attack that it is only what common sense would have told us in the first place), and indeed, the most sensible view might well be to assume that the stated positions of the three types of adolescent influence responses mentioned are too blunt for useful analysis. Each may be only a necessary condition for the indicated behavior; for prediction one needs to know more. Of course it would be better to know more, and for more refined analysis it is essential; nevertheless there may be summary trends, rather weakened by cross currents, which each of these adolescent states might reflect. At least many people have thought so, and it is worth examining further.

---

[1] See Russel Middleton and Snell Putney, "Political Expression of Adolescent Rebellion," *American Journal of Sociology* 68 (1963), pp. 527–535; Eleanor E. Maccoby, Richard E. Matthews, and Anton S. Morton, "Youth and Political Change," *Public Opinion Quarterly* 18 (1954), pp. 23–29.

METHODS AND CAUTIONS

We are talking about how a situation at one stage of a person's life affects his later behavior; in this case the later behavior ranges from only a few years later to some fifty-five years later. There are two ways to proceed: the best way is to capture and record youthful experiences at the time they occur and to observe how the subjects thus studied behave five, ten, or more years later — the longitudinal study. We cannot do this, at least not now. The other way is to take people at various stages in their lives and ask them about their youthful experiences. As is well known, there are grave deficiencies in this method: people's memories are faulty, often systematically distorted by some irrelevant bias; a bad report on childhood may stem from frustrating later experiences; parents may be unjustly blamed or may benefit from a conventional compulsion to say only good things about parents and family, and so forth. Nevertheless, since the questions are important, and other methods are not immediately available, the retrospective report is often used. This retrospective method serves as the basis for the following study.

In 1959 and 1960 Gabriel Almond and Sidney Verba arranged to have responsible survey organizations in each of five countries interview a sample of about 1,000 in each country on a range of issues dealing with patterns of citizenship. Included in these surveys were questions on political participation (voting, following public affairs in the media, talking politics, membership and leadership of various voluntary associations); on attitudes toward various governmental acts, on preferred methods of influence, if any; on various more general opinions of human nature; on patterns of partisanship; and, what is crucial for our purposes, memories of influence and family life during adolescence (age 16). These authors have interpreted their data in *The Civic Culture*[2] and they have generously made their basic data available on cards distributed through the Inter-University Consortium for Political Research. It is these data that I employ for the following analysis of United States and German patterns.

THE TYPOLOGY AND ITS VALIDATION

How shall we isolate those who were, or retrospectively feel that they were, appropriately influential as adolescents, those who were not and resented it, and those who were not and accepted this lack of influence as appropriate? There are two questions in these cross cultural surveys which will guide us:

> As you were growing up, let's say when you were around 16, how much influence do you remember having in family decisions affecting yourself? Did you have much influence, some, or none at all?

---

[2] Princeton, N.J.: Princeton University Press, 1963.

In general, how much voice do you think children of 16 should have in family decisions? (Great deal, some, little, none.)

By cross analyzing the answers to these questions we arrive at . . . four types (Table 1).

TABLE 1. BASIC TYPOLOGY OF ADOLESCENT INFLUENCE AND PERCENTAGE OF NATIONAL SAMPLES IN EACH TYPE

		"As you were growing up, let's say when you were around 16, how much influence do you remember having in family decisions affecting yourself? Did you have much influence, some, or none at all?"	
		Much or some	None
"In general how much voice do you think children of 16 should have in family decisions?"	Great deal or some	Influentials U.S. = 65% (577) Ger. = 42% (349)	Rebels U.S. = 15% (137) Ger. = 14% (120)
	Little, none	(Privileged) U.S. = 12% (111) Ger. = 18% (153)	Submissives U.S. = 8% (67) Ger. = 26% (214)

It is worth spending a moment to consider the meaning of this cross analysis. The two questions deal respectively with perceived own influence at age 16 and whether or not 16-year-olds in general should have influence. We assume that if a person feels that in general 16-year-olds should be influential, he will extend this to his own case: if he had influence, he will think this appropriate, and we call him an "Influential." On the other hand, if a person believes that 16-year-olds generally should be influential and perceives his own situation as one lacking in influence, he will be resentful, and we call him a "Rebel." Yet there are many who think 16-year-olds should have little or no influence in the family: 20 percent of the American sample and 44 percent of the German sample. We would assume that those who believed this and perceived their own situation as lacking in influence would be much less resentful, indeed, would feel it was appropriate for them to submit to this proper situation, hence the term "Submissive." The fourth logical category — those who feel that 16-year-olds generally should not be influential, but perceive their own situation as having been influential — we term "Privileged." The logic of this situation is somewhat obscure and the predictions as to how such people might behave uncertain, hence I will limit my analysis to the other three types.

One other observation is in order. Many people are reluctant to criticize their parents or express dissatisfaction with their behavior even though they feel this rather intensely. Our typology avoids an open criticism, such as that implied in the question, "Were you satisfied or dissatisfied with the amount of influence you had in family decisions when you were 16?" Thus, although 18 percent of the American sample were willing to say that they were "dissatisfied," only 7 percent of the German sample responded accordingly. We would expect our measure of "rebellion" to correlate with these answers, but to capture some people with resentments who could not say so. And we would expect, unfortunately, to lose some natural Rebels for whom the logic of their answers was obscure to them, or for some other reason. The question, of course, is whether or not this measure is, in fact, capturing the sets of attitudes and beliefs which one might properly think to be associated with the term "Influential," "Rebel," "Submissive," as described above. To find this out we can examine the way the three types respond to other questions about influence situations in their youth (Table 2).

TABLE 2. VALIDATION OF ADOLESCENT INFLUENCE TYPOLOGY: PERCENTAGE OF EACH TYPE WITH CERTAIN ATTITUDES ABOUT THEIR OWN INFLUENCE IN THEIR FAMILIES AND ABOUT PARENTAL UNDERSTANDING

	Dissatisfied with amount of influence in family		Better not to complain about disliked decisions		Complaints affected parents' decisions		Never did complain		Parents understood respondents' needs	
	%	(N)	%	(N)	%	(N)	%	(N)	%	(N)
United States										
Influential	14%	(79)	18%	(104)	73%	(442)	18%	(104)	85%	(489)
Rebel	46	(63)	64	(88)	18	(25)	43	(59)	55	(76)
Submissive	16	(11)	70	(47)	13	(9)	64	(43)	78	(52)
Germany										
Influential	3	(12)	11	(38)	84	(295)	25	(89)	85	(299)
Rebel	23	(28)	52	(62)	31	(37)	57	(69)	50	(60)
Submissive	8	(17)	53	(114)	23	(49)	54	(116)	68	(147)

Chi squares for all subtables (by question in each country) are significant beyond the 1% level; differences between Influentials and Rebels are all significant beyond 1% level; differences between Influentials and Submissives are significant at the 1% level in seven of the ten cases; differences between Rebels and Submissives are significant at the 1% level in six out of ten cases.

As a validation of the typology, and ignoring for the moment the cross cultural differences, this pattern holds up fairly well in both the United States and Germany. It will be observed that the Influentials in both countries have the least dissatisfaction with their family influence, the least sense that the best policy was never to complain, the greatest confidence that their complaints would make a difference; they did, in fact, complain most frequently, and, as a correlate or cause of these attitudes believed that they were best understood at home.

On the other hand, the Rebels were most dissatisfied with their influence in their families and, although they were surprisingly sanguine about being understood, nevertheless had less confidence than the others in this respect.

Finally, the Submissives had the least confidence that any complaint would affect family decisions, and, perhaps for that reason, felt it was better not to complain. Moreover, in the United States they did actually complain the least. On the other hand, because they were more likely than the Rebels to believe they were fairly well understood by their parents, they may have felt not only that it was useless, but that it was also unnecessary. Their state of dissatisfaction with their influence was, in any event, very like that of the Influentials, and very unlike that of the Rebels.

THE SENSE OF INFLUENCE: CAUSES AND EFFECTS IN TWO CULTURES

As we examine the causes and political consequences of these adolescent experiences in the United States and Germany, two general observations are in order. In the first place, for some of the reasons observed above with regard to the method employed (retrospection), and the ambiguity of the theory, we would not expect large differences to occur; we are grateful for patterned indications of the direction of the forces at work. Second, in comparing the effects in two cultures we are much more struck by the similarities than by differences, although one significant difference in the political meaning of adolescent rebelliousness will be presented at the end of the paper.

As may be seen in Table 1, there are more Influentials in the United States sample, and more Submissives in the German sample, while there are about the same proportion of Rebels in both. The difference in sense of influence in adolescence in the two countries is in the direction which the literature would suggest and which the Almond-Verba report led us to believe, but the similarity in rebellion is somewhat surprising. On the one hand Germans are, by many reports, more accepting of authority, but on the other hand, it has been suggested by Erikson that the German boy, at least, tends to rebel against his father in adolescence, and then to return to the fold later.[3] As indicated above, we sought to avoid relying on an explicit expression of dissatisfaction for our measure (the Rebels, it will be recalled, are those who felt 16-year-olds *should* have some influence but felt that *they had none*) in order to tap *latent* rebellion. Many more Americans express dissatisfaction with their adolescent influence situation than do Germans, but at this latent level of strain, there seems to be about the same proportion in each country. Now let us turn, in order, to some of the causes and consequences of each of these three adolescent influence situations.

THE GENESIS OF THE THREE TYPES

What is it that produces these three postures toward adolescent influence? In neither country does the rural-urban difference or size of town have any consistent effect, even when this is a measure of the place where one was brought up. We do not have available data on the family income during adolescence but if current income is any

[3] Erik Erikson, *Childhood and Society* (New York: Norton, 1950), pp. 289–294.

reflection of this, there is only a very moderate tendency for the better-off to have experienced this sense of appropriate influence—and this only in the United States. There is no clear pattern among occupational groups; at least status of current occupation seems almost irrelevant, when controlled for education. Curiously, there is no consistent difference between men and women in Germany, and in the United States there is only a slight difference. There, it is the women who feel more satisfied with their adolescent influence *and* who feel that others should have this too.

The things that do make a difference are education, age, and, to some extent, religion, with education the strongest and most persistent influence in both countries (Table 3, A). The more education he has the more likely a person is to recall having influence in the family as an adolescent and to wish this for others, too. Submissives tend to have the least education, with Rebels somewhere in between. This means that, at least in retrospect, those who were going to school at age 16 were more influential in their families than those who were working, but more important, those who came from homes where the parents sent their children on to higher education probably were, in fact, better treated. There is, too, the possibility that adolescents who continue their education are more responsible and reasonable — their complaints are worthy of attention. (Since occupation is so tenuously related to our typology, it seems unlikely that higher adult status leads to a selectively more favorable memory of adolescence; we may accept the patterned relationship to education as reflecting true adolescent situations, at least to some extent.)

A person's age tells us two things of relevance here; it tells us something about him *now*, and it tells us something about the historical period of his youth. In general, one would expect that the process of aging would have roughly similar effects in the United States and in Germany; therefore the fact (Table 3, B) that there is no relationship between age and feelings about adolescent influence in the United States for two of the three educational levels suggests that the very real influence in Germany has something to do with historical change and changing family patterns. In Germany, the older a person is the more likely he is to be a Submissive or a Rebel and the less likely to be an Influential. In effect, whether or not he approves of adolescent influence in general, the older he is, the more likely he is to feel he did not have much himself. And this progression occurs over the pre-Nazi, Nazi, and post-Nazi period. One wonders if increased adolescent influence is a necessary product of what has been called "modernization," that is, increasing urbanization industrialization, and per capita wealth.

On all educational levels in both countries religion makes a difference (Table 3, C); Protestantism, as contrasted with Catholicism, is associated with a sense of appropriate adolescent influence. The obverse is also true, in both countries, at every educational level except higher

TABLE 3. RELATION OF EDUCATION, AGE, AND RELIGION TO ADOLESCENT INFLUENCE TYPOLOGY: PERCENTAGE OF DEMOGRAPHIC GROUP IN EACH TYPE, WITHIN EDUCATIONAL LEVELS

	Primary education	At least some secondary education	Secondary education	Some higher education
A. Education[a]				
United States				
Influentials	56%		80%	88%
Rebels	25		16	9
Submissives	19		4	3
(Total N)	(251)		(369)	(161)
Germany				
Influentials	45%	77%		
Rebels	19	11		
Submissives	36	12		
(Total N)	(563)	(120)		

	18-35	36-60	61+	18-35	36-60	61+	18-35	36-60	61+	18-35	36-60	61+
B. Age[b]												
United States												
Influentials	55%	63%	47%				88%	78%	62%	94%	84%	86%
Rebels	32	19	30				11	19	25	6	12	9
Submissives	13	18	23				1	3	13	0	4	5
(Total N)	(22)	(123)	(106)				(160)	(157)	(52)	(66)	(73)	(21)
Germany												
Influentials	60%	45%	27%	90%	72%	54%						
Rebels	16	20	20	8	12	15						
Submissives	24	35	53	2	6	31						
(Total N)	(164)	(280)	(119)	(49)	(58)	(13)						

	Protestant	Catholic	Protestant	Catholic	Protestant	Catholic	Protestant	Catholic
C. Religion[c]								
United States								
Influentials	60%	44%			83%	71%	92%	87%
Rebels	23	27			14	24	5	10
Submissives	17	29			3	5	3	3
(Total N)	(179)	(52)			(264)	(75)	(102)	(32)
Germany								
Influentials	51%	39%	84%	64%				
Rebels	18	20	8	18				
Submissives	31	41	8	18				
(Total N)	(283)	(252)	(73)	(39)				

[a] Chi squares for the United States are significant beyond the 1% level for the entire table and for each paired comparison of types separately. For the German data the entire table and the paired comparisons between the Influentials and each of the other types show chi squares significant at the 1% level.

[b] Chi squares for the United States data are significant at the 1% level for the secondary education group where each paired comparison of types is also significant at the 1% level; other groups not significant and pairs not generally significant. The German data are significant at the 1% level for the primary education group, and almost at the 2% level for the secondary education group; paired comparisons of Influentials and Submissives are significant at the 1% level, others somewhat lower.

[c] Chi squares for the United States data are significant at the 10% level for the primary and secondary education groups but are not significant for the higher education group; in the primary group, the paired comparison between Influentials and Submissives is significant at the 5% level; in the secondary group the comparison between the Influentials and the Rebels is significant at the 5% level; in the German sample, the data for the primary and secondary educational groups are significant at the 5% and 10% levels respectively. The paired comparisons between the Influentials and the Submissives are significant at the 1% and the 10% levels; the comparison between the Influentials and the Rebels is significant at the 5% level for the higher educated sample.

education in the United States, Catholics are more likely to be Submissives, or Rebels—in this limited adolescent sense. In some manner not easily explained, the Reformation and its modern tradition seems to have given greater freedom and authority to its youth. It would be interesting to have this measure over time,[4] for the evidence on a related quality, the need to achieve, suggests that what was once a substantial difference between Catholics and Protestants in Germany, at least, has now become much less important.[5] Perhaps it is true that in some respects the Catholic Church has been "protestantized," but the difference between Catholic and Protestant adolescent family influence persists.

THE CENTER OF FAMILY AUTHORITY

But, after all, it is in the intimate relations between parents and children that the sense of appropriate influence is generated, and this, of course, is the area where it is hardest to get good information. Is it the father-dominated home (at least where he is seen to make the important decisions), the mother-dominated home, or the home where both are seen to be coordinate in authority where rebellious or submissive feelings are born? The pattern turns out to be rather complex, and, indeed, in Germany it is very difficult to discern any pattern to the answers at all. But in the United States, though not in Germany, one thing is clear: homes in which the parents shared authority were more likely to produce Influentials and least likely to produce Rebels than any other pattern of parental authority. And this is true regardless of the sex of the respondent or of the dominant parent. While the tendency is apparent in the lower educated group, it only achieves statistical significance in the two thirds of the sample with more than primary education. Perhaps in the United States parents who share power between themselves also share it with their children.

We have presented evidence in Table 2 showing that adolescents in the United States are more willing to express dissatisfaction with their status at home and are more likely to complain to their parents if something bothers them. Perhaps it is also the case that American wives and mothers are more likely to exercise independent influence in the home; after all, Germany is, by repute, a nation marked by father-domination[6] (and the United States by mother-domination). Yet the evidence runs against this hypothesis. There are only the most tenuous differences between perceptions of father-domination or of mother-domination in the two countries. Although it may be true that "shared power" is exercised differently in the two countries (perhaps in

---

[4] See, for example, *ibid.*, p. 247.
[5] David C. McClelland, *The Achieving Society* (New York: Van Nostrand, 1961), pp. 360–362.
[6] See Bertram H. Schaffner, *Father Land, A Study of Authoritarianism in the German Family* (New York: Columbia University Press, 1948).

Germany this represents a coalition to minimize adolescent influence), it is not at all clear why Germans should misperceive who it is that makes the important decisions in their households any more than Americans. Hence we accept this indication of similar patterns of parental dominance, tentatively, as a valuable modification of current socialization beliefs about both countries. . . .

REBELS

The Rebels, it will be recalled, are those who had little experience of influence as a youth and resent it. One might expect them to become radicals, but would they express this radicalism as a protest against their parental group tradition, lower income moving right and higher income moving left (unorthodox) or against the national status quo "establishment" tradition, possibly moving towards some radical extreme? Perhaps there are national differences in this respect, although our United States findings are largely heuristic here for they do not achieve statistical significance. The data suggest that, if anything, the American Rebel is more likely to be Democratic than his matched group member who is an Influential. But this is important, if at all, only as a possible contrast to the rather interesting German pattern. Compared to the Influentials, the German Rebels are *not* generally more leftist. A finer economic breakdown reveals that a middle income Rebel group is exactly modal in its partisanship and an upper income group is very slightly more rightist. But perhaps the Rebel is more likely to be unorthodox, in the sense that whatever his group tradition may be, he tends, more than others, to violate it, or transcend it. Eliminating the cross pressured groups (lower income Catholic and upper income Protestants) in order to isolate groups where the influences of religion and social status reinforce each other, we can compare the Rebel pattern with the pattern of the Influentials in the two countries. The result is a surprise; instead of being less orthodox, we find the Rebels *more* orthodox, according to these data. Among the Rebels, higher income Catholics are more likely to support the Christian Democratic party than the Influentials, and lower income Protestants are more likely to support the Socialists.

Obviously, since this was partially unexpected (but see item 6 in the introductory comments), the reversal of one relevant theory and a marked difference between the two national patterns requires the search for new theoretical considerations. What could account for this pattern? One very good possibility is that it is an artifact of the measures, but their fine performance according to (some of) our predictions in the validation tests above makes this a little less likely. The possibilities that the pattern could happen by chance are higher than one would like, but still it is only one chance in about fourteen that sampling variation is the correct interpretation. Perhaps there is a clue in Erikson's statement to the effect that the German male adolescent tends to be more rebellious (more than Americans) against his parents, but then, returns to the fold and shapes himself in the parental mold, becomes a father like his own father. That is, guilt over the rebellion may be great enough to create a counterforce to restore the Rebel to the parental tradition.

There are indications in our data that this may, in fact, be the case. Expectations are different, different standards are employed, but also, most probably Germans find the *overt expression* of criticism of their status in the home a more difficult thing to do. This is supported by the fact that the measure of latent dissatisfaction and rebellious feelings uncovered as many covert Rebels among the German population as in the American population. Latent rebellious feelings come more easily to the surface in the United States: 46 percent of the American Rebels expressed open dissatisfaction with their adolescent influence while only 23 percent of the German Rebels did so (Table 2). These are indications of suppression of critical feelings which might reasonably be interpreted as reflecting guilt. This guilt, then, could be the force which during the course of maturation, brings a person back into the parental fold, political and otherwise, with some of the force of a compulsion. Hence the Rebels are more orthodox than the Influentials and they over-conform.

SUMMARY AND IMPLICATIONS

. . . The strong relationship between adolescent influence and education at first suggested that more education simply creates in the educated person a sense of generalized influence in society, a sense that is projected back into adolescence: the later educational experience affects memories of the earlier adolescent experience. Probably this is true, but since occupational status (which should create a similar sense of influence) is not related to these memories, other factors must be important as well. I would hazard the guess that the family that values education also values children and children's opinions. These are correlate values. Second, the child who drops out of school early is a different kind of child from the one who persists in his education. The "complaints" of the one who goes on may be more worth listening to.

Why is it that there is a strong relationship between age and adolescent influence in Germany but much less in the United States? Could it be that the United States, without the residue of a feudal order to be broken and overcome through difficult historical trauma, passed through the last fifty years with far less change in social relationships than is true of Europe and especially Germany? McClelland has found that modernizing societies are more "other-directed" than static societies, their members more sensitive to each other's opinions.[7] Almond and Verba have found that the American is far more trusting of others

[7] D. C. McClelland, *op. cit.*, pp. 192–197.

than the German, Italian, or Mexican.[8] Part of the modernizing process, then, is an increased acceptance of the opinions, influence, and trustworthiness of others. And this includes adolescent sons and daughters. The age differences in Germany may, perhaps, reflect this aspect of modernization.

I have discussed the idea that the strong relationship in both cultures between Protestantism and adolescent influence is part of the general Protestant movement to set men free from institutional (including family) restraints. If a man can directly influence God, without intercession of another (church) authority, he may properly influence lesser authorities, such as parents. But does this also work the other way? Is the Protestant Reformation in part a product of the growing sense that youth can modify paternal authority? Kardiner says that religion is in large part a projection of social relations.[9] If this is so, what shall we say of the religious changes which the modern revolution in social relations may bring about?

These are the indirect influences of society on adolescent freedom and authority; they work through parental behavior. In the United States, at least, where the parents share authority with each other, they also share it with their children. But in Germany this is not so clearly the case. Does this mean that joint parental decision-making in Germany is more like a joint adult management of affairs in which children do not participate? In Germany fathers and mothers are seen as jointly deciding how to vote more often than in the United States, where they are seen as more often making this decision individually (though, of course, they usually do agree).[10] The particular nature of the family solidarity in Germany may include a set of constraints which the German child, imbued with a familistic loyalty and even ideology, views as appropriate. Thus the "togetherness" of German family decisions implies something different from what is implied by the joint decisions of the American family. Perhaps there is more freedom for the German child when the parents do *not* decide matters jointly. "Divide and rule" is a maxim that children as well as emperors can learn.

[8] G. A. Almond and S. Verba, *op. cit.*, p. 267.
[9] Abram Kardiner, *The Psychological Frontiers of Society* (New York: Columbia University Press, 1945), pp. 38–46.
[10] Unpublished data from the Almond and Verba study.

PHILIP E. CONVERSE
and GEORGES DUPEUX

Socialization into Apathy: France and America Compared

The simplest models of inter-generational political socialization make two assumptions: major political institutions remain stable from generation to generation, and parents are ready to give their children, formally or informally, cues for adult political behavior. The comparative study of politics calls attention to the fact that these assumptions, natural enough to American society, are not necessarily met elsewhere. The study by Converse and Dupeux draws attention to the unwillingness of parents to discuss party politics in front of their children in France, and the related instability of partisan labels from generation to generation.

When we consider the character of partisan ties felt by citizens in the two countries, we strike upon some contrasts of great magnitude. We have seen that when Americans are asked to locate themselves relative to the American party system, 75 per cent classify themselves without further probing as psychological members of one of the two major parties, or of some minor party. In France, somewhat before the elections, less than 45 per cent of those who did not refuse to answer the question were able to classify themselves in one of the parties or splinter groups, while another 10 to 15 per cent associated themselves with a more or less recognizable broad *tendance* ("left," "right," a labor union, etc.). The cross-national differences of 20 to 30 per cent are sufficiently large here to contribute to fundamental differences in the flavor of partisan processes in the two electorates. For a long time, we wrote off these differences as products of incomparable circumstances or of reticence on the part of the French con-

From Philip E. Converse and Georges Dupeux, "Politicization of the Electorate in France and the United States," *Public Opinion Quarterly*, XXVI, Spring, 1962, pp. 1–23. Reprinted by permission.

cerning partisanship, most of which was being expressed not as refusal to answer the question, but as some other evasion. As we grew more familiar with the data, however, these differences took on vital new interest.

The hypothesis of concealed partisanship was very largely dispelled by a close reading of the actual interviews. It is undeniable that nearly 10 per cent of the French sample explicitly refused to answer the question, as compared with a tiny fraction in the United States. However, we have already subtracted this group from the accounting. Beyond the explicit refusals, the remarks and explanations which often accompanied statements classified as "no party," or as "don't know which party," had a very genuine air about them which made them hard to read as hasty evasions. No few of these respondents were obviously embarrassed at their lack of a party; some confessed that they just hadn't been able to keep track of which party was which. The phrase "je n'y ai jamais pensé" was extremely common. Others indicated that they found it too hard to choose between so many parties; some indicated preferences for a specific political leader but admitted that they did not know which party he belonged to or, more often, had no interest in the identity of his party, whatever it might be. Others, forming a tiny minority of the nonparty people, rejected the notion of parties with some hostility.

It became clear, too, that people reporting no party attachments were distinct on other grounds from those who willingly classified themselves as close to a party. On our vertical involvement dimension, for example, they tended to fall in the bottom stratum of the least involved, just as the paper-thin stratum unable to choose a party in the United States consists heavily of the least involved. Demographically, these nonparty people were disproportionately housewives, poorly educated, young, and the other familiar statuses which tend to be uninformed and uninvolved.

Among actual party identifiers in France there was further interesting variation in the character of the party objects to which reference was made. A very few linked themselves with small new ideological splinter groups which had developed during the political crises of 1958. For these people, it was not enough to indicate that they felt closest to the Radical-Socialists, for example: they had to specify that they were Mendesists or anti-Mendesists, Valoisiens, and the like. Most identifiers suffered no difficulty in seeing themselves as "Radical-Socialists," completely shattered though the party was. Others, perceiving the system even more grossly, linked themselves only with a broad *tendance*. On involvement measures these groupings showed the expected differences: the grosser the discrimination, the lower the involvement.

In other ways as well it was clear that the extreme ideological fractionation of parties in France has few roots in the mass population, members of which simply pay too little attention to politics to follow the nicer discriminations involved. When asked whether the number of parties in France was too great, about right, or too few, 97 per cent of those responding said there were too many parties, and less than 1 per cent said there were too few. In response to an ensuing question as to the desirable number of parties, the mean of the number seen as optimal was 3.5 for the handful of adherents of the new ideological splinters, 3.0 for the partisans of the traditional mass parties, and less than 2.8 among those who had formed no party attachments. Perhaps the most apt expression of the problem of partisan fractionation and discrimination came from the naïve respondent who opined that France should have two or three parties, "enough to express the differences in opinion."

The fact that large proportions of the French public have failed to form any very strong attachments to one of the political parties should not be taken to mean that these people are totally disoriented in the French party system. In particular, a sensitivity to the gulf separating the Communist Party from the remainder of French parties does pervade the mass public. There seems to be less confusion as to the identity of the Communist Party than for any of the other parties; and for the bulk of non-Communists, the Communist Party is a pariah. There are some nonidentifiers who appear to shift from Communist to non-Communist votes with abandon, and were all of these votes to fall to the Communists in the same election, the Party would undoubtedly exceed its previous high-water mark in its proportion of the French popular vote. At the same time, however, one cannot help but be impressed by the number of respondents who, while indicating they were not really sure what they were in partisan terms, indicated as well at one point or another in the interview that they were not only non-Communist but anti-Communist. In other words, were the descriptions of party adherents to proceed simply in terms of a Communist, non-Communist division, the proportion of ready self-classifications would advance considerably toward the American figure, and would probably exceed that which could be attained by any other two-class division in France.

Nevertheless, the limited party attachments outside the Communist camp in France retain strong theoretical interest, as they seem so obviously linked to a symptom of turbulence which is clearly not an elite phenomenon alone — the flash party. With a very large proportion of the electorate feeling no anchoring loyalty, it is not surprising that a new party can attract a large vote "overnight," or that this base can be so rapidly dissolved. Furthermore, there is a problem here that is peculiarly French, in that the low proportion of expressed attachments cannot simply be seen as a necessary consequence of a multiparty system per se. . . . Fairly comparable data from Norway, where six parties are prominent, show party attachments as widespread as those in the two-party United States.

The French sample was asked further to recall the party or *tendance* which the respondent's father had supported at the polls. Here the departure from comparable American data became even more extreme (Table 1). Of those Americans in 1958 having had a known father who had resided in the United States as an American citizen, thereby participating in American political life, 86 per cent could characterize his partisanship, and another 5 per cent knew enough of his political behavior to describe him as apolitical or independent. Among comparable French respondents, only 26 per cent could link fathers with any party or with the vaguest of *tendances* (including such responses as "il a toujours voté pour la patrie"), and another 3 per cent could describe the father's disposition as variable or apolitical. In other words, among those eligible to respond to the question, 91 per cent of Americans could characterize their father's political behavior, as opposed to 29 per cent of the French.

TABLE 1. RESPONDENT'S CHARACTERIZATION OF FATHER'S POLITICAL BEHAVIOR, BY COUNTRY, 1958 (IN PERCENTAGES)

	France	United States
Located father in party or broad *tendance*	25	76
Recalled father as "independent," "shifting around," or as apolitical, nonvoting	3	6
Total able to characterize father's political behavior	28	82
Unable to characterize father's political behavior	68	8
Father did not reside in country or was never a citizen		3
Did not know father; question not asked about father surrogate	4	6
Refused; other		1
	100	100
(N)	(1,166)	(1,795)

It goes without saying that differences of this magnitude rarely emerge from individual data in social research. And they occur at a point of prime theoretical interest. We have long been impressed in the United States by the degree to which partisan orientations appear to be passed hereditarily, from generation to generation, through families. It has seemed likely that such transmission is crucial in the stability of American partisan voting patterns. Therefore, we find it startling to encounter a situation in which huge discontinuities seem to appear in this transmission.

What do the French responses concerning paternal partisanship really mean? As best we can determine, they mean what they appear to mean: the French father is uncommunicative about his political behavior before his children, just as he is more reserved in the interviewing situation than Americans or Norwegians. It seems highly unlikely, for example, that Franco-American differences in recall represent French concealment: large numbers of the French willing to speak of their own party preference are unable to give the father's preference of a generation before, and explicit refusals to answer, while attaining

10 per cent or more where own partisanship is at stake, are almost nonexistent for paternal partisanship.

Furthermore, we have come to reject the possibility that the bulk of the Franco-American difference is some simple consequence of the more fluid and complex French party system. Responses to a similar question in the Norwegian multiparty system look like our American results, and not like the French. Nor is there reason to believe that the Frenchman has trouble finding comparable modern terms for the party groupings of a generation ago. As we have observed, the respondent was invited to give a rough equivalent of his father's position in terms of *tendance*. Moreover, where there are any elaborations of "I don't know" captured in the interview, the consistent theme seemed to be that the respondent did not feel he had ever known his father's position ("je n'ai jamais su"; "je ne lui ai jamais demandé"; "il ne disait rien à ses enfants"; "il n'en parlait jamais"). Finally, if special problems were occasioned on the French side by the changing party landscape over time, we should certainly expect that older French respondents would have greater difficulty locating their fathers politically than would younger respondents. They do not: the tabulation by age in France shows only the slightest of variations attributable to age, and these lend no support to the hypothesis (e.g., slightly less knowledge of father's position for children under thirty) and are variations which may be found in the comparable American table as well.

If we accept the proposition, then, that there are basic discontinuities in the familial transmission of party orientations in France, all of our theory would argue that weaker party attachments should result in the current generation. The data do indeed show a remarkable association between the two phenomena, once again involving differences of 30 per cent or more. Both French and Americans who recall their father's partisanship are much more likely themselves to have developed party loyalties than are people who were not aware of their father's position. Of still greater importance are the more absolute Franco-American similarities. Setting aside those people whose fathers were noncitizens, dead, apolitical, or floaters, or who refused to answer the question, we can focus on the core of the comparison (in percentages):

	Know father's party		Do not know father's party	
	France	U.S.	France	U.S.
Proportion having some partisan self-location (party or vague *tendance*)	79.4	81.6	47.7	50.7
Proportion that these are of total electorate	24.0	75.0	63.0	8.0

Where the socialization processes have been the same in the two societies, the results in current behavior appear to be the same, in rates of formation of identification. The strong cross-national differences lie in the socialization processes. In other words, we have come full circle again: we have encountered large national differences but have once again succeeded in moving them to the marginals of the table. This is our best assurance that our measurements are tapping comparable phenomena.

Partisan attachments appear therefore to be very weakly developed within the less politically involved half of the French electorate. While undoubtedly a large variety of factors, including the notoriety which the French parties had acquired in the later stages of the Fourth Republic, have helped to inhibit their development, more basic discontinuities of political socialization in the French family appear to be making some persisting contribution as well.[1] Of course, similar lack of party attachment does occur among people indifferent to politics in the American and Norwegian systems as well; but the strata of unidentified people are thinner in these systems and do not extend greatly above that layer of persistent nonvoters which is present in any system.

The link between an electorate heavily populated with voters feeling no continuing party attachments and a susceptibility of "flash" parties is an obvious one. It must be recognized at the outset, of course, that such phenomena arise only under the pressure of social, political, or economic dislocations occurring in some segment of the population, thereby generating an elite which wishes to organize a movement and a public which is restive. This means that even a system highly susceptible to such phenomena is not likely to experience them when it is functioning smoothly: their prevalence in postwar France cannot be divorced from the severe dislocations the society has been undergoing. Once misfortunes breed discontent, however, the proportions of partisans in an electorate is a datum of fundamental significance. One can-

---

[1] Among other factors, an alleged paucity of voluntary associations acting vigorously to mediate between the mass of citizens and centralized authority in France has often been cited as a crucial differentium in the quality of the political process between France and the United States. See William Kornhauser, *The Politics of Mass Society* (Glencoe, Ill.: Free Press, 1959). If such differences do exist, they may well have some bearing on the prevalence of partisan attachments, for it is clear intranationally, at least, that high rates of participation in nonpolitical voluntary associations and strong partisan attachments tend to co-occur at the individual level (although it is much less clear whether this represents a causal progression or two aspects of the same stance toward community life). In other contexts, however, it has been argued that ostensibly nonpolitical associations of mass membership in France tend to play more vigorous roles as parapolitical agents than do comparable associations in the United States, which so often tend to regard political entanglement with horror. Both views have some appeal on the basis of loose impressions of the two societies, and are not in the strictest sense contradictory. However, their thrusts diverge sufficiently that a confrontation would seem worthwhile if either can be borne out by any systematic evidence. Where grass-roots participation in expressly political associations is concerned, we have seen no notable differences between the nations in either membership rates or rates of attendance at political gatherings.

not fail to be impressed by the agility with which the strong partisan can blame the opposing party for almost any misfortune or deny the political relevance of the misfortune if some opposing party cannot conceivably be blamed. Hence, where partisans are concerned, misfortunes do relatively little to shift voting patterns. Independents, however, have no stake in such reinforcements and defenses and move more massively in response to grievances. In France, the institutions which conduce to a multiparty system make the organization of new party movements more feasible from an elite point of view than it is likely to be under two-party traditions. At the same time, the presence of a large number of French voters who have developed no continuing attachments to a particular party provides an "available" mass base for such movements. This available base is no necessary concomitant of a multiparty system, but is rather a peculiarity of the current French scene.

RONALD INGLEHART

Generational Change in Europe

While parents can exercise a strong influence upon the political attitudes of young people, their influence is not deterministic. Ronald Inglehart's study of the attitudes of young Europeans toward European integration shows clearly the degree of change that can take place from generation to generation on an important issue. The article not only indicates what historical events are likely to account for these differences, but also projects forward the implications of these changes for European political systems.

I hypothesize that important changes in political socialization may have been taking place in recent years, as a result of the postwar European movement, the increases in trade, exchange of persons, and the erection of European institutions. If this is the case, we might expect to find differences between adults and youth in their orientations toward European integration. To test this hypothesis, I made a secondary analysis of two cross-national studies of adult attitudes, made in 1962 and 1963. I will compare these data with material which I collected in 1964 and 1965 through surveys of the school populations of France, The Netherlands, West Germany and England.[1] My sampling technique consisted of selecting several schools in each country which were considered representative of the important social and economic groups, on consultation with educational authorities in the respective countries. Self-administered questionnaires were given to all members of specific classes in these schools, under the supervision of a teacher.[2] The questionnaires incorporated a number of items from the two adult surveys just mentioned. The data indicate that a gap does exist between adults and youth in relative degree of "Europeanness."

In response to the question, "To what extent are you in favor of, or opposed to, the efforts being made to unify Europe?" adults compared with youth (ages 13–19) as shown in Table 1.

Among youth of the three European Community countries, this is about as near to a unanimous verdict as one is likely to come in survey research. The response is overwhelmingly favorable to European unification by a majority which swamps all differences of social class, sex, religion, etc. Among adults in these three countries, a substantial de-

---

From Ronald Inglehart, "An End to European Integration?" *American Political Science Review*, LXI, 1, 1967, pp. 91–97. Reprinted by permission.

I wish to thank Samuel Barnes, M. Kent Jennings, Warren Miller and David Segal for their valuable criticisms of an earlier draft of this article. I am also grateful to Karl Deutsch for generously giving access to research reports from his study. The interpretations reached here are, of course, my own.

[1] The data collection was supported by a Fulbright grant, with additional aid from the Dutch Ministry of Education. The analysis has been supported by a National Science Foundation Cooperative Fellowship.

[2] Total numbers of questionnaires obtained are as follows: France: 700; The Netherlands: 3,100; West Germany: 700; England: 500. Each social type is not included in proportion to its occurrence in the overall population. In order to correct for this fact, I will base my comparisons on samples which are weighted to compensate for the relative shortage of working-class students. I weighted our SES groups according to the proportions of manual to non-manual occupations indicated in the adult surveys (approx. 2:1). My estimates, therefore, can only be regarded as a spot check on the overall distribution of attitudes. I resorted to this approach because funds did not permit obtaining a probability sample, and no alternative data were available. In a more extensive analysis, I examine other factors which seem to influence support for European integration, and attempt to control for them also. See Ronald Inglehart, "The Socialization of 'Europeans'" (unpublished Ph.D dissertation, University of Chicago, 1967).

TABLE 1. OVERALL PERCENTAGE "STRONGLY FOR" OR "FOR" EUROPEAN UNIFICATION

	Netherlands	France	Germany	Britain
Adults 1962	87%	72%	81%	(65%)[a]
Youth 1964-65	95	93	95	72

[a] In the three most recent surveys in which this question was asked of British adults (1955, 56, and 57) the percentage favorable ranged from 64% to 66%.

gree of hesitation exists, especially in France; it virtually vanishes among the younger generation. English youth is far from unanimity, but does give a fairly solid majority in support.

The foregoing question merely indicates support or opposition to European "unification" as a general idea. What happens when we pin our respondents down to specific measures? A series of questions was asked concerning concrete proposals for European integration. We find that the favorable percentage declines in every case; a strong majority gives lip service, at least, to the general idea of "unification" but is less emphatically in favor of given specific proposals. A factor analysis of our secondary school data revealed that a number of these responses clustered together, evidently indicating a "Europeanness" dimension. Using the four highest-loading items which are common to both surveys, . . . the responses of youth with those of adults in 1963 are compared in Tables 2 and 3.

The Netherlands (in which the adult population already displayed a relatively high level of support for European integration) shows a relatively small age group difference; but over the four measures, our samples of French and German youth show pronounced increases in Europeanness relative to the adults in those countries. English youth lag behind here, as in our other comparison, although there is an indication of some increase in Europeanness relative to the adult popula-

TABLE 2. PERCENTAGE "FOR" FOUR PROPOSALS: ADULTS VS. YOUTH

	Netherlands	France	Germany	Britain
1. "Abolish tariffs?"				
Adults	79%	72%	71%	70%
Youth	87	83	89	74
2. "Free movement of labor and business?"				
Adults	76	57	64	52
Youth	64	65	75	65
3. "Common foreign policy?"				
Adults	67	50	60	41
Youth	80	71	74	56
4. "Use 'our' taxes to aid poorer European countries?"				
Adults	70	43	52	63
Youth	82	68	72	57

TABLE 3. AVERAGE PERCENTAGE "FOR" FOUR MEASURES

	Netherlands	France	Germany	Britain
Adults	73%	56%	62%	57%
Youth	78	72	78	63
Difference	+5	+16	+16	+6
Normalized Difference[a]	19	36	42	14

[a] Normalized according to the Effectiveness Index described by Carl I. Hovland et al. "A Baseline for Measurement of Percentage Change" in Paul F. Lazarsfeld and Morris Rosenberg, The Language of Social Research (Glencoe, 1955), pp. 77-82.

TABLE 4. AVERAGE PERCENTAGE "FOR" FOUR MEASURES, BY AGE GROUP

Age groups	Netherlands	France	Germany	Britain
55 and over	70%	47%	52%	49%
40-50	73	58	63	57
30-39	71	59	64	61
21-29	72	58	67	60
16-19 (youth sample)	77	72	78	63

tion of Britain.[3] Striking as these generational differences are, they become even more interesting when we break down the adult responses according to age group as in Table 4.

In the Netherlands, the most notable feature of this pattern is its stability among different age groups. Dutch youth are more European than the oldest adult group (55 and over), but the difference is one of only 7 percentage points: an average of 77% "For" among the teenagers, as compared with 70% among the oldest group. The gap between the "55 and over" Germans and the teen-age Germans is much larger: fully 26 percentage points separate the two groups, building from a base of 52%. This seems to confirm other findings of striking differences among age groups reported for that country. One hears less talk of a "generation conflict" in France, yet in regard to the European issue, my data indicate that among the French there is almost as great change from middle-agers to teen-agers as in the case of Germany: an increase of 25 percentage points in over-all support of the four European integration measures. The increase from oldest to youngest age group in England is intermediate: 14 percentage points.

While the average levels of support for these concrete proposals are considerably below the landslide approval of European "unification," we might tentatively draw the conclusion that the youngest generation in each of these countries is significantly more favorable to European

[3] Does this imply that youth is more cosmopolitan than adults as a general rule? Not necessarily. The example of the Hitler youth might be cited as an indication that the reverse relationship is also possible. My interpretation is simply that, because of the specific influences present in their early socialization, this *particular* crop of youth has been oriented in a more European and less nationalistic direction than preceding age cohorts.

integration than the group 55 and over — the age group which now holds most top-level positions of political power in these countries. Two relative discontinuities are particularly interesting in the age-group pattern: first, we notice that in France, Germany and Britain, the "over 55" group is markedly less European than the group immediately bordering it: there is a sharp drop of 8 to 11 percentage points. On the other hand, we find no sizeable gap between the oldest *Dutch* group and the next younger group, in regard to Europeanness. Indeed, the "over 55" group in that country is within 2 points of the "21–29" group. This contrast between Dutch stability and the rather sharp changes in the age group patterns of her neighbors cannot readily be interpreted in terms of a life cycle explanation and it leads us to a very interesting alternative interpretation.

The age group which was 55 and older in 1963 was at least 10 years old at the end of World War I. These individuals were exposed to the period of intense nationalism which preceded that war, and to the powerful fears and suspicions the war aroused during a relatively impressionable stage of life. Alone among these four countries, Holland did not participate in World War I — nor was she deeply involved in the preceding great-power rivalries. If one's concept of nationality tends to be established early in life,[4] then the sharp decline in Europeanness which we find among this age group in each country *except* The Netherlands might be attributed to a residue from experiences in childhood and youth. It seems plausible that the effect of a major war on one's feelings of trust and kinship with the "enemy" people (e.g., the French toward the Germans) is strongly negative.

The "over 55" group in France, Germany and Britain had a powerful dose of the influences of World War I in its early years: the corresponding group in Holland was much less affected by them. And the next younger group (this time in all four countries) also shows less of the effect which we might attribute to that period: the median year of birth for this group is 1916. The oldest members of the younger group would have had some exposure to World War I (and their Europeanness would be lessened accordingly); but to a large extent this group was too young to be directly aware of World War I, and had reached adulthood before the outbreak of World War II. Karl Deutsch reports a phenomenon which seems to fit in with this interpretation. Drawing on data from a series of elite interviews in France, he reports:

> Typically, age accounts for less than 5 per cent of the variance in the answers found. Within these limits, the "middle elites" — those in their fifties and hence the generation of the 1930's and World War II — tend

---

[4] See, for example, Jean Piaget, "Le développement chez l'enfant de l'idée de patrie et de relations avec l'étranger," *Bulletin Internationale de Science Sociale*, UNESCO, 1961, pp. 3, 605, 621. Piaget concludes that the concept of nationality is fully developed by age 14. Cf. Robert Hess, Judith Torney and David Jackson, *The Development of Basic Attitudes and Values Toward Government, Part I* (Chicago, 1965), p. 380; and Gustav Jahoda, "Children's Ideas about Country and Nationality," *British Journal of Educational Psychology*, June, 1963.

to differ from both their elders and juniors, who in turn often resemble each other. This middle elite group is somewhat more nationalistic and more closely identified with the de Gaulle regime. The junior elite — those under 50 — are more internationalistic, more in favor of alliances, and still more opposed to an independent foreign policy for France.[5]

While Deutsch refers to the relatively nationalistic group as "the generation of the 30's and World War II," they might also be described as "the generation of World War I": in their fifties in 1964 (the time of the interviews), the Great War was probably felt as *the* important event of their childhood. They were 4 to 14 years old at the War's end. The next younger group was unaware of the war, while most of the older group had already passed through their most important years of political socialization by that time.

Moving down the age group tables, we notice little further increase in Europeanness among the adult population. This would be surprising if we were to work on the assumption that younger people are naturally more open to new ideas (a favorite assumption of intuitive life-cycle interpretations). Again we would attribute this peculiarity to the psychological residue of a major event — in this case, World War II. The median year of birth of the youngest adult group is 1938: by 1945, its members were 3 to 11 years old, and had experienced Blitz, Occupation, and devastation during the most impressionable years of life. The "European" atmosphere of the post-war years should *also* have made a relatively great impact on this youngest adult group — but apparently not enough to make them significantly more European than the older adult groups.

Except for the oldest group, none of the age groups discussed so far is a "pure" category from the standpoint of historical experiences. To some extent they overlap, containing individuals who were socialized during periods which we would consider optimal (from the standpoint of developing Europeanness) as well as individuals who were exposed to powerful negative influences during the years of childhood and early youth. The youngest group of all (those in the 16–19 year old category) do constitute a "pure" group in this sense. All of these individuals were born in 1945 or later; they have gained their first political perceptions in a world where European organization seems natural and right, and nationalism seems archaic and dangerous. It is among this youngest group that we find (as we did with the oldest group) a relatively great discontinuity from the level of Europeanness of the adjacent group. This discontinuity is most marked in France and Germany; it exists also in The Netherlands; but it is very slight in England. The latter finding may be highly significant. I conclude that at least two elements are necessary for the establishment of a strong sense of Europeanness:

1. The absence of divisive memories (but this is not enough in itself).

[5] Deutsch, "Arms Control," *American Political Science Review* 60 (1966), p. 358.

2. A sense of positive participation in substantial common activities. Britain has not participated in the institutions of the European Community. Youth in the other three countries, however, have grown up with some awareness of a common endeavor, and this may explain, at least in part, their greater degree of backing for European integration measures.

I. AGE COHORT AND HISTORICAL PERIOD

Projecting from the foregoing data, we might anticipate that the current generation of youth in these countries will manifest a relatively "European" outlook when they become adults, because this accords with conditions obtaining at that point in time when their basic political orientations were instilled. At this point, let me introduce an hypothesis which will make more explicit the relationship which I believe exists between certain distinctive aspects of the attitudes of a given age cohort and the period in which the group received its early socialization. The central element in this hypothesis is something which we might call "structural inertia" in concept formation. Taking this view, we would regard the socialization process as one in which perceptions become ordered into increasingly complex conceptual structures. Only a few of the infant's earliest perceptions — those related to basic needs — will give rise to subjectively important symbols. Most other stimuli will be disregarded as "noise." Subsequent perceptions which are regularly associated with these symbols may take on a derivative importance; these will tend to become relatively permanent, to the extent that a relatively large number of perceptions are associated together around a given basic symbol. To change a central part of the system would require a disassembly and reintegration of the whole structure. Accordingly, adult learning has been contrasted with infant learning as the "recombination of a smaller number of larger subassemblies of memories or habits. . . ."[6] When one has reached adulthood, only a very important event, making a deep and continuing impact on the individual's life, would justify the cost of such a conceptual reorganization.

My expectation on the basis of this hypothesis, is that the full impact of the post-war European movement has not yet manifested itself among the adult population. I would anticipate a time lag between certain types of major political outputs and the resulting feedback into the political system, because of the gap in time between the early political socialization of individuals,[7] and the point at which they become politically relevant. We might diagram the basis of this time lag as in Figure 1.

A major event (war, or the establishment of new political institutions let us say) occurs at time X — during the adult years of generation "1," bringing about a relatively superficial attitudinal change in that

[6] D. O. Hebb, cited in Karl Deutsch, *The Nerves of Government* (New York, 1963), p. 166.
[7] That is, the socialization which takes place in childhood and youth.

FIGURE 1. TIME LAG AND ATTITUDE DEVELOPMENT

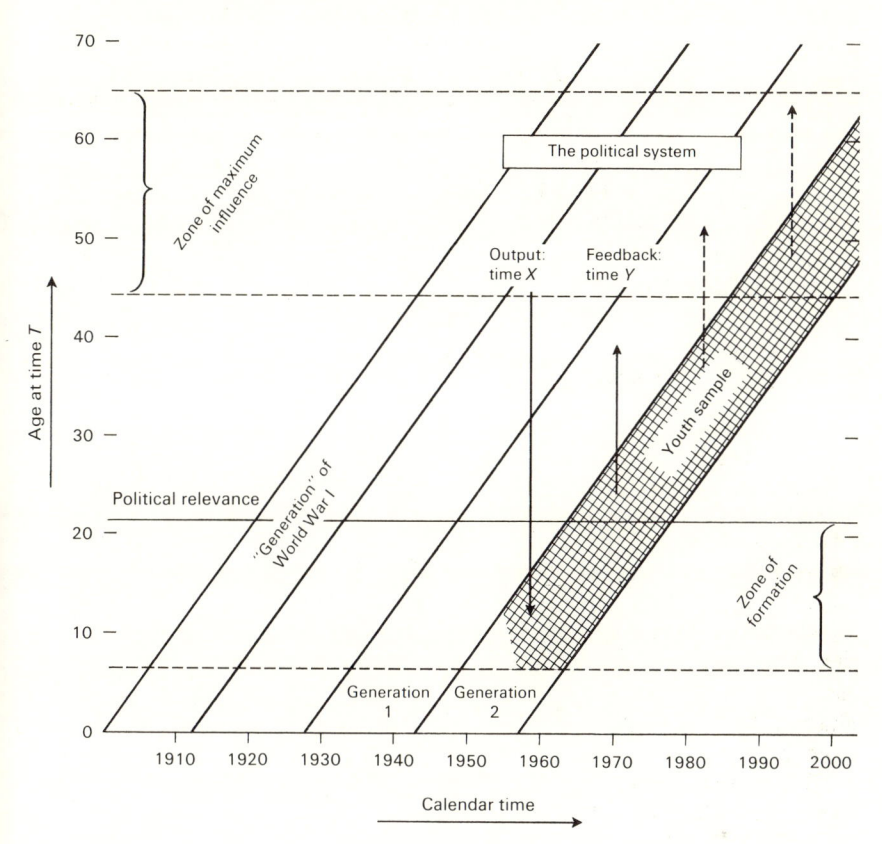

generation. It has occurred during the late childhood of generation "2" and influences the basic political orientation of that age group. Its political feedback, however, may not be felt until time Y, when that generation "surfaces" into political relevance. (This point is arbitrarily indicated as age 21.) Such a time-lag effect would only be expected to operate in connection with relatively early-established and persisting aspects of political socialization. Provisionally, I interpret these data on development of a sense of European political identity according to this model.[8]

---

[8] A parallel to the European phenomenon also seems to exist in the American context; it could be interpreted as due to a differential impact of this country's post-war internationalism on different age cohorts. A nation-wide survey of high school seniors and their parents in 1965 produced evidence of a possible intergenerational shift in the direction of more cosmopolitan political attitudes. Ranking the relative salience which four levels of government had for them (international, national, state and local), fully 65% of the students rated international politics in first or second place; only 42% of the parents did so. See M. Kent Jennings, *Pre-Adult Orientations to Multiple Systems of Government* (paper presented to the Midwest Conference of Political Scientists, Chicago, April 1966).

It is, of course, impossible to predict with certainty what attitudes a given age group will express in a decade or two. My interpretation would be far more convincing if I were able to support it with longitudinal data based on national probability samples made at *several* different points in time. This is a goal for further research. On the basis of the evidence we have examined, however, we might infer tentatively that the younger generation has a stronger *tendency* to support the concept of a federal Europe than do older age groups in these countries. The Europeanness of the youth samples presumably represents a basic orientation, rather than a re-orientation in conformity with current experience.

II. DECAY OR STABILITY IN AGE GROUP DIFFERENCES?

We find age group differences, then, as predicted by our model. But will these differences persist? From the perspective of the exceptionally stable American political community (which has experienced a relatively slowly changing political consensus for about a century) one may be tempted to assume that these age-group differences will decay — that by the time the current European youth are as old as today's adults, they will hold the same attitudes. To be sure, a life cycle interpretation may provide a valid explanation for many or most of the age group differences which have been found in survey research, especially among societies which are not undergoing rapid social change. On the other hand, it is clear that this is not true in *all* cases, even in Western societies.[9]

The relative importance of decay in age group differences probably varies according to at least three sets of circumstances: (1) The type of attitude involved. Preferences in popular music, for example, may be very largely governed by life cycle factors; political party preference, or matters of even more fundamental self-identification may be much less so. (2) The age at which the given orientation is established. According to our concept of structural inertia, those attitudes which are earliest established should be hardest to change. Orientation toward the political community seems to be established relatively early in life. (3) The causes of the given set of age group differences: are they attributable to different reactions to the same environmental conditions at different points in the life cycle, or are they due to different conditions of early socialization? If the latter, we might expect decay to be relatively unimportant, particularly if the changed conditions persist.

If Europeanness were a matter of teen-age rebellion, for example, we might be justified in assuming that it would diminish with increasing

---

[9] There are indications that an age-specific pattern in American political party preferences may be linked to the differential impact which the Great Depression had on different age groups. These differences apparently have not decayed. See Angus Campbell, Philip E. Converse, Warren E. Miller, and Donald E. Stokes, *The American Voter* (New York, 1960), pp. 153–156.

maturity. Our interviews gave little indication that Europeanness was regarded by youth as a form of rebellion.[10] On the contrary, it seemed to be generally regarded as an enlightened and highly respectable orientation. Analysis by social status reinforces this impression; far from being a deviant position, "Europeanness" is likely to be found among those of higher status and those who are most integrated into the community. My interpretation links the age group differences which seem to exist regarding Europeanness with the following differences in the conditions of early socialization:

1. Absence of a major intra-European war from the younger individuals' experience.
2. A marked increase in intra-European transactions, with a possible reduction in the psychological distance between the groups concerned.
3. Development of European institutions which perform important functions and are widely regarded as beneficial.

All these factors have distinguished the early socialization of European youth from that of the older generations. Moreover, they continue to operate; we might well argue that their impact is likely to *increase* rather than disappear as the current crop of youth grows older. These do not appear to be transient stimuli, felt only at a certain stage of life, but persisting factors. Although they probably reach their greatest degree of effectiveness in orienting (presumably malleable) children, they may also have some effect in resocializing adults in the same direction. The fact that adult age cohorts appear to have become somewhat more European during their mature years suggests that one might reverse the question about decay, and ask "How much *more* European are these younger people likely to become by the time they are 30 to 40 years old?"

---

[10] The relative Europeanness of the youth in our samples probably springs from naiveté or adolescent rebellion to only a very limited degree. The fact that they have a relatively pessimistic (and perhaps realistic) view of how long it will take for Europe to become "unified" — and the fact that they have a level of knowledge which compares favorably with that of adults — tends to make an explanation in terms of naiveté somewhat untenable. Our interviews indicated, moreover, that rebellion is not an important theme in connection with European integration. Despite the widespread prevalence of a stereotype of youthful rebellion, the available evidence suggests that it is important only in exceptional individual cases, as far as political views are concerned. See M. Kent Jennings and Richard G. Niemi, *Family Structure and the Transmission of Political Values* (paper presented at the 1966 annual meeting of the American Political Science Association, New York City, Sept. 6–10). Cf. Eleanor Maccoby et al., "Youth and Political Change," *Public Opinion Quarterly* (Spring 1954), pp. 23–29.

FRANK A. PINNER

Students in the Postwar World

University education in European societies has long been the privilege of a very small proportion of young people. It affords the promise of success in later life, but it does not guarantee this success. The conditions in which studies are conducted increase anxieties, for students must spend many years preparing for examinations, with very little contact with their professors, and often with considerable difficulties in financing their studies. (Britain is the exception to this generalization.) In such circumstances, it is hardly surprising that students organize to advance their aims as a distinctive social group, and feel ambivalent about the institutions of their elders. Frank Pinner's study of student organizations in Continental societies is particularly valuable, in that the author brings personal knowledge and time perspectives to the discussion of contemporary student demonstrations. A native of Germany, he studied at the University of Berlin and the Ecole Libre des Sciences Politiques, Paris, before proceeding to America to take his Ph.D. at the University of California, Berkeley, in 1954.

For leaders and activists, participation in an organization or movement constitutes an important part of life, while the involvement of sympathizers is much less complete and demanding. Sympathizers

Abridged from Frank Pinner, "Tradition and Transgression: Western European Students in the Postwar World," *Daedalus*, 93, 1, 1964, pp. 142–155. Reprinted by permission of *Daedalus, Journal of the American Academy of Arts and Sciences.*

I am indebted to the Institute for Advanced Studies and Scientific Research, Vienna, Austria, whose facilities I was able to use while gathering materials for this study. I also gratefully acknowledge the support of the Harvard Center for International Affairs which helped defray the research expenses. The data on Belgium and the Netherlands, gathered in 1962–63, were obtained with the support of the Institut de Sociologie, University of Brussels, whose cooperation I have greatly appreciated. I am most grateful to Harro Dietrich Kähler for reviewing the article, particularly my interpretation of the German events; and to Nancy Hammond for perceptive editorial advice.

may find themselves in general agreement with an organization's point of view, or they may participate in demonstrations because of an acute sense of crisis that calls for immediate action. Rarely, however, do they share the ideological commitments of leaders and activists. . . .

In general, students may be aroused when they see a major injustice being committed or when their personal interests are at stake. The specific issues that are thought to compel moral resistance or legitimate defense vary from country to country. They are probably determined more by cultural traditions and political antecedents than by the student's position in the university and society. The Algerian war can be regarded as a prototypical case: It stirred strong feelings of revulsion against the atrocities committed by the French authorities in Algiers and, at the same time, threatened the students with the possibility of military service in an unpopular war. . . .

For the student leader or activist, the organization is a way of life, and the movement is likely to have a significance that goes far beyond specific issues featured for public consumption and arousal. No student expects to remain a student forever, and no matter how he looks upon his organization, it must in some way permit him to pass from his current status to a different one, and from his present role to others. A student trade union, for example, cannot have the same significance for its active members as an industrial union has for its workers. The worker normally expects to spend his life in a particular occupation or trade, and his union aims to make that life as rewarding as possible.

Two broad possibilities are open to the student: He can either prepare himself to occupy a position in society, or commit himself to a restructuring of society that would make new roles and new positions available. Student organizations follow this dichotomy: "Socializing" organizations educate their members so they will be prepared for their future roles in society, while "transgressive" ones aim for social and political change.

Some socializing organizations prepare the student mainly for his future occupation, while others prepare him for status positions in society. The latter will be termed *traditional,* because they help to mold future social and political elites by inculcating traditional values. In this process, systematic indoctrination tends to be of secondary importance.

All traditional organizations — for example, the *gezelligheidsverenigingen* (social associations) in Holland and the *Korporationen* in Germany and Austria — have certain objectives and techniques in common. An esprit de corps is fostered in these groups by their selectivity in recruitment, by pre-emption of the student's time (particularly during his early years of study), and by elaborate rituals that emphasize the uniqueness of the particular group and the distinctiveness of the social stratum to which it belongs. Conceptions of hierarchy and its importance are fostered both within these organizations and without. Sharp social distinctions tend to separate the older students from younger ones inside the organizations, and "older" or "better" fraternities from less prestigious ones on the outside. Specific orientations toward conflict are generated through institutionalized behavior designed to challenge the wit or the courage of the young student.

There are telling differences between the Dutch and the Germano-Austrian fraternal organizations. The Germanic *Korporation* is usually a small group, having up to fifty active members. Conflict between fraternity brothers is minimized and considered undesirable, while conflict with outsiders is ritually encouraged. In Holland, on the other hand, the *gezelligheidsverenigingen* are generally larger structures comprising several hundred active members, and all challenges of the young members originate *within* the organizations. The archetypical, although no longer the most widely accepted form of conflict in German student fraternities is the *Mensur*, a modified and relatively harmless form of the duel, in which the contestants' steadfastness and ability to take adversity without fainting or flinching are tested. In the Dutch fraternity, the challenge consists primarily in a matching of wits, a degenerate form of the medieval disputation. The novice is challenged further by having his opinions contradicted and ridiculed on every occasion in order to make him realize that his views are without foundation and that he still has to learn.

These practices are clearly related to different role images. The German image of a worthy member of the elite still retains some of the attributes of the military aristocracy whose standards were eagerly adopted, often in their most corrupt form, by the middle classes in the second half of the last century. The Dutch role image is that of the *academicus*, a respected member of an urban society in which economic success rests upon cleverness in business and the ability to maintain a certain decorum.

In both Holland and Germany, the most prestigious fraternal organizations contain unexpectedly high proportions of students in the fields of medicine and law; here role images are the clearest, and pre-industrial forms of practice are jealously preserved. The less prestigious an organization is, the larger is its share of students preparing themselves for business or teaching. A social-science student is seldom a member of a fraternity. In the nontraditional organizations (which have been labeled *transgressive* above), the situation is reversed. A student of medicine is a great rarity, while sociologists, psychologists, and political scientists are encountered in proportions totally out of keeping with their relatively small representation in the university populations. The role images of social-science students, whose curriculum leads to no clearly defined career, are bound to be vague or nonexistent, and their choice of specialty betrays some critical attitude toward society.

Thus, for the typical members of transgressive organizations, role images are either unavailable because of the uncertainty of their professional future, or unacceptable because of their opposition to the traditional system of social roles. These organizations all tend to transgress social boundaries. By declaring in the Charter of Grenoble that "the student is a young intellectual worker," the French UNEF [*Union Nationale des Etudiants de France*] proposed to abolish the boundaries separating intellectuals from workers and young people from the world of work and responsibility. The alliance of Christians and Marxists that has governed the UNEF during most of its existence was itself an act of transgression for which both the young Communists and the young Catholics were disciplined by their Party or church.

In Germany, the most sacrosanct boundary (even though West German authorities officially and strenuously object to its existence) remains the Berlin Wall and the border fortifications separating the two republics; accordingly, the most extreme act of transgression consists of crossing that line by establishing links between the East and the West. Most of Germany's political student organizations and, to some extent, its official student representations have done this repeatedly, to the great dismay of their elders in political parties, government, and university administrations. These tendencies have become strongest and, for the official leadership, most embarrassing in Berlin, symbol of the East-West conflict. The perennial free-speech conflict at the Free University of Berlin has constituted the students' attempt to obliterate the traditionally strong distinctions separating student and professor in Germany. The charter of the university, written deliberately as a democratic response to the suppression of academic freedom in the East, had explicitly defined the new institution as a "community of scholars and students" (*Lehrende und Lernende*) and installed student representatives with voting rights in most of the university's decision-making organs. Thus, the students' demands once more struck particularly sensitive nerves in the administrations of the university and of the city.

To some degree, a social role system always reflects the system of social segregation — the division of society into groups constituted on the basis of social class, religion, ethnicity, and so forth. A wish to change the system of social roles may lead to the belief that the system of social segregation needs to be changed. Young people tend to be greatly concerned with the choice of roles, because it is through them that they try to establish their identity. In each age group, some young people will reject both the present and future roles that society assigns to them. During certain periods such young people may come to reject not only these roles, but also the group structure that corresponds to them. Clearly, such transgressive tendencies are less likely when social boundaries effectively limit the social horizon. Thus, the German youth movement, which arose at the end of the nineteenth century as a protest against urban life and the corruption of middle-class society, never got beyond a program of inner renewal through communion with nature and through cultivation of the horde spirit. The movement failed to ally itself with the organizations of young workers that appeared at the same time as part of the socialist movement, since the boundaries between social classes were too sharply drawn and too much taken for granted.

Transgression seems to occur when the members of a movement perceive the future — their own or that of their group — as either particularly barren or particularly promising. To the young Russian intellectuals of the late-nineteenth and early-twentieth centuries, for example, all avenues toward a rewarding future appeared blocked. The chances were slim that they might become effective members of their society as either professional men or social or political leaders. Thus, they felt the need to ally themselves with other groups of the population in order to achieve the downfall of a regime that frustrated all legitimate ambition. Young intellectuals in colonial countries have often reacted in a similar manner to the strict limitation of their opportunities. As nationalists aiming to achieve the independence of their country, they frequently transgress lines of class or caste in order to ally themselves with other social classes.

The second condition of transgression — the perception of an expanding social universe — is often associated with the end of a war or with pre-revolutionary gains in economic well-being and political freedom. After the end of the Napoleonic wars and again in the period preceding 1848, sizable groups in German universities attempted to ally themselves with other groups in the population. At the end of World War II, French students who had shared the experience of the resistance movement with young people from all walks of life intended to remain actively engaged in a common effort of all young people to rebuild and reshape their country. The Charter of Grenoble expresses their aspiration to play a role in a process of social transformation made possible by the common experience of a catastrophic past and the common hope for a brighter, more humane future. Toward the end of the last decade, the thaw following Stalin's death and the growth of modern trends in Roman Catholicism once again encouraged optimism concerning the possibility of productive co-operation among groups previously separated by social and ideological barriers. Herbert Marcuse, to whom many leaders of the Berlin movement look for intellectual guidance, has repeatedly expressed this philosophy of hope by pointing to society's tremendous technological potential and to the need for a new social structure capable of realizing that potential. Such rising expectations have made for discord between youth groups and their parent organizations and have furnished the impetus for the spread of the trade-union movement from France into Belgium and the Netherlands.

Depending on the conditions just discussed, one transgressive movement may differ from another in important ways. If frustration and despair preside at its birth, its members are apt to display tendencies toward ideological orientations that help to interpret and to render psychologically tolerable the marginal and precarious situation of the membership while strengthening its internal cohesion. Unable to hope for success in the present or the immediate future, such a movement will look forward to a total destruction of the social fabric, and the only payoff in the present will be the stubborn and self-reinforcing hope for the *dies irae*. It may adopt conspiratorial attitudes and practices and thus accentuate its separateness from society. Hence, it may be called an "ideological protest" movement.

A transgressive movement born of optimism will, on the other hand, tend to de-emphasize ideological divisions and stress the values that unite its members and followers. Thus, the UNEF emphasized the value of social obligation, an element common to the philosophies of Marxism and Catholicism, rather than the individualistic liberalism that had dominated the Third Republic. Since a movement of this kind seeks achievements in the present, it must take a position on specific current issues. This is not to say that such a movement is necessarily "reformist," in the sense that term has acquired in Marxist literature. During the period when the so-called *syndicaliste* wing was in command, most of the UNEF leaders were profoundly critical of the socioeconomic and political order, but thought that this system could be transformed radically if young intellectuals, in alliance with other progressive groups in the population, could actively participate in the process of policy formation by assuming responsible roles in society. For this reason, such a movement is best designated as "role seeking." Indeed, a central point in the internal debates of the UNEF has been the search for an adequate definition of the student's role.

By their very nature, the two types of transgressive movements are bound to have different political effects. Having nothing better to do, ideological protest movements often exhaust themselves in internal debates and in sporadic but mostly ineffectual action. In revolutionary situations, however, they are likely to furnish dedicated leaders for a popular movement. Role-seeking movements, on the other hand, are impatient: They constantly search for points of contact with other groups and with the happenings of the day, and they are likely to experience periods of discouragement if such points are not found.

DISSIDENCE

Role-seeking movements are frequently alliances of dissidents from established parent organizations. If young Communists and Catholics in UNEF work together in their student trade union, they rarely do so with the approval of their parent organizations. Both the Catholic and Communist hierarchies tend to regard their student groups as auxiliaries whose main tasks are spreading the organizations' beliefs, attracting young supporters, and preparing them for their future role as full-fledged members. The youth organizations, however, tend to insist on autonomy in their beliefs, actions, and alliances. The last of these demands regularly meets with the determined resistance of the parent hierarchy, which feels that their young supporters are likely to be lost to the organizational opponent.

Both the *Jeunesse Etudiante Chrétienne* (JEC) and the *Union des Etudiants Communistes* (UEC) have suffered repeated crises precipitated by the adult organizations' attempts to regain control of student groups that had, in their opinion, gone too far afield. The JEC experienced its first major crisis in 1956, when the Catholic hierarchy forced the dissolution of the *Association Catholique de la Jeunesse Française*

(ACJF), and its second in 1965, when the officers of the JEC were forcibly removed from their positions. In both cases, the point at issue was the role of the so-called "lay apostolate." The hierarchy insisted that the sole task of young people in Catholic Action was to evangelize their milieu and to combat godlessness by spreading the teachings of the gospel. The JEC leaders countered these demands by saying that Christian charity means helping others to understand better their own situations. They held that the success of evangelism depends on the lay apostle's ability to participate in the struggles of his social group and generation, and that such participation necessarily requires close co-operation with non-Catholics, particularly Protestants and Communists.

The crisis of the UEC lasted from 1962 to 1966. The ideological issue, which initially served to disguise more prosaic concerns with organizational control, dealt with the Marxist concept of class. Contrary to the wishes of the Party, the UEC had written a programmatic statement which described students as a progressive force in society. In a full-scale discussion of this definition, the Party theoreticians pointed out that most students belong to the bourgeoisie or petite-bourgeoisie and are, therefore, not to be considered natural allies of the working class. To these doctrinal objections, the president of UEC had a rather unorthodox answer: He affirmed that a person's class membership is not determined by what he is, but by what he does; that because most students act as progressives, they belong to the progressive forces in society. This debate with the Party leadership enabled the young Communists to increase their prestige among the students and, thereby, to play a greater role within the UNEF. Continued efforts by the Party's Central Committee to recapture control of the Communist student organization did, however, succeed in the end. The Party was aided in its efforts by a general resurgence of political sectarianism during the mid-sixties. The UEC soon became prey to intensive internal squabbles among "Italians" (followers of Palmiro Togliatti), neo-Stalinists, neo-Trotskyites, Maoists, and a variety of opposition groups within each of these major denominations. By 1965, the Party regained control of the organization, and, as a result, most of UEC's talented leaders withdrew.

Similar phenomena of dissidence and transgression are clearly observable among the student groups of German political parties. The SDS, currently the most influential left-wing student organization, was originally the official student group of the Social-Democratic Party. Because of continuing disagreements over German rearmament and contacts with East Germany, the Party created a second organization in 1960. In 1961, the Party declared that membership in the SDS was incompatible with Party membership, thus excluding in effect the entire SDS membership and withdrawing all subsidies. This separation from the Party eventually redounded to the political benefit of SDS, which could now ally itself with other left-wing groups and thus become the most vocal and most effective member of the "extra-parliamentary opposition."

The *Sozialistische Hochschulbund* (SHB), the successor of SDS as the official Social-Democratic student organization, has traveled approximately the same path as SDS. From a rival, it has become an ally. The organization opposes the Party on nearly all important issues, such as support of NATO, projected emergency legislation (which would suspend basic rights whenever the government declared a national emergency to exist), and the current policy of coalition with the Christian-Democratic Party.

Nearly everywhere, the student organizations of political parties are to the left of the officialdom, often considerably so. Commonly, the disagreement is over the kinds of associates the group may select for political company. Thus is replayed, in political terms, the old drama of parents and children, with the parents trying to restrict and the children trying to widen the range of their contacts. The Dutch socialist students, organized in a club called *Politeia*, are far to the left of the Labor Party and tend to associate with elements much further to the left; the student trade-union movement has given them increased opportunity to do this. A recent revolt in the socialist student organization of Austria has given control to a group that rejects the establishmentarianism of the Socialist Party, takes a self-consciously "Marxist" stand, and tends to embarrass the Party leadership by exposing its bureaucratic tendencies.

The recurrence of dissident movements and of periods during which control of the adult organization is restored has its origins in the rapid changes in the memberships of youth organizations. Once rebellious leaders of a youth group have been disciplined or removed by the parent organization, the group usually experiences a severe loss in members, vitality, and influence. When the crisis is over and new members begin to join the youth club, the process of dissidence is apt to start all over again. Organizational memories are short, in any event, where "generations" span only a few years. New recruits join a party-related group for the same reasons as their predecessors did: Politics may appear to them as an opportunity to participate responsibly in making social decisions. Once they discover that the party will not admit them to full citizenship in the organization, renewed efforts toward organizational independence and transgressive tendencies are likely to occur.

EFFECTIVENESS AND STABILITY

Among student groups with social or political interests, the party-related or church-affiliated organizations are usually the least effective. This indicates that students do not see the need for special political or religious student organizations if these have nothing more (and possibly less) to offer than the parties or churches themselves. Before 1962, the numerically rather weak political and religious student organizations at the University of Amsterdam had joined forces in order to present candidates at student elections and to allocate seats among themselves. Indeed, shortly before the student trade-union movement came into being, these groups had managed, with the help of some of the more modern fraternal organizations, to elect a socialist as president of the student council. The tide was obviously turning in the direction of greater political engagement on the part of students and of greater support for political action. Yet, the formally independent student trade-union movement, rather than the political groups, reaped the benefits of this change of mood in the student population. A similar development is observable in Germany, where the influence of SDS is clearly out of keeping with its numerical strength. SDS leaders claim, probably with some justification, that separation from the Social-Democratic Party helped rather than hindered their activities.

Clearly, role-seeking movements can be more effective than conventional political-party or religious organizations, particularly if effectiveness is defined as the ability to mobilize student masses; and that, after all, is the measure of success most commonly applied by leaders. A role-seeking movement that has been able to set masses into motion will sometimes even be able to gain the limited support of traditional groups, as happened in France during the campaign against the Algerian war, in Holland on the occasion of protest against the reduction of student government scholarships, and in Germany during the recent controversies and demonstrations in Berlin.

In spite of this ability to lead student masses into action, the role-seeking movement is typically unstable. If political circumstances do not furnish issues that can engage widespread interest, or political repression seriously inhibits mass action, the movement will find itself in serious difficulty.

The process can be most easily demonstrated in France. The campaign against the Algerian war carried the UNEF to its apogee. The organization had proved its ability to organize strikes and demonstrations and to play a significant part in uniting the French trade-union movement in opposition to the government's war policies. Internal factionalism had been reduced to a minimum. At the end of the war, the organization found itself without an issue and seized upon the disastrous conditions in the French universities. In the fall of 1962, the UNEF organized a series of protest strikes and demonstrations against government neglect of higher education. This campaign collapsed by 1963, however, because the government rapidly initiated a building program and created new centers of higher education. After this crisis had passed, the leadership attempted a systematic analysis of the possible bases of a stable student trade-union movement. The result of their "reflection" was the so-called *orientation universitaire*. The theoreticians of this strategy argued that a student trade union must concern itself chiefly with the problems students encounter as they do their work of studying, and that the chief objective must be the transformation of the social structure of the university in order to make it an agent of change in society.

These theoretical considerations resulted in the establishment of the *groupes de travail universitaire* whose collapse indicated to the UNEF leadership that a trade unionism based on "university work" could not be achieved, and that a restructuring of the university, let alone of society, through action from within was an impossible goal. The Catholic student movement lost much of its influence on the destinies of the UNEF at this time, and the UNEF became the arena for sectarian squabbles among a variety of more or less dogmatic factions, most of them committed to one or another Marxist doctrine. By 1966, the UNEF had lost half of its membership (in spite of rapidly increasing enrollments), probably because of the antagonisms within the organization and the ill-conceived campaign of strikes and demonstrations against the government's university reform.

By comparison, traditional movements exhibit much greater stability. Indeed, viability and continuity are the chief principles that inform the structure of traditional organizations. The German *Korporation* is prototypical of such structures.

With virtually no exception, all *Korporationen* consider themselves *Lebensverbände* (unions for life), so that it is, in principle, impossible for a member to resign. At the end of his studies, the fraternity "brother" becomes an *Alter Herr* (old gentleman). He is expected to remain in contact with his *Korporation* and, above all, to make financial contributions to it. In almost all cases, the *Alte Herren* own the house and other assets of the fraternity, and in many of them they can vote on important issues. Thus, by material contributions and by their emphasis on tradition, the *Alte Herren* — more perhaps than the active members — insure the continuity of the *Korporationen*. Indeed, the rather surprising comeback of these fraternities in postwar Germany is due almost entirely to the zeal of the *Alte Herren,* many of whom began to rebuild their organizations and to recruit new members during the Allied occupation when the *Korporationen*, burdened by their pro-Nazi past, were still illegal. From 1950 to 1966, the *Alte Herren* fought and financed a series of court battles to force the official recognition of the *Korporationen* by the universities.

Party- and church-related organizations, insofar as they are loyal to their adult sponsors, enjoy similar, although not quite so extensive, advantages. These groups are, however, probably less stable than the fraternities, because the commitment of the adult sponsors is less personal and is often merely a reflection of political and organizational necessities. Even so, the most effective pressures in party- and church-related organizations operate in favor of the traditional ideological positions and comply with official policy. While intellectual disagreement is frequent, officers of such organizations avoid steps that might lead to a break with the parent organization, for this entails loss of subventions, office space, and various other forms of support. Political student leaders who find themselves at odds with the policies of their party also tend to argue that independence from the party would condemn the student groups to political ineffectiveness and that, so long as the bonds are not broken, the students have at least a chance to expose their views within the party councils and thus to work for a modification of party policy.

STUDENT ORGANIZATIONS AND HISTORICAL CHANGE

The changing fortunes of student organizations are doubtless related to historical events. The parallelisms in the rise and fall of student organizations in the same country and in different ones are too striking for this not to be true. At the end of World War II, most students believed that the old exclusive fraternities would never be resurrected. In the Netherlands, plans had been laid for social organizations and clubs open to all, and the revival of *Korporationen* in Germany and Austria seemed inconsistent with the establishment of republican regimes. Yet, as the structures of social relations became stabilized, the old forms of traditional organizations reappeared and largely regained lost ground. There have been changes, to be sure. The German *Korporationen* now officially endorse the Republican regime that they had vigorously combated throughout the life of the Weimar Republic, and anti-Semitism is just as officially banned. In Holland, a variety of less exclusive social fraternities and sororities have developed alongside the traditional *Corps,* and the *Corps* itself is at pains to deny accusations of status-consciousness. The extent to which the traditional organizations have been reconstituted and their traditions reinstated reflects rather faithfully the extent to which the social distinctions of the prewar era have re-emerged.

Not only in France, but also in Holland and Austria, the first years following the war saw the initial efforts at creating role-seeking movements. Their first blooming was to be short, for the rigidities introduced into all political systems by the Cold War and the painful dissolution of the colonial empires gave little encouragement to such movements. The UNEF survived under the management of its more moderate, apolitical wing, while organized activity of students reached a low in the other European countries. A resurgence of role-seeking movements occurred toward the end of the fifties as the colonial wars subsided and the thaw in the Communist and Catholic worlds made social and national boundaries seem less forbidding. Yet the movement was soon to encounter new obstacles: the reappearance of international tensions and the determination of governments and university administrations to set limits to a movement that tended to interfere with the structure of authority.

As a result, transgressive student movements everywhere have now assumed a more ideological and sectarian character. This retreat may be temporary, but for the moment the belief in the malleability of the social structure has weakened, and more and more militants have become convinced that social change can only be achieved through violence. This posture is bound to reduce the popularity of transgressive organizations among students. At the same time, a polarization of minorities on the right and left might occur, producing all the disruptive effects such a change entails.

The great sensitivity of student movements to the political atmosphere of each period is doubtless a result of the rapid turnover in members and leaders. A generation of leaders usually lasts no more than three years, and the memory of student organizations, particularly of the nontraditional ones, rarely stretches further back than the preceding generation. Those who grew up in a movement under yesterday's leadership and who today realize its shortcomings and defects are likely to look for new ideas and strategies, unbridled by vested interests or long-standing intellectual commitments. Only the traditional organizations attempt to maintain continuity. To the extent that they are able to place their members in leading social positions, they tend to insure a certain uniformity over time of the character of social and political elites.

CHAPTER
FOUR

Social Structure and Voting Alignments

Cumulatively and at any time, the influence of a variety of institutions of socialization can be said to place people in a more or less complex social structure. Usually class differences are regarded as the chief dimension in social structure. The term "class" is a relatively high-level abstraction, with many of the advantages and disadvantages of a shorthand label. The development of modern European societies from a feudal basis has meant that class concepts are widely understood and in a number of respects appropriate. Yet deducing political behavior from class position presents many difficulties.

The first difficulty is that class is usually defined, for practical purposes, in terms of a single characteristic, an individual's occupation. Many people, especially the young, the retired, and widowed women, have no full-time occupation and a substantial number occupy jobs that are on the ill-defined border between the working-class and the middle-class. It is assumed that occupation is very highly correlated with a wide range of social attributes and attitudes. While there is usually some correlation between class position and political outlooks, in most of the Anglo-American societies, it is always imperfect and sometimes very weak. Moreover, occupation may appear most influential when in fact it does little more than reinforce outlooks developed in the family, e.g., when a child from a Labour-voting working-class English home follows his father to work as a coal miner at the age of 15 and votes Labour at the age of 21.

While occupational differences, like age and sex differences, are inevitable in all modern societies, these are not necessarily the only divisions within a society. In many countries, religion is less a belief system uniting people than a source of division between Protestants and Catholics, or Christians, indifferents, and anti-clericals. Language, ethnic, and racial distinctions can also serve to divide societies on political as well as social grounds. In such situations, social structure is multidimensional: individuals have a status reflecting religious, linguistic, or racial attributes, as well as a status reflecting their occupation. A relatively small proportion of a population may have the full cluster of attributes associated with an ideal-type worker, but many will have an imperfectly crystallized status, that is, they may rank higher on one attribute than on another. In such circumstances, it is important to assess which dimension of social structure most affects politics, as well as which provides an individual with his higher and lower statuses.

In comparative political analysis, the first task is to investigate whether dimensions of social structure are present, or are politically salient. For instance, all European societies have not had to face the division along color lines that has time and again been a major source of political conflict in America. Divisions along religious lines exist in most major European societies, as well as in America, yet only in France and Italy are they predominant politically. Clericalism and anticlericalism and not class provide the primary basis of political division there. Britain is unique in that the majority of its people are *only* divided on occupational grounds. One strong inducement to a two-party system is that about two-thirds of the total population of the United Kingdom, while divided into working and middle classes, are united in having an urban residence, a Protestant religion, and an English, as against a Scottish or Welsh, identity. In Germany, the two largest social groups constitute less than half the population, because of the division of society between Protestants and Catholics as well as between classes.

Social scientists have most frequently examined the relationship of social structure and politics through the study of voting behavior. Early findings emphasizing the importance of class position for party loyalties have undergone substantial revision and modification. One important change has been the emphasis placed upon the individual's ability to modify environmental influences through mechanisms of selective perception. Social structural phenomena seen as important by sociologists may not be regarded as equally important by voters. A second major modification is that political scientists have come to see that while some parties, under specified conditions, may represent a single cell of a complex society, parties may also play an independent and creative role, and their leaders may successfully solicit electoral support by aggregating groups in very different positions within society.

An exhaustive bibliography of electoral studies concerning European countries could easily consist of several hundred titles. Nevertheless, the balance, however impressive it may seem, is in one sense disappointing. In survey research, whatever the sampling method used, results are finally analyzed by taking into account the characteristics of the individuals interviewed and, with rare exceptions, without considering the social context in which these individuals live. However, social context has an important influence on individual behavior; this is commonplace in sociological textbooks but, paradoxically, has been more or less forgotten in the last twenty years by many very active researchers. A different method of research, analysis of the relationship between series of aggregate data by commune and other administrative units, has resulted in a number of descriptive-type publications. The analysis of aggregate data permits one neither to infer individual behavior from collective properties nor to analyze motivations. The survey method has particularly flourished in the United States and in Great Britain, and aggregate analysis in continental Europe. On the one hand, there was the danger of the ecological fallacy and, on the other hand, that of the individualistic fallacy. Now, with computer facilities, it is easier than before to combine, in electoral studies, aggregate data and survey data.

Bibliography

The best introduction to the voluminous literature on the formation of political attitudes in European societies can be found in S. M. Lipset and Stein Rokkan, editors, *Party Systems and Voter Alignments* (New York: Free Press, 1967). It includes chapters on England by R. T. McKenzie and Allen Silver, on France and Italy by Mattei Dogan, and on Germany by Juan Linz. Considerable comparative discussion of this problem can also be found in S. M. Lipset, *Political Man* (New York: Doubleday, 1960). Robert Alford's *Party and Society* (Chicago: Rand, McNally, 1963) spans continents in an analysis of class, religion, and regional influences upon party loyalties in Britain, America, Canada, and Australia. For an analysis of changes in class structure, see S. M. Lipset and Reinhard Bendix, *Social Mobility in Industrial Society* (Berkeley: University of California Press, 1959). For the influence of social context upon individual behavior, see Mattei Dogan and Stein Rokkan, editors, *Quantitative Ecological Analysis in the Social Sciences* (Cambridge, Mass.: M.I.T. Press, 1969), particularly the introduction and chapters by Juan Linz, Erwin Scheuch, and Philip Converse.

Notable national studies include David Butler and Donald Stokes, *Political Change in Britain* (New York: St. Martin's, 1969); Richard Hamilton, *Affluence and the French Worker in the Fourth Republic* (Princeton University Press, 1967); J. H. Goldthorpe, D. Lockwood, F. Bechhofer, and J. Platt, *The Affluent Worker: Political Attitudes and Behaviour* (Cambridge University Press, 1968); John Bonham, *The Middle Class Vote* (London: Farber and Farber, 1954), which is a good secondary analysis of survey data; S. Tarrow, "Political Dualism and Italian Communism," *American Political Science Review* (March 1967); M. Janowitz and D. R. Segal, "Social Cleavage and Party Affiliations: Germany, Great Britain and the United States," *American Journal of Sociology* (May 1967); and S. M. Lipset, P. F. Lazarsfeld, A. H. Barton, and J. Linz, *The Psychology of Voting: an Analysis of Political Behavior*, in G. Lindzey, editor, *Handbook of Social Psychology*, Vol.II (Reading, Mass.: Addison-Wesley, 1954), a comparative synthesis.

S. M. LIPSET

The Changing Class Structure and Contemporary European Politics

The concurrent appearance of working-class political organizations and demands for universal suffrage have made the relationship between class structure and party loyalties an enduring theme of European political sociology. Because the relation was assumed to be based on the economic disadvantages of workers, the post-war rise in standards of living throughout Europe has had major implications for theories of class politics. In his wide-ranging European survey, S. M. Lipset discusses both the causes and consequences of social change. It is important to note his qualification that, as class is not the only basis of party loyalty, so a decline in ideologies of class need not mean the end of all ideological conflicts in European politics.

During the 1950's commentators on both sides of the Atlantic began to depict western society by terms such as "The End of Ideology," "the post-industrial society," and the "post-bourgeois society." While emphasizing different themes, these commentators agreed that the growth of bureaucracy and "affluence" in western industrial democratic society has made possible a social system in which class conflict is minimized. Such a pattern in European society is relatively new. Much of the history of industrial society was a story of class-conscious politics and violent controversy between proletarian and bourgeois ideologists. Marxists viewed such tensions as inherent in a capitalist culture. That the United States, the most powerful capitalist state, lacks a strong socialist movement was viewed as a cultural lag, an inheritance of the period of an open land frontier that served as a "safety valve" for the

Abridged from S. M. Lipset, "The Changing Class Structure and Contemporary European Politics," *Daedalus,* 93, 1, 1964, pp. 271–87, 244–96. Reprinted by permission of *Daedalus,* Journal of the American Academy of Arts and Sciences.

tensions of industrialism. Presumably once this safety valve was gone, the European model of class-conscious politics would emerge.

In fact, history has validated a basic premise of Marxist sociology at the expense of Marxist politics. Marxist sociology assumes that cultural superstructures, including political behavior and status relationships, are a function of the underlying economic and technological structure. Hence, the most developed industrial society should also have the most developed set of political and class relationships. Since the United States is the most advanced society technologically, its superstructure should be more likely to correspond to the social structure of a modern industrial society than the "less" developed economies of Europe. In addition, one might argue that the absence of a traditional feudal past should mean that the United States has been most likely to develop the pure institutions of a capitalist industrial society. Hence, as an unpolitical Marxist sociology would expect, instead of European class and political relationships holding up a model of the United States' future, the social organization of the United States has presented the image of the European future.

The linkage between level of industrial development and other political and social institutions is obviously not a simple one. Greater economic productivity is associated with a more equitable distribution of consumption goods and education — factors contributing to a reduction of intra-societal tension. As the wealth of a nation increases, the status gap inherent in poor countries, where the rich perceive the poor as vulgar outcasts, is reduced. As differences in style of life are reduced, so are the tensions of stratification. And increased education enhances the propensity of different groups to "tolerate" each other, to accept the complex idea that truth and error are not necessarily on one side.

An explanation for the reduction in the appeal of total ideologies (*Weltanschauungen*) as simply derivative from the social concomitants inherent in increasing economic productivity is clearly oversimplified. T. H. Marshall has suggested that such extreme ideologies initially emerged with the rise of new strata, such as the bourgeoisie or the working class, as they sought the rights of citizenship, that is, the right to fully participate socially and politically. As long as they were denied such rights sizable segments of these strata endorsed revolutionary ideologies. In turn, older strata and institutions seeking to preserve their ancient monopolies of power and status fostered conservative extremist doctrines.

The history of changes in political ideologies in democratic countries, from this point of view, can be written in terms of the emergence of new strata, and their eventual integration in society and polity. The struggle for such integration took the form of defining the place in the polity of the old preindustrial upper classes, the church, the business strata and the working class. The variation in the intensity of "class conflict" in many European nations has been in large measure a function of the extent to which the enduring economic struggle among the classes overlapped with the issues concerning the place of religion and the traditional status structure. Such controversies usually were perceived in "moral" terms involving basic concepts of right versus wrong, and hence they were much more likely than economic issues to result in sharp ideological cleavage and even civil war. The continuance of extremist movements in nations such as Germany and the Latin countries of southern Europe may be traced to the force of moral sentiments inherent in concerns for traditional status or religious privileges. Where such issues were resolved without becoming identified with the economic class struggle, then as Marshall suggests intense ideological controversy declined almost as soon as the new strata gained full citizenship rights.

Still a third factor related to the general decline in ideological bitterness has been the acceptance of scientific thought and professionalism in matters which have been at the center of political controversy. Insofar as most organized participants in the political struggle accept the authority of experts in economics, military affairs, interpretations of the behavior of foreign nations and the like, it becomes increasingly difficult to challenge the views of opponents in moralistic "either/or" terms. Where there is some consensus among the scientific experts on specific issues, these tend to be removed as possible sources of intense controversy. As the ideology of "scientism" becomes accepted, the ideologies of the extreme left and right lose much of their impact.

But whatever the long-run sources of the reduction of the appeal of total ideologies (and there are short-run factors as well, such as the impact of wars both hot and cold), the fact remains that there has been a reduction in the intensity of class-linked political struggles in most of Europe. This paper surveys developments in the economies, social structures and political parties of European societies which are relevant to an analysis of such trends. Within the context of a broad comparative analysis it also deals with the sources of deviations from these trends. The analysis thus seeks to define the elements in the changing structures which make for a lessening or persistence of class ideologies in different parts of Europe.

CLASS AND POLITICAL CONSENSUS AFTER 1945

The "miracle" of the postwar economic growth of Europe has been well documented. A combination of circumstances — the depression crises, prolonged experience with state economic intervention and planning under fascism or wartime regimes, the sharp increase in approval of socialist or welfare state concepts during and immediately following the war and the need for some years after the conflict to plan for and even furnish the capital for capital investment — resulted in a far greater amount of planning and government involvement in spurring economic growth than had existed in any democratic state before 1939. The nationalization of businesses in France under the first de Gaulle regime surpassed the most grandiose ambitions of Third Republic Socialists, and systematic planning emerged in the early fifties.

The Austrian economy is characterized by large-scale government ownership. Italy retained and even expanded the considerable government economic sector developed under Fascism. In Germany, the numerous dependent war victims and the presence of refugees from the East, comprising more than one quarter of the population of West Germany, involved the state in welfare and other expenditures that took a large share of the gross national product for many years. And in Britain, the Labour government undertook an elaborate program of nationalization and welfare expenditures.

In almost all of these nations, therefore, two general events of considerable significance for class behavior have occurred. On the one hand, many of the political-economic issues that occasioned deep conflict between representatives of the left and of the right were resolved in ways compatible with social-democratic ideology. On the other hand, the dominant strata, business and other, discovered that they could prosper through economic reforms that they regarded a decade earlier as the rankest socialist measures. The socialists and trade unionists found that their formal structural objectives, in many cases, had been accomplished with the cooperation of their political rivals. The need for government planning for economic growth and full employment was generally accepted; the obligation of the state to provide welfare services for the ill, the aged and other dependent groups was viewed as proper by all parties; and the right of the trade union and political representatives of the workers to participate in decisions affecting industry and politics also was increasingly coming to be accepted. Domestic politics in most of these societies became reduced to the "politics of collective bargaining," that is, to the issue of which groups should secure a little more or less of the pie.

The transformation in class attitudes as reflected in political and interest group behavior is most noticeable in northern non-Latin Europe and among the socialist and Roman Catholic political parties. Large-scale extremist or avowedly authoritarian parties have almost completely disappeared north of France and Italy, with the exception of Finland and Iceland. The Norwegian and Austrian socialists who subscribed to a relatively left-wing Marxist view before World War II are now clearly moderate social-democratic parties. The latter take part in what has become a stable coalition regime with the bourgeois People's party. The parties of the three German-speaking nations, Switzerland, Austria and Germany, have given up any adherence to Marxism or class war doctrines and are little concerned with any further expansion of the area of state ownership of industry. The 1959 Godesberg Program of the German party explicitly revoked the traditional policy of public ownership of the means of production. . . .

On the right, one finds that those parties which still defend traditional European liberalism (laissez-faire) or conservatism (social hierarchy) are extremely weak. The Scandinavian Liberals and Agrarians now accept much of the welfare state. Many Scandinavian bourgeois politicians, in fact, propose that their countries adopt Swiss and Austrian political practice, a permanent coalition of all parties in which collective bargaining issues are fought out and compromised within the cabinet. The Roman Catholic parties, on the whole, have accepted the welfare state and economic planning, and have even supported increases in government ownership. They willingly participate in coalitions with socialist parties in many countries. Roman Catholic trade unions, once the bitter rivals of the so-called free or socialist unions in most Roman Catholic countries, either participate in the same unions as the socialists, as in Germany and Austria, or cooperate closely with the socialist unions, as in the Benelux nations. Issues concerning the relationship of church and state, particularly as they affect education and family legislation, still separate the left wing of the Roman Catholic parties from the Socialists, but these are not of grave moment as compared to their agreement on economic and class matters. In Germany the traditional base of the opposition to a democratic regime, the regions beyond the Elbe, the homeland of the Junkers and feudal social relationships, is no longer part of the nation. West Germany today is physically and socially largely comprised of regions and classes which historically have shown a willingness to sustain modern socio-economic and political systems. Although once playing a major role in politics, the civil service and the army, the old aristocracy today participate little in these institutions.

Reactionary parties in postwar Europe have tended on the whole to be peripheral movements based on the outlying regions and strata which have not shared in the rapid economic growth, which find themselves increasingly outside of the new cosmopolitanism and which have lost out in the relative struggle for influence and status. Thus in Norway the Christian party, which seeks to further traditional values, is clearly a provincial party based on the lower middle classes of the rural and provincial communities. Poujadism was the classic case of a movement appealing to the *resentments* of declining strata; its base was the backward parts of France which had been losing population, and the *petite bourgeoisie* whose relative position in French economy and society had worsened with the growth of the metropolis and large business and government. In Italy, the Monarchists and Neo-Fascists have recruited strength from roughly comparable groups, a pattern that has also characterized the support of the Austrian Freedom party.

Not unexpectedly, studies of the attitudes and behavior of the entrepreneurial strata in various parts of Europe suggest that the managerial groups in the traditionally less developed countries of Europe, such as France and Italy, have been the most resistant to yielding their historic autocratic and paternalistic view of the role of management. "In general, France and Italy have been characterized by a large number of small enterprises, looked on by the family as a source of personal security and conducted in an atmosphere of widespread absence of trust." The resistance to accepting trade unions as a legitimate part of the industrial system is greater in these nations than anywhere else in democratic western Europe. And consequently, the presence of extreme views of class and industrial relations among leaders of workers and management has contributed to resisting the pressures inherent in industrialization to stabilize such relationships. The available evidence would suggest that Italian industrialists may be more resistant to accepting a modus vivendi with trade unions and the planning-welfare state than are the French, although, as shall be noted, the relative situation is reversed among the worker-based Communist parties of these countries. It is difficult to account for these variations other than to suggest that Fascism as practiced in Italy for two decades conditioned many Italian businessmen to a pattern of labor-management relations that they still long for. Conversely, however, Fascism spared the Italian Communists the experience of having to repeatedly purge the various levels of leadership of a mass party. The party could emerge after World War II with close intellectual links to its pre-Fascist, and more significantly pre-Stalinist, past and with a secondary leadership and rank-and-file whose major formative political experience was the Resistance rather than the Comintern.

Class conflict ideologies have become less significant components of the political movements supported by the middle classes in Germany, Italy and France. In Germany and in Italy, the Christian-Democratic type parties, with their efforts to retain the support of a large segment of the unionized working classes, have made a trans-class appeal in favor of moderate changes. As compared to pre-Fascist days, they have gained considerably at the expense of older, more class-oriented, more conservative parties. The classically liberal Free Democratic and Liberal parties receive about 7 per cent of the vote in each country. In France, the Christian Democrats (MRP) were not able to retain the massive upper and middle class conservative vote which the party inherited in the first elections of the Fourth Republic, as a result of the traditional right's being discredited by its involvement with Vichy. And large-scale anti-labor and anti–welfare state parties arose in the late forties and fifties. The Gaullism of the Fifth Republic, however, has replaced such parties in the affections of the conservative and business part of the electorate. Gaullism is oriented to a trans-class appeal designed to integrate the lower strata into the polity, and it supports economic and social reforms which foster economic growth and reduce class barriers.

Looking at the policies of business toward workers and their unions, it would appear that Germany first, and much more slowly and reluctantly, France and Italy, in that order, have been accepting the set of managerial ideologies characteristic of the more stable welfare democracies of northern and western Europe. . . .

THE INTEGRATION OF THE WORKING CLASS

But if the evidence drawn from developments in various parts of the continent suggests that the secular trends press for political moderation, for the politics of collective bargaining, it is also important to note that these trends do not imply a loss of electoral strength for working class–based parties. In fact, in all European countries varying majorities of the manual workers vote for parties which represent different shades of socialism. As the workers have become integrated into the body politic, they have not shifted from voting socialist to backing bourgeois parties. If anything, the opposite seems to have occurred. In the Scandinavian nations, for example, "all evidence indicates that social class explains more of the variation in voting and particularly more of the working class voting than some decades ago. This has occurred simultaneously with the disappearance of traditional class barriers. As equality has increased the working class voters have been more apt to vote for the worker's own parties than before."

A comparative look at the pattern of working class voting in contemporary Europe reveals that with the exception of Holland and Germany, the leftist parties secure about two thirds or more of the working-class vote, a much higher percentage than during the depression of the 1930's. The two exceptions are largely a by-product of the Roman Catholic–Protestant cleavage in their countries. The traditionally minority German and Dutch Roman Catholics have considerable group solidarity, and the Christian Democratic and Roman Catholic parties in these countries secure a larger working class vote than occurs anywhere else on the continent. Close to 70 per cent of German Protestant workers vote Socialist, as do "humanist" and moderate Calvinist Dutch workers, as opposed to the conservative Dutch Calvinists, who are more like the Roman Catholics. The leftist working class–oriented parties have increased their strength in much of Europe during the 1960's. . . .

Greater national wealth and consequent lower visible class differentials, therefore, do not weaken the voting strength of the left as compared with the right; rather, their effects become most evident in the decline of ideological differences, in changes in the policies advocated by different parties. The leftist parties have become more moderate, less radical, in the economic reforms which they espouse. A look at the political history of Europe indicates that no mass lower class–based political party, with the single exception of the German Communists, has ever disappeared or significantly declined through losing the bulk of its votes to a party on its right.[1]

The loyalties once created in a *mass* left-wing party are rarely lost. . . . But if workers have remained loyal to the parties of their class on election day, they show much less commitment to these parties the rest of the year. All over Europe, both socialist and Communist parties have complained about losses in membership, in attendance at party meetings and in the reading of party newspapers. Such changes

---

[1] Although the German Communists secured about 16% of the vote in 1932, they were never as large as the Social-Democrats. The latter always retained their status as the predominant party of the workers. Hence even the German case is not a real exception.

attest to the growth of what French intellectuals are increasingly coming to describe as the problem of *dépolitisation*. Another phenomenon illustrating these trends is the growing tendency of all the working class organizations to place less emphasis on traditional *political* doctrines and to put more stress on representation of concrete interests. Roman Catholic trade unions also are increasingly reluctant to intervene directly in politics.

In discussing the implications of changes such as these, a number of French political analysts have argued that what is occurring in France, and presumably in some other countries as well, is not so much a decline in political interest (*dépolitisation*), as of ideology (*déidéologisation*). . . .

There are many ways in which the more pragmatic orientation of Europeans manifests itself, but the changes in trade union behavior are most noticeable. As already noted, in a number of countries socialist and Roman Catholic unionists are cooperating as they never did before World War II. The fact of such cooperation reflects the extent to which both have moved away from ideological or political unionism toward pragmatic or even, in the American sense of the term, "business unionism." In Italy and France, the trend toward a *syndicalisme de contrôle* is furthered by the emerging patterns of plant unions and supplementary factory contracts. Such organization and negotiation for the first time involve the unions in dealing with the concrete problems of the factory environment such as job evaluation, rates, productivity and welfare. The pressures in this direction have come primarily from the non-Communist unions, though the Communist unions have also increasingly come to accept such institutions, more in Italy than in France. The increase in economic strikes as distinct from political ones, though often resulting in an overall increase of the strike rate, has been interpreted by some observers as reflecting the integration of the workers into the industrial system; an economic strike is part of a normal bargaining relationship with one's employer. Some have suggested that the Italian strike wave of 1961 and 1962 was perhaps the first of this type since the war in that country.

The two major strikes of 1963, those of the coal miners in France and of the metal workers in Germany, are also notable for the extent to which each resembled a typical American strike flowing from a breakdown in collective bargaining. Each strike was ended by a negotiated settlement in which the unions secured more than they had been offered initially. Neither turned into a political strike, though the governments were directly involved in the negotiations. . . . These strikes in Italy, Germany and France may signify the beginning of a new era in labor relations — one in which strikes are recognized as part of the normal bargaining relationship rather than an embryonic civil war the outbreak of which is threatening to leadership on both sides.

The relative weakness of traditional leftist ideology in western and southern Europe is suggested also by various attitude surveys. These studies indicate that the actual sentiment favoring a "socialist solution" to economic or social problems is much lower than the Socialist or Communist vote. It again demonstrates that people will vote for such parties without commitment to the once basic ideological values of these parties. . . . A comparative analysis of attitudes toward ownership of industry in seven European countries based on interviews in the spring of 1958 reported strong sentiment favoring public ownership of industry only in Italy, the nation which has the largest support for radical ideologies in the form of large Communist and left-Socialist parties. . . .

The ideology of the "open society" in which competent individuals can succceed seems to have permeated much of Europe, a phenomenon which may also contribute to a reduction of class tension. Thus surveys in a number of countries which inquired as to the chances of capable individuals rising socially in their country found large majorities which reported their belief that the chances were good. The percentages of respondents saying that chances were good were 90 in Norway, 88 in England, 72 in West Germany, and 70 in Belgium. The one European country covered in this study in which the proportion of those who were optimistic about mobility was less than half was Austria, but even there the positive answers outweighed the pessimistic ones, 49 per cent to 34 per cent. Italy and France were not covered in this comparative study. However, another set of surveys which inquired as to careers one would recommend to a young man found that the Italians ranked second only to the English in suggesting high status professional occupations (62 per cent). The strongest French preference seemed to be for careers in the civil service, an orientation which distinguished them from all other European nations except the Belgians. It should be noted also that the Italians and the French were least likely among the citizens of eleven European countries to recommend a career as a skilled worker or artisan to a young man.

There is some direct evidence that modernization results in a positive attitude by workers toward their occupational situation. A French study of the consequences of modernization in textile factories in northern France brings this out clearly. The author notes that the workers view the effects of technological innovation as a "good thing," that they see it as resulting in an increase in employment, greater possibilities for social mobility and increased earnings. The findings of French factory surveys with respect to worker reaction to modernization are paralleled in a report on the comparative strength of the Communist party in five large Italian factories which varied in their degree of modernization. The less modernized the plants the larger the proportion of workers who belonged to the Communist party, holding size of plant constant.

But if workers react positively to working in modernized, more bureaucratic work environments, if they see these as offering greater opportunity for higher earnings and mobility, if job satisfaction is actually higher in many of these, the fact remains that when one looks at the sources of left-wing strength, either in voting or in union membership, and in the extent to which men agree with "anti-capitalist" attitudes, such strength is to be found disproportionately in the larger factories and the larger cities. This seeming contradiction points up an interesting relation between the variables linked to the overall characteristics of a national political class culture and the same variables operating within a given society. As noted above, nations with a high level of industrialization and urbanization tend to have a low level of ideological conflict. But within nations, whatever the level of intensity of political controversy, larger factories and cities tend to be the strongholds of the left politics dominant in the country, Communist, Socialist or Democratic. Trade unions also are generally stronger in large factories in large cities. It would seem that while greater industrialization and urbanization with consequent greater national wealth make for a more stable polity, *within* any system these social factors are conducive to fostering working class political and trade union strength.

How might we account for this? In part it may be related to the fact that the large factory environment sustains fewer informal relations between members of different classes, reducing the possibility that the members of the lower class will be influenced personally by the more conservative and more prestigeful members of middle and higher classes such as owners, managers and supervisors. And the more concentrated the members of a lower class are in a social environment, the easier it is for common class attitudes to spread among them and for representatives of class-oriented parties or other organizations to reach them and activate their antielitist sympathies.

But though the emergence of large social environments that are class homogeneous facilitates the spread of lower class–based movements, the same factors operating in the social structure as a whole become linked with other tendencies operating to reduce class friction. On the working class level these involve a rise in standards of living, educational levels and opportunity for upward social mobility within industry. In all countries with large Communist movements (Italy, France and Finland), within any given structural environment, the better-paid workers are more moderate in their political views than the poorer ones. Modernization reduces the sources of worker hostility to management by altering the sources of managerial behavior. These trends involve a decline in the family-owned corporation and in the domination of the economy by the *patron* type who sees himself as all powerful, and the rise within the management strata of a corporate leadership characterized by a division of labor and by the requisite of formal higher education. Accompanying the growth in large systems is a consequent increased emphasis on universalistic and achievement values, on judging individuals on the basis of their specific roles as worker or manager. As management's resistance to formalizing the labor-management relationship gradually declines, union labor's commitment to an ideological view of unionism, as distinct from a business or pragmatic view, is also reduced.

THE NEW MIDDLE CLASS – THE BASE FOR EMPLOYEE POLITICS

The emergence of the new middle class — the increasingly large layer of clerks, salesmen, technicians, middle management, civil servants — has served to introduce as a major factor in the European polity a group which itself is so exposed to conflicting pressures from the left and the right that it can contribute to stabilizing class tensions. A broad middle class has a mitigating position because it can give political rewards to moderate parties and penalize extreme parties on both sides — right and left. Its members wish to obtain more for themselves and their offspring; they advocate universalistic equality in the educational and other aspects of the status-allocating mechanisms; they often uphold the extension of the welfare state. Yet their position among the relatively privileged in status and possession terms makes them supporters of political and social stability, of the politics of collective bargaining. And the larger a proportion of the electorate and the labor force formed by the new middle class, the more both the left and the right must take this group into account in determining their own policies. The political and trade union influence of the new middle class is largely thrown on the side of pressing for greater opportunity, not greater social equality. The unions of the middle class are interested in maintaining, or even extending, the income gap existing between themselves and the manual workers. They often abstain from affiliating to the same central federation as the manual unions, and many of them are led by men who back "liberal" rather than labor parties. In some countries of Europe, and in Israel in recent years, there have been strikes by unions of salaried professionals in order to widen the gap between themselves and manual workers. However, interest in income differences apart, these rapidly growing new middle classes press the political system toward consensus because as employees they favor many of the same statist policies that were long pressed by the representatives of the manual workers. Otto Kirchheimer in fact has argued that it is the very growth of these strata, who form the mass base of the "bourgeois" parties, that is largely responsible for the decline of ideology.

It is important to recognize that the bourgeois parties are no longer bourgeois in the classic sense of the term. That is, the proportion of those who are self-employed, or who have close ties to the self-employed on the land or in the town, is an increasingly small part of the electorate. Most large parties now represent employees, manual or nonmanual. And while these strata differ in their orientations to many issues, they are also united on many welfare concerns. Recent Swedish political history is an apt illustration of this point. The dominant Social-Democrats were experiencing a secular decline in support, largely, according to survey analyses, because the white-collar segment of the population was growing relative to the manual sector. The party introduced a major reform, an old age pension of 65 per cent of salary, in large part because their electoral researches had suggested such a proposal would be popular not only with their traditional manual supporters but with many white-collar workers. The proposal ultimately carried in referendum, and the party increased its national vote substantially. Even more significant, perhaps, is the fact that the Liberal party, which accepted the general principle of the enlarged pension, gained enormously at the expense of the Conservatives, who took a traditional position against high taxes and against increases in the functions of the state. This suggests that the political struggles of the future will increasingly take place between parties representing the status concerns and economic interests of the two employee strata, and that the parties drawing heavily from the self-employed will continue to lose influence. . . .

The dominant structural trend in Europe involves the final triumph of the values of industrial society, the end of rigid status classes derivative from a pre-industrial world, and increasing emphasis on achievement rather than ascription, on universalism rather than particularism, and on interaction among individuals in terms of the specific roles played by each rather than in terms of their diffuse generalized statuses. The heightening standard of living of the masses gives them greater market power and enables them to affect much of culture and societal taste. All these changes imply the emergence of a somewhat similar social and political culture, one which increasingly resembles the first advanced industrial society to function without institutions and values derivative from a feudal past, the United States. And as has been indicated earlier, this should mean the end of class-linked severely ideological politics.

Yet there is one major force which in a number of countries has rejected this view of European social change and which has done its best to block these trends — the Communist party. It is clear that the very existence of powerful Communist movements in countries like France and Italy has been a major force perpetuating the institutions and values of the old society. In countries in which the Communists are the largest working class party, in which they secure around a quarter of all votes, it has been difficult to elect a progressive government to office. If governments must secure a majority from the non-Communist three quarters of the population, they have to rely in large part on the conservative and traditionalist elements. The fact that one quarter of the electorate, constituting one half or more of the social base of the "left," have been outside of the political game inevitably gives a considerable advantage to the conservatives. In effect, by voting Communist, French and Italian workers have disfranchised themselves. Thus not only does a mass Communist party serve to fossilize the ideological orientations characteristic of a pre-industrial society among the working class, it contributes to preserving pre-modern orientations on the right. . . .

The tension between equality and inequality is endemic in modern industrial democratic society. The dominant strata will continue the attempt to institutionalize their privileges, to find means to pass on to their kin and offspring the privileges they have gained. This conflict, however, does not mean that one or the other tendency must triumph, or that the strain will destroy or even necessarily weaken the social fabric. The predominant character of modern industrial democracy, as a free and evolving society, is in part a result of the chronic tensions between the inherent pressures toward inequality and the endemic emphasis in democracy on equality.

The current wave of writings that somehow see in the growth of affluence in the western world the emergence of a peaceful social utopia — which will not require continued political struggle between representatives of the haves and of the have-nots — ignores the extent to which the content of these very concepts changes as society evolves. As Marshall* has pointed out, ever since the beginning of the industrial revolution almost every generation proclaimed a social revolution to elevate the lower strata. "From the 1880's to the 1940's people were constantly expressing amazement at the social transformation witnessed in their lifetime, oblivious of the fact that, in this series of outbursts of self-congratulation, the glorious achievements of the past became the squalid heritage of the present."

But in spite of the progress leading one generation to proclaim the significance of recent social improvements, only a few years later others are arguing that the present conditions of the poor, of the lowly, are intolerable, that they cannot possibly be tolerated by free men who believe in equality. And as Marshall indicates, such phenomena do not "mean that the progress which men thought they made was illusory. It means that the standards by which that progress was assessed were constantly rising, and that ever deeper probing into the social situation kept revealing new horrors which had previously been concealed from view." One may ask with Marshall whether the concept of the affluent society will have any longer life than some its predecessors.

In large measure, the problem of the lower strata is now seen as that of "cultural deprivation." It is clear that in all countries, variation in participation in the intellectual culture serves to negate the dream of equal opportunity for all to mount the educational ladder; consequently, access to the summits of the occupational structure is still grossly restricted. In Sweden, for example, in spite of thirty years of Social-Democratic government providing free access to universities together with state bursaries, the proportion of working class children taking advantage of such opportunities has hardly risen. Few commodities are distributed as unequally in Europe as high school and university education. The simple improvement in economic standards of living, at least at its present pace, does little to reduce the considerable advantages held by the culturally privileged strata to perpetuate their families in an equally advantaged position. And socialist parties in a number of countries are beginning to look for ways to enhance the educational and cultural aspirations of lower class youth. Here, then, is the most recent example of the conflict between the principles

* [T. H. Marshall, "Citizenship and Social Class," in his *Sociology at the Crossroads* (London: Heinemann, 1963). — Editors' note.]

of equality inherent in citizenship and the forces endemic to complex stratified society that serve to maintain or erect cultural barriers between the classes. The latter operate as a consequence of the differential distributions of rewards and access to culture, and must be combatted continually if they are not to dominate. . . .

As a final comment, I would note that not only do class conflicts over issues related to division of the total economic pie, influence over various institutions, symbolic status and opportunity, continue in the absence of *Weltanschauungen,* but that the decline of such total ideologies does *not* mean the end of ideology. Clearly, commitment to the politics of pragmatism, to the rules of the game of collective bargaining, to gradual change whether in the direction favored by the left or the right, to opposition both to an all powerful central state and to laissez-faire constitutes the component parts of an ideology. The "agreement on fundamentals," the political consensus of western society, now increasingly has come to include a position on matters which once sharply separated the left from the right. And this ideological agreement, which might best be described as "conservative socialism," has become *the* ideology of the major parties in the developed states of Europe and America. As such it leaves its advocates in sharp disagreement with the relatively small groups of radical rightists and leftists at home, and at a disadvantage in efforts to foster different variants of this doctrine in the less affluent parts of the world.

RICHARD ROSE

Class and Party Divisions: Britain as a Test Case

Generalizations about class structure do not translate easily or accurately into descriptions of the political divisions of particular countries, for in each the configuration of non-class and class influences can produce significant variations on this familiar sociological theme. The conceptual looseness of a phrase such as class politics makes it necessary to specify the particular po-

litical significance of class when analyzing a country and to verify that its influence is actually as predicted. The following study of the significance of class in British politics defines clearly the different ways in which class might be significant, and then marshals precise forms of data to test general hypotheses.

Political divisions are inevitable in modern industrial societies, but social scientists disagree about the sources, signs and significance of such divisions. Students of comparative Western politics, while noting that differences in race, religion, language and regional identifications may be of special significance in particular national contexts, have usually emphasized the primary importance of class for political divisions. In such studies, Britain is often the prime empirical example of a political system based on class divisions. . . .

Characteristically, interpretations are more often incommensurable than irreconcilable, since they are based upon partial and sometimes reductionist criteria for examining the various ways in which class structure may influence partisan divisions. In this study, class will be considered in terms of its developmental and contemporary significance for the three main functions of political parties — recruiting political leaders, mobilizing voters and influencing policies concerning the allocation of resources and values. . . . Except where noted, the working-class is operationally defined as all individuals who are either manual workers or members of families primarily dependent upon a manual worker for support. Special attention is given to working-class influences upon the Labour Party, since this is the relationship that could, on a simplistic assumption, permanently sustain single-party dominance in Britain.

I

Choosing a date at which to begin developmental analysis is always a problem, because of the persistence of influences over time. Stein Rokkan (1968) has argued that the bases of party divisions in many European countries today can only be understood by examining social cleavages extending as far back in time as the Reformation. Analysis of this sort is both possible and profitable in terms of English history (Lipson 1953). Theories of class and politics, however, posit the primacy of activities occurring as a consequence of industrialization. Hence, a suitable point at which to begin this analysis is about

Abridged from Richard Rose, "Class and Party Divisions: Britain as a Test Case," *Sociology*, II, 2, May, 1968, pp. 129–162. Reprinted by permission.

This article was written while the author held an American Social Science Research Council fellowship for the study of problems of the legitimacy of regimes, and the ideas were thought through while he was a guest at the Institute of Political Studies, Stanford University. The facilities of the University of Strathclyde Survey Research Center proved invaluable for data analysis.

the 1850's, the point at which England had become a modern industrial society in terms of a wide variety of economic and social indices of modernization; it had not yet become a "modern" political system, however that term is defined (Rose 1965b). By this time, most of the great crises that disrupt regimes in many societies even today — the crises of identity, legitimacy, penetration and integration — had already become part of the past in England. Moreover, the regime had also managed to adapt to some extent to the pressures causing civil unrest among workers and middle-class citizens during the early 19th century transition to industrialism. Hence, at the point at which this essay begins, there remained "only" the problem of how the new working-class would actively participate in politics. The passage of the Reform Act in 1867 made the workers the majority of the enfranchised. Because of early franchise reform and the previous removal of many fundamental political problems still widespread in Europe, one might expect that class would quickly dominate political divisions in England. Yet such was not the case with any of our three criteria for judging political divisions — recruitment, voting and policy.

The recruitment of working-class people into political leadership roles is not important as an index of policy outlooks, but rather, as an index of the symbolic importance of persons who "represent" their electors in a social as well as electoral sense. The importance of recruiting candidates who are symbolically representative of a social group is most often noticed today in America, where Negroes, Jews and other members of minority groups are nominated on such grounds. Yet, it is important to recall that the origins of the Labour Party lay more in demands for working-class representation in Parliament than in any specific programmatic or ideal goals (Pelling 1965; Epstein 1962).

The data about working-class representation in Parliament, a clear and appropriate index of recruitment to political leadership, concerns the Labour Party exclusively, in view of the unwillingness of Liberals and Conservatives at any time to nominate working-men for Parliament in more than token numbers. Four periods can be clearly distinguished (Table 1). During the pre-Parliamentary phase from 1867 to 1906, working-men were increasingly able to assume positions of leadership in class-specific organizations such as the trade unions and Co-operative societies, yet they were usually rebuffed in efforts to secure Liberal

TABLE 1. THE CLASS COMPOSITION OF THE
PARLIAMENTARY LABOUR PARTY, 1906–1966

Average		Working-class background %	Labour MPs in Commons N	%
1906-1918	4 elections	89	38	7
1922-1935	6 elections	71	162	26
1945-1966	7 elections	36	317	50

Sources: Thomas, 1957; Guttsman, 1963; Harrison, 1960; Ross, 1955; and Butler, 1952 et seq.

TABLE 2. WORKING-CLASS MEMBERSHIP OF LABOUR CABINETS, 1924-1967

Year	Cabinet size N	Working-class N	Working-class %
1924	20	11	55
1929	19	8	42
1945	18	9	50
1950	18	9	50
1964	23	6	26
1966	23	4	17
1969 (December)	21	1	5

Source 1924-1950: Epstein, 1962, p. 144; cf. Guttsman, 1963, p. 242.

party nominations. In 1906, the success of the new Labour Party brought about the return of a working-class bloc of MPs. The Parliamentary Labour Party remained almost exclusively a working-class party until the election of 1922, when it became a party including a substantial minority of upper- and middle-class MPs. A fourth phase began in 1945 and has continued since: the Parliamentary Labour Party has become a body of predominantly middle-class politicians, with a substantial minority of working-class MPs. At Cabinet level, patterns of recruitment are broadly similar. (See Table 2.). No Labour Cabinet has ever been exclusively working-class, but ministers from working-class backgrounds formed about half the members of the MacDonald and Attlee Cabinets of the 1920's and 1940's. In Harold Wilson's Cabinets, the proportion of working-class members has been much lower; this is not a simple function of changes in working-class membership of the Parliamentary party. In all periods, the conclusion is the same: even in times of a Labour government, working-class men have rarely found themselves in important political offices.

The biographies and autobiographies of early Labour leaders emphasize the importance these men gave to symbolic representation of the working-class. Their lesser concern with policy is succinctly summed up in Henry Pelling's judgment:

> All along there is little doubt that most of the non-Socialist trade union leaders would have been happy to stay in the Liberal Party — which most of them had belonged to in the past — if the Liberals had made arrangements for a larger representation of the working class among their Parliamentary candidates. (Pelling 1965:222)

Once in Parliament, working-class MPs were ready to support the First World War and accept token offices in Cabinet, sufficient to show that working-men could hold office, if not make decisions. It is noteworthy that five of the eight Labour MPs given office in the wartime Coalition left the Labour Party in 1918 to fight as "National Labour" candidates. In the 1920's the Labour Party, by contrast with the German Social Democrats, welcomed as Labour candidates politicians from upper- and middle-class backgrounds, many with the social attributes of men born to rule (Wertheimer 1929). Dowse notes, "In changing their allegiance the ex-Liberals did not change their opinions" (1961: 84). A substantial number left the party by 1931 (Cline 1963). . . . Not until Ernest Bevin and Herbert Morrison entered the Coalition government of 1940 did working-class Englishmen hold major office and authority on the same basis as those who had been born and bred to rule. . . .

The concept of political socialization provides a better explanation for the behaviour of working-class leaders than such emotive terms as "careerist" or "class traitor." Working-class leaders were positively integrated in British society, thereby absorbing prevailing cultural norms (Steed 1906; Allen 1956). Working men tended to imitate or defer to their betters, for there was no other model immediately visible to them. . . . The greater a working man's interest in politics, the greater his awareness of the established order and, by implication, the less the likelihood that it seemed capable of radical transformation. While failure to gain political advancement might lead working-class politicians to reject the status quo, by definition, such men were far from office. Working-class leaders who achieved office were potentially subject to strains arising from very considerable upward social mobility. In practice, many men were so well integrated into conventional social values that they found no difficulty in adapting their life styles and, in some cases, their political views, as they rose. It is noteworthy that any insecurity was usually resolved by an individual over-identifying with the conventions of the ruling strata rather than by reacting against them. . . . Working-class parliamentarians were not alone in their readiness to accept society as they found it. On the few occasions at which industrial disputes threatened the stability of the system, trade union leaders too proved ready to defer to the national interest as defined by conventional leaders, rather than press class interests further. (See Symons 1957.)

The development of a more or less cohesive pattern of working-class voting loyalties was inhibited by two factors. The generic influence which modern social scientists refer to as "culture lag" was anticipated by Bagehot in comments on the importance of the 1867 Reform Act:

> A new Constitution does not produce its full effect as long as all its subjects were reared under an old Constitution, as long as its statesmen were trained by that old Constitution. It is not really tested till it comes to be worked by statesmen and among a people neither of whom are guided by a different experience (1872: 260–61).

Modern research on the formation of party loyalties through intergenerational socialization in the family has amply supported Bagehot's dictum on the relationship of macro-political change to micro-political behaviour. A situational influence of great importance was enfranchisement of industrial workers before the development of Socialist and Labour institutions. New voters first went to the polls when corruption and traditional influences were still widespread. Actions by Conservative and Liberal party organizers, plus trends in society and communication, brought about the creation of nationwide parties claiming the long-term loyalty of the vast bulk of the electorate by the 1890's (Stokes 1967; Lloyd 1965). Thus, before a Labour Party was organized, the great bulk of working-class voters were already integrated into patterns of support for parties which neither claimed to be nor acted like working-class spokesmen. This situational handicap was later greatly lessened by the Liberal Party splitting and collapsing in the decade after 1916. Given the importance of class-specific institutions in British society, it is hardly surprising that working-class people, seeking a means of orienting themselves in the resulting vacuum, should tend to choose a party with strong class attributes.

The hypotheses put forward in the preceding paragraph can be tested indirectly by reference to election results and to survey data. Firstly, it is implied that the longer the Labour Party has been established, then the better its average electoral fortunes should be, up to some unknown ceiling figure for a Labour vote in Britain. Electoral trends since 1906 confirm this hypothesis.

Average Labour vote, 1906–1910 elections   5.8 per cent
Average Labour vote, 1918–1935 elections   31.1 per cent
Average Labour vote, 1945–1966 elections   46.5 per cent

A second test is the hypothesis that older voters are less likely to favour Labour than are younger voters, since older voters will have had more exposure to political socialization influences of the period in which Labour was a minor party. Data from Gallup Poll studies at the time of the 1964 election show that older working-class men and women are less likely to be Labour than are voters in younger age categories (Table 3).

Divisions on policy outputs may involve symbolic conflict about values or substantive differences in material outcomes when party control of government shifts. Both types of division are important (Rose 1965a: 207 ff). Because these differences involve comparison with the performance of a second party, the degree of conflict is a function of the policies of a working-class party and of its opponents' adaptability. A simple typology involves the following distinctions: institutional divisions (no symbolic or substantive differences); nominal divisions (symbolic but not substantive differences); opportunistic divisions (determined by which party is in office and in Opposition); covert divisions (substantive but not symbolic difference); persisting and bargainable divisions (symbolic and substantive differences, capable of incremental adjustment through periods of office and opposition);

TABLE 3. WORKING-CLASS VOTING BY AGE AND SEX, 1964 (PERCENTAGES)

Age	Men Con.	Men Lab.	Men Other	Women Con.	Women Lab.	Women Other
21-24	21	68	11	23	52	25
25-29	17	67	16	26	65	9
30-34	27	62	11	29	59	12
35-44	22	66	12	27	56	17
45-49	29	63	8	28	64	8
50-64	26	61	13	35	48	17
65 plus	32	50	18	39	47	14

and, persisting and irreconcilable divisions (symbolic and substantive differences involving radical shifts in outcomes when control of government changes hands). The advantage of this crude typology is that it is more discriminating than those familiar but woolly terms "consensus" and "cleavage."

In judging the extent of symbolic divisions between the parties in the past, formal and official statements of policy intentions are much more likely to represent the mainstream of party opinion than the writings of individual and often atypical Socialists. Until 1918, the Labour Party symbolized primarily the institutional separation of working-class politicians from a Liberal Party whose policies they generally endorsed, inside and outside Parliament. In 1918, the party became committed to Socialism, albeit in a form which emphasized co-operation between workers by hand and by brain, thus introducing conflict only with the handful of rentiers and aristocrats. Until 1931, party divisions were nominal, symbolically important but substantively of little account in the decisions of the two MacDonald governments. In reaction to the 1931 debacle, Labour policy emphasized persisting and bargainable differences with opponents; those who insisted on irreconcilable conflicts often left or were expelled from the party. In the 1940's the wartime Coalition showed the extent to which the Labour Party would bargain, just as nationalization and the creation of the National Health Service by the Attlee Government emphasized persisting and substantial differences. The triumph of the Morrisonian doctrine of consolidating change and, simultaneously, the Conservative Party's acceptance of change in the 1950's tended to make party divisions nominal or covert in the period of "Butksellism" (Hoffman 1964). It is noteworthy that many of the most important symbolic divisions between the parties have not involved economic issues but foreign policy, a subject in which the interests of all classes in peace have been presumptively the same.

In the absence of survey data covering the early part of the century, generalizations about symbolic divisions within the mass population must be treated cautiously. The high turnout of voters in all classes in default of Labour candidates before 1914 indicates that working-class electors did not then sense any great gulf between their own loyalties and those of the Liberals or Conservatives. At the three elections of 1906–1910, turnout averaged 83.4 per cent. The derisory polls of extremist candidates in the inter-war period, whether Communist or Fascist, are an additional indicator of low social tensions, especially by comparison with European states at this time. From a wealth of post-war survey data, the most important finding to note . . . is the failure of partisan identifications to exert a negative influence on social relations (Almond & Verba 1963).

Divisions concerning material outputs are difficult to assess for two reasons. First, given the complex nature of the policy process, any findings showing a simple correlation between a party's control of government and a pattern of policy may in fact be caused by any number of other variables. Secondly, the differences in the constraints upon the governing party and the Opposition party make it impossible to say

TABLE 4. WELFARE EXPENDITURE IN BRITAIN, 1850-1950

Year	Expenditure £000	As percentage of natl. income	Per capita in constant 1900£ £ s. d.	Per £1 average income, constant 1900 £ £ s. d.
1850-51	7,000	1.2	5 3	2¾
1870-71	12,000	1.3	6 3	3
1890-91	23,425	1.7	12 8	4
1900-01	36,500	2.1	17 7	5
1910-11	59,314	2.9	1 4 9	7
1920-21	163,676	3.0	1 9 5	7¼
1925-26	202,089	5.2	2 8 7	1 0¼
1930-31	255,921	6.7	3 8 5	1 4
1935-36	327,949	8.2	4 10 5	1 7¾
1947-48	648,021	6.8	4 0 5	1 4
1949-50	1,162,000	10.7	6 0 8	2 1¾

Source: Stirling, 1952

with certainty what an Opposition would have done if, contrary to fact, it had been in government at a given time. Yet some sort of rough judgment must be hazarded, given the great theoretical and practical importance of the question. In analysing divisions concerning a class party, government expenditure concerning welfare measures provides relevant empirical evidence, in view of the extent to which working-class people are likely to benefit from welfare expenditure and the extent to which class interests may be in conflict on this issue. By contrast, the significance of nationalization for most working-class people is extremely difficult to assess.

The first point to note is that welfare expenditure has been increasing steadily since 1850, and that this secular trend was well established before Labour became a major party (Table 4). For example, Stirling's calculations show that from 1850–51 to 1920–21, just before Labour became a major party, expenditure on welfare services per head of population increased more than fivefold in terms of constant prices. Expenditure continued to rise subsequently, not only at times of Labour governments, but equally, at times of a Conservative government. The secular increase in welfare expenditure has been a response to many pressures independent of governmental control, such as the effects of war upon the need for services and upon the capacity of the government to raise additional revenues (Peacock & Wiseman 1961). Comparisons with patterns of welfare expenditure in European countries with Socialist parties, and with America and Canada, lacking such parties, make it clear that to a considerable extent increases in welfare expenditure are a concomitant of industrialization, occurring without regard to the nature of partisan divisions within a society (Briggs 1961). To say this is not to deny all importance to partisan-oriented decisions of government, but rather to emphasize that differences between the parties on policy outputs are most likely to be matters of degree and of timing, and that these differences do not necessarily depend upon the presence of a strong Labour party. Moreover, the most intensive conflicts in Britain since industrialization and democratization have not concerned economic issues, but rather, as on the Continent of Europe, have concerned nationalism (Ireland), religion (Ireland, Church disestablishment and education), and the Constitution (House of Lords reform and women's suffrage). By contrast, Home Secretaries and historians looking for evidence of extra-constitutional working-class activities have had little to show for their efforts.

In the development of the modern party system in Britain, inconsistency is the most striking feature of the role of class. Class has been of unequal significance for the three main functions of the Labour Party, and changes in class influence over time have tended to be in opposite directions. . . . The developmental pattern of working-class political activity in Britain has not involved a drive toward hegemony, but rather a pursuit of specific and limited goals by people with a clearly developed sense of what Perry Anderson has called "corporateness" (1965: 34), class-specific institutions and patterns of behaviour "within a social totality whose global determination lies outside it."

II

In analysing contemporary Britain, the wealth of survey data about voters makes it sensible to look first at the significance of class for electoral support. The comparison of voting in Britain with voting in other industrial societies emphasizes that over time and space Britain is a society in which occupational class is especially important as the basis of partisan divisions (Alford 1963). Conventionally, this phenomenon is interpreted in terms of a theory of cultural and class determinism. Class is regarded as the basis of political divisions in all industrial societies; the lack of intense class conflict in Britain is explained by peculiar or unique cultural characteristics, absent in societies such as France or Germany (Shils & Young 1953; Beer 1965). Yet the phenomenon can also be explained by a theory which posits a hierarchy of social divisions, with class less likely to cause intense conflict than non-class social cleavages, because many economic considerations that so influence class relations can be settled by incremental bargaining, whereas considerations concerning religious, racial or ethnic differences tend to inhibit bargaining and incremental adjustments. The second theory emphasizes the multi-dimensional composition of social relations; events in Britain can then be explained as a consequence of a society composed of people the great majority of whom lack major differences on religious, racial or similar grounds.

The class theory may be invalidated by showing that class is not the sole or overwhelming base of party divisions in modern, industrial societies. In operational terms, a class party can be defined as a party making a programmatic appeal to class interests, and recruiting a large bloc of candidates and voters on class-specific grounds. The extent to which class parties dominate a political system may be roughly measured by the proportion of the vote such parties poll at a general election. The relevant universe is 14 European countries, omitting those "British offshoot" countries studied by Alford. Class divisions are pre-eminent in Britain and Scandinavia, but only in Britain do nine-tenths of the electorate differ along the single dimension of class. In the area that Almond has identified with the Continental political culture (1956), class is only one among a number of sources of partisan divisions, including religion, nationalism, linguistic groupings and urban-rural cleavages. . . . Moreover, a high proportion of voters in class parties within a nation correlates with the persistence of the regime and, by implication, its legitimacy. In the seven societies with the highest amount of class division, only one, Finland, has been disrupted by a civil war or major extra-constitutional challenge since 1919. Reciprocally, in the seven nations ranking lowest in class divisions, all but the Netherlands have had their regimes overthrown or challenged by extra-constitutional action since 1919.

In addition to the preceding data, the compositional theory can be supported by testing the positive proposition that non-class cleavages can override social cleavages in the determination of partisan support. In terms of this study, the most appropriate test concerns possible deviations within the working-class. Comparative analysis suggests the need to test the following five hypotheses:

1.1 *Where religious loyalties are strong, working-class voters will deviate from overall patterns of class voting.*

Northern Ireland provides strongest support for this hypothesis. Even in Belfast, with its early industrialization and persisting high unemployment, the bulk of the vote is cast for Unionist and Nationalist parties making an appeal on religious and nationality grounds (Barritt & Carter 1962). To argue that evidence from Northern Ireland is unimportant because of the small size of Ulster is to give implicit support to the compositional theory, for it is an admission that if Ireland formed a larger part of the United Kingdom, it would produce a proportionately greater strain. To argue that Northern Ireland "really" does not constitute a part of Britain also supports the compositional theory, for it is a reminder that the only civil war fought in the United Kingdom in industrial times was settled, not by cultural compromise, but by the expedient of altering the boundaries determining the composition of the Kingdom. Within Britain, Gallup data on the party affiliation of Catholics provides clearcut support for the religious hypothesis (Table 5). The absence of a Gallup measure of regular church

TABLE 5. WORKING-CLASS VOTING BY RELIGION (PERCENTAGES)

Religion	Total adherents	Con.	Labour	Other
Church of England	64	32	55	13
Church of Scotland	7	29	64	7
Non-Conformist	10	29	49	22
Roman Catholic	10	17	73	10
Other	4	30	46	24
None	5	24	49	27

attendance makes it impossible to assess properly the importance of religion for voting among the minority of working-class persons actively involved in Protestant religious activities. Other studies have emphasized this factor as important, especially among working-class Anglicans (Birch 1959: 111–112). Of special significance are findings in Scotland, where nationality might be expected to be as important as religion. In fact, the apparently high Labour support among the Scottish working-class is almost entirely due to the substantial minority of Roman Catholics in its composition. Among working-class Presbyterians in Scotland, 60 per cent favoured Labour and 27 per cent the Conservatives in 1964, virtually the same as in England; among Roman Catholic workers in Scotland, Labour was favoured by 74 per cent, with 11 per cent Conservative (Cf. Budge & Urwin, 1966).

1.2 *Where nationality differences exist, working-class voters will deviate from overall patterns of class voting.*

Strongest support for this hypothesis is also found in Northern Ireland, where working-class Irish Catholics consistently give large majorities to a Nationalist Party so extreme that it has been hesitant to accept the title of a *Loyal* Opposition. It is reasonable to interpret the pro-Labour voting of British Catholics, the great bulk of whom have an Irish ethnic identification, as primarily a nationalist vote against the Conservative and Unionist party, rather than a sign of positive affection for a Labour and Socialist party, a pattern uncharacteristic of Catholics in the Republic of Ireland or anywhere else in Europe. Within Great Britain, nationality differences are especially strong in Wales; in 1964, Welsh working-class voters divided in the proportion of 79 per cent Labour as against 12 per cent Conservative (cf. Morgan 1964).

1.3 *Where peasants are numerous, voters will deviate from overall patterns of class voting.*

The term peasant is not conventionally used in Britain, for most agriculture practiced today is on large holdings remote from the condi-

TABLE 6. RURAL FRINGE SUPPORT FOR NON-CLASS PARTIES, 1959-66

Election	Con.	MPs Lab.	Lib.	Liberal candidates	Average vote percentage	Nationalists candidates	Average vote percentage	Average Lib. & Nat. all constituencies percentage
Scottish Highlands								
1959	4	1	1	4	34.1	1	15.0	21.6
1964	2	1	4	6	38.9	1	14.1	35.3
1966	2	2	3	6	37.5	1	20.5	35.1
Rural Wales								
1959	2	6	2	7	32.5	8	11.5	32.0
1964	2	6	2	8	29.3	10	9.5	32.9
1966	2	7	1	7	27.9	10	9.5	29.0

tions of the Continental peasantry. In North Wales and in the Scottish Highlands, however, there remain crofters and agriculturalists whose economic and social conditions approximate those of the isolated agriculturalists, fishermen and lumbermen whose distinctive political behaviour has been noted by Lipset in Continental countries (1960: 231–35). In these areas, both Liberal and Nationalist candidates stand. Analysis of voting patterns in these Welsh and Scottish constituencies at the last three elections, a grouping taken to avoid the impact of freak circumstances of candidature at one election, shows a degree of support for non-class parties higher than Scandinavian countries (cf. Table 6). Moreover, a detailed ecological study by Kevin Cox (1967) of Wales has shown how marked are variations in voting as between rural North Wales and urban South Wales.

1.4 *Where regional differences exist, working-class voters will deviate from overall patterns of class voting.*

Because of the convenience of using geographical terms to refer to differences in the social composition of different parts of Britain, many discussions of voting behaviour often emphasize seemingly regional differences (Pelling 1967). Within England, some degree of difference can be found between regions in working-class support for the Labour Party (Table 7). The differences are relatively small and the regional boundaries relatively gross; hence, one ought to be cautious in claiming that the hypothesis is confirmed. Further grounds for caution exist in survey data showing little support for the hypothesis, independent of religious influences on Merseyside and Clydeside, in the seven largest conurbations in Britain, where localized sub-cultures might be expected to be stronger than in regions defined more broadly.

TABLE 7. WORKING-CLASS VOTING BY REGION (PERCENTAGES)

Region	Lab.	Con.	Other
Wales	79	12	9
Northern England	65	28	7
North-West England	63	24	12
Scotland	61	24	15
English Midlands	58	31	11
Eastern England	56	27	17
Greater London	55	29	16
Southern England	54	27	19
Yorkshire—E and W Ridings	54	27	19
South West England	52	27	21

1.5 *Where colour differences exists, then working-class voters will deviate from overall patterns of class voting.*

This hypothesis should ideally be tested by separate reference to white and coloured working-class voters. The recency of coloured immigration and the relatively small numbers of immigrants in proportion to the host population does not yet make this test practicable by national surveys. The result in Smethwick at the 1964 general election proved that race *could be* important to white working-class and/or middle-class voters in an area of heavy coloured immigration; the pattern of voting in 1966 indicates that such cases are likely to be few rather than numerous (Cf. Deakin 1965, 1966). . . . The behaviour of individuals born and socialized in Britain after moving to such multiracial societies as Southern Rhodesia suggests that the political culture of Britain does not make for conciliation when compositional features of society are not overwhelmingly favourable to whites.

The foregoing analysis of the party affiliations of seemingly deviant groups shows that, where they exist, in four out of five tests non-class divisions are important in modifying partisan allegiances within the working-class. Barring intermittent acts of violence in Ulster, non-class cleavages remain minor enough within the United Kingdom so that they do not create difficulties for class-based parties or the regime. Yet if the social composition of Britain today approximated that of the pre-industrial United Kingdom, then 19th century controversies in religion and education would have been fought against an Established Church representing a limited minority of the population, and the rise of Irish nationalism would have occurred in a Kingdom one-quarter of whose population was Irish and another fifth Scottish or Welsh. In contemporary and comparative terms, one might imagine a Britain with more than 5 million Negroes, as in proportion to America, 17 million Roman Catholics, as in Ulster, and 22 million Welsh speakers, as in proportion to Flemish speakers in Belgium. In such cases, it would be difficult to conceive that the resulting party divisions would resemble those in Britain today; instead, a situation such as in the Netherlands, Belgium, or France would no doubt be regarded as natural, as class divisions are regarded here today.

Intensive examination of data concerning the voting loyalties of the entire British working-class is important in order to see under what circumstances and to what extent various definitions of the working-class are empirically significant in understanding party divisions. Three different approaches will be considered. The simplest involves the use of occupation as the sole indicator of class. . . .

The simple relationship between occupational class and voting at the 1964 general election shows, as at every election since 1945, that the middle class, and particularly the upper middle class, has been more cohesive in voting Conservative than the working-class has been Labour (Table 8 and Gallup Poll 1966). . . . In order to concentrate attention upon divisions within the "hard core" working-class, persons in the intermediate category of shop and personal service workers are omitted from subsequent analyses, as are the 5 per cent of Gallup respondents not assigned to any class.

Given the degree of unexplained variance, the safest method of proceeding further at this stage is to examine, one at a time, the impact of working-class occupation plus a wide range of other variables. . . . The first set of hypotheses concerns the importance of subjective, psychological factors operating in conjunction with occupational position.

TABLE 8. VOTING BY OCCUPATIONAL CLASS IN BRITAIN, 1964

Occupational class	Percentage of total	Con.	Lab.	Other
Professional	7	64	21	15
Business	7	75	11	14
Office workers	14	56	27	17
Shop; personal service	12	46	37	17
Skilled workers	29	33	52	15
Semi-skilled workers	14	25	64	11
Unskilled workers	12	21	65	14
Unclassified	5	39	40	20

2.1 *Workers subjectively identifying with the working-class are more likely to vote Labour than non-identifiers.*

Gallup data show that 65 per cent of persons whose objective and subjective positions were both working-class voted Labour, 24 per cent higher than the figure for manual workers without such an identification. It is important to note that the data also strongly support the converse of this hypothesis. Middle-class identifiers in the working-class divided 31 per cent Labour and 53 per cent Conservative.

2.2 *Workers interested in class-salient issues are more likely to vote Labour than other workers.*

This hypothesis assumes that a worker concerned with issues lacking class salience, e.g., defence or foreign affairs, will be less likely to align his vote with the party of his class than a worker concerned with such class-salient issues as labour relations or economic affairs. Notwithstanding the plausibility of this hypothesis, the data reject it. Working-class voters naming economic affairs and industrial relations as important issues do not differ significantly from the total. Moreover, workers naming international affairs as an important issue divide 36 per cent Conservative and 49 per cent Labour, and those concerned with defense as an issue divide 41 per cent Conservative and 49 per cent Labour.

2.3 *Workers showing higher levels of political involvement are more likely to vote Labour than other workers.*

This hypothesis assumes that subjective involvement in politics is more likely to make an individual align himself with the party of the majority of persons in his class. Three different indices are available — interest in the election, perception of important differences between the parties, and concern with the personal impact of the election result. On all three indices, the most involved members of the working-class differ hardly at all from a cross-section of all manual workers. The most straightforward inference from this data is that as involvement in politics declines, the inclination of workers to show a preference for either of the two major parties also declines.

A second set of hypotheses can be developed, which assert the importance of material influences by combining the occupational index with another economic sub-system measure. . . .

2.4 *Workers belonging to a trade union are more likely to vote Labour than are non-union manual workers.*

This hypothesis is supported by survey data, for among working-class respondents in a union (or in a family where the head of the household held a union card) 65 per cent favoured Labour and 22 per cent favoured the Conservatives, as against a Labour bias of 49 per cent to 35 per cent among non-union workers. Direct personal involvement in union activities appears to add little to Labour voting, since the difference in Labour support as between male respondents in trade unions and housewives whose only contact with a union is through their husband is but 7 per cent. . . .

2.5 *Workers who are more prosperous are less likely to vote Labour than those who are less prosperous.*

The thesis of working-class prosperity as a motive for voting Conservative was very popular after the 1959 general election (see, e.g., Butler & Rose, 1960) but since then has been subjected to criticism on various grounds by Goldthorpe and Lockwood (1967) and by Nordlinger (1967). . . . The omission of a direct question concerning income on Gallup surveys is an unfortunate handicap; earnings can only be inferred from questions concerning motor car and telephone ownership. These indices show that workers owning motor cars in 1964 divided 49 per cent Labour to 36 per cent Conservative, compared to a division of 60 per cent Labour and 26 per cent Conservative among non-vehicle owners. . . . Workers with telephones divided 49 per cent favouring the Conservatives as against 38 per cent favouring Labour. The findings are striking, although interpretation is difficult. It would be safest to infer that the fact of high wages is less immediately important than goods purchased with wages and their relation to life styles. . . .

2.6 *Workers with personal capital are less likely to vote Labour than those without capital.*

This hypothesis is accepted not only by persons on the extreme left, but also by business propagandists for wider ownership of company shares. Gallup data provide one suitable indicator — home-ownership. This is a good index, since home-ownership, even if only of a terrace house or a pre-1914 building, is a form of capital investment within the financial means of a large number of manual workers. The implications of home-ownership differ, say, from the implications of automobile ownership, since it implies responsibilities, e.g., calculating for future repairs, taxes, and maintenance, more acceptable to "respectable" workers than to the "rough" working-class. In 1964, the tendency of working-class home-owners (or, more properly speaking, mortgage-holders) to vote Labour should have been increased by the salience of the housing issue and Labour's image as a party which would keep interest rates down. Notwithstanding this situational consideration, the data show that at that election, 43 per cent of working-class home-owners voted Conservative and 42 per cent favoured Labour, compared with 64 per cent of working-class tenants supporting Labour and 22 per cent the Conservatives.

A third set of hypotheses concern the inter-action of occupational class and social and environmental characteristics. These hypotheses assume, like the American concept of *socio-economic* status, that the combined impact of social and economic influences is likely to be more important than influences derived solely from the economic system.

2.7 *Working-class men are more likely to vote Labour than working-class women.*

In support of this hypothesis, one could advance a "depth psychology" argument that Labour was a more "masculine" party, or a simple sociological assertion that first-hand experience of the work situation is more likely to increase class-oriented voting than is the situation of a housewife. While there is a sex bias toward Labour among men, when one controls for age, sex becomes of limited theoretical interest (Table 3). It can, of course, be of considerable practical importance in election results (Gallup Poll, 1966). The Almond-Verba study suggests that the similarities are evidence of the willingness of men and women to discuss public affairs in the home on a basis approaching political and sex equality (1963).

2.8 *Workers who read pro-Labour papers are more likely to vote Labour than those who do not.*

The data concerning this hypothesis, obtained from a 1967 National Opinion Polls survey, show strong relationships between newspaper reading and partisan preference, within both the middle-class and the working-class (Table 9). The problem is choosing between alternative

TABLE 9. VOTING BY CLASS AND NEWSPAPER READERSHIP, 1967 (PERCENTAGES)

Newspaper	N	Middle class (ABC1) Con.	Lab.	Other	N	Working class (C2DE) Con.	Lab.	Other
Times	(51)	59	21	20	(22)	—	—	—
Guardian	(67)	30	30	40	(16)	—	—	—
Telegraph	(308)	69	13	18	(80)	59	30	11
Mail	(292)	66	17	17	(282)	46	40	14
Sketch	(70)	80	10	10	(176)	42	39	19
Express	(406)	64	16	21	(692)	37	42	21
Mirror	(270)	42	34	24	(964)	27	53	20
Sun	(48)	35	50	15	(251)	14	73	13
None	(121)	48	26	26	(272)	28	49	23
Totals		58	21	21		30	51	19

Source: National Opinion Polls, July 1967.

explanations: (1) the editorial policy of a worker's paper tends to determine his party preference; (2) party preference tends to determine choice of newspaper; or (3) both party preference and choice of newspaper tend to be determined by a common set of underlying factors. Given the importance of inter-generational socialization influences on party preference and, by implication, on choice of newspaper, evidence that political news is not of substantial interest to most newspaper readers, and evidence of selective perception of political news, then it would be safest to accept the third explanation in default of further data. At most, newspaper reading may be important in reinforcing previously determined partisan commitments.

2.9 *The larger the proportion of workers in an area, the greater the proportion of workers voting Labour.*

This assumption concerning increased residential inter-action of workers with each other can best be tested by looking at the voting patterns of council house tenants, since council estates form communities or neighbourhoods most likely to intensify face-to-face contact; moreover, these estates are readily identifiable by residents and those outside as working-class areas, with very few middle-class residents. Among working-class council tenants, 70 per cent favoured Labour and 20 per cent the Conservatives. Tenants in private housing, by contrast, divided 59 per cent Labour to 24 per cent Conservative, almost exactly the overall class average, thus indicating that spatial segregation, rather than the status of a tenant, is the chief influence here. The impact of segregation can also be seen in the fact that among the ambiguously stratified personal and service workers on council estates, a majority, 53 per cent, favoured Labour and 33 per cent the Conservatives, a major deviation from the pattern of that group as a whole. . . .

2.10 *Workers with above-average education are less likely to vote Labour than workers with minimum education.*

Within the tenth of the working class with above-minimum education, Labour loyalties are weak. A total of 40 per cent in this group favoured the Conservatives and 41 per cent Labour in 1964. Analysis in terms of sex differences shows marked contrasts between men and women. Working-class men with further education favoured Labour as against the Conservatives, 46 per cent to 32 per cent. By contrast, educated women, most of whom will be in the working-class by virtue of their husband's occupation, favoured the Conservatives as against Labour, 50 per cent to 34 per cent. Educated women in the working class are motivated perhaps partly by aspiration and partly by frustration in actively favouring the Conservatives.

Collectively, the hypotheses concerning compound influences upon working-class voting show that insofar as factors in addition to occupation are important, they are more likely to depress working-class support for Labour than increase it. This gives a little support to Parkin's thesis (1967) that the cultural strength of Conservatism is so great in Britain that even within the working-class many voters are impervious to class appeals for party loyalty. . . . A second point of considerable importance is that the bulk of influences of special strength — e.g., Welshness, Catholicism and telephone ownership — tend to affect only a very small fraction of the working-class. . . .

Many of the problems investigated in the foregoing hypotheses are ignored because class and party loyalties are so often discussed in terms of an ideal-typical working man and his wife. In such circumstances, analysis begins with the postulation of a category of individuals all of whom have a large conglomeration of experiences and attributes in common, from a distinctive pattern of child-rearing by a working-class Mum to the special burial customs of the Co-operative Society. Attitudes and behaviour are then predicted and explained by deduction. While ideal-type figures can be heuristically valuable, they will cause confusion if their quasi-empirical nature is not subjected, sooner or later, to empirical test. . . .

Gallup Poll data includes a wide variety of attributes relevant to the ideal-type or idealized worker. In order to avoid reducing the category to an esoteric group possessing, say, up to twelve specified characteristics, four attributes commonly ascribed to working-class people besides occupation have been selected as the operational indicators of the "ideal typical" worker: subjective identification with the working-class, trade union membership or membership in a family whose head is in a union, only the minimum of education, and residence in rented property. These attributes are drawn from several sub-systems of society, but sub-systems in which class is presumed to be of constant influence. . . . Investigation shows that the ideal-type worker constitutes only one-quarter of the "hard-core" working-class (Table 10). . . . The attribute most likely to disqualify a respondent is lack of trade union membership within the family, a connection usually assumed to be of fundamental importance in theories of working-class political action. If allowance is made for individuals with at least three of the four ideal-type attributes, another 40 per cent of working-class respondents

TABLE 10. IDEAL-TYPE CHARACTERISTICS AND WORKING-CLASS VOTING

Category	Percentage of working-class	Con.	Lab.	Other
All characteristics (manual worker; subjectively working-class; tenant; t.u. family; minimum education)	26	14	75	11
All but trade union family	22	22	62	16
All but tenant	10	27	61	12
All but subjectively w-c	7	24	66	10
All but minimum education	1	(56)[a]	(34)[a]	(7)[a]
Lack two or more characteristics of ideal-type worker	34	44	40	16

[a] N = 27

can be said to approximate the ideal-type figure; more than one-third of the working-class remain clearly remote from this category. In all, 14 per cent of the total electorate falls in the pure working-class category, and another 22 per cent in the group approximating the ideal-type. Ideal-type workers are disproportionately Labour, but possession of all the classic attributes of class makes the group no more significantly Labour than either of two non-economic attributes—Welshness or Roman Catholicism (Cf. Tables 10, 5, and 8). Moreover, the absence of at least two of these four re-inforcing characteristics is positively associated with Conservative inclinations. . . .

The foregoing test of compositional and compound hypotheses has made it clear that subjective, psychological involvement appears less important as an influence upon working-class voters in Britain than appears to be the case in the Michigan analysis of party identification in the United States (Campbell *et al.* 1960). Among the most important influences subsidiary to occupational class, only one, subjective middle-class identification, is clearly attitudinal; the remainder refer to gross socio-economic characteristics or cultural influences such as Catholicism or Welsh nationality. One might speculate that in a country with a stable, strong class structure — in Weber's terms, "transparent" — then objective social characteristics are likely to be more important than in America, where the extremely complex nature of the social structure allows an individual's perception of his place in society to be more fluid, and parties too are less clearly class-oriented. . . .

In analysing the significance of class for political recruitment in contemporary Britain, one must avoid the fallacy of assuming that a whole constellation of attitudes and policy preferences can be deduced from data on social origins (Edinger & Searing, 1967). The most and the least that such data can supply is evidence of symbolic values in working-class representation. The use of such gross indices as occupational class and education can be justified, however, given the system of selecting parliamentary candidates in this country, because such attributes are immediately recognizable when nominating potential Members of Parliament.

Working-class politicians are now in the minority in the Parliamentary Labour Party, but they continue to form a large category by comparison with America and Canada, which lack a major working-class party. (Cf. Table 1 and Kornberg & Thomas 1966.) The proportion among Labour MP's is declining, however. . . . At Cabinet level, working-class representation is even less significant than in the parliamentary party as a whole, and the downward trend has extended very far (Table 2).

The question then arises: Are Labour MPs symbolically representative of any social group? The data in Table 11 show that the Parliamentary Labour Party is becoming representative of university graduates. Among new Labour MPs in 1966, 68 per cent were graduates, compared to a figure of 42 per cent for the whole PLP in 1964 (Butler & King, 1966:210). The position in terms of Labour Cabinet ministers is intensified. In autumn, 1967, 81 per cent of members of the Cabinet

TABLE 11. UNIVERSITY MEN IN THE HOUSE OF COMMONS, 1906–1966 (PERCENTAGES)

Year	Labour	Conservative	Liberals and others	Total
1906	0	57	49	49
1910 (Jan.)	0	58	48	52
1910 (Dec.)	0	59	45	51
1918	5	49	33	39
1922	15	48	40	39
1923	14	50	43	37
1924	14	52	48	43
1929	19	54	57	38
1931	17	55	53	51
1935	19	57	55	47
1945	32	58	62	42
1950	41	62	58	51
1951	41	65	75	54
1955	40	64	100	53
1959	39	60	100	52
1964	46	63	78	53
1966	51	67	77	58

Sources: 1906-1910: Thomas 1958: 38-39
1918-1945: Ross 1955: 424
1950ff.: Nuffield election studies

TABLE 12. UNIVERSITY MEN IN LABOUR CABINETS, 1924–1967

Year	Cabinet	All universities N	Percentage	Oxbridge N	Percentage of university men
1924	20	6	30	5	84
1929	19	7	37	4	57
1945	20	10	50	5	50
1950	18	9	50	6	67
1964	23	13	57	11	85
1966	23	14	61	11	79
1969 (Dec.)	21	17	81	11	65

were graduates; 11 of the 17 were from Oxford (Table 12). The most striking feature of this evidence is the convergence of Labour and Conservative patterns of symbolic representation. Notwithstanding the relatively great obstacles that most youths from Labour homes face in attaining a higher education, the proportion of Labour Cabinet ministers with a degree is now about on a par with that in Conservative times, and the proportion of MPs with a degree is becoming more nearly equal between the parties. Within the Conservative ranks, it is almost certainly true, although difficult to demonstrate statistically, that the value placed upon the *content* of a university education is increasing, as against the *status* of having a degree from or having matriculated at a prestigious institution. The trend can readily be explained as a reasonable response of the parties to the growing complexity of government, and the resulting need for politicians to have the functional competence expected of a graduate and not of working-class men who left school at 14.

Class is not declining in symbolic importance, but rather the class favoured for ruling has been redefined. No longer are MPs expected to represent an occupational class or a traditional upper status group. Instead, they represent a class defined in terms of achieved merit and presumed performance qualities. In the contemporary social structure, however, this new "ruling class" constitutes a minority of less than 4 per cent. It is ironically relevant that this is about the same proportion of the population as has had a public school education or otherwise qualified for inclusion in the traditional upper status classes. Political recruitment thus continues to emphasize government by a class so defined that workers and their children are unlikely to be included. . . .

Judging the significance of class for policy outputs in contemporary Britain is particularly difficult at the time of writing, because the Labour government is only part-way through the life of a Parliament. Government spokesmen can argue that the subsequent years will differ from those since 1964. At the symbolic level, the most notable feature of policy discussions is the absence of conflicts. In opposition in the 1960's, Labour shifted from Socialism to technocracy, but in office, the technocratic style has been abandoned as opportunistically as apparently it was adopted. At both the 1964 and 1966 elections, Labour campaigns emphasized men not measures. The campaign slogans — "Let's Go with Labour" and "You Know Labour Government Works" — were not only devoid of class-conflict implications but also of policy implications. In both foreign and economic policy, the government has pursued policies which have often resembled those of its Conservative predecessor. In short, symbolic partisan divisions, barring an abrupt change in the Conservative Party, appear at most to be nominal or opportunistic.

In assessing material policy outputs under a Labour government, figures on welfare expenditure are available for the first part of Labour's rule. In terms of constant prices, welfare expenditure has risen under the Wilson government. But it also rose under Conservative government from 1951–1964.* Examination of short-term fluctuations suggests that welfare expenditure tends to rise in advance of a general election. For example, the Conservatives prior to the 1964 election were as ready as Labour to promise greater benefits to the electorate in the late 1960's (*Cmnd.* 2235, 1963). The figures for the first two years of the Labour government may therefore be interpreted as a response to pre-election pressures, given the anticipation of a second poll, rather than as a clearcut disjunction resulting from a change of party in office. Events since the 1966 election, such as the Labour Government's policies on the £, on bank rate, unemployment and trade union legislation further suggest that differences on policies between Labour and its Conservative predecessors may be less great in the end than once was expected. . . .

* [See Table 14 in the original text — Editors' note.]

In contemporary Britain, class appears to be most significant for the mobilization of the electorate, of some significance in the recruitment of politicians, and almost certainly of least importance in decisions about policy outputs. . . . The existence of class differences in politics, however, is a very different thing from the existence of class conflicts. . . .

The most important implication of this case study, evidenced by the test of culture and compositional theories, is that social structure is likely to be more important than national culture in determining party divisions. In this context, however, social structure means far more than division into occupational groupings; it also includes divisions into racial, religious, nationality and peasant groupings. Among these groups, there is a strong suggestion of a hierarchy of influences, with class less important for party divisions than non-class determinants of the composition of society. Moreover, whether one looks at modern British history or the modern history of France, Germany or Italy, it appears that non-class divisions are much more likely to lead to the repudiation of a regime than are class divisions. Without going so far as to argue that class-based parties help create and maintain legitimacy, one can emphasize that such divisions are entirely consistent with the existence of a fully legitimate regime. It would be tempting to explain this simply as the consequence of full employment and rising prosperity buying off potential discontent. But this cannot be done in Britain since the legitimacy of the regime has persisted through periods of high unemployment and disastrous diplomacy as well as through times of peace and prosperity.

An additional implication is that the behavioural significance of stratification models may vary considerably from sub-system to sub-system of society. There is, for example, a better fit between membership in the occupational working-class and subjective working-class identification, or between level of education and a working-class occupation than there is between a working-class occupation and voting. These findings are, of course, consistent with the distinctions that Weber made between class, status and party. With a few exceptions such as Runciman (1966), writers have tended to assume that bases of stratification salient for behaviour in one sub-system have the same significance when translated into another field. Each model, like each social science discipline, captures only a part of the complexities of social relationships.

BIBLIOGRAPHY

Alford, Robert R. 1963. *Party and Society*. Chicago: Rand, McNally.
Allen, V. L. 1956. "The Ethics of Trade Union Leaders." *B. J. Sociol.* 7: 314–336.

Almond, Gabriel A. 1956. "Comparative Political Systems." *Journal of Politics* 18: 391–409.
Almond, Gabriel A. and Sidney Verba. 1963. *The Civic Culture*. Princeton: University Press.
Anderson, Perry. 1965. "Origins of the Present Crisis." In P. Anderson and R. Blackburn (eds.), *Towards Socialism*. London: Fontana.
Bagehot, Walter. 1955 (reprint of the 1872 edition). *The English Constitution*. London: Oxford University Press.
Barritt, D. F. and Carter, C. F. 1962. *The Northern Ireland Problem*. London: Oxford University Press.
Beer, Samuel H. 1965. *Modern British Politics*. London: Faber.
Birch, A. H. 1959. *Small-Town Politics*. London: Oxford University Press.
Blondel, Jean. 1963. *Voters, Parties and Leaders*. Harmondsworth: Penguin.
Briggs, Asa. 1961. "The Welfare State in Historical Perspective." *European Journal of Sociology* 2: 221–258.
Budge, Ian and Urwin, D. W. 1966. *Scottish Political Behaviour*. London: Longmans.
Butler, D. E. 1952. *The British General Election of 1951*. London: Macmillan.
Butler, D. E. and King, Anthony. 1966. *The British General Election of 1966*. London: Macmillan.
Butler, D. E. and Rose, Richard. 1960. *The British General Election of 1959*. London: Macmillan.
Campbell, Angus et al. 1960. *The American Voter*. New York: Wiley.
Cline, Catherine Ann. 1963. *Recruits to Labour*. Syracuse: University Press.
CMND. 2235. 1963. *Public Expenditure in 1963–64 and 1967–68*. London: H.M.S.O.
Cox, Kevin. 1967. "Geography, Social Contexts and Welsh Voting Behaviour: 1861–1951." Brussels: International Political Science Association, mimeograph.
Deakin, Nicholas (ed.). 1965. *Colour and the British Electorate 1964*. London: Pall Mall Press.
Deakin, Nicholas et al. 1966. "Colour and the 1966 General Election." *Race* 8: 17–42.
Dowse, Robert E. 1961. "The Entry of the Liberals into the Labour Party, 1910–1920." *Yorkshire Bulletin of Economic and Social Research* 13: 78–88.
Edinger, Lewis J. and Donald D. Searing. 1967. "Social Background in Elite Analysis." *American Political Science Review* 61: 428–445.
Epstein, Leon. 1962. "British Class Consciousness and the Labour Party." *Journal of British Studies* 2: 136–150.
Gallup Poll. 1966. "Voting Behaviour in Britain, 1945–1964." In Rose, Richard (ed.), *Studies in British Politics*. London: Macmillan.
Goldthorpe, John H., David Lockwood, et al. 1967. "The Affluent Worker and the Thesis of *Embourgeoisement*." *Sociology* 1: 11–31.
Guttsman, W. L. 1963. *The British Political Elite*. London: MacGibbon & Kee.
Harrison, Martin, 1960. *Trade Unions and the Labour Party Since 1945*. London: Allen & Unwin.
Hoffman, J. D. 1964. *The Conservative Party in Opposition, 1945–51*. London: MacGibbon & Kee.
Kornberg, Allan and Norman Thomas. 1965–66. "Representative Democracy and Political Elites in Canada and the United States." *Parliamentary Affairs* 19: 91–102.
Lipson, Leslie. 1953. "The Two-Party System in British Politics." *American Political Science Review* 47: 334–358.

Lloyd, Trevor. 1965. "Uncontested Seats in British General Elections, 1852–1910." *The Historical Journal* 8: 260–265.
Morgan, R. 1965. "Is Wales a Region?" *Parliamentary Affairs* 18: 458–462.
Nordlinger, Eric A. 1967. *The Working-Class Tories*. London: MacGibbon & Kee.
Parkin, Frank. 1967. "Working-Class Conservatives." *B. J. Sociol.* 18: 278–290.
Peacock, Alan T. and Jack Wiseman. 1961. *The Growth of Public Expenditure in the United Kingdom*. Princeton: University Press.
Pelling, Henry. 1965 ed. *The Origins of the Labour Party, 1880–1900*. Oxford: Clarendon Press.
Pelling, Henry. 1967. *Social Geography of British Elections, 1885–1910*. London: Macmillan.
Rokkan, Stein. 1968. "The Structuring of Mass Politics in the Smaller European Democracies: a Development of Typology." *Comparative Studies in Society and History* 10: 173–210.
Rose, Richard. 1965a. *Politics in England*. London: Faber.
Rose, Richard. 1965b. "England: a Traditionally Modern Political Culture." In Pye, L. W. and Verba, S. (eds.), *Political Culture and Political Development*. Princeton: University Press.
Ross, J. F. S. 1955. *Elections and Electors*. London: Eyre & Spottiswoode.
Runciman, W. G. 1966. *Relative Deprivation and Social Justice*. London: Routledge.
Shils, Edward and Michael Young. 1953. "The Meaning of the Coronation." *Sociological Review* 1: 63–81.
Steed, Wickham. 1906. "The Labour Party and the Books that Helped to Make It." *Review of Reviews* 33: 568–582.
Stirling, J. 1952. "Social Services Expenditure during the last 100 Years." *Advancement of Science* 8: 379–392.
Stokes, Donald. 1967. "Parties and the Nationalization of Electoral Forces." In Chambers, W. N. and Burnham, W. Dean (eds.), *The American Party Systems*. New York: Oxford University Press.
Symons, Julian. 1957. *The General Strike*. London: Cresset.
Thomas, J. A. 1958. *The House of Commons, 1906–1911*. Cardiff: University of Wales Press.
Weber, Max. 1948. *From Max Weber*, edited by Gerth, H. H. and Mills, C. Wright. London: Routledge.
Wertheimer, Egon. 1929. *Portrait of the Labour Party*. London: Putnams.

APPENDIX

All Gallup Poll data discussed in this study, unless otherwise noted, are drawn from samples conducted by the British Institute of Public Opinion on behalf of the *Daily Telegraph* shortly before the 1964 general election. This is a very good election to select for analysing voting behaviour, because electoral support of the two parties closely approximated the average division of votes between the two parties in the seven elections from 1945 to 1966. . . . The author is indebted to Dr. Henry Durant, William Gregory and R. J. Whybrow of the Gallup Poll for making the data available, and for acceding so courteously and generously to various requests for information since 1959.

KLAUS LIEPELT

The Infra-Structure of Party Support in Germany and Austria

The maintenance of stable political outlooks throughout a lifetime is dependent upon the contemporary environment, as well as upon youthful experiences that initially give direction to these attitudes. The analysis of Klaus Liepelt is concerned primarily with social structure influences upon political loyalties. The author employs a sophisticated statistical technique, tree analysis, to ascertain the most important influences that combine to maintain traditional partisan attachments, and those that allow for the movement of some voters between parties. Comparisons between Germany and Austria illustrate the extent to which there is greater fluidity in German society today than in Austrian society.

This contribution represents an experiment in using survey data from Germany and Austria to explain the socio-economic differences in the left vs. conservative voting balance of the two countries.[1] Comparison between these two countries is eased by the fact that there are few cultural and no language differences. Data based on interview surveys can easily be matched; and in this particular case comparability is increased by the fact that the questionnaire items used were to a large extent identical in both countries.

Abridged from Klaus Liepelt, *The Infra-Structure of Party Support in Austria and West Germany*, International Conference on Comparative Electoral Behavior, Ann Arbor, Michigan, 1967, 26 pp. Reprinted by permission.

[1] For Germany, a total of 12,676 cases were used which were collected by the Bad Godesberg *Institut für angewandte Sozialwissenschaft* during a one year period in 1963/64 and involved seven national surveys. For Austria, a total of 4,704 cases were reanalyzed which were collected by the Vienna *Institut für empirische Sozialforschung* during the winter of 1965/66, involving three national surveys.

The data were approached with an analysis scheme that is also at an experimental stage. A design was chosen that would allow for weighting the different factors associated with voting in the two countries. In order to identify the socio-economic groupings that are relevant for voting behavior, and, at the same time, to maximize the meaningful reduction of unexplained variance in party affiliation, the so-called tree technique[2] was applied which allows for a non-symmetric splitting of social groups in a process of ordering and dichotomizing of variables.[3]

The two Germanic-language countries show many similarities. (See Table 1.) In fact, they both seem to follow similar patterns of development, with Germany being a few years ahead of the neighbor country. Although the per capita rate of the Austrian gross national product is lower than that of Germany, both countries have shown similar rapid growth rates during the post-war period. Further, in 1961 almost half of the GNP in both countries still originated from industry (45 percent, 48 percent) while the United States for example relied much more heavily on the service sector of the economy. . . . The Austrian economy still relies more heavily on its agricultural segment than the German economy: Percentages of self-employed persons are higher, of working-class people lower in Austria than in Germany. More people live in villages and small towns, and the Austrian percentage of industrial employment is below the German figure. But still, in both countries agricultural production does not yet follow the Anglo-American patterns of marginality.

Much different, however, is the group structure of German and Austrian politics. While in West Germany the gap between the Socialist and the non-socialist parties has narrowed from election to election during the last 15 years, there have been few changes in the post-war two-party balance of Austria. Even in the 1966 election it was only a loss of 1.4 percentage points that tipped the scales and ousted the *Sozialistische Partei Österreichs* (SPÖ) from its share in government. Although Austria is predominantly Catholic and less industrialized than Germany, it took the conservative-Catholic *Österreichische Volkspartei* (ÖVP) two decades to gain an absolute parliamentary majority. Although Germany still has a high percentage of industrial workers and although the Protestant half of the population outnumbers the Catholic segment, the *Sozialdemokratische Partei* (SPD) is still well below a parliamentary majority. A two-party balance does not yet exist in Germany.

---

[2] The operations involved have been discussed in general terms by John A. Sonquist and James N. Morgan, *The Detection of Interaction Effects,* Survey Research Center, University of Michigan, 1964.

The specific model applied was that of Philip Stouthard and J. H. G. Seegers. See J. H. G. Seegers, "De Contrasgroepen-Methode: Nadere Uitwerking en een Tweetal Toepassinger," *Sociale Wetenschapen,* 1964, No. 3, pp. 194–225.

[3] The ordering of variables and their dichotomizing was based on the results of computer operations at the Institut für angewandte Sozialwissenschaft. The results of the "tree" analysis on the German data are discussed under different aspects in Klaus Liepelt and Alexander Mitscherlich (eds.), *Thesen zur Wählerfluktuation,* Frankfurt/M., Europäische Verlagsanstalt, 1967.

TABLE 1. STRUCTURAL DATA: WESTERN GERMANY AND AUSTRIA

Criteria	Definitions	Western Germany	Austria	United States
Social structure				
Catholics	percentage of total population, 1961	44%	89%	
Employment in industry	percentage of working-age population, 1961	32%	28%	
Workers	percentage of total labor force, 1964, 1961	46%	41%	
Self-employed, helping family members	percentage of total labor force, 1964, 1961	20%	29%	
Inhabitants of cities over 20,000	percentage of total population, 1961	55%	40%	
Economic structure				
Gross national product	per capita, in US $, 1963	1,400	900	2,900
GNP originating in agriculture	percentage of total gross national product 1960/61	7.0%	11.0%	4.0%
GNP originating in industry	percentage of total gross national product 1960/61	45.0%	48.0%	33.0%
Growth rate of GNP	average annual growth per capita, 1950-1960	6.2%	7.3%	1.8%
Communications structure				
Daily newspaper circulation	per 100 population, 1960	31	20	33
Radio sets	per 100 population, 1962	29	29	97
Television sets	per 100 population, 1962	13	5	32
Telephones	per 100 population, 1962	13	11	43
Private cars	per 100 population, 1963	14	9	36
Group membership				
Union membership	absolute, 1964, 1961	7.5 Mill.	1.5 Mill.	
	percentage of wage and salary earners	35%	63%	
Socialist party members	SPD 1966, SPÖ 1966 absolute (approx.)	700,000	720,000	
	percentage of Socialist votes at last election	5.5%	37%	
Catholic-Conservative party members	CDU/CSU 1965, ÖVP 1966 absolute (approx.)	380,000	650,000	
	percentage of Conservative votes at last election	2.5%	30%	
Other party members	FDP 1965, FPÖ 1966 absolute (approx.)	95,000	30,000	
	percentage of liberal votes at last election	3.0%	12%	
Voting patterns (Germany 1965, Austria 1966 national elections)				
Eligible voters	absolute, approx.	38.5 Mill.	4.9 Mill.	
Turnout	percentage of eligible voters	87%	94%	
Socialist votes	percentage of valid votes, SPD, SPÖ	39.3%	42.6%	
Catholic-Conservative votes	percentage of valid votes, CDU/CSU, ÖVP	47.6%	48.4%	
Liberal votes	percentage of valid votes, FDP, FPÖ	9.5%	5.3%	
Other votes	percentage of valid votes, other parties	3.6%	3.7%	
Trends in Socialist votes				
Election results (SPD, SPÖ)				
1953, 1953		28.8%	42.6%	
1957, 1956	percentage SPD, SPÖ of valid votes	31.8%	43.0%	
1961, 1962		36.2%	44.0%	
1965, 1966		39.3%	42.6%	
Spread	difference between highest and lowest value	10.5	1.4	
Highest change rate	maximum change from election to election	+4.4	-1.4	
Average change rate	average of differences between percentages	3.5	0.9	

Sources: Wahlhandbuch 1965, Österreichisches Wahlhandbuch, World Handbook of Political and Social Indicators, census documents.

By all that we know from the models of voting behavior, we should have assumed that social structure would favor the Socialists in Germany rather than in Austria. There has been a considerable increase in SPD votes lately, but it was preceded by enormous gains of the *Christlich Demokratische Union* (CDU/CSU)[4] which has thwarted almost all the smaller parties on the right of the Socialists. In Austria, the two major parties after the war shared political power and reestablished an unique system of two-party politics. By contrast, the German two-party system developed only slowly during the post-war period; it has still not reached the equilibrium point. With other words, the differences in the voting patterns of Western Germany and Austria cannot merely be explained in terms of general political predispositions of certain socioeconomic groups.[5]

Socialist strength in Austria might be due to the fact that the SPÖ membership figures are almost identical with the membership figures of the German SPD (about 750,000). While in Germany about 5.5 percent of the Social Democratic voters are party members, the percentage in Austria has reached the unique level of 37 percent. As voting to a large extent is not an individual but a household affair, the high percentage of the SPÖ vote could almost be inferred from its membership structure.

However, the ÖVP also commands considerable membership support. With about 650,000 dues-paying members among the three *Bünde*,[6] the conservatives in Austria have to a large extent managed to overcome the difficulties which middle-class parties generally meet when they try to tie their public support more closely to the party. As a result of this, the ÖVP can claim about twice as many members as its German sister party CDU/CSU. . . .

This infra-structure of party support may explain why the left vs. conservative proportion has in Austria been very stable for many years.[7] In the Austrian case both major parties control a large membership, while in Germany neither of them does. Hence, the question still re-

---

[4] In a landslide victory in 1953, the CDU increased its share from 31.0 percent to 45.2 percent.

[5] Instead of the Federal Republic as a whole, we might have taken Austria's neighbour state Bavaria as a point of comparison. In respect to the German Federal average, this state shows a less industrialized structure, and its population is predominantly Catholic. Consequently, the SPD share is below, the CSU share above the Federal average. While the social structure of Bavaria is closer to the Austrian than to the Federal average, the political discrepancy is even wider. Which of the two reflects the "proper" structural behavior?

[6] ÖVP membership is made up of membership in one out of three professional organizations of farmers, employees and employers: the *Bauernbund* (300,000), the *Arbeiter- und Angestelltenbund* (275,000), the *Wirtschaftsbund* (75,000).

[7] Even the loss of 1.4 percentage points which the SPÖ experienced in 1966 as the most extreme change observed before the 1970 upset, must partly be seen as a direct consequence of internal party differences. After a conflict with the SPÖ leadership, Franz Olah, formerly Chairman of the Trade Unions and Minister of the Interior, with a party of his own (DFP) appealed to the right wing of the SPÖ and polled 3.3 percent.

mains unanswered why and how the deviant proportions in the voting balance came about.

The different patterns of party support and party membership are not a post-war affair. They date back to the pre-1933 period. Whereas the SPD in 1930 claimed a membership of only 1,008,000 for the whole German Reich, the SPÖ figures were already above 700,000. . . .

CONSTRUCTION OF VOTER TYPOLOGIES

By simultaneously trying out 32 socio-economic and ecological criteria that have been said to be independent variables in the voting process, we discovered that the spectrum of Austrian party support can be slightly better explained by socio-economic factors than the German scene. Computer analysis produced an optimal combination of categories and variables and a maximal reduction of the initial variance in respect to a dependent variable defined as preferences for the Socialist parties.[8]

In the German case, the initial variance was reduced by 23.7 percent, and in the Austrian case by 31.2 percent. The German result represents a combination of only 5 variables; the Austrian tree combines 7 variables. (Cf. figures 1 and 2.) Three variables proved altogether sufficient to reduce the initial variance by 20.2 percent in the German and by 21.4 percent in the Austrian case.

In both countries these variables reflect ties to large scale organizations that integrate the individual or groups of individuals into the partisan arrangements of the political community. These are the Catholic Church on one side and the organized labor movement on the other. These organizations fulfill this function only insofar as the individual is continuously exposed to their messages.

In respect to the Catholic Church, religious denomination is not enough; it is church attendance that, in the first step, sets off 36 percent of the Austrian electorate with a mere 15 percent SPÖ preference Another 10 percent of the electorate contains 83 percent SPÖ supporters: . . . this group is the readership of the SPÖ party newspapers. Another 2.5 percent of the electorate, with a 63 percent SPÖ preference, among the active Catholics were identified as readers of the socialist press. . . .

Among those who neither go to church nor are exposed to the daily

---

[8] . . . The reader should note that in the Austrian tree all available cases were used while in the German analysis only those 9,493 respondents were included who stated their party preference. This was done for technical reasons. Trial runs have shown that the outcome would not have been different had the "no answer" groups been included in the German or left out in the Austrian case. The percentage of SPD supporters among the total sample (36 percent) was slightly lower than the respondents with SPÖ preferences. Comparisons should therefore not be made between absolute figures but rather between groups.

Parts of the analysis have also been done by taking preferences for CDU/CSU and ÖVP as the dependent variables. There were slight differences in the rank order of the variables, but no changes in the overall picture.

188 KLAUS LIEPELT

FIGURE 1. VOTER TYPES: AUSTRIA

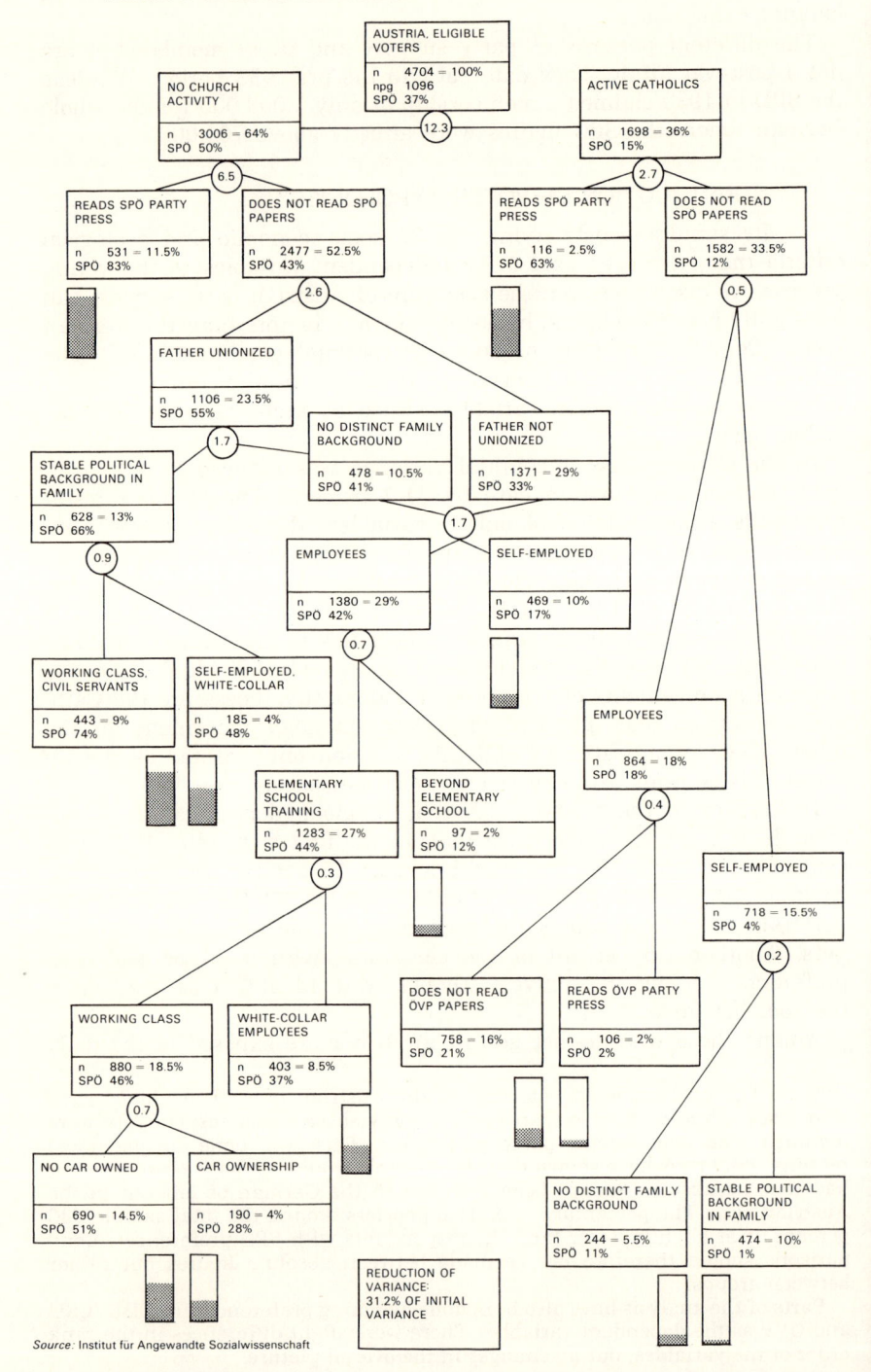

Source: Institut für Angewandte Sozialwissenschaft

PARTY SUPPORT IN GERMANY AND AUSTRIA 189

FIGURE 2. VOTER TYPES: GERMANY

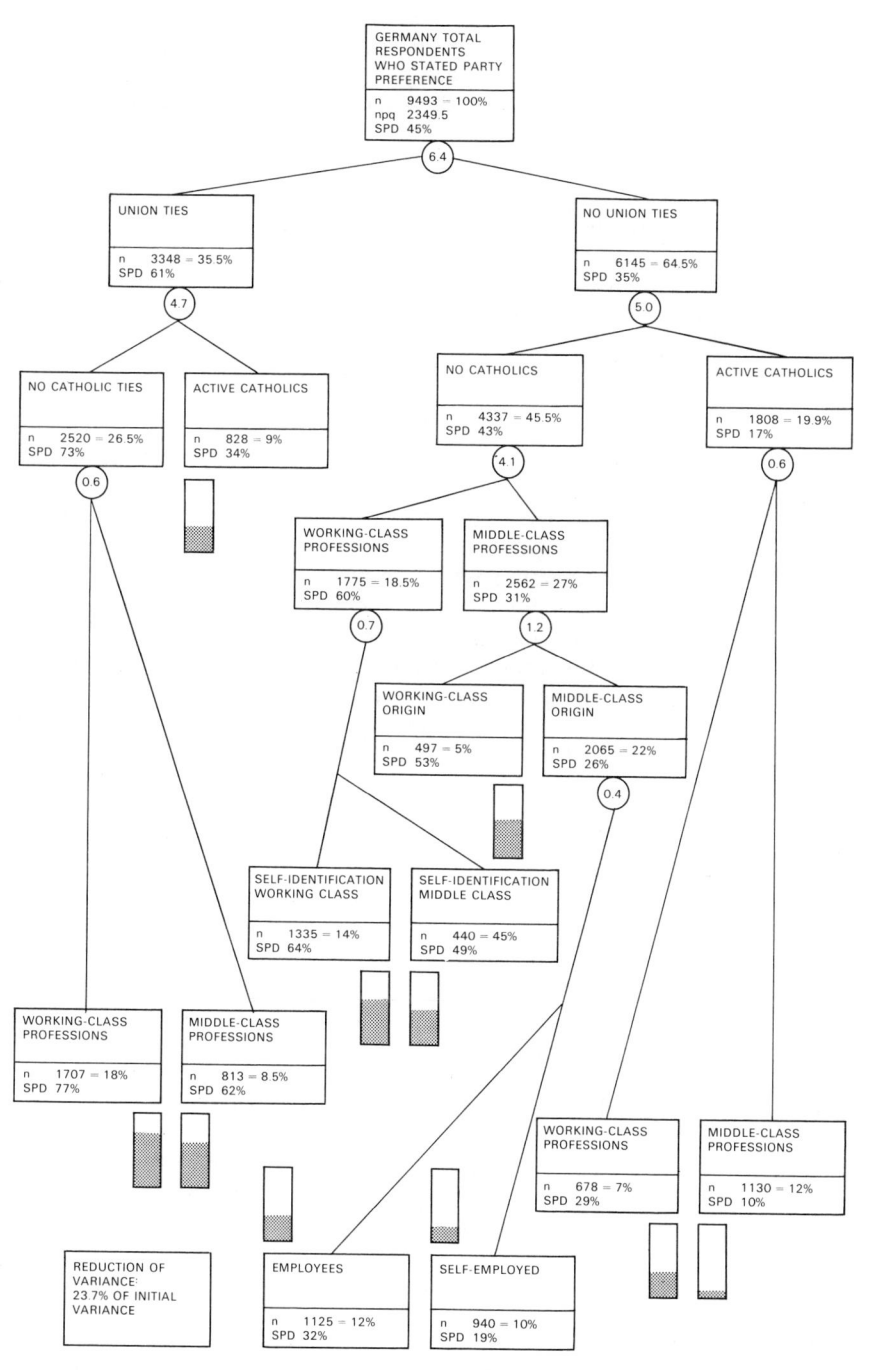

```
                    GERMANY TOTAL
                    RESPONDENTS
                    WHO STATED PARTY
                    PREFERENCE
                    n    9493 = 100%
                    npq  2349.5
                    SPD  45%
                         (6.4)
         ┌───────────────┴───────────────┐
   UNION TIES                        NO UNION TIES
   n   3348 = 35.5%                  n   6145 = 64.5%
   SPD 61%                           SPD 35%
        (4.7)                             (5.0)
   ┌─────┴─────┐                    ┌─────┴─────┐
NO CATHOLIC   ACTIVE           NO CATHOLICS   ACTIVE CATHOLICS
TIES          CATHOLICS        n  4337 = 45.5%  n  1808 = 19.9%
n  2520=26.5% n  828 = 9%      SPD 43%          SPD 17%
SPD 73%       SPD 34%              (4.1)            (0.6)
   (0.6)
                              WORKING-CLASS    MIDDLE-CLASS
                              PROFESSIONS      PROFESSIONS
                              n  1775 = 18.5%  n  2562 = 27%
                              SPD 60%          SPD 31%
                                  (0.7)            (1.2)
                                              ┌────┴────┐
                                        WORKING-CLASS  MIDDLE-CLASS
                                        ORIGIN         ORIGIN
                                        n  497 = 5%    n  2065 = 22%
                                        SPD 53%        SPD 26%
                                                          (0.4)
                              SELF-IDENTIFICATION  SELF-IDENTIFICATION
                              WORKING CLASS        MIDDLE CLASS
                              n  1335 = 14%        n  440 = 4.5%
                              SPD 64%              SPD 49%

WORKING-CLASS   MIDDLE-CLASS
PROFESSIONS     PROFESSIONS
n  1707 = 18%   n  813 = 8.5%
SPD 77%         SPD 62%

                                              WORKING-CLASS   MIDDLE-CLASS
                                              PROFESSIONS     PROFESSIONS
                                              n  678 = 7%     n  1130 = 12%
                                              SPD 29%         SPD 10%

REDUCTION OF    EMPLOYEES         SELF-EMPLOYED
VARIANCE:
23.7% OF INITIAL n  1125 = 12%    n  940 = 10%
VARIANCE         SPD 32%           SPD 19%
```

Source: Institut für Angewandte Sozialwissenschaft

press of the socialist movement, family ties come in. Where the respondent's father was a union member and the respondent still shares his view, SPÖ preferences are high (63 percent). This gives us another 13 percent of the electorate who are part of the informal communications network that is spread over the society and that works to sustain the inherited value systems.

At this point, we have explained 24.1 percent of the variance; two-fifths of the electorate are left who have personal contacts neither to the Catholic nor to the working-class realm.

The same observations can be made for Germany although the institutional arrangements are somewhat different. One-third of the German voters live in households that have membership ties to a labor union. Here the SPD preferences are almost twice as high than among the other two-thirds of the electorate; with this split, the initial variance was reduced by 6.4 percent. Another 5 percent of the variance will be explained by branching off one-fifth of the electorate who have no union ties but are practicing Catholics. Here the SPD percentage is at a minimum, quite similar to the Austrian case. There is only one difference: the group of active Catholics in Austria is considerably larger than in Germany. . . . A group of active Catholics was then identified among the union membership where only one-third have SPD preferences; this split accounts for another 4.7 percent of the variance. By now, 16.1 percent of the initial variance has been explained. . . . It should be noted that the Protestant church evidently does not play as important a role in the promotion or prohibition of support for the Social Democratic Party as has frequently been suggested.

After the majority of the eligible voters in Germany and Austria have been grouped under spheres of influence, a variable comes in that has long been considered the starting point of empirical analysis in voting behavior: occupational class. Among the respondents who have personal ties neither to the socialist camp nor to the various Catholic groups, the employer-employee distinction explains only another 1.7 percent of the Austrian variance. In Germany, 4.1 percent is explained by a split between blue- and white-collar occupations.

Immediately after this split, other variables indicate that voting is a matter of group integration rather than an individual decision on clearly perceived interests. Where the group contacts are not directly absorbed by large scale organizations that matter in the political process, they are handed down from one generation to the next. Among that segment of the German working class which is not organized, self identification makes the difference. The split carves out those workers (4.5 percent of the electorate) who seem to aspire to middle-class values and behavior. Among this latter group, SPD preferences are lower.

Tradition also matters among the large non-organized segment of the middle class. A minority of 5 percent comes from working-class homes. Among those, SPD preferences are considerably higher than among middle-class people from middle-class origin. . . . Social mobility is relevant only where the integrative network of the large-scale organizations is not operative. It works both ways: working-class people who aspire to upward mobility tend to accept the presumed political behavior of the middle classes; middle-class people who have climbed the ladder tend to adhere to the political traditions of their social origin.

This finding was less clear in the Austrian case. Instead, a minority of working-class people showed up who have no group ties but own cars and don't care much for the SPÖ. We will call them "consumer-workers"; their social role as consumers appears more important than their occupational role. . . .

Comparing the Austrian and German picture, it can be stated that the higher degree of stability in the Austrian political scene is certainly due to political organization. Even among active Catholics, readership of ÖVP papers (daily circulation: 160,000) and an unbroken family tradition tend to tighten the value systems of political Catholicism.

Although the distribution of party support may be different, the forces that are operative are similar in Austria and Germany. Quite a few variables did not show up in the analysis at all: income, skill, sex, position in the life cycle are already to a great extent explained by the interest group arrangements which the society provides for its individuals.[9]

DESCRIPTION OF THE VOTER TYPES

The tree technique has opened up the possibility of looking into the change and stability patterns of the relevant voter groups in Germany and Austria. To prepare for such analysis, the end groups of the voter trees were labeled and presented for comparison.[10]

. . . The German data formed eleven groups with an SPD preference that varies from 65 to 11 percent. The Austrian sample was broken into twelve groups with an SPÖ strength ranging from 83 to 1 percent. Although the operational definitions turned out to be slightly different, and although there are marked characteristics for each nation, the group structures show similar traits.

---

[9] Older women, for example, are more likely to vote conservative because their contacts to the sphere of work are low, particularly if the husband has died; they are more likely to go to church. This again makes for a smaller percentage of socialist voting among this portion of the electorate. There are quite a few further observations that could and should first be explained in terms of the social infra-structure made up for organized group interests than in terms of administrative categories. It should be noted that it was left to the analysis which occupation criteria should be used, the occupation of the respondent or of the head of the household; the computer decided in favor of the household's head.

[10] For Tables 2 to 6, from Austria the same data are used as above. From Germany a sample of 8,252 cases collected during the pre-election period in 1965 was used. Further analysis includes respondents who did not state a party preference. The switch to data of 1965 was made in order to have the pre-election situation represented in both countries.

Table 2 contains the operational definitions with the general distribution figures of voters and party members. Table 3 exhibits selected criteria on the social and political composition of the different groups.

About two-fifths of the electorate (Germany 41 percent, Austria 39.5 percent) belong to population segments where *traditional left attachments* prevail. The SPÖ preferences average 66 percent, while the SPD preferences are considerably lower (58 percent). Another fifth of the electorate (20.5 percent in each country) belongs to groups with *middle-class attachments* who have neither Catholic nor union ties. In this segment, socialist preferences are generally low; the SPÖ still scores better than the SPD (27 percent vs. 20 percent).

The remaining two-fifths of the electorate, however, split differently in Germany and Austria. While in Germany the population segment with *traditional Catholic attachment* encompasses less than a quarter (22 percent) of the electorate, it is much larger in Austria (33.5 percent). In both countries, socialist preferences are at a minimum (Germany 13 percent, Austria 12 percent) among this group.

Thus little is left in Austria for groups with *multiple attachments* who, according to the consensus and cleavage theorists, should promote changes among the electorate. By our definitions, in Austria only 6.5 percent of the eligible voters appear to be in touch with influences from different value systems of the society. In Germany, the comparable group amounts to 16.5 percent.

Although it is likely that the "multiple attachment" concept will provide indicators for the degree to which traditional forces are in unchallenged control of certain segments of the electorate, it would be too easy to consider merely one factor — even if it is the outcome of tree analysis. In all social groups, deviant political behavior can be observed, and we must assume that deviancy here is a reflection of some multiple attachments undercutting traditional social arrangements.

The four basic segments of the political society include groups that are quite different from each other.

1. In Austria, among the groups with *traditional left attachments*, there is one hard core element which is not measurable by survey technique in Germany. More than half a million eligible voters are daily readers of a socialist newspaper. Their SPÖ preferences are 83 percent. It is irrelevant in this respect, if we take readership as an index of integration into the value system of the labor movement, or as an influencing factor. We have isolated a rather homogeneous group with *strong political ties* to the left.

This group . . . reflects the fact that party membership is a unique dimension in Austria. More than two-thirds of the SPÖ voters of this highly politicized segment of the left are party members. . . . Its social profile also reflects the structure of the Socialist Party. Highly represented are the blue-collar professions, the civil servants and persons in high positions. Underrepresented or almost absent are those groups that are traditionally organized in one of the three middle class *Bünde*: white-collar employees, business and farmers. (See Table 2.) . . .

This uniquely politicized pillar of Austrian society is supplemented

TABLE 2. PARTIES AND VOTER GROUPS IN GERMANY AND AUSTRIA

Voter groups	Operational definition Germany	Operational definition Austria	Party members SPD	Party members SPÖ	Sympathizers SPD	Sympathizers SPÖ	Sympathizers SPD	Sympathizers SPÖ	Eligible voters Germany	Eligible voters Austria	Socialist preferences Germany pre-Sept. 1965	Socialist preferences Austria Winter 1965/66
Traditional left attachment												
Strong political ties	No church attachment		79%	76%	66%	69%	23%	10%	41%	39.5%	58%	66%
Left tradition	no comparable group unionized workers	reads SPÖ-paper blue-collar, left family tradition	—	38	—	25	—	1	—	11.5	—	83%
Working-class tradition	non-union workers	workers, no family ties	45	18	33	19	9	2	18	9.5	65%	74%
Middle class with left tradition	unionized, white-collar	white-collar, left family tradition	5	14	17	20	7	5	12	14.5	51%	51%
Multiple attachment												
Catholics with left tradition	attends Catholic church unionized	reads SPÖ-paper	29 10%	6 6%	16 15%	5 7%	7 18%	2 4%	11 16.5%	4 6.5%	53% 33%	48% 41%
Consumer workers	working class, but middle-class identif.	car owner-ship	2	4	4	4	5	1	5	2.5	31%	67%
Upwardly mobiles	father worker	no comparable group	3 5	2 —	5.5 5.5	3 —	5.5 7.5	3 —	5.5 6	4 —	34% 34%	28% —
Middle-class attachment	no working-class professions, no church attachment, no union ties												
Lower middle class	free professions, shopkeepers	self-employed	7% 4	11% 6	11% 7	13% 8	23% 12	21% 6	20.5% 10.5	20.5% 8.5	20% 23%	27% 37%
Urban middle class	white-collar employees	self-employed or more than										
Farmers	farmers and dependents	elementary training	3 0	5	3 1	5	6.5 4.5	15	6 4	12	18% 13%	15%
Traditional Catholic attachment	attends Catholic church, no union ties												
Catholic blue-collar	working-class occ.	employees	4% 1	7% 6	8% 4	11% 9	36% 10	65% 23	22% 7	33.5% 16	13% 20%	12% 21%
Catholic middle class	middle-class occ.	self-employed	3	1	4	2	26	9	15	5	10%	11%
Strong political ties	no comparable group	Cath. family tradition	—	0	—	0	—	33	—	12.5	—	1%
Eligible voters			100%	100%	100%	100%	100%	100%	100%	100%	36%	37%

Austria: Reanalysis of pre-election surveys conducted during Winter 1965/66 by the Institute of Empirical Social Research, Vienna, 4,706 cases.
Germany: Reanalysis of pre-election surveys conducted during Spring and Summer 1965 by the Institute of Applied Social Research, Bad Godesberg, 8,134 cases.

by another group of similar size that has no daily contact with official party channels but which is still safely embedded in the *left tradition*. Working-class people and civil servants[11] whose homes have formerly been politicized by union membership, exhibit a party preference pattern which is very similar to that of the "strong political ties" group. With 74 percent socialist preference and with one-third of the SPÖ voters being party members, this group adds another 18 percent to the total SPÖ membership. Their behavior patterns show a high degree of politicization: there is a strong tendency toward political discussion. . . . They do not question the inherited convictions although they may, more than their elders, be inclined to reinforce their beliefs by social contacts among each other rather than by waiting for a central message.

Groups of this kind will be found in most industrial democracies. There is a German equivalent which encompasses 18 percent of the electorate. However, the lack of a similarly strong party or union organization makes the German "left tradition" group less homogeneous, with a 65 percent SPD preference among unionized households. (Table 2.)

For German society, this group fulfills a similar function of catalyzing working-class notions that are continuously reinforced by the union organizations. It is not very important what the union organizations' particular policies may be. Membership evidently provides the social platform on which "left" policy notions are being promoted to the larger community.

Similar patterns may be observed among that small segment of the *middle class which is tied to left traditions*. In Germany, they amount to about 11 percent of the total electorate; in Austria they are considerably smaller (4 percent), as the civil servants are included in the "left tradition" group. Socialist preferences are at the 50 percent level in both countries, and the social and communications profile resembles that of the "left tradition" groups: political discussion at home and at work place is at a maximum level. (Table 2.) Another quarter of the total SPD party membership was found in this white-collar group, so that about three-quarters of the SPD membership are tied in with unionized households.

However, the traditional left segment of the society is not wholly politicized. A considerable portion consists of blue-collar workers who are neither union members nor church activists. By their life situation, they are exposed to the political traditions of the left, and — in the German case — they identify with them. Socialist preferences are 51 percent in both countries. The political involvement of this group with *working-class traditions* is far below average in both countries, and non-voting is a frequent pattern. This group represents the lower skill and income segment of the working class. In addition, the proportion

[11] The Austrian analysis has lumped the civil servants with the working class, which, for this country, makes good sense.

of older people, non-employed dependents, non-urban residents and women is higher than in any other group of the traditional left. (Table 2.)

Left ballots seem to result only partly from personal experience with the work sphere. Contacts with *opinion* leaders who are more closely knit into the large-scale organizational structure, may help to mediate and to substitute for party preference traditions. This group amounts to 12 percent of the German and to 14.5 percent of the Austrian electorate. The tendency to vote for the conservative party is only slightly higher here than it is among the more engaged segments of the left.[12] (Table 2.) But as motivations are less intense, competing values may result in abstention. . . .

2. The groups with *traditional Catholic attachments* are larger in Austria than in Germany. But the SPD and SPÖ score equally low (13 percent, 12 percent). . . .

The SPÖ strength is matched by a Catholic group with *strong political ties* which encompasses 12.5 percent of the eligible voters. Of these 600,000 church-going Catholics who either read ÖVP party papers or, by their family, are tied into the organizations of political Catholicism, only 1 percent exhibits a preference for the Socialist Party. (Table 2.) This group, similar to the one on the socialist side, reflects the membership structure of its party. . . . The membership of the *Bauernbund* is predominant in the profile of Austrian political Catholicism: 56 percent of this group are farmers; 25 percent are professionals and small shopkeepers; only 17 percent belong to the blue- and white-collar groups.[13] . . . An equivalent group does not exist among the German electorate.

In Germany, the integrative mechanism of political Catholicism is based on the more or less formal organizations that have developed around the Church community. The impact of these forces is particularly strong among the middle-class occupations. As the *Catholic middle classes,* in Germany as well as in Austria, reflect a combination of the conservative and Catholic interests that are represented by the same party, their behavior toward the socialists is distinct: among the middle-class professions, the SPD scores 10, the SPÖ 11 percent. . . .

As the *blue-collar groups with Catholic ties* have more intensive contacts with the sphere of work, their traditional attachment tends to be weaker, and the socialist percentage is higher (SPD: 20 percent, SPÖ: 21 percent).

---

[12] Our work on the support of the German rightist party NPD has shown that the proportion of potential NPD voters among the non-organized working class, particularly among its non-skilled segment, is markedly higher than among the unionized groups.

[13] It may be noteworthy that 58 percent of the country's farmers are among this group of Catholics with "strong political ties." Of the Austrian farmers, 80 percent are church-going Catholics; the total population average is 33 percent.

But to both groups, church attendance means about the same thing, as does union membership or identification with the working class, to the traditional left. It is not the Sunday sermon that ties these voters to the Christian parties, but rather the life they live. Of this life, Church is an integral part; so for their basic orientation it does not really matter what policies the church may pursue toward the political parties.

3. In our analysis, a traditional *middle class attachment* applies only to that portion of the middle class which has not been absorbed by Catholic or union attachments. For this group, no institution was found that would in a similar way promote a one-party group structure. As there was no religious barrier in Austria and since the German CDU/CSU has managed to incorporate diverse religious and vocational elements under the fold of a progressive conservatism, the ÖVP and CDU have successfully prevented the socialists from making inroads into a segment of society that might sooner than the Catholic or the left sectors lose its one-party preponderance.

On the base of the value system that still prevails among the non-organized middle classes, third parties have managed to survive or even reappear. The German *Freie Demokratische Partei* (FDP) pulls more than half of its support from this segment; and the proportions are similar for its Austrian counterpart FPÖ. The rightist *Nationaldemokratische Partei* (NPD) has also done surprisingly well among this group. However, the German experience shows that voters who leave these small parties favor the CDU by a ratio of 5 to 2. At present, in both countries middle class attachments appear to be still strong enough to let non-socialist preferences prevail. Naturally, the socialist percentages are a little higher among the white-collar employees than among businessmen and farmers. Particularly, the SPÖ scores well among the lower middle class (37 percent), while the SPD mobilizes here only 23 percent. Among the self-employed part of the middle class, socialist percentages were similarly low in both countries.

4. In both societies, we have found three distinct value systems that are linked to partisan politics. Where one predominates, there is a one-party bias. Where they merge, the party structure should be less imbalanced. While in Germany a relatively large proportion of the electorate (16.5 percent) exhibits *multiple attachments*, such voters are almost non-existent in Austria. Even of the two small groups that were labelled that way, one exhibits a middle-class, the other a traditional left voting structure.

The small segment of the Austrian working class (4 percent of the electorate) that we have termed *consumer-workers* shows distinctive traits of deviance. Young workers of the cities, with a relatively high standard of living and a certain amount of personal independence, and who talk politics more than the rest of the non-organized working class, seem to have left the fold of their traditional party. Only 28 percent of them are still SPÖ-inclined. . . .

The German consumer-workers, 5.5 percent of the eligible voters, do not exhibit such an extreme social profile. However, a disproportionately high percentage of them work in the service professions. It is likely that their personal contacts with people of middle class status has not induced them to talk politics at the work place, but rather provided a particular way of viewing their own life situation. Middle class identification has established a slight CDU preponderance.

On the other hand, a middle class group of similar size was found which predominantly holds industrial jobs, and frequently talks about politics at the work place. The contact with working class people and the traditions of their own families have prevented these people from completely assimilating to the voting habits that seem to be in line with middle class status. There was no comparable group in Austria.

Simultaneous attachment to Catholic and working class traditions is not frequent; in Austria they appear to be almost mutually exclusive. About 100,000 eligible voters are practicing Catholics and simultaneously read an SPÖ paper. About half of them are members of the socialist party; two-thirds are SPÖ voters. With the exception that church attendance and SPÖ membership more frequently coincide in villages and small towns, this group shows the traits of the highly politicized segment. In Germany, the profile of the Catholic union members is similar to that of the non-Catholic segment of the unionized working class. But in their voting behavior, the unionized Catholics are split between the CDU and SPD. This group encompasses about 5 percent of the total electorate.

In both countries, the impact of the formal and informal arrangements that promote the three relevant value systems is clearly discernible. The SPÖ and SPD mobilize about two-thirds of their electoral support from the traditional left segments of the society; only about one-fifth of their voters originate from those two sectors that are the domains of their competitors.

With their membership, the German Social Democrats and the Austrian Socialists are even more confined to the traditionally left groups; more than three-quarters of SPÖ and SPD party members belong to that segment.

Support for the two Christian Parties however shows a different structure. The Austrian People's Party is confined almost exclusively to the two sectors of the society where it predominates; two-thirds of the ÖVP voters come from the large segment of traditional Catholicism; one-fifth is polled among the groups with middle class attachments. Only 10 percent of the ÖVP support is recruited from the traditional left.

In contrast, the support of the German Christian Democrats is much more evenly distributed. They poll only 36 percent of their voters from the Catholic realm, another 23 percent are recruited in the middle classes. Another quarter (23 percent) of CDU support is found among the left segment of the electorate; the rest comes from the groups with multiple attachments. (Cf. tables 3, 4, 5, and 6.)

TABLE 3. SOCIAL PROFILE OF VOTER GROUPS: AUSTRIA

Voter groups	Total cases N	SPÖ preference %	Men %	Above 50 years %	Employed persons %	Persons living in villages %	Income below S 2000 %	TV owners %
Traditional left attachment	1850	66						
Strong political ties	532	83	55	56	53	15	23	40
Blue-collar, left tradition	443	74	45	35	63	12	16	32
Working class, without tradition	690	51	45	56	52	16	38	25
Middle class, left tradition	185	48	41	29	71	6	10	39
Multiple attachment	306	41						
Active Catholics, strong left ties	116	67	52	48	55	28	27	25
Consumer-workers	190	28	51	23	71	14	8	46
Middle class attachment	968	27						
Lower middle class	403	37	42	44	58	11	12	37
Middle class (incl. farmers)	565	15	50	47	63	21	14	45
Traditional Catholic attachment	1582	12						
Employees	758	21	40	46	49	33	32	26
Self-employed	244	11	40	52	60	47	29	34
Strong political ties	580	1	47	50	67	66	30	25
Eligible voters	4706	37	46	45	58	26	24	33

Reanalysis of 4,706 cases of pre-election studies conducted by the Institute of Empirical Research, Vienna, during Winter 1965/66.

TRENDS IN THE ELECTORAL BALANCE

Although the electoral systems of both Germany and Austria are based on the same three types of organized interest, they vary in some decisive details.

While the overall size of the groups who have traditional left or middle class attachments is about the same in both societies, the Catholic sector is considerably larger in Austria. On the other hand, in Austria a population segment which is exposed to mixed attachments is almost completely missing. In Germany, the groups which show a multiple interest structure today amount to about 16.5 percent of the electorate, and there is a tendency that some of these groups expand at the cost of the traditional ones.[14]

Group support of Austrian politics is highly structured. Each of the two big parties has an organized membership to a maximum degree. In contrast, German politics is marked by the absence of similarly large groups of organized supporters. Although there are distinctive roles that provide direction to the less politicized segments, they are much weaker

[14] We suggest that the multiple attachment groups increase while mass consumption patterns expand. David Segal's analysis of U.S. data seems to indicate that the segment of the American society which might be labeled with the multiple attachment concept is considerable.

than in the Austrian case. Unionized employees and active Catholics cannot replace the involvement of an engaged party membership.

Compared to Austria, the infra-structure of German party support is much more "relaxed" — although both have in no way reached the American pattern, if they ever will. In Austria, considering the size of the social groups, the Christian-conservative party is in a favored position. However, by a more thorough organization of the traditionally left groups and by a relatively high amount of additional support from the lower middle class, for about two decades the Socialists had managed to make up for their structural unequality.

Where all resources — including the non-voter potential — have been mobilized, the electorate is in a continuous state of alert. It can easily be seen that, under these circumstances, major shifts in the voting alignments are unlikely. It took an internal crisis within the Socialist Party to tip the scales. However, as the margin required for change is slim, it might just happen that deviance in a small population segment will result in a long-term change of the balance of forces. For example, further emancipation of that emerging working-class splinter which today exhibits particular consumption orientations, would already create a situation which the SPÖ might be unable to compensate by traditional resources. . . .

Social structure is less unfavorable to the SPD than it is in Austria to the SPÖ. But still, there is in Germany a slight preponderance in favor of the combined middle-class and Catholic segments. The Ger-

TABLE 4. SOCIAL PROFILE OF VOTER GROUPS: GERMANY

Voter groups	Total cases N	Men %	Above 50 years %	Employed %	Service occ. %	Village %	Pessimists %	SPD preference %
Traditional left attachment	3349	55	36	59	28	17	14	58
Unionized workers	1499	59	33	64	17	15	15	65
Non-union workers	962	52	44	48	14	26	15	51
Unionized white-collar	888	52	34	64	61	9	11	53
Multiple attachment	1316	50	36	61	31	19	12	33
Unionized Catholics	389	53	31	67	30	20	12	31
Consumer-workers	459	45	38	58	45	16	11	34
Upwardly mobiles	468	51	37	58	19	23	13	34
Middle class attachment	1662	48	42	55	43	20	15	20
Employees white-collar	864	39	32	59	55	13	9	23
Self-employed urban	499	56	52	54	50	15	15	18
Self-employed rural	299	59	56	49	0	50	28	13
Catholic attachment	1792	44	43	54	32	35	11	13
Working class	583	40	47	47	13	42	9	20
Middle class	1209	46	41	57	41	32	12	10
Total	8134	50	39	57	33	22	13	36

Question is: What percentage of men, old people, etc. is in the respective voter group?

TABLE 5. POLITICAL PROFILE OF VOTER GROUPS: AUSTRIA

Voter groups	Total cases N	SPÖ preference %	Talks politics At home %	Talks politics At work %	SPÖ-sympathizers[a] For Klaus %	SPÖ-sympathizers[a] Party members %
Traditional left attachment	1850	66				
Strong political ties	532	83	76	36	13	68
Blue-collar, left tradition	443	74	69	40	22	46
Working class, without tradition	690	51	48	29	28	32
Middle class, left tradition	185	48	75	48	27	47
Multiple attachment	306	41				
Active Catholics, strong left ties	116	67	74	31	23	49
Consumer-workers	190	28	55	40	36	32
Middle class attachment	968	27				
Lower middle class	403	37	57	30	32	34
Middle class (incl. farmers)	565	15	64	28	19	33
Traditional Catholic attachment	1582	12				
Employees	758	21	53	27	25	31
Self-employed	244	11	41	17	(30)	(19)
Strong political ties	580	1	61	22		
Eligible voters	4706	37	60	31	23	46

[a]Percentages refer to SPÖ-sympathizers, not to eligible voters.
Reanalysis of 4,706 cases of pre-election studies conducted by the Institute of Empirical Research, Vienna, during Winter 1965/66.

man Social Democrats have in recent years considerably increased their electoral strength, but they have not exhausted the potential in the traditionally left segments of the society. In fact, the amount of support which the SPD draws from the hard core working class groups has not much changed over a decade. It has been, and still is, well below the percentage which the Austrian SPÖ seems to have mobilized under different historic conditions. . . .

The SPD share did increase, however, among groups who have not traditionally voted for this party. These voters are not so much the hard core Catholic or middle class elements; we find them rather on the fringes of these traditional groups. Between 1961 and 1965, SPD percentages particularly rose among the unionized white-collar group (+13 percentage points); among the upwardly mobiles (+17); and the unionized Catholics (+9); while the CDU undid former losses particularly among the groups with middle class attachments (+19) and among the consumer-workers (+16).

On the left and in the Catholic segment, involvement patterns of the Austrian kind are missing. So it could happen that the SPD improved its lot among Catholic voters.[15] However, if we use our definition of

[15] Of the 1.4 million by which the SPD vote increased in the 1965 Federal Election 1.0 millions came from the four States with predominantly Catholic

TABLE 6. POLITICAL PROFILE OF VOTER GROUPS: GERMANY

Voter groups	Total cases N	SPD preference %	Talks politics at Home %	Talks politics at Work %	TV-informed %	SPD preference For Erhard %	SPD preference Firm voter %	SPD preference Party member %
Traditional left attachment	3349	58	69	47	66	12	67	11
Unionized workers	1499	65	71	52	70	8	70	12
Non-union workers	962	51	55	34	60	14	67	
Unionized white-collar	888	53	80	53	67	17	59	
Multiple attachment	1316	33	68	44	66	17	51	6
Unionized Catholics	389	31	65	46	65	17	54	5
Consumer-workers	459	34	72	37	68	17	54	5
Upwardly mobiles	468	34	69	48	64	18	45	8
Middle class attachment	1662	20	74	36	59	18	52	6
Employees white-collar	864	24	76	43	60	18	49	5
Self-employed urban	499	18	72	33	60	17	53	9
Self-employed rural	299	13	70	22	52	(23)	(65)	(0)
Catholic attachment	1792	13	68	35	53	24	50	4
Working class	583	20	55	33	47	25	53	1
Middle class	1209	10	75	36	55	22	47	6
Total	8134	36	70	42	62	14	61	9

Question: What percentage of voters talk politics, are informed by TV, or what percentage of SPD sympathizers show particular patterns in the respective voter group?

Catholic attachment, it turns out that these gains were considerably smaller than has frequently been assumed; also the hard core proved rather stable. In recent years, the party balance in Germany did not so much change among the hard core groups but rather in segments where multiple attachments predominate. As a matter of fact, the infra-structure of German politics is characterized by a gradual weakening of the classic hard core groups.[16] The processes which are inherent in the mass consumption economy seem to reflect themselves in electoral undercurrents.

If, in the years to come, German society should produce a close to equilibrium two-party situation, it is unlikely that these changes would develop by mobilization and organization of the hard core elements on the left. The increase of multiple attachments, brought about by a con-

---

population; of the 1.2 million CDU-increase again 1.0 million came from the six States with Protestant predominance. Survey analysis has shown that the SPD gains in the Catholic regions occurred not so much with the church-going Catholics themselves but rather with their neighbors, while CDU gains in Protestant areas were marked in the traditional middle class and a few related marginal groups.

[16] Further tree-analysis of the church-going Catholics for example has shown that among the unexplained variance exposure to the new mass media matters the most.

sumption society, is likely to change the one-party nature of traditional group structure. Analysis has shown that, on this score, Germany is well ahead of Austria, but still far behind the United States.

JOSEPH LOPREATO

Social Mobility and Political Outlooks in Italy

The tendency of adults to have a set of life experiences duplicating that of their parents is subject to a number of important exceptions. One of the most significant on theoretical grounds is the rise to middle-class status of children of manual workers. This can come about from the ambitiousness of a youth or his parents. It can also be a response to economic pressures, for an expansion of middle-class jobs increases the probability of individual mobility. In European societies working one's way up from the bottom to the top has not been expected and positively valued as in America. Hence, it is important, as Joseph Lopreato has done, to test American research findings about inter-generational political behavior patterns in a European context. He does this with data from Italy.

This is an exploratory study of the political consequences of upward mobility. The essay consists of: (1) a brief summary of major findings in this area together with a formal statement coordinating given explanations of the findings; (2) a tentative test of one particular aspect of the theory; and (3) a concluding formal statement

Joseph Lopreato, "Upward Social Mobility and Political Orientation," *American Sociological Review*, XXXII, 4, 1967, pp. 586–592. Reprinted by permission of the American Sociological Association.

This study is part of a larger project supported by grants from the Social Science Research Council, the Fulbright Program, and the National Science Foundation. Thanks are due to Leonard Broom and Janet E. Saltzman for helpful comments on an earlier draft of the paper.

that purports to do fuller justice to the available findings in this area of sociology.

THE STATE OF THE EXISTING THEORY

Concentrating on intergenerational movement across the manual-nonmanual line, students of social mobility have repeatedly found that upward mobility "results" in political "conservatism" for the majority of the achievers.[1] The explanation advanced for this finding is the alleged tendency of the upwardly mobile to emulate their former social superiors, otherwise known as the "pervasive influence of contact with superior status on attitudes and behavior."[2] Such tendency, however, varies between the United States and Europe, as represented by Germany, Finland, Norway, Sweden, Great Britain, and Italy. In both Europe and the United States the upwardly mobile are more frequently conservative than their class of origin. However, in Europe they are more "radical" (more likely to be Socialist or Communist) than their class of destination, whereas in the United States they are more conservative (more likely to be Republican) than their class of destination.[3]

Why such variations? Barring fleeting suggestions that both "rightist" and "leftist" political orientations may represent "alternative reactions" to the status discrepancies entailed by the experience of mobility,[4] no

---

[1] Seymour M. Lipset and Hans L. Zetterberg, "A Theory of Social Mobility," in Lewis A. Coser and Bernard Rosenberg, eds., *Sociological Theory*, New York: The Macmillan Company, 1964 (2nd edition), p. 456; S. M. Lipset, *Political Man*, Garden City, New York: Doubleday and Co., Inc., 1959, p. 257; S. M. Lipset and Hans L. Zetterberg, "Social Mobility in Industrial Societies," in S. M. Lipset and Reinhard Bendix, *Social Mobility in Industrial Society*, Berkeley, California: University of California Press, 1959, p. 70.

[2] Lipset, *op. cit.*, p. 258.

[3] The findings for Germany, Finland, Sweden, Norway, and the United States are reported by Lipset and Zetterberg in Lipset and Bendix, *op. cit.*, p. 67. For Great Britain, see R. S. Milne and H. C. Mackenzie, *Straight Fight*, London: The Hansard Society, 1954, p. 58. The Italian data, previously unpublished, are my own. They are as follows:

Party choice	Nonmanuals Old-timers	Nonmanuals New-comers	Manuals
Communist, Socialist, Social Democratic	27	39	46
Republican, Christian Democratic	20	19	17
Liberale, Monarchic, Neo-fascist	15	4	2
None	38	38	35
Total	100	100	100
(N)	(233)	(104)	(291)

[4] Lipset and Zetterberg in Coser and Rosenberg, *op. cit.*, pp. 454–456. Strictly speaking, of course, they are not alternative reactions but different degrees of the same "consequence" of mobility: political conservatism. Stated otherwise, upwardly-mobile Europeans maintain a political link with their class of origin more frequently than their American counterparts.

attempt has been made to explain them. The tendency has been instead to take the American case as given, assume it to be the normal case, and then seek to explain the European case by reference to the American. In a generally convincing statement, Lipset and Zetterberg have speculated, for instance, that upward mobility in European countries entails greater status discrepancies, and hence greater difficulties in class readjustment, than in the United States. Specifically,

> Given the much wider discrepancy in consumption styles between the European and American middle and working class, one would expect the upwardly mobile European of working-class origin to have somewhat greater difficulties in adjusting to his higher status, and *to feel more discriminated against* than his American counterpart. . . .[5]

An attempt to summarize briefly the logical structure of the preceding argument yields the following set of propositions:

1. If there is upward mobility, then the "newcomers" are likely to emulate the political behavior of the "old-timers" — the more prestigeful — of their class.
2. However, if there is upward mobility, then there are also status discrepancies. Specifically, the newcomers are likely to encounter difficulties in raising a working-class consumption style to a middle-class level, and to feel discriminated against by the old-timers of the class.
3. The effect of status discrepancies is to weaken the influence of the emulation factor.
4. Status discrepancies are greater among middle-class Europeans of working-class origin than among their American counterparts.
5. Therefore, middle-class Europeans of working-class origin are more likely to retain a working-class political orientation and hence are more likely to be leftist than their American counterparts.

BASIS OF CONFIRMATION

Whatever its validity, the above explanation still leaves unanswered the crucial question of why upwardly-mobile Americans are even more conservative than those whose middle-class position is of long standing. Yet the factor of "status discrepancies" is highly suggestive and deserves empirical examination. This paper is primarily addressed to the modest job of examining the extent to which the factor of status discrepancies is relevant to an explanation of political differences in one European country, Italy. The data are drawn from a national survey of 1,569 male family heads interviewed by DOXA of Milan between December 10, 1963 and January 15, 1964.

The first step is to isolate the elements in terms of which the factor of status discrepancies is explicable. An examination of the above

---

[5] Lipset, *op. cit.*, p. 254. (Italics provided.) See also Lipset and Zetterberg, in Lipset and Bendix, *op. cit.*, p. 68.

theory reveals that these elements are *discrepancies in consumption styles* and *feelings of discrimination*. They will be the focus of two sets of propositions that guide this study.

With respect to "discrepancies in consumption styles," we predict that within the middle class:

I. (1) The newcomers (the upwardly mobile) have a lower consumption style than the old-timers.
(2) As the newcomers attain the consumption level of the old-timers, they become comparable to them in political orientation.

With respect to "feelings of discrimination," the approach will necessarily be more circuitous. It is predicated on the assumption that people who suffer status rejection are likely to interpret it as an expression of a tendency in the stratification system to restrict inter-class relations. With this in mind, it is predicted that:

II. (1) The newcomers are more likely than the old-timers to perceive restrictions in inter-class relations.
(2) Among the newcomers, those who perceive obstructions to inter-class relations are politically more leftist than those who do not perceive such restrictions.
(3) Finally, those who do not perceive impediments to inter-class relations are politically alike — whether old-timers or upwardly mobile.

I. Consumption Patterns. (1) The data in Table 1 concern the first prediction regarding variations in consumption style. They show that middle-class Italians whose fathers were themselves in the middle class do indeed enjoy a significantly higher style of life than middle-class individuals of working-class origin. Thus, considering a list of 10 consumer items, we note marked differences between the two groups: while 40 percent of the old-timers own at least nine of the items in question, only 25 percent of the newcomers are so fortunate. The evidence would seem to indicate that the upwardly mobile are having some difficulty in raising their style of life to a middle-class level, and our first prediction is therefore upheld.

TABLE 1. PERCENTAGE DISTRIBUTION OF CONSUMER ITEMS OWNED, BY POSITION IN THE MIDDLE CLASS

Number of items owned	Position in the middle class	
	Old-timers	Newcomers
0-4	11	16
5-8	49	59
9-10	40	25
Total	100	100
(N)	(233)	(104)

Note: χ^2 significant at the .01 level, using a one-tailed test of significance.
Items considered: automobile, refrigerator, washing machine, telephone, television, radio, vacuum cleaner and/or buffer, electric or gas stove, toilet with bath, running water.

(2) The second prediction reasons that if differences in consumption patterns are to be taken as indicative of the causes of differences in political orientation, it must be demonstrated that as middle-class individuals of working-class origin attain the consumption level of the old-timers of the class, they become comparable in political orientation as well. Some evidence to this effect has already been presented in a Swedish study by Zetterberg.[6]

My own information (Table 2) casts doubt on the alleged influence of style of life on the political orientation of the upwardly mobile. Contrary to expectation, the achievers in the middle class continue to surpass the old-timers of the class in left-wing party preferences even when a high level of consumption style has been achieved. This is not to say, of course, that variations in style of life leave political orientation totally unaffected. Among both newcomers and old-timers, an enriched consumption level is associated with a certain conservative tendency. However, such improvement is more likely to reduce left-wing orientation among the more established members of the middle class than among the new arrivals. The result is that the upwardly mobile actually increase their leftist lead over the old-timers.

TABLE 2. PERCENTAGE DISTRIBUTION OF POLITICAL ORIENTATION, BY NUMBER OF CONSUMER ITEMS OWNED AND POSITION IN THE MIDDLE CLASS

Political Orientation	0-8 Items Owned Old-timers	0-8 Items Owned Newcomers	9-10 Items Owned Old-timers	9-10 Items Owned Newcomers
Left-wing[a]	49	68	32	61
Conservative[b]	51	32	68	39
Total	100	100	100	100
(N)	(84)	(47)	(60)	(18)

Note: χ^2 significant at the .05 level both within the 0-8 items category and within the 9-10 items category. Excluded from this and all following tables are those cases for which information is either unavailable or unclassifiable.
[a]This includes Communist, Socialist, and Social Democratic parties.
[b]This includes Christian Democratic, Liberale, Monarchic, and Neo-fascist parties.

From the data presented so far, it is evident that, although the upwardly mobile do not enjoy the high life style of the old-timers of their class, differences in consumption patterns do not account effectively for differences in political orientation between the two middle-class categories. Having controlled for consumption level, we still find the achievers to be politically more leftist than their new class peers.

This finding is supported by another interesting set of data. Follow-

---

[6] Reported in Lipset and Bendix, *op. cit.*, p. 68. Related findings are reported for the United States by Patricia S. West, "Social Mobility among College Graduates," in Reinhard Bendix and Seymour M. Lipset, eds., *Class, Status and Power*, Glencoe, Ill.: The Free Press, 1953, pp. 465–480.

ing convention in this area of sociology, I have conceived of the class structure dichotomously; I have accordingly assumed "the middle class" to be a homogeneous entity. This procedure is, of course, convenient, but it does not do full justice to the reality of the case. What we term "middle class" represents in fact a rather wide spectrum of social differences. The findings in Table 1, for instance, suggest rather strongly that the newcomers are more likely than the old-timers to be in the lower reaches of the middle class. Indeed, dividing the class between those who exercise managerial or decision-making functions and those engaged in "routine" non-manual occupations, we find that, whereas 65 percent of the old-timers belong to the former and 35 percent to the latter, the corresponding figures for the newcomers are 46 and 54 percent, respectively.

If we now related these differences to differences in political orientation, it could further be shown that among newcomers as well as old-timers, high position in the middle class is associated with a conservative political orientation more frequently than low position. Nevertheless, after controlling for position in the class, the newcomers continue to be more leftist than the old-timers. This fact can best be appreciated from the following data which show the "routine" contingent among the newcomers to be significantly (0.02 level) more leftist than its counterpart among the old-timers:

	Routine old-timers	Routine newcomers
Left-wing	48%	74%
Conservative	52%	26%
(N)	(50)	(35)

Taken together, the findings in the present section suggest that if the factor of status discrepancies is relevant to an explanation of political orientation among the upwardly mobile in Italy, consumption level is too crude an indicator of that factor. It is more likely that the status discrepancies of the upwardly mobile consist of a significant gap between their class position and a set of cultural *intangibles* that are expected of that position. Put otherwise, it would seem that the *social distance* between the once-proletarians and the old-timers of the middle class is not easily bridged through occupational achievements and objective aspects of life style. Perhaps due to a long national tradition of aristocracy, Italian — very likely European — middle classes today are still heavily permeated by an upper-class atmosphere. As a result, they are keenly sensitive to the nuances of class behavior, and the occupationally successful children of the working class may find it particularly trying to gain the social recognition and acceptance that their economic achievement would warrant. Whatever their present education, position, or wealth, one fact is not easily concealed: they were socialized within the working class. From there, they are likely to have brought into their new class situation evident traces of a "vulgar" upbringing that must be distasteful to the old-timers of the class, devoted as they are to the art of what an historical-minded journalist once termed "*domenichino* snobbery."[7] Under the circumstances, the postulated tendency to imitate superior status is weakened, early political socialization asserts itself the more forcefully, and political affiliation with the class of origin is more readily retained.[8]

II. CLOSURE IN CLASS RELATIONS. (1) The findings and discussion so far highlight the importance of feelings of discrimination as a possible influence on the political orientation of the upwardly mobile. Consider now the data in Table 3, which compare the achievers to the old-timers of the middle class on the basis of the following question: "In your opinion, do those who belong to a given social class tend to restrict their relations with persons belonging to another social class?" The findings bear out the third prediction. Despite their actual experience of mobility, the upwardly mobile are significantly more likely than the old-timers of their class to perceive a tendency toward closure in the stratification system.

TABLE 3. PERCENTAGE DISTRIBUTION OF PERCEPTIONS CONCERNING RESTRICTIONS IN INTER-CLASS RELATIONS, BY POSITION IN THE MIDDLE CLASS

| Class restric- | Position in the middle class | |
tions perceived	Old-timers	Newcomers
Yes	57	68
No	43	32
Total	100	100
(N)	(203)	(88)

Note: χ^2 significant at the .05 level, using a one-tailed test of significance.

It may be noted that the research question was broadly stated. It did not single out any one particular class, such as "the middle class" or the "higher classes," for assessment concerning a possible tendency to restrict out-class relations. My underlying assumption is that the perceptions produced by the question reflect personal experiences. This, it would seem, is not a query that can be answered in the abstract. Again, although conceivable, it is hardly likely that a higher class would feel excluded by a lower class. Hence it is reasonable to assume that the achievers' responses reflect their experiences of discrimination suffered at the hands of the old-timers of their new class, both while moving from a working-class position to their present one and in the process of adjusting to the new position.

(2) Table 4 examines data revelant to the fourth prediction and

[7] *Domenichino* is the Italian word for that peculiar type of servant who in recent centuries enjoyed the privilege of accompanying his lord on his Sunday (*domenica*) walk. This unusual honor was the source of grotesque ostentation on the part of the *domenichino* in relation to other members of the populace.

[8] For the influence of early political socialization on political orientation, see Herbert H. Hyman, *Political Socialization,* Glencoe, Ill.: The Free Press, 1959.

TABLE 4. PERCENTAGE DISTRIBUTION OF POLITICAL ORIENTATION AMONG NEWCOMERS, BY PERCEPTION OF INTER-CLASS RESTRICTIONS

Political orientation	Class restrictions perceived	
	Yes	No
Left-wing	73	40
Conservative	27	60
Total	100	100
(N)	(41)	(15)

Note: χ^2 significant at the .02 level, using a one-tailed test of significance.

further shows the pertinence of feelings of discrimination for explaining the political orientation of upwardly-mobile Italians. In keeping with the prediction, the table demonstrates that those newcomers who perceive tendencies toward closure in class intercourse are also significantly more leftist in political orientation than those who view social contact as unhindered by class differences. Among those who attest to class closure, preferences for parties of the left are almost three times as frequent as conservative preferences. Conversely, three-fifths of those who perceive free inter-class contact also favor the conservative side of the political spectrum.

(3) Table 5, finally, upholds the fifth prediction, demonstrating that when the newcomers do not perceive hindrances to inter-class relations — in other words when they are not the object of social rejection, according to my interpretation — they are almost exactly like the old-timers of their class in political orientation. In both groups, about two-fifths show a preference for parties of the left, while the other three-fifths choose conservative parties.

A REFORMULATION OF THE THEORY

The evidence presented in this paper lends plausibility to *one aspect* of the theory as it was stated above. The concept of status discrepancies, explicated in terms of feelings of discrimination, does indeed help explain the political orientation of upwardly-mobile individ-

TABLE 5. PERCENTAGE DISTRIBUTION OF POLITICAL ORIENTATION AMONG PERSONS WHO DO NOT PERCEIVE INTER-CLASS RESTRICTIONS, BY POSITION IN THE MIDDLE CLASS

Political orientation	Position in the middle class	
	Old-timers	Newcomers
Left-wing	42	40
Conservative	58	60
Total	100	100
(N)	(59)	(15)

Note: χ^2 not significant.

uals in one European country.[9] The theory as a whole, however, requires and deserves more attention than it has received so far. There is at least one major difficulty in it that is especially worthy of clarification. One could hazard the impression that in its present form the theory reflects an American ethnocentrism. European achievers, it argues, feel rejected by their new class peers more than their American counterparts. That may well be true. But does the lesser status difficulty of upwardly-mobile Americans explain the fact that they are more conservative than the old-timers of their own class? Obviously not. The question becomes all the more compelling if one notes that the American case stands alone against multiple European cases. In short, the theory behaves as if the European instances were to be explained away as exceptions to the American rule. The opposite, however, more nearly does justice to the logical substance of its postulates.

The normal case to which the underlying logic of the theory addresses itself is one in which the two fulcrums of the construct — "status discrepancies" and "emulation of superior status" — are both operative in producing a given political behavior. In Europe the known facts are indeed consistent with this logic: the upwardly mobile bestride class of origin and class of destination in their political stance. The case is different in the United States where the strength of the emulation factor seems to be so overpowering as to produce political "overconformity."[10] Why?

On this I can only speculate in this paper. The answer may lie in an alleged characteristic of American society widely discussed in American literature. In his essay on "Social Structure and Anomie," Merton discusses some interesting implications of the "American Dream." This ethos is presumably built on certain cultural axioms enjoining individuals to recognize that success can always be realized if one but has the requisite abilities and the perseverance to strive. By implication, the citizen ought not to blame anyone but himself in case of failure. According to Merton,

> ... the culture enjoins the acceptance of three cultural axioms: First, all should strive for the same lofty goals since these are open to all;

[9] In the absence of empirical data, Miller has argued that it is uncertain whether the upwardly mobile are "the most resentful, frustrated groups in society." S. M. Miller, "Comparative Social Mobility," *Current Sociology*, 9 (No. 1), 1960, p. 16. Although the present findings are far from providing an answer to this question, they do suggest that middle-class Italians of working-class origin feel rejected by those whose middle-class position is of long standing, and that such feeling may be strong enough to retard their political socialization into their new class.

[10] It is interesting to note that in a broader context, upwardly-mobile Americans do take a mid-course position. Blau, for instance, finds in a study of interpersonal relations that many beliefs and practices of the upwardly and of the downwardly mobile are intermediate between those of the "stationary highs" and those of the "stationary lows." Peter M. Blau, "Social Mobility and Interpersonal Relations," *American Sociological Review*, 21 (June, 1956), pp. 290–295.

second, present seeming failure is but a way-station to ultimate success; and third, genuine failure consists only in the lessening or withdrawal of ambition.[11]

The point to be made here is this: given the extreme emphasis on success, combined with the individual responsibility for non-fulfillment, the fear of failure is likely to be a constant threat to one's sense of security. Conversely, the experience of social success is likely to give the achiever enormous satisfaction and a deep sense of psychological relief. So profound indeed is the sense of relief, so great the joy of having avoided personal disaster, that the achiever is quite likely to develop what Melvin Tumin has termed a "cult of gratitude," an attitude of deep appreciation toward the social order for making the present pleasures possible.[12] Such gratitude is then expressed through an "over-conformity" to the prescribed behavior of the middle class, specifically, by voting disproportionately for the party that is loudest in proclaiming the reality of the American Dream and the old American virtues: self-reliance, individualism, and faith in the existing social order.[13]

The fact that the United States has not fully digested the immense intake of European immigrants may, of course, add to this possible consequence of the cult of success. Handlin has suggested that most immigrants have accepted the United States as the land of opportunity. And so it has been, for them especially. Whatever their difficulties of acculturation, in the New World they found economic conditions that far excelled those in the old country.[14]

In view of the foregoing findings and considerations, I shall conclude with an effort to reformulate and expand the theory presented at the beginning of this paper. Let us begin with a necessary premise:

Premise: Political behavior among most normal adults is in large part determined by early political socialization.

1. If there is upward mobility, then there are status discrepancies and difficulties in gaining social recognition from the old-timers in the class of destination.
2. If there is upward mobility, then the newcomers are likely to emulate the behavior of the old-timers — and thus more prestigeful — of their class.
3. Emulation varies directly with the emphasis on social success and achievement.
4. The likelihood of retaining political links with the class of origin (avoiding resocialization):
   (a) increases with the degree of status discrepancies, namely,

---

[11] Robert K. Merton, *Social Theory and Social Structure*, Glencoe, Ill.: The Free Press, 1957 (second edition), p. 139.

[12] Melvin M. Tumin, "Some Unapplauded Consequences of Social Mobility in a Mass Society," *Social Forces*, 36 (October, 1957), pp. 32–37.

[13] This "latent function" of the "American Dream" seems to be a reasonable complement to the latent functions discussed by Merton. *Loc. cit.*

[14] Oscar Handlin, *The Uprooted,* Boston: Little, Brown and Company, 1951.

rejection — real or imagined — by the old-timers in the class of destination;

(b) decreases with the strength of (1) the emphasis on achievement and (2) the tendency toward emulation.

Assuming now that,

A. status discrepancies (experienced social rejection) are greater among middle-class Europeans of working-class origin than among their American counterparts;
B. the emphasis on success and achievement is "excessive"[15] in the United States but not in Europe;
C. emulation of higher status can be as disproportionate as the emphasis on success and achievement;

then it follows that:

5. Middle-class Europeans of working-class origin are more leftist than their new class peers and more conservative than their class of origin.
6. Middle-class Americans of working-class origin are more conservative than both their class of origin and their class of destination.

[15] In the sense that it represents a "threat to one's sense of security."

CHAPTER
FIVE

Political Parties

Because history is so important in European politics, it is striking that the major parties in Europe today are of such recent creation or re-creation by comparison with American parties. The Democratic Party traces its ancestry back more than 150 years to Thomas Jefferson, and the Republican Party was founded in 1854. In the four countries surveyed, only the British Conservatives could claim anything comparable in the way of lineage; the national party organization was founded in 1867 upon an earlier parliamentary base. The German Social Democrats were founded in 1875, but only briefly during the 1920's were they a governing party until the formation of the Grand Coalition in 1966. The Labour Party became a major party in Britain in the early 1920's, and the French Communist Party also became important then. The Communist Party of Italy had only a clandestine organization between the wars, in opposition to Mussolini's one-party Fascist regime. Like the Christian Democrats in Italy, the Christian Democratic Union in Germany and the various Gaullist groups, such as the UNR (*Union pour la Nouvelle République*), only achieved electoral prominence after 1945.

The foundation of these parties was a consequence of the failure of pre-existing party systems. The British Labour Party came forward at the end of World War I, because the Liberals, a major party in the preceding half-century, had split badly during the war, a large portion forming a coalition with the Conservatives under a Liberal Prime Minister, David Lloyd George. Anti-Conservative supporters gradually coalesced around Labour. The entrance of Italy into World War I intensified political divisions and led to a Fascist triumph in 1922. The collapse of Fascism in the defeat of Italy in World War II was the basis on which the contemporary Italian party system was founded. In Germany, the contemporary party system emerged from the successive wreckages of the imperial system of the Kaiser's Reich, the centrifugal pluralism of the Weimar Republic in the 1920's, the totalitarian system of the Nazis, and military occupation. In France, competitive party politics flourished (some would say excessively so) in the period of the Third Republic from 1875 to 1940. The climax, however, was defeat and occupation by Germany. In the Fourth Republic, founded in 1946, the old parties that emerged found themselves in competition with two new parties, a Gaullist group, then called the RPF (*Rassemblement du Peuple Français*) and a middle-of-the-road Christian Democratic Party, the MRP (*Mouvement Républicain Populaire*). The coup d'état of 1958, leading to the establishment of the Fifth French Republic, revived a loosely organized Gaullist group and dealt shocks to parties that had previously shown great powers of persistence.

The political problems that have faced European parties in this century have put a high premium upon the ability to survive. One way in which parties have survived is by intensive organization on a scale known in America only in machine politics. Socialist and Communist parties have been pre-eminent in stressing the nationwide formation of small cells, where regular, face-to-face contacts reinforce lines of communication with party headquarters, or even sustain party loyalties in the event that party headquarters are closed by police or an invading army. Catholic parties have been able to draw upon the very considerable organizational capacities of the Church. Its ubiquitous parochial organization, community significance, and involvement in political issues have made it possible for Catholic-sponsored parties to form quickly and to gain substantial electoral strength in France, Germany, and Italy. In the United Kingdom, parties have been primarily electoral in intent; only in Ireland has party politics shaded into armed conflict. On the Continent, however, parties organized with ample reminders that elections were not the only means of settling disputes. Mass demonstrations, general strikes, civil war, and guerrilla war against a native or foreign authority were all recognized alternative forms of contest. All the men now in high positions in these countries have themselves lived through times when the verdict of a ballot box was a remote worry. In such circumstances, politicians could not rely upon the use of electoral institutions nor can the civil administration of the regime be relied upon. Only the party — in constitutional or extra-constitutional ways — could provide the security and power necessary to achieve their ends.

The principles for which European parties stand, like the principles of American parties, are a mixture of old and new themes, some of recurring relevance and some anachronistic or ephemeral. Issues of church and state, of national identification, of protecting the peasantry, and of providing welfare for industrial workers were not born yesterday, nor will they disappear tomorrow. Americans who doubt this may consider the contemporary importance attached in the United States to controversies about public funds for parochial schools, relations between black and white and North and South, farm price supports, and government grants to the urban poor. Yet, as argued in several selections in this volume, European parties since the war have devoted much more attention to electoral competition and bargaining for office in coalition governments than to creating or intensifying conflicts between ideological *Weltanschauungen*. Some writers have praised this trend as a sign of progress, marking the acceptance by all political groups of common standards of peaceful political disagreement. A small number, both young and old, have criticized this as a demoralizing denial of absolute principles and absolute ends. The demonstrations that occurred in France, Germany, Italy, and Northern Ireland in 1968 are a reminder that party systems cannot assure that all political conflict remains within the limits implied by free elections.

Bibliography

In the literature of comparative party politics, two classics draw especially upon the formative years of European party systems. Robert Michels' *Political Parties* (1912) concentrates primarily upon Continental Socialist parties. M. I. Ostrogorski's *Democracy and the Organization of Political Parties* (2 vols.: 1st English language edition, 1902) is a comparative study of British and American parties. For an important reinterpretation of the meaning and the motivation behind Michels' study of "the iron law of oligarchy," see John D. May, "Democracy, Organization, Michels," *American Political Science Review* LIX: 2 (1965).

The pioneering post-1945 comparative study of political parties is Maurice Duverger's *Political Parties: Their Organization and Activity in the Modern State* (1st English language edition, 1954). The analysis there has been subjected to strong criticism in Aaron Wildavsky, "A Methodological Critique of Duverger's *Political Parties*," *Journal of Politics* XXI: 2 (1959), and F. C. Engelmann, "A Critique of Recent Writings on Political Parties," *Journal of Politics* XIX: 3 (1959). Very useful comparative volumes, collecting articles by specialists in several countries include: S. M. Lipset and Stein Rokkan, editors, *Party Systems and Voter Alignments* (New York: Free Press, 1967); Robert A. Dahl, editor, *Political Oppositions in Western Democracies* (New Haven: Yale University Press, 1966); Joseph LaPalombara and Myron Weiner, editors, *Political Parties and Political Development* (Princeton University Press, 1966); and Sigmund Neumann, editor, *Modern Political Parties* (University of Chicago Press, 1956). Useful information about now defunct parties of the Fascist type in the inter-war period can be found in H. Rogger and E. Weber, editors, *The European Right: A Historical Profile* (Berkeley: University of California Press, 1966). For smaller European countries, see Stein Rokkan, "The Structuring of Mass Politics in the Smaller European Democracies: A Developmental Typology," *Comparative Studies in Society and History* X: 2 (1968). In the great majority of European countries, elections employ some form of proportional representation. The machinery and its implications are analyzed in Douglas Rae, *The Political Consequences of Electoral Laws* (New Haven: Yale University Press, 1967), and W. J. M. Mackenzie, *Free Elections* (London: Allen & Unwin, 1958). A very useful record of the electoral rise and fall of parties can be found in Stein Rokkan and

Jean Meyriat, editors, *International Guide to Electoral Statistics* (Paris: Mouton, 1969).

The literature on party politics is substantial in nearly every European society, in English and in other languages. In the contemporary academic literature about British party politics, R. T. McKenzie's *British Political Parties* (New York: Praeger, revised edition, 1963) is outstanding, because in addition to a wealth of historical and institutional detail, it contains a controversial general thesis about power within parties. The thesis is challenged on several points in Richard Rose, "Complexities of Party Leadership," *Parliamentary Affairs* XVI: 3 (1963) and "The Variability of Party Government: a Theoretical and Empirical Critique," *Political Studies* XVII: 4 (1969). The best introduction to party politics in France is Philip Williams' *Crisis and Compromise: Politics in the Fourth Republic* (New York: Anchor, 1964). Scholarly introductions to German party politics can be found in Arnold J. Heidenheimer, *Adenauer and the CDU* (The Hague: Martinus Nijhoff, 1960), and Douglas A. Chalmers, *The Social Democratic Party of Germany* (New Haven: Yale University Press, 1964). Intensive studies of parties include Sidney Tarrow, *Peasant Communism in Southern Italy* (New Haven: Yale University Press, 1967); Samuel H. Barnes, *Party Democracy: Politics in an Italian Socialist Federation* (New Haven: Yale University Press, 1967); Donald L. Blackmer, *Unity in Diversity: Italian Communism and the Communist World* (Cambridge: M.I.T. Press, 1968); Robert H. Evans, *Coexistence: Communism and Its Practice in Bologna, 1945–1965* (University of Notre Dame Press, 1967); René Remond, *The Right Wing in France from 1851 to de Gaulle* (Philadelphia: University of Pennsylvania Press, 1966); Francis De Tarr, *The French Radical Party from Herriot to Mendès-France* (Oxford University Press, 1961); Mario Einaudi and François Goguel, *Christian Democracy in Italy and France* (University of Notre Dame Press, 1952); Thomas H. Green, "Communist Party in France and Italy," *World Politics* XXI, 1968; Raphael Zariski, "Intra-Party Conflict in a Dominant Party: The Experience of Italian Christian Democracy," *Journal of Politics* XXVII: 1 (1965), and "The Italian Socialist Party: A Case Study in Factional Conflict," *American Political Science Review* LVI: 2 (1962).

RICHARD ROSE
and DEREK URWIN

Social Cohesion, Political Parties and Strains in Regimes

The classification of political parties and party systems in terms of theoretically meaningful criteria is one of the persisting problems in the literature of party politics. Many writers assume that parties can be classified along a single left-right continuum of class differences. This belief leads them to describe varied groups as "class parties" without citing reliable or valid evidence. As the following article shows, religious, linguistic, and nationalist divisions have also been significant in developing contemporary party divisions. Moreover, differences in the social bases of parties influence the effect of party systems upon the stability of regimes.

I

In many models of competitive politics, parties are presented as the resultant of social forces; their existence is derived from social divisions. The model is simple, general and pervasive. Yet reality is much more complex. In practice, party leaders are free to choose whether they wish to depend upon any particular social group, and which group this will be. Hence, the primary concern of this paper is the social cohesion of political parties, rather than the political cohesion of social groups.

The most important characteristics to study in a wide-ranging comparative analysis are those which, on a priori theoretical grounds, are most likely to be translated into political issues. In their magisterial

---

Abridged from Richard Rose and Derek Urwin, "Social Cohesion, Political Parties and Strains in Regimes," *Comparative Political Studies*, II, 1, April, 1969, pp. 7–67. Reprinted by permission of the publisher, Sage Publications, Inc.

review of social change and party divisions in modern Europe, Lipset and Rokkan (1967, pp. 9ff.), distinguish four main social sources of party divisions — religious conflicts, territorial-cultural conflicts, divisions between rural and urban industrial interests, and divisions between workers and employers within industrial society. The non-deterministic nature of these divisions is emphasized by the fact that the potential permutations of social divisions are far greater than the actual number of parties in Western nations. (Cf. Rokkan, 1968, pp. 180ff.) . . .

The Lipset-Rokkan analysis provides an operationally manageable multi-dimensional description of social structure. It does not reduce all social phenomena to class phenomena, nor does it generate a model of society so complex that many cells have trivial numbers and trivial meaning. *Religious* divisions may exist between adherents of different churches, between pro- and anti-clerical groups, or between practicing believers and uninvolved secular indifferents. *Regional* territorial divisions take note of spatial clustering or dispersion as an important electoral consideration. *Communal* divisions arise if, and only if, a country includes substantial numbers of people speaking different languages or if the population is divided in terms of its ethnic or national identification. Divisions between *rural and urban* groups reflect problems of an early stage of commercialization or industrialization, when those in the modern sector of the economy are in conflict with traditional, agrarian groups. The conventional *class* divisions of contemporary social science are derived from urban conditions, differentiating industrial workers and the middle class. Four of these five divisions must exist in all modern states; divisions along communal lines need not have survived to the present day.

If a party is to be considered socially cohesive in terms of any of the foregoing structural characteristics, the following conditions must be met:

1. The measure must concern a positive attribute, rather than the absence of an attribute. For instance, "non-Southerners" are not regionally cohesive in America.
2. To avoid double counting, the measure must be logically independent of other characteristics. . . .
3. The measure must vary substantially within a society. Where a characteristic is invariant or nearly so, as in the case of Catholicism in the Republic of Ireland, it is a basis for national cohesion, cutting across partisan lines. . . .
4. The number of categories into which a given variable is divided should be kept low. Failure to do this would make it unlikely that any party should be considered cohesive. . . .
5. The incidence of a given social characteristic among a party's supporters should be high. As a general rule, two-thirds must share an attribute for a party to be considered cohesive on this point. If a party is regarded as cohesive on two attributes, then individuals with both of these should be the most numerous

group. . . . When a characteristic is held by more than 50 per cent but less than 83 per cent of the population, a party is normally regarded as cohesive on this point only if its degree of homogeneity exceeds the national average by 17 per cent, the same figure by which 67 per cent exceeds 50 per cent. . . .

This measure of cohesiveness makes it valid to characterize parties in terms of social bases, even when the parties are less than entirely successful in mobilizing the support of all of a social group. For instance, a Communist Party supported by only 10 per cent of the working class can hardly claim to be *the* working-class party in a country. On the other hand, if 90 per cent of the vote that it obtains comes from workers, it can be said to be *a* working-class party. . . .

Nationwide survey findings usually provide the best data for identifying the social characteristics of party supporters. In measuring regional distinctiveness, use of aggregate data eliminates the problem of sampling error. . . . Where no survey data were available, classification is attempted, if possible, on the basis of other information, since surveys are not the only source of valid and reliable judgments. This seemed better than implying that because no survey data are available, two-thirds of the supporters of the Belgian Christian Social Party were not practicing Catholics.

The universe for comparison is defined by a political characteristic — competitive parties — and a social characteristic — a high level of socio-economic development. These embrace the societies conventionally referred to as Western, although they range in space across three Continents from Finland to the antipodes. The universe cuts across culture areas and is sufficiently large for Anglo-American, Scandinavian, and Continental European sub-groups to be noted. Iceland, Luxembourg, and Switzerland have been omitted because of insufficient data. Northern Ireland is included because it has a high degree of political autonomy and a distinctive social structure and party system; moreover, data from it could not be reasonably assigned to either the Republic of Ireland or Britain, the two states claiming jurisdiction over the territory.

Political parties are defined as cross-local groups running candidates for office in the chief legislature of the central government. Within each country, all parties are included for which data are available. In the absence of theoretical criteria distinguishing between parties big enough to be counted and those small enough to ignore, this seems the best course. Given the recency of nationwide surveys, nearly all classifications are based upon data from the 1960's. . . . Because of major changes in the French party system since the war, French data refer to parties of the Fourth Republic only. . . .

II

In their developmental study, Lipset and Rokkan (1967) seem to suggest that all the social divisions discussed are of substantial or roughly equal importance. In an earlier work, however, Lipset has argued, "On a world scale, the principal generalization which can be made is that parties are primarily based on either the lower classes or the middle and upper classes." (1960, p. 220.) . . . Contrary to Lipset's assertion, religion, not class, is the main social basis of parties in the Western world today. (Table 1.) A total of 35 parties in 11 different countries are cohesive because of a common religious or anti-religious outlook among their supporters. . . . Among the religious parties, 18 (28 per cent) have supporters with a positive religious commitment; 17 (26 per cent) have supporters who are indifferent or anti-clerical. Of the 17 secularly based parties, 15 are in countries where the Catholic church is either the sole church or a major one.

Occupational class is important as a source of cohesion among 33 of the 76 parties analysed. Among 25 formally working-class parties, 20 draw two-thirds or more of their support from manual workers. The five parties that fail to achieve a cohesive working-class basis do not fail because of a statistical middle-class appeal; the Australian DLP, the Canadian NDP, the French Socialists, the old Italian PSDI, and the Irish Labour Party are all relatively small. The three societies without a nationwide class party are the United States, Ireland and Canada.

At least four different types can be distinguished among the 12 parties outside the working class cohesive on occupational grounds. None of the so-called "right" parties in the Anglo-American group draws two-thirds or more of its vote from the middle class, nor do any of the major Continental parties. The six urban middle-class parties are Scandinavian — the Conservatives in each of the four countries, and the Finnish Liberals and the People's Party in Sweden. A second category is the secular middle-class party; the Dutch Liberals are the only one so classified here, but other parties, such as the French Radicals and the German FDP, show clear tendencies in this direction. They differ from traditional conservative parties because they are libertarian, i.e. anti-clerical, in social terms. The category is distinctive enough to form a Liberal International and to secure recognition as a *tendance* from supra-national European institutions. (Cf. McCallum Scott, 1967.) It stands sharply in contrast to "illiberal" parties based on pro-clerical middle-class supporters. (Cf. Rogger and Weber, 1965.) While no party is classified as such here, it is appropriate that an Italian party, the Liberals, most nearly approximate the type, being cohesive in terms of middle-class support and pro-clerical in tendency. . . . Each of the four Scandinavian countries provides an example of a party based on rural support. . . . The historical failure of farmers everywhere to "give rise to" their own class parties is theoretically very significant, for farmers have been at least as distinctive occupationally, in life style, and in spatial segregation as industrial workers. In France and Italy, this can be explained in terms of divisions cutting across urban-rural contrasts (Dogan, 1967, pp. 141ff.), but such circumstances are not pervasive in Western countries.

Communal nationalism in past European history has led to such large-scale movements of populations and changes in state boundaries

TABLE 1. PARTIES AND COHESIVENESS

Parties N	Country	Hetero-geneous	Single claim religion	Class	Mutually reinforcing loyalties
3	Australia	Lib.	DLP	Lab.	—
3	Austria	FPO	OVP	—	SPO: religion/class
5	Belgium	—	Lib.	—	Volks-Unie: religion/language/region Comm.: religion/class/language/region Soc.: religion/class Christian: religion/language/region
3	Britain	Con. Lib.	—	Lab.	—
5	Canada	Lib. NDP	—	—	Con.: religion/language Soc. Credit: religion/language/region Creditiste: religion/class/language/region
5	Denmark	Radical	—	Left Soc. Soc. Venstre Con.	—
6	Finland	—	—	Comm. Soc. Agrarian Liberal Con.	SPP: language/region
6	France (Fourth Republic)	—	SFIO RAD MRP RPF IND	—	PCF: religion/class
3	Germany	CDU	FDP	—	SPD: religion/class
3	Ireland	Fianna Fail Fine Gael Labour	—	—	—
8	Italy	PSDI MON	DC PRI MSD	PLI	PCI: religion/class PSI: religion/class
6	Netherlands	Farmers	Cath. ARP CHU	—	Soc.: religion/class Lib.: religion/class
3	New Zealand	National Soc. Credit	—	Lab.	—
3	Northern Ireland	—	Unionist	—	Lab.: class/region Nat.: religion/ethnic/region
6	Norway	Lib.	Christian	Lab. Centre Con.	Comm: religion/class
6	Sweden	—	Christian	Con. Peoples Centre Soc.	Comm.: religion/class
2	U.S.A.	Democrat Republican	—	—	—
76	Totals	19	18	20	19 Religion = 17 Class = 13 Region = 8 Communal = 8 45

that linguistic or ethnic communalism is not today a major source of social cohesion for parties in Western countries. In 10 countries, there is no numerically substantial basis for a communal party. Communal differences of measurable size exist in Belgium, Britain, Canada, Finland, Northern Ireland, Norway and the United States. In these countries, a total of eight parties have cohesive communal followings — three each in Belgium and Canada, the Swedish People's Party in Finland, and the Nationalists in Northern Ireland. . . .

In terms of electoral mechanics, regionalism could easily "give rise to" parties, because of the value of clustering votes in securing representation in nearly every electoral system. As the Irish Nationalist Party demonstrated in Britain before World War I, even a relatively small group, given regional segregation, can achieve a substantial influence in a two-party [sic] system. In multi-party systems where coalition governments are usual, this is even more true. Yet only eight of the 76 parties examined show regionally cohesive support, notwithstanding the relatively large areas used here to delimit regions. In seven cases, regional cohesion runs parallel with communal cohesion. . . .

This review of the cohesion of Western parties tends to substantiate multi-causal as against mono-causal explanations for party support. (Cf. Tables 2–5.) The Lipset-Rokkan typology over-emphasizes the importance of communal and regional divisions in contemporary politics, for each was a base of cohesion for only eight of the 76 parties examined. The earlier Lipset emphasis on class under-estimated the significance of religion; it provides common ground in 35 of 65 parties examined, whereas class is the common factor in 33 of 76 parties. The figures for class cohesion would be reduced by four if agrarian parties were excluded as unrelated to urban, industrial societies. The joint importance of religious and class divisions is emphasized by the fact that 56 of the 57 parties showing some social cohesion were cohesive on religious or class grounds or both. The one exception is the Swedish People's Party in Finland. . . . In theory, the 76 parties examined here could have been cohesive on more than 300 points. In fact, they showed cohesion on a total of 83 points; 19 parties were not cohesive in terms of *any* major social characteristic. Four broad types of parties can be distinguished.

1. *Heterogeneous* parties draw votes in such a way that their supporters share no major social characteristics in common. The 19 parties in this category are dispersed through 12 of the 17 countries studied. Heterogeneous parties are institutions aggregating demands of different social groups. While their leaders must accept that electoral competition will set limits to their strength, efforts will be made to be as inclusive as possible. . . . Kirchheimer has argued (1966, pp. 192ff.) that rising standards of living have so reduced social differences that major European Socialist parties are all becoming catchall or heterogeneous in their appeals for votes. It is important to note that none has been successful; the only heterogeneous parties with Socialist leanings are the relatively

TABLE 2. BRITAIN

	Labour (46%)	Conservative (42%)	Liberal (8%)
Religion			
Church of England, 64%	61	69	64
Other Protestants, 22%	22	22	26
Roman Catholics, 9%	12	6	6
Other, none, 5%	5	3	4
Gallup, 1966b: 8			
Occupation			
Middle, 32%	17	47	51
Intermediate, 15%	12	18	16
Workers, 53%	71	35	33
Gallup, 1966b: 9			
Urban/Rural			
Conurbations, 35%	36	32	29
Boroughs, 21%	23	21	11
Small towns, 20%	20	21	25
Mostly rural, 24%	26	20	34
Gallup, 1966a: 27			
Regionalism[a]			
Greater London, 30%	28	31	38
South and Southwest, 15%	12	17	25
Midlands and East Anglia, 22%	24	23	12
Northern England, 32%	36	29	23
Gallup 1966a: 22-23			
Communalism[b]			
England, 85%	83	88	89
Scotland, 10%	10	9	7
Wales, 3%	7	3	4
Northern Ireland			
Gallup, 1966a: 22			

Sources: Gallup, 1966a: Election '66, aggregate analysis of 1966 election results. Gallup, 1966b: The Gallup Election Handbook, survey data analysis of 1964 election random samples. N = 5,028.

[a] These regional figures report variations within England only (see Communalism).
[b] In 1966 the Scottish National party obtained 5% of the Scottish vote and 0.4% of the United Kingdom total, contesting 23 of 71 Scottish constituencies. The Welsh Nationalists won 4.2% of the Welsh vote and 0.2% of the United Kingdom total, contesting 20 of the 36 Welsh seats.

small Canadian New Democratic Party, the Irish Labour Party, and the old Italian PSDI.

2. *Single-claim* parties are those whose supporters have one but only one social characteristic in common.

(a) Religious and anti-clerical parties are the best examples of this category; 18 were found in this analysis. Such parties tend to give unique importance to church-state issues, such as education. On other matters, they are unlikely to have clearly defined policies, because their support is otherwise heterogeneous. (Cf. Burks, 1952.) Religion is primary, not only in terms of priority but also because it is the one thing that holds supporters together.

(b) The 20 class parties are the other empirical example of single-claim parties. . . .

3. *Mutually reinforcing* loyalties are found in parties whose supporters share two or more social characteristics. In this study 19 parties

TABLE 3. FRANCE (FOURTH REPUBLIC)

(1956 Election)	Comm. 26%	Soc. 15%	Radical 15%	Christian 11%	Gaullist 23%-1951	Cons./Ind. 15%
Religion						
Practicing Catholic, 41%	6	14	30	88	76	67
Nonpracticing, 59%	94	86	70	12	35	33
Lipset, 1960: 245						
Occupation[a]						
Business, middle, 34%	20	34	39	35	47	35
Workers, 31%	60	35	20	25	28	18
Peasants, 35%	20	30	41	40	24	47
Stoetzel, 1955: 116						
Urban/Rural						
5000 plus	52	50	40	47	55	45
Under 5000	48	50	60	53	45	55
Williams, 1958: 452						
Regions						
Paris and North, 21%	28	19	28	20	24	16
West, 26%	11	19	17	25	25	25
East, 25%	22	29	15	28	25	23
Center-South, 28%	39	34	40	27	26	36
Institut National Survey, 1956						
Communalism						
Not relevant as a basis of distinctiveness						

Sources: S.M. Lipset, Political Man, (1960), p. 245, survey by Institut National D'Études Demographiques, 1956. N = 1469. Secondary analysis of the same survey was also used to obtain regional divisions; J. Stoetzel, "Voting Behaviour in France," British Journal of Sociology, VI (1955), surveys by IFOP, circa 1952. Exact N and date not given; P. Williams, Politics in Post-War France (1958), surveys by IFOP, 1952, N not given.

[a] Occupational categories in France are not standardized, and the proliferation of strata makes it particularly difficult to draw simple class lines.

draw support from people who share several things in common, typically, working-class and anti-religious characteristics. Parties of mutually reinforcing loyalties begin to resemble the ideal-type picture that a sociologist is likely to sketch of a party. The greater the number of social characteristics in common, the easier it is too for party leaders to perceive the character of their support and to predict supporters' reactions. . . .

III

The utility of classifying parties in terms of their social cohesion can best be evaluated by testing hypotheses about the relationship of different types of cohesion to other features of party activity. Inevitably, the data used for these tests will vary in precision from hypothesis to hypothesis, because of the nature of the problems considered. . . .

Implicit in much sociological discussion of parties is the hypothesis that social groups "give birth to" political parties. The statement is as implausible empirically as it is metaphorically unnatural. If each permutation of four major groups in a society gave birth to a party, then each society would have 16 parties. In fact, in the 17 countries surveyed, the average number of parties catalogued is 4.5. There are, as it were, many infertile groups, miscarriages or political abortions in efforts to create parties. . . .

The formation of parties with social cohesion would seem to reflect a "demand-push" for political representation from social groups. It could be expressed in this form: H.1: *The stronger the social integration of a group, the more likely it will be to stimulate the formation of a political party.* Tested in a religious context, one would propose H1.1, that the existence of a significant Catholic population is the most likely source of party formation. The Catholic Church stands for a distinctive form of social integration, enrolls members in parallel organizations and has cadres of men distributed territorially in ways specially suited to facilitate nationwide political organization. In nine of the eleven countries in which Catholicism is a religion with substantial numbers of adherents, Australia, Austria, Belgium, Canada, France, Germany, Italy, the Netherlands and Northern Ireland, there is a cohesive party based on practicing Catholics. In Ireland, all parties agree in supporting the special position of the Church, and in the United States, Catholics can appear as a distinctive political sub-group in a heterogeneous Democratic party. The reactive influence of the Catholic Church is also noteworthy, for in seven of the nine countries with Catholic-based parties, there also exist anti-clerical or Protestant-based parties. In heavily or exclusively Protestant countries, one would not expect to find religious parties, for Protestantism is a more individualistic religion and its churches are less likely to provide a nucleus for social integration. In the six overwhelmingly Protestant countries, pro-religious parties exist

TABLE 4. GERMANY

	Socialist SPD (39%)	Christian CDU (48%)	Free Democratic FDP (10%)
Religion			
Protestant, 50%	58	39	71
Catholic, 46%	37	59	25
Other, none, 4%	6	2	4
Churchgoing, 41%	25	58	29
Not regular churchgoer, 59%	75	42	71
Liepelt, 1967b			
Occupation			
Professions and business, 20%	8	27	42
Employees and civil servants, 34%	32[a]	38	38
Workers, 46%	61	36	20
Liepelt, 1967b			
Urban/Rural			
100,000 plus, 30%	38	25	27
500-100,000, 31%	30	30	41
Under 5000, 39%	32	45	32
Liepelt, 1967b			
Regionalism			
North, 22%	23	20	24
West, 37%	51	45	43
South, 31%	26	35	33
Statisches Bundesamt, 1966: 6-10			
Communalism			
Not relevant as a basis of distinctiveness			

Sources: Liepelt, 1967b, unpublished surveys by Institut für Angewandte Sozialwissenschaft, 1967. N = 6143; Statisches Bundesamt, 1966, official report of 1965 federal election.
[a] The SPD is classified as homogeneous on class grounds in view of the blurring of manual/nonmanual distinctions in the very large intermediate category of Angestellte and Beamte and the very low support for the SPD in the unambiguously middle-class groups.

TABLE 5. ITALY

(1963)	Comm. PCI 26%	L. Soc. PSI 14%	Soc. PSDI 5%	Rep. PRI 1%	Christ. DC 41%	Lib. PLI 6%	Monarch 1%	Neo-Fasc. MSI 4%
Religion								
Proclerical, 55%	11	21	44	8	72	57	36	33
Anticlerical, 45%	89	79	56	92	28	43	64	67
Poggi, 1968: 32, 43, 52, 57								
Occupation								
Middle class, 35%	10	17	44	38	39	80	31	43
Manual workers, 46%	87	76	41	54	25	13	46	48
Independent farmers, 19%	3	7	15	8	36	8	23	9
Dogan, 1967: 158; Poggi, 1968: 19[b]								
Urban/Rural								
Urban, 37%	36	42	44	29	32	55	48	44
10-39% in agriculture, 32%	32	32	32	33	34	24	26	28
40% plus in agriculture, 31%	32	26	24	38	34	21	27	28
Barberis and Corazziari, 1968: 425								
Regionalism								
North, 49%	45	55	59	39	49	56	38	32
Center, 20%	25	19	17	27	17	17	12	26
South, 21%	20	17	17	16	23	15	42	28
Islands, 10%	10	8	7	19	11	12	18	14
Communalism								
Not relevant as a basis of distinctiveness								

Sources: Poggi, Le Preferenze Politiche degli Italiani, 1968 (Religion), Doxa survey, 1958. N = 1028 men; Dogan, "Political Cleavage and Social Stratification in France and Italy," in S.M. Lipset and S. Rokkan, 1967: 158, estimates from aggregate results, ecological analysis and survey data; Poggi, 1968 (Occupation), 1963 data. N = 1537 men; Barberis and Corazziari, "Strutture economiche e dinamica elettorale," M. Dogan and O. Petracca, editors, Partiti Politici e Strutture Sociale in Italia , 1968, aggregate results, 1963; Regionalism calculated from aggregate election results reported by province, 1963.

[a]Proclerical Italians are those scoring 7–14 points on a cumulate index of religious involvement (see Poggi, 1968: 30).

[b]Calculations for the five largest parties — PCI, PSI, PSDI, DC and PLI — are taken from Dogan, and for the three smaller parties, from Poggi, who lists data separately for these parties. The Ns are small. Agricultural workers and tenant farmers are grouped with manual workers, in view of the existence of a rural proletariat in Italy.

only in Norway and Sweden; it is significant that these parties are small and based on fundamentalist sectarian-type doctrines.

H1.2: *Industrial workers are most likely among class groups to stimulate the formation of one (or more) political parties.* By comparison with the middle class, which extends from clerks through bankers to traditional leaders, or farmers, whose social isolation makes difficult coordinated political action necessary in founding a party (cf. A. Campbell et al., 1960, Ch. 15), industrial workers are *relatively* homogeneous. In fact, there are working-class parties in 15 of the 17 countries surveyed; Ireland and America are the only exceptions. Smaller middle-class parties exist in four Scandinavian countries, Italy and the Netherlands. In none of the major industrial societies has the middle class formed its own party. . . .

H1.3: *The size of a communal group affects its social integration and its significance for party formation.* The larger it is, the weaker its integration, because it more nearly approximates a cross-section of a population, with many points of differentiation. The smaller the group, then the more a sense of "minority consciousness" is likely to increase its social integration. If the group is a large minority, its relative size may cause the majority group to discriminate, fearing domination, and by reaction, increase the minority's integration. A very small minority may be easily assimilated and lose its sense of social integration, as well as being numerically weak for electoral purposes. Sizable communal minorities exist in Northern Ireland, Canada and Belgium, where the Flemish majority is de facto treated like a minority (cf. Lorwin, 1966); and there are communal parties in each of these countries. . . .

H1.4: *Heterogeneous parties are formed by the initiatives of specially skillful broker politicians.* Times of political crisis or rapid social change provide the best circumstances in which brokers can work. In non-crisis times, there seems less a priori reason why groups of people with no common social attributes should come together in a party. The evidence to test this parsimonious hypothesis is less easy to marshal. In America, Ireland and Germany, the heterogeneous parties can trace their formation back to times of civil war or national collapse, but this is not so elsewhere. . . .

Once a party is formed, its situation is not dissimilar to a firm in oligopolistic competition. Within a somewhat protected market, leaders of political parties face a continuing dilemma. As the size of a party's vote increases, supporters tend to become increasingly heterogeneous in their characteristics and form increasingly difficult coalitions to manage. The more socially homogeneous the supporters become, the more limited is the party's potential and actual support within a society. . . . Two hypotheses concerning these variations can be easily tested with electoral data:

H2.1: *The electoral strength of a party varies inversely with its cohesiveness.* This assumes that as a party becomes more restricted in the characteristics of its members, its electoral appeal will also be constricted. Reciprocally, parties that exist as coalitions of social groups will be most interested in expanding their coalition, inasmuch as electoral success is the raison d'être of the existing coalition. Tested by reference to the average vote for each type of party in its last three national elections, the hypothesis is confirmed. Heterogeneous parties average a vote of 25 per cent, whereas parties of mutually reinforcing loyalties average only 19 per cent of the vote. (Cf. Table 6.)

TABLE 6. PARTY SHARE IN OFFICE

Type	% Share in office	% Average vote
Heterogeneous parties	30	25
Single-claim religious	26	18
Single-claim class	23	24
Mutually reinforcing loyalties	12	19

H2.2: *The elasticity of support for a party varies directly with its cohesiveness.* This hypothesis assumes that people identifying with a party of mutually reinforcing loyalties will be relatively stable in their voting because of the inter-action of political and social influences. Reciprocally, individuals whose only tie to a party is of a political nature will be more likely to defect from a party, or to be attracted to it for one election and then defect. Calculation of the average postwar inter-election fluctuation for all elections each party has contested provides some support for the hypothesis. The average fluctuation in the vote for heterogeneous parties has been 3.8 per cent of the total national vote; the average fluctuation for single-claim religious parties, 2.2 per cent, for single-claim class parties 2.1 per cent, and for parties of mutually reinforcing loyalties, 2.4 per cent. The evenness in the fluctuations for cohesive parties suggests that the degree or type of cohesion is less important than that there be *some* social reinforcement for party identification. The small average fluctuation in the support for all types of parties is a reminder that the rewards for seeking additional votes — whatever strategy is tried — are likely to be meager. This is especially true in multi-party systems, where small fluctuations in voting strength have only a marginal influence on coalition-making and not the all-or-nothing effect evidenced in predominantly two-party systems. As the rewards for seeking new voters are small relative to strains placed upon existing supporters, the incentive upon leaders to play for safety by maintaining a stable following is likely to be great. . . .

In examining the significance of social cohesion for party programs, i.e., statements of political intentions, it is important to avoid two reductionist assumptions: social characteristics are readily and automatically translated into party demands, or, party demands bear no relationship to the social interests of their followers. Sharing a common religion or class identification gives people an identifiable interest, but the interest need not be readily converted into a political issue. It is the task of party politicians to create consciousness of these characteristics and to demonstrate their political salience, if they are successfully to propose programmatic solutions for the problem they define. . . .

Variations in social cohesion should directly influence the character of parties' programs. As a general hypothesis, one would propose H.3: *The greater the social cohesion, the greater a party's concern with ideology* (i.e., programmatic coherence); and, conversely, H3.1: *Heterogeneous parties show less concern with ideology than do cohesive parties.* These hypotheses cast a fresh light upon the discussion of the "end of ideology" (Bell, 1961) or the difference between what LaPalombara and Weiner have described as pragmatic and ideologically oriented parties (1966, pp. 36ff). Leaders of heterogeneous parties will have a strong pragmatic inducement to adopt programs which are non-ideological (i.e., lacking in coherence), because of the difficulty in developing an ideology immediately relevant to the daily life-situation of their varied supporters. By contrast, leaders of parties whose supporters have related and clearly discernible mutually reinforcing loyalties will have a pragmatic inducement to adopt an ideological program, for it will reinforce support. . . . Once adopted, there is a pragmatic inducement for party leaders to maintain the ideology, for efforts to reduce ideological commitments in seeking an expanded electoral appeal are likely to be resisted in a disruptive fashion by existing supporters. . . .

Leaders of clerical parties will have a formal commitment to an ideology, but one which is only partially relevant to problems of this world. Insofar as religious beliefs concern affairs of state, then the party will tend to be ideologically rigid on the pragmatic ground that their religious commitment is their raison d'être. Increasingly, issues such as church schools are of limited importance on the agenda of government. In economic affairs, single-claim religious parties are unlikely to be ideological, for support is drawn across class lines. The pragmatic thing for such parties is to show considerable programmatic flexibility or incoherence. In Almond's terms (1960, pp. 34ff.) these parties articulate interests on some issues, and aggregate very disparate interests on other issues. If occupational similarities are a valid index of a wide set of social characteristics and, therefore, of a potential *Weltanschauung*, single-claim class parties should be ideologically rigid. Insofar as occupational position is a specific role, which is viewed instrumentally, then one would expect leaders of such parties to adopt pragmatic policies. In some cases, these might be consistent with ideological positions, e.g. redistributive tax policies, but this need not necessarily be so.

Testing this set of hypotheses is difficult, because social scientists have done surprisingly little work in measuring the programmatic content of parties. . . . An approximate index of party flexibility involves assessment of the period of time a party has spent sharing office since World War II. The assumption is that ideological parties will be sufficiently committed to principles that they will readily accept long periods in opposition and be less willing to adapt their programs to fit into coalition government, which is found in the great bulk of the countries analyzed. Reciprocally, heterogeneous parties will be more committed to power as an end or an "ideology," and therefore, readier to accept office in coalition. The specific index of "share in office" employed is that developed by Blondel (1968, pp. 190ff.). It gives weight to the length of time in office and, on a ten-point scale, to the degree of control that a party has in forming the government. Blondel's figures have been updated to December, 1968. Judged by their share of office, parties are distributed as hypothesized. (Table 6.)

Heterogeneous parties enjoy, on the average, about two and one-half times the power of parties with mutually reinforcing loyalties. This is not simply a function of differential electoral support, for heterogeneous parties are much more successful in gaining office than single-claim class parties, even though both types poll about the same vote. . . .

In the foregoing tests, single-claim class and religious parties have appeared similar in all but one case. The test of average voting strength showed class parties with 24 per cent of the vote, compared to 18 per cent for religious parties. Single-claim religious parties are slightly more successful in sharing in office than class parties. There is therefore no necessary reason to distinguish these parties in testing electoral hypotheses. However, separation is desirable to see if the difference between a religious and a class base of support has important implications for parties in relation to political systems.

IV

Because political parties give organizational form and *political* meaning to social differences, their activities can have major consequences for the regimes of which they are part. . . . For example, Huntington has postulated that the most important function a party can perform, particularly in a one-party state, is the institutionalization of support and compliance with a regime. (1968, Ch. 7.). . . These functions are normally discussed in terms of benign examples, especially the United States since 1865. . . . Yet parties can have as their aim the decomposition of the regime. . . . If the Netherlands is an example of parties acting benignly to maintain a regime, then the Weimar Republic in Germany can be instanced as an example of parties making a positive contribution to the repudiation of a regime. . . .

In order to analyze the significance of different degrees and types of party cohesion for regimes, we need a means of summarizing statements about individual parties in a form relevant to a description of party systems. The conventional discussion of numbers of parties does little to clarify such problems, for calculations of numbers tell us nothing about the content of the claims of parties, or the competing direction in which parties would like to lead a government. . . .

A multi-dimensional geometry of party systems, applicable cross-nationally and cross-culturally, can be developed from a few simple components. If a party possesses a particular attribute, e.g., it is socially cohesive in terms of religion or class, it can then be placed at a *point* in space. If two parties in a society are cohesive in contrasting values of an attribute, we can connect the two points they occupy to form a *dimension*. . . . In cases where three, rather than two alternatives are possible, then we can place parties on three points within a single *plane*. A plane surface connects three forms of an attribute without treating them ordinally. . . . Applying this analysis to the seventeen countries studied here yields the following classification of party systems:

1. Systems *without any major points of orientation* are those lacking even one party cohesive in terms of one major social characteristic. The United States and Ireland are the two countries . . . lacking stable points of reference in terms of large fixed social clienteles.
2. A *unipolar* party system (if the term be allowed) occurs when a

party or parties are cohesive on a single pole, but no other party is cohesive in the complementary form of the social attribute. In such a circumstance, one party has a fixed reference point, but the other parties can be located only by the statement "Not there." This gives them less clarity of clientele, but much more tactical and strategic flexibility. Such systems exist in Britain and New Zealand. . . .

3. In the seventeen countries surveyed, no empirical example was found of the often invoked ideal type, a *one-dimensional bi-polar* system, with working-class parties at one pole, and middle-class parties at the other.
4. When parties take three different forms of a social characteristic, then a *single-plane* party system exists. Denmark conforms almost exactly to this requirement, for four of its five major parties are class-based; the Radical party is heterogeneous.
5. *Two-dimensional* party systems include some parties cohesive on class and religious grounds. In two-dimensional party systems, the median party is cohesive in terms of a single social characteristic; the average number of points of cohesion is 1.05. These systems are Germany, Austria, Italy, France, the Netherlands, Sweden, Norway, and Australia.
6. *Three-* and *four-dimensional* party systems are also found in the present analysis. Finland is a poor example of a three-dimensional party system, inasmuch as the five largest parties in the system are cohesive only in class terms. Canada, Northern Ireland, and Belgium are proper four-dimensional systems.

The average number of parties, 5.1, is greater in two-dimensional systems than in systems of one dimension or less, 3.1. But the average number of parties does not grow as the number of dimensions along which parties can differ increases. In three- and four-dimensional systems, the average number of parties is 4.8, slightly less than in two-dimensional systems. This means that when the number of politically salient social divisions increases, each party tends to become cohesive on more points. In party systems of two dimensions, the average party is cohesive on 1.05 points, reflecting many single-claim parties. In more complex party systems, the average party is cohesive on 1.83 points, with a typical party that of mutually reinforcing loyalties. . . .

The weight of different types of parties in a system is more important than their number. The weight of parties can be indicated by their electoral success, and the weight of social divisions by the total vote for parties cohesive on each of the major social characteristics analyzed here. The weight can thus run from 0, when all parties are heterogeneous, to 400, when all parties are cohesive on all four measures. In view of the weakness of regionalism and the absence of communalism in many societies, a weight of 200 would be very high and anything above 100 would indicate that at least two social divisions were of substantial importance. Table 7 shows the weight of social divisions in

TABLE 7. PARTY SYSTEMS BY WEIGHT AND TYPES OF COHESION

Weight	Country	% Hetero.	% Class	% Religion	% Com'l.	% Region
A. Heterogeneous or class cohesion						
0	U.S.A.	100	—	—	—	—
0	Ireland	97	—	—	—	—
41	New Zealand	58	41	—	—	—
48	Britain	50	48	—	—	—
48	Australia	49	41	7	—	—
79	Denmark	15	79	—	—	—
84	Norway	10	75	9	—	—
102	Finland	—	90	—	6	6
103	Sweden	—	98	5	—	—
B. Religion and class cohesion						
88	Germany	48	39	49	—	—
113	Netherlands	5	34	79	—	—
125	France	—	26	99	—	—
133	Italy	7	47	86	—	—
134	Austria	5	43	91	—	—
C. Religion and communal cohesion						
85	Canada	62	5	37	37	6
163	Northern Ireland	—	20	77	23	43
209	Belgium	—	31	94	42	42

(Weight calculated from most recent election result, except for the Fourth French Republic, where the 1951 result was used, as the RPF was a major party. Figures may not sum to 100 per cent because of the omission of minor parties.)

each party system. The average weight of class divisions in the 15 systems where they appear is 48 per cent; of religious parties in 12 systems, 53 per cent, and of heterogeneous parties in 12 systems, 42 per cent.

What looks like cohesion in terms of an individual party looks like fragmentation in terms of a total political system, for the greater the weight of cohesive parties, then the more the parties institutionalize social divisions. Differences in the weight and types of social divisions produce three clusterings of countries. All the Scandinavian countries and five of the seven Anglo-American countries have party systems where heterogeneous and/or class parties are taking nearly all the vote. The Continental European countries plus Canada and Northern Ireland are systems in which non-class divisions are predominant. . . .

Strains in regimes are evidenced by limited support for and/or compliance with the basic political laws of a regime (see Rose, 1969). Carried to the extreme, such strains result in civil war and the repudiation of a regime. . . . Among the seventeen countries studied here, no significant political strains threaten the regime in Britain, Australia, New Zealand, Denmark, Norway, Sweden, and the Netherlands. France is the only society that has had a regime overthrown since the war. Germany, Italy, and Austria, however, have yet to demonstrate that their governing party can be succeeded in office by an opposition party without major strains. Moreover, all three of these regimes were established by military occupation. Belgium, and two Anglo-American societies, Canada and Northern Ireland, have parties challenging the regime and/or the boundaries of the state. Finland has had a major civil war in the lifetime of most voters, and also retains a strong Communist Party. In Ireland and America, civil war experiences are part of the historical past, but the issues involved — the independence of all parts of Ireland from Britain, and the place of the Negro in American life — have not been settled. In all, seven regimes are subject to no significant strains, and ten regimes subject to some. The following hypotheses assume that parties affect strains in a regime by the way in which they institutionalize support from particular types of social groups.

H4.1: *If all parties lack social cohesion, then regime strains are likely to be relatively high.* . . . In a regime in which all parties are heterogeneous, as Richard McCormick notes (1967, p. 113) in a perceptive study of American parties, "the strain on the political system at the level of the parties may be disruptive." Insofar as the disruption of parties increases strains in a regime, then indirectly an exclusively heterogeneous party system may create major political difficulties. This hypothesis does not seem to be confirmed by contemporary Western experience. The major strain placed upon the American regime in its history has arisen from communal (Negro) or regional (Southern) problems. In Ireland the regime was of uncertain legitimacy in the 1930's and, arguably, as late as the mid-1950's, when extra-constitutional Republican parties succeeded in winning parliamentary representation. . . .

H4.2: *If class cohesive parties predominate, then regime strains are likely to be relatively low.* This hypothesis assumes that class cohesion makes for bargaining politics. Class is defined by occupation, an economic characteristic, and reflects the significance of market considerations. (Cf. Weber, 1948, pp. 181ff.) While social scientists have argued that these economic considerations ought to lead to political conflict, it would be more parsimonious to assume that economic differences should lead to economic conflicts. These may be conducted strictly through economic actions, such as strikes and labor-management bargaining, and/or they can be conducted by workers using the political power of massive numbers to offset the economic power of massive capital, concentrated in a group which is small in regard to the electorate. Economic controversies are typically expressed in terms of money, and money is a continuous variable capable of indefinite subdivision for purposes of providing incremental adjustments in the distribution of economic benefits. In other words, it is something that it is very easy to bargain about. . . . A second feature of economic differences is that they are capable of non-zero sum settlements. Economic growth makes is possible to settle disputes about earnings by increasing the real standard of living of all major sections of society. . . . Insofar as occupational position defines status, this too need not involve zero-sum conflicts between fixed groups, for the criteria of status may change, or be incommensurable between groups, and an individual may undergo mobility between occupational groups more easily than mobility between communal or religious groups.

Class-based parties do predominate where regime strains are low. Of the seventeen countries, Sweden is the society where class parties most clearly are pre-eminent; it is also an example of a regime which has suffered the fewest strains in the past troubled half-century. (Cf. Rustow, 1955.) In three more countries, class parties take more than 50 per cent of the vote; these are the other three Scandinavian countries. Only in Finland has the regime been subject to any strains in the recent past. In three more societies — Britain, New Zealand and Australia — class parties and heterogeneous parties compete for votes. All three are societies where no significant regime challenge exists. Incipient problems in Britain take the form of communal movements in the Celtic fringes and, in Australia, of a religious-oriented party. . . . The orderly character of government in societies where class parties are predominant is not only a function of the content of economic issues, but also, perhaps, of the fact that the related status differences result in a social system where members of different classes or *stande* have a clear awareness of what their reciprocal rights and obligations are. (Cf. Nordlinger, 1967.)

H4.3: *If parties cohesive on religious grounds predominate, then regime strains are likely to be relatively high.* This hypothesis derives from the fact that claims of religious and anti-clerical groups tend to be non-bargainable. An educational system, for example, either gives instruction consistent with Catholic doctrine on faith and morals, or it does not. It is worth noting that the decision is not made by the parties but by the church. Church-state conflicts also tend to take the form of zero-sum conflicts: the power that the state gains is taken from the church, or the powers that the church gains are taken from the regime.

Religious divisions are pervasive in France, Belgium, Austria, Italy, the Netherlands, and Northern Ireland, and of primary importance in Germany and Canada. The position of the regimes in these eight countries supports the hypothesis. One of the major causes of the fall of the Fourth French Republic was the inability of the parties favoring the regime to form a durable coalition because they differed on religious issues (Williams, 1964.) In Austria, the downfall of the First Republic was a direct consequence of clerical and anti-clerical conflicts. Religious divisions were important too, in helping to create openings for Nazism in Germany. (Cf. Blankenburg, 1967, pp. 139–153; Edinger, 1968, pp. 65–68.) The problems and downfall of these regimes cannot be explained in terms of class conflict for, as Lorwin has shown (1958), historically class divisions have not been *politically* strong in these societies. In Northern Ireland, religious divisions are the base of the conflict about the existing regime. In Belgium and Canada, religious differences are reinforced by communal differences. (See *infra*, H4.4.) The Netherlands is exceptional, in that religion is important yet the regime has suffered no major strains because of this. The exceptional position of the Netherlands seems explicable in terms of the tri-partite religious division, which has placed a high premium upon bargaining as the price of any form of government. Historically, Protestants and

Catholics submerged differences to protect both religions against secular attacks. Today, bargains are difficult to strike (e.g., in coalition formation), but remain necessary since no religion can hope to dominate. (Cf. Lijphart, 1968; and Daalder, 1966.)

The importance of religion, as against class, is most clearly demonstrated by comparing countries where the weight of social divisions is approximately equal, but for contrasting reasons. The weight of religious divisions in France, Austria, Italy, and the Netherlands is virtually the same as the weight of class divisions in the four Scandinavian countries; the total weight of strains is not a different order in the two groups (see Table 7). Strains on regime have been much greater where religion has weighed heavily in the scales. . . .

H4.4: *If communal parties predominate, then regime strains are likely to be relatively high.* Communal issues are non-bargainable. For example, children must be taught either in French or in Flemish as their first language of instruction, and, a flag cannot be British on one side and Irish on the other. A linguistic conflict is also likely to be a zero-sum conflict, for the use of one language in an area is inevitably regarded as a deprivation by the speakers of the other language. Linguistic conflict can be diminished by spatial segregation, but this, in turn, increases the likelihood of demands for political autonomy, culminating in the disruption of a multi-national state, and its replacement by separate regimes for each of two nation-states. Since communal identifications tend to be ascriptive, individuals caught in a communal dispute have little chance of resolving difficulties by personal mobility — except to leave the boundaries of a state, or change them.

Communally based parties are significant in three countries — Canada, Northern Ireland, and Belgium. All three societies have parties seeking to disrupt the state and placing major strains upon the regime. When religion and class were major issues, Belgians disagreed, but about issues which cut across communal loyalties, bringing some Flemish and Walloons together. The increased significance of communal issues has led to increasing disruptive tendencies in the major parties, and also, in the streets of Belgian cities. (Cf. Lorwin 1966.) In Canada, the growing strength of Quebec separatism has also led to increasing political strains upon the federal regime, symbolized by the creation of a new, non-British flag, and a spate of political initiatives designed to reduce tensions between the French and English-speaking communities. (Cf. Schwartz, 1967.) . . .

H4.5: *Regional cohesion, independent of communalism, is not a source of regime strains.* This hypothesis assumes that regional demands are bargainable *as long as* they are stated in a context accepting the existing boundaries of a state. In such situations, regional demands involve the use of central government power to redistribute benefits as between say, the North and South of Italy, or to allow a particular group to enjoy the advantages of both large- and small-scale administration, as in American federalism. . . . Regionally cohesive parties are found in four societies, the three societies where communalism is important, plus Finland. In Finland, regionalism is of little importance, involving a small minority of Swedish speakers on the west coast of Finland. . . . The absence of regional divisions elsewhere in the 17 countries surveyed, including a number where regimes have been subject to strains, suggests that regionalism, *by itself,* is not an independent influence. In the absence of communalism, parties are likely to perform the function of integrating different regions into a national political system, for cross-local and cross-regional bases of support are necessary if a party is to become electorally successful. . . .

Since divisions based on classes occur historically late in the development of modern nations, class parties may well become important by default, in the absence of other, earlier social divisions. The one major European country omitted from this study — Switzerland — shows that communal, regional and religious divisions can be contained by parties without disrupting a regime. Nonetheless, specifying all the circumstances that make Swiss politics work only underscores the likelihood that in most countries where religion, language and ethnic identity are important, some parties are likely to organize supporters in ways placing major strains upon regimes.

BIBLIOGRAPHY

Almond, G. A. (1960) "A Functional Approach to Comparative Politics," in G. A. Almond and J. S. Coleman (eds.), *The Politics of the Developing Areas.* Princeton: Princeton University Press.

Blankenburg, E. (1967) *Kirchliche Bindung und Wahlverhalten.* Olten & Freiburg: Walter-Verlag.

Blondel, J. (1968) "Party Systems and Patterns of Government in Western Democracies." *Canadian Journal of Political Science* 1: 180–203.

Burks, R. V. (1952) "Catholic Parties in Latin Europe." *Journal of Modern History* 24: 269–286.

Campbell, A., P. Converse, W. Miller, and D. Stokes (1960) *The American Voter.* New York: Wiley.

Daalder, H. (1966) "The Netherlands: Opposition in a Segmented Society," in R. A. Dahl (ed.), *Political Oppositions in Western Democracies.* New Haven: Yale University Press.

Edinger, L. J. (1968) *Politics in Germany.* Boston: Little Brown.

Huntington, S. P. (1968) *Political Order in Changing Societies.* New Haven: Yale University Press.

Lijphart, A. (1968) *The Politics of Accommodation: Pluralism and Democracy in the Netherlands.* Berkeley: University of California Press.

Lipset, S. M. (1960) *Political Man.* New York: Doubleday.

Lipset, S. M. and S. Rokkan (eds.) (1967) *Party Systems and Voter Alignments.* New York: Free Press.

Lorwin, V. R. (1958) "Working Class Politics and Economic Development in Western Europe." *American Historical Review* 63: 338–351.

Lorwin, V. R. (1966) "Belgium: Religion, Class and Language in National Politics." Pp. 147–187 in R. A. Dahl (ed.) *Political Oppositions in Western Democracies.* New Haven: Yale University Press.

MacCallum Scott, John H. (1967) *Experiment in Internationalism.* London: Allen & Unwin.

McCormick, R. P. (1967) "Political Development and the Second Party System." Pp. 90–116 in W. N. Chambers and W. D. Burnham (eds.), *The American Party Systems.* New York: Oxford University Press.

Nordlinger, E. A. (1967) *The Working-Class Tories.* London: MacGibbon & Kee.

Rogger, H. and E. Weber (eds.) (1965) *The European Right.* London: Weidenfeld & Nicolson.

Rokkan, S. (1968) "The Structuring of Mass Politics in the Smaller European Democracies: A Developmental Typology." *Contemporary Studies in Society and History* 10: 173–210.

Rose, R. (1969) "Dynamic Tendencies in the Authority of Regimes." *World Politics* XXI: 4.

Rustow, D. A. (1955) *The Politics of Compromise.* Princeton: Princeton University Press.

Schwartz, M. A. (1967) *Public Opinion and Canadian Identity.* Berkeley: University of California Press.

Williams, P. M. (1964) *Crisis and Compromise.* London: Longmans.

MAURICE DUVERGER

The Eternal Morass: French Centrism

Ministerial instability in France (103 governments under the Third Republic, 22 under the Fourth Republic) has often been denounced without considering its causes and by exaggerating its effects. Actually, the instability of cabinets was accompanied by a stability of ministers and even by a certain immobility of policies. This paradox is explained by the fact that, except in rare circumstances, the French government rested on center majorities. The French political vocabulary is very significant in this regard: "conjunction of centers," concentration, convergence, the juste milieu, *the third force, center-left, center-right, etc. Maurice Duverger's exacting analysis of the causes of this centrism and of its effects is an example of a study that can illuminate the depths of a political system without the aid of quantitative materials.*

Why, in a country such as France, where opposition between the right and left is readily proclaimed as fundamental, do the right and left of both basic political tendencies so rarely succeed in uniting as they do in Great Britain? Why is each basic tendency inclined to split almost continually into extremists and moderates? Why is the French government most frequently based upon a morass, that is, a loose alliance of center parties which forces the extremes into opposition? To these fundamental questions there are no obvious or satisfying answers. It seems that two principal factors have played a role: the multiparty system on the one hand and the "trauma" of 1789 on the other. However, these two explanations remain conjectural and insufficient.

THE CAUSES OF CENTRISM

A regular alliance of moderates and extremists on the right and on the left is only found in those countries with two-party systems. Elsewhere, as in Scandinavia, the Netherlands, or Weimar Germany one often sees the formation of a loose alliance of center parties. The multiparty system provides the center-right and center-left with room to maneuver. Each side can either form a coalition with the extremists of its own tendency or unite with the moderates of the other side. Center parties can form "reversible alliances," which are impossible for the extremists, since those in the center enjoy a much greater freedom of movement. In a multiparty system, the power of a party depends not only on the number of parliamentary seats it controls but also on its position in the spectrum of parties — the central position being the most advantageous.

Moreover, in a coalition of center parties the strength of each depends as much on its ability to reverse alliances as on its position in the spectrum. Under the Third Republic before 1914, the center-right (republican) could scarcely unite with the extreme right (monarchist) while the center-left (radical) could unite with the extreme left (socialist); that tipped the scales of the center alliance toward the center-left. Under the Fourth Republic, on the other hand, the center-left (socialist) could hardly ally itself with the extreme left (communist) after 1947, while the center-right (radical and Christian democrat) could ally itself with the right: whence the power of the center-right in the "third force."

The multiparty system stems from various factors. In France the succession of constitutional regimes has contributed to the division of both the right and the left. In 1848, those persons who would have joined the Tory party in Great Britain split into Legitimists, Orleanists, and Bonapartists in France. Among the latter two groups, there were also

Abridged from Maurice Duverger, "L'éternel marais: essai sur le centrisme français," *Revue française de science politique,* February, 1964, pp. 38–48. Translated into English by Allen Rozelle. Reprinted by permission.

some liberals. Other liberals gathered under the republican banner. In England all liberals would have supported the Whig party. More important, however, has been the French electoral system. Though the great conflict between conservatives and liberals, which dominated the first part of the nineteenth century, was being replaced by the struggle between capitalists and socialists, the basic two-party system of European politics was yielding everywhere to a three-party system. Only in Great Britain with its single, majority ballot were the liberals eliminated and the two-party system maintained.

Such an electoral system is very effective in preventing the very divorce between moderates and extremists on each side which is the basis of the loose center alliance. The electoral mechanism forces revolutionaries and reformers, ultra-conservatives and the "intelligent right" to live together. If English socialists on the far left tried to establish an extreme left-wing party such as the PSU (Parti Socialiste Unifié) or a Communist Party, the chances of British socialism winning an election or forming a government would collapse. If Lord Beaverbrook's friends organized a dissident faction, the Conservatives would see all hopes of power disappear. An alliance of center parties presupposes a less unifying, less simplifying electoral system than the single ballot. However, a second ballot or a system of proportional representation is not sufficient to result in a center alliance. The proof is that in other continental European countries, which do not use the British electoral system and have multiparty systems, center alliances are less frequent than in France. In many respects, moreover, French multiparty politics is as much the consequence of the center alliance as its cause. The essential reason for French political tendencies to sink into a morass must be sought elsewhere.

The origin probably lies in the trauma of 1789 and the reaction of 1814–15. In most other western European countries the conflict between liberals and conservatives did not take on a revolutionary character. It went on within the framework of contemporary institutions. The extreme left sometimes wished for revolution, but it was never capable of carrying it out. Under such conditions it seemed preferable to unite tacitly with the reformist left rather than retreat into isolation, a course of action which would accomplish nothing concrete. For the reformist left such a union was possible so long as the extreme left had no blood on its hands, was not too frightening, could not really use the fear it inspired, and was not too powerful. Certainly the conflict between moderate liberals and "radicals" was often bitter during the nineteenth century — sometimes bitter enough to cause schisms — but the break was never as profound or as definitive as it was between Jacobins and other liberals in France after 1793.

At the moment when modern political evolution was beginning in France, the extreme left was catapulted into power by a revolution without really wanting it (in 1789, no one wanted the Republic). The course of events drove that revolution to extreme measures which struck fear not only into conservatives but also into reformist liberals. The

Republic of 1792 was much too far ahead of contemporary social structures and mentalities to have had any chance of lasting. Even the Terror was incapable of prolonging it, but recourse to the Terror split the liberals, isolating the implacable, intransigent Jacobins from the moderates. The latter, profoundly shocked by the methods of the Jacobins and yet tainted themselves by Jacobin radicalism, went to great lengths to dissociate themselves from the extremists and for several decades relegated them to a ghetto analagous to the one occupied by the Communists after 1947.

The violence of the left in 1793–94 was repeated by the right in 1814–15: after the red Terror a white Terror, which created the same difficulties within the conservative party. The memory would not last as long, however; the moderate right would always have less horror of the ultra-conservatives than the liberals would of the Jacobins. The excesses of the well bred are always less shocking than those of the lower classes. Open-minded conservatives split with the extremists because of the latter's obstinacy in using ineffectual methods: such was the case in 1873 when the "fusion" failed. Nostalgia for brutal reaction and the sword within a certain faction of the right kept it divided just as the nostalgia for revolution within a certain faction of the left kept it divided.

Thus separated from their extremist factions, the center-right and center-left naturally tended to unite, first because it was the only means of achieving power and because they both rejected the use of violence and wanted to establish a minimum of consensus. The first true coalition of center parties did not occur until 1830, after the failure of the Restoration had followed that of the Revolution. Only such an alliance was capable of recreating an embryo of social order at the moment when France seemed torn into two irreducible, political tendencies, between which coexistence was virtually impossible. The partisans of the Old Regime and those of the Revolution were in agreement on absolutely nothing; the regime wanted by the former seemed unbearable to the latter and vice versa. The shocks of 1789 and 1814 had shattered the national community. Neither the right nor the left could govern according to its principles without crushing its adversary; that is, half the country. Only a compromise between moderates on both sides could reestablish a certain stability.

On the whole, the Empire was the first attempt at such a compromise. That republican monarchy, based on the plebiscite and papal consecration, tried to conciliate the two legitimacies. The July Monarchy followed a similar route by enthroning a king produced by a revolution and a parliamentary vote, but born of royal blood. More clearly than the compromise of 1804, that of 1830 stood on the loose alliance of two centers. Orleanism brought together those conservatives who were determined to make something of their power as well as reformist liberals. The regime collapsed because of a rupture in the equilibrium between those two elements. As the aging king was sinking into immobility, by according predominance to the center-right, the center-left unintentionally unleashed the Revolution of 1848, which went far beyond their original, elementary objective.

The compromise of 1830 was reestablished in 1875 on rather similar terms between the same political tendencies. The monarchists, Orleanists, and moderate republicans reached an agreement to set up a parliamentary regime very similar to that under Louis-Philippe, only without a king. Forty-five years after the beginning of the July Monarchy, the center of gravity had shifted from the center-right to the center-left. However, the struggle between conservatives and liberals had gradually ceased to be fundamental. After 1877, the return of the monarchy and its aristocratic privileges became impossible. By then another conflict had occupied the center stage — the struggle between capitalists and socialists — and it had already spilled more blood than both the Revolution of 1789 and the white Terror.

As in the earlier struggle, the one between capitalists and socialists developed with more violence in France than elsewhere. The harsh awakening of June 1848 after the idyll of February and then the fierce repression of the Commune engendered a profound bitterness in the ranks of the new left and shaped the conviction among many that nothing could be gained by legal means within the framework of a bourgeois regime. Throughout the rest of western Europe revolutionary socialists were far outnumbered by reformist socialists. Of the revolutionaries, the most realistic decided to conclude alliances with the reformists, thereby giving birth to some of the great political parties. In France the memory of 30,000 capital executions in 1871 turned the best militant workers against reformism and confirmed them in their anarchistic or revolutionary syndicalism. Their heirs entered into political action only when they found a party radically opposed both to the bourgeois order and to reformism — the Communist Party. Just as violence had split the liberal left in two, so it divided the socialist left. This time, however, the schism was not caused by violence perpetrated by the left but rather by violence against it.

The capitalist right was no more united than the conservative right had been, but for slightly different reasons. Everywhere in Europe the appearance of the socialists drove the old liberal left toward the center. In France the division of the old left into moderates and Jacobins retarded that evolution because the latter resisted the change. In their revolutionary nostalgia they resembled the socialists, and that kept them in the center-left. Thus before 1914, the new right was comprised of a mixture of all the old conservatives, extremists, and moderates (Legitimists, Orleanists, Bonapartists) on the one hand, and on the other hand of the moderate republicans of the Republican Federation or the Democratic Alliance. Though those groups claimed to represent the center-left, they actually formed the center-right. The real center-left consisted of the radicals, and the extreme left of the socialists. The former were already playing a skillful game of political see-saw between leftist electoral alliances and center parliamentary alliances.

While the Communist Party was developing, the radicals slipped from center-left to center-right (the popular republicans and the Christian radicals would follow the same course after 1945) and in turn the socialists took over the center-left. Within the right, ex-conservatives and ex-liberals merged without the former ever completely losing their nostalgia for violence. If a strong man emerged — preferably military, a marshal or general (or even a colonel like La Rocque) — they were ready to desert the Republic, leading their liberal friends with them, as in 1851. That latent extremism continued to prevent a fusion between the right and the radical center or the MRP (*Mouvement Républicain Populaire*, a Christian Democratic party). Similarly, on the left the extremism of the communists forestalled any unification of the socialist family.

THE CONSEQUENCES OF FRENCH CENTER POLITICS

The loose center alliance had one great advantage: it made compromise possible between apparently irreconcilable opposites. It permitted the two halves of France, who dreamed of annihilating one another, to live together. It provided a democratic framework for that existence, which only an iron fist could have provided otherwise. Center politics of the English type with its alternation of power from right to left can work only if each side respects the other when the latter controls the government. The violence of the antagonisms in France during the nineteenth and early twentieth centuries prevented the growth of any such respect. From that time only a loose alliance of center parties has been able to allow France's free institutions to function, on the condition that the center parties have been strong enough to command a majority. Whenever they were too weak, only a dictatorship prevented the right from crushing the left or vice versa. Such is approximately the significance of the First Empire and to a lesser extent, of the Second.

The development of center parties and their regular collaboration permitted the creation of parliamentary regimes in France — regimes which probably represented the maximum possible democracy at the time: the July Monarchy in 1830 and the Third Republic in 1875. Without the center coalition, parliamentary government could not have been established in France. It functioned well as long as the coalition could be maintained and could control a majority. The Orleanist monarchy was based on the "exact middle" (*juste milieu*), the Third Republic on the "concentration," and the Fourth Republic on the "third force." In each case strictly rightist or leftist majorities were only temporary, existing under the exceptional circumstances of war or crisis. To this day, the loose center alliance has been the basis of democracy in France.

However, it has also produced certain poisons which have weakened that democracy. First of all, it has erased the boundaries between parties. Certainly in Great Britain the difference between a moderate Laborite and a progressive Conservative is not very great, but despite everything, the difference is easily recognized by public opinion because each belongs to a clearly delineated political entity. Consequently, political battles are relatively clear to the public. In France the center coalition has obscured if not wiped out both the distinction between moderates and extremists on the right and the left and the distinction between center-right and center-left to such an extent that all parties now comprise a sort of continuum whose elements are as difficult to separate as the different colors of the spectrum. . . .

Nevertheless, the lines of separation are clearer today (for example, between communists and socialists and even between socialists and parties farther to the right) than they were during the nineteenth century. Such political confusion is a permanent consequence of the loose center coalition. It even tends to erase the distinctions between right and left. In theory the two associated centers are clearly distinguished one from the other: the center-right whose members accept certain reforms in order to stay afloat and thus conserve the essence of the existing order; the center-left whose partisans want to replace the existing order gradually by successive reforms with an entirely new order. In practice, whenever they are faced with concrete problems, the distinctions tend to disappear. The center-left is naturally inclined to restrain its reformist urge not simply in order to continue collaborating with the center-right but also because any change is difficult and because it is always easier to maintain the existing order than to modify it when one is in power.

This phenomenon is thus another consequence of the loose center alliance: it tends to give preponderance to the center-right within the center majority. Any reformist in power is dangerously tempted to put off reforms because of practical difficulties. Whenever all the factions of the left govern together, the most extreme prevent the most moderate from following that natural inclination. When Labour is in power in Great Britain, the left wing prods the right — if it can be called that — and thus prevents it from delaying reforms indefinitely by pleading the practical difficulties of applying them. In a center coalition, on the other hand, no group pressures the center-left to implement the reforms it wants in principle. On the contrary, the center-right checks any reformist bent; its braking action combines with natural inertia and the problems inherent in any change to limit the center alliance to the task of administering the existing order. At the boundary between the center-right and center-left it is difficult to distinguish those who accept reforms to consolidate the status quo from those who see in reforms a means of taking another step toward further transformations. The two centers disagree on their long-range goals but agree at the governmental level where grand horizons are always somewhat obscured by the conduct of daily affairs.

Thus everything conspires to trap center governments in immobility. In this respect, the alternation of power between the two centers, based on their respective strengths within the coalition and on their ability to establish reversible alliances, is more apparent than real. According to parliamentary and ministerial arithmetic, a certain pendulum movement exists between center majorities dominated by the center-left and others controlled by the center-right. In reality, scarcely anything is involved other than personalities and vocabulary; center coalitions always tend toward the center-right. Sometimes there are center governments distraught at their inability to effect reforms, which they thus promise for the future, and sometimes there are center governments which are delighted by their immobility and show no desire to escape it, but neither moves very much in fact. The alternation of power between the two sides concerns words more than acts.

BLENDING THE LANGUAGE OF THE LEFT AND THE ACTIONS OF THE RIGHT

Even in matters of language the differences tend to disappear. The governments of the center-right are generally as reformist in word as the governments of the center-left. The center coalition thus tends to rest on a dual equilibrium: in its actions it is securely anchored to the practical conservatism of the center-right; in its proclamations it is no less clearly oriented toward the reformism of the center-left. This tendency of all French parties to pass themselves off as more "radical" than they are gives the center coalition a leftward-moving appearance behind which conservative policies continue almost without interruption. The fact that the center-left presents itself as leftist (the SFIO or *Section française de l'internationale ouvrière*, the Socialists, today), the center-right as center-left (the Radicals and the MRP), and the right as center-right (the independents and the UNR or *Union pour la Nouvelle République*, the Gaullist party) facilitates that camouflage as well as the confusion of party lines.

Whenever the pressure from the left is too strong, the center coalition can only survive at the expense of a few reforms. However, they usually only involve issues of secondary importance, and conforming with the views of the center-right, they do not threaten the essence of the existing order. Even in its suppositions, the real orientation of the center majority leans to the center-right. Reforms are enacted not because they fit into any comprehensive plan for the complete transformation of society, but because they must be enacted if the coalition is to survive. The habits which the center-left has acquired from its participation in center majorities cause it to act as a brake within leftist coalitions on those rare occasions when they are formed. Such was the case in 1924–26, 1932–34, and 1936–38. Ultimately, the center-left reaches the point where it considers any reform as dangerous and thus unconsciously acquires the viewpoint of the center-right. At the same time it retains its leftist vocabulary, which the right uses as an excuse to continue its attacks. The center coalition thus tends to become a mixture of leftist slogans and rightist political action.

For this reason the left feels frustrated. But to a certain extent so does the right. By almost always bringing the centers into power and relegating the extremes to opposition, the French morass engenders a spirit of alienation in both the right and the left. There is a dissociation between practical politics and theoretical politics. The latter has very little to do with reality. Intellectuals on the right and the left have little influence on the governing politicians of their own persuasion. New ideas on both sides develop within a closed circuit without directly affecting those who hold power. There are thus two separate realms of politics: on the one hand, the parties in power which resemble one another more and more and which collaborate most of the time to run the country; and on the other hand, the opposition parties, which are confined to dialectics and agitation.

In Great Britain, whenever the Labour Party is in power, it is dominated by moderates, but its leftist factions are still considered part of the family; they are not shunned by the ministers and the government. On the contrary, leftist members are always included in the government. They have the impression of influencing policy — and they do in fact. They do not feel doomed to impotence or, to use a Marxist term, alienated. In France, the left finds itself in a similar situation only on those rare occasions when leftist governments are in power. The same difference applies to the rights of the two countries: in England extremists feel a part of moderate Conservative majorities, whereas in France, they are forced to fend for themselves.

The reciprocal isolation of governing politicians and ideologues is harmful to both. Denied contact with ideas and ideologies and losing sight of distant goals by concentrating on immediate affairs, governing politicians condemn themselves to immobility and turn to financial deals: Orleanist speculations, Bonapartist public works, and republican railway construction created the context of center coalitions under successive regimes. At the same time, the extremists on both sides are pushed into opposition and thereby get the impression of having been betrayed by their moderates. While the intermingling center-right and center-left collaborate to govern the country, the revolutionaries and reactionaries, denied any other means of action, intensify their opposition on a theoretical plane. Growing extremism and rigorous idealistic political purity correspond to moderation and the constant confusion of daily politics.

Cut off from the responsibilities of decision, the doctrinaire extremists naturally tend to harden their revolutionary or reactionary attitude, which is further fed by their revulsion at the politico-financial dealings of the center coalition. The general evolution of western societies in the twentieth century, which tends to reestablish a consensus between the right and the left and to lessen the probability of reaction or revolution, has been slowed in France by the separation between governing politicians and doctrinaire extremists, which the loose center coalition has caused. After having permitted France to overcome its deep political divisions and allowed it to establish a minimum of consensus between almost irreducible political antagonisms, the politics of the French center has since exercised the opposite influence: it has retarded the creation of a deeper political consensus.

Whenever extremists hold sway over moderates within each political tendency — right or left — the sort of pendulum action of British politics is not possible, and a loose center coalition springs up to prevent a bloody succession of brutal revolutions and reactions, red terrors and white terrors. On the other hand, whenever the moderates become stronger than the extremists within each tendency, their union on the right and the left helps strengthen the position of the moderates over the extremists by forcing the latter to act within the framework of a large party which must keep in touch with millions of voters, by associating them with the responsibilities of power, and by giving them an awareness of the difficulties and practical conditions of political action. Under such circumstances, a loose center coalition loses its raison d'être and becomes more harmful than useful.

One might wonder if the French political situation is not on the eve of such a change and if, rather than being eternal, the morass, which has characterized French politics for 170 years, is not destined for an early end.

ROBERT T. McKENZIE

Parties and the British Constitution

The American practice of separating the legislature from the executive is unknown in Europe, for the conventions of parliamentary government compel a prime minister to have the support of a majority in the legislature or resign. The rise of disciplined political parties in Britain has made the prime minister of the day able to appeal to partisan loyalties and political self-interest, so that formal votes of confidence may be won even when no such confidence exists in practice. This phenomenon, however, raises constitutional questions about the relationship between party leaders in office and the extra-parliamentary party organization. In the concluding chapter of British Political Parties, *Robert T. McKenzie summarizes the implications of his lengthy study of modern parties and the workings of British government.*

The distribution of power within British political parties is primarily a function of cabinet government and the British parliamentary system. So long as the parties accept this system of government effective decision-making authority will reside with the leadership groups thrown up by the parliamentary parties (of whom much the most important individual is the party leader); and they will exercise this authority so long as they retain the confidence of their respective parliamentary parties. The views of their organized supporters outside Parliament must inevitably be taken into account by the party leadership because of the importance of the rôle these supporters play in selecting candidates, raising funds, and promoting the cause of the party during elections. But, whatever the rôle granted in theory to the extra-parliamentary wings of the parties, in practice final authority rests in both parties with the parliamentary party and its leadership. In this fundamental respect the distribution of power within the two major parties is the same.

. . . Both major parties have consistently exaggerated the differences between their party organizations with a view to proving that their own is "democratic" and that of their opponents is not. The Labour Party customarily argues that the Conservative Leader rules his party with the iron hand of an autocrat; that he is not subject to the effective control either of his followers in Parliament or of the mass organization of the party outside Parliament. Labour spokesmen claim that, in contrast, their own party is fully democratic because their party leaders are subject to annual re-election (at least when the party is in opposition) and both the Leader and the parliamentary party, they claim, are ultimately responsible to the annual conference of the party. The Conservatives habitually reply that the Labour Party in Parliament is in fact subject to the control of a tight-knit clique of party managers at the party head office and of a group of trade union oligarchs; these party "bosses," the Conservatives charge, manipulate the affairs of the party in their own interest and are in no way responsible to the electorate. The Conservative spokesmen draw a sharp contrast between this state of affairs and the position in their own party, where the parliamentary Leader (who is subject to the control of the electorate) is assigned full responsibility for the affairs of the party although (the Conservatives add) he gives due weight to the views of his party followers both inside and outside Parliament.

All of these descriptions of the power structures of the rival parties, proffered by the parties themselves, are fundamentally misleading. The Conservative statement of the position within their own party is perhaps the least misleading of the four views summarized above. (Although . . . the Conservative Leader plays nothing like the almost dictatorial rôle Conservative literature would seem to suggest.) But the Conserva-

Abridged from R. T. McKenzie, *British Political Parties*, 2nd Ed., pp. 635–649 (London: Heinemann, 1963). Originally published by Heinemann Educational Books, Ltd. Published in the United States by Frederick A. Praeger, Inc. Reprinted by permission.

tive view of the Labour Party and the Labour Party's own picture both of itself and of its opponents are highly misleading.

Some part of the confusion about the power structure of the parties arises . . . from a careless use of terms and a failure to distinguish between several autonomous organizations which are loosely associated together for common political purposes. Two parliamentary parties face each other in the House of Commons: they are correctly called "the Conservative Party" and "the Parliamentary Labour Party." Each is an autonomous organization which is aided for electoral purposes by a mass organization of its supporters: the Conservatives by "The National Union of Conservative and Unionist Associations," the Parliamentary Labour Party by a body properly known as "The Labour Party." At the regional and national level each of the mass organizations is sustained by a professional staff, the Conservative Central Office and the Labour Party head office. The mass organizations are best understood as voluntary associations of the politically-active members of the population who are prepared to work for the return to office of one or other of the parliamentary parties. Each mass organization represents a reservoir of largely voluntary and unpaid labour of the sort which is indispensable in the era of the mass electorate. All other functions of the mass organization are, and must remain, subsidiary to their primary task as vote-getting agencies. They can and do exact a certain price for their labour; they expect to be, and are, listened to by their leaders. Like Bagehot's constitutional monarch, the annual party conference has the right to be consulted, the right to encourage, and the right to warn. But this is not to say that the members of the mass organization have the right, under the British parliamentary system, to control or direct the actions of their parliamentary leaders.

The evolution of the British political parties in the era of the mass electorate has witnessed two striking developments, both of which reflect the ascendancy and the primacy of Parliament. Until well into the nineteenth century the Conservative Party was no more than a grouping of a few hundred Members of Parliament and Peers who were associated together for sustaining (whenever it proved feasible) a Conservative cabinet. They had neither a professional staff of any size nor a mass organization of voluntary supporters in the country; nor did they need them. They were able to rely for the most part on the allegiance and authority of the squirearchy and the generous financial contributions of a section of the business community to provide the very considerable financial resources which were required to win elections in the days of widespread political corruption. Two developments forced the Conservative Party to transform itself. The first was the rapid expansion of the electorate, especially in 1867 and afterwards; and the second, the drastic tightening of the electoral laws against corruption. Even if the Conservatives had not themselves become aware that these developments would force a transformation of the party, the initiative of the Liberals under Joseph Chamberlain would certainly have forced them to do so. In any event, a combination of pressures forced the Conservative Party to devise a mass organization of voluntary supporters to sustain the Conservative cause and to secure votes at elections. Disraeli and Lord Randolph Churchill provided a new statement of Toryism which succeeded in attracting a wide range of popular support, and a number of hard-working party managers did the job of building the National Union as the co-ordinating agency of Conservative activity in the country.

It was by no means certain (when Ostrogorski wrote at the end of the century) that the National Union or the Central Office (or both) might not manage ultimately to become the controlling influence in the affairs of the Conservative Party. Parliament might, as Ostrogorski feared, ultimately be supplanted by the caucus. But . . . this has not happened. Effective control of the affairs of the Conservative Party remains in the hands of the Leader thrown up by the parliamentary party and those he chooses as his associates; they retain their authority as long as they retain the support of their followers in Parliament. The National Union remains what it was declared to be in its earliest beginnings, a "handmaid" to the party in Parliament, although as befits a more democratic age, it has fairly frequently talked to its masters in a way that no Victorian domestic servant would ever have dared to do. The Conservative Party has been transformed since the mid-nineteenth century; it now has a large popular organization which labours on its behalf between and during elections; but the working of the parliamentary party has been remarkably little affected.

A combination of factors has helped to ensure the autonomy of the Conservative parliamentary party. The first has been the sharp awareness of the dangers of extra-parliamentary control on the part of the leaders of the party. The party had existed in Parliament long before it found it necessary to call its mass organization into being. Its leaders, familiar with the rules and conventions of cabinet government, were instinctively aware of the dangers of allowing the extra-parliamentary party to claim a decisive voice in the affairs of the party. Moreover their authority has been reinforced by the fact that the party has been so frequently and continuously in office during the modern period. (In the 77 years since 1886 the Conservatives have been in opposition for only 21 years.) While the Leader of any party is Prime Minister, and his principal colleagues constitute a cabinet, there can be no debate as to where, in principle, final authority in the party lies. In practice, the party's activists outside Parliament may on occasion become so bitterly hostile to policies of the parliamentary leadership that they can play a considerable part either in changing those policies or in overthrowing the existing Leadership. (This was certainly the case in 1922 when Austen Chamberlain, then Conservative Leader in the Commons and a member of the Lloyd George coalition, failed in his attempt to carry the Conservatives into a permanent alliance with the Lloyd George Liberals.) But, in general, party Leaders in office (whether Conservative, Liberal or Labour) have little to fear from their activists outside Parliament.

In addition, the traditional Conservative concepts of leadership and discipline have tended to discourage (although not to eliminate) the possibilities of rebellion. In all normal circumstances revolt against their leaders is furthest from the minds of even the most militant Conservative party workers. Subtle considerations of social deference towards their leading parliamentarians (especially when they are the Queen's ministers, as they tend to be for so much of the time) reinforce the party's own view that it is the prime duty of "followers" to sustain rather than to attempt to dominate their leaders. Except in comparatively rare circumstances, therefore, the Conservative extra-parliamentary organization does no more, so far as policy-making is concerned, than to fulfil its appointed rôle within the party organization: that is to offer advice (which may or may not be acted upon) to the party's parliamentary leaders.

This should not be taken to mean that the National Union has played a wholly insignificant part in the affairs of the Party. It loomed very large indeed in the great controversies over Tariff Reform before the First World War; it had to be taken seriously into account during the struggle over the Irish Treaty in 1921 and during the downfall of the Coalition in 1922. Baldwin was frequently in trouble with his followers outside Parliament and had to pay close attention to their views during the period of the General Strike and during the great debates on the future of India in the early 1930s.

Since 1945 the National Union appears to have had an explicit influence on party policy only on rare occasions. (As it did for example in the matter of the 300,000 houses issue.) . . . This may have been one consequence of the post-war "democratization" of the party undertaken by Lord Woolton. The annual conference is manifestly more representative of rank-and-file Conservative support in the country than ever before; right-wing ideological dogmatism has been much less in evidence than it was, for example, in Baldwin's day. But, in addition, for the twelve years after 1951 the party leaders constituted the government of the country and this in itself assured their absolute ascendancy within the party assemblies.

The transformation of the Labour Party in the half-century of its existence has been in one sense diametrically different from that of the Conservatives, although the end product is in certain important respects strikingly similar. While the Conservative Party in Parliament created a mass organization to serve its purposes, Labour began as a movement in the country which created a parliamentary party to give the working class a voice in the House of Commons. A gathering representing some hundreds of thousands of organized trade unionists and a few thousand members of socialist societies decided in 1900 to co-operate together for this purpose. They soon found it necessary to instruct their representatives in Parliament to form themselves into what amounted to a parliamentary party. This body began increasingly to resemble the other great parliamentary parties as it came to rival them in size and strength. By the time the Parliamentary Labour Party had taken office in 1924 its transformation was almost complete. By accepting all the conventions with respect to the office of Prime Minister and of Cabinet government it ensured that effective power within the party would be concentrated in the hands of the leadership of the PLP. When the party has been in power this proposition has been self-evident and largely unchallenged. Each of the two governments formed by MacDonald and by Attlee wielded not one whit less authority than other governments in comparable circumstances; nor were they in any sense subject to external direction by the party outside Parliament. Indeed, if the Labour Party had been as continuously in office as the Conservatives have been, it is highly likely that the issue of external control of the Parliamentary Party would be as nearly dead in the Labour Party as it is with the Conservatives.

But even with Labour so continuously in opposition the autonomy of the PLP and the authority of its leaders has been demonstrated beyond question. From Keir Hardie to Gaitskell the Leaders have repeatedly refused to accept external direction. They have taken the view expounded by Morgan Phillips, the former Secretary of the Party, " . . . the Parliamentary Party could not maintain its position in the country if it could be demonstrated that it was at any time or in any way subject to dictation from an outside body which, however representative of the Party, could not be regarded as representative of the country."[1] And it was particularly significant that, on the day of his election as Leader in 1963, Harold Wilson stated that he did not consider himself bound by the Labour Party conference resolution demanding withdrawal of the American Polaris base from Britain because that resolution had not been accepted by the Parliamentary Labour Party.

The Labour Party's devices for ensuring the ascendancy of the Parliamentary Party and its leaders . . . are infinitely more complex than those which obtain in the Conservative Party. But basically they have depended on the existence of a bond of confidence between the parliamentary leaders and a sufficient number of leading trade unionists to command preponderant support for the policies of the party leadership at the party conference. During most of Labour's history it has been overwhelmingly clear that the initiative in the main areas of policy-making (with the possible exception of industrial relations) has lain with the parliamentary leaders rather than with their trade union allies; the latter appear tacitly at least to have recognized that the leaders of the PLP, as a potential cabinet or "Shadow Government," cannot appear, even in opposition, to be reduced to the rôle of political spokesmen for the trade union movement or for the Labour Party conference, with its dominant trade union block vote.

. . . In all normal circumstances, Labour's parliamentary leaders (who, like their Conservative opposite numbers, will take into account the currents of opinion within all sections of the party in the course of determining their policies) are likely to be sustained by majority sup-

[1] M. Phillips, *Constitution of the Labour Party*, London, 1960, p. 4.

port within the PLP and the NEC, and in *both* the trade union and the constituency sections of the mass organization. Except on the rarest occasions in the history of the party it has been a Centre-Right majority in the PLP which has carried the day against a Left minority within each of the constituent elements of the party.

The left-wing activists in the constituencies have been repeatedly disillusioned on discovering that the party's rhetoric about "inner-party democracy" bears so little relation to its practice. R. H. S. Crossman, one of the recent heroes of the activists, has summarized the situation, as the militants tend to see it, with cruel precision:

> ... Since it could not afford, like its opponents, to maintain a large army of paid party workers, the Labour Party required militants — politically conscious socialists to do the work of organizing the constituencies. But since these militants tended to be "extremists," a constitution was needed which maintained their enthusiasm by apparently creating a full party democracy while excluding them from effective power. Hence the concession in principle of sovereign powers to the delegates at the Annual Conference, and the removal in practice of most of the sovereignty through the trade union block vote on the one hand, and the complete independence of the Parliamentary Labour Party on the other.[2]

The only occasion when the party's policy-decision mechanisms broke down completely was in 1960–61 when, on a major issue of policy, the party leadership was unable to win preponderant trade union support in the conference (although at Scarborough in 1960 two-thirds of the constituency delegates supported the parliamentary leadership). And in this profoundly important test case a sufficient number of the dissident unions subsequently reversed themselves in the following year to ensure that the next party conference would fall in line again with the Parliamentary Party.

Thereafter the autonomy of the PLP could hardly any longer be in dispute. But what was in dispute was whether the party could continue to cling to a policy-decision process which conveyed the *public* impression that Labour's parliamentary leaders (and therefore the alternative government) were repeatedly on the point of destruction at the hands of their more militant "supporters." In fact, of course, Gaitskell emerged from the struggle of 1960–61 a more powerful figure in his party than all but a very few Leaders of any of the main parties in this century. And this helped enormously to enhance his personal standing as a prospective Prime Minister. But the opinion polls and other evidence strongly suggest that the Labour party has suffered grave electoral damage as a consequence of its bitter public quarrels. Yet, incredibly enough, the party has made no move even to re-examine its decision-making processes in almost half a century.

Friction between parliamentary parties and their supporters outside

---

[2] R. H. S. Crossman, in his Introduction to the Fontana edition of Bagehot, W., *The English Constitution* (1963). To trace the gyrations in Crossman's own position, see p. 626 above, and n. 2.

Parliament is no doubt inevitable; the parliamentarians, in determining their policies, must take many factors into account and, whatever weight they may give to the views of their active supporters on particular issues, they cannot allow themselves to be reduced to the rôle of spokesmen of the active minority who control their extra-parliamentary organizations. The Labour party endowed itself with a party constitution which raised this danger in sharpest form. Yet the leadership group of the PLP, while paying lip-service to the theory of inner-party democracy, has repeatedly and consistently refused to accept direction from its extra-parliamentary supporters.

Setting aside the party myths and the inter-party propaganda it is clear that the primary function of the mass organizations of the Conservative and Labour parties is to sustain two competing teams of parliamentary leaders between whom the electorate as a whole may periodically choose. When the electorate has made its choice, the leaders of the successful team don the garments of authority which are provided under the Cabinet system and they retain this authority so long as they retain the confidence of their followers in Parliament (and, of course, of the electorate). Their followers outside Parliament become little more than a highly organized pressure group with a special channel of communication directly to the Leader, the Cabinet and the parliamentary party. Any disposition to take advantage of this special relationship is normally more than neutralized by feelings of pride and loyalty to their leaders and by an anxiety not to embarrass them in the execution of their duties or to provide aid and comfort to the rival team, who are eagerly preparing to overthrow them at the forthcoming election. Most governments at one time or another find it advisable to make concessions on some issue of policy to the clearly expressed views of their followers outside Parliament. But they make such concessions much more frequently to their followers *in* Parliament, on whose day-to-day support in the division lobbies the government depends, than they do to their followers in the country whose allegiance is tested normally only at five-yearly intervals. While the parliamentary party is in opposition it tends to listen more readily to the voices of its supporters in the country; but even while in opposition no major parliamentary party in the modern period has allowed itself to be relegated to the rôle of spokesman or servant of its mass organization.

Ostrogorski's fears notwithstanding, the institution of Parliament has survived almost unimpaired into the age of mass electorates and of mass parties. One of the few significant developments has been the decline of the independent Member of Parliament (although this has been a much less spectacular process than some have maintained)[3] and in addition, the diminishing freedom of action accorded to the independently-minded members of both of the great parties. As each parliamentary party has developed a vast, cumbersome, but highly organized appendage outside Parliament, the flexibility of parliamentary parties

---

[3] See D. E. Butler, *The Electoral System in Britain, 1918–1951*, pp. 153 ff.

has undoubtedly declined. The parliamentary leaders can be virtually certain that the withdrawal of the whip by the parliamentary party, if it is followed by expulsion from the mass organization, will result in the political death of the apostate concerned. In this respect it may be argued that the growth of the mass party has greatly increased the rigidity of party relationships in the House of Commons.

In such circumstances it would appear to be more than ever important that minority groups within each of the great parties should be given reasonable scope for expression of their views and for an opportunity to convert their fellow party members both in the House of Commons and in the mass party outside to their own point of view. Admittedly no party can tolerate a fully organized "party within a party"; this was shown conclusively by Labour's experience during the period 1929–31 . . . which culminated in the break with the ILP. It is largely because of this experience that the Labour Party has viewed all attempts to organize minority opinion within the party as an intolerable threat to its own survival. There are clearly-defined limits beyond which organized minorities cannot be permitted to go if the parent party is to function as a coherent contender for office. But the Labour Party appears to lean towards a dangerously rigorous conception of party discipline which sometimes appears to resemble the Communist conception of democratic centralism. If both major parties become too grimly intolerant of honest differences of opinion among their followers on major matters of policy then there are real grounds for concern in a period in which the prospects for minor parties and independent candidates are so poor. The danger has been more evident in the case of the Labour Party; but in another form it is no less real in the case of the Conservatives. They have found it less necessary to rely on rigid codes of discipline; this may be in part a reflection of the fact that ideological disputes culminating in threatened party splits are rare. But . . . the Conservatives have tolerated a type of constituency discipline applied to certain of their MPs which has been almost as harsh in its effects as the disciplinary codes imposed by the PLP. If the two great parties together are to dominate the whole political life of the community, then it is essential that every encouragement should be given to the expression of honest political differences within each. These differences become a source of concern only if they threaten the ability of a party to form and sustain a government. Short of this, intra-party differences must be welcomed as an indispensable means of preventing the sort of intellectual sclerosis which appears at times to threaten the two great parties of this country.

Apart from these particular sources of concern, one must face the more fundamental question as to whether the present system of party organization in Great Britain deserves the label "democratic." Because the party leaders in Parliament do not hold themselves directly responsible to the members of the party outside Parliament it is sometimes alleged that this proves that both great parties are "undemocratic." Or, as some would argue, it provides a triumphant vindication of the "iron law of oligarchy" associated with the name of Robert Michels. Certainly the analysis in Parts I and II of this study has shown that there is ample evidence of the working of what Michels calls the "technical" and "psychological" factors which tend to ensure the emergence of, and the retention of power by, a small group of leaders in each party. But evidence has also been provided (it is perhaps more extensive in the history of the Conservative Party than in the Labour Party) of revolts against the party leaders which have culminated in their overthrow. The "law of oligarchy" is certainly not an "iron" law. Parties are usually content to be led; but this is largely because there is no other way in which they can operate. This does not mean, however, that party leadership groups can ignore with impunity the moods and aspirations of their followers; they must carry their followers (and above all their followers in their parliamentary party) with them. And to do so, they have to take into account at every stage the clearly-defined currents of opinion within their party. Blind appeals to loyalty (either to the person of the Leader or to the party itself) are frequently resorted to, and often they achieve their purpose. But they are rarely successful in bridging a real gulf when one does develop between the leaders and their followers.

Another factor must be taken into account in assessing the relevance of Michels' theories. Largely no doubt as a result of his own continental background, Michels appeared to assume that a "democratic" political party ought ideally to be under the direction and control of its mass membership. Michels suggested that this relationship never proves feasible in practice because of the operation of his law of oligarchy. But in the British context there is another reason of greater importance: the conventions of the parliamentary system (which have been accepted by all parties, including the Labour Party) require that Members of Parliament, and therefore parliamentary parties also, must hold themselves responsible solely to the electorate and not to the mass organization of their supporters outside Parliament. In other words, a crude application of Michels' theories would ignore what might be termed the division of labour within British political parties. It would ignore the fact that the primary function of the mass organizations is to sustain competing teams of potential leaders in the House of Commons in order that the electorate as a whole may choose between them. All other functions (involving attempts by the mass organizations to influence the formulation of policy and the emergence of leaders within the parliamentary parties) are, and must remain, subsidiary. The mass organizations may be permitted to play some part in these respects; but if they attempted to arrogate to themselves a determining influence with respect to policy or leadership they would be cutting across the chain of responsibility from Cabinet, to Parliament, to electorate, which is fundamental to the theory of the British parliamentary system.

But Michels apart, many of the other criticisms of the alleged undemocratic nature of party organization reflect a persistent belief in what might be termed the classical conception of the democratic process.

In a penetrating analysis of the shortcomings of this classical conception, Joseph Schumpeter has shown how little relation it bears to the democratic process as it has evolved in Britain and most other political democracies.[4] In the late eighteenth century it was assumed that the democratic process would ensure the triumph of the common good by permitting the people themselves to decide issues through the election of representatives who assembled to carry out "the people's will." The electorate, it was assumed, might be called on to pronounce on certain major issues (perhaps by means of referenda); all other issues would be decided by a committee (Parliament) elected by the whole adult population. The function of the members of this committee would be to voice, reflect or represent the will of the electorate. Lip-service is still paid to this classical conception of democracy even by many who are aware of the extent to which it has proved unworkable. The study of the psychology of political processes has revealed the importance of the extra-rational and the irrational elements in social behaviour. The parallel development of the arts of political propaganda has enabled political leaders to exploit the irrational element in human behaviour and to manufacture what is often a purely synthetic "general will"; so much so that some are prepared to argue, with Schumpeter, that the will of the people is the product and not the motive power of the political process.

It has also become increasingly evident that the classical theory attributed to the electorate an altogether unrealistic degree of initiative; it came near to ignoring completely the importance of leadership in the political process. It is no doubt more realistic to argue that the essence of the democratic process is that it should provide a free competition for political leadership. The essential rôle of the electorate is not to reach decisions on specific issues of policy but to decide which of two or more competing teams of potential leaders shall make the decisions. The democratic process ensures that there will be a periodic opportunity for the electorate to review the record of the decision-makers who currently hold office; and, if the electorate wishes, it may replace them with an alternative team. The competing teams usually offer broad declarations of policy respecting their long-range goals; they may also promise to introduce specific items of legislation; or alternatively they may, like the National Government formed in 1931, ask only for a "Doctor's Mandate" to do whatever they may subsequently decide to be necessary in the national interest. In the formulation of electoral programs the mass party usually plays some part, although in both the Conservative and Labour Parties final decisions in this regard rest with the parliamentary leaders. These leaders are bound to be concerned mainly with their own conception of the national interest and with the competing demands of various interest groups which may or may not be adequately reflected within their party organizations. But one thing

---

[4] J. A. Schumpeter, *Capitalism, Socialism and Democracy*, London, 1952, pp. 250 ff.

is certain: initiative in the formulation of policy cannot possibly come primarily from the several millions of party supporters or from the electorate as a whole. The active party workers must devote themselves primarily to sustaining the teams of candidates for leadership between whom the electorate may choose (although the interest group system enables those elements in the electorate who wish to do so to press their views and demands on the team that secures office).

The mass organizations of the Conservative and Labour Parties have, of course, additional functions which have been examined in some detail in the course of this study. They serve as a two-way channel of communication between the leaders of the parliamentary parties and their supporters in the country; when the parliamentary party is in office its mass organization plays a vital rôle in explaining and defending the work of the government and in keeping it informed of currents of opinion in the country. A further function of the mass political organizations is to provide a means whereby the politically active individuals in the community can play some part, however limited, in influencing both the formulation of party policy and the emergence of party leaders. And for those citizens who seek to play a more influential part in the political life of the community, participation in the mass organizations provides an excellent preliminary training for parliamentary candidature and eventual entry into Parliament.

Seen from the viewpoint of society as a whole, mass political parties of the kind that have emerged in Britain fulfil an invaluable set of functions. By exposing the electorate to a cross-fire of political argument and debate they stimulate public interest in the essential business of "attending to the arrangements of society." The mass parties also fulfil an important integrating function. They are one of the main channels through which interest groups and both organized and unorganized bodies of opinion can bring their views to the attention of parliamentarians. The parliamentary leaders in turn must weigh and evaluate the views that are conveyed through these and other channels. Inevitably these views are taken into account in the formulation of parliamentary policy.[5] Lord Bryce saw American parties as "brokers" whose primary business it was to serve various interests and to reconcile them. In the much more homogeneous society of Britain the mass parties are inevitably less preoccupied with this task; they do nevertheless play an important rôle in integrating the diverse and sometimes conflicting interests and opinions in the community. But this study has been concerned not with the broad social function of parties but with their internal structure and the distribution of power within each. And no emphasis on the auxiliary functions of the mass organizations outside Parliament can be allowed to obscure the basic proposition that the mass parties are primarily the servants of their respective parlia-

---

[5] For a fuller statement of the present writer's views on the rôle of interest groups in the political system see R. T. McKenzie, "Parties, Pressure Groups and the British Political Process," *The Political Quarterly,* Jan.–Mar., 1958, pp. 5–16.

mentary parties; that their principal function is to sustain teams of parliamentary leaders between whom the electorate is periodically invited to choose.

If this is a fair description of the realities of the democratic process then it should be evident that the two major British political parties are well suited to play an appropriate rôle in this process. They have managed to avoid most of the serious pitfalls into which party organizations in many other countries have fallen. The ideological conflict between the parties is not so great as to threaten the survival of the democratic process itself; yet it is great enough to ensure that the members of the mass organizations of the two main parties will work willingly for the victory of their cause without seeking illicit material rewards for their efforts. The autonomy of the two great parliamentary parties is almost completely unimpaired, although each of them has devised a system of consultation with its mass organization which ensures that the latter will not be so exasperated with its impotence as to refuse to fulfil its function as a vote-getting agency. Each major party has organized a professional machine which works alongside the mass organization and ensures the latter's efficiency without appearing too obviously to dominate it. Neither of these machines has in any way threatened to become the real centre of power within its respective party organization. Both great parties have tapped large-scale financial resources without becoming completely beholden to those who provide the funds; neither party in office has sacrificed its conception of the national interest in order to serve the purposes of those sections of the community which finance its operations.

Reference has been made throughout this study to serious shortcomings in each of the major party organizations; there is plenty of scope for the reformer in both the Conservative and Labour Parties. There may also be scope for those who seek to modify or to transform other aspects of British parliamentary democracy. But an extensive review of the working of British party organizations inspires neither alarm nor gloom; sixty years after Ostrogorski wrote there appears to be no reason to conclude that events have justified his pessimistic expectation that the parliamentary system was unlikely to survive the emergence of the mass party. It might be argued, indeed, that the parliamentary system gives every appearance of outliving the age of the mass party; there is much evidence to support the view that the traditional electoral activities of the mass party, including the conduct of public meetings, canvassing and the rest, are now of declining importance in influencing the outcome of elections. It seems likely that the really effective electioneering of the future will rely increasingly on the newer mass media of radio and, above all, of television. Perhaps in retrospect it will be evident that the mass party saw its heyday during the period when the extension of the franchise had created a mass electorate, but there was as yet no effective means of reaching the voters in their own homes. But meanwhile, there can be no doubt that despite the many new problems it created, the mass party did not fulfil the gloomy expectations of its early chroniclers. Perhaps the most apt conclusion for this study can be borrowed from Lord Bryce's foreword (written in 1902) to the first edition of Ostrogorski's *Democracy and the Organization of Political Parties*. Bryce had praised Ostrogorski's work very highly, but he questioned his preoccupation with "the pathology of party government." Bryce concluded: "In England, happily for England, the party organizations have not ceased to be controlled by men occupying a position which makes them amenable to public opinion, nor have they as yet departed far from those traditions in which the strength of English free government lies." Bryce's observation is equally valid to-day.

GERHARD LOEWENBERG

The Remaking of the German Party System

In one lifetime, the median German voter has seen his political system change greatly, from the instability of the Weimar Republic of the 1920's through Hitler's Reich to a seemingly stable system in which two major parties seek the spoils of office. Accounting for these changes presents major challenges to social scientists. Are they the consequence of economic or social change common to many lands? Are they the consequence of particular cultural factors? Or, do specifically political conditions primarily account for events in Germany in the past half-century? The theory appropriate to one phase of this history need not necessarily fit other phases. Gerhard Loewenberg summarizes the record of these changes and of theories of change. He concludes by emphasizing the importance of political influences, not least the four-power military occupation brought about by the failures of generations of German politicians.

Within the last 40 years the German party system has undergone remarkably rapid and fundamental changes. In the last normal pre-Hitler election in 1928, 15 parties won seats in the Reichstag. The Weimar Republic, in Sartori's terms, was a clear case of a "pluralistic polarized polity."[1] Five and one-half years later, the Nazi regime had outlawed or caused the dissolution of all political parties but one. The resulting one-party state survived for only a dozen of the 1,000 years for which it had been planned and was in turn followed by an interregnum of no-party military government. A famous directive issued to General Eisenhower in April, 1945, stated:

> No political activities of any kind shall be countenanced unless authorized by you.[2]

But after four months of government without political parties, the military occupation began to authorize their reappearance; within three years an even dozen were again on the scene. While informed observers then unanimously anticipated the re-creation of an "extreme pluralism," what Sartori calls "moderate pluralism" developed instead. Between these two types of party system Sartori finds all the difference in the world. He associates extreme pluralism with "centrifugal drives . . . ideological rigidity . . . marked cleavage at the elite level . . . the absence of real alternative government . . . [and] the growth of irresponsible opposition. . . ." It produces a "political system badly fitted for the absorption of change." By contrast, he believes that "whenever a situation of moderate pluralism is stabilized, orderly change is likely, and the party system is able to perform a cohesive and integrative function."[3]

It is the purpose of this article to examine and explain the profound changes which have taken place in the German party system and in the process to test various theories of party system change. The most commonly held hypothesis — that party systems merely reflect basic social and economic "realities" — does not adequately explain the German case. The most basic social and economic changes which occurred in Germany after the advent of political parties came with the industrial revolution in the latter part of the nineteenth century. The resulting urban, industrialized society was entirely consistent with an "extreme pluralism" in the party system which in many respects had antedated industrialization; in fact, the complexity of Germany's post-industrial social and economic structure was generally regarded as a

---

From *Polity* I, 1, 1968, pp. 87–113, with footnotes abridged and a new concluding paragraph by the author. Reprinted by permission.

[1] Giovanni Sartori, "European Political Parties: The Case of Polarized Pluralism," in Joseph LaPalombara and Myron Weiner, eds., *Political Parties and Political Development* (Princeton, 1966), p. 153.

[2] JCS 1067 (April, 1945), reprinted in Beate Ruhm von Oppen, *Documents on Germany Under Occupation* (London, 1955), p. 19.

[3] Sartori, *op. cit.*, pp. 137, 159–61, 175.

mainstay of extreme party multiplicity. Only the dramatic *political* changes of 1933 and 1945 disrupted this pattern of pluralism.

The explanations of party systems in terms of political culture are even less convincing, especially for the rapid German development since 1919, for they would imply that

> we could possibly have on record three types of German political culture, namely, fifteen years of cultural fragmentation, ten years of monolithism, and now an integrated and moderately pluralistic political culture.[4]

At best, a much more refined — and verifiable — concept of political culture than that generally employed would be necessary to make such a hypothesis tenable for Germany.

Finally, the hypothesis that electoral systems determine party systems is not persuasive in the German case either. For despite appearances to the contrary, proportional representation, which was generally regarded as a cause of the fragmentation of the party system during the Weimar Republic, has been essentially maintained in the postwar period. Under the Weimar regime, parties received one seat in the Reichstag for every 60,000 votes they attracted nationally; in the Federal Republic, the number of seats each party receives in the Bundestag is also directly proportional to the popular vote it has won nationally, although a 5 percent minimum vote is now required for parliamentary representation. This is, admittedly, a new and important qualification. One must nevertheless remember that the fragmented German party system established itself nationally during the Bismarckian Empire, when a system of elections in single-member constituencies with two ballots was in effect and that fragmentation diminished while the essentials of proportional representation remained in effect. No simple relationship between proportional representation and extreme pluralism can therefore be established for Germany.

The sharp discontinuities in the development of the German party system do not seem to correlate readily either with socio-economic or with "cultural" change, nor in any simple manner with the advent of proportional representation. Quite obviously, however, party system change has been associated with changes in the political regime: with the accession of Hitler to power and the rule of military government. It is the thesis of this article that these political factors are the critical variables in the change of the German party system. Socio-economic factors are intervening variables; they were necessary but not sufficient to produce changes in the party system. To support this hypothesis, we will first examine the pattern of social and economic change in Germany and then consider the policies of the Nazi regime and of the military government affecting political parties, indicating how the interaction between these factors can account for the emergence of the new German party system.

---

[4] *Ibid.*, pp. 165–66.

I. ECONOMIC AND SOCIAL CHANGE

The industrialization of Germany occurred very rapidly during the 43 years between the founding of the second Empire and the First World War. "On the eve of the founding of the Reich," the authoritative economic history by Stolper notes, "Germany's economic character was predominantly agricultural, but the process of industrialization had begun." In 1860, German pig iron production was only half a million tons, less than one seventh of British and about 60 per cent of French production. By 1910 Germany produced 15 million tons of pig iron, 50 percent more than Britain, and nearly four times as much as France. In 1913 Germany produced seven times as much coal and lignite as she had 42 years earlier; she had pulled even with British production, which had been three times as great as Germany's in 1871. These dramatic economic developments were of course accompanied by social changes. In 1871, 64 percent of the population lived in towns of under 2000 inhabitants; by 1910, three fifths of the population was urban, an almost complete reversal. By the first World War two thirds of the working force were engaged in industry, commerce, or service trades. "After the founding of the Reich," Stolper writes, "agriculture and industry exchanged their relative importance in Germany's economic life. . . . Within a few years Germany had joined the ranks of the leading industrial nations."

However, these economic developments, far from reducing the number of existing political parties, added to them. By 1871 a multiplicity of conservative, liberal, and regional parties already existed in the various German states; they persisted in the face of industrialization, national unification, and the introduction of universal manhood suffrage. These developments, particularly the growth of an industrial working class, merely generated support for two new parties: the Catholic Center party, founded in 1871, and the Social Democratic party, organized in 1875. Economic modernization thus only accentuated the pattern of extreme pluralism. In excluding the party leaders in the Reichstag from cabinet positions, the constitution of the Empire did nothing to encourage the amalgamation of parties for purposes of gaining power. But the Weimar Constitution, which opened the way to party government, did not produce a reduction in the number of parties either. On the contrary, the radicalism of the 1920's merely added new formations to the party system.

It has long been recognized that the industrial revolution left many of the traditional social structures intact in Germany. Despite the rapid economic development of the late nineteenth century, class, region, church, and family continued to be very influential, preserving traditional values amidst economic change. The German party system reflected these older social groups, while also expressing new ones in the form of parties representing specifically economic interests. On the eve of the Nazi dictatorship, therefore, the German party system, like the German social system, still exhibited great continuity with the pattern existing 60 years earlier at the founding of the Empire, although the German economy had been profoundly changed.

Only the coercive political measures of a totalitarian regime finally destroyed the traditional party system. Within half a year of coming to power the Hitler government outlawed all party organizations except that of the Nazis; some parties, including the powerful Center, had disbanded themselves even before the final decree. The persecution of party leaders forced many into exile or concentration camps; before the collapse of the regime in 1945, particularly in its final months after the unsuccessful attempt on Hitler's life in July, 1944, a large number of the old party leaders were executed.

Less deliberately, but nonetheless powerfully, the Nazi regime destroyed some of the traditional social structures which had supported the multi-party system. The social consequences of Nazism have recently been explored by two authors, a historian and a sociologist, who have each made efforts to assess the Nazi regime in the perspective of long-term social change in Germany. Both reach the same conclusion: Nazism destroyed much of the traditional social structure which had until then resisted the influence of economic modernization. Although Nazi ideology abounded with nostalgic references to traditional German values, Nazi reality "was the very opposite of what Hitler had presumably promised and what the majority of his followers had expected him to fulfill."

> In 1939 [writes historian David Schoenbaum] the cities were larger, not smaller; the concentration of capital greater than before; the rural population reduced, not increased; women not at the fireside but in the office and the factory; the inequality of income and property distribution more, not less conspicuous; industry's share of the gross national product up and agriculture's down, while industrial labor had it relatively good and small business increasingly bad.[5]

Ralf Dahrendorf, postwar Germany's most perceptive sociologist, has explicitly placed the Nazi era in the mainstream of German social development. He believes that industrialization failed to democratize Germany because its economic changes had been assimilated to traditional German political and social structures. It failed to make citizens out of subjects, failed to alter the pattern of political decision making by authority, failed to produce a democratic political elite, and failed to alter the preference for private over public virtues.[6]

> Neither in the sense of a society of citizens nor in that of one dominated by a confident bourgeoisie did a modern society emerge. In order to establish the political institutions of liberal democracy in the society

---

[5] David Schoenbaum, *Hitler's Social Revolution: Class and Status in Nazi Germany 1933–1939* (New York, 1966), p. 298.

[6] Ralf Dahrendorf, *Society and Democracy in Germany* (New York, 1967), pp. 387–388.

that did emerge, a social revolution was necessary, but the Weimar Republic held up rather than realized that revolution. . . .[7]

It is his bold conclusion that

> National Socialism completed for Germany the social revolution that was lost in the faultings of Imperial Germany and again held up by the contradictions of the Weimar Republic. . . . Brutal as it was, the break with tradition and thus a strong push toward modernity was the substantive characteristic of the social revolution of National Socialism.[8]

Like Schoenbaum, Dahrendorf notes "the contradiction between the ideology and practice of National Socialism." Regardless of what the Nazis proclaimed, they had to "break the traditional, and in effect antiliberal, loyalties for region and religion, family and corporation, in order to realize their claim to total power. Hitler needed modernity, little as he liked it."[9]

The conclusions of Schoenbaum and Dahrendorf point to the sharp differences between prewar and postwar German society. Nazi *Gleichschaltung* and the population movements prompted by the war and the occupation effectively loosened traditional regional ties. Defeat and occupation destroyed the political existence of Prussia, and its feudal pattern of landholding. They destroyed German industry and created the need for a second industrial revolution. To lead it, a new managerial elite developed, the values of which differed sharply from those of its aristocratic predecessor. This new industrial management preferred enterprise and competition to monopoly and cartel. According to Lipset, where paternalism had governed the relationship between owners and workers, "the set of managerial ideologies characteristic of the more stable welfare democracies of northern and western Europe" began to prevail.[10] The growth of a large "service class" attenuated the simple two-sidedness of class distinctions.[11] The rapid growth of economic prosperity helped in any case to integrate the working class into society to the point where its members no longer took a class view of voting alternatives. In short, the second industrial revolution had far more profound social consequences than the first, because it took place against a background of the social disintegration of the old order which had been caused by Nazism and the war.

Dahrendorf bases his interpretation on the conviction that "contrary to the beliefs of many, the industrial revolution is not the prime mover of the modern world at all."[12] Instead, social change is the chief

---

[7] *Ibid.*, p. 397.
[8] *Ibid.*, pp. 402, 403.
[9] *Ibid.*, pp. 402 ff.
[10] Seymour M. Lipset, "The Changing Class Structure and Contemporary European Politics," in Stephen R. Graubard, ed., *A New Europe?* (Boston, 1964), p. 344.
[11] Ralf Dahrendorf, "Recent Changes in the Class Structure of European Societies," in Graubard, pp. 310–318.
[12] Dahrendorf, *Society and Democracy in Germany*, pp. 46 ff.

determinant and social change did not correspond with economic modernization in nineteenth-century Germany. The social structure of the Empire developed "faultings" which prevented systematic change until the Nazi revolution upset the precarious edifice.

The distinction between economic and social change is indeed important in the case of Germany. But to emphasize this distinction Dahrendorf focuses unduly on the influence of Nazism on German society. There is important evidence to suggest that social, like economic, change occurred in Germany over a long period. Family structure, for example, apparently began to change as early as the pre-World War I period. Well before the crises of the 1930's, the "authoritarian family," a favorite explanation of Germany's authoritarian politics, showed signs of yielding to a pattern of mixed family authority under the impact of the long-term forces of industrialization and urbanization. There is also evidence that the advent of women's suffrage in 1919 began a process of change in the political role of women. The sharp social criticism to be found in much of the literature and drama of the 1920's also gives signs of the erosion of the traditional social pattern.

But in contrast to these social changes, the multiple party system remained remarkably stable. The fragmentation along ideological, regional, religious, and class lines to be found in the voting pattern of 1928 bears marked similarity to the pattern of a generation earlier. The tenacity of this distribution of political attitudes in the face of profound changes in both the social and economic substructure of politics casts doubt on any simple correlation between economic, social, and political change. Recent studies of political socialization give one explanation for the absence of such simple relationships. They show that in a modern society, there is no direct transfer of attitudes from the family to the political domain; the two worlds are apparently too dissimilar.[13]

In his emphasis on social change as the basis of modernization, Dahrendorf fails to make explicit the role of political factors in determining the pace and the shape of social change. It is, of course, implicit in his whole interpretation that Nazism, a political force, brought long-delayed social changes to a head, and that the West German regime is giving Germany's changed social structure a shape entirely different from that given it by the East German regime. As he writes, the Nazi revolution "gave German society an irreversible push, which exposed it to totalitarian dangers and opened it to liberal changes at the same time."[14]

Thus it seems clear that social changes alone can no more account for changes in the German party system, than can economic changes. A marked discontinuity characterizes German modernization, between rapid economic change in the late nineteenth century, gradual social

---

[13] Gabriel A. Almond and Sidney Verba, *The Civic Culture* (Princeton, 1963), pp. 373–74.

[14] Dahrendorf, *Society and Democracy in Germany*, p. 403.

change throughout the twentieth century, and abrupt political changes after 1933. It is just this discontinuity which permits us to distinguish between economic, social, and political determinants of the German party system. Because the German party system remained stable for so long in the face of economic and social transformation, while changing so basically within the relatively short period of time since 1933, a study of this party system must seek the critical variable in the political domain.

II. POLICIES OF THE ALLIED MILITARY GOVERNMENT

The heritage of 12 years of totalitarian government was not only a changed social environment, but also a sharply interrupted party tradition, and a regime of foreign military occupation with its own externally-determined objectives for the party system. The Soviet military government sought to re-establish a party system which would mobilize the entire electorate, including its anticommunist elements, while enabling the Communist party to dominate the political process. By licensing only four political parties — only three remained after the enforced Communist-Socialist fusion — and eventually requiring them to enter elections on a single slate, Communist hegemony was fully achieved in the Soviet zone of occupation.

The political objectives of the Western Allies in their zones were entirely different. Initially, they were wholly subordinate to military security. Military government was to restore law and order by making use of available German administrative personnel; it was to "permit freedom of speech and press, and of religious worship, subject to military exigencies and the prohibition of Nazi propaganda"; and it was to purge Nazis from public positions.[15]

As the actual occupation of Germany proceeded, it became apparent that military government would have a far more profound influence on German politics than had been anticipated, like it or not. German government had collapsed so completely in the wake of unconditional surrender that military government was compelled to make basic decisions affecting political reconstruction immediately upon its arrival. In the absence of pre-established policy, improvisation ruled.[16]

Everywhere, German personnel had to be recruited to man essential administrative services. The only policy requirement was that former Nazis were to be excluded. But for identifying non-Nazis, little explicit guidance had been provided. In many cases military government units

---

[15] CCS 551, quoted in Paul Y. Hammond, "Directives for the Occupation of Germany: The Washington Controversy," in Harold Stein, ed., *American Civil-Military Decisions* (Birmingham, Ala., 1963), p. 329.

[16] *Ibid.*, pp. 389–391; 422–423. Hammond shows that the absence of policy was due to Roosevelt's procrastination, the sharp controversy between the views of the State and Treasury Departments, and the Army's traditional view that a military government should not unnecessarily disturb the political structure of the occupied country; see pp. 319, 348–388.

did have lists of old Weimar politicians who could be trusted, although these lists were often useless since prominent political survivors were hard to find. Nevertheless, on the basis of these lists the men who had been the mayors of Cologne and Munich before 1933, Konrad Adenauer and Karl Scharnagl, were reappointed to these posts. In predominantly Catholic regions, as a rule of thumb, the advice of the clergy was sought, leading, for example, to the selection of Fritz Schäffer as the first Minister-President in Bavaria. Many old Bavarian and Center party politicians were appointed in this way. In Protestant areas where church advice was not similarly trusted, there was a tendency to rely on political outsiders, frequently intellectuals, such as Ludwig Bergsträsser and Carlo Schmid. Specialists who had been in private life during the Nazi period were also frequently recruited, such as the business consultant Ludwig Erhard. In most cases, the earliest appointees went on to develop prominent political careers, favored by an early start at a formative moment. In this way military government strongly influenced the composition of the new political class. Without seeking any specific political objectives, the military occupation facilitated the re-establishment of political leaders from the strongest of the center parties of the Weimar Republic and the entry into political life of intellectuals and other professionals who had not previously had political experience.[17]

Improvisation likewise governed the revival of political parties. During the first four months of occupation the formation of parties was prohibited, but political activity of many kinds was nevertheless allowed. "Freedom of speech, press, and religious worship will be permitted" and "all religious institutions will be respected," read the relevant United States military directive.[18] As a result, military government destroyed the spontaneous attempts to form new political groupings which occurred in several German cities immediately after Nazi forces were driven out. These "antifa" organizations, composed usually of Social Democrats and Communists, were quickly disbanded.[19]

However, informal organizing activity by surviving leaders of the Weimar parties was permitted. The best preserved of these, the Social Democratic party, which had been outlawed by the Nazis but had continued an underground and an exile existence, was soon being reorganized. Kurt Schumacher, a prominent SPD leader who had spent most of the Nazi period in a concentration camp, established an SPD city committee in Hanover almost immediately after the Allies had

[17] Lutz Niethammer, "Amerikanische Besatzung und bayerische Politik (1945)," *Vierteljahrshefte für Zeitgeschichte*, XV (1967), pp. 164–65, 173, 179–80; Harold Zink, *The United States in Germany, 1944–1955* (Princeton, 1957), pp. 170–75; F. Roy Willis, *The French in Germany, 1945–1949* (Stanford, 1962), pp. 185–90.

[18] JCS 1067, *op. cit.*, p. 19.

[19] Niethammer, *op. cit.*, p. 190; Leonard Krieger, "The Inter-Regnum in Germany: March–August 1945," *Political Science Quarterly*, LXIV (1949), pp. 513–14; 517–18; Lewis Edinger, *Kurt Schumacher, A Study in Personality and Political Behavior* (Stanford, 1965), p. 95.

driven the Nazis from the city in April 1945, even before the final surrender.[20] The next largest Weimar party, the Catholic Center, had ignominiously disbanded itself in July, 1933, after having approved Hitler's enabling law.[21] But some of its surviving leaders were meeting soon after the surrender to plan a new Christian Democratic party. In Berlin, Cologne, Frankfurt, and Munich they were joined in varying numbers by Catholic and Protestant clergy, Catholic intellectuals, and political conservatives, and considering the creation of a new, interdenominational center party.[22] Their efforts were supported by the Catholic church, as Social Democratic efforts were supported by labor union leaders. In this early period, these major interest groups provided an important organizational nucleus for political activity since open party organization and a party press were banned. The informal organizing activity of these early months gave a head start to certain groups which they never again lost.

The early period of military government improvisation came to an end with the unilateral decision of the Soviet military authorities to permit within their zone "the formation and activity of all antifascist parties having as their aim the final extirpation of all remnants of fascism." In rapid succession, the Communist, Socialist, Christian Democratic and Liberal parties were licensed in the Soviet Zone. Continued prohibition of political parties in the Western zones became untenable. On August 2, at Potsdam, the four Allies agreed that "local self-government shall be restored throughout Germany on democratic principles and in particular through elective councils," and that "all democratic political parties . . . shall be allowed and encouraged throughout Germany." This obliged the Western Allies to begin licensing political parties in their zones, with the only requirement that they be "democratic." But since parties had to be established before electoral competition could take place, it was nearly impossible to determine the commitment to democracy on the part of applicants. In practice, "democratic" was therefore equated with "antifascist."[23] Most of the non-Nazi parties which applied were eventually licensed. However, the need to license parties compelled the Allied military governments to develop some explicit procedures and policies and these had a pronounced effect on the parties which first entered the field.

Both the French and the American military governments insisted that parties in their zones be formed first on the most local level of government; this was the level at which elections would first be held. Such a requirement was to assure that the parties have "grass roots." Almost everywhere the Communist party was first in line for a license,

---

[20] Edinger, *op. cit.*, p. 71.

[21] Erich Matthias and Rudolf Morsey, *Das Ende der Parteien 1933* (Düsseldorf, 1960), pp. 353–367; 395–417.

[22] Arnold J. Heidenheimer, *Adenauer and the CDU* (The Hague, 1960), Ch. 2.

[23] Dolf Sternberger, "Parties and Party Systems in Postwar Germany," *Annals of the American Academy of Political and Social Science*, CCLX (November, 1948), pp. 11–22.

easily qualifying as "democratic" by the going definition. Social Democrats (SPD) and Christian Democrats (CDU) as well as a liberal Free Democratic party (FDP) followed suit, so that four parties were in the field in nearly all localities for the first local elections, exactly those four which had had a head start in establishing themselves during the earlier period of the party ban. The United States military government screened applicants for licenses for their political backgrounds, the sources of their funds, and their proposed party statutes, in order to prevent the establishment of neo-Nazi parties. Eventually the requirement that parties must have a democratic organization and must account publicly for the sources of their funds found its way into the German constitution and became the basis for outlawing both the Communists and a radical right-wing party.

Although the French barred what appeared to them to be minor, regional parties, the British and American authorities did not practice such discrimination. In the British zone, a traditional Lower-Saxon State party (later to become the German party) was licensed, and, after some delay, so was a successor to the old Center party; the Americans licensed the Economic Reconstruction Association, an idiosyncratic creation of a right-wing Bavarian leader, and also the Bavarian party, which had notable Weimar antecedents but which applied too late to participate either in the constituent assembly or in the first state legislature.

The disenfranchisement of former Nazis kept nearly six percent of otherwise eligible voters from participating in the earliest state elections; modifications of these restrictions by 1948 provided an electoral base for an extreme right-wing party, which explicitly denied Nazi sympathies, but was nevertheless given a hard time by the occupation authorities, gaining sporadic recognition only in the British and parts of the American zones.

The Allied military governments agreed not to license any parties specifically appealing to refugees and expellees from the East. They feared the revanchism such groups might exhibit, and were anxious to assimilate the newcomers into West German society. Because of variation in policies and applicants among the zones of occupation, therefore, only the four parties first licensed were able to operate in all of western Germany, and only these four eventually presented candidates in all states for the first parliamentary election in 1949.[24]

The sequence of party formation also varied somewhat among the zones. The United States military government began licensing political

[24] Richard M. Scammon, "Political Parties," in Edward H. Litchfield, ed., *Governing Postwar Germany* (Ithaca, 1953), pp. 475–80; Seymour R. Bolten, "Military Government and the German Political Parties," *Annals of the American Academy of Political and Social Science*, CCLXVII (January, 1950), p. 55; F. Roy Willis, *op. cit.*, pp. 190–96; Raymond Ebsworth, *Restoring Democracy in Germany; The British Contribution* (London, 1960), Ch. 2; James K. Pollock and James H. Meisel, *Germany Under Occupation: Illustrative Materials and Documents* (Ann Arbor, 1947), p. 144. Ossip K. Flechtheim, *Dokumente zur parteipolitischen Entwicklung in Deutschland seit 1945* (Berlin, 1962), Vol. I, pp. 33, 38, 51.

parties on August 27, 1945, the British and French following in October and December of that year. The Americans were also quickest to respond to the pressure to hold elections, permitting the first local governments to be elected on January 20, 1946; in the British and French zones this did not take place until September. On the basis of these local elections, all three military governments appointed consultative assemblies which, in the British and French zones, drafted state constitutions, and in the American zone formulated an electoral law for the election of constituent assemblies. These appointed bodies, at best reflecting party strength in the sometimes hasty rural and municipal elections, established the ground rules for subsequent statewide election contests. By that time each of the four initially licensed parties had state-wide (and informal national) organizations, before they had ever submitted themselves to electorates above the purely local level.[25]

In working out the first postwar electoral laws, the appointed German assemblies mostly opted for proportional representation, the system in effect in the Weimar Republic, and the safest system for parties uncertain of their respective strengths. Only in the British zone did Allied military government intervene with a preference for a single-member constituency system with plurality voting. As a result, a mixed system was established there which later became the model for federal legislation on the subject.[26] The constituent assemblies themselves, dominated by the four parties first licensed, wrote one restriction on proportional representation into most constitutions. This provided that parties failing to receive five (or ten) percent of the votes would be denied their proportional share of seats. This restriction was obviously motivated by the desire of the earliest parties to secure their advantage, even though it could also be justified as a barrier against splinter parties. During the Weimar Republic, attempts to enact minimum clauses in various German states had been declared unconstitutional by the Supreme Court as violations of the principle of equality before the law. Deliberately inserting them in the state constitutions in the postwar period would prevent the possibility of invalidation by the courts.

That a similar provision found its way into the federal electoral law was a direct consequence of military government intervention. The Main Committee of the Parliamentary Council, which drafted the Basic Law of the Federal Republic, had by a narrow 11 to 10 vote defeated a provision permitting minimum clauses. The argument, strongly pressed by representatives of the minor parties, was that such clauses destroyed the equality of the vote; that argument was bolstered by the assertion that in any case such details had no place in a national constitution. Two days after adopting the text of the Basic Law, the Parliamentary Council enacted an electoral law for the first parliamentary election, which accordingly contained no minimum clause. However, the military

---

[25] Dolf Sternberger, "Parties and Party Systems in Postwar Germany," *op. cit.*, pp. 25–26.
[26] Ebsworth, *op. cit.*, ch. 3.

governors, who had other reservations about this law, registered their objections to the Ministers-President of the German states; the Parliamentary Council had by then adjourned, and these chief executives of the states were the only German authorities in existence, pending the first federal elections. Having listed their specific reservations, the military governors added, somewhat disingenuously, that they were "prepared to consider such [other] modifications of the law as may be proposed by the Ministers-President. . . ." There was reason to believe that the Ministers-President, all of whom belonged to the three largest parties and most of whom were accustomed to minimum clauses in their own states, would be less partial to an unrestrained proportional representation than the Parliamentary Council had been. Indeed, within two days the Ministers-President responded with several recommendations to modify the proportional elements of the law; among these was a proposal that parties which failed to receive five percent of the votes or at least a single victory in a single-member constituency were to receive no seats. The military governors approved these recommendations on the day they were made and authorized the Ministers-President to promulgate the revised law. When sharp SPD and FDP criticism of the intervention caused the Ministers-President subsequently to hesitate about their authority to alter the work of the Parliamentary Council, the military governors took the responsibility for the result "in virtue of our supreme authority."[27]

The minimum clause which was thus inserted into the German electoral system had a profound effect on the fortunes of the parties. It slightly favored the three largest, but, above all, eliminated the smallest parties, as effectively as a system of plurality voting in single-member constituencies would have done.[28] It was eventually declared constitutional by the Federal Constitutional Court, which asserted that equality of the vote required equality in the counting of each ballot, not in its efficacy. After all, it was argued, in the systems of plurality voting in single-member constituencies, which were accepted in Britain and America, it was taken for granted that votes cast for losing candidates were wasted in the sense of not affecting the outcome; a system of proportional representation which allotted no victories to parties receiving less than five percent of the votes was not violating the equality of the ballot in any other sense than that.

III. THE EMERGENCE OF THE POSTWAR PARTY SYSTEM, 1949

By the time the first general parliamentary election was held in August, 1949, 14 political parties were in the field, representing all the

---

[27] See John Ford Golay, *The Founding of the Federal Republic of Germany* (Chicago, 1958), Ch. 4, esp. pp. 145–47.
[28] Douglas Rae, *The Political Consequences of Electoral Laws* (New Haven, 1967), pp. 111–113.

major currents found in the Weimar political system, although in nowhere near their previous number; only the original four had candidates in every state. In the last normal election held during the Weimar Republic, in 1928, 41 parties had been in competition, 32 of these actually submitting national lists of candidates. While 11 parties won representation in 1949, 15 had won seats in 1928. The vote cast for anticonstitutional parties was vastly reduced. Communist strength was halved, from 10.6 to 5.7 percent; the vote for the extreme right, which might include 14.2 percent of the ballots cast for the German National People's party and 2.6 percent cast for the Nazis in 1928, had shrunk to an insignificant 1.4 percent cast for the German Right party in 1949.

The four parties which won the largest number of votes in 1949 corresponded exactly with the first four to be licensed in 1945, the same four which had dominated the consultative assemblies and the local and state elections. Of these four, the Communists suffered the special disabilities of association with the policies of the Soviet military government. But the other three, the Christian Democrats, Social Democrats, and Free Democrats, attracted a concentration of electoral support which greatly exceeded the strength of the first three parties in 1928. Furthermore, the electoral system substantially overrepresented these leading parties in Parliament, giving the three top parties an even greater concentration of parliamentary power. This was the direct consequence of the five-percent clause, which worked with special efficacy in 1949. In that year, with licensing of parties still in effect at the state level, and new parties on the verge of formation in anticipation of the end of military government, an exceptional number of candidates ran as independents or as representatives of locally-organized groups. Such splinter and independent candidates attracted 4.6 percent of the vote, but won only three seats, 0.7 percent of the total, a marked underrepresentation; their loss was the largest parties' gain. In sum, the three largest parties won less than three fifths of the seats in the Reichstag in 1928; they won over four fifths in 1949 (see Table 1).

Some of the contrasts between the voting patterns of 1928 and 1949 are attributable to traditional political differences between eastern and western Germany. The Catholic western sections of the country had always given above average support to the Center and less than average support to the Communists, Socialists, and conservative right. But the election of 1949 showed differences in electoral behavior beyond those which can be accounted for by traditional regional contrasts (see Table 2).

To what extent did the initial consolidation in the German party system and, in Sartori's terms, the decrease in its polarity and its centrifugal tendencies, result from the policies of the military government? To what extent were they the consequences of deeper social changes brought about by the Nazi revolution and by unconditional surrender? While an absolute distinction between these two factors cannot be drawn, some striking relationships between military government policies and electoral consequences can be set out.

TABLE 1. CONSOLIDATION IN THE GERMAN PARTY SYSTEM

Election year	1928	1949	1953	1957	1961	1965
Number of parties presenting candidates	41	14	15	14	8	10
Number of parties gaining parliamentary seats	15	11	6	4	3	3
Percent of votes won by three largest parties	56.1	72.1	83.5	89.7	94.3	96.4
Percent of seats won by three largest parties	58.7	80.1	91.0	96.6	100.0	100.0
Index of overrepresentation of three largest parties (ratio of percent of seats to percent of votes)	1.05	1.11	1.09	1.08	1.06	1.04

Sources: For the election of 1928, Statistisches Jahrbuch für das deutsche Reich, 1928 (Berlin, 1928), pp. 580-581.
For the elections of 1949-1957, Dolf Sternberger, et al., Wahlen und Wähler in Westdeutschland (Villingen, 1960), pp. 321-323.
For the elections of 1961 and 1965, Amtliches Handbuch des deutschen Bundestages, 4. Wahlperiode, p. 174; 5. Wahlperiode, p. 182 (Darmstadt, 1961, 1965).

TABLE 2. COMPARISON BETWEEN THE PARLIAMENTARY ELECTIONS OF 1928 AND 1949 (IN PERCENTAGE OF VALID VOTES CAST)

Tendencies	Parties	Germany 1928	West Germany 1928[a]	West Germany 1949
Extreme right	National Socialist (NSDAP)	2.6	3.3	
	German Right Party (DRP)			1.8
	German National People's Party (DNVP)	14.2	9.8	
Regional	Economic Reconstruction (WAV)			2.9
	German (Hannoverian) Party (DP)	0.6	1.2	4.0
	Bavarian (People's) Party (BP)	3.1	5.6	4.2
	Christian Social Union (CSU)			5.8
Christian center	Christian Democratic Union (CDU)			25.2
	Center Party (Z)	12.1	17.6	3.1
	German Middle Class Party	4.5	3.7	
Liberal middle class	German People's Party (DVP)	8.7	8.7	
	German Democratic Party (DDP)	4.9	4.7	
	Free Democratic Party (FDP)			11.9
Socialist	Social Democratic Party (SPD)	29.8	26.8	29.2
Extreme left	Communist Party (KPD)	10.6	8.6	5.7
	Others	8.9	10.0	6.2

[a] Includes returns for districts 13 through 27 and 31 through 34.

First, the initial ban which military government imposed on the formation of political parties, and then the abrupt decision to license them after all, gave advantages to those formations which were able to prepare informally during the period of party prohibition and were then able to take quick advantage of the lifting of the ban. This favored those groups able to build on the remains of a strong prewar organization (the Communists and Social Democrats), on a strong interest group (the Christian Democrats), or on a group of notable leaders (the Free Democrats).

Second, military government unquestionably gave these four parties additional advantages by relying on them in the early period to recommend office holders, who in turn established the rules of the coming electoral contests, before other parties could get into the field and before the relative strengths of the parties were tested in the first elections. These initial four parties therefore had a corps of leaders, processes of recruiting office-holders, patronage in state government, habits of bargaining with each other, an advantageous electoral system, and a visibility to the voter, before the other parties even obtained their licenses.

Third, military government refused to license extreme right-wing parties and special interest refugee parties, excluding them from the formative constitutional and electoral decisions and condemning them to a very late start in postwar politics. By the time these parties entered the field, after licensing ended in 1950, the disruptions of the immediate postwar period which they might have effectively exploited were already being overcome.

Fourth, the very process of licensing, varying among the zones, even where it was not used in a discriminatory fashion, put some brakes on the proliferation of parties.

Fifth, military government intervention in the process of drafting the first electoral law produced a modification of proportional representation which greatly favored the three leading parties.

And sixth, the east-west division of the nation, an indirect effect of military government, put the Communist party, which had been one of the originally favored four, in the very disadvantageous position of representing a foreign occupying power.

Yet despite the very real contrasts between the elections of 1928 and 1949 and the clear relationship between military government policies and party system change, most observers believed that the prewar party system had been re-established unaltered. Bemused by the relatively high number of parties, and their apparent congruity with the major parties of Weimar, one analyst concluded, in 1950, "that western military government has not engineered a social revolution in German political life; nor did it intend to do so. On the contrary, under the guidance of occupation authorities, the pre-Nazi political pattern and behavior have been restored almost intact."[29] Four years later, however,

---

[29] Seymour R. Bolten, *op. cit.*, p. 66.

this conclusion was no longer tenable. A further concentration of both electoral and parliamentary power in the hands of the three largest parties, and further signs that the other parties were in trouble, could no longer be ignored.

IV. THE CONSOLIDATION OF THE POSTWAR PARTY SYSTEM

Although military government ended in 1949, processes of change which it had set in motion continued, as the leaders of the strongest parties exploited their initial advantages to various extents. Before the election of 1953, the leaders of the governing coalition put through a strengthened five-percent clause. While in 1949 parties receiving five-percent of the vote in any state, or victory in one single-member constituency, were entitled to representatives from that state, five percent of the *national* vote or one constituency victory was now required to obtain proportional representation. Only 6 of 15 parties competing in that year met the more stringent requirement. Prior to the 1957 election, two of these unsuccessful contestants had merged and one had dissolved itself in vain attempts to concentrate strength in order to jump the five-percent hurdle; another merger before the 1961 election was similarly unsuccessful.[30] In that year five out of eight parties remaining in the competition garnered less than six percent of the vote among themselves; by 1965 less than 4 percent of the votes were cast for parties other than the top three (see Table 1). Clearly, all others had been reduced to nuisance status.

But if their demise was hastened by the electoral law, it was fundamentally caused by the skill with which CDU/CSU leaders read the signs of the social changes undermining the minor parties, and the success with which they appealed to the clientele of these groups. Unencumbered by the survival of a prewar party organization, the leaders of the old Center party had proven responsive to changes in the social climate from the start. In informal meetings held in various cities while the ban on party organization was still in effect, most of them had decided that the distinction between Protestantism and Catholicism had lost its political relevance. In ideological terms, they saw Nazism as the anti-Christ against which all others shared a common Christianity. In practical terms, they regarded the old conservative parties as too badly compromised with Nazism to recover quickly. They were convinced that a nondenominational Christian conservatism would have broad appeal. Their prompt decision to create a new Christian Democratic Union in place of the old Center party placed this new party in the ranks of the initially favored four. Supported by Catholic clergy and prominent

---

[30] U. W. Kitzinger, *German Electoral Politics: A Study of the 1957 Campaign* (Oxford, 1960), pp. 18–19, 38–56. Before the 1957 election, the Bavarian party and the Center party merged into the Federal Union, and the All-German People's party dissolved itself; prior to the 1961 election, the All-German Bloc merged with the German party.

Center and conservative politicians of the Weimar era, the CDU clearly met Allied licensing requirements as a democratic party. The experience of its leaders and the old ties among them gave the new party some of the advantages of its old predecessors without any of the mortgages to the past. The CDU had instant electoral success, not only in the Rhineland and, separately organized as the Christian Social Union (CSU), in Bavaria, the former bastions of Catholic political strength, but also in the areas of traditional conservative strength, in the Protestant north. A similar attempt to form a nondenominational Christian party in 1919–20 had failed, under the leadership of some of the same men, like Adam Stegerwald, who now, under different social conditions, succeeded.

But that social conditions alone were not decisive can be seen by the contrasting behavior of the Social Democratic party. Its organization had survived the Nazi regime, underground and in exile, and was promptly ready for reorganization in 1945, under leaders like Schumacher whose ideological convictions had not changed. Viewing the postwar scene through the prism of his Weimar experience, Schumacher was convinced that an unreformed social democracy was now destined to triumph. This caused him to resist Communist appeals for a Marxist amalgamation, but equally to refuse a moderation of the party program in order to extend its appeal beyond the working class traditionally supporting it.[31]

The contrast between the political perceptions of CDU and SPD enabled the former to exploit social changes far more effectively than the latter. Under Adenauer, the CDU took effective advantage of its position as a governing party, which the election of 1949 had given it. As the mobility of the population undermined the specifically regional appeal of the Bavarian and the German parties, for example, leaving them with only a general conservative appeal, the CDU was able to compete with these parties as a broadly-based conservative movement promising access to national power which the smaller parties could not offer. As rising prosperity and labor shortages facilitated the rapid absorption of refugees and expellees into German society, the CDU was able to attract voters from this group by a ritual support of their claims to their national homelands in the East, and government policies in aid of resettlement in the West. Thus, between 1949 and 1953, the Bavarian party fell from 4.2 to 1.7 percent of the vote, the German party from 4.0 to 3.2 percent, and the All-German Bloc, the expellees' party, which had been prohibited in 1949, appeared in 1953 with 5.9 percent, barely above the minimum. By 1957 none of these parties could win parliamentary representation on their own. The beneficiary of their demise was the CDU/CSU, which went from 31 percent of the vote in 1949 to 45 percent in 1953 and 50 percent in 1957.

In causing the reabsorption of the minor parties, the electoral system and the breadth of CDU/CSU appeal restored and even strengthened

---

[31] Lewis Edinger, *op. cit.*, Ch. 5.

the pattern of large party dominance which had existed in the very first postwar elections for the state constituent assemblies and legislatures. Because of the demise of the Communists, who received only two percent of the votes in 1953 and were outlawed by the Federal Constitutional Court in 1956, a concentration of strength among three parties replaced the earlier concentration among four. Except for that, the pattern in the early 1960's strongly resembled the pattern which had first emerged in 1946–47 (see Table 3).

TABLE 3. PARLIAMENTARY ELECTIONS IN THE FEDERAL REPUBLIC OF GERMANY, 1946–1965 (PERCENTAGE OF VALID VOTES AND NUMBER OF ELECTED MEMBERS)

	1946-47[a]	1949	1953	1957	1961	1965
Christian Democratic Union/ Christian Social Union	38.5	31.0 139 seats	45.2 244 seats	50.2 270 seats	45.3 242 seats	47.6 245 seats
Social Democratic Party	35.7	29.2 131 seats	28.8 151 seats	31.8 169 seats	36.3 190 seats	39.3 202 seats
Free Democratic Party	8.2	11.9 52 seats	9.5 48 seats	7.7 41 seats	12.7 67 seats	9.5 49 seats
German Party[b]	2.6	4.0 17 seats	3.2 15 seats	3.4 17 seats	2.8 0 seats	
Bavarian Party		4.2 17 seats	1.7 0 seats			
All-German Bloc (Expellees)			5.9 27 seats	4.6 0 seats		
Radical left[c]	9.3	5.7 15 seats	2.2 0 seats		1.9 0 seats	1.3 0 seats
Radical right[d]	0.4	1.8 5 seats	1.1 0 seats	1.0 0 seats	0.8 0 seats	2.0 0 seats
Other parties and independents	5.3	12.2 26 seats	2.4 2 seats	1.3 0 seats	0.2 0 seats	0.3 0 seats

[a]First state constituent assembly or legislature elections.
[b]Merged with All-German Bloc in 1961; previously had stand-down agreements with CDU to enable it to win single-member constituencies.
[c]Communist Party in 1949 and 1953; German Peace Union in 1961 and 1965.
[d]German Right Party in 1949; German Reich Party in 1953-1961; National Democratic Party in 1965.

Only the striking success of the CDU/CSU finally caused the Social Democrats to reconsider their position. In Bad Godesberg, in 1959, they adopted a new program in which socialism received a most pragmatic formulation: "as much competition as possible — as much planning as necessary. . . ." At the same time, the SPD began to emulate the CDU's emphasis on personalities in election campaigns and to abandon its opposition to the foreign policy which successive CDU/CSU governments had developed. In the elections of 1961 and 1965 the SPD began to receive new sources of support, particularly from professionals and white-collar workers, even in rural and Catholic areas.

Undoubtedly, the attempt of those parties which had been initially favored in the postwar period, to mobilize the entire electorate, and to maintain their early advantage, was facilitated by a social climate which weakened the old partisan commitments. "The mass integration party," Kirchheimer observed, "product of an age with harder class lines and more sharply protruding denominational structures, is transforming itself into a catch-all 'people's' party."[32] Total party membership in the postwar period did not rise beyond four percent of the population; in 1920 it had been as high as 15 percent. By comparison with their Weimar predecessors, the postwar parties concentrated on winning votes, at the expense of winning and politicizing members. To maintain a broad appeal, they aggregated a wide range of interests, at the expense of articulating any particular demand clearly. After Adenauer's electoral triumph in 1953, it was clear to the two largest parties that the highest office of government, the Chancellorship, was directly at stake in the elections, and they correspondingly emphasized personalities over program in their campaigns.

In weakening regionalism, denominationalism, and class consciousness as the sources of political divisions, social changes were therefore responsible for creating new opportunities for political party organization. But the exploitation of these opportunities undoubtedly depended on two major political factors: the disruption of the traditional party organizations by the Nazi regime and the new ground rules for party organization and competition set by Allied military government.

The violent impact of Nazism on the German party system had not hit every part of the political spectrum equally. On the left, Communist and Socialist party organizations had survived the Nazi regime, in exile, and were ready for reorganization in 1945; in the center and on the right, the old parties had disbanded themselves voluntarily, and efforts at postwar party organization started from scratch. Ironically, this enabled a new center party to adapt itself quickly to a changed social environment, while the Social Democrats were condemned to suffer from the inertia of the past. Ironically too, military government influenced the party system in complex and substantial ways, although its original purposes had merely been to destroy the Nazi party and to provide military security for the Allied armies of occupation. In setting the conditions for the revival of a party system, military government policies, quite unintentionally, permitted those social changes which had long been in progress to manifest themselves in a new party pattern, while restricting the influence of certain short-term social factors which, unchecked, might have reinforced the traditional party fragmentation. But no matter how accidental the consequences of Nazism and military government, without the changes in the political structure which they produced there is no reason to believe that social

---

[32] Otto Kirchheimer, "The Transformation of the Western European Party Systems," in Joseph LaPalombara and Myron Weiner, eds., *op. cit.,* p. 184.

changes alone would have had any greater impact on the party system after 1945 than they had had after 1871 or 1919.

V. CONCLUSION

In the sixth general parliamentary election in 1969, nearly 95 percent of the votes were cast for the three largest parties, and nearly 89 percent were given to the CDU/CSU and SPD alone. For the third election in a row, only three parties gained parliamentary seats. Clearly, the number of parties competing in the system has been reduced. There has been a marked change from extreme to moderate pluralism. The formation of a coalition between the CDU/CSU and the SPD in 1966 drew attention to another attribute of the new party system. That the two largest parties were able to govern together, as they did between 1966 and 1969, signifies the absence of "polarity" in the system. "Centrifugal drives . . . ideological rigidity . . . [and] marked cleavage at the elite level," which Sartori associates with extreme pluralism, are no longer in evidence, and "the party system is able to perform a cohesive and integrative function." When the election of 1969 was followed by the creation of an SPD-FDP coalition with the CDU/CSU going into opposition, an alternation of the major parties in office took place for the first time, indicating the existence of a "real alternative government" and the possibility of "orderly change," two further characteristics which Sartori associates with moderate pluralism. Thus, twenty years after the establishment of the Federal Republic of Germany, the profound changes which had taken place in the German party system were fully apparent.

The attempt to explain these unusual changes tests some of the common hypotheses regarding party system change. Because economic and social changes had long preceded the changes in the party system, while specific discontinuities in the political framework attended these changes, it is possible to demonstrate that political factors were the critical variables. This is not to deny that changes in the party system reflected fundamental social and economic changes. It only asserts that the response of the party system to economic and social changes was possible only because Nazism had disrupted the traditional party system, and because the fiat of an externally imposed regime — Allied military government — had created new political conditions for the development of a party system. The social changes which Nazism brought to a head had been going on for half a century, without basically affecting the party system. Only the destruction of that party system under totalitarian coercion and the establishment of new ground rules for party competition by the occupation regime permitted social change to work its political effect.[33]

---

[33] The general advantages and disadvantages of studying military occupation as a "particular type of planned political change" are discussed by Robert E. Ward in a report on a conference on "Military Occupations and Political Change" in *Items*, XXI (1967), pp. 25–29.

The development of the German party system suggests a more general, though tentative, hypothesis. Party systems, like all institutional systems, may have considerable inertia which slows their response to social change. Voting habits, vested interests in existing organizations, and constitutional and legal rules may all promote the maintenance of the established party system and create a lag between political and socio-economic change. The explanation of party systems in terms of socio-economic systems may therefore overlook critical variables. The legal and institutional framework of political life may well have so great an influence on political behavior that it determines the particular effects which the social and economic environment has on politics.

OTTO KIRCHHEIMER

The Waning of Opposition in Parliamentary Regimes

In Western nations, party politics implies competition between parties, and competition implies opposition to as well as support for the government of the day. The alternation of parties in office in the United States and the norm (if not always the reality) of a pendulum-like swing between parties in Britain is not matched in the record of Continental European societies. From the point of view of government, the multiplicity of parties is perhaps of less importance than the character of the Ins and Outs. As Otto Kirchheimer shows, government by a coalition of parties results in major changes in the operations of party government. Moreover, opposition by parties so committed to principle that they will not sink their differences in coalition is opposition of a type different from that by politicians who value office above all else.

Political opposition is an eternal paradox. It postulates the principle that impediments to political action may be wholesome and are therefore to be protected. But what is the chance of institutionalizing such limitations? The parliamentary regime, and the favorable climate it created for the rise of the political party as a vehicle for the exercise of both governmental and opposition functions, has been one of the more felicitous inventions in the limited field of political institutions. But contemporary parliamentary institutions, working as they do in the framework of mass democracy, obey different laws and pressures from those governing their predecessors half a century or a century ago. Reinvestigation of the meaning of opposition under the conditions of the present age may be in order. For the sake of preciseness these remarks will be restricted to European parliamentary regimes, omitting the role of opposition under presidential regimes, which obey somewhat different political and, as the case may be, social considerations.

I should like to put up three models, two of which pertain to the forms of political opposition. First is the "classical opposition" under the parliamentary form of government, developed from the practices of eighteenth-century England. Second is what might be styled "opposition of principle," bent not only on wrenching power from the government of today but on ending once and for all the system on which that government rests. The third is a counter-concept to the other two; it relates to government under various forms of cartel arrangements among political organizations operating within the framework of parliamentary institutions.

I

If we look only at definitions we might regard Messrs. Eden in 1946 and Gaitskell in 1956 as the linear descendants of Edmund Burke and Charles Fox. Burke's 1770 formula,[1] describing a party as a body of men united for promoting the national interest, by their joint endeavors, on the basis of some particular principle on which we all agree, seems quite acceptable as a definition for the minimum of coherence needed to carry through an effective opposition. But we should not claim more for Burke or for Bolingbroke, his predecessor in the field of manufacturing political ideologies, than is due to them. For both of them, the Archimedean point of party was still "connexion, affection, and friendship" in the face of possible political adversity.[2] It needed the injection of a less savory character, John Wilkes, into the placid waters of eighteenth-century aristocratic politics to start the enlarging

---

Abridged by the editors from Otto Kirchheimer, "The Waning of Opposition in Parliamentary Regimes," *Social Research*, XXIV, 2, Summer, 1957, pp. 127–156. Reprinted by permission.

[1] Edmund Burke, "Thoughts on the Causes of the Present Discontents," in *Works*, World's Classics ed., vol. 2, p. 82.

[2] To cite but one out of many, see H. Butterfield, *George III, Lord North and the People* (London 1949).

of faction to party and the assertion of more than evanescent group interest. But it is important to recall that this transition from the aristocratic parliament of the eighteenth century via the alternation of conservative-liberal governments of the nineteenth century, with their restricted basis of urban middle-class and landowning strata, to the present-day mass-democracy dichotomy of conservatives and labor has taken place in the framework of parliamentary institutions and their game of government opposition.

What are the bases for this game of alternation? John Morley, the Victorian, considered the right of the defeated group to publicly maintain its principles after they were rejected by the majority to be the foundation of the opposition's functioning.[3] By the end of the 1850's, however, Walter Bagehot had already shown that this continuous right of vindicating solutions rejected by the electorate presupposes that the participants in the political game consist of moderate elements. "An ultra-democratic parliament" could not preserve such a state of affairs. There each class would speak its own language, unintelligible to the others, and an "immoderate ministry" and "violent laws" would be the consequence.[4] John Stuart Mill applied similar considerations specifically to the conditions of a society resting on well organized groups. Competition must be a competition of ideas as well as of interests, because without a competition of ideas and the duty to listen to them the victory of the momentarily more powerful group would always be a foregone conclusion.[5]

To this day the British system and the practices of most of the Dominions of English stock are well within the range of these considerations. On the social and economic level there is continued agreement either on major objectives or, at least, on the mutually permissible range of change. If this agreement no longer existed, it would be rather doubtful whether parliamentary government could be maintained along traditional lines. This would raise questions to which, as a contemporary Australian author puts it, "the current focus of politics hardly suggests an answer."[6] But the experience of the last decades seems not to have confirmed Harold Laski's well known notions on "the bridgeable abyss" between Conservatives and Labour, on which he laid so much stress in his analysis of the British parliamentary system in the 1930's.[7]

In an age when foreign policy may determine the very existence of a nation, parliamentary government also presupposes a high amount of opposition confidence in the government's sense of direction in reacting to situations that have to be handled without prior parliamentary discussion; at a minimum it presupposes a complete and unfaltering

---

[3] See John Morley, *On Compromise*, 2nd ed. (London 1877) p. 209.

[4] Walter Bagehot, *Works and Life*, vol. 5, p. 269.

[5] John Stuart Mill, *Representative Government*, Chapter 5; see also G. Burdeau, *Traité de science politique*, vol. 3 (Paris 1950) p. 327.

[6] L. F. Crisp, *The Parliamentary Government of the Commonwealth of Australia*, 2nd ed. (London 1952) p. 121.

[7] Harold Laski, *Parliamentary Government in England* (New York 1938).

belief in the majority's sincerity, if it decides to make grave (but in its own mind unavoidable) changes. The Conservative attitude toward the Labour Party's abandonment of India may in this connection be compared with the sea of hatred and mutual recrimination recently produced in comparable circumstances in France. The government-opposition game further presupposes conditions in the army and the civil service which make for firm control and responsiveness to the civilian government. Both army and civil service must leave behind them the idea of forming social-political blocs of their own, warring and coalescing at will with other forces, thus upsetting and falsifying the delicate balance of forces between opposition and government.

If all these conditions are met the respective roles of government and opposition become both clearly defined and constitutionally sacrosanct. As a ceaseless critic, the opposition will try both to wring concessions from the government and to force changes of policies. As the alternative government, it will try to focus public opinion on the possibility and desirability of a speedy change via the electoral process. On the other hand, it is the government's duty to give the opposition full opportunity to carry through its function. To exercise their correlative rights and duties, both majority and opposition are therefore equipped with prerogatives, weapons, and sanctions. The official and salaried position of the leader of the opposition, the practice of informing and conferring with him, the opposition's right to debate topics chosen by itself, the differentiation between the normal function of opposition and obstruction, and the majority's right to use cloture and guillotine to break such obstruction mark the different phases in the institutionalization of opposition.

The government-opposition duel, moreover, does not interrupt the government's relations with the social and professional groups that by tradition and inclination belong to what one may call the clientele of the opposition party. Acceptance of the claims of the opposition's clientele may be limited both by policy considerations and by prior incompatible obligations toward groups closer to the heart of the government. Within these limits, however, the test of the political skill of a new cabinet may often be found in its dexterity in dealing with and acquiring the confidence of the social strata belonging traditionally to the other flock. This is of the utmost importance as each party competes for the support of voters among the strata that are to a large extent among the opposition's traditional clientele.

The more skillful (or simply lucky) the government, the greater the opposition's quandary in developing what would amount to a policy alternative, and the more intensively must the opposition rely on purely tactical attitudes, taking its cues from the frequent boners that any far-flung administration is bound to commit at one time or another. Like its predecessors of former centuries, it will often pursue opposition for opposition's sake, but its scope of action is now many times enlarged, commensurate with the infinitely larger and more complex administration on which it can focus and pounce for criticism. But though the opposition's writ now extends further, its rewards may be as subject to caprice as those of its predecessors. No longer does caprice take the form of a king's whims and the accompanying reshuffling of party connections, which within the lifetime of a single parliament could bring victory to the opposition. Now, more often than not, the opposition has to wait for the decision of the sovereign electorate, possibly some years distant, to get another chance at power. Even then, the electorate may simply react to momentary situations or persevere in following long-standing social images, neither necessarily connected with the labors of the opposition, real or inconsequential as they may have been. This strong factor of chance, the difficulty in foreseeing which element in a given situation will determine the voters' choice, is inherent in the game of political competition and strengthens the camaraderie of all those participating actively in the political lottery.

While the players are the parliamentary leaders, the game is no longer played for the parliamentary theater alone, but for the quite different audience of mass democracy — the wholesale consumer, or the interest groups, and the retail public, the individual voter. The stage acting is essential only to get the show before the mass audience, the voter. In such circumstances resoluteness and energy are needed to prevent opposition from degenerating into mere routine, and to relate it to the lives and expectations of a political clientele. The energetic inclinations of the opposition leader are the weaker the more he has come by habit, or just occupational disease, to react as part of the overall governmental machine. He may fall easy prey to the comfortable belief that his political chances increase by minimizing rather than by magnifying the policy differences between opposition and government.

If this should happen, the opposition that exists within every opposition is what becomes the moving force of the country's political machinery. The irregulars rather than the official leadership will strive to inquire into the deeper reasons for the party's last defeat, clamor for the overdue great inquest, shout for reformulations of principles and goals, and redraw the battle lines between government and opposition. The local party worker may be uninformed, the voter inarticulate; yet such gadflies may force on the recalcitrant party leadership a sharper differentiation between official opposition and governmental policies. They may, at times, run ahead of both leaders and voters, or sometimes even run amok. Their attitudes may lead the whole organization into the political wilderness, but that danger may be no greater than the disorganization threatening from total surrender to the government.[8] . . .

Why did not the government-opposition pattern of parliamentary government implant itself more firmly into the mores of the major continental countries of Europe? One decisive reason is that the monopoly of final political decision so long remained beyond the grasp

---

[8] This quintessence of a long political career is drawn by L. S. Amery, *My Political Life*, vol. 1 (London 1953) p. 416.

of political parties. Until the middle of the nineteenth century, and often much longer, opposition remained "institutional opposition." To some extent parliament as a corporate entity formed the opposition to the government. In such circumstances parliament had to fight for recognition of strictly limited influence against the representatives of more traditional powers, arrayed against it under the cloak of the crown. And even after this system ended — in France in 1869, in Italy in 1871, and in Germany in 1917 — political decisions often remained subject to what one may call an *avis préalable,* or a veto exercised, as the case might be, by the army, the upper bureaucracy, or central-bank institutions.[9] With parliament bereft of decisive power and unable to concentrate political decisions in its own hands, strata of the people which had little chance to make their voices heard through other channels turned toward groups that promised remedial action by supplanting the political system as a whole. Hence arose what I should like to call the "opposition of principle."

II

Speaking of the opposition of principle, one thinks mostly of the last decades' totalitarian parties, and is inclined to forget that European socialism of the 1880's, 1890's, and the 1900's posed similar, though less insoluble, problems. The opposition of principle assumes that realization of its program requires full political power — or at least its intentionally or unintentionally ambiguous statements may be interpreted by its more moderate competitors in this fashion. At times the opposition of principle may be insignificant, and it may never have the chance to seize political power except with the help and as an instrument of foreign backers. At other times it may loom large enough to deflect competition partially or completely from the rules of the parliamentary game, and may force the parliamentary parties into a kind of compulsory cartel and even abdication of their powers into the hands of other institutions — the army, the police, the bureaucracy. In a sense, therefore, the opposition of principle makes its own analysis and prophecy come true. By postulating the uselessness of the whole parliamentary game it may, by its very existence, threaten the parliamentary parties enough to force them into abandoning many of the rules of the parliamentary game.

In these circumstances the meaning of both government and opposition deviates markedly from the classical model. Parliamentary opposition in its classical sense presupposes both the possibility and the preparedness to form an alternative government willing and able to grant its presumptive successor in the opposition the same privileges it enjoyed itself. The very character and goals of an opposition of

[9] On the role of the Bank of France under the Third Republic see Otto Kirchheimer, "Political Compromise," in *Studies in Philosophy and Social Science,* vol. 9, no. 1 (1941).

principle limit its parliamentary chances. It threatens the existence of the other parties, and forces its competitors into preventive and defensive measures. New and discriminatory differentiations between loyal and disloyal opposition are introduced into the parliamentary game. There may be discriminatory constitutional changes, but even outside the sphere of explicit derogation from constitutional rules, new differentiations may be introduced. The votes of the opposition of principle, though counted correctly according to constitutional rules, may be weighed differently in counting votes of confidence or no-confidence. Special rules and usages may be adopted to exclude the members of such an opposition from partaking in parliamentary functions and administrative positions.

Whatever the justifications for these precautions, they inevitably distort political reality by denying adequate representation to those who, for better or worse, insist on giving these parties their confidence. Parliament may continue to provide the basis for the exercise of governmental functions, and not be paralyzed into inaction as in the classic case of pre-Hitler Germany. But its representative function and its possibility of giving expression to the various currents of opinion are bound to suffer.

Thus one test of a democratic political system is the degree to which such opposition of principle, if it has reached some magnitude, may eventually be integrated into the existing political order without forcibly dissolving it or liquidating it or substantially weakening the pursuit of the legitimate interests it represents. Such integration is the more difficult the more elections and parliament are visualized from a purely instrumental viewpoint as a possible, but by no means exclusive, field of political manoeuvre. European experience in the first half of this century contains numerous examples of both alternatives. Each case of failure or half failure has left the parliamentary system of the country weaker and less able to form the basis for the exercise of political leadership.

III

We come now to the third model: the elimination of major political opposition through government by party cartel. What I have in mind here are not the national or national-unity governments of war and crisis vintage. By their very definition they are exceptional occurrences. Moreover, two of them, the MacDonald government of 1931 and Doumergue's attempt in 1934, were nothing but transparent endeavors to hide an attempt at political realignment and to cash in on the possible goodwill of the national-unity label. Rather, I have in mind the more than temporary abandonment of the government-opposition relation in contemporary Austria.

Between the end of World War I and the 1934 civil war Austria had a record of bitter and incessant struggle between two major parties, both resting on an amalgamation of social class, political creed, and religious conviction, with a third party too small and inconsequential to play a balancing role. After a relatively short period of coalition between the two major parties immediately subsequent to World War I, the Christian Social Party entrenched itself firmly in the saddle of national government. For over a decade its socialist competitor hovered uneasily between the position of a parliamentary opposition and that of an opposition of principle. After World War II approximately the same party constellation emerged, with the two major parties dividing more than eighty percent of the total vote almost evenly between themselves. In view of the difficult situation of Austria, occupied by both Eastern and Western powers, and the republic's historical record of political frustration and abiding suspicion, the parties decided on a carefully prearranged system of collaboration.[10]

Renewed after the 1956 election, this system has outlasted the occupation. Neither party has been willing to leave the conduct of public affairs in the hands of its competitor or of a civil service working exclusively under its competitor's direction. The two parties proceeded with a detailed parceling out, among their adherents, of all cabinet posts and the majority of the significant administrative positions. This involved explicit understandings on many issues, on appointments, on the filling of regional, local, and semi-governmental jobs, and on the elaboration of legislative programs.

This procedure has led to significant changes in the function of parliamentary institutions in Austria. The inconsequential right-wing and left-wing opposition parties have kept their freedom of parliamentary action. But the members of the two big parties can exercise their normal parliamentary prerogatives — what is now called "acting within the coalition-free area" — only with the permission of the partner party. It would jeopardize the functioning of the cartel agreement to allow party caucuses or individual backbenchers to oppose bills proposed by the government or to introduce motions themselves without previous clearance with the cartel. The area free of the binding rule of the coalition government is predetermined neither by general criteria nor by preestablished subject matter. In each case the parties' possibility of taking back their freedom of action rests on a particular agreement between the coalition partners. Major parliamentary criticism is thus relegated to the status of opposition by joint license.

What have been the consequences of this cartel arrangement? Curiously enough, the restricted exercise of parliamentary opposition has not dried up the competition between the two major parties for the votes of the new voters, of potential switchers from each, and of the declining reservoir of third-party voters. In effecting this competition in face of the stringent rules of the cartel agreement, both partners have been quite ingenious in discovering and profiting from any opportunity for competition. A minister may utilize the key position assigned to

---

[10] See Bruno Pittermann, "Oesterreichs Innenpolitik nach dem Staatsvertrag," in *Die Zukunft* (July 1955) p. 88.

him, under the coalition pact in order to carry through some controversial policy by administrative fiat, thus trying to create a fait accompli in favor of his own party. On the other hand, if a party has to agree to a compromise particularly distasteful to its clientele, it will be allowed to make enough parliamentary and extraparliamentary noises to convince its clientele of the intensity of its reluctance. This then leads to a new kind of built-in opposition which the Austrians themselves have baptized *Bereichsopposition,* meaning opposition to what is happening under the agreed-upon jurisdiction of the other party. . . .

What about the compatibility of the different social-economic orientations of the partners of a coalition government? How are the views of the proponents of extensive state intervention and of an important planned sector made compatible with the endeavors of those who want a so-called free-market economy? The problem looks more formidable in theory than it is in practice. All governments operate within the limits and necessities of their period, which rarely allow either a consistent interventionist or a consistent free-market pattern. The most arduous adherents of a free-market economy have steadfastly followed a policy of protection and interventionism in the agricultural sector, with the Austrian government assuredly no exception to this rule. Everything is therefore a matter of degree and compromise; and these compromises have to be carried out irrespective of whether they are forced on a classic one-party alternation government, by the needs of multifarious political clienteles, or on a coalition government, where the various currents are represented by distinct parties. Changes rarely spring Minerva-like from Zeus's head at the prompting of program builders who got the ear of the public at election time. More often than not it is the imperative requirement of a new societal situation which makes such programs sprout and be adopted by all those who want either to stay or to get a fresh start in the political business. What at first looks like a clear-cut dichotomy is mostly in point of fact a continuum.

A more fundamental objection to the Austrian-type cartel agreement, and one that has been voiced against similar tendencies of some present-day German state governments, rests on the resulting absence of the opposition's control function. Each party may have an interest in covering up the inefficiency, waste, and corruption of its partner. Hence arise all the problems of institutionalized reinsurance practices. Neither public opinion, to the extent that such an animal exists independently of interest groups closely tied in with the major parties, nor the small opposition of principle represented in parliament has enough breadth of action, inside knowledge of the administration, or authority with the public at large to compensate for the absence of a major parliamentary opposition group. Control is mutual control in the matrix of a government acting within the confines of the coalition agreement; the party and parliamentary discussion sets the frame for the compromise effected inside the government. . . .

In France, transfer of votes to and from the opposition of principle is of greater importance than the internal transfer of votes among the various parliamentary groups. Acting in this fashion, however, the voter largely abdicates the role assigned to him under the classical government-opposition scheme, namely, to participate in the arbitration of conflicting leadership claims among parties operating within the framework of the regime. Thus the vote determines at best the margin that the groups loyal to the regime retain to form and reform their ephemeral alliances, and influences to a lesser degree the process of cabinet forming.[11] This insensitivity of government formation toward popular currents allows the opposition of principle to contest the moral title of the government to represent the country, thus confronting the *pays légal* with the *pays réel*.

There may be neither abiding suspicion, leading to a watertight voluntary cartel, nor crisis of the regime, leading to a compulsory or near-compulsory cartel arrangement: coalition government may be simply a consequence of a well established multiparty system, as in present-day Holland, Weimar Germany, or interwar Czechoslovakia. But whatever the reason for the coalition arrangements, their establishment and practices are all bound to lead to deviations from the classical norm. The major government party may be concerned mainly with dislodging one partner or switching coalition partners. The opposition parties too may fight on various fronts; without the possibility of setting up a government of their own, they may concentrate energy on improving tactical chances of government participation. This purpose may involve subtle modulations of policy in regard to various governmental or other opposition parties. The possible variations and combinations are of great variety. Neither of the constellations is conducive to a sharp differentiation between government and opposition policies. The tortuous ways of the multiparty government and of multi-opposition tactics are the province of the political professional. The public at large looks at the results, while the more loyal party public may judge also by intentions.

Nevertheless, a multiparty coalition government need not be congenitally weak, nor need a divided opposition be impotent. Everything depends on the character of the various participants and their leadership, and on the temper of national political discourse and action. The maxim "where all govern, nobody governs" does not correctly describe all relevant factual situations. Prewar Czech and postwar Dutch governments, though they were difficult to assemble, show a reasonable record of stability and efficiency.[12] On the other hand, multiparty government in the larger countries has more often than not been weak. The difficulty in bringing together various factions, the limited minimum program to which the coalition partners are willing to subscribe,

---

[11] Some of these problems are discussed in R. A. Aron, "Electeurs, partis et élus," in *Revue française de science politique* (April–June 1955) p. 304, and in Philip Williams, *Politics in Post-War France* (London 1954), especially p. 358.

[12] On the Dutch experience see H. Daalder, "Parties and Politics in the Netherlands," in *Political Studies*, vol. 3, no. 1 (1955) p. 1.

and the concomitant attempts to restrict the mandate given to the parties' representatives in the cabinets inevitably provoke sharp counter-thrusts. Each cabinet minister will try to assert his maximum independence of his group, emphasize the dignity and independence of his office, and make the most of his assertion that he is His Majesty's or the nation's representative. He will therefore fall in most eagerly with the higher ranks of the bureaucracy who might liberate him from the embraces and demands of his party.

Such "liberation tendencies" are not restricted to representatives of multiparty coalition governments. But the fact of having been carried to power by a strong party, whether within the frame of the classic two-party system or as participant of a strong and stable coalition, enhances the chance that a minister will be willing and able to implant his party's value scale and program. Ministers of a weak coalition government are more predisposed to become instruments in the hands of their official advisers. It is in such cases that the always latent nineteenth-century antinomy, with parliament opposing the administration as an intrinsically inimical institution — so well known from the practice of presidential regimes — has a tendency to become universal. But unless the parties want to be relegated to the role of political prayer mills, this can be only a transitional and, from the viewpoint of the parliamentary regime, uncomfortable solution.

Political opposition as a continuing function presupposes the existence of a yardstick for governmental performance. The opposition on principle need not bother to unearth such a yardstick, as the very existence of the government is sufficient proof of its wickedness. In contrast, opposition within the confines of the parliamentary system presupposes some semblance of coherence if at least some vestige of a rational alternative to the government's policy is to be preserved.

This coherence may have its roots in program, ideology, and tradition. To be sure, coherence is always threatened, if for no other reason than the fact that in our day and age both government and opposition are always faced with unforeseen and unforeseeable situations requiring immediate action without their catechism offering satisfactory or, indeed, any answers. Gone are the days when a man could make up a program at the outset of his career to last all his life.[13] But coherence is more likely with a party that has a tradition and some hold over its clientele, and therefore can afford the luxury of convictions, than with a marginal group whose survival, depending on the outcome of the next election, requires that it make its decisions on exclusively tactical grounds. The freedom of movement of the first is principally determined by the objective requirements of the situation it encounters when it comes to power; the latter is subjected to all the additional impediments stemming from its uneasy and always imperiled relations with its more comfortable competitors. To the extent that coalition government and multifarious opposition rest on quickly shifting and purely

---

[13] See the instructive remarks of M. Ostrogorski in *Democracy and Political Parties*, vol. 1 (New York 1902) p. 22.

tactical alignments, they provide only an indistinct focus for the exercise of governmental responsibility and the complementary function of parliamentary opposition.

IV

The question arises whether this desiccation of the opposition function that has here been followed through a number of variations can be attributed to more or less technical factors, and hence could be reversed by technical changes in election procedures or parliamentary rules. . . . It seems unlikely. There is no meaningful connection between the form of the electoral system, the practices and malpractices of government formation, and the crisis of the concept of political opposition. It may be more rewarding to look into the incongruities between continental party systems and the social realities of the twentieth century.

Continental European parties are the remnants of intellectual and social movements of the nineteenth century. They have remained glued to the spots where the ebbing energy of such movements deposited them some decades ago. The more violent twentieth-century eruptions, fascism and communism, have surged much further, but in flowing back have petrified rather than envigorated the existing system. Postwar attempts at rationalization have produced some new variations, but have not eliminated the basic heritage of the parties. They were built around combinations of nineteenth-century class, occupational, and religious, or, as the case might be, anti-religious interests. How does this heritage relate to the most important stages of twentieth-century transformation?

From the viewpoint of political dynamics, the most important change is probably the emergence of a substantial new middle class of skilled workers, the middle ranks of white-collar people, and civil servants. All their work is done under instruction from superiors. Similarities of situation, thought processes, and expectations outweigh still existing traditional distinctions. Their consumption expectations, resting on the concept of increasing prosperity, as well as the demands they address to the community at large for sufficient protection against institutional and personal hazards of life, are identical. The cleavage that separates them from the more successful elements of the older independent middle classes — the artisans and peasants of medium-size holdings, both with enough capital equipment to profit from technological progress — is diminishing. The technological revolution is changing the outlook of these tradition-bound and conservative groups at the same time that it reduces their size. Increasingly enmeshed in the fortunes of the national economy, they now raise claims, identical with those of the new middle class, for guaranteed real-income levels and participation in social-insurance schemes. To this extent the struggle between the independent old middle class and the employed new middle class is more a struggle for similar goals than a clash of incompatible programs.

To the extent that all major parliamentary parties are permeated by the opinions and attitudes of these groups, strategic on account of both their size and the compactness of their professional organizations, one may justifiably say that diminished social polarization and diminished political polarization are going hand in hand. As Beatrice Webb expressed this particular phenomenon forty-odd years ago, "the landslide in England towards Social Democracy proceeds steadily, but it is the whole nation which is sliding, not the one class of manual workers."[14] We are faced with a somewhat languishing system of interparty competition which in many cases is even overshadowed by intraparty competition, the attempt of the various interest groups represented in one party to have an official party stand adopted that is maximally favorable to them.[15] The parliamentary party has thus become in a double sense a harmonizing agency. It harmonizes first the conflicting claims within its ranks, and on this basis participates in interparty adjustments on the governmental level.

The same harmonizing tendencies are potently reenforced by the contemporary opinion-forming process. The rise of the nineteenth-century party was inseparably linked with the growth of newspapers as vehicles for the creation and expression of public opinion. The newspapers, being politically oriented, and helping aspirants for political power to obtain recognition and spread their doctrine, were the handmaidens of emerging parliamentary government. Twentieth-century media of communication are not primarily politically oriented. They are business enterprises bent on maximizing profits from huge investments by catering to the inclinations and aspirations of a presumed near totality of readers and listeners, rather than appealing to an educated elite. They interlace the consumption expectations of their readers and listeners with the interests of their backers and advertisers. In order to fulfill this dual mission they preserve a maximum of neutrality, not only between the possibly conflicting interests of the various advertisers but also between the prejudices of the various strata of their readers and listeners. Resting on a presupposed harmony of interests among advertisers, financial backers, readers, and listeners, they are using the Hays-office technique of neutralizing and playing down divisive elements or transferring elements of conflict from the domestic to the international scene.[16] The rise of consumer-oriented public-opinion formation has been one of the most powerful elements in the

---

[14] Beatrice Webb, *Diaries, 1912–1924* (London 1952) p. 18.

[15] These trends appeared earliest and in the most succinct form in Sweden. See Herbert Tingsten, "Stability and Vitality in Swedish Democracy," in *Political Quarterly*, vol. 26 (1955) pp. 140–51: "As the general standard of values is so commonly accepted, the function of the state becomes so technical as to make politics appear as a kind of applied statistics." See also his statements (p. 148) on the nature of political parties.

[16] For a partial analysis see Jacques Kayser, *Mort d'une liberté* (Paris 1955). S. Diamond, *The Reputation of the American Businessman* (Cambridge, Mass., 1955), brings out very well the importance of mass communication for the maintenance of consensus in the functioning of society.

reduction of the political element to the semi-entertainment level.[17] Thus objective factors of social development and conscious efforts join in breaking down barriers between some strata of society and in creating what has been rather prematurely styled a unified middle-class society. . . .

Moreover, the same process that has created a new middle class and lessened the distance between the old and new elements has everywhere uprooted diverse other social strata, and has so far failed to assign them a satisfactory position within the new society. The main victims of this process of transformation have been older people whose income has not kept pace with inflation, small peasant holders, small artisans and retailers without the capital to modernize their shops, and white-collar elements, economically outflanked by many groups of manual workers and unable to acquire a new feeling of "belonging" to compensate for the meagerness of their occupational existence. These changes, too, have indelibly marked the present party system. These strata form a steady source, even in present favorable economic circumstances, for a predominantly but not exclusively right-wing opposition of principle. By the same token, they are an element in the petrification of the traditional parliamentary parties.

To compete with the opposition of principle for this substantial vote, the parliamentary parties find it useful to fall back on their nineteenth-century heritage. This heritage may vary widely: with the socialists it may mean an occasional harking back to the class basis of political structure and its promise of a classless society; with the vaguely Christian catch-all parties, in vogue after the war, it may mean the concept of spiritual brotherhood or a specific religious appeal, transcending the cleavages of the day; and with the liberal or radical socialist parties it may refer to the autonomy claim of the non-collectivized individual, raised against both church and state. What we are here concerned with, however, is not the content of the often interchangeable doctrines but their survival as an element in keeping together or bringing again together the various elements of formerly unified groups, now torn asunder in the process of social transformation, employing here the unity of the working classes or there the image of a self-reliant independent middle class.

To be sure, not all — or even most — members of status-threatened disadvantaged and dissatisfied groups join the ranks of the opposition of principle. But this is probably less significant as indicating the continuing attraction of the parliamentary party than as emphasizing the fact that the primarily consumption-oriented thought process of their more fortunate brethren has become for them a natural habit. They momentarily accept the parliamentary party not because it struggles to uphold a lien on their grandfathers' social vision, but because they

---

[17] The role of the "lowest common denominator" in the news presentations of the movie industry is forcefully analyzed in H. M. Enzensberger, "Die Anatomie einer Wochenschau," in *Frankfurter Hefte* (1957) vol. 12, pp. 265–78.

grant some advance credit to its promise to give a high priority to their material claims. Mistrustful of the more remote if all-embracing solutions of the opposition of principle, they accept the parliamentary party's arbitration regarding the extent to which their claims can at present be honored without conflicting with other weighty claims. But some claims have to be honored here and now if their loyalty to the parliamentary party is to last.

In the final analysis it is this urgency of group claims which militates against the parliamentary party's breathing for any length of time outside the precincts of government. It has greatly weakened the party's desire to don the robes of parliamentary opposition, as this would lessen its effectiveness in the adjudication of group claims, which in our time has become its raison d'être. If a party chooses voluntarily to go into opposition — which happens under conditions of a multiparty state — it does so for purely tactical reasons, in order to fasten the burden of unpopular policies on some political competitor, or in order to be free to outbid the opposition of principle by espousing some manifestly inflated group claims.

The rise of the consumption-oriented individual of mass society thus sets the stage for the shrinking of the ideologically oriented nineteenth-century party. After the unlimited extension of the party concept, first in the traditional *Weltanschauungs* party and more recently in the totalitarian movement, its recent reduction to a rationally conceived vehicle of interest representation becomes noticeable. By and large, European parliamentary parties are reducing their special ideological and material offerings. Instead, they substitute a demand for a wide variety of ever expanding community services, open on a basis of equality to whole categories of citizens. Unlike the totalitarian movements they are not equipped to overrun the state machine; at best they aspire to participate in the rewards and premiums it offers. In reminiscence of tradition, or more likely as a planned investment in a public career, individuals may still become party workers. But the tendency for the party to exercise a brokerage function for specific interest groups is present, and is likely to become more accentuated as time goes on. Thus the non-professional in politics is destined to be relegated to a back seat. The interest group, however, as distinct from the individual party member, manifests a loyalty that is limited and contingent. Not only may this loyalty be transferred to more useful political groups, but support may be given simultaneously to groups competing in the political arena.

The modern party is thus forced to think more and more in terms of profit and loss. To it, opposition scarcely relates to the sum total of style, philosophy, and conduct of government, but concentrates on some concrete measure where the government decision may reflect a balance of forces disadvantageous to the interests the party represents. This does not mean that in other instances the balance may not be more favorable, or, even more important, that participation in administrative implementation could not redress the balance in its favor. In such circumstances government participation becomes a matter of necessity; the party would consider it an unmitigated evil if it were excluded for any length of time. But it is also worth while to look at the other side of the coin. While government participation furthers the claims of the party's backers, it also allows the party to assert its own authority over them. The radiation of state authority involved in the party's moving from the brokerage stage to the position of an arbitrator removes the party from many suffocating embraces and carries it beyond the confines of its interest configurations.

The party's alertness in first pursuing and then arbitrating the claims of its clientele is not necessarily related to an equally clear-cut vision of the processes of history at large. The modern party man knows where he has to take his stand if the roll call concerns a question of taxation of consumer cooperatives or an increase in maternity benefits. There are few guideposts to enlighten him as to the best course on EDC or the recognition of Communist China. A roll call of contemporary politicians of many countries and parties would show only a tiny minority who could meaningfully relate the broad canvas of international politics to their domestic objectives. In addition, the more freedom of decision in the realm of foreign policy has narrowed down in the last decade, as a consequence of international developments, the more difficult becomes the offering of foreign-policy alternatives. No parliamentary opposition in Great Britain, France, Italy, or Germany can, without evoking the specter of incalculable and frightening consequences, propagandize a reversing of alliances as a goal and consequence of its coming to power. This lack of realistic alternative solutions leads to a certain sterility and artificiality in the foreign-policy arguments of parliamentary opposition parties, which for better or worse are tied to the geographic location, to the prevailing social system, and consequently also to the international engagements of their countries. . . .

The demise of the opposition is not tantamount to the complete dismantling of the European party, relegating it to some form of procedural device to be used for every comer to fight particular and eternally changing issues, as the stereotype of the political party in the United States would have it.[18] Other factors still favor some measure of party cohesion. One is the existence of an opposition of principle, threatening the continuation of present political patterns. Another is the fact that there are fairly constant elements — slurred and overlapping though they may be — determining which type of interest a party may pick up.

Thus the parliamentary party may continue as a relatively stable

---

[18] Interesting material for comparisons between reality and stereotype can be found in L. D. Epstein, "British Mass Parties in Comparison with American Parties," in *Political Science Quarterly,* vol. 71 (1956) p. 97.

entity. But the unifying and leveling element of the mass media and a certain lessening of social polarization mark a definite stage in the decline of this delicate part of our political heritage, the classic parliamentary opposition. It is in this sense that the Austrian practice of coalition pacts with built-in opposition devices commands interest. It presents a limited survival and revival of the opposition concept at a time when opposition ideologies either have come to serve as handmaidens of total and revolutionary social and political change or are becoming downgraded to the role of relatively meaningless etiquettes and advertisement slogans within the framework of interest representation.

ERWIN K. SCHEUCH
and RUDOLF WILDENMANN

The Professionalization of Party Campaigning

The growing importance of electoral victory to politicians has had major implications for the development of parties as campaign organizations. Often, this trend is denounced as the advent of "the politics of admass" or "the Americanization of campaigning." It is best described neutrally in the title that Erwin Scheuch and Rudolf Wildenmann have given their discussion of German campaign practices. It is appropriate that thorough attention has been given to professionalized campaigning in Germany, since it has for generations been a stronghold of well-organized political parties.

At first sight election contests in three constitutional systems as different as the United States, England, and the German Federal Republic exhibit a striking similarity today. In all these countries, though to the least extent in England, the planning of an election campaign is dominated by professional experts in propaganda. Commercial advertising and public relations agencies have gone far to replace the activity of individual party members, amateurs at propaganda. At one time these voluntary helpers of the parties were the cadres of the election campaign troops, and the response of the party members determined the substance of campaign propaganda. Today, party headquarters, above all in Germany, try to fend off this unwanted help, since it tends to be motivated by ideological beliefs. In election contests, the contents of the propaganda appear to be designed like advertisements for branded consumer goods, with appeals aimed at group characteristics and stereotypes.

The professionalization of propaganda has also influenced the preliminary approach to the voters which precedes the formal election contest. In the years leading up to the opening of the campaign, especially about twelve months before, there is now much research into the behavior patterns and attitudes of the voters. All major parties make use of market research surveys as a matter of routine. These studies are supplemented by special inquiries which often claim for themselves the pretension of being "depth-psychological." It was reported, for example, that about forty opinion surveys were commissioned by the Christian Democratic Union in preparation for the 1961 election campaign. Modern campaigns are first planned on the basis of such information. Moreover, by means of secondary analysis of surveys with third-generation high-power computers, sophisticated typologies and models of the electorate are developed. The techniques used include simulation and multivariate tree analysis.

When at last the voters become aware that a campaign has commenced, the greater part, and perhaps the most important part, of the campaign is already over. The last, the most varied, and the most entertaining weeks of the campaign, resembling the promotion of consumer goods, usually serve only to reinforce existing political sentiments. In this phase of the election contest, non-political means must be used in efforts to influence the outcome.

It is characteristic of the modern election campaign that a carefully worked-out conception underlies it, even though the theory may not be impressive intellectually. The most diverse measures are considered one after another. It is necessary, for example, to decide whether the propaganda should be full of ideas; only after this is determined are ideas sought. In the development of underlying strategies, there are assumptions about necessary laws governing election campaigns.

From Erwin Scheuch and Rudolf Wildenmann, *Zur Soziologie der Wahl*, pp. 50–54 (Westdeutscher Verlag, 1965). English translation by Derek Urwin and Richard Rose. Reprinted by permission.

The strategy to which parties today appear to be committed is that political action and unplanned events preceding the pre-election campaigns are decisive. Thus, campaign planning can really begin with the evaluation of the results of the previous election. The decisions arising from this affect the legislative program of a government during its term of office, even though there is a danger that such a concern with electoral tactics devalues politics as a meaningful business. Electoral considerations can affect foreign policy (because of domestic reactions) as well as internal affairs.

The practices of campaign management in Germany are not unique. In fact, German parties have assimilated developments from other industrial societies. The 1959 election in Britain began initially with the political and economic measures taken by the Conservative government in 1957. These measures were intended to make the pound secure and then produce a pre-election boom in prosperity. The strategy made it possible for the Conservatives to campaign successfully in 1959 on the slogan, "Life's better with the Conservatives; Don't Let Labour Ruin It," a slogan colloquially phrased as "You've Never Had It so Good." (The strategy broke down in 1964, as the most important part of the pre-election plan — entry by Britain into the Common Market — could not be brought off.) In the United States, Lyndon Johnson laid foundations for his massive 1964 majority in the pre-election period, as he or his publicists represented Barry Goldwater as a man wanting war; during the campaign, Goldwater did much to reinforce this image.

Despite cross-national similarities in campaigning, differences still remain. Some are the result of the political culture, such as the stress upon the rules of the game in England. Above all, differences arise from the institutional framework within which competition for office takes place. In Britain, party competition focuses upon a single problem: securing a majority of Members of Parliament in order to form a Cabinet. In the United States, the heterogeneity of the population, along with the sharing of powers and elective offices with local and state governments, contributes much to the autonomy of individual politicians, as well as to their dominance of administrators. They often conduct campaigns very much in terms of local or sectional interests. In Germany, it is sometimes important to campaign with a view to establishing a favorable position for coalition negotiations with third parties after the results are in. This gives the potential supporters of third parties a special significance to the parties. In short, similar techniques can have different consequences, according to institutional and party circumstances.

In the election campaigns in Germany prior to 1961, the parties had made differential use of modern techniques of campaign management. The CDU — or rather, the leadership of the CDU — decided in 1953 to plan a "scientific" election campaign. By the time of the 1957 contest, they had obtained a certain sovereignty in the use of new campaign techniques. At this point, the Social Democratic Party for the first time tried to emulate the CDU, but with a lesser degree of proficiency;

it resembled the CDU in 1953. It might appear paradoxical that a party like the SPD, which had taken great pains since its foundation to develop methods of political agitation, should find it so difficult to accept the instruments of modern campaign management. But the SPD had specialized in agitation to the politicized, and not in propaganda to those electors whose decisions are seldom determined by deep political beliefs. It was easier for a party like the CDU, whose connections with the world of commerce and advertising are closer, to modify its campaign strategy in this respect.

The success of the CDU in 1957 contributed to the tendency of politicians in all parties to see the result of an election as the result of better advertising of manufactured articles. The research staffs of the parties perceived more accurately the limits of influencing voting behavior through advertising and propaganda techniques, for they were increasingly conscious of the difference between selling consumer goods and winning adherents to a party. This more sophisticated understanding has been slow to gain acceptance by the leadership of the parties.

The preparations for the 1961 election campaign were intended to repeat and improve upon the CDU election efforts of 1957. For the first time, in 1961 all parties were ready and able to employ the full technology of modern election campaign management, from opinion surveys to entertaining advertisements. The technical output of the campaigning groups tended to have a standardized appearance.

Two other elections were also used as examples in Germany: the British general election of 1959 and the American presidential election of 1960. Both elections, and especially John F. Kennedy's campaign, were followed and studied carefully by special observers from the major German parties. The fact that some conclusions drawn were wrong, e.g., ideas about the meaning of candidates shaking hands, did not affect the fact that the campaigns in Germany were modelled after these successful campaigns elsewhere.

The CDU undertook, in the eighteen months before the campaign, about as many surveys as it had commissioned in the six years between 1953 and 1959. This quantitative increase expresses only imperfectly the degree to which such data gained in importance for decision-making in the parties. It is noteworthy that while the CDU and the FDP (Free Democrats) commissioned surveys by commercial agencies, the SPD preferred to use a closely connected institute for opinion research founded in Bad Godesberg after the 1957 election contest. The CDU, like a consumer goods firm, entrusted two commercial agencies with the development of campaign propaganda. By contrast, the SPD, oriented toward large-scale industrial models, preferred to have its own research and propaganda staff, operating like many of the major industrial firms in Germany.

Since then, the campaign strategies and the types of organizations preparing research and planning public relations work have become more similar, both parties borrowing from each other. A law providing for the continuous financing of party activities from tax revenues enabled the major parties to set up research staffs plus quasi-independent research institutions. Traditionally, professional politicians on the Continent turned themselves into amateur campaigners as the time of elections came closer. There is some tendency now for professional campaign strategists to become amateur politicians. A stable balance between the different roles of professionals in politics is still to come in a process of trial with much error. The early 1960's was one sort of watershed: professional politicians tended to become consumers and mere executors of long-term campaign strategies. There are some indications that now the professional politicians on the Continent will try to reshape the system of the major mass media to better suit their needs. Were such a change in the institutional framework of politics successful, the role of professional campaign strategists would change again. The process of professionalization of party campaigning, however, is irreversible.

GEORGES LAVAU

Parties of Interests and of Abstractions

The translation of major social differences, particularly economic differences, into partisan divisions is sometimes denounced as contrary to the general interest, an abstraction as familiar rhetorically as it is difficult to define empirically. By contrast, parties based upon economic groups are making claims that are easily recognized and material. Moreover, those who support a party because it speaks for their interest are likely to remain loyal followers, for the economic interests of workers or businessmen do not fluctuate from election to election. In France, parties of special interests have been less prominent than parties claiming to represent the general will or particular ideals of French society, whether revolutionary or anti-revolutionary. Georges Lavau analyzes the consequences of such a party system.

A great number of political parties is in itself neither a sign nor a source of political instability. In comparison with their population, Switzerland, Denmark, and the Netherlands have a much larger number of political parties than France. These countries, however, have more stable party systems than the United States, which has only two parties. On the other hand, it has been maintained with a bit of exaggeration that there were only two or three political forces in France: the right and the left (order and movement), to which the center is sometimes added.[1]

Whatever the classification adopted, whether one uses the classification of groups in the National Assembly or a simplifying dichotomy, numbers of parties are not the thing that contributes to political instability. The fundamental vice of our party system is the penchant of parties for *abstraction*. If one compares the names of several French parties or groups from the Third or the Fourth Republic with several Swiss, Dutch, and Norwegian counterparts, one quickly realizes that unlike what occurs elsewhere, a French party rarely sets forth clearly its social raison d'être or states which social group, interests, or beliefs it intends to represent. It presents itself as an *abstraction* unsullied by any compromising relationship with a social class, an economic category, or a religious belief.

Judging from French party labels, even a very knowledgeable observer can scarcely presume to say whether the adjective "French" is an indication of a rightist party, for there is the *French* Communist Party, or whether a party "of the left" is in fact of the right. The terms "social," "socialist," and "popular" are but expletives used to make the title more euphonious.

This neutralization of party titles would simply be ridiculous if it were only camouflage behind which parties actually corresponded to specific social or ideological interests, but such is not the case. With the exception of the Communist Party, a French political party never represents one social interest, one economic category, one belief, or one political doctrine; it is neither a mixture nor a synthesis of those things but rather truly an *abstraction*, the analysis of which reveals an infinity of elements, originally very distinct and conflicting, which have been changed and deformed.

Take, for example, one of the most distinctive parties, the SFIO (the *Section française de l'internationale ouvrière*, the French section

---

Abridged and translated by Allen Rozelle and Mattei Dogan from *Partis politiques et réalités sociales: contribution à une étude réaliste des partis politiques* (Paris: A. Colin, 1953), pp. 138–150. Reprinted by permission. Cf. the analyses here with the article by Rose and Urwin, *infra.*, pp. 217–237.

[1] Such a reduction is a bit exaggerated because at the moment it is only with the greatest reluctance that one could classify both the Communist Party and the Radical Party under the same heading of the forces of movement; likewise, it seems a bit arbitrary to classify the parties of a "bonapartist" nature among the parties of order. Such classification is only admissible from an historical and dialectical point of view.

of the working-class International). From the point of view of class composition, this party contends that it represents the working class, but, compared with Anglo-Saxon labor parties or Scandinavian social-democratic parties, it has never been *the* party of the working class with the possible exception of its first few years. An examination of the party's leadership and parliamentary representation as well as of its electoral support shows that the SFIO is simultaneously a party of workers, civil servants, employees, professors, and even farmers. Never has the SFIO maintained relations with the CGT unions or with the CGT-FO unions as close as those between other European social-democratic parties and labor unions. Ideologically, the SFIO is socialist, but the question is, what kind of socialism? It is reluctant to declare itself overtly reformist like the British or Swedish labor parties, but at the same time it dares not proclaim itself frankly Marxist (though it does not wish to scrap the Marxist label). It is certainly not an agrarian socialist party (although it sometimes waves this flag in certain overseas territories). In a crisis, it saves face by referring to "Jauressism," that is to say, emotional and abstract words. Moreover, the SFIO not only represents socialism, but also (and not without contradicting itself at times) internationalism and jacobinism, anticolonialism and the policy of colonial assimilation (an unconscious form of colonialism), anarchism and state centralization, and rationalism with romanticism straight out of Rousseau's *La Nouvelle Heloïse*. A comparable examination could be made of the Radical Party, the Republican Federation, the Catholic Popular Republican Movement (MRP), etc. It is also extraordinary that there has never been a true peasants' party in France. . . .

Likewise there has never been a Catholic party, nor even more generally a Christian party. The Young Republic and the Popular Democratic Party, which could have formed the seed of one, declared themselves as such only timidly and never represented more than a narrow faction of the Christian population. The MRP has come close, but it is well known that it avoids the label of a clerical or religious party, and leaving aside the question of education (over which it has not seen fit to do battle), it has been quite successful on the whole.* Finally, it is hardly contested that the MRP is much less the party of Catholics than are the Christian Social Party in Belgium and the Christian Democratic Party in Italy.

In every country, the "middle classes" constitute the group which most objects to expressing itself through a well-defined, political movement, but almost nowhere does this tendency seem to be as pronounced as in France. It is still a fairly sizeable part of the middle classes who fill the ranks of the Liberal parties in Great Britain and Belgium, the *Folkpartiet* in Sweden, and the Radicals in Denmark. In France, on the contrary, the Radical Party, which is too often represented as *the* party

---

* [The MRP went out of existence early in the life of the Fifth Republic. — Editors' note.]

of the middle classes, is far from having even a quasi-monopoly. It applies only in certain regions (southwest and southeast) and especially in the small provincial cities, where it seems to have a lien on the middle classes. In other regions, in Paris, and in the other large cities, the Radical Party often has to fall in behind the Gaullisto, the Independents, the MRP, or the SFIO.

We have dwelt on this examination of the *abstract* character of French parties because we consider its consequences to be of fundamental importance. Except for the Communists, without doubt every Frenchman considers it fortunate that his parties do *not* represent particular classes, economic interests, or faiths. Dedication to universalism is considered the touchstone of the democratic nature of political parties, and the curse placed on the Communist Party rests partly, whether one admits it or not, on the fact that it is not afraid to proclaim itself a class party.

In countries where political life involves only two parties or evolves under the control of a dominant party, it is normal, but not ineluctable, that the one or two parties should be high level aggregations of diverse political tendencies, groups, and traditions. Such is the case of the Liberal and Conservative parties in Canada and the Republican and Democratic parties in the United States. And such will remain the case at least as long as opposition of economic and social structures is masked or neutralized by other antagonisms of a regional, racial, or traditional, e.g. Whigs and Tories, nature. When those antagonisms blur or collapse, as in Great Britain, at least one of the parties takes on a pronounced class character. As long as this point is not reached, only pressure groups can fill the gaps left by the parties and perform the function of representation. However in a multi-party system, especially where the expression of various tendencies is favored by proportional representation, such discord between interest groups and sociologically determined currents of thought and political parties is neither normal nor fortunate.

One can certainly challenge the advisability of religious parties because they can involve a dangerous confusion of spiritual demands and mundane alternatives. They can lead to a confusion of two spheres of life which manifests itself less by a spiritualization of the temporal than by a questionable temporalization of the spiritual. Especially in an age when faith is questioned and when masses profess no religious belief, religious parties cannot escape the risk of representing a social group or even a class, even though the spiritual message from which they take their strength is universal.[2] However, it appears indispensable to us that parties correspond to clearly determined economic and social *realities*. To be more precise, the closer the party system conforms to the divisions and contours of the social structure, the healthier it is,

---

[2] For example, it is inadmissible for a Christian party to adopt a policy hostile to the independence of colonial peoples, a policy in no way supported by the teachings of Christianity, even if not explicitly contradicted by them.

because it is more realistic. A party system which differs markedly from the real is a mystery; it offers citizens only alienation by abstractions. Politics is not a kind of cerebral activity; nor is it an art for the elect or an abstract science of economic conditions within which humanity works out its destiny. It is action in the world — and action transforming it. It is through his work that man acts on the world, and it is in the work-place relations that economic and social structures are born.

French parties along the spectrum from the SFIO to the Gaullist RPF are unreal. They correspond to none of the realities which shape the daily existence of man. Frenchmen are workers, peasants, shopkeepers, from Alsace, Valois, or Dalecarlie, and not "Democratic Alliance," "Assembly of the Republican Left," or "Radical and Radical-Socialist"! This unreality is why Frenchmen use their ballots as other peoples consult mediums; the parties are spirits and there is no question of asking them to make sense. Politics springs from marvels and magic; it is a form of escapism which holds no hope for a better world; it is an addiction, a game of grand quarrels about clericalism, liberty, peace, etc. The end and justification of politics is its formalism. Contacts with French Communist workers (themselves victims of another sort of mystification) indicate that what attracts them to their party is precisely that it alone gives its faithful the impression of participating in their reality, and of basing its action on the transformation of the real world through politics.

The consequence of this situation is twofold. First, parties stuffed with abstractions and contradictions can rarely decide on a clearly defined, political line. From this fact stem splits, disagreements, and a reluctance to confront true problems. Second, no government coalition can rest on alliances of well-defined interests, since the parties themselves lack clarity: it is the source of unstable coalitions simultaneously supporting anti-clerical education policies and the civilization of Christian values; rearmament and the struggle against inflation, or job protection and the fight against social security.[3]

In the French political debate, no party — with the exception of the Communist Party — can state without lying or betraying itself that it speaks for such and such a clearly-defined interest or group.[4] This creates perpetual ambiguity and encourages the pretense of speaking

---

[3] We do not criticize coalitions in themselves, but rather coalitions based on nothing and offering no clear option. In this respect, it does not seem to us that Danish and Swedish coalitions incur the same reproaches. In Denmark, the coalition of Agrarians and Conservatives is an alliance of agricultural and commercial interests; it reflects fairly well the Danish economic structure. In Sweden, the already old alliance of Agrarians and Labor is symbolic of coordinated action by the two portions of the population who are manual workers.

[4] Moreover, reality enters in more or less occult ways. Certain parliamentary groups are in fact linked to fairly specific economic interests (there were some celebrated examples of this under the Third Republic), and it is well-known that if the rules of the National Assembly prohibit lobbies for wine, beets, automobiles, etc., the field is clear for "study groups," which pursue the same objectives under another name.

for the general interest, public opinion, the French people, or the average Frenchman. These are fetishes. Just as the average Frenchman is an abstraction, so the general interest is but a fiction conjured by jurists to mask private interests whose preeminence they wish to legitimize.

As far as elections are concerned, the idealistic nature of French parties appears to us to be one of the primary reasons for the variation of their electoral power, especially since the creation of the RPF. When one compares the number of votes received between 1945 and 1951 by the SFIO, the MRP, the Radicals, and the various moderate parties, with those received during the same period by all the Swiss, Scandinavian, and Dutch parties (excluding the Communist parties), it can be said that electoral strength varied more among parties in France than elsewhere. One reason seems to be that where parties correspond to clearly defined economic and social groups, variations are necessarily weak because those groups have stable support from well-defined groups in society, at least over short periods. The movement of votes only represents the unsteadiness of marginal groups, or of individuals who are not entirely integrated in a social group.[5]

In Parliament, the unreality of French parties manifests itself on the one hand by their fragility and on the other by the confusion they perpetuate.

Fragility: It is truly surprising to hear so many persons criticize French parties for their "monolithic nature" since, with the exception of the Communist Party, they all suffer from a cruel lack of cohesion and a perpetual tendency to explode — a tendency they can overcome only by becoming stagnant. This fragility is evident in the large number of ephemeral party alliances which sometimes fail to last out a legislative term: from 1881 to 1940, but especially during the last twenty years of the Third Republic, it is virtually impossible to calculate the number of small groups that appeared and disappeared for no apparent reason.

Confusion: Even more than the number of parties, fragility makes coalitions difficult to form and condemns them to a short life. Between a peasant party and a worker party, bargaining can be long and hard before agreement is reached; once concluded, however, it normally remains effective because each party overwhelmingly represents the interests in question. When parties simultaneously represent all and nothing and, to make things worse, "the public interest," nothing is ever fixed. There is always uncertainty about the nature of the heterogeneous electoral following behind the parties, and the parties themselves can only rarely define their intentions clearly. Excluding the case of majorities clearly oriented toward the right or the left (and such majorities are necessarily rare since an ambiguous situation is created as soon as they include Radicals and Popular Republicans), no party

---

[5] The class character of Labour would explain the remarkable stability of the distribution of votes in Great Britain since 1945, while the sudden shocks caused by the elections in the United States could be explained by the mystifying nature of American parties.

can feel truly at ease in a coalition regardless of the policy of the coalition. The histories of the Radical Party, the MRP, and the SFIO illustrate quite well such inhibitions. (One dares not speak of parties being distraught; only certain lower-level party activists could feel that, for legislators are too thick-skinned.)

In the more general and essential realm of governmental action, the idealism of our political life is the cause of its impotence. It is there that the source of political instability is to be found, and not in a few tumults at the National Assembly or in the obstruction of its work; such disorders are only external signs of a more profound weakness.

French parties are criticized for being too numerous (which is true only with regard to what they represent: virtually nothing real), for being too subtle (but they are only artificial), for being too doctrinaire (but a label is needed to hide the emptiness of the bottle), and finally for lacking an understanding of the general interest (but they all offer themselves as the ideal image of the whole nation). In truth the major complaint that can be made of the French party system — and it contains the key to understanding the imbalance of our political life — is that it is not healthy because it wallows in idealism and angelic purity.

A final qualification is necessary. There are other countries where parties have little to do with reality. It could be maintained that such is always the case at least for center parties; it is certainly true of the large, traditional parties of the United States and Canada. In their case, however, two facts redress the balance, if only partially; first, the para-political action of pressure groups, which represent social groups and very precise interests, reintroduces reality into the political life; second, federal structures, by creating the conditions for party decentralization, permit them to correspond to local and regional realities which are truer than the abstractions which the parties are compelled to represent at the federal level.

In France, these two corrective factors scarcely exist. American and Canadian pressure groups have no exact French counterparts. Certainly there are various influential groups such as the truckers, the beet-growers, the Education League, and the League for the Rights of Man, but besides the fact that their activities are considered shameful and carried on in ways almost unknown to the public, their numbers are limited because associational life remains very weak in France. Federalism cannot play any insignificant role because there are no federal structures. The French political system is still dominated by centralization and by an extraordinarily unitary conception of the state.

CHAPTER SIX

Pressure Groups

The basic premise of pressure group politics — the political power of economic interests and social groups — has always been accepted in European nations, originating in medieval societies where political power, economic resources, and social honor were closely intertwined. In such circumstances, politics was not only a case of conflict between groups, but also an activity in which a man's multiple interests might well be in conflict with each other. For instance, the issues of the Reformation faced kings and bishops with institutional conflicts between church and state and a personal conflict between interests in this world and the next.

The theory and practice of pressure group politics is not, however, easy to trace through the centuries. In France, Germany, and Italy, political philosophers endorsed the belief that there was a general interest, above and apart from the outcome of group conflict that James Madison extolled in *The Federalist*. In Germany, the claims of the state, standing over against particular groups, were considered especially strong. In Britain, the 18th century philosophy of interests was replaced in the 19th century by a liberal belief in the virtues of individual activity: British politicians became hesitant to admit openly the existence of pressure groups, although in practice they continued to discuss pending legislation in language that sounded suspiciously like that of American pressure politics. On the Continent, by contrast, interest groups often pressed claims in extremist form, whether they were Socialist or syndicalist proponents of a general strike for workers' control, or businessmen making contributions to a Fascist party in hopes that this would create an orderly society in which they could prosper with state patronage and assistance.

Since World War II, all European governments have become more intimately and pervasively involved in the socio-economic conditions of ordinary citizens' lives, and they have tried to operate a mixed economy welfare state with authority derived from democratic procedures.

While definitions of democracy vary cross-nationally, in each society it is assumed that democratic government requires consultation with the accredited representatives of affected groups before legislation is passed affecting them. In short, pressure group spokesmen have become legitimate participants in politics, as well as major beneficiaries of government policies.

To note similarities between contemporary European and American pressure politics is not to suggest that American concepts or experiences can automatically be matched in European countries. The nature of the interests advanced are often very different. For example, in no European society is there a prohibition of connections between church and state, such as is found in the First Amendment to the United States Constitution. The church is perceived as a pressure group, with special interests and demands to make in such fields as education and social welfare, and with a following of some electoral importance. The weight of religious interest groups is different in Italy, Germany, France, and Britain. In Italy, religious pressures have been strong and successful, with a Christian Democratic party in power continuously since the war. In France, anti-clerical pressure groups have tended to be stronger. In Germany, regional differences, a federal constitution, and government by a mixed Protestant-Catholic Christian Democratic Union has reduced friction. In England, religious interests are only occasionally important, when legislation concerns matters such as divorce or abortion. In part, this is because the Prime Minister appoints the head of the English Church, the Archbishop of Canterbury, and in part it is because of the secularization of English society.

There are well organized business interest groups in all European countries. In France, Germany, and Italy, the continued importance of peasant farmers and of small shopkeepers means that there is a strong counterweight to the influence of "big" business. Trade unions are particularly well organized in Britain, where about 40 per cent of the labor force belongs to a union, and the majority of trade union members regularly pay a small membership contribution to the Labour Party. The actions of the Labour Government since 1964 emphasize, however, that party politicians can use such close ties to influence unions, as well as to be influenced by them. In Germany, there are three principal trade union groupings, one appealing primarily to manual workers, another to white collar workers, and a third to civil servants. While trade unionists tend to sympathize with the Social Democratic party, the CDU has been successful in obtaining some union support too. In France and Italy, both party and religious differences divide the labor movement; in each country there are union federations dominated by the Communists, the Socialists, and the Catholic Church. Singly and collectively, the unions are much weaker in France and Italy than in Britain and Germany.

The division of nominally economic interest groups along clearcut ideological lines is a very striking example of a major feature of the history of European pressure groups: the extent to which organizations nominally established to represent specific interests are often associated with broad ideological movements or parties. These lead them to define their interests in terms of abstract and even rigid principles, as well as in terms of material demands capable of settlement by bargaining.

BIBLIOGRAPHY

Good introductions to the comparative study of European pressure groups, especially written to take account of American similarities and differences, can be found in Joseph LaPalombara, "The Utility and Limitations of Interest Group Theory in Non-American Field Situations," *Journal of Politics* XXII: 1 (1961); and Gabriel Almond, "A Comparative Study of Interest Groups and the Political Process," *American Political Science Review* LII: 1 (1958). "Comparative Political Finance," a special issue of the *Journal of Politics* XXV: 4 (1963), edited by Richard Rose and Arnold J. Heidenheimer, is especially useful as an introduction to material connections between political parties and interest groups. *Interest Groups on Four Continents,* edited by Henry W. Ehrmann (Pittsburgh University Press, 1958), brings together the views of scholars from a wide range of countries, including France, Germany, and Britain.

Walter Galenson, *Trade Union Democracy in Western Europe* (University of California Press, 1962), makes a very useful distinction between unified trade unionism, as in Great Britain and Scandinavia, strong but divided unionism, as in Belgium, Holland, and Austria, and divided but weak unionism, as in France and Italy. See also W. Galenson, editor, *Comparative Labor Movements* (New York: Prentice-Hall, 1952). A detailed comparison between labor movements, images of labor leaders, and collective bargaining relationships is in Joseph A. Raffaele, *Labor Leadership in Italy and Denmark* (University of Wisconsin Press, 1962).

In addition to the articles reprinted here, one might refer specifically to these studies for each of the four countries: *Britain:* Samuel H. Beer, *British Politics in the Collectivist Age* (New York: Random House, 1965), S. E. Finer, *Anonymous Empire* (London: Pall Mall, 2nd edition, 1966); Allen Potter, *Organized Groups in British National Politics* (London: Faber, 1961); and Richard Rose, *Influencing Voters* (New York: St. Martins, 1967), a study of party-pressure group relations. *France:* Henry W. Ehrmann, *Organized Business in France* (Princeton University Press, 1957); Val R. Lorwin, *The French Labor Movement* (Harvard University Press, 1954); Gordon Wright, *Rural Revolution in France* (Stanford University Press, 1964); and Bernard E. Brown, "Pressure Politics in the Fifth Republic," *Journal of Politics* XXV: 3 (1963). *Germany:* Gerard Braunthal, *The Federation of German Industry in Politics* (Ithaca: Cornell University Press, 1965); Herbert Spiro, *The Politic of German Codetermination* (Cambridge, Mass.: Harvard University Press, 1958); Charles Frye, "Parties and Pressure Groups in Weimar and Bonn," *World Politics* XVII: 4 (1965); and Louis P. Lochner, *Tycoons and Tyrants: German Industry from Hitler to Adenauer* (Chicago University Press, 1954). *Italy:* Joseph LaPalombara, *The Italian Labor Movement: Problems and Prospects* (Ithaca: Cornell University Press, 1957); Daniel L. Horowitz, *The Italian Labor Movement* (Harvard University Press, 1965); Gianfranco Poggi, *Catholic Action in Italy* (Stanford University Press, 1967); Michael P. Fogarty, *Christian Democracy in Western Europe, 1820–1953* (University of Notre Dame Press, 1957); Leicester C. Webb, *Church and State in Italy, 1947–1957* (Melbourne University Press, 1958); and Richard A. Webster, *The Cross and the Fasces* (Stanford University Press, 1960).

ROY MACRIDIS

Interest Groups in Comparative Analysis

Each of the articles in this chapter illustrates that pressure groups cannot be studied in isolation from other parts of a political system, notwithstanding the intrinsic interest of many things that lobbyists do. The political significance of a group depends not only upon the activities it undertakes, but also upon the reactions these acts produce from men in power. Roy Macridis's survey of the field draws an ironic conclusion: the comparative analysis of pressure groups is primarily valuable in identifying cross-national differences in more general political processes. These differences, in turn, can explain many variations in the actions of pressure groups in different lands.

. . . Group theory assumes the existence of organized groups or interests that can be defined in objective terms; labor, business, and agriculture are some of the more obvious and frequently studied ones. It is further assumed that their members have a common perception of the interest involved which accounts for the very formation of the group and its organization and articulation. . . . Descriptive and comparative study immediately presents us with extreme variations in the organization, cohesiveness, membership strength, forms of action and patterns of interaction among these groups. It reveals some striking differences in the manner in which interest groups in various political systems relate to the political parties and the political processes.

To attempt to explain such differences in terms of a group theory is impossible. Why, for instance, are agricultural groups so well organized under the National Farmers Union in England, to which more

Excerpted and reprinted by permission of the author and publisher from *Journal of Politics* XXIII: 1 (1961). pp. 34–38.

than ninety per cent of the farmers belong, but dispersed and relatively unorganized in the United States and France? Why are more than eighty-five per cent of all manufacturing concerns in England represented in the F.B.I. [Federation of British Industries], while not more than six per cent are represented in the N.A.M. [National Association of Manufacturers]? Why do more than fifty per cent of the British workers belong to trade unions which are almost all represented in their peak organization, the T.U.C. [Trades Union Congress], while in France membership remains low and articulation of labor interest dispersed in at least four trade union organizations? Why is it that in England interest groups avoid large publicity campaigns and center their attention on the party and the cabinet, while in the United States interest groups perform important publicity and propaganda functions through the media of communications and center their efforts on the electorate and the legislature, primarily, but French interest groups shun publicity and center their activities upon the legislature and the administration?

A number of answers can be given to these questions in the form of propositions to be carefully investigated, but I submit that none of them are researchable in terms of group analysis. The answers are often given (without adequate evidence, to be sure) in terms of other categories: the American political system *with multiple foci* of decision-making, for instance, makes the legislature and more particularly individual legislators more susceptible to pressure either directly or indirectly; *the diffusion of power* in the political party in the United States makes any effort to control or influence the party unrewarding for pressure groups. The same answer applies to France, where it is often pointed out that "interest" and "interest groups" are divided and subdivided and lose their "objective" or "real" interest *because of political reasons:* the workers, the farmers, the teachers have no spokesmen and no cohesive and disciplined interest articulation because they are divided into a number of "political" or "ideological" families. As for group interaction, again the differences are striking: in some cases, groups interact within a given political party and compromise their differences; in other cases, compromise is made outside of the political parties, or is not made at all, leading to immobility; elsewhere compromise is made impossible by virtue of the fact that interests are "colonized" by ideological parties so that interest groups mirror the ideological divisions of the society instead of causing them.

In all cases the reasons advanced for a given pattern of group organization, action and interaction derive from categories other than group analysis would suggest: the formal organization of power; the cohesiveness or dispersal of political power; the two-party or multi-party configuration; the "climate of public opinion"; the intensity of consensus or lack of same in given political systems. Garceau rightly points out that groups and group interaction must be seen "in context" rather than as independent raw forces of politics struggling against each other. Alfred de Grazia observes that "whether a particular interest group has much or little power depends upon its place in the total way of life of the population. . . ."[1] Sam Eldersveld points out that ". . . we need a research design to test propositions about indirect influence and vertical relationships if we are really interested in analyzing influence. Such a design must recognize assumptively the extent to which interest groups in America are *interwoven* with the social, economic and cultural system."[2] Henry Ehrmann in his study on French business groups points out in discussing Max Weber's observation — according to which interest can often bring order into the dynamics of the society — that "interests assume that function only where their implementation accepts the restraints which commonly shared political and social values will impose. . . . Where, as in France, consensus on such values is largely absent, the lack of integration will communicate itself to all of the stages of the political process and will . . . impede the emergence of a setting in which simultaneously ascertained interests could further the establishment of an equilibrium."[3]

The shortcomings of group analysis as an explanatory theory may be further illustrated by borrowing from the conclusions of authors interested in comparative study or who did field work in foreign political systems. Professor Ehrmann writes in his introduction to *Interest Groups on Four Continents*: "The political system, as well as the social structure, will often decide whether claims raised in the name of special interests will be successful or not; it may determine the "style" used by pressure groups when raising their demands."[4] Professor Georges E. Lavau, after indicating in detail the fragmentation of many French interests because of ideological reasons, points out that "This hostile ideological and moral climate surrounding pressure groups in France reacts in turn upon their behaviour. . . ." He indicates that some pressure groups if *not politicized* play an aggregative and integrative role that the French political parties do not play. This is, for instance, the case with some peak organizations that include a variety of professional groups. "Since it is [their] function to arbitrate or mediate possible conflicts between different member organizations, this role confers upon [them], in the eyes of the administration and the politicians, a considerable dignity."[5] In fact one of the most pervasive efforts of the French interest groups is to liberate themselves from a divided political culture and be able to organize their membership on the basis of interest alone. That they fail more often than they succeed is an in-

---

[1] Alfred de Grazia in "Unofficial Government, Pressure Groups and Lobbies," a special issue of *The Annals of the American Academy of Political and Social Science* CCCXIX (September, 1958), p. 115.

[2] "American Interest Groups," in Henry W. Ehrmann, editor, *Interest Groups in Four Continents* (Pittsburgh, 1958), p. 187.

[3] Henry W. Ehrmann, *Organized Business in France*, p. xii.

[4] Henry W. Ehrmann, "The Comparative Study of Interest Groups," in *Interest Groups in Four Continents*, p.1.

[5] See his excellent article — the best in the English language — "Political Pressures in France," in *Interest Groups in Four Continents*, pp. 61, 78.

dication of the importance, and what is more, the independence, of political and ideological factors.

Professor Samuel Finer accepts Samuel H. Beer's emphasis upon the British "consensus" and the general agreement of the British leadership on a number of policy issues as a factor that shapes and structures group action. He adds that such beliefs are brought together in English political life by the myth of "public interest" which provides a yardstick in terms of which interest claims are judged. The image of the national interest acts as a cohesive force.[6] Professor Beer in an excellent analysis points to the parallel development in Great Britain of well-organized and integrated political parties with well-organized national interest groups.[7] For the purpose of our discussion this parallelism between interest organization and party organization is striking and one cannot avoid the conclusion that British interests gradually evolved a pattern of organization and cohesiveness *that corresponds to* and *parallels* the highly centralized and cohesive political system; that perhaps their "style" of action was conditioned by the cohesiveness of the political culture and the organization of political parties very much as the dispersion of the French interest groups may well have been shaped by the diversity of the French political culture and multipartism.

Joseph LaPalombara points out bluntly that many interest groups in Italy (and the same applies to France) operate within the political sub-cultures of the system (communist, catholic, socialist, etc.), resulting in an enormous proliferation (and the same applies to France) of pressure groups.[8] Writing on Swedish pressure groups, Gunnar Heckscher points out that ". . . there is hardly any point at which this term [politics of compromise] seems more definitely warranted than with regard to interest organizations: an equilibrium is maintained chiefly through the willingness of each of them to make concessions in order to achieve important results. . . ." But why? Because "the pluralistic character of the Swedish society is openly accepted on all sides."[9] Back we come to the general values of the community in terms of which the role of pressure groups and pressure group action and interaction can be explained.

Jean Meynaud, in his comprehensive study of French pressure groups in France,[10] comes very close to a very important theoretical insight

---

[6] Samuel E. Finer, "Interest Groups and the Political Process in Great Britain," in *Interest Groups in Four Continents*, p. 143.

[7] Samuel H. Beer, "Group Representation in Britain and the United States," in *The Annals of the American Academy of Political and Social Science* CCCXIX (September, 1958), pp. 131–140.

[8] "The Utility and Limitations of Interest Group Theory in Non-American Field Situations," *Journal of Politics* XXII (February, 1960), pp. 29–49.

[9] Gunnar Heckscher, "Interest Groups in Sweden," in *Interest Groups in Four Continents*, p. 170.

[10] Jean Meynaud, *Les Groupes de Pression en France*, particularly Chaps. 1 and 5.

when he points out that the fragmentation of parties, like the fragmentation of the groups, has its origin in the divisions in the public mind. Political ideologies and religious considerations destroy the unity that would result from objective professional and interest considerations. A number of organizations mushroom *within the same* professional sector because of ideological reasons. One might hypothesize indeed that this parallelism between the political system and the interest configuration is true everywhere. *Wherever the political governmental organization is cohesive and power is concentrated in certain well-established centers, the pressure groups become well organized with a similar concentration of power and vice versa.*

HARRY ECKSTEIN

The Determinants of Pressure Group Politics

Fascination with the details and machinations of pressure group activities leads many students to evaluate them in isolation. In practice, the political influence of pressure groups can never be divorced from a consideration of the reaction that their activities cause in other parts of a political system. In a bargaining process, pressure groups may be as much the objects of influence as the wielders of it. Not the least of the virtues of Harry Eckstein's approach to the subject is that he sets out clearly the importance of the interaction of pressure groups, parties, and government in the British political system. The chapter forms an introduction to a study of the efforts of the British Medical Association to oppose the introduction by a Labour Government of a National Health Service. The doctors' lobby was spectacularly unsuccessful in preventing the introduction of a scheme providing extensive and free medical care.

PROBLEMS

Case studies never "prove" anything; their purpose is to illustrate generalizations which are established otherwise, or to direct attention towards such generalizations. Since this is a case study of the political activities of the British Medical Association it may be well to state at the outset the broad principles it illustrates. These principles are formulated in answer to three questions:

1. What are the determinants of the *form* of pressure group politics in various political systems? What factors determine the principal channels and means through which pressure groups act on government and the character of the relations between the groups and organs of government?
2. What are the determinants of the *intensity* and *scope* of pressure group politics? "Intensity" here refers to the fervour and persistence with which groups pursue their political objectives as well as to the relative importance of political activities in their affairs; scope, to the number and variety of groups engaged in politics.
3. What determines the *effectiveness* of pressure groups? From what principal sources do they derive their power vis-à-vis other pressure groups and the more formal elements of the decision-making structure, such as parties, legislature and bureaucracy? . . .

DETERMINANTS OF THE FORM OF PRESSURE GROUP POLITICS

CHANNELS. By the "form" of pressure group activities I mean, first, the channels of action on which such groups concentrate. The most important, and the most obvious, determinant of the selection of channels for pressure group activity, in any political system, is the *structure* of the decision-making processes which pressure groups seek to influence. Interest groups (or any other groups) become pressure groups because they want to obtain favourable policy decisions or administrative dispositions; hence, obviously, they must adjust their activities to the processes by which decisions and dispositions are made. To cite a very simple example: in Great Britain the National Union of Teachers is one of the larger and more active pressure groups on the national level, while in the United States teachers' groups play only a very minor role, if any, in national politics;[1] the reason is simply that

---

Abridged from Harry Eckstein, *Pressure Group Politics: The Case of the British Medical Association*, pp. 15–39 (© 1960 by Harry Eckstein). Reprinted by permission of the publishers, Stanford University Press and George Allen & Unwin Ltd.

[1] V. O. Key, Jr., *Politics, Parties and Pressure Groups* (Thomas Y. Crowell Co., N.Y., 2nd ed. 1947) does not even mention them. David B. Truman's encyclopaedic *The Governmental Process* (Knopf, N.Y., 1951) mentions the National Education Association (p. 452), but does not bother to describe its activities.

British educational policies are made and administered by the national government, while in the American federal system this is not the case, except only in the most indirect sense. But this is perhaps too simple an example. Pressure groups tend to adjust the form of their activities not so much to the formal (constitutional) structure of governments as to the distribution of effective power within a governmental apparatus, and this is often something very different from formal structure; in the competition for influence they cannot afford to be deceived by political myths. Hence their activities are themselves one of the more reliable guides to the loci of effective power in any political system, whenever the "political formula" of the system — as Lasswell and Kaplan call it[2] — does not indicate these loci correctly.

Not only the structure of the decision-making process but also the decisions which emerge from it — the *activities* of government — influence the predominant channels of pressure group politics, and this just because decisions have a reciprocal effect on the structures that make them. The most obvious example is the devolution of decision-making powers from legislatures to bureaucracies in this age of the social service state, both through the direct delegation of legislative powers and the indirect influence which bureaucrats enjoy over decisions still formally taken by legislatures.

Finally, the dominant channels of pressure group politics may be determined by certain *attitudes,* the most obviously important being attitudes toward pressure groups themselves. Where, for example, the pursuit of corporate interests by political means is normatively reproved — where "liberal" individualist assumptions[3] are deeply ingrained — pressure groups are likely to work through more inconspicuous channels and with more unobtrusive means than where corporate politics are normatively tolerated. But even attitudes not directly concerned with pressure groups may, indirectly, affect the form of their activities, at any rate if the attitudes have a bearing on the distribution of effective decision-making power. For example, a broad consensus on major policies — the sort of policies usually made by cabinets and legislatures — will tend to shift the major arena of political conflict, hence the major efforts of pressure groups, toward the administrative departments.

Basically, it is always the interplay of governmental structure, activities and attitudes which determines the form of pressure group politics (in the sense of channels of participation) in a given society. These factors may, of course, pull in different directions. Usually, however, they do not — chiefly (1) because the attitudes which bear directly upon a society's structure of decision-making (constitutional myths) and the attitudes which bear upon it indirectly (e.g. attitudes

---

[2] Harold D. Lasswell and Abraham Kaplan, *Power and Society* (Routledge, 1950), p. 126 ff.

[3] The term "liberal" is used in accordance with S. H. Beer, "The Representation of Interests in British Government," *American Political Science Review,* Sept., 1957, pp. 628 ff.

underlying governmental activities) tend to be integrated, and (2) because the activities of government and non-"constitutional" attitudes (such as attitudes on policy) generally have an important bearing on the decision-making structure itself. In Great Britain, at any rate, all three factors pull in a single direction: toward the concentration of pressure group activities on the administrative departments.

Pressure is concentrated upon the executive in Britain, first, because of the logic of cabinet government in a political system having two highly disciplined parties; such a system simply precludes any consistently successful exertion of influence through members of Parliament, or, less obviously perhaps, through the political parties. Secondly, pressure is focused on the executive because the broad scope and technical character of contemporary social and economic policies has led to a considerable shift of functions to the bureaucracy; not only that, but the decision-making powers usually exercised by administrative departments are, generally speaking, of much more immediate and greater interest to British interest groups than the kinds of decisions made in Cabinet and Parliament.[4] Attitudes, finally, lead in the same direction. There does not exist in Britain any profound prejudice against corporate politics, against the organization of opinion by "interested" groups; this makes possible extraordinarily free, easy, open and intimate relations between public officials and lobbyists (using that term in a purely descriptive sense).[5] Attitudes in Britain also tend to shift pressure toward the executive in more direct and obvious ways: for example, because the lack of inhibitions upon delegating legislation gives to the administrative departments powers which legislatures more jealous of their functions than the British Parliament are likely to exercise themselves;[6] and because there has in fact existed in Britain a consensus on general policy, shifting political conflict to matters of technique and detail, that is, matters generally dealt with by administrative departments.[7]

All this, of course, applies to pressure groups only in a general sense — to predominant and characteristic modes of pressure group activity rather than the activities of every particular pressure group. Whether any particular pressure group will concentrate on the executive or some other part of the governmental machinery and political apparatus of a society depends on certain factors additional to the broad variables

[4] Farmers, for example, are likely to be rather more interested in the annual price reviews than in broad agricultural policies, doctors more interested in conditions of service under the Health Service than in general medical policy. That, at any rate, is what the behaviour of the National Farmers Union and British Medical Association suggests.

[5] See S. H. Beer, "Pressure Groups and Parties in Britain," *American Political Science Review*, March, 1956, pp. 6 ff.

[6] In Britain, after all, the process of delegating legislation hardly involves delegation in any real sense, but rather a shift of responsibility from ministers as leaders of Parliament to ministers as heads of administration. . . .

[7] For a fuller discussion of this point, see Beer, "Pressure Groups," Part III. . . .

I have sketched. For example, the power base of the group certainly plays a role in the matter. A group which commands a large number of votes will tend, other things being equal, to exert pressure on elected members of the decision-making structure; a wealthy group on party organizations; a group in command of specialized knowledge on the specialists in the governmental structure, chiefly the bureaucrats. But, to repeat, this is so *ceteris paribus,* not under all circumstances. It is very likely to be the case, for example, where there exists a relatively even distribution of power among representatives, party oligarchy and bureaucracy; or it may be the case where the group has only one power base which can be effectively brought to bear only in one direction. Both these cases, however, are unusual. In the ordinary instance, speaking metaphorically, the power base of the group will do little more than deflect the momentum of its pressure off the idealized path prescribed by governmental structure, activity and relevant attitudes. The ultimate aim of pressure groups is always to bring power to bear where it will produce intended consequences, and this makes the power structure of government a more decisive desideratum than the power base of the group. . . .

One should add that the factors which induce pressure groups to use certain channels of influence also have effects upon their internal organization and the means they use to exert political pressure. Pressure groups tend somehow to resemble the organizations they seek to influence. Take two examples, one American, the other British. Not only does the American federal system guide political pressure into certain channels, as in the case of teachers' organizations, but it impedes the formation of national associations as such. The American Bar Association, for instance, has a very small membership and was relatively late in getting under way compared to state and local legal associations. Why? Simply because training and admission to the profession — the two political concerns which most often lead to the formation and growth of professional associations — are controlled by state governments, not the federal government.[8] In broader terms, the formal dispersion of authority in government inhibits the concentration of membership in voluntary organizations, a fact with far-reaching consequences, because the "density" of members affects many aspects of a pressure group's activities (such as its political effectiveness and the extent to which it can participate in genuine negotiations with public authorities).

In Britain we can see equally clearly the effect of informal governmental power relations on the organization and tactics of pressure groups. As long as Parliament held the centre of the political stage — as long, that is to say, as political conflicts centred on parliamentary policies — interest groups tended not only to act chiefly through "interested" MP's but to be ephemeral, one-purpose organizations, chiefly

---

[8] Truman, *The Governmental Process,* p. 95.

concerned with raising a large volume of public support for important legislative changes. Nowadays, however, they possess much greater continuity and engage in a much wider variety of political activities, for their interests are being constantly affected by governmental actions. The public campaign has been replaced largely by informal and unostentatious contacts between officials, and interest groups themselves have become increasingly bureaucratized (in short, more and more like the government departments with which they deal), for only bureaucratic structure is appropriate to the kinds of negotiations groups nowadays must carry on to realize their interests. The changing pattern of policy is not alone responsible for this. The shift of power from Parliament to the Cabinet and from the Cabinet to the administrative departments is equally important. These shifts have not been simple adjustments to new policies but are the results of many other factors, such as the professionalization of the civil service and the development of large, disciplined, national parties (paralleled by the development of large, national interest group organizations in place of the much greater decentralization of vested interest organizations in the nineteenth century).

The striking correspondence of governmental organization and the internal organizations of pressure groups in most countries may of course be the result of a still more basic factor: deeply established "constitutional" attitudes (an aspect of what Bentley called the "habit background" of societies) which dictate forms of organization and power relations (structures of authority) not only in government but also in voluntary associations. For the present purpose, however, it is sufficient to point out the similarity and to suggest that it is a product both of social norms and calculations as to where and how group pressure can be exerted most effectively.

There is then a two-fold relation between the channels of pressure group activity on one hand and structure of government, pattern of policy and political attitudes on the other: structure, policy and attitudes decide the channels pressure groups will use predominantly to exert influence, and the nature of these channels in turn affects pressure group organization and tactics.

CONSULTATIONS AND NEGOTIATIONS. By "form" of pressure group politics, I do not mean channels of influence only but also the kinds of relations which predominate among groups and governmental bodies. Leaving aside the intimacy and easiness of these relations (which has already been touched upon), we may distinguish here between two polar extremes — consultations and negotiations — granting that most concrete relations involve both to some extent. Negotiations take place when a governmental body makes a decision hinge upon the actual approval of organizations interested in it, giving the organizations a veto over the decision; consultations occur when the views of the organizations are solicited and taken into account but not considered to be in any sense decisive. What decides whether one relationship or the other plays a significant role in government-group relations? The determining factors again are structure, policies and attitudes.

Structure is important because genuine negotiations can take place only if governmental decision-making processes and patterns of action within pressure groups are of a certain kind. Above all, those who speak for the public authority and those who speak for the interest group must be able to commit those whom they represent; otherwise their deliberations will have only a kind of consultative value, whatever their intentions. Negotiations, then, demand the concentration of authority on both sides, as well as the vesting of considerable discretionary authority in the negotiators. Indeed, the latter presupposes the former. Genuine negotiations between governmental bodies and pressure groups are not likely to take place when a decision must be obtained from a large number of bodies before it has force — as in the American separation-of-powers system — so that decisions are made in effect by negotiations among governmental bodies themselves; and how can there be any negotiations when the negotiators have no discretion, no room to manoeuvre, to make concessions, to meet unexpected gambits and pressures? From both standpoints, an effective cabinet system like the British clearly permits negotiations more easily than a balance-of-power system like the American. It is also necessary, of course, that there should be on the side of the group a formal organization that can speak for most of the members, rather than many competing organizations, or organizations unable to mobilize a sizeable majority of group members. This also is the case in Britain more often than in America.

Policies and attitudes in Britain reinforce the tendency of governmental and group structure to produce negotiations as the dominant form of pressure group politics. The policies of the social service state, for example, demand technical knowledge which, frequently, the members of some interest groups (doctors, for example) are best able to supply. In any case, they often require the positive co-operation of interest groups if they are to be effectively carried out; and what is more natural than to give the groups a direct voice of some sort both in the formulation and administration of policies which cannot be administered without their support?

Among attitudes making for negotiations between government and pressure groups in Britain three are of particular significance. One is the widespread belief (in this case both in Britain and America) that technical experts (practitioners) have some singular competence even in regard to the social policies and administrative forms that touch upon their fields of practice, competence which politicians and bureaucrats do not possess. The second (certainly without an American counterpart) is the persistent "corporatism" in British social attitudes, the still lingering anti-individualist bias which Beer has labelled the "Old Whig Theory of Representation";[9] by this is meant a conception

---

[9] Beer, "Representation of Interests," p. 614 ff.

of society as consisting primarily not of individuals but of sub-societies, groups having traditions, occupational and other characteristics in common. Where Lockean liberalism is the dominant political myth, decisions of government are supposed to be the result of conversations, as it were, between individuals (electorate) and sovereign (state); the intervention of groups is considered inherently pernicious or at best something merely to be tolerated.[10] Where corporatistic attitudes persist, on the other hand, functional representation — that is, the representation of corporations (in the sociological, not legal, sense of the term) rather than individuals — is not only tolerated but insisted upon; governments tend to be regarded not as sovereigns in the Austinian sense but, in the pluralistic sense, as corporations among many other kinds of corporations. Hence the frequent normative insistence on negotiations between government and "voluntary" associations on matters of policy; in Britain, at any rate, a policy regulating, say, farmers, embarked upon without close conversations between government and farm organizations, would be considered to be only on the margins of legitimacy, whether highly technical in character or not. Indeed, close conversations are not enough. Note, for example, that in the debate on the second reading of the National Health Service Bill of 1946 — the stage at which the most general policy considerations raised by a bill are discussed — the opposition hinged its case upon a motion alleging the failure of the Ministry of Health to *negotiate* the proposed Service with the medical profession; this despite the fact that plenty of talks (consultations) between the Ministry and the profession had taken place and that technical details were not at issue. And to the survival of the Old-Whig Theory of Representation we may add the concomitant survival of what might be called the Old Tory Theory of Authority: the tendency both in British government and British voluntary associations to delegate inordinately wide powers to leaders and spokesmen, to ratify decisions taken by leaders almost as a matter of form, which affords such leaders a wide range of manoeuvre when they come face to face in negotiations.

Consultations and negotiations are not, of course, the only "practices" through which pressure groups act upon government. In fact, these two concepts may be useful for characterizing pressure group activities only in political systems which have two, not in the least universal, characteristics: a high degree of differentiation between pressure groups, parties and formal decision-making offices, and relatively great ease of access by pressure groups to the formal decision-making offices. Where these conditions do not exist, pressure group activity will inevitably assume other forms. In multi-party systems, where parties and pressure groups are not sharply differentiated (that is to say, where many parties are pressure groups that merely call themselves parties

---

[10] For the best discussion of the origin and development of these attitudes, see Otto Gierke, *Natural Law and the Theory of Society* (Cambridge University Press, 1934).

and sometimes behave like parties) decisions will often be made, not by negotiations between pressure groups and formal decision-making officers, but by negotiations among the pressure groups themselves. In such countries, the basic assertion on which contemporary "group theorists" in political science have built their model — that politics is "the allocation of social values through group conflict" — comes much closer to a full description of political decision-making than it does in countries where political parties perform their integrating function effectively and where the formal structure of decision-making represents something more than the myths of the dominant groups in institutionalized form. On the other extreme, where groups are effectively segregated out of the formal political process — prevented from having access to formal offices — the chief form of pressure group politics will be intrigue, or violence; perhaps, however, it would be better in this case to speak of the cessation of politics rather than of a particular form of it.

DETERMINANTS OF SCOPE AND INTENSITY

To discover the factors on which depend the scope and intensity of pressure group activity, it is necessary to bear in mind just what sort of political activity pressure group politics is. As I define it, pressure group politics . . . involves, on the one hand, the *political* promotion of interests and values, that is, the attempt to realize aspirations through governmental decision-making; on the other, it involves something less than an attempt by the group to become itself the government, or even to seize for itself certain political offices which are vitally concerned with its goals. That, at any rate, is how we generally differentiate pressure groups from parties, or political movements, or purely political "associations" (like the parliamentary associations which antedate the advent of mass parties in Great Britain). Moreover, pressure groups, normally, are not solely engaged in political activities; even in the case of "promotional" groups (groups seeking to achieve not their own interests but what they conceive to be broader social values) political activities rarely exhaust the full range of activities of the group. Pressure group politics, then, represents something less than the full "politicalization" of groups and something more than utter "depoliticalization"; it constitutes an intermediate level of activity between the political and the apolitical. In accounting for the growth and development of pressure group activity, therefore, we must simultaneously account for two things which are, at first sight, nearly paradoxical: how groups come to seek the political promotion of certain of their goals, yet are kept from attempting to promote them by the capture of authoritative offices or from pursuing politically all their objectives. I shall concentrate on the first of these problems. . . .

THE POLITICAL MOBILIZATION OF GROUPS: POLICY. As governmental structure is the most obvious determinant of the form of pressure group activities, so the activities of governments are the most obvious determinants of their entrance into politics. British pressure groups have been so much discussed recently[11] for the simple reason that welfare state policies have, so to speak, generated such groups in large number (that is, transformed groups into "pressure groups"), or, where they already existed, intensified the pressures they exert. This is clearly due to the fact that private associations now have much more to gain or lose from governmental decisions than in the past: farmers their incomes, doctors the conditions in which they practice, businessmen a host of matters, from capital issues to raw materials.[12] The state in Britain today disposes directly of 40 per cent of the national income; and that fact speaks for itself. We may regard political systems as amalgams of potential and actual pressure groups: groups which from a political standpoint are merely "categoric" groups and groups which have actually been drawn into politics, chiefly through the impact of public policies, either policies actually adopted or policies which are "threatened." In short, we can usefully stand Bentley on his head to supplement Bentley right side up; if interaction among politically active groups produces policy, policy in turn creates politically active groups.[13] . . .

ATTITUDES. Attitudes influence the scope and intensity of pressure group politics not only because they determine policy but also because pressure groups generally require some sort of legitimation before they come into play in the political process. The obstacle to legitimacy may be internal or external, so to speak; it may arise either from the convictions of group members or those of non-members, particularly if the latter occupy positions of power, that the political promotion of the group's collective interests is somehow illegitimate. Trade unions, for example, play a more significant political role today than in the nineteenth century, both in Britain and the United States, not only because they are larger and better managed, but also because they are more widely accepted and because they themselves are more reconciled to action within the operative political system. To consult with trade union leaders is no longer tantamount to conspiracy; nor do trade union leaders any longer regard political participation in democratic government as a kind of class treason, or as a trespass upon

[11] For a list of publications on the subject, see Samuel E. Finer, *Anonymous Empire* (Humanities Press, 2nd ed., 1966), p. 148, and Sir Ivor Jennings, *Parliament* (Cambridge University Press, 2nd ed., 1957), esp. Ch. II, Sec. 4 and Ch. VII, Secs. 1 and 2.

[12] How much such groups stand to gain or lose emerges most strikingly in the pioneering *Report of the Committee on Intermediaries*, Cmd. 7094 of 1950.

[13] The extension (or contemplated extension) of government policy is not, of course, the only factor which tends to draw groups into politics. Perhaps equally important is the desire to obtain legislation in order to impede rival groups or to regulate relations within the groups, e.g. the promotion by trade associations of retail price maintenance legislation or by professional associations of licensing regulations.

alien domain. Of course, the legitimacy of a group is not absolutely decisive in determining whether it will play a political role or not. Conspiracies do occur where negotiations are prohibited, but the difficulties in such cases are so great that "illegitimate" groups may find it desirable to leave politics alone, or impossible to find channels through which to act. The attitudes which legitimate pressure groups or deny them legitimacy usually constitute the fundamental political ethos of a society, such as the long prevalent liberal belief that economic actors should act upon each other through the spontaneously adjusting mechanics of the market rather than though the political process.[14]

Legitimacy in this case need not mean legitimacy in regard to political action only; a group may be prevented from taking an intense part in politics by much more general attitudes: for example, a prejudice against corporate organization as such. S. H. Beer has pointed out[15] that the major occupational interests — business, labour, and agriculture — are far more thoroughly and monolithically organized in Britain than in the United States, and related this fact to the profound influence of liberal "atomism" in America and the survival of the older corporatistic theory of society in Britain. These differences in organization are marked by differences in the groups' involvement in politics and administration. The sub-groups of larger societies may, however, have significantly different attitudes toward organization as well as political action itself. Thus, while it is true, broadly speaking, that British attitudes are more corporatistic than American attitudes — and that, as a result, British pressure groups "even if compared with American examples . . . are numerous, massive, well-organized and highly effective"[16] — it is also true that British professional groups resist corporatization as much as, if not more than, their American counterparts. The British Medical Association, for example, has not until very recently (when special factors compelling corporatization have been at work) managed to outstrip the American Medical Association in proportion of doctors enrolled in it. This is just one facet of a much broader behaviour pattern; another facet of this pattern is the resistance of the British medical profession to all corporate forms of practice, in partnerships, group practices and especially health centres. Both reflect a profound bias against association. . . .

Attitudes may determine the intensity of group politics in still another way. Even when they permit intense political activity by a group,

---

[14] Not only groups but also their interests require legitimation; indeed, *felt* interests may be themselves functions of the value structure of a society. (See John Plamenatz, "Interests," *Political Studies*, February 1954.) Attitudes may therefore restrict group politics either by ruling out all political activities by the groups or by prohibiting activities of certain kinds or in pursuit of certain goals.

[15] In "Group Representation in British and American Democracy," *The Annals of the American Academy of Political and Social Science*, CCCXIX, September 1958, *passim*.

[16] Beer, "Pressure Groups and Parties in Britain," p. 1.

they may keep that activity from assuming certain forms, i.e. limit the group's range of political activities. Some groups which play a legitimate role in government may be prevented, by normative attitudes no less than considerations of expediency, from openly associating themselves with a political party or taking a part in electoral campaigns;[17] again, certain groups such as professional associations — may have deep inhibitions against anything that smacks of trade unionism (any sort of bargaining, for example); still others may be prevented by their internal ethics from using certain instruments of pressure, such as strikes and boycotts, or certain kinds of publicity. . . .

STRUCTURE. Of the three basic determinants of pressure group behaviour which I have stressed, perhaps the least manifest determinant of their political mobilization is governmental structure; nevertheless, it also plays a role. Key, for example, argues that a two-party system stimulates the formation of pressure groups because special interests cannot find consistent champions in any party which must continuously appeal to a great many interests. That, however, strikes me as an over-simplification. The parties in a two-party system may themselves be composed of wings and sub-groups which consistently espouse certain interests, making them, as Key himself has pointed out, more like multi-party systems in fact than they seem in form.[18] This is certainly true of American parties. It may also apply to British parties, for both Labour and the Tories include certain enduring subgroups which stand for special, chiefly economic interests. The point that should be made surely is that two-party systems do not encourage all interest groups to seek political channels outside of the parties but only groups having certain characteristics; and rather than maintaining that multi-party systems discourage the formation of organized pressure groups because the parties themselves are freely available to special interests, one should argue that (just because of this) many "parties" in such systems are themselves pressure groups in disguise, but pressure groups more fully politicalized than those we find in two-party systems.

Somewhat more persuasive is Truman's argument that certain groups are likely to pursue their goals through politics when the structure of government gives them important advantages over others and when they are in a relatively weak position in the "market," that is, in spontaneous adjustment to other groups. His chief case in point is that of American farmers who have a relatively weak bargaining position on the market but are over-represented in both state and national legislatures.[19] Rural areas in many other countries tend to be over-represented

---

[17] Note, for example, that the British Legion stopped its efforts to influence elections when threatened with the withdrawal of royal patronage because of its forays into party politics. See Graham Wootton, "Ex-Servicemen in Politics," *Political Quarterly*, vol. 29, no. 1, pp. 34–5.

[18] Key, *Politics, Parties and Pressure Groups*, p. 177 and Ch. 10.

[19] Truman, *The Governmental Process*, pp. 87 ff. and 107.

too, which may help to explain the relatively great readiness of farm groups everywhere to seek out government interference in their market relations.

This argument may, however, be stated much more broadly: governmental structure affects the scope and intensity of pressure group activity chiefly because expectations of success govern the political mobilization of groups, and whether or not a group can be successfully influential is determined at least partly by the structure of the government on which it acts. . . . Governmental structure may determine not only the influence of particular pressure groups (and therefore whether or not they will actually organize for politics) but also whether pressure groups in general can effectively translate their demands into policies (and therefore whether or not large numbers of them will be active, or whether political activity will play a large role in their affairs). I have in mind here the difference between systems like British cabinet government, which are highly effective in making decisions, and systems like the American or highly fragmented parliamentary systems, which seem more effective in frustrating them. The first kind of system is more likely to induce the political mobilization of groups than the second, if only because government offers them a reasonable chance of action — any sort of action. . . .

INHIBITIONS ON POLITICAL MOBILIZATION. If certain attitudes, elements of governmental structure, and the impact of governmental policy, adopted and threatened, account for the political mobilization of groups, what inhibits them from mobilizing on a full scale once they decide to become politically involved? Clearly, the relevant factors are the ways in which groups define their goals and evaluate their chances in the political arena, and the extent to which an existing governmental apparatus appears capable of satisfying their demands without being changed or captured. Each of these considerations, however, requires some elaboration.

There are conditions when government itself, not the detailed products of government, is the primary concern of politics, most clearly of all when new states are in the building or old forms of government widely discredited. Such conditions are obviously inhospitable to pressure group politics, for they awaken much more profound political concerns. Intensive pressure group politics then presupposes as its most fundamental condition a stable and widely accepted political apparatus — political consensus. To "press" upon a government is itself, in a way, a form of commitment to it; profoundly disaffected groups will rarely stoop to sully themselves by dealing with an abominated system. This accounts for the curious impression one gets in societies widely committed to their governments both of intense politics and political apathy; intense politics, because the society seems split into myriad groupings, loosely, if at all, associated, all busily seeking to exert influence, to capture opinion, to enlist decision-makers; political apathy, because no fundamental issues are ever raised and people seem remarkably uninterested in what looms, in other societies, as decisive political activity: elections, for example. The simple reason for this apparent paradox is, of course, that political activities do not possess decisiveness intrinsically but only in terms of what people want to be decided: if the chief political question is one of the very location of formal power, then elections (or violence) become decisive; if political questions involve less fundamental issues — the detailed uses to which formal power is to be put — then influence-wielding, i.e. pressure group politics, becomes decisive. Consensus does not imply the cessation of politics, but it does imply a shift of political concerns to issues best dealt with through the unobtrusive interplay of semi-politicalized groups; in "consensual" systems, therefore, fully politicalized groups will perform certain routine functions but only rarely absorb primary allegiances. Lack of consensus in a society will make almost every group join fully politicalized organizations, or try to become themselves such organizations, or wash their hands of politics altogether. Politics will become no concern of theirs, or all of their concern. . . .

Whether groups will define their goals as being fully political or, as do pressure groups, only partially political may depend also on still more fundamental characteristics of a society. A high degree of pressure group activity presupposes logically a high degree of social differentiation. It is difficult to envisage intensive pressure group politics in relatively primitive societies, not only because basic political questions loom relatively large in them these days, but also because the vast multiplicity of criss-crossing groups existing in more advanced societies does not exist (at least to the same extent) in the less advanced. Group politics in such societies tends therefore to define goals of very wide concern, and associations tend to absorb wide segments of society; in such a situation group politics becomes almost by definition social politics.[20] The communications system of a society also plays a fundamental role, at any rate in deciding the very possibility of association as a preliminary to political mobilization. But apart from such absolutely fundamental and obvious (perhaps tautological) conditions, the extent of politicalization of groups is primarily a reflection of the degree of consensus among them. In that sense, the existence of a multiplicity of pressure groups is a sign of health in the political organism, not, as the muckrakers thought, a symptom of disease.

Within consensual systems, however, different groups have different propensities to act in politics, depending on contingencies like those operating in non-consensual systems. Very large groups and very wealthy groups may be encouraged to play a direct role in party-political conflict, as do British trade unions — although one gets the impression nowadays that their identification with Labour is a cultural lag from

[20] "Primitive" here is not meant as a synonym for non-western or industrially underdeveloped. It stands, in Durkheim's sense, for a low level of social differentiation, and there are many ways in which societies may be differentiated. But the economic division of labour being one of them, economic underdevelopment is at least a loose and imperfect synonym for the term.

days of more profound political disagreements, and that they yearn (many at any rate) for looser forms of political engagement. Stable two-party systems also discourage full political involvement, although such party systems may themselves be, at bottom, products of consensus. Finally, groups may become disenchanted in the process of pressure politics if the resolution of group conflicts is consistently against their interests — if, in the political market, their power to compete is small, due to their objective characteristics or the structure of government on which they act. In that case, however, they are more likely to become fully alienated from the political system rather than fully involved in it. In any case, the market of political competition tends to become so widely disjointed in highly consensual systems that almost any groups can get "satisfactions" out of it; that is to say, groups which are relatively weak in absolute terms (in size, wealth, prestige, etc.) may, due to wide agreement, simply not have to confront significant opposition in their political affairs. Despite that, however, calculations of the chances of a group's effectiveness help to decide not only whether the group becomes politically active at all, but also the extent to which it carries its political activity. What then determines the effectiveness of pressure groups?

DETERMINANTS OF EFFECTIVENESS

Factors determining the effectiveness of pressure groups may be classified under three headings: (1) attributes of the pressure groups themselves; (2) attributes of the activities of government; (3) attributes of the governmental decision-making structure. Perhaps operative attitudes constitute a fourth category, since the ability of a group to mobilize opinion certainly enhances its chances of success in any political system in which opinion matters. . . .[21]

GROUP CHARACTERISTICS. Certain characteristics of groups are likely to determine decisively their effectiveness under almost any pattern of policies or structure of government (popular government, of course): for example, physical resources, size, organizational cohesiveness, and political skills. Physical resources means wealth, first and foremost: wealth to contribute to party treasuries, wealth for "buying" the goodwill of influential persons, wealth with which to advertise and circularize, and so forth. Other resources, of course, are useful too; for example, the possession by a group of a journal or newspaper,

---

[21] Truman identifies three factors which determine the extent to which a group achieves "effective access" to the institutions of government: "(1) factors relating to a group's strategic position in society; (2) factors associated with the internal characteristics of groups; and (3) factors peculiar to the governmental institutions themselves." (Truman, *Governmental Process*, p. 506.) (1) and (2) are grouped under (1) above; the determining role of public policy is not considered by Truman, at any rate not as explicitly as the other factors.

especially a popular newspaper, or (in a rather different sense of the term "resource") the fact that it has members in influential positions. Among useful resources must be included also the prestige of the group: the capital of public support, so to speak, which it can command regardless of the substantive policies it espouses. Certain groups possess not merely legitimacy to participate in decision-making processes, but also a sort of special privilege to determine the outcome of these processes; this is true especially of groups possessing technical competence in fields where there is a wide gulf between the professional and the layman, although any high status and prestige can usually be converted into political profit, if only through the day-to-day influence of "opinion leaders."

The size of the group may itself be reckoned among its resources, although brute size is never likely to be of crucial account. Rather we should speak of the politically effective size of a group: its ability to make its quantitative weight felt. This is partly a matter of the other resources it commands — its wealth, prestige, whether it has easy access to public opinion and to influential persons — but still other considerations enter the equation as well. One of these is organizational cohesiveness, and this is a function of a great many variables. Does the group possess any formal organization at all? Is the membership split among a large number of such organizations or concentrated in an omnibus organization? Is membership perfunctory or the result of genuine commitment to the formal organization? Do members in fact participate in organizational affairs? Are their personal interactions frequent and persistent? Do they have important conflicting loyalties outside the group? Are their interests really compatible? Can the leaders mobilize disciplined and loyal legions in times of crisis? The answers to these questions will determine whether membership statistics can in fact be translated into influence.

Among the skills which enable groups to achieve their political objectives we must therefore reckon the internal political and administrative skills of their leaders. Some groups, to be sure, are more cohesive than others in their very nature: if, for example, they have no cultural or ideological inhibitions against close association (unlike businessmen in a truly "liberal" society, or doctors in a country having a deep tradition of individual practice, as in Britain); if their members do have largely identical, at any rate easily comparable, interests; if they are concentrated in small areas; if status considerations or the nature of the members' work lead to social as well as occupational identification among the members.[22] But here, as in everything else, art can guide and support nature.

The nature of the objectives sought by a group may also be a deter-

---

[22] Note, for example, the decisive role of the printers' high status among manual workers and of the peculiar nature of their work in producing solidarity and comradeship in the International Typographical Union. S. M. Lipset, et al., *Union Democracy* (Free Press, 1956).

minant of effectiveness, but chiefly because this factor affects the other internal group characteristics mentioned. I have in mind here primarily the difference between groups agitating for their own corporate interests and groups dedicated to social causes not necessarily arising out of their members' self-interest — "interest groups" as against "promotional groups," as S. E. Finer calls them. The former generally have a more disciplined membership, more affluent treasuries, tighter bureaucratic organization, a more permanent and indeed also more active clientele. Their officers tend to acquire great skill in propaganda and negotiations, and they frequently have their own private channels of propaganda — journals and press departments, for example.

POLICY. As there are many kinds of resources which constitute political capital, so there are many kinds of organizational forms and political skills which may be turned to account in the decision-making process; *which* is likely to exercise a decisive influence depends largely on the setting in which the group functions. Generals cut a wider swath in war or cold war than in peace; groups that want money spent have a relatively hard task in times of inflation and retrenchment. The pattern of policies enforced in a political system is an important determinant of the effectiveness of pressure groups simply because it is one of the situational elements which selects among the objective attributes of groups those which are of special political account. Take two examples. A policy may demand, in its formulation or administration, some skill or knowledge over which members of a special group have, or are believed to have, a monopoly; this is increasingly the case in the age of the social service state. Again, it may be impossible to carry out a policy without some sort of active support by the group; what use, for instance, is an agricultural policy without co-operative farmers? In either case, the pressure group concerned may not get exactly what it wants, but the need for knowledge and co-operation at least acts as a limit on what can be imposed upon it; usually, of course, the group's influence is much more positive than that.

Policy may also impinge upon the effectiveness of groups in another way: by affecting their size and the resources they command. When a group is subjected to public regulation and control its members are more likely to join organizations which press the group's interests. They are more likely to contribute to group treasuries; to tolerate specialization of leadership and administration in their organizations; to sublimate differences of interest and attitude for the sake of common ends, and to respond in a disciplined way to group decisions. Policy, in short, may make it easier to mobilize the potential power of groups by accelerating tendencies toward corporatization and by making for greater cohesiveness within the organized groups.

GOVERNMENTAL STRUCTURE. Finally, the effectiveness of pressure groups is also determined to some extent by governmental structure. There is, for example, a great difference between systems in which power is concentrated and those in which it is dispersed. In American government, groups can ordinarily get what they want, at any rate if they want something important, only by obtaining favourable decisions from a large number of bodies: legislatures, legislative committees, executive officers; this, as has been repeatedly pointed out, favours defensive pressure groups, those that want to maintain the status quo, by promoting delay and inaction as such. But while under effective cabinet government it is much easier to obtain positive decisions at all levels, from Parliament to the lowliest interdepartmental committee, such systems inhibit many manipulative activities familiar in systems where power is widely dispersed (senatorial courtesy, for example) which give minor groups useful entrées into politics and means for getting "positive" decisions.[23]

On a somewhat lower level of generalization, the influence of pressure groups may also be affected by electoral systems. Under proportional representation sheer weight of numbers is likely to be a matter of importance, while under the single-member system the distribution of members will be an important factor determining the "effective size" of a group; a group the members of which are strategically posted in a large number of doubtful constituencies will be able to exercise influence disproportionate to its size in simple quantitative terms. So also will a group which derives special advantages from distributive anomalies in an electoral system; a case in point are American farmers, who are benefited not only by the over-representation of agricultural districts in the House of Representatives, but even more by the peculiar system used to elect the Senate. The National Farmers Union of England and Wales failed in its original aim to play a role like that of the American farm bloc in British politics, partly because of the existence of two highly disciplined parties in Great Britain, but partly also because the British electoral system never favoured farmers as much as the American system.

Third, there is a relationship between the effectiveness of pressure groups and the character of the administrative structure upon which they act. A close "clientele relationship" between group and administrative department always tends to give the group important advantages over others, if only by obtaining for it a permanent spokesman within the structure of government; it has been argued, for example, that in America the air lines have important political advantages over other public carriers because they have a public regulatory agency all to themselves (the Civil Aeronautics Board) while the other carriers all come under the jurisdiction of the Interstate Commerce Commission, within which there is consequently a stiff, often self-defeating, struggle

---

[23] These points are usually made to contrast cabinet systems and separation of power systems, but they apply equally to coalition *v.* single-party governments, i.e. unstable *v.* stable parliamentary systems. In regard to the opportunities it offers to pressure groups, both to gain access to decision-making bodies and to realize their objectives, French government is probably more like American than British government.

for power. Much depends also on the power which a given administrative department can exert on behalf of its clients within the executive structure. Administrative systems are not merely tools for executing policy, but are themselves structures of power; they influence (often make) policy, and within them different departments carry different degrees of weight, depending on the political positions of their heads, the broadness and significance of their functions, and their traditions. In British government, there certainly is a world of difference between important departments like the Treasury, Supply, and the Board of Trade on one hand and Education and Pensions on the other. Whether a pressure group can carry great weight in government obviously depends on the power of the agency through which its weight is exerted, as indeed do also certain aspects of the form of its activities — for example, the extent to which its relations with government have the character of genuine negotiations; normally a President of the Board of Trade can negotiate far more easily than a Minister of Education, if to negotiate means to take decisions by bargaining with pressure groups. Finally, we should add to clientele relations between groups and departments, clientele relations between groups and legislative committees. Similar considerations apply, although the absence of specializing standing legislative committees makes this point inapplicable to Britain.

SUMMARY

To sum up the argument in very general terms, pressure group politics in its various aspects is a function of three main variables: the pattern of policy, the structure of decision-making both in government and voluntary associations, and the attitudes — broadly speaking, the "political culture" — of the society concerned. Each affects the form, the intensity and scope, and the effectiveness of pressure group politics, although in each case the significance of the variables differs — structure, for example, being especially important in determining the form of pressure group politics, policy especially important in determining its scope and intensity.

HENRY W. EHRMANN

Interest Groups and the Bureaucracy in Western Democracies

The rise in state intervention in the mixed economy welfare state has brought interest groups and governments much closer together everywhere in the Western world. The growth in government subsidization and regulation of social activities has made the goodwill of government administrators an important asset to many groups. Reciprocally, government officials require cooperation from interest group leaders if they are to intervene successfully in their affairs. Henry Ehrmann describes the consequences of these changes for European systems of government.

"... In everyday affairs, domination is primarily administration."
Max Weber, *Wirtschaft und Gesellschaft*

The preoccupation of political scientists with the activities and the influence of interest groups can lead to a realistic understanding of the political process only if we also acquire an understanding of the institutions through which the groups are compelled to function and of the milieu in which they move.[1] This comparative essay is concerned with the interaction of public administration and interest groups since policies originated by them mirror rather distinctly both the plural patterns of power and the functional specialization which exist in countries of a highly developed economy. In such societies the resolution of even the most important issues is transferred from the general level of policy-making downwards to a combination of institutions

From Henry W. Ehrmann, "Les groupes d'intérêt et la bureaucratie dans les démocraties occidentales," *Revue française de science politique,* September, 1961, pp. 541–568. The author supplied the abridged English-language version. Reprinted by permission.

[1] Cf. M. Fainsod, "Some Reflections on the Nature of the Regulatory Process," *Public Policy,* I (1940), p. 298.

among which the administrative bureaus are most prominent. The "separate whirlpools of policy formation" which have been described as typical of the United States exist elsewhere as well.[2] Moreover the subsystem in which public servants and group representatives meet offers frequently a glimpse of a counter-system to representative democracy.

In the modern welfare state political power is increasingly substituted for economic power and problems whose solution was previously left to private initiative have become public issues. Pressed for manifold decisions for which they are ill-equipped parliament and frequently also the political executive entrust discretion to the bureaucrats (1) as holders of the technical knowledge that is needed to bring about the intended political results; (2) as wielders of the instrumentalities of economic and social planning where neither the legislator nor the executive know exactly which ultimate results are desirable; (3) as conflict resolvers who are, at least implicitly, asked to break a deadlock between contradictory claims and values especially when the legislature has embodied its own doubts and hesitations into the law.[3]

The diminished role of parliament has been paralleled usually, if somewhat unexpectedly, by a decrease in the weight of the political executive. Where Ministers used to tell the civil servants what the public would not stand for, the bureaus are now in direct contact with an organized public, viz., the interest groups. If a high degree of governmental controls has increased the power of Ministers and of their departments, such power is counterbalanced by their dependence on outside organizations. From the perspective of the bureaucracy interest groups are audience, advisors, and clients, foremost participants in the process of bargaining over governmental policy. From the perspective of pressure politics the administrative bureaus are a decisive center of power although this does not mean that for the interest groups their contacts with the bureaucracy have everywhere replaced other forms of influence.

In all Western democracies the consequences of such a configuration are discussed in fairly similar terms. Is there a danger, it is asked, that the groups, acting through a subsystem over which external controls have weakened, exercise an inordinate amount of influence, or can the civil service because of its disinterestedness, knowledge and permanency be relied upon to act as a check on group influences?[4]

[2] Cf. E. S. Griffith, *Congress. Its Contemporary Role* (New York: New York University Press, 1951), p. 112; and H. J. Spiro, *Government by Constitution* (New York: Random House, 1959), p. 340.

[3] Cf. W. A. R. Leys, "Ethics and Administrative Discretion," *Public Administration Review*, III (1943), p. 23.

[4] In France pioneering studies on the subject have been undertaken by J. J. Meynaud. Cf. especially "Les groupes d'intérêt et l'administration en France," *Revue française de science politique*, VII (1957), pp. 573–593; and his *Les Groupes de Pression en France* (Paris: A Colin, 1958), pp. 203–216. Since it can be assumed that to readers of [*Revue française de science politique*] the situation in France is known better than that in other countries, this paper pays somewhat scant attention to France. My article, "French Bureaucracy and Organized Interests," *Administrative Science Quarterly*, V (1961), pp. 534–555 may be considered as complementary to the present one.

OBJECTIVES OF GROUP-BUREAUCRACY CONTACTS

Today extensive consultation between group leaders and civil servants is generally considered as a "fundamental democratization" of the administrative process.[5] If in Europe official collaboration with the groups is praised openly only since the war, European administrators have practiced it for as long a time as Americans. The British may describe what they are doing as a mere form of courtesy or of good manners, the Germans may praise it as a necessary departure from the methods of the *Obrigkeitsstaat*. What matters is that there exists by now in all countries widespread agreement on the propriety and convenience of continuous consultation both when the bureaus are drafting legislation and when they administer enacted laws. "We should be very loath to make any recommendations which might have the incidental effect of impeding or restricting liaison between Government Departments and the public":[6] this conclusion reached by a British Committee set up inter alia to investigate the role of interest groups as intermediaries, would today be echoed almost everywhere.

The administrator turns to the group leader in order to obtain an understanding for the practices and customs of that part of the society that is affected by his ruling. Without the benefit of a sounding board the official feels that he is unable to correctly forecast the results of his actions. What at first has been merely useful, soon becomes necessary.[7] Where the sources of official information, statistical and otherwise, are as notoriously insufficient as in France and Italy, many bureaus must rely constantly on the data provided by trade associations, trade-unions or other groups. But also in other countries the administration is compelled to utilize the groups as technicians and experts rather than as partisan advocates even though their advice may be that of an expert *engagé*.[8] Information flows in either direction. The groups frequently serve as channels for those explanations of its policy which the administration wishes to communicate to the public but feels it cannot convey directly. Where, as in France, important interest groups pay little attention to the cultivation of outside contacts, the bureaucracy complains that it has altogether inadequate means of conveying and interpreting its programs.[9]

---

[5] Cf. K. Mannheim, *Man and Society in an Age of Reconstruction* (London: Paul, Trench and Trubner, 1940), p. 44.

[6] *Report of the Committee on Intermediaries* (London: H. M. Stationery Office, 1950), p. 69.

[7] Cf. Political and Economic Planning, *Advisory Committee in British Government* (London: Allen and Unwin, 1960), pp. 99–105; and A. Leiserson, *Administrative Regulation: A Study in Representation of Interests* (Chicago: University of Chicago Press, 1942), p. 53.

[8] Cf. J. Meynaud, *Technocratie et Politique* (Lausanne: Études de Science Politique, 1960), p. 38, and J. LaPalombara, "The Utility and Limitations of Interest Group Theory in Non-American Field Situation," *The Journal of Politics*, XXII (1960), p. 47.

[9] For details, cf. H. W. Ehrmann, *Organized Business in France* (Princeton: Princeton University Press, 1957), pp. 257 ff. For the situation in Great Britain, cf. *Report on Intermediaries, op. cit.*, p. 69.

Even more important than the channeling of information is the general decentralization of governmental functions which the group-bureaucracy relationship affords. Where the administration lacks technical knowledge or considers its apparatus inadequate for the performance of incumbent tasks, yet hesitates to add more bulk to the governmental machinery, the burden of executive responsibility may be shifted to well organized interest groups. In the United States such an abdication of administrative functions to a wide variety of licensing boards gives to the groups powers that are often not better controlled than those of medieval guilds. In the field of labor relations and social insurance most European democracies practice the "self-government" of unions and management.

Where organs of consultation and cooperation are lacking, the administration will frequently create them. In all countries, especially in the wake of war-time or emergency controls, the need of the bureaucracy for contacts with groups has been stimulus for the organization of interests. Some of the large confederations or *Spitzenverbände* owe their existence to the initiative of the government.[10]

If such are the main objectives of the cooperation between group and bureaucracy, it is natural that in the eyes of the administration not all groups are equal. It will prefer those that have given proof of representing the wishes of their membership, those whose information has been found reliable and whose staff is not only competent but also attuned to style and working methods of the civil service. Were it only because of their search for rationality civil servants will most of the time prefer to deal with large-scale organizations: "their representatives can usually appreciate the larger view even when they disagree with it, and they have a surer and more intellectual approach to what is politically and economically feasible."[11] With some exceptions only groups which represent such sectional interests as industry, agriculture or labor will be admitted to regular consultation or be used for the decentralization of administrative departments.

POINTS OF GROUP ACCESS

Either on their own initiative or prodded by the Ministry with which they have dealings, the groups will shape their organizational structure so as to resemble the institutions they wish to influence. The resulting parallelism between the structure of public administration and of interest groups does much to facilitate informal and continuous group access. Wherever the government regulates multiple aspects of the national economy, an increasing functional specialization leads to the consolidation of clientele administrations animated by a clientele

---

[10] For examples, cf. W. J. M. Mackenzie, "Pressure Groups in British Government," *British Journal of Sociology*, VI (1955), p. 144.

[11] B. Chapman, *The Profession of Government. The Public Service in Europe* (London: Allen and Unwin, 1959), p. 318.

orientation. The groups find greatest satisfaction in their contacts with what the French call the "vertical" administrations which correspond to the sponsoring departments in Great Britain, to the regulatory commissions or clientele administrations in the United States. As technical advisors to these agencies they shape much of the actual regulatory process; as public they make the administrator fully aware of the point of view taken by the interests they represent. Natural alliances between bureau head and group leader are formed; if necessary they are directed against such "outsiders" as other administrations and the rival interests they may sponsor, against the political executive or against parliament. In the United States the mutual support of groups and clientele administrations has often complicated if not obstructed the efforts of the President and of Congress to make the government serve broader public interests.[12] Usually both agencies and groups have a common interest in the continuation of vigorous regulation; the prestige if not the survival of both may depend on it.

If other civil servants grow sometimes extremely critical of the mentality and the rulings of their colleagues in the clientele agencies, it can be answered that the conditions they criticize appear endemic in any agency performing such tasks. They are the natural outgrowth of the process of regulation, of its organizational structure and of the underlying philosophy of functional representation. Yet it cannot be denied that in many countries the point has been reached where the trend towards specialized organizations runs afoul of the need for a macro-economic policy.[13] The narrower the clientele, the less capable becomes the administrative agency of resisting pressures. When the government tries occasionally, as has been the case in Western Germany, France and Great Britain, to remedy the prevailing situation by combining administrations, the violent protests that have come from the interest groups are an indication of what they stand to lose.

More amply discussed than other phases of group influence is the cooperation in which organized interests and administrations engage in order to prepare legislation. Especially in such small countries as Sweden and Switzerland, Belgium and the Netherlands, all known for their frank acknowledgement of a pronounced pluralism, the bureaucracy, when drafting bills, leans heavily on a constituency composed of interest groups. The *Vernehmlassung* in Switzerland and the *remissyttranden* in Sweden not only enable the groups to comment

---

[12] Cf. C. Hyneman, *Bureaucracy in a Democracy* (New York: Harpers, 1950), p. 64. For the interesting, somewhat abnormal situation that arose in the United States while Mr. Benson was Secretary of Agriculture, see J. L. Freeman, "The Bureaucracy in Pressure Politics," *The Annals of the American Academy of Political and Social Sciences*, CCCIXX (1958), p. 17.

[13] Cf. L. L. Jaffé, "The Effective Limits of the Administrative Process: A Revaluation," *Harvard Law Review*, LXVII (1954), p. 1113. The same point is made for England, after much praise for interest group consultation, by L. Tivey and E. Wohlgemuth, "Trade Associations as Interest Groups," *The Political Quarterly*, XXIX (1958), p. 71.

extensively and at every stage on the legislative proposals of the government; their opinions, if they have not already modified the bills, are also transmitted to parliament. Often the collaboration between bureaucracy and groups will result in unanimous agreement on bills which parliament is then asked to endorse. To be sure, complaints that parliament is most of the time confronted with a fait accompli are quite common. "Le Parlement passe de plus en plus pour un décor dans lequel on apparaît quand les jeux sont faits," remarks a Belgian author, and a British author concludes that "if Whitehall (i.e. the Bureaucracy) can claim the monopoly of knowledge and the agreement of the interested parties . . . (it is strengthened) at the expense of Westminster (i.e. parliament)."[14] Although the practices that have become widespread in all of Western Europe can hardly be reconciled with classical theories of democratic representation, parliament knows full well that it will never be able to match the bureaucracy group effort in its attention to detail. The more thoroughly group opinion has been explored beforehand the less need will there be for amendments, costly in time and effort, by members of parliament. Besides being indicative of the general decline of parliamentary opposition,[15] this situation had to be accepted by the elected representatives when it became apparent that to an increasing extent the citizen prefers the concrete involvement in interest group activities to the identification with political parties.

The fact that in the Third and Fourth Republics the legislative process has remained, and in the United States still remains more traditional has compelled the interest groups to divide their efforts between the bureaucracy and the parliamentary committees. The American Congress, it is true, is better equipped than European parliaments to collect expert and group advice. Since the French constitution of 1958 has all but squashed the amending power of the National Assembly as extravagant, groups have, except in extraordinary situations, deserted the couloirs of the Palais Bourbon and are cultivating now almost exclusively the administrative bureaus.[16]

FORMS OF GROUP ACCESS

One can easily exaggerate the difference between situations in which the bureaucracy negotiates with pressure groups and where it

[14] Cf. W. J. Ganshof Van Der Meersch, *Aspects du Régime Parlementaire Belge* (Bruxelles: Librairie Encyclopédique, 1956), p. 129; and K. C. Wheare, *Government by Committee* (Oxford: Oxford University Press, 1955), p. 67; see also E. Gruner, *Die Wirtschaftsverbände in der Demokratie* (Erlenbach-Zurich: Rentsch Verlag, 1956), pp. 97 ff.
[15] Cf. O. Kirchheimer, "The Waning of Opposition in Parliamentary Regimes," *Social Research*, XXIV (1957), pp. 127–156.
[16] Why the circumstances surrounding the parliamentary deliberations of the law on the new status of the private schools proved an exception to this generalization, cannot be discussed here.

merely consults them. It is generally impossible to measure the relative influence that groups exert over administrative decisions. But how much influence is exercised will depend less on the label describing the exchange than on the eagerness with which the decision-maker seeks advice and negotiation and on the persuasiveness with which both are offered.[17]

More important is a distinction between formal, institutionalized consultation and informal contacts. Both exist in all countries, but their legal significance and actual effect may be very different. The so-called advisory committees usually attached to a specific administration are everywhere, whatever other functions they may fulfill, an instrumentality of interest group influence. In Great Britain a recent census of such committees counted 484 on the level of the central government alone, more than one-fourth of them attached to the Ministry of Agriculture, that of Supply and the Board of Trade.[18] The very proliferation of such committees forces many governmental departments to constantly "keep in touch"; at almost every step it is necessary to take into account a large number of reasons and arguments.

In most cases interest groups propose committee members for nomination or nominate them outright. For these groups there is therefore no need for hammering at the doors of the Ministries; they are constantly being invited in and have acquired the status that stems from being immensely useful. They also may acquire the inside information that enhances their position in regard to their own membership. This however does not change the fact that the advice which the groups tender may not present to the bureaucracy sufficient alternatives for action.[19] Where the acceptance of the committee's advice has become habitual, because the bureaucracy hesitates to formalize any decision for which the groups concerned do not want to take the responsibility, the groups are in fact vested with administrative authority. In most countries it seems to take particular courage to by-pass agricultural organizations, which contributes to an inflation of the group-ego. Yet it is still true that frequently the outcome will depend on the forcefulness of the administrator to whom the committee reports.

Being less useful, the larger and less technical committees have also less weight. This explains in part why the various Economic Councils have never fulfilled the expectations of pluralists and administrators who hoped that the councils would, by combining the advantages of

---

[17] Cf. H. Simon, "Decision-Making and Administrative Organization," *Public Administration Review*, IV (1944), pp. 24–25; and LaPalombara, *op. cit.*, p. 39.

[18] Cf. P.E.P., *op. cit.*, listing (pp. 193–217) all existing committees as well as the major nominating bodies, mostly interest groups.

[19] For parallel criticism of the situation in the United States and in France, see C. Wirtz, "Government by Private Groups," *Louisiana Law Review*, XIII (1953), p. 440, and G. Lavau, "Political Pressures by Interest Groups in France," H. Ehrmann (ed.), *Interest Groups on Four Continents* (Pittsburgh: University of Pittsburgh Press, 1958), pp. 82–84.

expertness and publicity, relieve the pressures of the lobbies. In countries such as Germany and Great Britain, where they once existed, they have been abandoned. The French experience remains inconclusive, and the same must as yet be said about the Dutch Economic Council although as an institutionalized representation of the "Estates" the latter seems to have become an effective "shadow parliament."[20]

Besides the official committees which are used by the administration as seals of democratic legitimacy, informal face-to-face contacts remain important for the groups since they are more interested in the substance than in the form of power. In countries like France and Finland where the fragmentation of interests is pronounced, the flight into informal and confidential contacts often follows the breakdown of communications in the more or less publicly conducted committees.[21] But informal daily contacts are also usual in the United States and Germany. In Great Britain they have been described as forming the very basis of a "quasi-corporatism." In Sweden a "Thursday Club" brings together high civil servants, representatives of industry and finance to engage in serious planning business over the dinner table.[22]

Formal as well as informal consultation will have some of the consequences which resulted when in the United States the Tennessee Valley Administration found it necessary to bargain with local centers of power for their support.

Such cooperation led unavoidably to an acceptance by the T.V.A. of the entire pattern of Southern economic, race and class relations.[23] Almost any bureaucracy which in order to ensure its own stability makes outside organizations part of the policy-making administrative structure, will find that in the process the groups may succeed in modifying the character and even the role of governmental instrumentalities. The regular consultation of groups, indispensable as it might be, is likely to lead to commitments which have restrictive consequences for official policy and the behavior of authority.

A far-reaching "colonization" of the bureaucracy occurs where groups determine the personnel policy of the administration and where therefore personal relations have become institutionalized in a somewhat drastic fashion. Here differences between various countries continue to

---

[20] Cf. H. Daalder, "Parties and Politics in the Netherlands," *Political Studies*, III (1955), pp. 1–16; but see for France, H. Seligson, "An Evaluation of the Economic Council of France," *Western Political Quarterly*, VII (1954), pp. 35–50.

[21] For a report on Finland revealing striking similarities to the French situation, see L. Krusius-Ahrenberg, "The Political Power of Economic and Labor-Market Organizations: A Dilemma of Finnish Democracy," Ehrmann (ed.), *op. cit.*, pp. 33–59.

[22] For England cf. S. H. Beer, "Pressure Groups and Parties in Britain," *The American Political Science Review*, L (1956), p. 9; for Sweden, cf. H. Thorelli, "Formation of Economic and Financial Policy: Sweden," *International Social Science Bulletin*, VIII (1956), p. 270.

[23] Cf. P. Selznick, *TVA and the Grass Roots* (Berkeley: University of California Press, 1949), pp. 12, 265 and *passim*.

exist. In Great Britain one considers "sinister" what has become common practice in Western Germany. In France there are at most social sanctions against the civil servant who has incurred the displeasure of an interest group, and if a group wishes to see a particular *fonctionnaire* put in charge of a certain assignment, it must act surreptitiously. In Belgium, on the other hand, outside pressure on promotions, though no longer on appointments, remains strong and gives the groups an effective lever on decision-making. In Italy the influence of groups affiliated with the dominant Christian Democracy seems to loom large in the thinking of civil servants about their career.[24] Whether or not the non-existence of life-tenure makes the Swiss civil servant amenable to pressures coming from a particularly well developed network of interest groups, has not been investigated so far. Cases of group leaders entering the administration are known in the United States as well as Sweden, though presumably in Sweden interest group personnel will sever all of their former connections.

It is not easy to find a common denominator for the factors which in different countries have made it possible to operate, as it were, from within the administrative hierarchy. The degree of and the belief in the political neutrality of the civil service is obviously an important factor. In Germany, the politization of the bureaucracy, though it had started earlier, reached its apogee in the Third Reich. Denazification, the distrust by the occupying powers of the civil service, and the rapid re-emergence of the interest groups after the war while political parties were still discredited, combine to explain a situation in which certain groups consider certain administrative jobs their fief. Some bureaus have been described as "feudal dukedoms," and administrative autonomy is threatened wherever the civil servant knows that he occupies his post because of the *satisfecit* of an interest group.[25] In the United States some of the regulatory commissions have come under the sway of the economic forces they were set up to control partly because presidential appointments of commissioners have drawn freely on interest representatives who were presumably considered to possess expert knowledge. The result has been in many cases a perversion of the law which the regular courts can seldom correct.[26] In Belgium the politization of promotions is a legacy of ideological, religious and cultural-linguistic conflicts. There, as well as in Italy, the colonization of parts

---

[24] These and other data on Italy and Belgium are gleaned, with the permission of the authors, from unpublished reports by Professors V. Lorwin and J. LaPalombara submitted to the Conference held in September 1960 under the auspices of the Social Science Research Council.

[25] Cf. T. Eschenburg, *Herrschaft der Verbände?* (Stuttgart: Deutsche Verlagsanstalt, 1956), pp. 16 ff.; and W. Weber, in *Der Staat und die Verbände* (Heidelberg: Verlag Recht und Wirtschaft, 1957), p. 22. For the influence of German veterans' organizations on the recruitment of the officers' corps in the new army cf. K. W. Deutsch and L. J. Edinger, *Germany Rejoins the Powers* (Stanford: Stanford University Press, 1959), p. 96.

[26] Cf. James M. Landis, *Report on Regulatory Agencies to the President-Elect* (Washington: Government Printing Office, 1960), esp. pp. 11–17.

of the administration is effected through the political parties which may act as agents for the groups. It would be an unwarranted generalization to expect this to be true in all political systems where interest groups are massively involved in party affairs or at least in party finances, since the case of Great Britain clearly refutes such an assumption.

Whether or not the groups succeed in "boring from within" tactics or whether their access to decision-making is confined to other channels is quite obviously determined by the framework of the institutions and by the traditions within which the groups operate.

CONTROLS OF THE BUREAUCRACY-GROUP RELATIONSHIP

In all democratic systems administrative decisions are subject to a variety of administrative, political and judicial controls.[27] The decisive question seems to be how deeply the available controls can penetrate into the subsystem in which groups and bureaucracy interact.

The fact that different Ministries vary in their outlook on the desirability or the danger of group influence determines the nature of certain intra-administrative controls. The competence of an administration and its position in the hierarchy may generate enough independent power to change decisions that have been made elsewhere, e.g., by clientele agencies or in another administrative environment where groups have weighed heavily. The Treasury (in the United States together with the Bureau of Budget) seems to fulfill this role in many countries; in such different systems as those of Great Britain and France it exercises its prerogatives in very similar fashion. For all their differences in style (persuasion here, haughtiness there) Treasury and *Rue de Rivoli* are always waiting to turn something down, to be the guardians of the general interest in a universe seething with special interests and to use budget compliance as a means of administrative-political control. Even in Sweden where a curious 18th century tradition of keeping executive policy separate from routine administration compels the groups to work on both levels, the budget is the main device of curbing the autonomy of the Central Administrative Boards in charge of administration proper.[28] But everywhere treasury controls are somewhat blunted by the fact that if they are carried too far, an overcentralization of final decision-making is bound to occur.

The way in which intra-bureaucratic arbitration is organized has a bearing on pressure group activities. Muddled responsibilities may transform the dialogue between group and regulatory agency into a colloquium between private and public bureaucracies. In such a situation the best informed, i.e., usually the best organized groups can play on intra-bureaucratic feuds and peddle information from one agency

---

[27] For reasons of space the effectiveness of judicial controls in various countries cannot be examined here. Moreover this is as yet a largely unexplored question.

[28] Cf. Thorelli, *op. cit.*, pp. 262–264.

to another. Should the lack of effective arbitration leave the situation so unsettled that administrative immobility sets in, the groups will either be happy with a status quo that serves them well or they will have to appeal to forces outside the bureaucracy. In any country difficulties of reaching decisions on the ministerial level are likely to impede long-range programming by officials which in turn might make the bureaus listen with more benevolence to short-term causes pleaded by the groups. Such a situation arose in England during the last period of the war-time coalition; it has been chronic in Finland and during much of the Fourth Republic. On numerous occasions the French bureaucracy took major political decisions under the cloak of an administrative ruling and more than once under pressure from organized interests — the "solution" of the Moroccan crisis in 1953 is a well-known case in point.[29]

The point has been made that where a strong and disciplined legislature exercises political controls the civil service is in a better position than elsewhere to hold the dam against special interests, for otherwise the interests penetrate the bureaucracy and undermine its neutral, instrumental character.[30] A comparative inquiry seems to suggest that while such a penetration occurs everywhere, its effects depend on many factors besides the ability of parliament to articulate and aggregate group demands. Where parliament is organized so as to function, usually through committees, as a body for intensive legislative initiative and even current administration, this will have its repercussions for the structure and the workings of the subsystem. In the United States and the now defunct French Republics the interaction between committee chairmen, bureau heads and clientele groups provides a different field for group activities from that existing in Great Britain or other countries where parliament is concerned with the discussion of broad policy issues rather than with influencing legislation.

If it is true that the British official has to sustain relatively few pressures coming directly from Westminster, this does not mean that existing controls will always shield him from direct group intervention. Only in rare situations can he protect himself against group demands by obtaining appropriate directives from his Minister. On the other hand many French civil servants maintain that during the years of the Fourth Republic they were perfectly capable of insulating themselves from parliamentary pressures transmitting demands emanating from interest groups. They considered themselves safe from such intervention just because the National Assembly did not muster efficient parties which might have aggregated interests behind the closed doors of a caucus or an executive committee meeting. Since it was well-known which deputies were the appointed spokesmen of particular special

---

[29] Cf. Meynaud, "Les groupes d'intérêt," *op. cit.*, p. 584.
[30] G. Almond, "A Comparative Study of Interest Groups and the Political Process," *American Political Science Review,* LII (1958), p. 280. For the situation in the United States, see J. L. Freeman, *The Political Process. Executive Bureau–Legislative Committee Relations* (Garden City, N.Y.: Doubleday & Co., 1955).

interests, it was easy to discredit their *démarches* in the governmental bureaus. Undoubtedly the contempt which many French civil servants harbor for the politician is much greater than that of his British or American colleague and results in bureaucratic unwillingness to grant a sympathetic hearing to most deputies.[31] Developments in the Fifth Republic are contradictory. Certain groups, especially those representing small and marginal interests, which in the past had an easy access to parliament and its committees, were compelled to seek other channels, some of them leading through the ministerial *cabinets*. But at least so far one cannot conclude that the drastic transformation of parliamentary functions has had any clear influence on the relationship between groups and bureaucracy.

There is evidence that in all Western democracies political and technological developments led to a weakening of controls over the administration. Though the civil servant is steadily gaining ascendancy over the politician, his own autonomy does not always increase correspondingly. In the absence of a clear political impulse the bureaucracy finds it often necessary to lean heavily on the interest groups for advice and cooperation and subsequently identifies itself more easily with their demands.

BUREAUCRATIC MENTALITY AND ENVIRONMENT AS FACTORS IN GROUP ACCESS

Which are the factors making civil servants personally amenable or resilient to group influence? From the angle of the old controversy as to whether the high civil service should be turned over to the expert-technician or to the amateur-generalist there is evidence that the latter knows better how to defend himself against special interests. For Max Weber the absence of emotional involvement distinguishes the administrator from the politician.[32] But the technically trained bureaucrat in charge of highly specialized regulation becomes frequently as committed to causes as his clients and seems incapable of the stoical realism and open-mindedness which his generalist colleagues are proud to push to the point of professional agnosticism. In France the state engineers, distributed through many agencies and excellently trained though they are, are regarded by their colleagues to be least capable of thinking in terms of long-range generalized interests and therefore easily swayed by the pleadings of articulate groups. The strong identification of the administrator with his agency and its clientele will be lessened by the mobility which a unified civil service generates more easily than a highly stratified bureaucracy whose *grands corps* are fairly strictly separated.

[31] Cf. R. Grégoire, *Réflexions sur le Problème des Réformes Administratives* (Paris: Cours ENA, 1951), p. 23.
[32] Cf. the significant quotations from various writings by M. Weber in R. Bendix, *Max Weber, an Intellectual Portrait* (Garden City, N.Y.: Doubleday & Co., 1960), p. 421.

In many countries civil servants, rather than being men of ideas, pride themselves on enjoying a freedom from ideas.[33] But then interests may be more convincing than political doctrines and the civil servant might judge the vagaries of party politics more severely than the concrete and closely reasoned arguments of interest groups. Does the character training to which monarchical and aristocratic traditions in Great Britain and Sweden are still submitting the civil service elite have an immunizing effect?[34] The French scoff at it. But they admit that their pre-war training which provided solitary preparation for mastery, left the official without sufficient initiation in the skills of negotiation, so important in dealings with interest groups. The almost exclusively legalistic training of the German and Italian civil servant, while satisfactory to the generalists' orientation, tends to provide the administrator with a perspective which leaves the concrete content of administrative issues indecisive and confused. A focus on the abstract might create a void into which interest group leaders can move to press their demands.[35]

Because of the controls they exercise over other sectors of the bureaucracy, the differences in attitude of the officials of the British Treasury and the French Ministry of Finance are noteworthy. The British staff is lacking specialized training but is now imbued with a practical philosophy: Keynesian thinking. The French Inspectorate of Finance (and there are close parallels to its outlook in Belgium) is highly trained in the techniques of public finance but so preoccupied with monetary considerations that, at least until recently, a philosophy of economic development was alien to its members.[36] It appears that the Treasury control is more effective when it is called upon to arbitrate between conflicting claims. The *Rue de Rivoli* has, especially in an inflationary situation, the tendency to turn down everybody until its defenses are breached from without.

It is sometimes argued that the degree to which an administrative agency is permeable to organized interests is a function of its age: the more recent administrations, especially those established in the wake of war-time and post-war controls are said to lack the traditions of autonomy and to be as yet too unsure of themselves to develop the standards that are needed in their relationship with interest groups. This seems to be an unwarranted generalization.[37] In most countries an enumeration of Ministries, noted for granting easy access to inter-

---

[33] Cf. C. H. Sisson, *The Spirit of British Administration and Some European Comparisons* (Oxford: Blackwell's, 1959), p. 23.

[34] Cf. Chapman, *op. cit.*, p. 93.

[35] A point developed by LaPalombara in his unpublished paper, *op. cit.*

[36] For England, cf. S. H. Beer, *Treasury Control* (New York: Oxford University Press, 1956), pp. 58, 95. For France, P. Lalumière, *L'Inspection Générale des Finances* (Paris, 1959).

[37] For France this hypothesis is advanced by Meynaud, "Les groupes d'intérêt," *op. cit.,* p. 580. For Italy it is rejected by LaPalombara, "The Utility," *op. cit.*, p. 44.

est groups, includes old-time administrations as well as newer ones. It is still the specialized clientele agency, whether new or old, which is most given to quasi-corporatist practices. Hence function and not age seems to be the decisive factor.

For the time being it rather appears that the younger generation of civil servants is more fully aware of the problems inherent in their contacts with organized interests. Whether they are correct when they boast of having developed a mentality and techniques that ensure a greater autonomy to the bureaucracy remains to be seen. In Saskatchewan[38] and in France the conjuncture of political circumstances and of thorough reforms in the training of top administrators could be a reason for change. But one notes also in Holland a more frankly technocratic orientation of the younger civil servants: if they have acquired the political skill which is necessary in their contacts with interest groups, they have even less sympathy than their elders for the professional politician.

Social cohesion and strongly developed corporate life make undoubtedly for bureaucratic autonomy. Frequently however, the social origin of the top-bureaucrats facilitates feelings of kinship with groups outside the administration and notably with a milieu that dominates the private sector of the economy. These attitudes, noted equally in France and in Great Britain, have their impact on the relationship between officials and those who come to represent in their bureaus the major interests of the nation. In Western Germany the business elite and their professional spokesmen are much closer to the foreign service and the military than both are to the political elites presently ruling the country.[39] Similar affinities based not only on social origin and education but also on manners, style and outlook exist now elsewhere when most of the influential interest groups are employing a personnel that is particularly attractive for the civil service and that has been described in the United States as the "counter-elite of the private governments."[40] There is nothing involved here that could be characterized as collusion. But administrators are likely to be receptive to proposals which stem from sources comparable to those from which their own attitudes and values have been derived.[41]

The professional aspirations of the civil servant may include plans for a switch to private employment. In both France and the United States this phenomenon is particularly frequent and provokes strikingly

---

[38] For observation on Saskatchewan, see S. Lipset, *Agarian Socialism*, quoted here from R. Merton et al. (eds.), *Reader in Bureaucracy* (Glencoe, Ill.: The Free Press, 1952), p. 228.

[39] Cf. Deutsch and Edinger, *op. cit.*, pp. 99–100.

[40] H. Morgenthau, "Our Thwarted Republic," *Commentary*, XXX (1960), p. 484. The entire article is a sharp attack on the place of interest groups in the American political system of today.

[41] Cf. R. W. Gable, "Interest Groups as Policy Shapers," *The Annals of the American Academy of Political and Social Sciences*, CCCIXX (1958), p. 91.

similar attitudes both before and after the transfer takes place.[42] The official who looks forward to a business career is generally able to develop during his term of office a concept of independent public service without thereby spoiling his chances for a change in employment. Nevertheless the fact that he who regulates today expects to spend his later days representing the other side, is apt to be reflected in the general outlook of the civil servant. In general the *pantouflard* will be employed in an activity with which he was familiar while in government service, if he is not simply now doing what he was previously called upon to control. He is almost always hired because of his expert knowledge of public administration, its personnel, its methods and policies. When he calls on his former colleague to transact business with him the cordiality of their contacts will greatly further the symbiosis of officialdom and private interests.

STANDARDS FOR THE DEFENSE OF THE PUBLIC INTEREST

It has become evident from the foregoing that the political efforts of interest groups directed at influencing administrative decisions show a great deal of uniformity in all Western democracies. Held against existing similarities the effect of diverse political institutions of sharply different political cultures pales in comparison. It remains quite true that the degree of political homogeneity of a society, and the consensus achieved by its citizens will have an important impact on the way in which private conflicts are taken into the public domain and group claims are transformed into public policy. The general effect which the interest group system has on the political process in countries like France and Italy may still be very different from that produced in Great Britain or the Scandinavian countries. But where they interact with the bureaucracy (and at least as long as they interact), group leaders even in countries with a fragmented, isolative political culture[43] will show a somewhat unexpected degree of consensus and of loyalty to the rules of the game.

To seek a hearing in governmental bureaus, to act as advisor and consultant implies on the part of the groups at least a momentary, but probably a lasting commitment to the political system, the acceptance of common values include the acknowledgment of the fact that every social service state controls a large share of the national income through administrative decisions and that it is the proper role of the bureaucracy to adjust conflicting group claims. The more regularly such an arbitration occurs, the more will even the temporarily

---

[42] The description of the American situation by Jaffé, *op. cit.*, pp. 1132ff., could be taken as an exact portrayal of the mentality of the *pantouflard* in France.

[43] For an interesting typology of different countries of Western Europe cf. Almond, *op. cit.*, p. 274.

dissatisfied groups have confidence in the stability of the state, however much they may decry, as they did for instance in the Fourth Republic, the instability of governments. In the perhaps extreme case of Sweden the general standard of values is so commonly accepted and the function of the state has become so technical that politics appears to administrators as well as to groups as a kind of applied statistics.[44] But also in societies where distrust frequently destroys the basis of pragmatic behavior, mutual fears of group leader and officials of being manipulated by the other side will subside. A high degree of agreement on basic issues coupled with a high degree of concern with narrowly delimited policies impinging mostly upon technical fields creates an atmosphere in which there is a premium on moderation.[45]

It is true that in order to participate in the bargaining process of the subsystem a group must be confident that its demands can be handled there. Any group that has major demands upon society and state will go elsewhere than to the bureaucracy: it may turn to the party system, transform itself into a party if the parties fail, or take to violence. The British and German trade-unions early in the century, Dorgères in the Thirties, Poujade in the Fifties are examples of such attempts of translating political power into economic power. Just as the "time for law has not yet come while opposite convictions still keep a battle front against each other,"[46] the administration cannot fulfill its function as a mediating authority in regard to groups which give expression to fundamental discontents. Where the disruption of the consensus divides the community into armed camps, the bureaucracy risks being transformed into a battalion of one of the armies.[47] But the situation is fundamentally different when permanently organized groups seek, through their own bureaucracies, the assistance of officialdom to translate their economic power into favorable regulations.

In that process the administrator is faced with the task of utilizing, if at all possible, the currents of special interests with which he is surrounded, for the discovery of the public interest.[48] It is significant that in all Western democracies practitioners and theorists of public administration discuss the concept of the public interest in very similar terms, though in Anglo-Saxon countries their terminology might be colored by Bentham, while elsewhere it is influenced by Rousseau.[49] The way in which the bureaucrat will assess his role in discovering the "x-factor in the political equation," namely the public or general interest, is highly significant for his self-image and thereby for his

---

[44] Cf. Thorelli, *op. cit.*, p. 272.
[45] Cf. H. Eckstein, *Pressure Group Politics. The Case of the British Medical Association* (Stanford: Stanford University Press, 1960), p. 156.
[46] O. W. Holmes, *Collected Legal Papers* (London: Constable, 1920), p. 295.
[47] Fainsod, *op. cit.*, p. 322.
[48] Cf. P. Herring, *Public Administration and the Public Interest* (New York: McGraw-Hill Book Co., 1936), p. 134 and *passim*.
[49] Cf. the discussion on Bentham and Rousseau by a British and a French observer in Ehrmann (ed.), *op. cit.*, pp. 278–280.

dealings with organized interests. One finds in most countries a variety of schools viewing the search for the general interest in a different light. There are those who believe in the ability of the expert-technician to distill the Public Will from a rationalization of the decisional process with apparently little room left for discretion. There are also the "philosopher-administrators" whose creed, whether they admit it or not, comes close to an organic theory of the state since they trust their intuition for a recognition of the common good even though the public which allegedly wills it, is unaware of its concrete content. Apostles of a political Darwinism may hold that the invisible hand will find a counter-lobby for each lobby, and that from the group struggle the public interest will spontaneously emerge.[50]

But of late, and especially since World War II, the sociological reality of the administrative process has been grasped more clearly and insights have spread which attribute to the bureaucracy less sweeping though not less exacting functions. In reality the official will have to select among the interests pressing on him some that are more readily identified with his concept of the public welfare than others. Here demands must be fused, their dormant interests must be awakened so that they can be opposed to others that have long been vocal. All this might, though it must not necessarily, increase for the bureaucracy its freedom of maneuver. The choices which it will communicate to the groups as well as to other parts of the political system, become an expression of the policy to which the administration is committed.[51]

Understood in this way the concept of public interest, rather than being, as it was considered earlier, a standard for administrative behavior, becomes the post-hoc label for the resolution of group conflict. Just as the interplay of interests is regarded as legitimate in a pluralist society, the form in which their claims affect administrative decision-making is legitimized by a reference to the public or common interest. Since the well-organized pressure groups which find recognition and, frequently, satisfaction in the subsystem are similarly structured in many countries, and since they also act similarly at least as long as they are addressing the bureaucracy, it can only be expected that the process of and the procedures for legitimization have many similarities from one country to the other.

This does not mean that in all Western democracies decisions reached in the bureaucracy-group system will produce identical results. It is true that everywhere and only with some exceptions, sectional interest groups are better at conservation than at development, more prone to protect vested rights than to face new problems. The power of the bureaucracy on the other hand may be utilized either to maintain an

[50] On the concept of the public interest and the various schools which have formed in regard to it, cf. G. A. Schubert, "The Public Interest in Administrative Decision-making; Theorem, Theosophy or Theory?" *American Political Science Review,* LI (1957), pp. 346–368; and F. Sorauf, "The Public Interest Reconsidered," *Journal of Politics,* XIX (1957), especially pp. 617, 628.

[51] Cf. Fainsod, *op. cit.,* p. 320.

existing equilibrium or to tilt the balances so as to create a new equilibrium. Which way the decision goes may, but need not, be decided in the subsystem. Whether special interests will in the end further or obstruct the achievement of a viable policy will depend not only on the degree of autonomy which the bureaucracy has preserved, but on impulses that come from other parts of the political system. Economic policies followed after the war in different European countries provide contrasting examples. In Sweden powerful and self-conscious interest groups were not less responsible for assuring economic stability than the government. In England governmental initiative, backed by a disciplined parliamentary majority, was needed to produce similar results. But in France organized business and labor, preying upon a weak political executive and upon parliament, inaugurated policies which for long years veered between the alternatives of inflation and recession.

SUBSYSTEM INTO NEO-FEUDALISM?

The generally smooth functioning of the group-bureaucracy subsystem contributes greatly to the efficiency of modern government; but also has its dangers, acute or latent, for the democratic process. In the eyes of those who doubt that there exists a metaphysical "general interest" and who admit that administrators can "find" the common good only by reference to the interests and demands which surround them, it is neither avoidable nor inherently bad that pressure groups have an impact on decision-making. According to this view the democratic process is not disturbed by the mere fact that the administration seeks legitimacy for its decision by group consultation and that the groups wish to see legitimacy bestowed on them by being admitted to the consultation-decision circuit. The decisive question is rather whether in concrete situations the sharing of power between groups and bureaucracy perverts the democratic method of formulating policies.[52]

A number of disturbing questions can nowhere be answered satisfactorily. On which basis are some groups admitted and others excluded? It is a truism that society is not vocal and that the expressed demands of society are usually the demands of vocal, organized groups.[53] In some countries there might be agreement as to which groups are representative of the publics in whose name they are speaking. Elsewhere this might be impossible if only for the fact that many sectional groups will try to identify their demands with the interests of the general public and will have successfully manipulated public opinion to lend verisimilitude to their claim. A decision by the administration to invite certain interest groups rather than others to take part in the regulatory process might reflect a state of tension

---

[52] Cf. Gable, *op. cit.*, pp. 92–93.
[53] Cf. L. Lancaster, "Private Administration and Public Administration," *Journal of Social Forces* (1934), p. 291.

between formal authority and social or economic power; it might deflect a possible threat coming from such powers. It might, however, also lead to policies quite different from those which a wider, but inarticulate, public would have approved.

In most countries the articulation of demands by the consumer "group" encounters particular difficulties. What these demands are is most of the time an unexplored mystery. To expect the administrator to be constantly mindful of the existence of unorganized consumer interests is probably unrealistic. Consumer demands or revolts used to assert themselves rather through political parties, and obviously most likely through opposition parties. Hence, the present-day decline of the role of political opposition in most democracies tends to consolidate from yet another side the relative weight of organized interests interacting with the bureaucracy.

Although serious conflicts are infrequent between groups and the administration, it should not be assumed that intra-group conflict is always solved benevolently nor that the interests of all group members are represented fairly.[54] The more efficient its own organization, the easier it becomes for the group to determine which interests will be expressed and which will be silenced. In fact when they sift and arbitrate between conflicting claims of their membership, interest groups fulfill an important political function. How satisfactorily they perform this role might depend upon procedures for accountability and in general on the social and political climate. But it is certain that the effects of such group activities can very seldom be controlled by the bureaucracy. (In France some efforts in this direction were made by the newer administrations when they sought to break the grip of group leaders who were all too devoted to the practices of economic malthusianism.)

The possible misrepresentation of member interests is all the more serious since even in countries where the functioning of parliamentary institutions is unimpaired, a creeping pluralism has rendered the right to an isolated existence very precarious. In many cases, of which the cartel situation is only one of the better known, an individual or a subgroup wishing to balk the decisions made in their name by the leadership of an interest organization can do so only at the risk of ostracism and economic ruin. Where citizens owe their livelihood and security to the groups, their primary loyalties will easily belong to the interest groups rather than to the state.[55] Thereby a situation reminiscent of feudal arrangements is created and these arrangements are solidly underpinned in the relationship between groups and bureaucracy.

What a Swiss writer has called the *Unio Mystica,* the merging of state and group power[56] is strengthened by the fact that at present in most countries group leaders and bureaucrats are frequently united by

---

[54] Cf. Jaffé, *op. cit.,* p. 251.
[55] Cf. Morgenthau, *op. cit.,* p. 481.
[56] Cf. F. Marbach, here quoted from E. Gruner, *op. cit.,* p. 109.

bonds of similar origin, education and outlook. The subsystem turns into a subsociety. Its members are drawn to each other by mutual respect which enhances the understanding of each other's position but also induces both sides to consider personalities, institutions and ideas outside the subsystem as a possible disturbance. This excludes, however, the wider public. By a frequently diffident attitude towards the public at large the amalgam formed by groups and bureaucracy assumes the characteristics of a counter-system to political democracy.

At least in countries of continental Europe administrators and group leaders are also likely to share feelings of hostility against politics and of disdain for the politician. Since their foremost standards are efficiency and effectiveness they may believe that by de-politicizing and presumably neutralizing decisions one can arrive at technically perfect solutions which are all but insensitive to the variations of the political conjuncture. Partly such a belief may simply reflect a middle-class distaste for political struggle; in the United States the preference of millions of citizens to participate in public life through civic groups rather than through party channels is another expression of this distaste. In their self-image the partners of the subsystem are cleansed of political motivations and are engaged in what has been correctly called a "non-traditional kind of engineered neo-corporatism."[57] It is indeed preferable to stress the non-traditional character of the phenomenon rather than to trace it in Great Britain to the old Whig theory of representation, in the United States to a grass-roots concept of democracy, in continental Europe to a revival of the *Ständestaat* or to catholic notions. The striking similarity in present-day attitudes is far more significant than their possibly differing historical derivation.

In their common resistance to politics the technicians who collaborate in the subsystem hope to bring about, among other desirable results, that close union of public and private decision-making which in France has recently been christened *économie concertée*[58] Objectively they may multiply states within the state and thereby reconstitute the technicalities of a feudal system.[59] Should under such circumstances administrative creativity collapse, political decisions would amount to little more than an endorsement of the lowest common denominator of what the affected groups are willing to concede. It may be unavoidable that in any modern state the administrative stream is frequently threatened by "the embolism of off-setting groups." But a mentality which disdains politics and strives for technical perfection "rejects the very solvents that would reduce the obstruction."[60]

---

[57] Cf. Spiro, *op. cit.*, p. 340.

[58] F. Bloch-Laine, *A la Recherche d'une "économie concertée"* (Paris, 1959). The author is however fully aware of the technocratic dangers inherent in such a constellation.

[59] Cf. M. Waline, "Les résistances techniques de l'administration au pouvoir politique," *Politique et technique* (Paris: Presses Universitaires, 1958), p. 173.

[60] Cf. E. Latham, *The Politics of Railroad Coordination, 1933–1936* (Cambridge, Mass.: Harvard University Press, 1959), p. 277.

Then the creative impulse needed to serve the ends of a broader public policy must come from outside the subsystem, most likely from the political executive or from parliament and its parties. In the end this amounts everywhere to the problem which has been stated by an American author: "How much decentralization can the political system stand before some redress in the form of centralized power becomes necessary to maintain or re-establish the equilibrium of the system as an integrating unit?"[61]

Two opposite, though not necessarily mutually exclusive, dangers arise. One might ask whether such redress will always be possible after bureaucracy and groups have been given near-unlimited opportunities for autonomous action. And after the equilibrium is re-established a government strong enough to check the deeply rooted neo-feudalism may at least in certain societies also be strong enough to destroy the freedom of all.

The ghost of Jean-Jacques Rousseau has not been laid.

[61] A. Leiserson, *Parties and Politics* (New York: Alfred A. Knopf, 1959), p. 304.

GIORGIO GALLI
and ALFONSO PRANDI

The Catholic Hierarchy and Christian Democracy in Italy

The position of the Catholic Church as a worldly as well as spiritual power in Italy has long been central to party divisions in Italian politics. The creation of an Italian Republic at the end of World War II confronted the Catholic Church with the threat of a Communist anti-clerical regime. In reaction against this possibility, the bishops used their influence to mobilize votes for the Christian Democrats, the country's other major party. Yet, as the article by Galli and Prandi shows, the involvement of bishops has subjected them to the compromises and dilemmas of party politics, as well as gaining them influence upon party politics.

The intervention of the hierarchy in Italian political life from 1945 to 1963 has been constant and, to all appearances, monolithic. This intervention has taken the form of continuous "religious education." Those who contested its legitimacy and protested against clerical intervention were told that the Church has the right to give Catholics an orientation to political life when the stakes are the future of religion and the conditions which the Church must enjoy in order freely to carry out its mission on earth.

To the minds of Pius XII and the Italian bishops, a strong communist party in Italy gave a particularly dramatic content to the democratic contest for power. There was no possibility of compromise between political forces, as there would have been if all had shared a common underlying system of values. From the communists and their allies, Catholics could expect, instead, a complete reversal of that social order based on the natural law of which the Church was the authoritative and divinely-constituted interpreter. This is the reason for the Church's violently anti-communist position, for its assertion that the proper foundation for the institutional edifice of the state and the proper inspiration for its laws and customs were Christian principles, and for its position that it is the duty of every Catholic to be present and active *as a Catholic* in public life.

In 1945 the young Italian democracy did not seem to the Church to augur a peaceful future. It seemed possible that even the Concordat and the Lateran Pact, which in 1929 had ended the 60-year-old conflict between the Church and the Italian state[1] might be called into question. Thus the Church, through the bishops and the Pope, appealed to the faithful, alerting them to the growing communist threat to religion. The Church feared absenteeism at the polls, apathy, and the indifference of the faithful to imminent religious-political dangers. It aimed at one principal objective: to see to it that *all* the Catholics voted and that they all voted for the same party. Thus the "Christian nation" would easily be victorious over the enemy, and the reins of power would be placed in the hands of men and forces who were devoted to the cause of religion and of the Church.

The best occasion for such admonitions was obviously the electoral campaign. The basic document of hierarchical intervention is the

Printed from an unpublished manuscript by Giorgio Galli and Alfonso Prandi, "Patterns of Political Participation in Italy" (1969), by permission of Instituto di Studi e Ricerche Carlo Cattaneo, Bologna, Italy.

[1] The best source in English on the Concordat and the Pact, and the relations between the Holy See and the Fascist regime which preceded and followed, is still D. A. Binchy, *Church and State in Fascist Italy*, R.I.I.A., London, 1941.

circular of the Consistorial Congregation which was addressed to all Italian bishops in August, 1945. It gave the following instructions:

> 1. In view of the dangers to which religion and the public well-being are exposed and whose gravity requires the unanimous collaboration of all honest men, all those who have the right to vote, of every condition, sex, and age, with no exceptions, are, in conscience, strictly obliged to avail themselves of that right.
> 2. Catholics may give their vote only to those candidates or those lists of candidates of whom one has the certainty that they will respect and defend the observance of the divine law and the rights of religion and the Church in private and in public life.[2]

The language, in spite of its typically ecclesiastical circumlocution, is explicit: the candidates who should have the votes of honest men (and thus of Catholics) cannot be other than those of the DC (the *Democrazia Cristiana*, i.e., the Christian Democratic Party).

In the 1946 elections for the Constituent Assembly the Catholics were admonished to vote as a block because it was imperative "to assure to the present and future generations the blessing of a fundamental law of the nation which is not opposed to sound religious and moral principles, but rather takes from them vigorous inspiration and proclaims them and wisely follows their lofty ends."[3]

In 1948, in the face of the threat from the communist and socialist Popular Front, the appeals became unprecedentedly dramatic, as if there were taking place in Italy an all-out battle which would decide the future of the Church itself. The Pope and bishops joined the fray with repeated admonitions to Catholics under penalty of sin to make proper use of their vote in order to overcome the socialist and communist enemy. Because it was perfectly clear that the mass support of the Church was going to the DC, other political forces (besides the red "enemy") contested violently, and not merely verbally, the intervention of the Church.

In these and other similar documents, the warnings and teachings of the Pope and the bishops were always prefaced by a statement of the reasons justifying such intervention, which are along the lines we have mentioned. This need for justification was felt not only vis-à-vis public opinion as a whole; symptoms of disturbance and perplexity began to appear also among the Catholics. Between 1945 and 1948, there were a number of Catholics, militants in the DC, who wished to keep the Church out of the political contest. There were others who failed to understand the reasons for the anticommunist alarm. There was even

---

[2] Circular of the *Sacra Congregazione Concistoriale* of August 29, 1945: *Sull uso del diritto di voto.* See the text in *Civiltà Cattolica* Notebook 2286 of September 15, 1945.

[3] From a letter from Pius XII to Cardinal Lavitrano on the occasion of the 19th Italian Catholic Social Week, which took place in Florence, October 23–October 28, 1945. The theme of the meeting was "Constitution and Constituency." See *L'Osservatore Romano*, October 22, 1945.

a movement (the "Christian left") which expressly favored the alliance between Catholics and communists. This movement was soon condemned by the Church and disbanded; some of its followers joined the Italian Communist Party.

But Catholic criticism of ecclesiastical intervention was especially strong from 1953 on. The bishops themselves began to speak of an increasing indifference to their warnings. The fact is that the hierarchy, which had earlier limited itself to strong recommendations to Catholics to vote as a block for the DC, began to have other worries. In the face of the threat to unity which was represented by the growing, and increasingly obnoxious, factional activity within the DC, the hierarchy reacted by trying to establish closer control over the actions of the party. It claimed the credit for making the DC a strong anti-communist bulwark and asserted that it must remain such without allowing itself to diverge from that goal, which allowed it to enjoy united Catholic support. In other words, the hierarchy was not content with mobilizing the Catholic forces for the DC, but thought it equally important to pronounce on the proper uses of such unity. When the results of the 1953 general elections proved a disappointment, the hierarchy felt even more called upon to devote its attention to what was going on within the party. Catholic unity was no longer enough if the party which it supported was divided and lacked a solid organization such as that which characterized the Communist Party. It was necessary that the best Catholics (that is, the members of Catholic Action) devote themselves even more to the party, strengthening it and making it more sensitive to the warnings of the Church.

Within the DC, disappointment of hopes caused organizational concerns. Beginning in 1954 with the secretaryship of Fanfani, the party turned to organizational activities in order to transform itself from a merely electoral party into a mass party. This implied the beginning of rigorous discipline which, except for certain later reservations about Fanfani's experiment, the bishops viewed with favor. In fact, they interpreted diversities within the party in traditional moralistic terms as merely the expression of immoderate personal pride and greed.

But when the DC began to discuss the "opening to the left" (an alliance with the socialists which would transfer them from the communist camp into the democratic one), the hierarchy denounced the plan as deplorable and dangerous. It saw little merit in the argument that a courageous policy of reform, such as could be conducted by a socialist-Catholic alliance, was the only final answer to the communist challenge. Pius XII remained firm in his anti-communist denunciations, and the bishops, in their turn, denounced the illusion, the falsity, and the impossibility of such coexistence. They did not hide their alarm over the possibility that certain Catholic factions might consider a dialogue or collaboration with Marxist forces. The bishops were alarmed because it seemed to them that a new movement was making progress, a movement which, in the name of social reform, actually represented

Marxist infiltration and engendered a feeling of rebellion against ecclesiastical authority.

The hierarchy took the opportunity offered by the 1958 general election to remind the Catholics that the Church's position concerning political commitment had undergone no changes. The Catholics must be and remain united. Ten years earlier the hierarchy had manifested no lack of faith in the DC. Now, however, the Catholics were not only invited to vote united, but to vote for DC candidates having a specific qualification — opposition to the daring designs of the leftists. According to the bishops, the parties of the left had since 1946 undergone no changes which called for the Church to reconsider its position toward them. The growing distance between the PSI (*Partito Socialista Italiano*) and the Communist Party (especially after destalinization and the events in Poland and Hungary) seemed to them to offer no good reason for the Catholics to modify their attitude toward the socialists: the latter would always be the allies and accomplices of communism.

Between 1958 and 1961, the tension between the Italian episcopate and the DC was at its maximum. More and more party members were in favor of opening a dialogue with the socialists in order to accelerate their separation from the communists; but the hierarchy, in stronger and stronger terms, denounced the DC's wooing of the socialists as the most serious of threats to Catholic unity. At times the warnings of the bishops even included threats to withdraw the support of the Catholic forces from the DC.

Episcopal pronouncements against the Catholic leftists were particularly severe in 1959 and 1960. The pressures that were regularly brought to bear on the party were explicit and sometimes openly provocative. It was during this period, for example, that Cardinal Siri (archbishop of Genoa and president of the Italian Episcopal Conference) wrote to the secretary of the DC (Moro) to dissuade him from continuing the "opening to the left" policy in parliament, that is, trying to form a parliamentary majority which included the socialists.

The episcopate did nothing but reiterate the positions which it had held for years. The only exception to this generalization was Cardinal Montini (the future Pope Paul VI, then archbishop of Milan). Although he also did not favor the "so-called opening to the left at the present moment and in the manner now being considered,"[4] in 1960 he admitted the possibility of guarantees which would be sufficient to allow for a change in the Church's negative attitude.

But in the autumn of 1958 John XXIII succeeded Pius XII as Pope. He appeared not to share the burning concern of his predecessors for events on the Italian political scene. The episcopate which previously had only to repeat, amplify, and adopt the position of the Pope was now

---

[4] Letter to the clergy of the diocese of Milan, dated May 21, 1960. The letter was not supposed to have been released to the public, but through an indiscretion it came to the attention of the press. See *L'Italia,* June 4, 1960.

left to its own discretion. It seemed that nothing had changed, but in reality Rome either left matters alone or suggested that such things should not be too much discussed.

In spite of the warnings and threats of the most alarmed and vocal of the bishops, the opening to the left was a constant theme for discussion by Catholics, both within and outside the DC. After the local elections of November, 1960, it finally began to be cautiously realized in the first center-left alliances in the governments of some large cities, such as Milan, Genoa, and Florence. This caused serious concern among the episcopate as is shown, for instance, by the Sicilian bishops' attack on the opening to the left of February, 1961. But the lack of a pontifical pronouncement weakened the voices of the bishops. The DC did not seem to fear that the *united* hierarchy would go so far as to excommunicate the party and advise the Catholics to withdraw their electoral support. Many bishops — most of them in fact — were silent. Did this signify acquiescence, resignation, prudence, or tolerance? Or did it indicate a reconsideration of the advisability of pastoral pronouncements about political questions? The bishop of Pesaro, who had most strongly denounced the opening to the left as going against religious teachings, wrote "We have concerned ourselves too much with politics, to the detriment of our ministry."[5]

In reality, John XXIII induced the episcopate to give more and more attention to general problems of the Catholic world and humanity. The calling of the Ecumenical Council and the encyclicals *Mater et Magistra* and *Pacem in Terris* created an atmosphere in which the politico-religious themes of the first fifteen post-war years sounded a jarring note. At last the bishops were silenced.

At its Naples Congress at the end of 1961, the DC got underway with the opening to the left; and in 1962 the PSI pledged itself to support the government, although it did not form part of the cabinet. The bishops still refrained from comment; in fact, many of them seemed to be worried lest their earlier thunderous pronouncements against the operation now be used to justify a break in the united Catholic front. And, to the extent that they discussed political questions at all, they returned to the theme of Catholic unity. That unity was said to be a blessing which was superior to the contingent decisions of the party and the various orientations of its currents. Cardinal Siri, one of the most explicit adversaries of the opening, in 1962 limited himself to encouraging the "coherence" of Catholics even "in the face of most dangerous and perplexing facts."[6] The opening to the left had become nothing but a source of perplexity, while it had formerly been condemned as something which would surely result in the breakup of Catholic unity.

[5] Pastoral letter for Lent, 1961. See *Lettere Pastorali de Vescovi Italiani, 1961*, Cittadella (Padova), 1961, pp. 422–442.
[6] Pastoral letter to the faithful of the Diocese of Senova for Lent, 1962. See *Lettere Pastorali, 1962–63*, Cittadella (Padova), 1964, pp. 771–811.

In short, the episcopate took refuge in caution and reserve. They seem to have been convinced of the difficulty, if not the impossibility, of imposing specific political preferences on the DC. There were no serious alternatives to the party, and thus it would have to be left to make its own decisions. The bishops did not wish to destroy Catholic unity; thus it was necessary to accept the opening as an accomplished fact. If the party desired the collaboration of the socialists, then it was the function of the priest to remind the faithful that they were not to compromise the teachings of the Church in any future legislative or executive agreements.

During the 1963 electoral campaign the official organ of the Italian episcopate advised that the Catholics must vote united and "make their choices with a watchful Christian conscience, knowing, if necessary, how to put their faithfulness to essential Christian principles and the requirements of the common good before personal opinions and particular interests."[7] Not a word about the center-left — in fact, it was fairly clear that "faithfulness to essential Christian principles and the requirements of the common good" here consisted in voting for the DC. Residual objections to agreements with the socialists were brushed aside as merely "personal opinions and particular interests."

Had the Italian bishops merely resigned themselves to their new role as guardians of Catholic unity, or had they really felt the impact of John XXIII and the significance of the council — and had they become aware of the dangers of their previous positions? Although we cannot answer these questions, we do know that a process of disengagement had clearly taken place and that it was reflected also in the Catholic Action groups which are directly controlled by the hierarchy.

There were, at any rate, important elements of continuity with the previous situation. In the eyes of the Italian hierarchy, the DC remains today the political force in which the Catholics may confidently place their trust. It is in the DC that the political unity of the Catholics manifests itself. Furthermore, it is the unity of the Catholics which allows the DC to maintain its position as the major political force in the nation.

---

[7] Communication of the C.E.I. of March 12, 1963. See *Civiltà Cattolica*, Notebook 2707 of April 4, 1963. Cf. the clarification of the meaning of the communication in *L'Osservatore Romano*, April 7, 1963.

PETER MERKL

The Structure of Interests and Adenauer's Survival as Chancellor

The distinction between pressure group and political party is difficult to make when groups organized to advance specific economic and social interests are formally affiliated to political parties. In Europe links are typically found between trade unions and Socialist and Communist parties. In Germany, the dominant Christian Democratic Union is, as its name implies, a federation of organizations representing distinctive economic, social, and religious interests. Peter Merkl's study of the re-election of Konrad Adenauer as German Chancellor following the 1961 federal election provides a very clear illustration of the way in which interest groups can so permeate a political party that the leader must give priority to his role as a broker between interests in order to survive.

In studies comparing the Bonn Republic with the Weimar Republic, few aspects of the former have received more attention from political scientists than its extraordinary political stability. Contrary to all expectations in the immediate postwar era, and under the same leadership, Germany's second try at parliamentary democracy has already outlasted the Nazi millennium and will soon have exceeded — successfully — the lifespan of its ill-fated democratic predecessor, the Weimar Republic. Interpretations abound which attribute the political stamina of the Bonn government to the economic prosperity of Western Germany, its Allied tutelage, its firm Western-oriented course, or its disenchantment with political extremism of either variety. Of particular interest to political scientists, however, are the theories which identify

Abridged from Peter Merkl, "Equilibrium, Structure of Interests and Leadership: Adenauer's Survival as Chancellor," *American Political Science Review*, LVI, 3, 1962, pp. 634–650. Reprinted by permission.

INTERESTS AND ADENAUER'S SURVIVAL AS CHANCELLOR 361

the political stability of the Bonn Republic with the "reign" of Konrad Adenauer from the beginning to this day.

At the time of the *Bundestag* elections of September, 1961, the octogenarian Chancellor had already governed the Federal Republic for three terms and there were abundant signs that his time was up. Having captured a majority of the *Bundestag* seats in the two previous elections, his Christian Democrats (CDU/CSU) now lost their absolute majority to the two opposition parties, the Free Democrats (FDP) and Social Democrats (SPD).[1] The FDP was willing to enter a coalition with the CDU/CSU, but its chairman, Erich Mende, definitely rejected Adenauer as the new Chancellor in favor of Ludwig Erhard or any other prominent CDU/CSU politician. A coalition between the CDU/CSU and the SPD was an unlikely choice for reasons we shall return to. During the campaign, Adenauer's popularity had slipped far from the heights of public veneration[2] and the press claimed that he was already beginning to confuse things and names in public speeches and had lost his zeal and touch for appealing to crowds.[3] Most damaging of all, a revolt against him was threatening in his own party where an opposition, the *fronde,* had formed since the presidential elections of 1959,[4] centering around Minister of Economics Erhard, *Bundestag* President Eugen Gerstenmaier, and the Hamburg deputies Bucerius and Blumenfeld.[5] At the height of the election campaign, Adenauer's internal enemies publicly attacked him, when the old Chancellor made the mistake of questioning the personal integrity of the SPD candidate, Willy Brandt, a few days after the outbreak of the Berlin crisis. They began to campaign for Erhard; and the ambitious Minister of Defense, Franz Josef Strauss (CSU), joined them in the last weeks before the elections. It was surprising that the CDU/CSU in spite of this internecine war managed to win a plurality at the polls.

Two days after the elections, therefore, when the 85-year-old Chancellor faced his Executive Board (*Parteivorstand*), angrily upbraiding his critics for showing him the door after twelve years of successful leadership, this seemed to be the end of the Adenauer era. Yet before the week was over, gasps of uncomprehending protest could be heard throughout the editorial offices of the German press. Cartoons appeared depicting Adenauer as a naughty child refusing to go to bed. Newspaper editors wrote the letter of resignation he should have written,

---

[1] The popular vote was distributed as follows: CDU/CSU 45.4% (1957: 50.2); SPD 36.2% (31.8); and FDP 12.8% (7.7).

[2] "Protest ist keine Denkmalsschaendung mehr," *Sueddeutsche Zeitung* (hereafter referred to as *SZ*), Sept. 13, 1961.

[3] *Der Spiegel,* Sept. 6, 1961, p. 17.

[4] On this occasion, Adenauer at first decided to go into semiretirement by running for the largely honorific office of Federal President. He changed his mind, however, when he learned that his successor as Chancellor would be Ludwig Erhard, of whom Adenauer declared in public that he lacked the ability and stature for this position.

[5] "Brandt alias Frahm," *Der Spiegel,* Aug. 23, 1961, p. 18.

and some compared him to the famous surgeon Sauerbruch who, stubbornly refusing to retire from the operating room because of his advanced age, had contributed to the death of several patients. Six weeks later, Adenauer had once more become Chancellor for at least another two years.

What had happened? Could Adenauer's survival against all odds be understood with the help of the various theories advanced by political scientists and other observers to explain his dominant role in West German politics? It is the intention of this study to reexamine these theories of Adenauer's leadership in the light of the revealing events accompanying the formation of his new coalition cabinet, and to supply a new explanation of this phenomenon of leadership and of the peculiarities of the West German political system which sustain it.

I

A cursory survey of the literature about the astounding stamina of Adenauer as a leadership figure shows a good deal of agreement among political scientists, journalists and other observers about the basic elements of his dominant role. Four major themes recur in most articles, books and comments about him: his personality, his international stature, his constitutional position and the plebiscitary character of West German democracy. . . .

These four elements of Adenauer's tenacious dominance in West German politics . . . are the basic conceptual tools offered in the endeavor to understand and explain Adenauer's survival against great odds in the almost seven weeks of bargaining over the new coalition government. His personality obviously had much to do with his success: his stubborn refusal to bow to the storm of public indignation and ridicule; the brazenness with which he seized the initiative both toward the public and within his own party;[6] the superior skill with which he outmaneuvered his chief rivals Erhard, Strauss and Gerstenmaier, and finally his future partners of the FDP. His international stature helped him little, although he lost no opportunity to show his own party leaders and the FDP negotiators letters and telegrams he had received from Washington. Later he insisted that he should be reelected soon, since President Kennedy was expecting him in Washington. His constitutional position also did not help him. It may on the contrary have made his prospective partners more wary of him: once they helped reelect him Chancellor, how could they be sure that he would retire at the agreed moment; how could they be certain of a reasonable measure of control over him short of forming a new coalition with the

[6] The morning after the Bundestag elections, Adenauer called a press conference without consulting his party in order to assert his leadership toward the public from the start. Three days later he disarmed his Party Executive Board so successfully that they appointed him as chief negotiator for the coalition talks, thereby prejudging the question of his continued leadership.

opposition? The charm of the "Chancellor effect" with the people had already worn thin and was used up even more rapidly by the refusal of the Old Man to resign while his people still respected and admired him. Only over his own party did his call for loyalty still have effect, especially after he had outmaneuvered the *fronde* and his most serious rivals.

Yet when one reviews the changing scenes and battles of the formation of the new Adenauer coalition, these four tools of analysis fall definitely short of explaining how and why Adenauer succeeded once more. They fail to explain, in particular, why Ludwig Erhard, the popular architect of the West German "economic miracle" and the choice for Chancellor of the people, of large parts of the CDU, the FDP and the CSU, did not press through his demand to become Chancellor. Nor can they make plausible the failure of the ambitious Strauss (CSU) to take control of the situation and either to end or to limit to a transitional one-year period the tenure of the Old Man. Nor do they make intelligible the similar failure of Gerstenmaier, the popular and experienced President of the *Bundestag*. These three men certainly did not fail for lack of trying. Least of all can the four elements mentioned above explain the slow but inexorable collapse of the position of Mende and his FDP who started out dictating the end of the Adenauer era and ended up content with little more than an empty gesture of compliance with their minimal request: to share the control over German foreign policy.

II

Dissatisfaction with these explanations leads us to probe further into the structure and substructure of the political system which made it possible for Adenauer to weather the storm facing him after the 1961 elections. The stability of his leadership, it is submitted, is the consequence of two structural aspects of the West German system which are linked together and will continue to favor anyone with the qualities necessary to become the leader of the CDU/CSU. This statement presupposes, of course, that the political camp to the right of the SPD will continue to enjoy a popular majority. One of the structural factors is the equilibrium among the group forces of which the CDU/CSU is composed. . . .

By equilibrium among the group forces we mean a relative state of balance among several pairs of distinct and antagonistic groups within the CDU/CSU which tends to operate in favor of the status quo. This state of balance need not be static or exclusive of the wax and wane of individual groups. There can be shifts of emphasis or orientation owing to the changing weight of individual groups. It is essential to this concept of equilibrium, however, that there is a consensus among the groups not to wipe out one another at times of superiority and to give each group its due voice, according to its size, in the formation of the policy of the whole organization. Such an equilibrial system will tend to operate similarly to the American system of the great sectional and socio-economic interests, or "veto groups": a candidate for leadership or a new policy, in order to be accepted, must not arouse the strong opposition of any one group. Once a leader or a policy has become accepted and managed to unify the whole system behind it, however, efforts at overthrowing the leader or the policy face the same obstacle: the opposition of a single group, albeit a small minority, can frustrate them once and for all.

The CDU/CSU indeed operates like such an equilibrial system. It is composed of a number of distinct and separate groups which oppose each other in pairs and yet are held together by a consensus mixed of mutual respect, Christian Democratic ideas about government and society, and the tangible advantages of party unity: organized labor and organized business, Protestants and Catholics, centralists and states righters, on the one side Big Business and Big Labor, and on the other, the *Mittelstand, i.e.* farmers, small business and the civil service. Members and voters of the CDU/CSU come from all layers of society. A web of associations from the Catholic labor organizations to business and farm organizations and the far-flung system of church organizations ties the party to all kinds of groups and social forces in West German society.[7] An elaborate system of party committees on several levels, moreover, channels the programmatic demands of labor, business, the *Mittelstand*, refugees, local government organizations, women and youth groups through Social Policy Committees, *Mittelstand* Policy Committees, and further committees on communal policy, and the women's and youth organizations, respectively, into the policy-making agencies of the party.[8]

As in our equilibrium model, this system has called for a leader who is basically uncommitted to any one group. While Adenauer could not help being a pronounced Catholic, a man of business associations and a former local government official of considerable reputation, he has remained far from becoming the herald of any of these groups. He has bent over backward to win the confidence of Protestants and to get along with organized labor and the states righters whose interests at times clash with those of the local government organizations. His role as a leader has been mainly that of a moderator and mediator among all the groups, a task which is also implicit in Christian Democratic thinking and in Catholic social philosophy.

This concept of leadership also implies a rather passive role in the

[7] For details, see Gerhard Schulz, "Die Organisationsstruktur der CDU," *Zeitschrift für Politik,* Vol. 3 (1956), p. 161. On the theory of parties of integration, see Sigmund Neumann, "Towards a Theory of Political Parties," *World Politics,* Vol. 6 (1954), p. 501 ff.

[8] Gerhard Schulz, "Die CDU — Merkmale ihres Aufbaus," in Max Gustav Lange, ed., *Parteien in der Bundesrepublik* (Stuttgart-Duesseldorf: Ringverlag, 1955), p. 143.

making of domestic policy. Under such circumstances, the leader is not expected to come up with an imaginative policy of his own. He fares better if he is content with being the broker of the policy trends developed by the dominant groups of his party, or the executor of the resultant of the parallelogram of forces among these groups. As has been noted by many an observer, Adenauer has never exhibited a pronounced conception of his own in domestic policy.[9] Only in foreign policy, he has a definite commitment to European unification and to the Western alliance.

Adenauer's broker role becomes evident especially if we review the spectacular changes in the economic policy of the CDU/CSU in the period during which he headed his party in the Bizonal Economic Council and later in the Bonn government. The CDU programs of Neheim-Huesten (1946) and Ahlen (1947) still advocated a planned economy and the socialization of the coal industry,[10] thereby reflecting both the hard times and the dominance of the labor wing within the CDU/CSU which at that time also frequently entered coalitions with the SPD. Then came the rise of Erhard's "social market economics," coalitions with the FDP and the Conservatives (DP), and the Duesseldorf Principles of 1949 in which the "regulated competition" of *ordo* liberalism[11] replaced the earlier socialism. In the following four years, the CDU/CSU dropped its labor orientation more and more while its business and *Mittelstand* wing came into full control. After 1952, Erhard and his free enterprise policy increasingly fell out of favor with the protectionist interests of Big Business, the *Mittelstand* and the farmers. This new trend of the CDU/CSU reached its climax with the postponing of Erhard's's anti-cartel bill until it was finally passed in an emasculated form in 1957, half a decade after it was first submitted.[12] But while the economic policy of the CDU/CSU thus traversed a half-cycle from socialism to recartelization, Adenauer remained party chairman and Chancellor without even once losing control, due to his lack of commitment and flexibility in domestic affairs.

With this party structure of the CDU/CSU and the corresponding leadership model in mind, we can reexamine the situation which Adenauer was facing after the elections of 1961. With his *Bundestag* majority lost, the Old Man had to choose between SPD and FDP as coalition partners. Apparently he preferred the latter because he would

---

[9] See the quotations in *Der Spiegel,* Sept. 27, 1961, pp. 64–5.

[10] See Wolfgang Treue, *Deutsche Parteiprogramme 1861–1961* (Frankfurt: Musterschmidt, 1961), pp. 183, 189; and Bruno Doerpinghaus und Kurt Witt, *Politisches Jahrbuch der CDU/CSU 1950* (Generalsekretariat der Arbeitsgemeinschaft CDU/CSU fuer Deutschland, 1950), pp. 226–9.

[11] *Duesseldorfer Leitsaetze,* July 15, 1949, Sonderdruck des Deutschland-Union-Dienstes. See also Carl J. Friedrich, "The Political Thought of Neo-Liberalism," *American Political Science Review,* Vol. 49 (June 1955), pp. 509–25.

[12] "Wege zur Sicherung des freien Wettbewerbs," *Das Parlament,* July 24, 1957, pp. 5–8.

have to share less power with a small party, if for no other reason. However, the FDP had campaigned with the slogan "No more one-party dominance in Bonn" and a promise not to enter a coalition with the SPD under any circumstances — thus encouraging a good many dissatisfied CDU/CSU voters to vote for the FDP instead. It appealed in particular to right-wing voters who had so far voted for Adenauer. Widely acclaimed as the real winner of the 1961 elections, the FDP interpreted its gains as a popular mandate to overthrow the Old Man. Favored by the conservative character of the Basic Law of the Federal Republic and by the position of strength he had created for himself, Adenauer could afford to ignore the popular clamor for his resignation. But the adamant refusal of the FDP and the insurgents within his own ranks were a serious challenge to his survival as Chancellor. Knowing the way in which his party operates, Adenauer apparently decided to tackle his internal opposition first. Once the CDU/CSU had committed itself to reelecting him Chancellor, the fear of losing face would keep it from backing down before the small FDP which would have no choice, therefore, but to accept Adenauer or to go into the opposition. We shall see how the equilibrial system of the CDU/CSU helped the Old Man to stifle his internal opposition.

The FDP had counted on the assurances of Erhard, Strauss, Gerstenmaier and the Hamburg deputies of the CDU to topple Konrad Adenauer. Mende's sharp rejection of Adenauer as Chancellor of the next coalition was to give the cue for this internal revolution. To be sure, a party leader who has headed the government for such a long time is likely to have accumulated supporters who owe their position to him, in this case men like the Minister of the Interior Schroeder, or the Foreign Minister von Brentano. Adenauer also had personal friends from his home state who were likely to support him even at a time of declining popularity, such as the banker Pferdmenges or the trade unionist Blank. Yet it was doubtful whether such supporters were numerous enough to continue him in office against overwhelming odds. As Gerd Bucerius, the most outspoken of the *frondeurs,* argued persuasively in his weekly magazine *Die Zeit* (Hamburg), Adenauer had come a long way from his peak in 1957 due to his age and immense burden of work. Unlike Erhard as a Chancellor, Adenauer's continued tenure of office would also cost the CDU/CSU very considerable concessions to the FDP in questions of personnel and policy.[13]

While Adenauer's "Chancellor effect" thus failed to save him at this crucial moment, the prospect of a coalition of the CDU/CSU with the FDP under Erhard set into motion the mechanics of the equilibrial system of the CDU/CSU. Wary of the economic and social policy of such an industry- and *Mittelstand*-dominated cabinet, the labor wing of the CDU/CSU utilized the general impasse to extract a number of concessions and promises from Adenauer in exchange for throwing its

---

[13] Dieter Schroeder, "Die Erben Adenauers muessen noch warten," SZ, Sept. 30/Oct. 1, 1961, p. 4.

weight against the attempts to remove him. The CDU/CSU labor wing in the *Bundestag* and in the extra-parliamentary party apparatus has always been a factor to be reckoned with[14] and has lately moved more into the foreground under the leadership of Hans Katzer, the Executive Manager of the Social Policy Committees of the CDU/CSU. According to press comments, Katzer received specific assurances regarding the extension of the Law of Savings Premiums, the "social discount" in the stock of further denationalized enterprises, an increase in the workers' share of productive capital, a reform of corporation law, higher sickness benefits and family allowances, a strong Cartel Office, and the establishment of an Economic and Social Council to extend labor co-determination above the plant level.[15] The labor wing would probably have preferred a coalition of the CDU/CSU wth the SPD, but, rather than upset too much the balance of the equilibrial system, it contented itself with a firm commitment to its program of social policy by a CDU/CSU-FDP government.

Adenauer clearly stood to gain from the motion of the CDU/CSU labor wing to restore the balance as long as he was known to be flexible enough to return to the earlier CDU/CSU tradition of Kaiser and Arnold if need be. At the same time, he wanted to avoid becoming dependent on his new allies. This was the Archimedian point from which he could unhinge his entire opposition and yet retain his freedom of choice. He resolved, therefore, to swing the equilibrial pendulum all the way to the left in order to be sure of a reaction: one week after the elections, he invited the SPD leaders Ollenhauer, Brandt and Wehner for an extended discussion of German foreign policy which they had already requested months before. There was no mention of a "black-red" coalition, but most observers understood that the Old Man was exploring his only logical alternative for a coalition as long as the FDP refused to accept him. The reaction came instantly: the two top officials of the *Bundesverband der Deutschen Industrie* came to see Adenauer and assured him that they did not want Erhard as Chancellor either. CSU chairman Strauss and the CDU/CSU Minister President of Baden-Wuerttemberg, Kiesinger, hastened to express their horror of a "black-red" coalition. Most important, industry spokesmen put the FDP under pressure not to drive Adenauer to such an "extreme step." At this point Ludwig Erhard gave in and made it known that he no longer expected to become Chancellor right away. From this we can also gather that the *fronde* was a personal faction rather than one of economic interest. Without their favorite candidate, the internal opposition against Ade-

---

[14] According to Dr. Juergen Domes of the Institut fuer Politische Wissenschaft at Heidelberg University, the labor wing of the Bundestag CDU/CSU is the most cohesive and well-organized group of the parliamentary party, second only to the CSU Landesgruppe. Its strength has been consistently at 23 or 24% of the total, excepting only the period from 1953 to 1957. It also constitutes the largest single group within the Party Executive Board of the extra-parliamentary party.

[15] *Der Spiegel,* Oct. 11, 1961, pp. 27–8.

TABLE 1. SCHEDULE OF NEGOTIATIONS OVER THE NEW COALITION

Time period	Moves
Sept. 17 (elections)–19	(1) *General orientation:* Adenauer seizes the initiative, meets the press and sounds out the FDP and SPD about a coalition.
Sept. 19–27	(2) *Stage-setting maneuvers:* (a) The labor wing of the CDU/CSU throws its weight behind the Chancellor in exchange for certain promises; (b) Adenauer invites the leaders of the SPD for a discussion of West German foreign policy; (c) Franz Josef Strauss tries to decree a compromise, a transitional Adenauer Cabinet, with the help of his CSU; (d) Representatives of West German business and industry appeal to Adenauer and put pressure on the FDP in order to prevent a "black-red" coalition. (e) Adenauer gains the support of his party (Sept. 27).
Sept. 28–Nov. 7	(3) *Actual negotiations:* (a) First phase of negotiations between a reluctant FDP and a self-confident Adenauer; (b) Second phase: Unsure of itself, the FDP *Bundestag* caucus calls on the FDP Main Committee to make the basic decision of accepting or rejecting Adenauer; (c) Third phase: Bitter wrangling over the coalition contract between the two parties; (d) Final phase: Pressed by Federal President Luebke's threat to take action, the CDU/CSU and FDP come to a compromise.

nauer collapsed and, a mere ten days after the elections, the Old Man received the unanimous endorsement of the CDU/CSU caucus in the *Bundestag*. Erhard took it upon himself, in fact, to persuade his party to reelect Adenauer once more.[16] . . .

III

Once the CDU/CSU was solidly behind Adenauer, he could return to his negotiations with the FDP. Before we can fully understand his final victory over this party, we have to draw into account the forces which have driven the multi-party system of Weimar Germany into a bipartite mold. There may be some doubt whether the long evident trend toward a two-party system in Western Germany was not reversed by the 1961 elections which cost the CDU/CSU its majority and brought a third party, the FDP, dramatic gains.[17] However, it appears that the FDP became a mere appendix of the CDU/CSU from the minute it

---

[16] See *SZ*, Sept. 25, 26 and 29, 1961.

[17] Some observers have called the West German party system a one or a one-and-a-half party system because of the seeming inability of the SPD to challenge the dominant position of the CDU/CSU. However, the West German situation appears to be more like the alternating periods of Republican and Democratic supremacy before and after 1932 in the United States than like comparable post-colonial examples. Cf. Heidenheimer, "Der starke Regierungschef . . . ," pp. 241 ff.

pledged itself not to enter a coalition with the SPD after the elections, because thereby it allowed itself to become a mere instrument of CDU/CSU voters who desired to register their protest against Adenauer without voting for the SPD. This FDP pledge automatically made the SPD the only alternative to continued CDU/CSU rule and, by implication, made the FDP a splinter of the CDU/CSU which had split off from the mother party over some grievance and now wished to coerce it to mend its way. If there had been any doubt about the dependence of the FDP on the CDU/CSU, it was quickly dispelled after the elections: for a while, there was still talk that the FDP would simply remain in the opposition, if it could not dislodge Adenauer from his post. Rumor had it that the FDP might prefer to do so in order to avoid the blame for some of the unpopular concessions which Western Germany might have to make with regard to Berlin and reunification.[18] But it soon became evident that the FDP had no such choice, quite apart from the lure of cabinet posts and patronage. It was driven by the same force which has reduced the number of political parties represented in the *Bundestag* from election to election, until in 1961 there were only two left to contend, the CDU/CSU-FDP and the SPD.

At first glance, the difference between the party systems of the Bonn and Weimar Republics is indeed striking and not easy to explain: the Weimar *Reichstag* was composed at times of more than thirty and never of less than eight distinct groups, of which none was able to get more than a third of the vote—except in the final Nazi landslide. There were the Communists, the Social Democrats, at least two middle-class Liberal parties, the Catholic Center, the Bavarian People's Party, the German Nationalists, and the extreme right, not counting the wax and wane of smaller groups in between. The new party system of 1945, by comparison, started significantly with the reappearance of the SPD and the foundation of the CDU/CSU as a broad "political rally to the right of the SPD," to which old Weimar politicians flocked, ranging from former left-wing Liberals (DDP) to the German Nationalists (DNPV). In comparison to these two great forces, SPD and CDU/CSU there was little else to report: even at the time of its origin, the FDP barely escaped the "rally to the right of the SPD."[19] The Communists did not for long outlast the Sovietization of East Germany. Neofascist parties died out or were outlawed almost as fast as they were founded. The refugees and other splinter groups of discontent failed to survive the economic boom. Regional parties like the Bavarian Party (BP) and the German Party (DP), once called Lower Saxonian Land Party (NLP), did not fare well in Bonn. With the benefit of hindsight, one

[18] *Frankfurter Allgemeine Zeitung* (hereafter referred to as *FAZ*), Sept. 21, 1961.
[19] See especially Hans Georg Wieck, *Die Entstehung der CDU und die Wiedergruendung des Zentrums im Jahre 1945*, and *Christliche und Freie Demokraten in Hessen, Rheinland-Pfalz, Baden und Wuerttemberg, 1945/46* (Duesseldorf: Droste, 1953 and 1959).

may say today that the trend toward a two-party system in West Germany was evident from the start.

What could have transformed the complex Weimar system into the far simpler system of the Federal Republic which in this way resembles the Anglo-American democracies? It was hardly the electoral system, a mixture of single-member district plurality with proportional representation, with the latter rather preponderant.[20] Nor can it be explained satisfactorily with the argument that the West Germans learned to shy away from political extremism, considering that most Weimar parties were not extremist in this sense. Even less plausible would be the statement that the German voters and politicians learned from the Weimar experience. The West German voters are not overwhelmingly in favor of a two-party system.[21] Nor would it be reasonable to expect such a self-conscious electoral conduct from any people, least of all the Germans whose interest in politics has been very low although their voting participation is high. Politicians also can hardly be expected to be motivated by such considerations: for years the FDP and other third parties have campaigned against the trend toward a two-party system and, at the *Laender* level, many CDU/CSU and SPD politicians favor their cause for practical reasons. The only frequently advanced argument which seems to have merit is that Adenauer's domineering role has tended to create two camps, one for and one against him. However, it should be noted that until 1961 the anti-Adenauer voters have always had other alternatives than to vote in increasing numbers for the SPD.

If these arguments fail to explain the change from the Weimar party system to the new bipolar trend, what others are available? A number. In particular, socio-economic and physical changes distinguish the Federal Republic from its predecessor. The Federal Republic is considerably smaller and economically more integrated than its predecessor. The loss of land and sectionalism, for example, removed the geographic basis of the bulk of German Nationalist support, and has softened the old states rights movements in various parts of the country. The dismemberment of Prussia and the new geopolitical situation at the fringe of the Iron Curtain, moreover, has further reduced the causes of faction which might arise from many alternatives of foreign policy. The class structure of Germany, finally, which was still basic to the Weimar social and party system, was subjected to a long series of

---

[20] For details, see James K. Pollock, "The West German Electoral Law of 1953," *American Political Science Review*, Vol. 49 (March 1955), pp. 107–30. Also Gerhard Loewenberg, "Parliamentarism in Western Germany: The Functioning of the Bundestag," *ibid.*, Vol. 55 (March 1961), pp. 87–102.

[21] When in February, 1956, the Institut fuer Demoskopie asked a national sample: "Would you welcome it if only the CDU/CSU and the SPD were left in Germany?", only 36% of the respondents answered yes. Forty per cent said no and 24% were undecided. *Jahrbuch der Oeffentlichen Meinung, 1957* (Allensbach: Verlag fuer Demoskopie, 1957), p. 260.

shattering experiences — the economic crises under the Weimar Republic, totalitarian and post-totalitarian reshuffling of rank and status, the impoverishment resulting from war, air raids and mass expulsion and, most recently, the socio-economic changes of a rapid economic boom. A few years after the end of the last World War, most Germans were fairly equal in economic terms, namely at the bottom of the economic ladder. The accumulation of wealth since that time has created a new society of status, expressed in the ownership of automobiles, washing machines, refrigerators and television sets, but hardly a society of class distinctions.[22] With the class lines went another important division of the Weimar party system. With most of the old causes of faction removed, a new alignment could form.

One should also mention the organizational changes among parties and interest groups in the direction of greater simplicity and unity which have occurred between the time of the Weimar Republic and its current successor. In the political field, the CDU/CSU now unites Catholics and Protestants, Conservatives and Liberals, and the FDP consolidated the remainders of the several Liberal parties. The cohesion of Adenauer's coalitions and especially the formidable size of the CDU/CSU itself forced the organized interests to coordinate their efforts and align their organizations behind the majority party and its leader rather than trying to have a separate little political party for every little interest. There was also the consolidation of interest groups as a consequence of Nazi regimentation. Under the Weimar Republic, the major and minor interest groups from the trade unions to the farm, business and professional organizations of all kinds were divided along numerous lines according to class prejudices, ideological convictions, geographical considerations, economic interests and political preferences which added up to "an infinitely differentiated labyrinth"[23] and contributed considerably to the political chaos. This complex interest group system was rudely forced into a highly simplified and rigidly controlled "corporative mold" by the Nazis. After 1945, the reconstituted groups tried to undo some of the enforced group consolidations, but by and large retained much of the newly found unity. In most cases they no longer found the issues that once divided them very pressing and appreciated the political advantages of unity in a free society. The result was an interest group system so powerful and well organized that the German political scientist, Theodor Eschenburg, has called the Fed-

---

[22] About the socio-economic changes since the 1920's, see Thomas Wellmann, "Die soziologische Grundlage der Bundesrepublik," *Deutsche Rundschau* (June 1953), pp. 591–600. Regarding the "status symbols," about 30% of West German households in 1961 had television sets and washing machines, mostly of the wringer type. Forty-two per cent had refrigerators and there was one automobile for about every ten persons or three families.

[23] Gerhard Schulz, "Ueber Entstehung und Formen von Interessengruppen in Deutschland seit Beginn der Industrialisierung," *Politische Vierteljahresschrift*, Vol. 2 (July 1961), 126.

eral Republic "a federation of associated interest groups, churches, county and city republics,"[24] and interest groups are said to be closer to the voters than the political parties.

It is against this new background of simplified interest and party politics that the rise of Adenauer and his CDU/CSU has to be understood as a bundle of mutually reinforcing processes which have led to this concentration of political power and interests. Somewhat comparable perhaps to Franklin Delano Roosevelt and his New Deal Democrats of the 1930, the rise of Adenauer and the CDU/CSU to their dominant position was less a success of personal mesmerism than a great alliance of important interests held together by the ingenious integrative system through which the CDU/CSU allows them to satisfy their demands. Where the party committees and the more informal devices for channeling demands were not considered sufficient "access" for the more "respectable" groups, in fact, Adenauer personally acted as the master integrator who would satisfy the group demands as he saw fit.[25] The dissatisfied groups and interests left out by this great rallying around Adenauer's pork barrel then tended to support the SPD as the only opposition party capable of doing something for them.

Many SPD voters, to be sure, are still motivated by traditional attachments. But we must guard against the fallacy of seeing in the new alignment a class alignment. Public opinion polls conducted in 1956 by the *Institut für Demoskopie* have shown that the magic word *bourgeois*, which once separated parties like the CDU/CSU and FDP from the SPD and revolutionary movements at both extremes, has a most hazy meaning for the man in the street. During the last federal election campaign it seemed, in fact, as if the new alignment had something to do with the participation in the great economic boom of Western Germany: those who felt the "economic miracle" had passed them by or was unjustly distributed voted SPD. The SPD also enjoyed the support of local government interests, especially in the big cities, of other consumer interests whom the Adenauer government forgot, and of the giant German Trade Union Federation (DGB) with which it has shared many goals. The bipolar arrangement of interests is both partially caused by and behind the new West German trend towards a two-party system.

IV

. . . Apparently, this new alignment of interests leaves no secure place for the FDP or for other third parties to the right of the SPD.

---

[24] *Herrschaft der Verbaende* (Stuttgart: Deutsche Verlagsanstalt, 1955), p. 87.

[25] As Drs. Wolfgang Kralewski and Rupert Breitling of the Institut für Politische Wissenschaft of Heidelberg University told this writer, this aspect of Chancellor democracy has become more and more prominent during the last term of Adenauer.

The FDP is even more dependent than the CDU/CSU on industrial, professional and *Mittelstand* groups — in other words, on the whole combine of interests behind the governing coalition. Their financial support is vital to the party, but the party's fate is not nearly as important to these groups as the fate of the CDU/CSU which is far too large to be ignored or circumvented in the striving for favorable government policies. A brief review of the history of the FDP in Bonn will show that this was not the first time that the ability of the FDP to maneuver freely between CDU/CSU and SPD was curtailed by the group sponsors and finance sources of the Free Democrats. . . .

Past precedents explain a good part of the fear with which the FDP views Adenauer, its anxiety to replace him with Erhard and its distrust of the CDU/CSU in general. The course of the negotiations over the new coalition between the CDU/CSU and the FDP likewise bears out the thesis that the FDP has very little choice: the real situation of the FDP revealed itself within a week after the elections encouraged Mende to his proud words "Never again Adenauer" and Strauss to his abortive attempt to force the Old Man into a compromise with the FDP. . . .

The erosion of the FDP position during the negotiations involved several distinct aspects. First of all, there was the question of the continuation of Adenauer as Chancellor. Then there were issues of coalition policy and of the FDP share of the personnel of the new cabinet. Finally, there was the controversial coalition contract between the two parties. . . .

V

. . . On November 7, 1961, six and one-half weeks after the elections to the *Bundestag*, Konrad Adenauer for the fourth time was elected Federal Chancellor. Of the 490 deputies present, not counting those from Berlin, he received 258 votes, a slim margin of eight more than he needed. There were 206 votes cast against him and 26 deputies abstained. Forty-nine deputies of his coalition parties either abstained or voted against him. The composition of this internal opposition in the new coalition government can only be guessed. About 15 FDP deputies may have voted no. Twenty abstentions were said to have come from the CSU. This leaves about eight no votes and six abstentions for the *frondeurs* and friends of the offended Erhard in the CDU. The size of this negative vote surprised many observers, although the press had often estimated Adenauer's secret enemies in the CDU/CSU to number between forty and fifty. If we compare this Chancellor election with the previous elections of Adenauer, it becomes quite clear that his margin of safety has not been so small nor his opposition so large since 1949. . . . We can also attempt similar comparisons of the size of his internal opposition in these election years, although we cannot say with certainty when deputies in the opposition parties crossed

TABLE 2. INTERNAL OPPOSITION AT CHANCELLOR ELECTIONS, 1949 TO 1961

Year	Coalition parties	Total coalition	Voting yes	Internal opposition	Total noes and abstentions	SPD deputies
1949	CDU/CSU - FDP - DP 139 52 17	208	202	None (?)	186	131
1953	CDU/CSU - FDP - DP - BHE 244 48 15 27	334	305	About 15	162	151
1957	CDU/CSU - DP 270 17	287	274	About 2	202	169
1961	CDU/CSU - FDP 242 67	309	258	49	232	190

party lines to support him and thereby made up a deficit in his own coalition parties (Table 2). But even a very rough estimate shows clearly that the opposition to Adenauer within the parties of the government coalition has never been as great as at this time.

CHAPTER
SEVEN

Political Leaders

Within any political system, social scientists may concentrate upon the few who lead or the mass who intermittently intervene decisively in political affairs. Many of the articles in preceding chapters analyze important features of mass publics and influences upon their attitudes and behavior. There are good sociological as well as normative reasons for believing that majorities are important in politics. There are also good reasons, though less congenial to democrats, to give special attention to the activities of that small proportion of people who have the opportunity to exercise political influence out of all proportion to their numbers. They are privileged by virtue of the positions that they occupy in society. The bases of potential influence take a variety of forms: high social status, wealth, educational attainment, professional skills, civil service position, and electoral success. Most of these positions exist in all cultures, but a few are distinctive, such as that of Etonians in England, Prussian officers in the old German Reich, Freemasons in the Third Republic of France, or Catholic bishops in Italy.

People who occupy such positions are often described as part of an *elite*. (The word "elite" and the word "elected" both have the same Latin root, *eligere*; the basis of selecting an elite, however, is usually very different from that of popular election.) The characteristics of prominent people have long been subject to minute scrutiny by everyone from gossip columnists to sociologists. From the study of the characteristics of elites, one can learn much about the qualities and performance skills that are valued generally in a society or by sub-groups within it. For instance, in the United States, the Democratic Party makes a special effort to nominate candidates from minority ethnic groups or the black community, just as in Britain about one-sixth of the seats in the House of Commons are held by trade union–sponsored MPs, whose principal claim to office is that their presence gives symbolic representation to workers. It does not, however, follow that people with prominent social characteristics will necessarily seek to convert these attributes into political power, or that they can do so if they try.

In recent years, American social scientists have been engaged in a long and lively controversy about the political importance of elite social groups. At one extreme can be heard the argument that some type of social advantage must necessarily carry with it political advantages. From the other extreme comes the rejoinder that as long as political influence is dispersed among a plurality of groups, then it is unreasonable to write about the concentration of political power in the hands of a few. The resulting research has shown that people with certain high status attributes or popular reputations for influence are not necessarily the ones who command the most political influence. It has also shown that political influence is not distributed equally and evenly within societies conventionally described as democratic.

The articles in this chapter are less concerned with the social origins of politicians than with the course of activities that lead them toward political office and the things that happen to them once in office. After all, no amount of youthful experience can prepare an individual, in a practical or an emotional sense, for the things he will face after becoming a party leader, a civil servant, or an expert whose opinion is sought by the government of the day. For the few who are called to high office, socialization into a political role is likely to be a more important determinant of political behavior than a host of experiences and attributes remote from government.

Bibliography

Classical European social scientists, writing when the debacle of World War I had not yet destroyed the political importance of old social groups, devoted much attention to political elites. Major studies of this sort include Vilfredo Pareto's *The Mind and Society* (1935), Gaetano Mosca, *The Ruling Class* (1939), Robert Michels, *Political Parties* (1912), and Max Weber's "Politics as a Profession," the last conveniently available in *From Max Weber,* edited by H. H. Gerth and C. Wright Mills (New York: Oxford University Press, 1946). Harold Lasswell's *Politics: Who Gets What, When and How* (New York: 1st edition, 1936; Meridian edition, 1958) is an American landmark. A recent survey of elite concepts, drawing heavily upon comparative data for illustration, is Suzanne Keller's *Beyond the Ruling Class* (New York: Random House, 1963). The controversy about political power and social position in American society is reflected in Floyd Hunter, *Community Power Structure* (Chapel Hill: University of North Carolina Press, 1953); C. Wright Mills, *The Power Elite* (New York: Oxford University Press, 1956); Robert A. Dahl, *Who Governs?* (New Haven: Yale University Press, 1961); and in all the literature that has grown up around these books. For the viewpoint of one of the editors of this reader, with British and American examples, see Richard Rose, *People in Politics: Observations Across the Atlantic* (New York: Basic Books, 1970), Chs. 4–6.

A very large amount of social science data are available about people of high standing in European societies. One can even find articles noting that the elite way to describe a mirror is to call it a looking-glass. (Cf.

Noblesse Oblige, edited by Nancy Mitford, Harmondsworth: Penguin, 1959, p. 26.) It requires considerable theoretical sophistication to pick one's way through large masses of data in order to select things of particular *political* relevance. An introduction to the European literature on this subject can be found in Dwaine Marvick, editor, *Political Decision-Makers* (New York: Free Press, 1961) which includes articles on Britain, France, and Germany. Selections which give more emphasis to psychological influences can be found in Lewis J. Edinger, editor, *Political Leadership in Industrialized Societies* (New York: Wiley, 1967). It includes special studies of all four countries covered in this reader. The footnotes in the original versions of the articles by Dahrendorf and Edinger and Searing reprinted here also contain references to a wealth of materials. The most detailed British study is W. L. Guttsman, *The British Political Elite* (London: MacGibbon & Kee, 1963). For France, see particularly the article by Mattei Dogan, in Dwaine Marvick, *op. cit.* For Germany, see Karl Deutsch and Lewis J. Edinger, *Germany Rejoins the Powers* (Stanford University Press, 1957), an excerpt from which is printed below (pp. 539–549). Daniel Lerner and Morton Gordon, *Euratlantica: Changing Perspectives of the European Elites* (Cambridge, Mass.: M.I.T. Press, 1969), summarize the results of five successive waves of interviews with opinion leaders and policy-makers in Britain, France, and Germany between 1955 and 1965. Lewis J. Edinger's *Kurt Schumacher: A Study in Personality and Political Behavior* (Stanford University Press, 1965) is a meaningful portrayal of the socialist leader, as is the portrait of de Gaulle by Stanley and Inge Hoffman, "The Will to Grandeur: de Gaulle as Political Artist," *Daedalus* (Summer 1968). See also Jean Lacouture, *De Gaulle* (New York: New American Library, 1966). Very well documented, even if somewhat sarcastic, Viansson Ponté, *The King and His Court* (Boston: Houghton Mifflin, 1965), describes de Gaulle's style, the rituals of the Elysée Palace, and gives short biographies of the outstanding Gaullist personalities.

On the parliamentary elite, see Austin Ranney, *Pathways to Parliament: Candidate Selection in Britain* (London: Macmillan, 1965). A detailed analysis of about 7,500 candidates for Parliament, 1918 through 1955, is Philip W. Buck, *Amateurs and Professionals in British Politics, 1918–59* (The University of Chicago Press, 1963). On the English public schools, see Rupert Wilkinson, *The Prefects* (London: Oxford University Press, 1964). See also Gerhard Loewenberg, *Parliament in the German Political System* (Cornell University Press, 1967), the first two chapters of which are devoted to recruitment and composition of the Bundestag. Gordon J. Di Renzo, *Personality, Power and Politics* (Notre Dame University Press, 1967) gives the results of interviews with more than 100 Italian MPs. For the Nazi and Fascist elites, as specialists on violence, see Harold D. Laswell and Daniel Lerner, *World Revolutionary Elites* (Cambridge, Mass.: M.I.T. Press, 1965).

RALF DAHRENDORF

The Evolution of Ruling Groups in Europe

Long established leadership strata in a society may appear as, or claim to be, the natural leaders of their country. The comparative analysis of political elites provides a simple means of differentiating between career characteristics considered "natural" in many nations, and features that are distinctive or unique to one. Ralf Dahrendorf's review of data from Britain, France, and Germany succinctly summarizes the way in which political leaders have risen to high office. He also relates changes in the recruitment of political elites to changes in the structure of power in modern European societies.

... Class is about power. While social and economic status affect the relations of power, these have their own peculiar characteristics and laws of development. By power, we shall mean what John Locke meant when he said: "Power, then, I take to be a right of making laws with penalties of death, and consequently all less penalties, . . . and of employing the force of the community in the execution of such laws, and in defense of the commonwealth from foreign injury."[1] To try a somewhat more modern formulation: power is the right to make laws, that is, norms binding upon those subject to them by virtue of the sanctions attached to them, as well as the right to execute these laws and to enforce the sanctions. This "making" of laws thus involves all three of the classical branches of government.

I find Locke's definition rather more useful than all modern attempts

Abridged from Ralf Dahrendorf, "Recent Changes in the Class Structure of European Societies," *Daedalus*, 93, 1, 1964, pp. 232–244. Reprinted by permission of *Daedalus*, Journal of the American Academy of Arts and Sciences.
[1] [Numbers in parentheses refer to bibliography at the end of the article.]

to define power in terms of "control over others," "the chance to find obedience," and the like.[2] But in quoting Locke, I have left out three short phrases which require brief comment. One is Locke's concluding optimistic requirement: "and all this only for the public good." It is hard to share this optimism today. Second, Locke specifies the making of laws by the addition "for the regulating and preserving of property." At least from Locke to Marx, property was the prime mover of all things social — and very nearly an obsession — for most social analysts. To us, it seems not only unlikely that it is property that moves the world, but also evident that laws can be made for many other purposes. Third, Locke is not really trying to define power in general, but, as he says, "political power." In our context, political power is only one — if the most general — of many aspects of power; it is power as it affects people in their position as citizens. But as clerks (in their occupational or economic organization), as laymen (in their religious organizations), as members of tennis clubs (in voluntary organizations), and in many other organizational contexts people also make laws that are sanctioned and executed; and it is a question of great empirical relevance how political power relates to that in other institutional orders of a society.

Regarding the structure of classes in contemporary Europe, four trends in the recent history of power require our attention. The first of these is closely related to the advancement of citizenship in the last half century. It is the transformation (in Max Weber's terms) of *Macht* into *Herrschaft*, that is, of personal power into institutional power.[3] Strictly speaking, personal power does not come under Locke's definition. It is not a right, but simply a capacity to make others do what one wants them to do. The relation of dependence constituted by personal power is tied to the individuals involved; thus, in a sense, it is not a social relation at all. Yet there have been such relations of personal power throughout history. Where they have taken the form of "charismatic rule" they have involved not two but hundreds and often thousands of people; perhaps there is an element of personal power in the genesis of every form of institutional power. However, there is a general trend in politics as well as in all other social organizations today to reduce the unbounded potentialities of control inherent in personal power to power vested in positions and incumbent on persons only for the duration of their occupancy of such positions. As a consequence,

---

[2] Among sociologists, the most widely quoted definition of power (*Herrschaft*) is Max Weber's: "Herrschaft soll heissen die Chance, für einen Befehl bestimmten Inhalts bei angebbaren Personen Gehorsam zu finden." (*Wirtschaft und Gesellschaft*, 4th ed., Tübingen, 1956, p. 28) This is not the place for conceptual discussions, but one of the disadvantages of this definition seems to me that it describes power in too personal a fashion ("command," "obedience").

[3] Unfortunately, terminology is not settled here in English. Numerous concepts — power, authority, rule, domination, dominion, imperative coordination, and others — compete, so that it seemed wisest to me to express the trend in question by adjectives.

the claim to charismatic rule becomes increasingly unlikely in modern social organizations.[4] At no time could the powerful really "do what they want" — as many would have it — although this notion is akin to that of personal power; but in modern Europe, their radius of action is much more limited still by the comparative neutrality of power exercised only within well-defined roles associated with social positions.

This domestication of power would of course not be very effective if it were not coupled with the development of mechanisms to control the exercise of power more effectively than can be done by unchanneled expressions of protest or agreement. The generalization of the "rule of law" is the second relevant trend in our context. Hobbes had, if not logic, then at least probability on his side when he claimed that the sovereign is exempted from the laws which, after all, he himself has a right to make. In actual fact, it can still be demonstrated by many instances that the law — that is, those who execute and enforce it — tends to become more lenient with people as they occupy positions closer to the source of the law. Prime ministers are unlikely to get tickets for speeding. At the same time, Laski was right in observing that the very paradox of the sovereign — the legislative, executive, and judicative — who is subject to his own law has come true in modern societies. The courts are open to all; and that means that everbody can find himself on either side of their disputes.[14, 18] Possibly, the rule of law is only part of a syndrome of control to which elections, parliaments, a free press, and other institutions of modern representative government also belong. In any case, the extension of these controls to most — though not all — European countries has changed the nature of class and class conflict profoundly.

A third modern development of power, although no less significant, is of a somewhat different kind. There are several reasons why, in the phase of industrialization, economic and political power tend to coincide in the sense of being held by the same group. In nineteenth-century Europe, industrialization created huge instruments of power in a sphere of life where many people had to spend almost the whole of their waking life, and at a time when the influence of the state was largely restricted to the tasks prescribed by Locke, that is, to "the regulating and preserving of property." Thus, the economically powerful tended to be all-powerful by the same token, and of course vice versa. Industrialization in the twentieth century is invariably the result of vigorous and direct action by the state. Thus, the politically powerful tend to be all-powerful, and vice versa. However, insofar as European societies have passed through this first stage of industrialization — whichever of the two forms intimated here it may have taken — neither of these coincidences holds true any more. Instead, everywhere there is a large, relatively independent machinery of political administration; and those who have

---

[4] Weber himself has often discussed the mutual exclusiveness of charisma and bureaucracy. However, I am here using Weber's so-called "types of power" in a rather different sense than was intended by Weber.

power in other institutions, whether economic organizations, churches, universities, trade unions or women's clubs, act as influence groups in the penumbra of political decision-making. Clearly, some of these influence groups are able to exert more pressure than others. This is true notably for the military and for the leaders of industry and labor; but none of these is exclusive in a world in which people's lives are no longer confined to one and only one sphere of organization.[5]

I have described the machinery of political administration as being large and relatively independent. In fact, the fourth important trend in the nature of power in European societies today is the seemingly ever increasing division of labor in the business of making, enforcing and executing laws. Where a comparatively small — and thus easily identifiable — group of people controlled the classical branches of public and private governments a century or even half a century ago, numerous positions of partial power have since come into being, many of them so apparently subordinate that it is hard to discover their relation to the exercise of power. The analogy to the division of labor is striking: in the exercise of power, too, one process has been subdivided into so many contributing part-processes that it is hard to discover the whole in any one of its individual parts. Just as in a modern shoe factory it is hard to answer the question, "Who makes the shoes?" it is hard to tell who, in the bureaucratic administration of a modern enterprise, church, trade union or state, holds the reins and in this sense has the power.

This last observation is indeed the main source of an interpretation of society which is today almost equally widespread among sociologists and ordinary citizens. In a word, this interpretation amounts to saying that the peoples of Europe have once again turned into "tribes without rulers." Since it is hard to localize power, power itself has disappeared. There is no longer a ruling class but only a market of veto groups, or the reduction of power to administration, or the transformation of power over men into power over things, or simply the power of the law. This of course is also David Riesman's conclusion with respect to the United States.[22] But, in one form or the other, a number of European scholars have followed Riesman or advanced similar interpretations on different grounds — although it is a striking fact that these are more numerous on the continent than in England, and, again, more numerous in German-speaking countries than in all others.[7, 9] I shall try to show that the alleged disappearance of power is as much of a myth as its opposite, the tightly-knit, conspiratorial "power elite" à la Mills.[21] But if there is any conclusion to be drawn already from this cursory analysis of some trends which have changed the structure of class in many European societies, it is that this structure has become rather more complicated today than it was as described by Marx and seen by many people

---

[5] Few theses of my book on *Class and Class Conflict in Industrial Society* (Stanford-London, 1959) have been more widely criticized than that of the "institutional isolation of industry and industrial conflict" in the modern world (pp. 267 ff.). Perhaps the preceding formulations can help to clarify this discussion.

throughout much of the last century. Class in Europe is no longer a matter of the antagonism of a small group of all-powerful rulers and a large mass of powerless subjects. Indeed, Europe can no longer be properly described as a "fairly rigid class society."

But these remarks can do little more than set the stage. Let us turn, therefore, to the principal characters in the new drama of class and power.

THE RULING GROUPS

Upon closer inspection, even Africa's "tribes without rulers" turn out to recognize some positions of power.[20] It would be very surprising indeed if this were different in contemporary Europe. As a matter of fact, our definition of power makes it quite clear where to look for the rulers; they are evidently those who have a say in the making, carrying out and enforcing of laws. For the purpose of the present analysis, I should like to restrict the definition of the ruling groups even further to those who, above all others, participate in making laws and in making those laws which concern every citizen as such.[3] Probably no more than about two thousand people in any given European society can be described as belonging to these groups. Among these, the following categories may be distinguished. (It must be understood that these distinctions are introduced purely for purposes of identification and are not meant to indicate lines of cleavage within the power elite.)

1. Incumbents of formal political positions of political power; that is, members of both houses of parliament, cabinet ministers, other ministers, undersecretaries of state (or their equivalent) insofar as their position is regarded as "political" in the sense that they are tied to a given government.
2. Incumbents of formal administrative positions of political power, including the highest civil servants as well as generals, diplomats and judges of the Supreme Court (or its equivalent).
3. Incumbents of other positions of political power.
4. Incumbents of positions of political influence.

What is the social origin, what is the recruitment of the ruling groups of contemporary European societies? If there is any general answer to this question, one of three first posed by Raymond Aron,[2] it would resemble the heading of a section of one of M. Dogan's studies of the French political elite: "from the republic of dukes to the reign of the middle class and lower-middle class."[8] Not all European countries are of course republics, and from the evidence we have there is some doubt as to the importance of the lower middle class as a reservoir of the ruling groups in our restricted sense, but the general trend observed by Dogan is certainly confirmed by studies in many countries. Throughout the last decades, there has been an increasing trend for the upper two thousand to be recruited from fathers in professional and commercial occupations rather than from the older agricultural and often aristocratic groups.[6]

Among members of parliament, this trend has had two complementary components. While the total figures given, for example, by M. Dogan for France[8] and W. L. Guttsman[12] and G. D. H. Cole[5] for Britain, M. Knight and H. Schmidt for Germany,[17] demonstrate the increasing importance of the urban middle class, their breakdown by parties shows a more complicated picture. It seems clear that among the conservative groups (the "right"), the proportion of deputies of aristocratic origin has declined fairly consistently in favor of what is generally called middle class origin. At the same time, a recent study by W. L. Guttsman in Britain indicates that the leadership of the Labour party has changed also. A slight decline in the proportion of Labour members of Parliament recruited from working class families was accompanied by a remarkable increase in the number and proportion of Labour M.P.'s whose own occupation must be described as middle class and who have received secondary or university education.[13] If this observation about the "left" is confirmed in other countries — as seems likely — it would indicate not only that politicians in general "follow a career pattern not dissimilar to that of other professionals,"[8] but also that parliamentarians of all groups have contributed to the invasion of "the middle class" (or its children) in positions of power.

However, parliamentary groups are only part of the ruling groups in our sense of the term. In fact, the studies cited themselves show that, in general, cabinets tend to consist of people of higher social origin than parliaments. In France and Germany at least, this would also be true for higher civil servants, diplomats, generals and judges. A certain degree of "democratization" is, however, discernible for these groups also. Among the higher civil servants of Britain, for example, 18 per cent were, in 1950, recruited from the manual census categories III, IV, and V, as against a mere 7 per cent in 1929.[16] In Germany, this trend was not quite as pronounced.[1] In fact, the administrative elites appear least affected by the social and, more surprisingly perhaps, the political changes since the 1920's. Thus, the trend toward recruitment from middle class families, while present everywhere, can be asserted only with reservations for Europe's ruling groups as a whole.

This conclusion is accentuated if we try to render the highly general term "middle class" more concrete. In many studies, this term has in fact replaced the older labels of "upper" or "ruling class" — a procedure which may in itself be symptomatic of the changing interpretation of status and power in Europe. In fact, the "middle class" that forms the main recruiting ground of the power elite of most European coun-

---

[6] Since D. R. Matthews published his little booklet on *The Social Background of Political Decision-Makers* (Garden City, 1954), there has been an ever increasing number of studies of this subject. At the same time, the question has rarely been asked what precisely these studies tell us. Thus we really know very little about the ways in which social background determines political behavior.

tries today, often consists of the top 5 per cent of the occupational hierarchy in terms of prestige, income and influence. From a study of over 2000 eminent people in France, A. Girard concluded that "plus de 68 pourcent des 'personnalités contemporaines' se recrutent dans 5 pourcent de la population, ou encore 81 pourcent dans 15 pourcent."[11] The same study shows that this conclusion holds a fortiori for the political power elite. A series of similar studies in Germany has consistently yielded the same result.[6] "Middle class" as the reservoir of ruling groups generally means fathers in one of the occupations included by M. Janowitz in the "upper middle class" of his stratification model (a category which, in the Federal Republic of Germany, comprises 4.6 percent of the population): "professional occupations, higher civil servants, independent businessmen with large enterprises, higher salaried employees."[15] In other words, the recruiting ground for the ruling groups of today is what we shall call the service class.

Which are the qualities that seem to assure success, and what are the modalities of the career? The transition from upper class to "middle class" origin — the answer to Aron's second question — would seem to imply a transition from ascribed to achieved status as the basis of personal success. For instance, the proportion of "dukes" with hereditary privileges has declined fairly consistently in the political elites of all European countries. Apart from the occasional "cabinet of barons" (Hitler's first cabinet in 1933), and of the permanently renewed peerage of Britain, aristocratic origin does not seem an advantage to speak of in the top power positions of Europe today. Once again, incumbents of formal administrative positions of political power are the most conservative group in these terms.

This also holds for a new type of ascriptive status less easily recognizable but equally effective: self-recruitment. In Germany, 7 per cent of all judges are the sons of judges, 8 per cent of all professors the sons of professors, very nearly one third of all higher civil servants are the sons of higher civil servants.[6] Girard's study in France confirms this conclusion, and Guttsman found in Britain that there is a considerable number of what he calls "political families" where political activity is inherited (although their number is apparently rather smaller among non-aristocrats than among aristocrats).[6, 12] Without doubt, the degree of self-recruitment varies from country to country as well as in the different segments of the power elite. It is not likely to be as great among members of parliament as it is among generals or diplomats. But self-recruitment — that is, the invisible hand of the family — certainly plays an even larger part in the careers of top people than it does in society in general.[7]

However, emphasizing this point should not make us overlook the

---

[7] All mobility studies since D. V. Glass's *Social Mobility in Britain* (London, 1954) confirm the conclusion that throughout society (with the deceptive exception of peasants, in whose case only one son can succeed his father) the most likely status of sons is that of their fathers.

fact that an increasing proportion of the members of Europe's ruling groups acquire their position by their own achievement, and that generally means by education. Nowadays, the road to the top almost invariably leads through a successful university career, or at least a secondary education. Of a sample of 250 members of the ruling groups in Germany in 1955, a mere 14 per cent had received primary education only, and 23 per cent either primary or secondary education, all others having at least started university studies.[10] Of the much larger sample studied by Girard in France, 5.1 per cent had received primary education only, 10.4 per cent secondary education, and no less than 84.5 per cent a "higher education."[11] In England, a university education is socially regarded as rather less important, but here too "the rise of the meritocracy" — as M. Young, an English sociologist, has called it — is unmistakable. The school is replacing the family as an avenue to the top.

To understand the modalities of the careers of top people, reference to the importance of a "good" or higher education is, however, too general to be of real interest. The important question is: is there any particular kind of education which helps the ambitious to make a success of their careers? While there is no type of education which guarantees entry to the upper reaches of the power structure anywhere in Europe, there are two types of institution which — with varying weight in the various countries of Europe — make success very probable, to say the least. One of these consists in especially prestigious schools, of which the English Public Schools are perhaps the outstanding example. Even today, the overwhelming majority of all conservative members of the British Parliament, and a not inconsiderable minority of Labour members, has been educated in Public Schools.[13] While the proportion of Public School boys has been decreasing among higher civil servants in the last decades, almost two thirds of all British higher civil servants had attended such schools even in 1950, and one out of five had been to one of the twenty best known and most expensive schools.[4, 16] There is no real equivalent to the Public Schools anywhere on the continent, although the four *grandes écoles* in France play a somewhat similar part. But the real continental equivalent to the Public School as an avenue to power is the study of law. Dogan demonstrates that lawyers are the most numerous occupational group in most European parliaments. For entry into the higher civil service a law degree is, in many continental countries, an essential condition. Even among captains of industry, it is not unusual to find lawyers, so we may conclude that a law degree is the most helpful single achievement for those Europeans who aspire to a place at the levers of power.

From W. L. Guttsman's study of British Labour leadership, it would appear that the most frequent career pattern of Labour cabinet members between 1924 and 1950 was "working-class background, with a career as an official of a trade union or other working-class organization."[12] Outside socialist groups, this kind of pattern has of course never been typical. But even so far as these groups are concerned, it would appear that the educational system, and more particularly the study of law (and in Britain, attendance of a Public School) is the new road to positions of power.

What is the rate of circulation or exchange of personnel in given elite positions; in other words, how much "job security" do members of ruling groups enjoy? I would like here to insert a question of my own among Aron's. "One of the essential characteristics of a legislative career is its insecurity." Dogan backs up his conclusion by solid evidence: "To sum up, 2,400 deputies out of 4,300 . . . or 55 percent, finished their legislative careers in electoral defeats."[8] The figure seems surprisingly high, and one would think that it did not hold in all political systems and at all times (although Dogan suggests that electoral systems other than that of the French Fourth Republic are even more sensitive to small shifts in voting preferences and, therefore, even more likely to unseat deputies). The rate of turnover of members of ruling groups is relatively high everywhere in Europe if we compare it with a time at which most top positions were held for life. (G. K. Schueller's study of *The Politburo* suggests that, in a thwarted fashion, tenure for life is still prevalent in totalitarian countries, where liquidation and death are the main causes of circulation.)[23] At the same time, there are clearly great differences between various elite groups as well as between times and countries. Not surprisingly, a circulation index developed by W. Zapf and applied to Germany shows a relatively high rate of turnover among political leaders, as against a very low one among what he (somewhat misleadingly) calls the "feudal elite groups," meaning church dignitaries, generals and large-scale entrepreneurs.[9]

In discussing the turnover of members of European political elites, we cannot omit the fact that most European countries have undergone, in the course of the last decades, at least one more or less violent change of political regime. Not all these changes have been as violent as the Spanish Civil War or military occupation, but in our context Mussolini's March to Rome and Hitler's rise to power in 1933, as well as the transition from the Fourth to the Fifth Republic in France, are no less important. In the last decades, relative political stability such as has been enjoyed by Sweden, Switzerland or Great Britain was the exception rather than the rule in Europe. Changes of political regime invariably involve changes of leading personnel. At the same time, it is not always a "counterelite" that replaces its predecessor entirely when political systems change. W. Zapf, who has studied samples of German ruling groups in our sense of the term in 1925, 1940, and 1955, has been able to show that: (1) there was rather less change between 1940 and 1955 than between 1925 and 1940, that is, less change between the Nazi elite and the present ruling groups than between the leaders of the Weimar Republic and the Nazis; (2) in both periods, change was most marked in what Zapf calls the "political elite," while there was considerably less turnover among both the "administrative elite" and the "economic elite." Clearly, these changes were of a very much higher order of magnitude in countries that had known "Quisling" regimes under German occupation during the war. Here, presumably, Dogan's conclusion can be generalized: "Two-thirds of the (French) deputies elected in 1951 and 1956 were also former members of the Resistance." In any case, the job insecurity of European men of power has been due as much to political upheavals as to patterns of circulation characteristic of the normal process of political development.

What is the manner of thinking, what is the conception of existence characteristic of this category? While there are numerous studies of the social origin and career patterns of elites in many countries, there is comparatively little evidence that bears immediately on Aron's last two, and perhaps most significant questions. Interview studies of leaders are as rare as interview studies of workers are frequent in Europe. Rather than trying to piece together a more or less literary image of Europe's rulers from scattered sources and materials, let me emphasize, therefore, two features suggested by sociological studies, both of which seem to me highly characteristic of trends in the social self-image of Europe's ruling groups. They are, of course, largely guesses which will have to be tested in further research.

When A. Girard asked his sample of French leaders to which factors they themselves ascribed their success, by far the most frequent answer was "hard work." No less than 78 per cent of those asked replied in terms of "travail, persévérance, ténacité, volonté, énergie." Perhaps the result of a similar survey a hundred years ago would not have been altogether different. It is evidently more pleasing to ascribe one's success to one's own effort than to factors outside one's control. Yet it seems to me an evident fact that the ruling class of Europe is no longer a leisure class, and that with ever shorter working hours for labor, the traditional relations between the working and the leisure classes have been reversed. In any case, a modern prime minister can hardly afford to stay in his castle (if he has one) for months at a time without bothering about the business of government, as Bismarck did; nor can a modern industrial manager spend half the year traveling around the world for fun before his retirement. Ambition and hard work are features characteristic of the ruling groups of today and their outlook on life.

Possibly this is one of the reasons for a second change in outlook suggested by recent studies. When M. Janowitz gave a sample of over 3000 Germans the choice to ascribe themselves to the upper, middle, working or lower class, only 1.9 per cent placed themselves in the upper class. Of these, no less than half must have done so in order to mislead the interviewer, since their actual occupations ranged from the small shopkeeper and the postman to the unskilled laborer. Of the 4.6 per cent placed by Janowitz in the "upper-middle class" on occupational grounds, more than 70 per cent preferred to describe their status as "middle class," and an additional 10 per cent as "working" or "lower class." In short, people at the top seem reluctant today to admit that they are at the top.[15] In fact, everybody who is "at the top" in terms of status, income or power is sure to know somebody else who, in fact or at least in his opinion, is placed even higher. Those who are by many workers described as "they," as being "above," themselves tend to think of society as a long ladder with many steps. And while without doubt they realize that they stand somewhere near the top of this ladder, they do not believe that they have reached the very top, and they would probably be as hard pushed as sociologists are to describe that peak of all ambition. In other words, the ruling groups of Europe today tend to be a rather self-conscious elite.

What is the coherence, what is the consciousness of solidarity among the members of this category? Several years ago, the English weekly *Spectator* started a discussion about the question of whether Britain is ruled by a small Establishment — a coherent set of powerful people — or not. If I am not mistaken, most English intellectuals seem inclined to believe in the reality of the Establishment and thus to subscribe to a variant of the conspiracy theory of society according to which a few invisible hands pull all the strings and monopolize the roads to power. The outside observer, on the contrary, is inclined to regard the very discussion of the Establishment as a symptom of the dissolution of the old upper class of British society. Yet it remains probable that the two thousand people with whom we are here concerned are a more coherent and solid social category in Britain than in most other European countries. Many of them have attended the same, or the same kind of, school and university; many of them belong to the same clubs, follow the same pastimes, meet and talk regularly, and feel part of the same "set." In this sense, the ruling groups of Britain do in fact tend to what might be called the "established" type.

Near the other end of the scale, we have the German case. The ruling groups of West Germany today are an almost perfect example of the "abstract" type: their unity exists nowhere except in the minds of some social analysts. In actual fact they are a highly heterogeneous and heteromorphous category. A career characteristic of a member of an established elite which leads him successively to being a university professor, director-owner of an investment trust, brigadier general and cabinet minister, and who may yet become an ambassador or director-general of the BBC, would be unthinkable in Germany, where every one of these "estates" has its own standards, interests and, above all, well-guarded boundaries. It is for this type of elite that the plural "ruling groups" is particularly appropriate, for ruling classes of this kind consist in fact of a plurality of competing and often hostile groups, the members of which are separated by great social distance.

In summarizing the evidence presented in this section, I would contend that the abstract type of elite, in Europe, constitutes the ruling class of the future. There are of course still remnants of the established elites of pre-industrial Europe, especially in countries like Spain or Portugal. There are also new kinds of establishment brought about, for example, by similar educational biographies (the "meritocracy"). But by and large, there is little indication that the ruling groups of the majority of countries in Europe really form coherent classes. They are anxious rulers, divided among themselves, uncertain of their position, and too hard-working to enjoy its rewards. In many ways, they have become indistinguishable from those one or two or three steps below them on the ladder of success.

BIBLIOGRAPHY

1. M. Albrow and W. Zapf, unpublished data gathered under the supervision of the author, available at the Sociological Seminar of the University of Tübingen.
2. Raymond Aron, "Classe sociale, classe politique, classe dirigeante," *European Journal of Sociology* I/2 (1960).
3. *Berichte aus dem Soziologischen Seminar der Universität Tübingen* 1 (1963).
4. T. J. H. Bishop, unpublished Ph.D. dissertation, University of London.
5. G. D. H. Cole, *Studies in Class Structure* (London, 1955).
6. Ralf Dahrendorf, "Deutsche Richter. Ein Betrag zur Soziologie der Oberschicht," *Gesellschaft und Freiheit* (München, 1961); "Eine neue deutsche Oberschicht? Notizen über die Eliten der Bundesrepublik," *Die neue Gesellschaft* IX/1 (1962).
7. ———— "The Education of an Elite: Law Faculties and the German Upper Class," published in *Transactions of the Fifth World Congress of Sociology* (German version published in *Der Monat* 166 [1962]).
8. M. Dogan, "Political Ascent in a Class Society: French Deputies 1870–1958," in D. Marvick (ed.), *Political Decision-Makers* (Glencoe, 1961).
9. L. J. Edinger, "Post-Totalitarian Leadership: Elites in the German Federal Republic," *American Political Science Review* LIV (1960); "Continuity and Change in the Background of German Decision Makers," *Western Political Quarterly* XIV (1961); and W. Zapf, unpublished Ph.D. dissertation, University of Tübingen.
10. Th. Geiger, *Aufgaben und Stellung der Intelligenz in der Gesellschaft* (Stuttgart, 1949).
11. A. Girard, *La Réussite sociale en France* (Paris, 1961); D. V. Glass, *Social Mobility in Britain* (London, 1954); B. Gleitze, *Wirtschafts- und Sozialstatistiches Handbuch* (Köln, 1960).
12. W. L. Guttsman, "The Changing Social Structure of the British Political Elite, 1886–1935," *British Journal of Sociology* LI/2 (1951).
13. ———— "Changes in British Labour Leadership," in D. Marvick (ed.), *Political Decision-Makers* (Glencoe, 1961).
14. Th. Hobbes, *Leviathan* (London-New York, 1934, new ed.)
15. M. Janowitz, "Soziale Schichtung und Mobilität in Westdeutschland," *Kölner Zeitschrift für Soziologie* X/1 (1958).
16. R. K. Kelsall, *Higher Civil Servants in Britain* (London, 1955); "The Social Background of Higher Civil Service," in W. A. Robson (ed.), *The Civil Service in Britain and France* (London, 1956).
17. M. Knight, *The German Executive 1890–1933* (Stanford, 1952); H. Schmidt, article in *European Journal of Sociology* IV/1 (1963).
18. H. Laski, *Grammar of Politics* (London-New Haven, 1934, 3rd ed.).
19. John Locke, *Second Treatise of Civil Government* (Chicago, 1955, new ed.).
20. D. Middleton and D. Tait, *Tribes Without Rulers* (London, 1958).

21. C. W. Mills, *The Power Elite* (New York, 1956).
22. David Riesman, *The Lonely Crowd* (New Haven, 1950).
23. G. K. Schueller, *The Politburo* (Stanford, 1951); *Statistisches Jahrbuch für die Bundesrepublik Deutschland 1958* (Stuttgart, 1958); M. Stein, *The Eclipse of Community* (Princeton, 1960).

LEWIS J. EDINGER
and DONALD D. SEARING

Social Background in Elite Analysis

The social characteristics of political leaders provide a simple index of attributes especially valued within the political culture of a society, for leaders can be recognized by diffuse social traits, as well as by their office. The emphasis in classical sociology upon the importance of position in the social structure has stimulated many studies of the social origins of political leaders. Often, these studies infer a set of political attitudes from the possession of given social characteristics. Instead of relying upon inference, Lewis Edinger and Donald Searing have drawn upon interview data as well as social background data to test the relationship between social position and political outlooks among French and German political leaders.

I. INTRODUCTION

... All political systems are more or less stratified and their elites constitute that minority of participating actors which plays a strategic role in public policy making. As the incumbents of such key positions they have a far greater influence than the masses in structuring and giving expression to political relationships and policy outputs at various

Abridged from Lewis J. Edinger and Donald D. Searing, "Social Background in Elite Analysis," *American Political Science Review*, LXI, 2, 1967, pp. 428–445. Reprinted by permission.

levels of authoritative decision making. They wield this influence by virtue of their exceptional access to political information and positions and their consequently highly disproportionate control over public policy making and communication processes which relate society to polity and governors to governed.

Usually exceeding no more than about 5 percent of the members of a political community, such elites not only know a good deal more about the internal workings of the pertinent system than do the rest of its members, but they can do a good deal more to give shape and content to general input demands and supports, as well as to formal governmental rulings at the national or sub-national level. Therefore, their behavior patterns represent a crucial dimension of behavior patterns in a political system, providing important clues to characteristics making it like or unlike other systems. . . .

By and large, applications of the social background approach [to elite analysis] have left unanswered the question of how and to what extent data of this nature actually can be used to forecast attitudinal distributions. Which social background variables best predict which attitudes under what conditions? Are all background variables presently used equally good attitudinal indicators? Might not some need to be refined, and should we not add others to our inventories? . . .

Fortunately a computer program has recently been developed by Theodore D. Sterling and his associates which meets our three criteria, and we have employed it in the following analysis. The program's *predictability* measure, which we have used throughout this article, is a *maximum likelihood estimator,* easily interpreted as the percentage of correct classifications of respondents which would have been made on dependent attitude x, by using independent background variables(s) Y. In other words, if background variable Y has a predictability of .70 for attitude x, and we had predicted the distribution of attitude x among this elite group on the basis of background variable Y, we would have been correct in seventy cases out of a hundred. This straightforwardness in interpretation seems to us a strong point favoring this procedure over currently employed statistical approaches to multivariate analysis. Therefore when we use the term "predict" in this paper, we are referring to this measure of classificatory accuracy in the data we are examining.

II. DATA

During the summer of 1964 eight American university professors conducted extended interviews with French and German national leaders in connection with a project directed by Karl W. Deutsch under the auspices of Yale University. The questions asked were designed to elicit the respondent's attitudes about his political system and its domestic and foreign policies, with particular reference to European integration and arms control issues.

After identifying seven elite groups believed nearest to the national political decision-making process (military, political, civil service, and business leaders, other key interest group elites, mass media leaders, and intellectuals in France, university professors in Germany), the names of individuals who were to be representative of their elite, as well as themselves political influentials, were sought from a panel of recognized experts in the politics of contemporary France and the German Federal Republic. This "reputational" sample was, in effect, largely based on "positional" criteria and the sample was subsequently enlarged by the addition of other incumbents of key offices.[1]

In response to letters requesting talks with the individuals thus selected, 44 per cent of the French and 74 per cent of the German leaders contacted agreed to be interviewed. This criterion of "self-selection" was further complicated by scheduling problems, but on the whole efforts to fill stipulated quotas for each of the six elite groups, and to contact the respondents believed to exercise the greatest influence from among those answering the initial letter, were quite successful. All told, the respondents interviewed included 147 French and 173 German leaders. . . .

III. MANIFEST ATTITUDES AND SOCIAL BACKGROUND

We asserted earlier that in practice the social background approach has tended to employ all background variables as though they were equally strong indicators for general elite attitudes. More importantly, in the absence of any assessment of the predictability of a *specific* attitude by *particular* background variables in the data, all background variables have often been treated as equally good indicators of that specific attitude. We sought to shed some light on [elite] assumptions by examining the relationships between social background variables and all manifest and latent attitudes of German and French elite respondents.[2]

Finding: While most social background variables showed some degree of association with manifest elite attitudes in the German case, some background variables were clearly better predictors of manifest attitudes than others.

Looking at Table 1 we see that 38 out of 40 background variables are predictors of at least one of the German elite's manifest attitudes. In order to compare the overall predictability of one background vari-

[1] The combination of reputational and positional approaches yielded an initial group of 441 French and 650 German leaders which for operational purposes was understood as representative of elites in both political systems.

[2] The number of latent attitudes (11) used was the same for both the French and German leaders. However, with regard to manifest attitudes less data were available for the French (39 attitudes) than for the Germans (48 attitudes). With regard to the biographical or social background data, there was considerably less data available in the French case (11 variables), than for the German (40 variables). We felt that for theoretical reasons it was worthwhile to utilize the greater body of German data, which will explain differences in our tables. Whenever the French and German respondents were compared, however, this was done using only the attitudes and background variables for which adequate data were on hand for both.

TABLE 1. GERMAN RESPONDENTS: RELATIONSHIPS BETWEEN SOCIAL BACKGROUND FACTORS AND SET OF 48 MANIFEST ATTITUDES, BY SCOPE, STRENGTH, AND PREDICTION RANGE[a]

Background factor	Number of attitudes predicted	Percentage of attitudes predicted	Strength (by mean)	Prediction range
1. Principal occupation, 1952-1964	12	25	.62	.39–.85
2. Present occupation	11	23	.62	.40–.85
3. Political party leader, 1964	9	19	.65	.39–.86
4. Political party affiliation, 1956	9	19	.61	.38–.79
5. Political persecution, 1933-1944	8	17	.51	.37–.65
6. Nazi political activity, 1933-1944	8	17	.61	.40–.83
7. Present political party affiliation	6	13	.69	.48–.80
8. Membership in two voluntary economic associations	5	10	.66	.50–.84
9. Religious affiliation	5	10	.57	.46–.77
10. Incumbent governmental office, 1956	5	10	.56	.41–.78
11. Political party leader, 1956	4	8	.56	.37–.78
12. Principal occupation, 1945-1952	4	8	.61	.59–.68
13. Region of Birth	4	8	.56	.39–.62
14. Size of town of birth	4	8	.48	.37–.63
15. Political party affiliation, 1933-1934	4	8	.59	.41–.73
16. Membership in one voluntary economic association	3	6	.55	.41–.67
17. Military service	3	6	.60	.51–.75
18. Level of political governmental office, 1956	3	6	.50	.36–.71
19. Number of years in present elite position	3	6	.50	.41–.64
20. Membership in one voluntary non-economic association	3	6	.68	.65–.71
21. Membership in three voluntary non-economic associations	3	6	.52	.44–.66
22. Principal occupation, pre-1933	3	6	.54	.38–.76
23. Political party affiliation, 1946	3	6	.55	.41–.74
24. Political party leader, 1946	3	6	.47	.42–.56
25. Social class background	2	4	.59	.57–.60
26. Highest academic degree attained	2	4	.57	.47–.66
27. Country of birth	2	4	.49	.38–.60
28. Principal occupation, 1933-1945	2	4	.64	.63–.64
29. Age	2	4	.59	.57–.61
30. Positions in two voluntary economic associations	2	4	.58	.51–.64
31. Level of political governmental office, 1946	2	4	.55	.53–.56
32. Membership in three voluntary economic associations	1	2	.78	—
33. University specialization	1	2	.73	—
34. Level of education	1	2	.41	—
35. Political party leader, pre-1933	1	2	.68	—
36. Membership in two voluntary non-economic associations	1	2	.46	—
37. Highest military rank attained	1	2	.61	—
38. Position in three voluntary economic associations	1	2	.84	—
39. Position in one voluntary economic association	0	0	—	—
40. Political party affiliation, pre-1933	0	0	—	—

[a] Scope is the number of manifest attitudes predicted at .05 level or better (48 possible attitudinal predictions). Strength is the mean of the background factor's attitudinal predictions at the above level. Prediction range specifies the lowest and highest attitudinal predictions made by the background factors at this level.
Number of respondents (N) = 173.
Number of attitudes = 48.

able with another, we have employed two indices: *scope,* which simply refers to the number of all attitudes the background variable predicted; and *strength,* which refers to the mean of all the background variable's attitudinal predictions.

By the *scope* criterion we find that 38 out of the 40 background factors did, in fact, allow us to predict at least one manifest attitude. But some background factors predicted far more such attitudes than others. The first two, both occupational categories, predicted eleven to twelve attitudes, while 30 other categories predicted only four or fewer.[3]

As to their *relative strengths* as predictors, some background factors clearly were more important than others, the range extending from .41 for the lowest to .84 for the highest. Moreover, in almost all cases, background categories were not steady predictors of those attitudes they did predict. The *prediction range* in Table 1 shows that many variables predicted some attitudes considerably better than others. To take an extreme example, principal occupation 1952–64, the background variable that predicted the greatest number of attitudes (i.e., had the widest *scope*) varied in its predictions between .39 and .85.

In sum, while the predictive strength of 16 background categories among the German elites was fairly high — .61 or better — the number of attitudes they predicted was generally very small. Moreover, an examination of the entire prediction matrix — too large to reproduce here — indicated that in most cases it would have been practically impossible to have forecast which background category would have predicted what attitude(s) of the German leaders.

Note that the five background categories which predicted the greatest number of German elite attitudes (*i.e., scope*)[4] were all related to adult socialization experiences during the preceding 14 years. On the other hand, level of education, a background variable often highly associated with attitudes in mass opinion surveys, was near the bottom of the scope scale. It predicted only one of the 48 elite attitudes. Another point worth noting is the type of attitudes that were most susceptible to probabilistic prediction. The four attitudes predicted by eight to twelve background categories were all associated with particularly salient political issues.[5]

---

[3] It is worth emphasizing that even the background variable predicting the greatest number of attitudes allowed us to do so for only twelve, that is, 25 percent, of all 48 attitudes.

[4] We use *scope* rather than *strength* as a summary measure because for purposes of the present discussion — demonstrating that some background variables have more relevance than others for elite attitudes in a national political system — the number of attitudes a background variable predicts seems more to the point.

[5] These were responses to the following interviewer questions: (1) What developments in domestic policy are likely to bring about a change in German foreign policy? (2) Would the recognition of East Germany ease international tension? (3) How would recognition of the Oder-Neisse line affect efforts toward German reunification? and (4) What is the greatest threat to German security at the present time?

Next, let us look at the French elite data and compare them with the German.

Finding: Among French elites, as among German, some social background factors were considerably better predictors of manifest attitudes than others, and some manifest attitudes were again more frequently predicted by background categories than were others.

While nine of the eleven French background factors predicted at least one French elite attitude in the data, Table 2 shows the differences in their relative *scopes*. Two were related to nine manifest attitudes, while six were related to only three or fewer attitudes. In predictive *strength* they varied between .64 and .77 for particular attitudes and the *prediction range* indicates that the same background categories were far from being steady predictors for the set of attitudes they did predict. As in the case of the German elites, however, when the background variables predicted attitudes, their strength was usually high, but their

TABLE 2. FRENCH AND GERMAN RESPONDENTS: RELATIONSHIPS BETWEEN COMMON SOCIAL BACKGROUND FACTORS AND MANIFEST ATTITUDES BY SCOPE, STRENGTH, AND PREDICTION RANGE[a]

Background factor	French respondents Prediction of manifest attitudes				German respondents Prediction of manifest attitudes			
	No. of attitudes predicted	Percentage of attitudes predicted	Strength (by mean)	Prediction range	No. of attitudes predicted	Percentage of attitudes predicted	Strength (by mean)	Prediction range
1. Present political party affiliation	9	23	.65	.53–.77	4	10	.68	.48–.75
2. Political party affiliation, France, 1958; Germany, 1956	9	23	.68	.50–.81	6	15	.60	.38–.75
3. Present occupation	6	15	.65	.49–.82	7	18	.68	.44–.85
4. Social class background	4	10	.75	.67–.80	2	5	.59	.57–.60
5. Size of town of birth	4	10	.64	.42–.86	1	3	.47	—
6. Principal occupation, France, 1958-1964; Germany, 1952-1964	3	8	.54	.48–.61	8	21	.66	.45–.85
7. University specialization	3	8	.67	.60–.75	1	3	.73	—
8. Level of education	2	5	.71	.63–.79	0	—	—	—
9. Age	1	3	.77	—	2	5	.64	.63–.64
10. Region of birth	0	0	—	—	3	8	.53	.39–.62
11. Principal occupation, France, 1945-1958; Germany, 1945-1952	0	0	—	—	2	5	.60	.59–.60

[a] Scope is the number of manifest attitudes predicted at .05 level or better (39 possible attitudinal predictions). Strength is the mean of the background factor's attitudinal predictions at the above level. Prediction range specifies the lowest and highest attitudinal predictions made by the background factors at this level.
Number of respondents (N) = French, 147, German, 173.
Number of attitudes = 39.

scopes, the number of attitudes they did predict, were low. Here too, it would for the most part have been difficult to have forecast which background factors would predict which attitudes.

Observe that the background factors with the widest scope (predicting in this case six to nine of all attitudes) were again associated particularly with adult socialization experiences — especially occupation and party affiliation. And again, level of education was a relatively poor predictor of elite attitudes.

In order to contrast these results with the German findings, let us look at those background variables and attitudes for which comparable results were available (see Table 2). While age and social class background had the highest predictive *strengths* for the French elites they were comparatively low in the German data. As we have already noted, party affiliation and occupation have relatively wide *scopes* for both French and German elite attitudes. On the whole, however, the rank orderings of all background variables by scope in the French and German social circles was highly dissimilar. The Spearman r^s is .16 for the two rankings.

But scope is a crude index, describing only the total number of attitudes a background variable predicted. It could be that the same background factor, at least, predicts the same attitudinal responses to identical questions for both German and French elite respondents. In our analysis, this might have been the case for 24 background-attitude combinations. But it proved to apply to only four of these: the same background factors generally predicted different attitudes in the French and German data.

Shifting our perspective from the background categories to the attitudes predicted, we find, as in the German case, that some attitudes were predicted by more background variables than were others: two attitudes were predicted by four to five background factors, but twenty of the remaining attitudes were not predicted by any background factors. None of these attitudes were among those most frequently associated with the same background variables in the case of the German elites. They did however touch upon extremely salient issues in French politics — just as the German attitudes most often predicted by German background variables were particularly salient issues in German politics.[6] This suggests that, generally, elite socialization experiences associated with social background factors may possibly be more

---

[6] Those attitudes predicted by more background variables (three to five) than other attitudes were responses to the following questions put by the interviewers: (1) Are you content with the present governmental system in France? (2) Are you satisfied with the government's foreign policy measures? (3) Which group or groups do you feel have gained in political power over the last few years? (4) Which features of French foreign policy, if any, are likely to remain after deGaulle? (5) Do you expect an appreciable change in the relations between France and the countries of Eastern Europe during the next few years? and (6) Is an independent nuclear deterrent necessary for a nation's prestige in the world?

strongly related to orientations toward highly salient issues than to orientations concerning issues of lower saliency. If this hypothesis should be sustained by further research, future analysis would require considerable discrimination among attitudes conditioned by the differential saliency of issues in various political systems and periods of time.

IV. NATIONALITY AND SOCIAL BACKGROUND

Nationality is frequently believed to be an important social background variable, with widespread and powerful effects on elite attitudes. However, its actual relationship to elite attitudes has infrequently been analyzed quantitatively and cross-nationally. Most studies focus on elites of the same nationality and do not include cross-national attitudinal responses to identical questions which permit comparison. But if all respondents are Germans, for example, there is no way to assess the relative importance of their "Germanism" for different attitudes.

The Yale group, however, did ask the same questions of French and German respondents, affording us an opportunity to compare the relationship between the nationality factor and manifest attitudes to similar relationships between other background variables and the same attitudes. To explore this problem we combined the French and German elite responses, and utilized nationality as a social background predictor of differential attitudes. We then compared our findings with those of other background factor predictions in the French and German groups treated separately.

Finding: Nationality had a significantly greater scope (i.e., predicted more attitudes) than any other background variable in either national group. However, its strength as a predictor was about the same as that of other elite background variables in Germany and below the average in France.

In *scope,* nationality predicted 85 percent of the manifest attitudes in the combined groups. When they were examined separately, no other social background factor proved a predictor for more than 25 percent of the same set of attitudes and most others predicted far less than that. But on the *strength* index, nationality had only a mean predictability of .60 for the combined groups; taken separately the average background variable for the German elites had practically the same mean predictability (.59) and for the French it was higher (.67).

The extremely wide scope of nationality as a predictor might lead us to inquire whether or not this factor affects the attitudinal predictions of other background factors. In other words, we are now interested in the relative impact nationality had on the relationships we have already observed between other background categories and manifest attitudes among French and German elites considered by themselves. The method for determining this is a simple control. When we examined the relationship between background variables and manifest attitudes in each country separately, we were controlling for nationality. By combining the two groups we no longer do so. Thus, if another background factor's prediction of an attitude now decreases in predictability or drops below the .05 significance level we have been using when compared to its predictability in the controlled samples, we can attribute this effect to nationality.

As shown in Table 3, nationality affected over 80 percent (36 out of 41 for the French and 30 out of 36 for the Germans) of the attitudinal predictions made by other background variables among the French and German elites. Those background factors less affected by nationality in their attitudinal predictions again referred to contexts of adult socialization experiences.

V. LATENT ATTITUDES AND SOCIAL BACKGROUND

The data provided through the Latent Attitude Instrument of the Yale Study present an opportunity to examine the social background

TABLE 3. FRENCH AND GERMAN RESPONDENTS: COMPARISON OF ATTITUDINAL PREDICTIONS BY BACKGROUND FACTORS IN SEPARATE NATIONAL SAMPLES CONTROLLED FOR NATIONALITY WITH ATTITUDINAL PREDICTIONS AFFECTED BY NATIONALITY IN COMBINED GROUP[a]

Background factor	French respondents — Number of attitudinal predictions in separate sample controlled for nationality	Number of these attitudinal predictions affected by nationality	German respondents — Number of attitudinal predictions in separate sample controlled for nationality	Number of these attitudinal predictions affected by nationality
1. Principal occupation, France, 1958-1964; Germany, 1952-1964	3	3	8	5
2. Present occupation	6	4	7	6
3. Political party affiliation, France, 1958; Germany, 1956	9	7	6	6
4. Present political party affiliation	9	8	4	3
5. Principal occupation, France, 1945-1958; Germany, 1945-1952	0	0	2	2
6. Region of birth	0	0	3	4
7. Size of town of birth	4	4	1	0
8. Social class background	4	4	2	1
9. Age	1	1	2	2
10. University specialization	3	3	1	1
11. Level of education	2	2	0	0
Totals	41	36	36	30

[a]The criteria for attributing a nationality effect to a background factor's attitudinal prediction are whether or not this predictability decreases or drops below the .05 level in the combined French-German group compared to its attitudinal prediction in the separate sample controlled for nationality.
Significance Level .05.
Number of Respondents (N) = French, 147; German, 173.

approach from yet another perspective. It enables us to consider — apart from manifest response patterns — eleven implicit attitudinal orientations, such as respondents' level of political affect, sense of involvement, level of information, resistance to new information (cloture), and alienation from the prevailing political order.

The Latent Attitude Instrument . . . coded the interviewer's intuitive judgements of response patterns. In that sense it provided ostensibly "softer" data than the actual responses coded in the Manifest Attitude Instrument and the social background information included in the Biographical Data schedule. In view of this we first sought to check its reliability as a source for data evaluating the respondent's orientations. Included in these latent ratings were questions requesting the interviewer to categorize each respondent's degree of information along an ordinal scale. If accurate, the interviewer's judgement should correspond roughly to the total number of "don't know" answers the respondent gave to explicit questions in the Manifest schedule. While such a reliability measure is by no means ideal, it seemed a reasonable and feasible estimate given the nature of the data.

We took the number of "Don't Know" answers given by each respondent as a percentage of the total number of questions put to him from the Manifest Attitude Schedule. Respondents were ranked from high to low according to this criterion, and the ranking was compared to a similar ranking of the same respondents according to their degree of information as estimated by the interviewer in the Latent Attitude Schedule. For the latent ratings of the German sample, we found seven ranking errors (4% error), and four ranking errors (3% error) in the French sample. This low percentage of error appeared to lend sufficient credence to the Latent Attitude ratings to permit us to employ these data in further exploration of the social background hypothesis.

Finding: For both the German and French elites there was considerable association between social background factors and latent attitudes, though not as much as between background factors and manifest attitudes. Again, some background variables proved better predictors of latent attitudes than others in the two sets of elites.

As shown in Table 4, in *scope* twenty-nine of the forty German background variables predicted at least one latent attitude, but only seven predicted more than two. Predictive *strength* varied considerably among different background factors (from .53 to .84), and also within each one, as indicated by the *prediction range*. The two background variables with the widest scope proved to be military service and principal occupation 1952–1964, whereas for the manifest attitudes, it was political party factors and present and past occupations that were the most frequent predictors. However, note that in both instances the highest predictors relate particularly to adult socialization experiences, while level of education is at the bottom, and the case of the latent attitudes does not even qualify as a predictor.

Among the French elite respondents, eight of the eleven potential background predictors for which data was available were related to at

TABLE 4. GERMAN RESPONDENTS: RELATIONSHIPS BETWEEN SOCIAL BACKGROUND FACTORS AND SET OF 11 LATENT ATTITUDES BY SCOPE, STRENGTH, AND PREDICTION RANGE[a]

Background factor	Scope of attitudes predicted	Strength (by mean)	Prediction range
1. Military service	6	.71	.55–.86
2. Principal occupation, 1952-1964	4	.67	.58–.78
3. Present occupation	3	.70	.62–.78
4. Political party leader, 1964	3	.70	.63–.79
5. Political party leader, 1956	3	.68	.62–.79
6. Membership in two voluntary non-economic associations	3	.60	.59–.62
7. Present political party affiliation	3	.69	.60–.78
8. Political party leader, pre-1933	2	.71	.64–.77
9. Political party leader, 1946	2	.68	.57–.78
10. Principal occupation, 1933-1945	2	.78	.77–.78
11. Membership in three voluntary non-economic associations	2	.67	.63–.70
12. Political party affiliation, 1946	2	.70	.64–.76
13. Age	2	.81	.77–.84
14. Level of political governmental office, 1946	2	.69	.59–.78
15. Level of political governmental office, 1956	2	.70	.62–.78
16. Principal occupation, 1945-1952	2	.69	.60–.78
17. Nazi political activity, 1933–1934	1	.77	—
18. Incumbent governmental office, 1956	1	.84	—
19. Highest military rank attained	1	.62	—
20. Highest academic degree attained	1	.53	—
21. Membership in one voluntary economic association	1	.61	—
22. Position in one voluntary economic association	1	.77	—
23. Membership in two voluntary economic associations	1	.55	—
24. Membership in three voluntary economic associations	1	.78	—
25. Position in three voluntary economic associations	1	.78	—
26. Political party affiliation, 1933-1944	1	.73	—
27. Political party affiliation, 1956	1	.78	—
28. Number of years in present elite position	1	.77	—
29. University specialization	1	.77	—
30. Religious affiliation	0	—	—
31. Social class background	0	—	—
32. Size of town of birth	0	—	—
33. Country of birth	0	—	—
34. Region of birth	0	—	—
35. Level of education	0	—	—
36. Position in two voluntary economic associations	0	—	—
37. Membership in one voluntary non-economic association	0	—	—
38. Principal occupation, pre-1933	0	—	—
39. Political party affiliation, pre-1933	0	—	—
40. Political persecution, 1933-1944	0	—	—

[a] Scope is the number of latent attitudes predicted at .05 level or better (11 possible attitudinal predictions). Strength is the mean of the background factor's attitudinal predictions at the above level. Prediction range specifies the lowest and highest attitudinal predictions made by the background factors at this level.
Number of respondents (N) = 173.
Number of attitudes = 11.

least one latent attitude (see Table 5). Once again the background factors varied in scope: two predicted four to five latent attitudes, while three predicted none. As with the German elites, strength varied — though not as much — among different factors (from .58 and .72) and again certain background factors generally predicted some attitudes better than other attitudes. In France too, the factors with the widest scope, present occupation and present political party affiliation, related to adult socialization experiences. These two thus proved to be among the strongest predictors of manifest as well as latent elite attitudes in both countries, while level of education, with equal consistency, was a very poor predictor. Note, however, that the comparison between the predictive scopes of the same latent attitudes by all identical French and German background factors in Table 5 shows their overall rank order to be quite dissimilar in the two countries.

TABLE 5. FRENCH AND GERMAN RESPONDENTS: RELATIONSHIPS BETWEEN COMMON SOCIAL BACKGROUND FACTORS AND LATENT ATTITUDES BY SCOPE, STRENGTH, AND PREDICTION RANGE[a]

Background factor	French respondents Prediction of latent attitudes			German respondents Prediction of latent attitudes		
	Scope (number of attitudes predicted)	Strength (by mean)	Prediction range	Scope (number of attitudes predicted)	Strength (by mean)	Prediction range
1. Present occupation	5	.68	.63–.74	3	.70	.62–.78
2. Present political party affiliation	4	.70	.66–.79	3	.69	.60–.78
3. Political party affiliation, France, 1958; Germany, 1956	3	.71	.65–.80	1	.78	—
4. University specialization	2	.59	.52–.65	1	.77	—
5. Social class background	2	.58	.50–.66	0	—	—
6. Level of education	1	.58	—	0	—	—
7. Age	1	.63	—	2	.81	—
8. Size of town of birth	0	—	—	0	—	—
9. Principal occupation, France, 1945-1958; Germany, 1945-1952	0	—	—	2	.69	—
10. Principal occupation, France, 1958-1964; Germany, 1952-1964	0	—	—	4	.67	.58–.78

[a] Scope is the number of latent attitudes predicted at .05 level or better (11 possible attitudinal predictions). Strength is the mean of the background factor's attitudinal predictions at the above level. Prediction range specifies the lowest and highest attitudinal predictions made by the background factor at this level.
Number of respondents (N) = French, 147; German, 173.
Number of attitudes = 11.

As with the manifest attitudes, differences in the comparative scope of a background factor do not preclude that it might have predicted the same latent orientations of both German and French elites. In our analysis this could have occurred eight times. In fact, however, only three such orientations — level of involvement, level of affect, and cloture of thinking — were predicted by the same factor in both countries, all three being predicted by a single one, namely present occupation.

To sum up, we found latent attitudes to show associative patterns similar to those for manifest attitudes among French and German elites. When predictions were made by the background categories their *strength* was acceptable and, in many cases, quite high. Predictive *scope,* on the other hand, proved rather limited, and indicated wide differences in the associative patterns in France and Germany apart from the consistency with which occupation and party affiliation turned out to be high predictors of latent as well as manifest attitudes.

Repeating our study of the nationality factor with the latent attitudinal data, we found nationality again to have an impressively broader scope than other background variables. Nationality was related to 73 percent of the latent attitudes, while on the average other French and German background factors were respectively related to only 16 and 13 percent of those attitudes. However, its strength, or mean predictability, was .63, below the average for other background predictors for the French (.65) and the Germans (.72). Once more we combined the French and German elites and compared resulting attitudinal predictions with those made by the same background variables when nationality was held constant. Here we found that nationality affected the attitudinal predictions of more than three-quarters of the background variables in both French and German cases, about the same proportion as with manifest attitudes.

VI. ATTITUDINAL COHESION AND SOCIAL BACKGROUND WITHIN NATIONAL ELITES

As a further step in our cross-national analysis, we reduced the ninety-eight questions in the Manifest Schedule to eight basic questions which could serve as a core for a comparison of attitudinal consensus and disconsensus among French and among German leaders. . . .

Finding: German elites displayed an exceptionally high attitudinal consensus, while French elites showed considerable dissension.

French leaders generally identified the positive features of their regime with its effective "leadership" and the contents of "policy-making." While in their orientation toward internal or external problems relating to the purpose of European integration French respondents divided approximately 5:3 in favor of an internal orientation, this division did not show up as a cleavage across any of the other dimensions.

Not surprisingly, the most significant elite cleavages in the de Gaulle

Republic were found to exist along the approbation/alienation, nationalist/supranationalist, and European/Atlantic dichotomous dimensions. Those who evaluatively (*i.e.*, instrumentally) and affectively (*i.e.*, emotionally) approved of the present governmental system, also tended to take a "nationalist" position on NATO strategy and to focus cognitively upon "European" as opposed to common "Atlantic" interests. This Gaullist position was opposed correspondingly on the same dimensions by the anti-Gaullists who were evaluatively and affectively more or less alienated from their political system.[7] In short, while the French respondents manifested high disagreement along the lines of Gaullist–anti-Gaullist questions, their agreement was usually in areas where leadership and foreign policy issues were less salient.

The German elites, in sharp contrast to their French counterparts, appeared highly consensual and integrated. The contrast between the two elite groups in terms of their integration may be seen clearly in Table 6, which summarizes the proportion of individuals within each sample who agreed with one another — that is, gave identical responses on one or more of our eight questions.

Looking at Table 6, we find that on three questions the German respondents demonstrate higher consensus than the French in taking a position by an average ratio of 4:3; on four through six questions the Germans show about twice the amount of agreement on a position than the French show.

TABLE 6. DEGREE OF ELITE CONSENSUS AND INTEGRATION AS MEASURED BY AGREEMENT ON MULTIPLE QUESTIONS

Number of questions	French N	French %	German N	German %
1	106	72	161	93
2	74	50	143	83
3	61	41	99	57
4	36	24	69	40
5	19	13	47	27
6	11	7	30	17
7	6	4	11	6
8	0	0	6	3

Elite Respondents

When the German respondents were in disagreement it was along the trust/non-trust and European/Atlantic dichotomous dimensions. However, these two divisions did not show up along any other dimensions; there were no cleavages across multiple questions, as in the French sample. Also, in contrast to the French, the German elites, on the whole,

---

[7] Moreover, these alienated elites are generally oriented beyond the boundaries of France: not only are they on the whole supra-nationalists, but their cognitive focus extends to a "larger European" and "Atlantic" outlook, *i.e.*, to a diffuse internationalism.

supported their political system and were strongly oriented toward structural, regime features rather than leadership and policy features. They manifested internationalist orientations in both NATO strategy and evaluative perceptions of prospective European union partners. But they were concerned more with internal — primarily economic — European problems than with world bi-polarism in their evaluations of the purpose of European integration.

In sum, whereas the German sample demonstrated a generally high degree of consensus along our eight dimensions, the French respondents seemed deeply divided on all of them. In France the most basic elite cleavages appeared related to approbation vs. alienation toward the political system, or, more specifically, to lie along dimensions which can be labeled Gaullist and anti-Gaullist.

In comparing the manifest attitudes over which there was high disconsensus among the French elites with those attitudes that were found to have been frequently predicted by social background factors, we found that they were not identical. This led us to hypothesize that, though the strength of social background predictions of manifest attitudes for the French group as a whole was relatively high, background variables would not be as strongly related to attitudes if we narrowed the focus from the entire national samples to intra-national groups in high agreement and disagreement.

To pursue this hypothesis, we divided our respective French and German leaders into two groups for each country — four altogether — which agreed internally and disagreed between each other on three attitudinal dimensions. The members of each group had in common that they all took precisely the same position on a number of questions, while the distinction between the two groups was that their respective members took exactly opposite positions on these questions. Thus, respondents within each agreed with each other but absolutely disagreed with all members of the other group. If all in Group I answered a question one way, then all members of Group II had answered it in the opposite direction.

Now, if social background factors are indeed strong indicators of elite attitudes they should clearly discriminate between groups within a country that are internally homogeneous in attitudes but in absolute disagreement with each other. As Groups I and II in each country are distinguished by the opposite attitudes of their members, if social background is highly related to attitudinal group membership, the two groups should have highly dissimilar backgrounds because they have dissimilar attitudes. Or at least, they should show greater dissimilarity in their backgrounds than would be found in the entire French and German elite samples when there are no internal controls for attitudinal group membership. On the three attitudes which define attitudinal group membership, common background characteristics should be highly associated with these attitudes, or at least more highly associated than in the entire elite samples.

Finding: (1) *In the German sample, background characteristics were more highly associated with attitudes in dichotomous groups than they* were for the German elites as a whole on the three responses. (2) In the French sample the relationships between background and attitude in dichotomous groups was less highly associated than they were for the entire French sample on the same three responses.

In Figure 1 the German background-attitude relationships are depicted by solid lines and the French by broken lines. It shows that among German elites background remained an adequate attitudinal indicator when they were divided into groups which agreed internally and disagreed with each other. Among the French exactly the opposite happened. With the exception of size of town of birth, significance of background decreased in relationship to attitude in the case of the two groups below what it was in the French entire elite sample. . . .

VII. CONCLUSION

This paper has attempted to make a modest contribution to cross-national comparisons of political systems in general and to the study of their leaders in particular. Analysis of the relationships between the

FIGURE 1. FRENCH AND GERMAN RESPONDENTS: DEGREE OF ASSOCIATION BETWEEN SOCIAL BACKGROUND AND SELECTED MANIFEST ATTITUDES OF DICHOTOMOUS GROUP MEMBERS COMPARED TO DEGREE OF ASSOCIATION BETWEEN THE SAME SOCIAL BACKGROUND AND ATTITUDE IN ENTIRE ELITE SAMPLES[a]

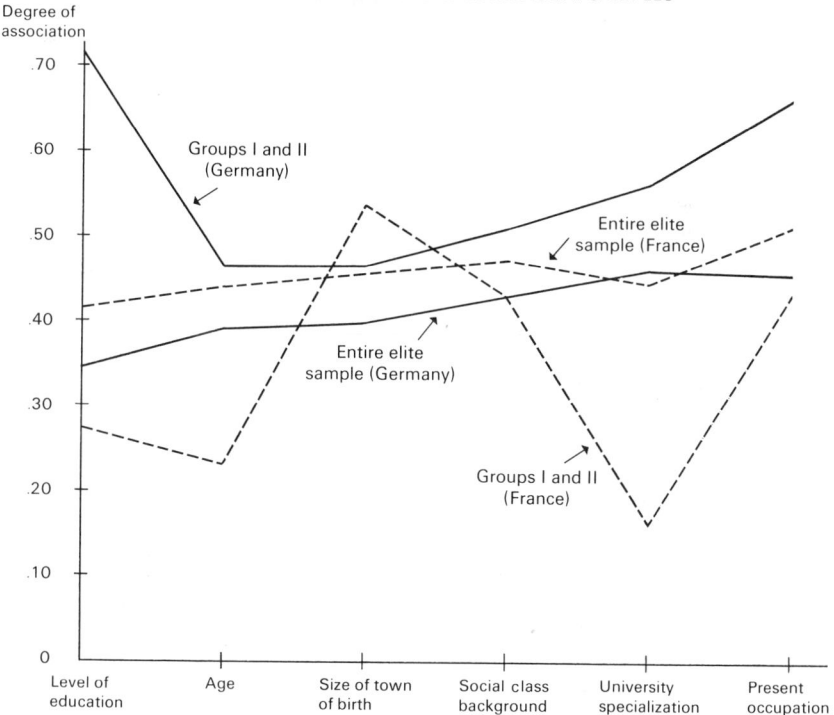

[a]Measure of association = Pearson's Contingency Coefficient.
Note: Groups I and II are in internal agreement but dichotomous in attitude.

TABLE 7. GERMAN RESPONDENTS: BACKGROUND FACTOR COMBINATIONS YIELDING HIGHEST PREDICTIONS FOUND IN DATA OF SELECTED MANIFEST ATTITUDES

Attitude predicted	Background factors in the combination and their relative contributions to the combined prediction						Combined predictions
1. Approbation — alienation toward governmental system	Social class background	.62	Political party leader — pre-1933	.62			.66
2. Policy, government — structure, regime orientation	Region of birth	.60	Principal occupation — 1952-1964	.60			.64
3. Secure, trust society — bad portents, distrust society	Highest degree attained	.50	Membership in two voluntary economic associations	.51	Political persecution, 1933-1944	.50	.57
4. Nationalist — supra nationalist	Membership in one voluntary economic association	.59	Membership in two voluntary economic associations	.59	Number of years in present elite occupation	.64	.70
5. European — Atlantic orientation	Military service	.51	Political party affiliation, 1946	.50			.58
6. Little European — larger European orientation	Highest degree attained	.49	Principal occupation, pre-1933	.60	Political persecution, 1933-1944	.56	.72
7. Internal problem — external problem orientation	Membership in one voluntary economic association	.68	Number of years in present elite occupation	.68			.68
8. Communist threat — no communist threat perception	Membership in two voluntary economic associations	.73	Present political party affiliation	.76			.80

social backgrounds of elites on the one hand, and their orientation patterns on the other, has obvious relevance for the study of sub-national and national, as well as supra-national political systems. For example, where nationality is a significant factor relating to elite attitudes, it may tell us a good deal about the cohesiveness of old and new national states and about the prospects for supra-national political entities. Strong relationships or, conversely, weak relationships, between attitudes and religious or age cohort socialization experiences may similarly reveal significant patterns of elite ties and cleavages within, between, and across political communities. . . .

At the present juncture, the background data that have been collected are often used undiscriminatingly for lack of conclusive evidence on the actual relationships between particular background variables and particular attitudes in different cultural circumstances. Our analysis suggests the following qualifications: (1) some background variables are considerably better predictors than are others[8] of attitudes within a single national political system; (2) some elite attitudes in a particular national polity are more frequently related to background variables than are others; and (3) relationships between social background and attitude vary from one national political system to another even within the same supra-national culture area.

---

[8] In the case of the data used here predictive strength often proved acceptable, but the scope of prediction was frequently lower than might have been expected and did not seem to conform to any obvious patterns beyond those we suggested rather tentatively. Moreover, the relevance of the diffuseness or specificity of the attitudes in question remained to be resolved. Despite our contrary findings in comparing latent with manifest attitudes among French and German elites, we suspect that quantitative forecasting may be more successful with diffuse than with specific attitudinal responses.

GIOVANNI SARTORI

The Professionalization of Italian MP's

The existence of well organized political parties in European countries makes party officials much more important than their American counterparts. The machinery for nominating and electing Members of Parliament tends to enhance further the power of party officials, both in selecting candidates and in distributing favored positions on the ballot in proportional representation elections. From data on parliamentary careers, Giovanni Sartori draws important inferences about the relative independence or dependence of men in important political posts.

I will look more closely at the phenomenon of the professionalization of politics to determine how far it is correct to speak of "party rule" in the various senses of the much-used Italian word *partitocrazia*, with particular reference to the type and degree of dependence of the deputy on his party.

"Professionalization" and "professional politician" are ambiguous terms. At least four aspects of "professionalization" must be distinguished: (1) the functional aspect, i.e., specialization, the acquisition of a specific skill; (2) the representative implication, involving detachment from one's social origins and therefore a disturbance of the sociological aspect of representation; (3) the personality aspect, involving the professional politician's lack of principles and opportunism; (4) the economic and occupational aspect, i.e., the fact that the professional politician has no other profession: he has to live off politics.

I shall be obliged to pass over the second problem and, again for brevity's sake, I shall take the third and fourth meanings together, even if the coincidence between the political opportunist and the politi-

From Giovanni Sartori, "Members of Parliament in Italy," in *Decisions and Decision-Makers in the Modern State,* pp. 169–173 (Paris: UNESCO, 1967). Reprinted by permission.

cian who must hold his job in order to live is only a probability, that is, even though generalization in this respect must be received with great caution.

The problem of professionalization may be reduced, then, to the two following headings: (1) the functional acceptance of the term, according to which the professional politician is an expert; (2) the economic acceptance — including its psychological implications — according to which the professional politician has no alternative means of subsistence: his choice is between political employment and unemployment. This is what raises the question of the deputy's dependence and allows the study at close range of the evolution of party rule (*partitocrazia*) under the parliamentary system.

The word "dependence" should, of course, be taken with a grain of salt. It cannot be compared or contrasted with the independence of the gentleman politician of bygone days. The amateur politician, the man who used to give his spare time to politics, has become, at the parliamentary level, a marginal case. In the second place, a representative is always "dependent" to some extent, if for no other reasons because considerations of ambition, prestige or status will induce him to hold on to his post. (This was true even of the gentleman politician despite his economic independence.)

Moreover, a deputy always depends both on the electorate that chooses him, and on the party that puts him up as a candidate. But which form of dependence is most felt? Which is prevalent?

In any event, the first problem is to what extent the professional politician is in the process of emerging as a predominant type of parliamentarian. From this angle my question is: what proportion is struck, amongst the Italian MP's, between semi-professional and professional politicians *stricto-sensu*? In the strict meaning because, by my definition, the professionalization of political man cannot be assessed merely in terms of time, that is, merely by ascertaining whether or not politics becomes a full time job. This criterion is far too loose and neglects the crucial point: whether politics is, for the politician, the *only* possible profession, or whether he had formerly a private profession to which he could eventually return. Here, it seems to me, is the decisive criterion which defines the "pure professional," and thereby the crucial shift which is taking place in a number of present-day representative bodies.

Let us begin with professionalization considered as specialization. A fair test of how far the professional politician thinks of himself as a specialist is provided by the permanence of deputies on parliamentary committees. In practice, a large part of the Italian parliament's work is done in committee, for most of our legislation is enacted by the committees without being presented to the Assembly.[1] And while it is open to question whether ministers should be specialists rather than gen-

[1] The pros and cons of the Italian system of committee legislation are discussed by A. Predieri in G. Sartori, ed., *Il Parlamento Italiano 1946–1963* (Napoli: ESI, 1963), pp. 205–261 *passim*.

eralists, the idea of acquiring expert skill in parliamentary committee work seems a sensible one.

Since each Italian legislature is divided into five sessions, the committees are renewed, at least formally, five times in each parliament, that is, every year. We have examined, therefore, the course of twelve sessions (first and second legislatures, plus the first two sessions of the third). By and large, the deputies do not seem interested in acquiring competence in any particular sector by staying put in the same committee. To be sure each party is interested in having on any given committee a permanent representative who will be its expert on the problems dealt with. It is also clear that certain deputies have special qualifications and get themselves appointed to a committee with the firm intention of staying there. However, the bulk of deputies do not appear to attach much importance to remaining on the same committee. In the three legislatures under consideration, out of 218 deputies having served for twelve sessons the permanent members amounted only to 20.6 per cent; and 49.8 per cent of this group had changed at least twice, that is, had served on at least three different committees. Let it be added that a fair proportion of the group of permanent members is made up of run-of-the-mill deputies who do not change principally because nobody thinks of asking them to. It is fair to conclude, therefore, that the desire to develop specialization through committee practice is hardly felt.

This is confirmed by the replies of deputies to the following question: "To what aspect of your parliamentary work do you attach more importance?" Only 14.6 per cent vaguely mentioned their committee work.

Moreover, the relationship between committees and the educational or professional background of their members appears very loose. To take one significant case, in 1960 the composition of the Finance and Treasury Committee was as follows: out of forty-five members, twenty-six had degrees and nineteen did not (while the overall proportion between university graduates and non-graduates is seven to three). Among the degrees, fourteen were in law, eight in economics, two in political science, one in engineering and one in mathematics; of the non-graduates, two had only an elementary school licence. The turnover is even more interesting. Of the forty-five members, eighteen had been elected in 1958 and were therefore serving on the committee for the first time. Of the remaining twenty-seven who had been deputies in at least one of the preceding legislatures, thirteen had never served on this committee, and five had done so on a temporary basis only. So we reach the conclusion that only nine members of the committee had been on it for any length of time; that is, only one-fifth of the committee in charge of the "control of the purse" was made up of experienced members.

From what has been said, it follows that the salient aspect of the professionalization of politics points to the situation of the man who lives off politics. How many professional politicians of this kind are to be found in the Italian parliament? Table 1 distinguishes among non-professional politicians (the equivalent of the former gentleman politician and of Weber's *nebenberufliche Politiker*), the semi-professional politicians (who still have, at least potentially, an alternative occupation), and the professional politicians.

Table 1 requires little comment. However, as regards the actual importance of non-professional politicians, we should note that they are mainly found in the small parties, which means that their weight in parliamentary decision-making is even smaller than that indicated by the percentages. The importance of the "semi-professional politician" must also be re-measured. Not only are the semi-professionals more numerous in the smaller parties than in the large; but as time goes on, and as election follows election, many semi-professionals become de facto professional, in the sense that they end up by finding themselves in a "no return" situation. By and large the curve of professionalization follows the curve of duration of parliamentary service. It is almost impossible in many cases to determine the point of no return, and therefore the caution is that professionalization could be greater than Table 1 would suggest.

TABLE 1. PROFESSIONALIZATION OF POLITICAL LIFE

Type of politician	Total %	Constituent Assembly 1946 %	1st legislature 1948 %	2nd legislature 1953 %	3rd legislature 1958 %
Non-professionals	7.1	9.3	5.9	5.5	4.5
Semi-professionals	64.6	67.8	68.0	60.9	57.2
Professionals	28.3	22.9	26.1	33.6	38.3

However, the trend to be kept in mind is the other one, the increase in the number of professional politicians who never had another occupation, that is, the increase in the proportion of party or trade union career men. There are, of course, different types of party men as indicated in Table 2.

Note the decline in the proportion of party leaders from 33.6 per cent in the Constituent Assembly to 23.0 per cent in the first legislature, explained by the disappearance of many of the old "notables" and also by the losses which the small parties suffered in the 1948 elections. The big names absent from the first legislature reappeared, however, in the second. Note also that the relatively high percentage in the leader category follows from the high number of parties.

TABLE 2. ASSOCIATION WITH PARTY

Career	Total %	Constituent Assembly %	1st legislature %	2nd legislature %	3rd legislature %
Party career at leadership level	22.7	33.6	23.0	25.5	23.8
No party career	20.6	24.4	21.4	17.7	12.9
Part-time party career	39.1	32.2	41.9	38.1	40.6
Full-time party career	17.6	9.8	14.7	18.7	22.7

An opposite trend is shown by the "part-time party career" category, which benefited from the defeat of the notables in the first legislature. The second legislature saw a decline in this group corresponding to the come-back of party notables. Also, the proportions of "non-party" and "party" deputies have been substantially reversed. The first have seen their ranks cut in half, while the latter have more than doubled.

From the data set out so far, particularly in Table 2, what conclusion can be drawn about the dependence or independence of deputies? While the MP's belonging to the first category — those having started from the top — are not necessarily professional politicians (even though most of them are likely to become entirely professionalized), this is surely the case with the members of parliament belonging to the fourth category, i.e., those having climbed the party ladder from the rank and file level. On the other hand, it should be kept in mind that not all professional politicians are necessarily "dependent." The party bosses, the leaders who not only wield sufficient power within the party to ensure their own re-election but also the power to decide who else should be re-elected (remember that we are considering a list system of proportional representation in which the party machine has a decisive say) — these party bosses are, in a very substantial sense, employers. Their position of strength in the party is equivalent to an independent position. Those who are in a position of dependence are the party or trade union officials who do not have any real share in basic decision-making, and in particular in the decisions affecting their own destiny. Between the party bosses and the party "creatures," there is the intermediate position of the semi-professional parliamentarian. He is independent, or potentially so because he can always fall back on his former or concomitant profession, but with rare exceptions, at least in large parties, he has little say in policy-making decisions. His position might be called one of passive independence. He may, if he wishes, resist the party directives, but he cannot impose his own directives on the party.

In Table 3 we distinguish, then, between active independence (party bosses), passive independence (semi-professional parliamentarians) and dependence (professional parliamentarians below the boss level). Naturally, these are highly hypothetical extrapolations. It is by no means certain that an independent situation produces independent, or at least "inner-directed" behaviour. Similarly, it is not inevitable that a dependent situation leads to passivity. Table 3 should consequently be interpreted in the light of these cautions. In other words, it focuses on a situation, not on actual behaviour.

TABLE 3. DEPENDENCE OR INDEPENDENCE OF DEPUTIES

Degree of autonomy	Total %	Constituent Assembly %	1st legislature %	2nd legislature %	3rd legislature %
Active independence	17.2	25.5	18.9	22.2	24.3
Passive independence	59.5	61.6	61.8	52.8	44.6
Dependence	23.3	12.9	19.3	25.0	31.1

As can be seen, the independent leadership of the various parties more or less maintains its position. It suffered an upset with the election of 1948 (the first legislature), but the balance was rapidly restored. Instead the diminution in semi-professional parliamentarians has been constant, and even more so the increase in deputies wholly dependent upon the party. Yet the distribution of these three groups is still such today as to allow a parliament as a whole a sufficient measure of autonomy.[2] A critical or turning point is surely looming, but it would be premature to conclude — I believe — that, in the Italian parliament, a situation of "dependence" already prevails over the opportunities of independent behaviour of members.

[2] Among other reasons because of the party-by-party breakdowns. Cf. for the details *Il Parlamento Italiano 1946–1963*, pp. 336–40.

MATTEI DOGAN

Charisma and the Breakdown of Traditional Alignments

Charles de Gaulle, founder of two French Republics, clearly had what Max Weber called a "charismatic" personality. One of its essential aspects, arising from a distrust of traditional political personnel, is a direct appeal to the masses of the population. Commenting upon his task in establishing a regime at the end of World War II, de Gaulle wrote, "I had to gather support among the people rather than among the elites, who tended to interpose themselves between the people and me." After his return to power in 1958, he once again sought to re-establish authority by direct appeals to the people in speeches and referenda, and, indirectly, by electoral pressures upon candidates for the National Assembly. This study is based on a content analysis of 2,100 election addresses issued by candidates to their constituents during the 1962 French general election. It was published before the desacralization of his authority in 1968, leading to de Gaulle's resignation from the presidency in 1969.

In the legislative elections of November, 1962, the majority of voters in effect pronounced either for or against President de Gaulle. Public opinion polls have left no doubt about this. In presenting themselves, the candidates did not give the impression of soliciting a parliamentary mandate but rather that of an American convention delegate charged with the nomination of a president of the republic. Nearly all the candidates defined their position, in one way or another, regarding the chief of state. In their electoral addresses more than three-quarters, regardless of their affiliation, mentioned his name. It could be said that General de Gaulle was omnipresent. He dominated the electoral campaign. Everything took place as if presidential and not legislative elections were taking place, with the candidates playing the role of "grand" electors.

The significance of these elections and the referendum extends beyond this: a charismatic phenomenon was evident.[1] All the conditions converged. First, the presence of a leader who was convinced that he represented national legitimacy, that he carried the destiny of France, and that he had a mission to fulfill. His disciples were ready to follow him against wind and tide. In the country, de Gaulle's prestige, which was considerable, transcended traditional cleavages. Institutions were powerless or ineffective, parties were diminished or discredited, and adversaries were profoundly divided.[2] Many politicians were compromised and the opposition was without a leader.[3] In the background was the specter of civil war, awakened by a *putsch*, barricades and violence. Economic prosperity, however, had attenuated the conflict between classes and favored the collective support of a man who did not identify with any class, who wanted to confer on the people, against

---

Mattei Dogan, "Le Personnel politique et la personnalité charismatique," *Revue française de sociologie,* VI, 1965, pp. 305–324. Abridged and translated into English by the author. Reprinted by permission of Les Éditions du Centre National de la Recherche Scientifique.

[1] The notion of charismatic power has been defined by Max Weber. In his fundamental work, *Wirtschaft und Gesellschaft,* see the sections on "charismatic authority," "the routinization of charisma," and "the transformation of charisma in an anti-authoritarian direction." (American translation by A. M. Henderson and Talcott Parsons, *The Theory of Social and Economic Organization* (Glencoe, Illinois: Free Press, 1947). On the role of the charismatic leader in a democratic regime and the legitimation of his power, one can consult Reinhard Bendix, *Max Weber, An Intellectual Portrait* (New York: Doubleday, 1962). A bibliography of recent studies of charismatic phenomena is given in an article by W. H. Friedland, "For a Sociological Concept of Charisma," *Social Forces,* 43, October 1964, pp. 18–19.

[2] In 1962, the opposition was divided, with more than 1,700 candidates out of a total of 2,172, or an average of four opposition candidates per seat. Only 21 percent of the mandates were decided in the first round of voting. In 1877, the adversaries of Marshal MacMahon practiced "Republican discipline": none of the 363 deputies who voted in defiance of the MacMahon government encountered another Republican in his constituency. For each official candidate there was only one opposing candidate, so that 98 percent of the seats were accorded in the first round of voting.

[3] No man like Gambetta was presented by the opposition.

the advice of the traditional political personnel, the election of the head of state, a reform considered democratic[4] and for a long time wished for by the majority of citizens.[5] In short, in the eyes of most of the citizens, there was only one alternative: "the Leader or Chaos."

In a study of de Gaulle's charisma, all of these points, as well as others, merit careful examination. Our aim, however, is limited to a single aspect: the perception of de Gaulle by the political personnel, notably the candidates, particularly those of the UNR. In our content analysis of the 2,172 electoral addresses, let us, as much as possible, quote the candidates themselves.[6]

A diversity of types revolved around the central personality: famous men or men hardly known; old campaigners or newcomers; followers from 1940 or young converts; opponents. or supporters; defenders of the institutions or disciples of the savior. Each played his role with conviction, respecting the rules of the game. The most famous were not the most applauded. From the defeat of many well known personalities, we can appreciate the amplitude of the charismatic phenomenon.

THE MASSACRE OF LEADERS

> Never in France has the President of the Republic aroused such enthusiasm.
>
> André Malraux[7]

The elections of 1958 were distinguished by the sweeping defeat of deputies seeking re-election: 344 were defeated and another 62 declined candidacy. In 1962 there were fewer victims: 184 were defeated and another 27 did not solicit renewal of their mandate. Without entering into the different reasons, it should be noted that, in 1962, according to a survey by the French Institute of Public Opinion,[8] the electorate was not hostilely predisposed to the deputies. When asked whether they would rather vote for a former parliamentarian or for a

---

[4] Cf. *Sondages, Revue Française de l'Opinion publique,* 2, 1963, p. 86, and 3, 1964, p. 13.

[5] In effect, according to a survey of the Institut français d'Opinion publique, just after the Liberation, the majority was favorable to the election of the president of the republic by universal suffrage. Cf. *Sondages,* December 1, 1945.

[6] Electoral addresses are public letters that the candidates send to each of the voters in their constituencies. The state, in order to assure to the candidates an equality of means during the course of the campaign, assumes the costs of paper, printing and distribution of the electoral addresses. Each candidate has the right to send two *"professions de foi."* Thus, during the legislative elections of November 18 and 25, 1962, more than two hundred million copies were distributed by the 2,172 candidates in the 465 constituencies of metropolitan France.

[7] André Malraux, discourse televised, October 30, 1962.

[8] Survey of IFOP, October, 1962. Cf. *Sondages, Revue française de l'Opinion publique,* II, 1963, p. 104.

new man, the majority of the sample (61%) did not indicate any preference. Of the minority, those preferring the former deputies were the more numerous (27% against 12%). Many agreed that it was "a good thing to be represented by a well known politician."

The result of the elections of 1958 and 1962 was the elimination from the political scene, particularly from the Chamber of Deputies, of an impressive number of representatives of the Fourth Republic. The Assembly was "skimmed." Excluding the two governments of de Gaulle, of which one inaugurated and the other closed the Fourth Republic, there was a succession of 17 prime ministers, who headed 23 Cabinets. Only four of these prime ministers were re-elected in 1962, and even for these four men the electoral battle was not always easy. René Pleven, who said "no" at the referendum, was elected in the first round, but he had only a single adversary, a Communist, as the other parties had considered his personal position too strong in his constituency. Perhaps the Gaullists slipped up. Paul Reynaud in the North, and Frédéric Dupont in Paris, to cite two examples, held what were considered impregnable positions: they were both beaten by opponents who benefited from the Gaullist label. Guy Mollet received fewer votes in the first round than a Gaullist who had just become active in local political life. In compensation, Gaillard and Pflimlin, the last two prime ministers of the Fourth Republic, easily defeated their Gaullist adversaries. Although he moved to a new constituency, P. Mendès-France was not able to regain a seat. André-Marie, who had been for a long time deeply rooted in his fief of Seine-Maritime, was beaten by a Gaullist. Defeated in 1958, Edgar Faure, Laniel, and Bourgès-Maunoury made no further attempts to face universal suffrage in 1962. René Mayer renounced political life, more or less voluntarily, in order to devote himself to European institutions. Pinay also renounced candidacy. Robert Schuman, as Queuille had done before him, preferred to retire from politics for reasons of age and state of health after 43 years in parliament. The Socialist leaders Blum and Ramadier were dead, "surrounded with *bourgeois* respect." Félix Gouin, victim of a famous scandal, did not seek re-election.

After the death of Edouard Herriot, the National Assembly had two other presidents. Both of them lost their positions as deputies in 1958: Schneiter without incident, and Le Troquer after the "ballet rose scandal." The leaders of the parliamentary groups fill another corner of the political cemetery. The leader of the Independents, Bertrand Motte, and the leaders of the MRP, Dorey and Simmonet, were beaten by Gaullist candidates. The president of the Socialist group, Francis Leenhardt, was eliminated, as well as the leader of the dissident Socialist party, Depreux.

What had become of the numerous ministers of the Fourth Republic? Of the 24 ministers of the Pinay Cabinet, which was one of the most distinguished, only five were present in the new Chamber. Of the 36 members of Guy Mollet's Cabinet, which had reigned the longest during the Fourth Republic, only half returned to the Chamber as deputies.

Excluding the Gaullists, there were only 37 former ministers of the Fourth Republic who were re-elected in 1962. Some of the victims of universal suffrage found refuge, however, in the Senate. Even among the Gaullists, leaders were defeated. In the elections of 1958 a leaflet distributed in millions of copies throughout all of France presented the Gaullist Party under the patronage of three great men: Debré, Michelet and Soustelle. In 1962, the first met a resounding defeat. The second was for some time no longer in the forefront, and the third was a conspirator taking refuge abroad. In brief, few former leaders in the Chamber were elected in 1962. Some rejoiced in this, perhaps; others grieved. The Socialist leader Guy Mollet commented in these terms on the defeat of some Conservative leaders: "It is unjust of the electorate."

Among the deputies of the Assembly elected in 1962, 166 were new men and 151 had begun their political careers with the Fifth Republic. There remained in the Bourbon Palace only 148 deputies from the Fourth Republic, less than one-third the total membership. The venerable institution had grown a new cover. Who were these new deputies?

THE DEPERSONALIZATION OF THE CANDIDATURES

For all action there must be a head, and as this head is a person, it is important that he receive the personal expression of confidence from all those involved.

Général de Gaulle[9]

If one asked the average elector to read the 2,172 electoral addresses, taking care to conceal the names of the candidates and their parties, he could quite easily identify the Communists and the Gaullists, but most likely he would be unable to distinguish among the Moderates, Radicals, Popular-Republicans, and Socialists.

Many Gaullist electoral addresses contained identical paragraphs, based upon a model furnished to the candidates by the UNR headquarters, which, for example, declared that "the parties led the Republic to the disaster of Dien Bien Phu in 1957" (sic). This error of three years in the date was reproduced all over France in 50 printings, a detail which indicates that the model was mechanically recopied.

The Gaullist candidates presented themselves as candidates who supported the new constitution, which was adopted by referendum the month before. "Confirm your *yes*" was the pervasive theme of their electoral addresses. It was General de Gaulle himself who inspired this: "You can confirm by your choice of men that in voting 'yes' you have made a choice as to your destiny." All of the Gaullist electoral addresses echoed this statement, so that the first round of the legislative elections appeared like a second round. "I want to thank again the electors who have replied 'yes' to the referendum." "I asked you to vote 'yes' and you have made it an overwhelming majority." "Be logical, vote for the only candidate of 'yes'; you must not let the benefits of your 'yes' be stolen."

[9] General de Gaulle, press conference of January 14, 1963.

Votes were often solicited not for oneself but for de Gaulle. "Vote for the only real candidate, General de Gaulle . . ."; "This election is of foremost importance for General de Gaulle"; "Vote for the candidate who has always given proof of his fidelity to de Gaulle." Numerous electoral addresses ended with "Long Live de Gaulle."

After having solicited votes in the name of the General, the candidates recognized in the second round of the legislative elections that the votes they had "collected" in the first were not accorded to them personally: "I know that the vote for me was a vote for General de Gaulle"; "In the name of General de Gaulle, I thank the electors . . ."; "I want to thank warmly and heartily the electors who have expressed through my modest person their affectionate attachment to the President of the Republic"; "I know, and I am not jealous, on the contrary, that your confidence has gone first and foremost to de Gaulle." Even important personalities such as Schmittlein considered themselves as simple intermediaries: "I know that these votes go beyond me to the man of the 18th of June, 1940, to the prestigious head of state who holds his hand firmly and assuredly on the rudder of the state." Vendroux, a brother-in-law of de Gaulle, stated after his victory at Calais: "I consider my personal success as only that of General de Gaulle."

Another sign of depersonalization: references to the candidate, his past, his career, his own personality (except when they emphasized his fidelity to General de Gaulle) were relegated to a second position in most of the Gaullist electoral addresses. In preference, often an entire page was devoted to a citation and photo of the President of the Republic. Among the Gaullist electoral addresses, there were fewer photos of the candidates themselves.

On the one hand, the candidate effaced himself to the point of being only a vote collector for General de Gaulle. On the other, he claimed for himself the most spectacular achievements: "I have respected the pledges I made: peace in Algeria, the resurrection of the State, the reorganization of finances. . . ." The achievements of the Fifth Republic were not presented without some demagogy, sometimes of an amusing nature. A candidate would thus declare in all seriousness, "In three years there has been more agricultural legislation voted upon than in the last fifty years."

The Gaullists made some concrete proposals but this was less a program in the traditional sense of the word than a simple list of what remained to be done. Doctrine was particularly avoided. It was considered a prerogative of the old parties: "I am not proposing to you a political doctrine but a program of action." Some Gaullist candidates were content with invoking the program of the party: "My program is that of the UNR." Or they would refer to the Plan: "The Fifth Plan gave a general summary of our Gaullist politics"; "Our program: to support the action of the President of the Republic."

Such avoidance of doctrine, is but one more proof of the depersonalization of candidatures under the shadow of a charismatic personality. Far from being a sign of weakness, this avoidance of policies assured the Gaullist party of greater cohesion, due, as Max Weber noted, to the satisfaction that a man experiences through dedicated action to the cause of a personality rather than to the abstract mediocrities of a program.[10]

Depersonalization seems to correspond to the idea that the electors themselves had of the role of deputies. The popularity of the deputies had already been weakened in their own constituencies, by the discredit of Parliament at the end of the Fourth Republic,[11] and the personal ascendancy of the chief of state. Many polls by the French Institute of Public Opinion have testified to this fact. In 1962, more than a quarter of the electors did not know the name of their representative and only half knew his name and party. A poll in October, 1962, revealed that only one person out of ten believed in the efficacy of parliamentarians in defending his socio-economic interests, whereas the majority reported confidence in the unions.[12] Yet this sentiment does not necessarily imply approval of the modest role left to the members of Parliament. On the contrary, with the exception of UNR sympathizers, the majority favored a more important role for Parliament.[13] On this point the electors and deputies of the parties agreed. Thus, the most powerful group in the Assembly was also the one least in favor of the omnipotence of Parliament over the government. In Great Britain such an attitude is not at all surprising: it results from the discipline of the parties. In France, it reflects the charismatic influence of a man.[14]

An analysis of some of the French Institute of Public Opinion surveys revealed that General de Gaulle attracted the confidence of most of the citizens without radiating it to the members of his government.[15] The distance which separates the personal prestige of the head of state and the credit of his government has often been stressed, and confirmed by the polls. There was a striking contrast between the criticisms of governmental politics and the unshakable confidence that the majority of the French gave to the person of General de Gaulle. The ministers, even the most important of them, evoked little interest from the public. None of them enjoyed great popularity.[16] To the person of the prime minister himself there was indifference. When Michel Debré left the

[10] Max Weber, "Politics as a Vocation," in M. H. H. Gerth and C. Wright Mills (eds.), *From Max Weber* (London: Routledge and Kegan Paul, 1952), p. 103.

[11] In August, 1958, three-quarters of the persons questioned by the Institut français d'Opinion publique denounced "bad parliamentarian morals." Cf. *Sondages*, IV, 1958, pp. 29 and 31. According to another survey of IFOP, carried out in September and December, 1958, among the persons who expressed an opinion, four out of five held that "the deputies are responsible for the poor functioning of the Fourth Republic." Cf. *Sondages*, IV, 1960, pp. 43 and 56.

[12] *Sondages*, II, 1963, p. 68.

[13] *Sondages*, II, 1962, pp. 75 and 76.

[14] Charismatic power is not incompatible with the party system. Cf. Max Weber, *Politics as a Vocation, op. cit.,* p. 106.

[15] *Sondages*, III, 1963, pp. 40 and the following.

[16] *Sondages*, III, 1963, p. 53.

government, two-thirds of the persons interviewed expressed neither satisfaction nor displeasure.[17]

One man, only one, symbolized the regime. Around him, from the summit to the base of the political pyramid, most of the candidates voluntarily effaced themselves before their leader.

FROM THE RESISTANCE TO THE GOVERNMENT

The man of 18 June, without whom most of us would not be engaged in political action, to whom we attach ourselves with gratitude, respect and fidelity.

J. Chaban-Delmas[18]

Max Weber commented that heroism in a military leader is often a determining factor in his charismatic authority. It is the image of the *"Premier Résistant,"* i.e., founder of the wartime Resistance, that was immediately mentioned by most French people when they were asked by IFOP in December, 1962, to give their opinion of the personality and achievements of General de Gaulle.[19] The prestigious leader of the Resistance became then head of state, drawing in his wake many comrades in arms. The UNR, like the RPF in 1947, was rooted in the Resistance. The UNR parliamentary group appeared twenty-five years after the Liberation as a resurgence of the spirit of Free France. It was principally from among the former members of the Resistance that the UNR selected the men who became the electoral representatives of de Gaulle. Apart from the Gaullist deputies who were less than 20 years old in 1944, most of the others — 130 out of 180 — had distinguished records in the Resistance or on diverse fronts during World War II. Among them 17 were decorated as *"Compagnons de la Libération."* Among these Resistants, some had joined General de Gaulle in London. Others had participated in the provisional government or the Consultative Assembly of Algiers. Others had fought in the Free French Army. The clandestine network of occupied France also furnished UNR staff. Some of these men had been prisoners of the Gestapo and in the concentration camps of Dachau, Sachsenhausen, Buchenwald, etc. Among the UNR deputies the proportion of ex-prisoners was lower than among the Communists and Socialists, who, with rare exceptions, had remained in France during the German occupation.

Although the Resistance constituted the principal crucible in which this generation of Gaullist deputies was formed, their own military actions were scarcely exploited in electoral addresses. Rarely was there reference to the candidates' heroic pasts. Mentioning the Resistance was intended above all to establish proof of long fidelity to General de

---

[17] *Sondages,* III, 1963, p. 48.
[18] J. Chaban-Delmas, speech at the Congrès national du mouvement des Républicains sociaux, November, 1955.
[19] Cf. *Sondages,* III, 1963, p. 35.

Gaulle. "Vote for a man who has supported General de Gaulle since June 19, 1940"; "Since his call of June 18, 1940, I have always followed de Gaulle"; "I have supported the actions of General de Gaulle since 1940"; "I have remained faithful for 22 years, and never denied my pledges"; "To vote for me is to vote for de Gaulle: I was one of the first to escape from occupied France and rejoin the Free French Army, where I performed 53 bombing missions"; "You know my past and my personal attachment to the First French Resistance."

As Converse and Dupeux have noted, "In spite of their differences, General de Gaulle and General Eisenhower have benefited from the same processes which are as old as the world: the popularity that a people reserves for victorious generals." In both countries, "People have been more attached to the personal qualities of these men and to their personalities than to their political ideas."[20] This is precisely one of the main characteristics of the charismatic personality.

THE FAITHFUL GAULLISTS

> We revive this great title: the Party of the Faithful. Yes, we are the Party of the Faithful, of those Faithful to the Liberator.
>
> Roger Frey[21]

Max Weber characterized charismatic authority as the personal devotion of subjects to the cause of a man, showing confidence in him because he displays prodigious and heroic qualities suiting him to leadership.[22] The electoral addresses of the Gaullist candidates fit this definition. One finds in them a whole range of proclamations of fidelity, and this fidelity to General de Gaulle is the common denominator: "You know me, a faithful Gaullist"; "I solicit your votes emphasizing my total fidelity to General de Gaullle"; "Help by your vote those who have never betrayed de Gaulle"; "Having always served de Gaulle, I appeal for your vote."

The true Gaullists were those who had always been faithful. Many specified that they had been Gaullists from the first hour, that they were not opportunists: "For more than 20 years, I have professed my devotion to de Gaulle"; "I haven't any special title to claim except that I have always been faithful to General de Gaulle"; "Member of the RPF, finally of the UNR, I am proud that I have never changed my opinion." It was not always easy to remain faithful, particularly during "the crossing of the desert," and those candidates who had been loyal did not forget to recall this: "Faithful to General de Gaulle in the most dramatic moments . . . you know, it is in these moments that Fidelity is precious. I have not betrayed . . ."; "In 1947, one of the first, he joined

---

[20] P. Converse and G. Dupeux: "Eisenhower et de Gaulle: les généraux devant l'opinion," *Revue Française de Science politique,* March, 1962, pp. 54–62.

[21] Roger Frey, speech at the Congrès national du mouvement des Républicains sociaux in November, 1955.

[22] Max Weber, "Politics as a Vocation," *op. cit.,* p. 79.

the RPF. In the difficult moments that followed, his fidelity to General de Gaulle never wavered."

There was no pity for opportunists: "In presenting myself before you in 1958, I said that many candidates are Gaullists because it is the style. But they were not yesterday, and they won't be tomorrow, because personal ambition alone will guide their line of conduct"; "The deputy that you elect must be a supporter of constructive politics and not a self-seeking chameleon"; "A majority of the deputies elected in 1958 under the flag of General de Gaulle changed their political mind, when there was no longer an imminent danger in Algeria. As the proverb says, 'the tempest past, the saint is forgotten.'" It was necessary to give General de Gaulle "a crew on which he can rely, a crew which won't sabotage the navigator."

The opposition parties insisted in their campaign on the danger for the Republic of a majority of "unconditional" Gaullists in Parliament. The candidates of the UNR did not defend themselves against this title. Above all, their program was to support without restriction "the liberator of the country," the "Savior of the Republic." Some were not even afraid to avow themselves "unconditionals": "Faithful at all times and unconditionally to the politics of General de Gaulle"; "Some ridicule the unconditional Gaullists, but let me tell you that I am one and I am proud of it. Fidelity in politics is a very rare virtue." Others turned against their adversaries with such formulas as "the unconditionals of Moscow," "the unconditionals of anti-Gaullism," or "the unconditionals of the old parties."

Self-devotion implied disinterest, "Serve in order to help de Gaulle reconstruct the country, not in order to serve oneself"; and also gratitude, "Acknowledgement is the memory of the heart." Often there was bitterness in the tone: "The ingratitude of those who had gone to Colombey as others go to Canossa, to ask General de Gaulle to protect them from the shock troops of the extreme Right."

De Gaulle appeared as the only man capable of dominating the situation: "Who besides de Gaulle could have saved the Republic at the time of the Algiers barricades, at the moment of the putsch?" "Only de Gaulle could have assumed this task, only de Gaulle could have accomplished it." He alone was able to "be at the helm of the ship of state during times of distress."

The man that is sought when all seems lost is the providential leader: "Without excessive passion . . . we recommended that you trust in the providential man." He led his people: "You have followed the thought of General de Gaulle." He symbolized "France adapting itself to the rhythm of the modern world." He embodied "the will of the French revival." He personified the nation: "This new face of France, it is General de Gaulle who has given it to her." He guided France "on the way to grandeur and prosperity." He would be the builder of a new Europe: "The genius of General de Gaulle will know how to shape it"; "The exceptional prestige of the chief of state in the world creates the indispensable conditions for the realization of a Europe in which France will play a preponderant role."

His gifts were superhuman. He was the sorcerer who magically dispels chaos: "The parties went to General de Gaulle in order to avoid civil war; he returned and stopped it with his bare hands"; "Three times he saved the Republic"; "Thanks to him the blood of our children no longer flows." This magician was irreplaceable: "The country will not find every five years a de Gaulle to put its house in order"; "De Gaulle must not be abandoned mid-way." What would happen if he left, if he abandoned the tiller? "We would fall back into the tragic difficulties of the past which have led us to the edge of the abyss"; "If he leaves, we will know new distress"; "We will know weakness, instability, interminable crises"; "We will return to anarchy"; "If he leaves, there will be a succession of miseries"; "There will be chaos, civil war and dictatorship."

Even his opponents were aware of the sacred character which was attributed to him by his followers. With the exception of the Communist Party, there were few criticisms of General de Gaulle in the electoral proclamations. Everyone had respect for him. A kind of taboo preserved the charismatic personality even in the camp of his adversaries. The Socialist leader, Gaston Defferre, saw de Gaulle as "a head of state with exceptional qualities, whose extraordinary stature dominated all French political men." Guy Mollet, a former Socialist prime minister, stressed, in his electoral addresses, that he "had been with de Gaulle in all the dramatic hours in which the Republic has been menaced: from 1940 to 1944; in 1958 against civil war, in April, 1961, against the attempted putsch. . . ." Paul Reynaud, the last prime minister of the Third Republic, recalled that none of the Republican parties "have ever asked for the resignation of General de Gaulle." Pleven, former prime minister, recognized "the contribution of the Fifth Republic and General de Gaulle. . . ." If the former Socialist minister Max Lejeune criticized Prime Minister Debré and the UNR for having "considerably reduced the rights of Parliament," he did not criticize de Gaulle. In a democracy, everyone reserves the right to oppose the head of state. This right, however, was not exercised without prudence: the opponents knew that a personal criticism of de Gaulle might be used against them.

CHARISMA, THE ELITE AND THE PEOPLE

> The chief of state has the majority of the masses behind him, but not that of the elite.
>
> Paul Reynaud[23]

By maintaining an equilibrium between institutions, constitutional systems usually satisfy the needs of the political community

---

[23] Paul Reynaud, declaration to the press. In his book, *Et après?* (Paris: Plon, 1964) it is stated, page 110: "If the majority of the masses are for him [General de Gaulle], the elites, that is to say the elected, are against him. Even most of the little country mayors do not favor him."

during normal periods. But in times of distress, of peril, the rules and routines of official institutions can become inefficient or inadequate. Men of exceptional talent are then required. Experience has shown that a leader with a charismatic vocation can only assert himself during a critical situation, a dramatic conjuncture.

General de Gaulle had twice taken the destiny of France into his hands, each time pushed by a grave national crisis. He left power in January, 1946, because, it was said, he could not stand "the yoke of the parties." In spite of the return of relatively normal conditions on the national and international scene, his strong personality excluded sharing the highest state responsibilities. The political elite, particularly the parliamentarians, once out of peril did not want to accord to any one man such extended powers. Historical precedents and democratic doctrines supported this refusal. The deputies were particularly unwilling to accept a reduction of their prerogatives. They could not put up with what they considered to be excessive authority. There had been a similar experience after World War I with Clemenceau, "the Father of the Victory."

Only when the rebellion exploded in Algiers, on May 13, 1958, only when the generals challenged the authority of the government, which was powerless to make them obey, only when military dictatorship was imminent and the shadow of a civil war loomed on the horizon, only then, in a climate of collective psychosis, did the deputies consent to call to power the man who appeared to be providential.

When the rebellion was smothered, the army neutralized, and the Algerian affair under control, no one explicitly spoke of a return to the old system. But disagreement between General de Gaulle and the majority of the political elite was not settled. If the project for the reform of the constitution had been submitted to the political elite (deputies, senators, mayors, municipal councillors) for approval, instead of to a referendum of universal suffrage, would it have been approved? It is not likely. Already the National Assembly had voted, in September, 1962, a motion of censure proposed by the leaders of the opposition and accepted by 280 votes against 200. One of the leaders had concluded with the apostrophe: "Mr. Prime Minister, go and say at the Elysée Palace that we are not so degenerate as to deny the Republic." In the Senate, where the opponents were the majority, president Monnerville had cried in alarm: "The constitution is violated, the people abused," and he had been acclaimed.

As for provincial leaders, most of them were men of the Fourth Republic and strongly attached to the old parties. In the local elections of 1962 the great majority of votes went to opponents, the UNR having received only 16% of the vote. The majority of the municipal councillors in the 456 towns of more than 9,000 inhabitants, who had been re-elected in March, 1959, were Communists, Socialists, Radicals, and other representatives of the left, or else Popular Republicans and moderate anti-Gaullists. Even in the small communes, the majority of municipal councillors belonged to the old parties. The Constitution of

1958 stipulated that the president of the republic had to be elected by about 76,000 deputies, senators, provincial representatives, mayors, municipal councillors, etc. If this clause of the constitution had been applied with de Gaulle as a candidate, it is very likely that he would not have been elected.

Besides, most of the public opinion leaders, writers, and journalists took positions against the government on the referendum. Most of the daily and weekly newspapers, in Paris and the provinces, supported the opposition (and their influence undoubtedly compensated to some degree for the state-owned radio and television which gave more time to government propaganda). For every Gaullist writer such as François Mauriac there were many writers such as Jules Romain who took positions against the projected Gaullist constitution. The same can be said of the other strata of the intellectual elite.[24]

On the contrary, the masses followed de Gaulle. His charismatic influence could be measured, in a way, by the difference between the results of the referendum and the results of the legislative elections. Schematically, and without taking into account abstentions, one can distinguish three categories of electors. The first voted "no" on the referendum and pronounced themselves at the legislative elections in favor of the opposition parties. The second voted "yes" at the referendum, and for the Gaullist candidates. It is the third category which interests us here. In spite of an attachment to other parties, these citizens were drawn by the charismatic influence behind de Gaulle. Certainly the voters of the right and center were more susceptible than those of the left, and women even more so. On the whole, the personal audience of General de Gaulle was twice as large as those of his UNR lieutenants.[25]

Whereas the deputies wanted to confine the president of the republic to the role of arbiter, the people recognized him as their leader. In 1877, the dissolution of Parliament had turned like a boomerang against Marshall MacMahon. In 1962, the motion of censure turned against the opposition. Such is the difference between an ordinary head of state and a charismatic power.

The force of the charismatic leader is nourished by the faith that the subjects have in his exceptional qualities, but he must renew his feats, as the prophet repeats miracles in order to prove that he is sent from heaven. In triumphing over successive difficulties, in re-establish-

---

[24] In the referendum of 1962, according to a survey by the IFOP, the majority of the electors with university training voted "no": 54%; the electors with average instruction: 36%; and those with only primary education, 32%. Cf. *Sondages*, 2, 1963, p. 93.

[25] In the United States, in 1952, the difference between the number of votes received by General Eisenhower and those accorded to the Republican candidates for the House of Representatives was 20%. See Warren E. Miller, "Presidential Coattails: a Study in Political Myth and Methodology," in *Public Opinion Quarterly*, 24 (4), 1955, pp. 353–368. See also the article by James C. Davies, "Charisma in the 1952 Campaign," in *American Political Science Review*, 48, December, 1954, pp. 1083–1102.

ing order as if by enchantment, he becomes less and less indispensable, irreplaceable, providential. Thus, the charismatic phenomenon obeys a dialectical law.

Put in power by exceptional circumstances, the charismatic leader accomplishes his mission by preparing for the return to a normal situation, one which does not require a charismatic personality. In a democratic regime the charismatic phenomenon cannot be permanent. After having personalized power, the leader institutionalizes it. He forges a new doctrine, he inspires a new school, he organizes a new order, inaugurating thereby a system of institutions which perpetuate his name. But the true charismatic leader does not have an immediate charismatic successor, at least in a democracy. At most, his heritage will be a new political class.

SAMUEL BRITTAN

An Elite Within an Elite

Within every European society, senior civil servants form a group of high status in the policy-making process, including many of the ablest of university graduates in the nation. The British civil service has traditionally had an especially high reputation; within it, the most important and able group is at the Treasury. Hence, Samuel Brittan's account of the work of the Treasury elite provides an excellent insight into the role of the civil service in government, a stratum often described as non-political but much more accurately described as non-partisan. As Brittan shows, the economic tasks delegated to such men are very relevant to the main lines of governmental decision-making. Yet the things that these officials do when they are "eliting" is very different from that rationality presupposed by power elite theories of politics.

The best introduction to the work of the Treasury is to glance at the Civil Service of which it is part.

The Fulton Committee, which reported in 1968, began its description with the words "Civil Servants work in support of Ministers in their public and parliamentary duties."[1] This statement is deliberately open-ended. The work involves preparing plans and advising on policy, drafting regulations or Parliamentary Answers and producing briefs for Ministerial speeches and conferences. There are motorways to be planned, weapons systems to be designed, and contracts to be placed. There are the less glamorous jobs such as collecting tax and running employment exchanges, which provide the public with its main impression of the Civil Service at work.

These examples could be multiplied over many pages. There is, however, an important distinction to be made at the outset. The Fulton Committee remarked: "Operating policies embedded in existing legislation and implementing policy decisions take up most of the time of most civil servants," While perfectly correct for most Government departments, this is much less true of the Treasury, most of whose work is concerned with policy of one kind or another. The boundary line between the two kinds of activity is, of course, a vague one. A Treasury official who recommends a change in credit restrictions to prevent consumer spending from diverging from the Chancellor's intentions is indeed suggesting new measures; but, from another point of view, he is trying to enforce an existing policy. The expression "economic management" indicates how blurred the distinction is.

Nevertheless, compared with other Ministries, the Treasury is clearly at the policy-making end of the spectrum. This characteristic became even more pronounced with the 1968 decision to hive off the responsibility for running the Civil Service on to a new department. . . .

The total size of the non-industrial Home Civil Service (excluding the Post Office) amounted to about 470,000 in 1968. The Treasury accounted for a very small fraction of this number; its total staff is likely to fluctuate around 1,000, depending on the precise allocation of functions between economic departments. By contrast the Ministry of Defence had 110,000 and the Health and Social Security Department had a staff of 70,000 members. The Inland Revenue had about 60,000, the Department of Employment nearly 30,000, the Ministry of Technology, Board of Trade, the Ministry of Public Building, the Customs and Excise, and the Home Office had in the neighbourhood of 20,000 each, while even the Ministry of Transport had about 8,000.

The smallness of the Treasury staff reflects, of course, its central policy-making functions and its relative lack of responsibility for detailed administration and casework. The figure of 1,000 quoted includes

---

From Samuel Brittan, *Steering the Economy*, pp. 3–4 and 23–35 (London: Martin Secker and Warburg, Ltd., 1969). Reprinted by permission.

[1] *The Civil Service*: Paras. 27 and 28, Cmnd 3638, 1968.

secretaries, messengers and typists. The number of officials in "administrative" and "economist" grades, on whom responsibility for policy largely falls, comes to around 150. . . .

The most highly regarded younger Treasury officials tend to circulate between the Treasury itself (where they will have done spells of duty in the Private Offices of Ministers and senior officials) and the very small staffs who make up the Cabinet Office and the Prime Minister's own band of personal secretaries. Mr. Harold Wilson made efforts to reduce the Treasury role in the staffing of both of these other offices; and it is not yet clear whether the new Civil Service Department will continue to be part of this inner circle. Nevertheless there is every sign that this nucleus, which in a very real sense has been the centre of the Government machine, will continue in being. The close personal contacts involved do have some use in short-circuiting a great deal of cumbersome and archaic protocol.

Despite these contacts, and a few personal friendships, Treasury officials do not see a great deal of each other socially in their own homes. A few senior officials, especially on the Overseas side, have to attend a large number of official lunches and cocktail parties, mostly to meet foreign visitors and Embassy representatives. But these officials are very much in a minority.

A handful of the more senior Treasury men do come together for more informal and private dinner discussions at one or two dining groups, chiefly the Political Economy Club and the Tuesday Club, where they are joined by a few selected academics and business figures and one or two very senior financial journalists.

More important nowadays are the links with the independent National Institute of Economic and Social Research. The contacts here are of a different kind, and perhaps not quite so near summit level. Clearly the Treasury and the National Institute will not always have identical views either on the economic situation or on the appropriate policies, but the occasional well-publicized disagreements give a false impression. The whole argument is conducted like an eighteenth-century battle, with the commanders on each side on the friendliest of terms. Both sides use forecasting techniques first developed in the Economic Section of the Treasury, and interchange of staff is frequent. Indeed the National Institute's widely quoted quarterly *Review* emerged as a direct result of the desire of Sir Robert Hall, the Government's Economic Adviser from 1947 to 1961, to have an independent check on the Treasury's forecasts. Allowing for all disagreements and frictions, the Treasury economists and the National Institute have more in common with each other than with any other group of laymen or economists in the whole of the country.

Another organization with which many Treasury men have connections is Nuffield College, Oxford, which specializes in politics, economics, and social studies. The Warden, D. N. Chester, used to be editor of a journal, *Public Administration*, to which many Civil Servants contribute, and its Fellows have included men such as Sir Donald Mac-

Dougall, now head of the Government Economic Service. Ministers and officials frequently come to dine at Nuffield, and Mr. Maudling, Mr. Heath, and Mr. Callaghan have all been Visiting Fellows.

Members of the Treasury, like members of any large organization, discuss some of their thorniest problems at informal and unrecorded meetings; but these are to prepare the ground for more formal sessions and for papers to be submitted to the Chancellor or to Cabinet Committees. Such papers try to harmonize conflicting views as far as possible, before submission to Ministers; and where different opinions have to be mentioned, no names are mentioned (with the possible exception of some of the senior economic advisers).

In the middle and lower reaches of the Treasury the only way to canvass an idea is to circulate a carefully drawn-up paper which will have to devote most of its space to a discussion of objections, snags, and loopholes; and the shrewder authors of Treasury papers will take careful verbal soundings before putting pen to paper to make sure the climate is right. The power of fashion is almost as great among officials and economists as it is among politicians. In any case anything that cuts across the work of several parts of the Department, still more if it affects other Ministries, is sure to present special difficulties. The atmosphere is one in which the highest marks are scored by those suggesting limited innovations which are simple to put into effect, and do not challenge the basic assumptions of existing policy.

Papers for Ministers are usually set out in a fairly simple, standardized form. If the subject is at all complex, there will often be a summary at the beginning, the adequacy of which may sometimes be open to question. Alternatively, the main paper will be kept short, and much of the information and analysis relegated to an appendix.

Decisions are usually taken around the long thin table in the Chancellor's room. Nearly all such meetings are with high-level officials. In the Foreign Office the expert on a particular region is present as a matter of course at highly secret meetings and personally interrogated by the Foreign Secretary. Most recent Chancellors, by contrast, have not met the real specialists who have actually written the papers discussed around their table.

One special Treasury characteristic is that it *normally deals with the outside world through other Departments,* which act as its eyes, ears, and arms. If Treasury economists want to find out how industry is feeling, they must enquire through the Board of Trade's regional officers; if they want to make a suggestion to the coal industry, they must go through the Minister of Power. Even chairmen of nationalized industries have been known to complain that they can only approach the Treasury through intermediate Ministries. Treasury officials are more likely (although the chances are not great) to visit Paris, Washington, or Brussels in the course of their official duties than Newcastle, Liverpool, or Glasgow. The Permanent Secretary and his immediate deputies might now and then see the leaders of the CBI, TUC or one or two very large firms; and there are more frequent encounters at business lunches and dinners. But most Treasury officials below this level see very little of industry or the City in the course of their professional duties.

As the Treasury is responsible for economy in Government spending *it feels bound to set a parsimonious example in its own activities.* The normal office amenities enjoyed by executives in any medium-sized commercial firm are often lacking. Principals writing papers on high state policy have no proper secretarial assistance, apart from the use of a common typing pool, and even have to correct their own carbons. The remarks in the Fulton Report . . . about the neglect of "working environment" apply with considerable force to the Treasury (and were also felt in the DEA at the end of the corridor). Anyone who has worked in the building will confirm Fulton's remarks about the shabby impression of many offices,[2] and the absurdity of senior officials "keeping their personal towels and soap in a drawer of their desk and walking the corridor with them."

More serious perhaps is a psychological atmosphere in which long hours of work, and a pressure of duties which give no adequate time for reflection, are seen as positive virtues. When Mr. Roy Jenkins became Chancellor he had the greatest difficulty in dissuading officials from working far into every evening as a matter of course.

In this respect Treasury practice reflects in extreme form more general conditions in the Administrative ranks of the Civil Service. One of the complaints that emerged most strongly from the Fulton survey of principals was excessive working hours, coupled with long journeys to and from work. Most of those interviewed were normally in the office from 9:45 a.m. to 7 p.m. and took home about five hours' work per week. But weeks of 55 hours in the office were not unusual; Private Secretaries expected to work a 60-hour week; and one Principal had worked 75 hours in Downing Street during the Rhodesian crisis. Many complained that they had little leisure time and that their circle of friends and interests had contracted. One wrote that the work was "not a job but a way of life. It demands most of one's time and energy and this pressure is kept up so that one can see people becoming paler editions of themselves." How far these rather worrying aspects reflect the disadvantages of metropolitan life for any ambitious young professional or businessman who cannot afford a house near his work, and how far they are a reflection on Whitehall, must be left for the reader to determine.

As far as the Treasury itself is concerned, its weaknesses arise directly from its virtues. One of them springs from the fact that it is a small organization of highly intelligent and sensitive individuals. As in most such organizations, members tend to be intensely loyal to each other and they will not query too deeply reports or recommendations which emanate from among their number, but have an instinctive reluctance to take seriously contributions from outside.

Added to this is a certain primness. Ministers below the rank of

---

[2] A stricture that applies with even greater force to journalism.

Chancellor are made to feel that they must show great diligence at the less attractive chores before they can be taken seriously. The Treasury insisted far longer than other Departments on the constitutional fiction that it had no policies of its own, but was simply there to advise Ministers. It takes the doctrine that everything is secret until it is publicly announced much more seriously than other Departments or overseas Governments with whom it may be negotiating, as a result of which the British case has too often been allowed to go by default (and British journalists have had to find out about it from overseas Governments). Not surprisingly the Treasury's public relations have been appalling — perhaps an endearing fault in the second half of the twentieth century.

MINISTERS AND OFFICIALS

The relationship betwen Ministers and Civil Servants, and the relative influences of the two groups on policy, is extremely difficult to state without distortion and it is a topic that Fulton avoided as far as possible. The view that Civil Servants are pliant mind-readers, executing policies which they have had no say in making, has always been absurd. The opposite view, that senior officials blatantly urge one single course of action on Minister after Minister is equally false, if stated in this crude form. The usual procedure, in the words of Sir Burke Trend, is to indicate "both the range of possible decisions open to Ministers and the probable consequences of adopting any one of these rather than any other." An American observer, Professor Samuelson, remarks that "it is all done in oh-so-subtle and pleasant a way as to make the Minister feel that he is enjoying Hegelian freedom — that delicious freedom which represents the cheerful recognition of necessity."[3]

The position, of course, varies with the personalities, and also the departments involved. The Treasury deals in issues which are both more technical and more abstract than those of any other Department. In this situation the dice are loaded against the conventional type of politician; and it is almost inevitable, as Lord Woolton remarked, that "the Civil Servants in the Treasury should have a very large, if not dominant say."[4]

One should not in this context overestimate the extent to which permanent Civil Servants are influenced by conscious views on policy. Like most other human beings, permanent officials want to get to the top in their jobs, and dislike avoidable complications and unpleasantness. They know they are judged not by their policy views, but by their ability to do a series of practical tasks, such as drafting reports on which committee members can agree, chairing difficult meetings, and above all else in getting documents "cleared" quickly with all the many interested parties.

[3] *Problems of the American Economy.*
[4] Lord Woolton: *Memoirs,* Cassell, 1959.

Much of this work is far more high-grade than the description would suggest, and calls for considerable finesse. Nevertheless, it is hardly surprising that shrewdness in matters of policy is only one of the qualities — and in itself neither sufficient nor necessary — required in a good Civil Servant. The sheer process of getting something out and agreed (or clearly disagreed) exerts a great pressure for orthodoxy and following precedent. The most valued man of all — as in other walks of life — is the one who can cope with a sudden flap.

The proliferation of new Ministries after the 1964 election, so far from being an improvement, in fact made committeemanship, appeasement, and face-saving even more important than they were before. A limited degree of informality and frank conversation on a personal basis is possible within departments before papers and positions are formalized, which is much more difficult when the same men are separated by a departmental wall.

One trouble is that officials at the top are too busy to think imaginatively about policy and are in fact dependent on policy papers originating in the middle or lower reaches of their departments. Yet all these lower officials are bound by the framework laid down from above. The net result is that policies change infrequently and slowly, and usually in response to, rather than in anticipation of, external disturbances. It is through institutional pressures of this kind, rather than ideological commitment, that characteristic Whitehall attitudes emerge.

Civil Servants are understandably irritated by any tendency to exaggerate their influence on Government decisions. They are conscious of the futility of a head-on clash with strongly held political beliefs and prejudices, and are conscious of the many occasions in which their advice has been rejected. On peripheral measures such as the abolition of Schedule "A" or the abolition of the business entertainment allowance, politicians are usually able to push through the measures which they think will please their supporters. On the major issues they may ignore the analysis presented to them and refuse to choose between alternatives. They may also prevaricate, or add verbal glosses; but the one thing they are rarely able to do, without expert assistance, is to question the analysis on which advice to them is based. Still less are they able to offer an intellectually credible alternative of their own. In the years preceding the 1967 devaluation, politicians interfered enough to prevent the Treasury policies from being carried out logically and consistently, but were not able to produce a substitute policy of their own.

It should be noted at this point that on many questions concerning foreign exchange markets and international finance, the Treasury has itself often been dependent on the Bank of England's expertise, and has stood in the same relation to it as Ministers normally do to departmental officials. Whereas the Treasury maintains the polite fiction of having no view other than the Chancellor's, this is not true of the Bank even in theory. In the last resort it has to obey his will; but, despite nationalization, it is an independent self-perpetuating entity with a distinctive viewpoint of its own. On issues like devaluation or exchange control it does not pretend to be impartial. It is professionally against them both.

The Bank of England has fewer inhibitions than Treasury officials about making its views public. The Governor's speeches occasionally criticize government policy with little attempt at concealment and frequently take sides in arguments over public policy. It is normally a good thing to bring policy arguments into the open instead of confining them to a closed circle. But the reason why the Governor of the Bank of England should have special privileges in this respect, denied to, say, the Permanent Secretaries of the Treasury and Board of Trade, have never been convincingly explained. The other unfortunate element is that Ministers often feel it imprudent to answer the Governor, fearing that a criticism of the Bank of England would damage sterling: it probably would.

The appointment of Ministers, especially Chancellors, who are at home in the arguments of their departments is, on balance, helpful. My own view is that there is no longer a place for a Chancellor who does not have a feeling for economic management. (The vague expression "feeling" has been deliberately used, to signify something more than the normal Front Bench politician can bring to the subject, but not necessarily amounting to academic or professional qualifications.)

Such appointments do not, however, solve all problems. A politician's life is utterly different from that of an academic specialist or official adviser; and he is unlikely to have the time or be in the mood for really rigorous study and analysis once he is in charge of a department. Considerable harm has resulted in some recent years from politicians in the highest positions who held exaggerated ideas of their own economic understanding.

REGULARIZING THE "IRREGULARS"

It was against this background that the recruitment of a few special advisers, to be appointed directly by Ministers, was widely recommended in the mid-1960's and endorsed by the Fulton Committee in 1968. A small number of such appointments had in fact been made by Conservative Ministers when they returned to office after 1951, but they did not become a pronounced feature of the Whitehall scene until Labour came back in 1964.

It was probably Mr. George Brown who first coined the term "irregular" for such appointees. In practice the distinction between "regular" and "irregular" was blurred at the edges. There were many temporary Civil Servants who had been "recommended" to the incoming Labour Ministers, but who might equally have been recruited by departments on purely professional grounds. Moreover, as time went on, some "irregulars" became established, whether technically or in spirit.

One argument for the "irregular" is that, as he does not owe his appointment to the Civil Service heads and his place in the hierarchy is less closely defined, he ought to be in a better position to question accepted departmental attitudes at the vital stage before policy alternatives are presented to Ministers. Outside critics, especially where the subject is technical rather than crudely political, have little opportunity of influencing policy in a specific way. Not having seen the confidential minutes of all meetings and not knowing the stage which departmental thinking has reached, they have little chance of making headway against a minister's official advisers. They can only hope to make an impact if they are taken into a department as "antibodies" and participate in the real discussions where policy is made. (Many of the established Civil Servants who were originally most opposed to the new recruits came to regard them as a stimulating influence.)

The whole concept of "irregular" advisers, who were specially prominent in the economic field, came under a cloud as a result of the Labour Government's disappointing economic performance in its first few years of office. The argument about who was really to blame is never likely to be resolved. . . . Whatever one's views on this historical episode, the very nature of much Civil Service work puts the "irregular" at a disadvantage. The scarcest commodity in Whitehall is information, and like all scarce commodities it is not freely exchanged. It is quite wrong to think that someone in another department (or even always in one's own) will give freely of his knowledge. Therefore those best able to find out what is really going on are off to a head start; and these are usually the established professionals.

Despite their pre-Fulton title, Administrative Civil Servants in the central policy-making departments such as the Treasury are not, on the whole, responsible for the detailed execution of policy. For this they are dependent on the men-on-the-ground in departments such as the Inland Revenue, Customs and Excise, Board of Trade, or Department of Social Security (or in a different category, the Bank of England). The really successful policy-making Civil Servant is the one with the knack of getting these less glamorous departments to produce ideas of their own, or to envisage in outline schemes which fit the long-established working habits of these departments. Such qualities may be regarded as aspects of the more obvious, but all-important, knack of knowing what buttons to press to make things happen in Whitehall. Clearly these qualities are by their nature more likely to be found among regular Civil Servants.

While "irregulars" inevitably run with leaden boots in any race against professionals, the Labour Government unnecessarily increased their handicaps in 1964 by putting the majority of them in newly created departments outside the traditional centres of power. Nearly all the industrial advisers seconded from leading management positions went initially to the Department of Economic Affairs. Not a single one was taken into the Treasury. The same applied to the Foreign Office, which, even under Mr. George Brown, was quite untainted by "irregulars."

Another difficulty about using "irregulars" profitably is that they are on the whole a phenomenon of newly elected Governments (or very occasionally new Ministers). This timing is a misfortune. For "irregulars" come in when they and their Ministers are very "green." They would be more useful several years later when Ministers have become part of the machine and their ideas have dried up. But that is just when lines of policy have already been established, when Ministers have discovered the wavelengths on which career Civil Servants work, and least feel the need for outside stimulation.

The really questionable assumption once made by reformist literature (including the first edition of this study) was that it would be desirable to strengthen the influence of politicians against officials. But it really is doubtful if the day-to-day horizons and public relations obsessions of most Ministers in any Administration are any more worthy of reinforcement than the intellectual conservatism of senior officials. Indeed in some ways the greatest criticism of conventional Civil Servants is that they let Ministers pursue too many ill-considered ideas, and do not sufficiently push forward unpalatable truths. Yet at the same time Ministers are terribly in the hands of the Civil Servants for the analysis of problems, and the enumeration of practical policy alternatives. Such is the inwardness of the system that both these statements can be simultaneously true. Perhaps at the root of it all is the view of the Civil Servant as a Court eunuch who has his own special kind of influence but must not presume to argue with his Ministerial overlord on equal terms.

The insulating mechanism is strengthened by the fact that a large number of the briefs put up to Ministers are not advice on matters of policy at all, but defensive briefs for use in speeches, meetings, negotiations, and even social occasions where Ministers may come under fire. The job of any Civil Servant, regular or irregular, in writing such briefs is, like that of a barrister, to put up the best case he can for the client, whether he believes it himself or not — and with imagination it is possible to put up a good brief for almost any policy under the sun. The constant exposure of Ministers to briefs of this kind encourages self-delusion, both on the strength of their case and on the degree of expert support it commands.

Despite all these weaknesses, temporary personal advisers appointed by Ministers are on balance desirable as the only practicable way of bringing fresh air into Whitehall in quantities or packages which have not been selected by the Civil Service itself. Fulton recommends that such appointments should be "regularized" on the clear assumption that they are temporary and that the person concerned has no expectation of remaining when there is a change of Minister. This is reasonable enough; but with the rate of Ministerial turnover of the 1960's, it may well be difficult to get good people to interrupt existing careers to take up such appointments.

Fulton, however, made the wrong concession to traditional opinion in dismissing the idea that Ministers should be served by a small personal *cabinet* on the French model. The virtue of such *cabinets*, which Fulton did not discuss at all, was that they would contain a mixture of regular and temporary officials, in proportions which would vary with the personality of the Minister. Such *cabinets*, apart from providing useful policy forums for the Minister, could widen the horizons of both types of official. The real knowledge about what is wrong with existing policies or institutions, and the most practical way of changing them, is often to be found not among outside academics but among the Young Turks within Departments. Ministerial *cabinets* might provide them with an outlet for their energies (even if the selection were in the nature of a lottery) which they lack under a strictly hierarchical system. More generally, they would provide some admittedly limited way of promoting younger officials to policy-making positions and helping them avoid the dead hand of the seniority system.

A permanent Civil Servant who became too closely identified with the *cabinet* of one Minister, might, it is true, find himself in an embarrassing position after a marked change of personality or political direction in his department. But such difficulties are not insuperable. There are posts, both in his own and other departments, which would be less politically sensitive, to which he could be transferred. More fundamentally, an ambitious and energetic official who wants to by-pass some of the rungs in the normal career ladder and take personal policy initiatives cannot expect to enjoy the opportunities without running the risks.[5]

THE SECRECY OBSESSION

One Whitehall characteristic not so far discussed, but far and away the most unattractive, is the *obsession with secrecy*. This is partly due to the Official Secrets Act, which makes it a criminal offence for a Civil Servant to communicate any note, document, or information to any unauthorized person. But it is also rooted in the doctrine that Ministers alone are responsible for policy and that the advice given to them is on a par with the secrets of the confessional.

For many years the economic forecasts which lay behind the budget and other acts of economic intervention were closely guarded secrets. Mr. Roy Jenkins's decision to publish in the 1968 Financial Statement a carefully abbreviated version was rightly hailed as a major step forward. But what appeared was only the tip of the iceberg. The analysis, argument, and differences of view which lay behind the figures presented were concealed; and so was the continuing re-examination of the outlook that goes on between the Budgets. Regular publication of the five-year forward projection of public expenditure, which the Treasury rolls forward annually, began in 1969, but not in such a way that Parliament could cost alternative options.

It is sometimes argued that certain economic predictions, for ex-

---

[5] A somewhat fuller discussion of the lessons of the post-1964 "irregulars" can be found in my chapter of that title in *Policy-Making in Britain*, edited by Richard Rose (New York: Free Press, 1969).

ample, ones that indicate a worsening of the balance of payments, would affect foreign confidence adversely. But if Britain is heading for a payments deficit, there will be no dearth of gloomy private forecasts for holders of sterling to read. By keeping silent, Treasury officials may keep British MP's in the dark. They will not reassure those who matter in New York, Paris, Frankfurt, Zürich, or the City of London. Even if they do succeed in glossing over the facts for a while, the public is likely to lose rather than gain from any increase in the ability of Ministers to postpone decisions.

Another objection is that a realistic prediction might differ from the Government's professed aims. Forecast wage increases might be higher than Ministers have publicly stated to be desirable. The fallacy behind such arguments is the belief that silence about a disagreeable prospect will help to change it.

The Fulton Committee agreed that "the administrative process is surrounded by too much secrecy." It drew attention to the Swedish system under which the files of any administrative office are open to the Press and public unless declared secret on grounds of military security, good international relations, or protection of individuals. Before policy is formulated in Sweden, a committee of inquiry is normally set up and its results published. This model could clearly not apply to some matters, for example a decision on Bank Rate. But the spirit behind the two systems is very different. Here again Fulton felt that it had to limit itself here to suggesting another inquiry.

The obsession with secrecy is harmful not only because it lowers the standard of public discussion, and prevents the real arguments which move Whitehall from being brought out into the open. Even more important is the creation of an inquisition atmosphere in the Civil Service itself. Peter Jenkins once explained in *The Guardian* that when a newspaper reporter happens to hit the mark, a "leak procedure" is usually set in motion in which all officials with access to the information are interrogated directly, or through their superiors, on "When did you last see your father?" lines. This practice has applied particularly to the central economic policy departments; and in the (frequent) periods of pathological Ministerial preoccupation with security these have been an almost weekly occurrence.

Sensitivity to so-called "leaks" became even greater after the change of Government in 1964. What made the whole procedure particularly intolerable was that the leaks often originated from Ministers, or others in a relatively invulnerable position; and the leak procedure had all the appearance of a search for scapegoats.

The result is a working atmosphere in which a disproportionate amount of time is spent making sure one's door is locked, that nothing is left on one's desk, and that there is nothing in the wastepaper basket which a literal-minded security officer will not report as an offence. Despite frequent admonitions not to overclassify papers, the habit is endemic, at least in the economic policy departments. Very often a "secret" classification on a paper is no more than a way of drawing attention to its importance; and a draft with no security marking has little chance of being taken seriously. It becomes more important to keep one's thoughts on policy confidential than to get them right.

Here is one of the main roots of the monastic isolation so often alleged of departments such as the Treasury. Whatever abstract encouragement may be given to the idea of the exchange of ideas with outsiders is more than offset by the need to avoid suspicion of "having said too much." This is best done by minimizing contacts. Such a system puts a premium on the type of official who is happy never to discuss his work once he has left the office, who makes a rigid division between his professional and personal life, and whose intellectual interests are totally divorced from his main work. The system encourages not versatility, but compartmentalization, which is something different. An example was the period *after* the 1967 devaluation, when public ignorance and suspicion of Government economic strategy was at its height; and where officials who could have helped to improve understanding were reduced to silence, lest they be accused of leaking some trivial piece of Whitehall guesswork.

In some areas of policy (of which the Budget is only the most notorious example) secrecy limits the exchange of information not only with the outside world but within departments. To safeguard security the smallest possible number of Civil Servants, whether regular or irregular, are brought in on many of the really key decisions; and a large number of officials, whose own work might have had a useful contribution to make to the discussion, are presented with a *fait accompli* arrived at during high-level huddles.

THE CRUCIAL ISSUES

Some of the grosser absurdities could be removed by the exercise of a sense of proportion and a sense of humour, and less devotion to the conspiracy theory of history by political leaders. Nevertheless, any major move towards more open government would soon come up against three constitutional conventions: the anonymity of Civil Servants, Ministerial responsibility, and collective Cabinet responsibility. It is arguable that all three need drastic modification.

The importance of official advice to Ministers remaining in all circumstances confidential is more often asserted than convincingly justified. Very often it is just an accident whether an outside committee, which publishes its report, or an interdepartmental committee, which does not, is appointed to advise a Minister. The traditional argument for confidential reports was that officials could only give of their best if they could speak frankly and without fear of public attack. It is equally arguable that the quality of advice would improve if officials had more often to defend it against expert outside criticism, whether in Parliamentary committees or more generally. Indeed some Civil Servants would positively welcome a chance to explain work which is so often buried from view, bowdlerized in Ministerial statements, or subject to ill-informed public criticism. The spirited counterattack by some of the Treasury economic forecasters during the Select Committee Enquiry of 1966–67 was a foretaste of what could happen

There must obviously be some limits to open government; it is not suggested that the Budget Committee should sit in public. But it is very doubtful if the right dividing line is between factual analysis and the policy advice which flows from it. Attempts to publish pieces of Whitehall analysis, with all hint of policy recommendation carefully removed, usually bear a castrated and intellectually impoverished look.

The real obstacle to more open processes often comes from Ministers, anxious to preserve the myth that all policy originates with them, and that only they can explain in public what their departments are doing. This myth becomes every day more difficult to maintain. With the proliferation of international and national economic organizations, officials are having to appear in public (or semi-public) more and more; and it becomes increasingly apparent that what they say is a mixture of their own professional analysis and the need to put the best face on Ministerial policy. The old relationship between Ministers and officials is disintegrating, but new principles of public accountability have still to be invented.

The most deeply rooted obstacle of all to more open Government probably arises from taking too seriously the convention of a plural executive, operating on the principle of collective responsibility. This convention also lies, incidentally, behind the excessive role of interdepartmental committees, and the difficulty of making one man clearly responsible for a project. For just as no Minister has jurisdiction over any other Minister, no official in one department can overrule an official in another; and in the last resort unresolved differences have to go right up to the Cabinet, or one of its Committees. If a greater amount of the analysis and advice coming to Ministers were published, it would soon become apparent — as it does in the USA — that more than one view exists inside the Government and that some Ministers have in the end prevailed over others.

CHAPTER
EIGHT

Centers of Power

In this century, constitutional forms of government have changed much more, and changed much more violently, than the structure of societies. Since the beginning of the century, Germany has been governed by an Imperial Kaiser, the Weimar Republic, Hitler's Reich, four different occupation armies and, since 1949, by two regimes, the West German Federal Republic, and, in East Germany, the Communist-run German Democratic Republic (the DDR, i.e., *Deutsche Demokratische Republik*). France has been governed by three Republics, one lasting from 1875 to 1940, another from 1945 to 1958, and a third from 1958. Between the third and fourth Republics there was an uneasy period of interim rule by German occupation forces, a pro-German anti-democratic government at Vichy, and resistance and liberation armies. Italy has gone from a constitutional monarchy, through Fascism and military occupation by Germans and Allies, to a republican and democratic form of government. Of the four major European powers, only Britain's regime has shown continuity throughout this century. But even Britain suffered a civil war from 1916 to 1921, leading to an independent Irish Republic, removing about one-twelfth of the United Kingdom's population.

These upheavals have important implications for contemporary social science theory: they demonstrate that the structure and process of government cannot be deduced or predicted in any kind of simple fashion from a study of social structure.

In Europe, as elsewhere, men who occupy strategic positions as civil servants and in the military, as well as elected office-holders, will always be important, especially when government activities penetrate so greatly into social affairs. European governments enjoy the advantage that the powers of the state have traditionally been regarded as great or without limitations. In the monarchical societies that preceded them, the king was not subjected to the limitations written into the American federal constitution. The monarch, rather than the people, was the source of sovereignty.

The study of political institutions in European societies was long handicapped by the dominance of lawyers and of legalistic interpretations of the governmental process. Moreover, even in Britain, where libertarian values are strong, there has long been a belief that the activities of the government should not be subjected to intense public and scholarly scrutiny, but should be treated discreetly. This contrasts greatly with the philosophy of "government in a goldfish bowl" that can be found in Washington. Hence, it is hardly surprising that many European social scientists have concentrated their attention upon such extra-governmental phenomena as parties, elections, and voting behavior.

Some of the difficulties of studying the processes of government are theoretical difficulties, shared with American social scientists. It is very easy to ask but very hard to answer the simple question: What do governments do? A liberal democrat might suggest that the principal function of government is to promote the general welfare of its people; a conservative might emphasize the importance of government maintaining the social status quo; and a radical could argue that governments ought to overturn the existing social order. If one retreats from such openly value-laden disputes to the more abstract language of social science, there is still no easy answer. Social scientists have ascribed a wide variety of functions to government. Some of these functions, such as maintaining a social equilibrium, are very general and abstract, whereas others, such as providing welfare benefits, are very precise. There is no agreed scholarly answer.

The recovery and growth of European economies in the past two decades, combined with growing American interest in sophisticated forms of public management of the economy, has emphasized the role of government as a director or participant in a more or less planned economy. The greatest attention has been given to the apparent success of French planning procedures, though there has been no general agreement about the extent to which particular institutional forms have caused desirable consequences. The German "economic miracle," while claimed as a victory for free enterprise, has also shown the importance of government undertaking the classical liberal task of maintaining a sound, stable currency. In Italy, the country's relative poverty by European standards, especially in the South, has faced the government with problems not entirely different from those confronting the so-called developing nations of Africa and Asia. The growth in prosperity and in productive capacity in the countries of the European Common Market in the 1950's and early 1960's gave the British a special interest in this subject when considering how they could compete or join with their neighbors. The concern intensified as the British pound came increasingly under pressure, leading up to devaluation in November, 1967.

Important as economic issues are — to ordinary people, as well as to economists and administrators — they are not the most important activities of government. A liberal would probably say that the most important activity of government is to secure the safety and liberty of the individual citizen against internal coercion as well as against external armies. A conservative would say that the most important task of government is to ensure its own survival — even at the price of repressing a substantial portion of its people. The twin themes of liberty and order are not necessarily in conflict, as modern English political history reminds us. But England in this, as in many other things, is a deviant case.

Ultimately, the study of government cannot be divorced from the study of the society that is to be governed. In the study of voting, emphasis falls primarily on extragovernmental concerns, just as in the study of foreign policy, emphasis is primarily upon activities within the institutions of government. Many of the most important general questions of politics concern the relationships between governors and governed. This is true when the process of government is visualized as an efficient mechanism for the feedback of popular demands and public policy. It is even more true, as the concluding article in this reader demonstrates, when the ties that bind government and governed break, and a polity approaches anarchy, as happened in France for a short time in May, 1968.

Bibliography

General discussions of the nature of government have been a staple of political philosophy since the time of Plato and Aristotle. Contemporary discussions by social scientists include: Gabriel Almond and B. Powell, *Comparative Politics* (Boston: Little, Brown, 1966); Robert Dahl, *Modern Political Analysis* (Englewood Cliffs, N.J.: Prentice-Hall, 1963); Robert Dahl and C. E. Lindblom, *Politics, Economics and Welfare* (New York: Harper, 1953); Karl W. Deutsch, *The Nerves of Government* (New York: Free Press, 1966 edition); David Easton, *A Systems Analysis of Political Life* (New York: Wiley, 1965); and Samuel P. Huntington, *Political Order in Changing Societies* (New Haven: Yale University Press, 1968). The viewpoint of one of the editors is found in Richard Rose, *People in Politics*, Chs. 7–8.

In all European democracies, with the exception of the French Fifth Republic, parliament is considered by the constitution as the first center of power. In reality, of course, the situation is much more complex, but it is understandable that parliamentary institutions have, in a sense, a priority in political science research. Two books on the British Parliament concentrate on the modest role of backbenchers in the House of Commons: S. E. Finer, H. B. Berrington, and D. J. Bartholomew, *Backbench Opinion in the House of Commons, 1955–59* (London and New York: Pergamon Press, 1961); and Peter G. Richards, *Honourable Members: A Study of the British Backbencher* (London: Faber & Faber, 1959). The British legislative process is examined in Bernard Crick, *The Reform of Parliament* (London: Weidenfeld & Nicholson, 1965), and in D. N. Chester and N. Bowring, *Questions in the House of Commons* (Oxford: Clarendon Press, 1962).

For the functioning of the French parliament during the Fourth Republic, the book by Philip M. Williams, *Crisis and Compromise* (London: Longmans, 1964), is a monument. See also a much shorter book by the same author, *The French Parliament, 1958—1967* (London:

Allen and Unwin, 1968). Two American political scientists, both from the University of Chicago, have analyzed the same problems and aspects of French politics during the Fourth Republic, particularly the causes of ministerial instability and the behavior of the parliamentarians. Their approaches and methods are contrasting: sophisticated factorial analysis by Duncan MacRae, Jr., *Parliament, Parties, and Society in France, 1946–1958* (New York: St. Martin's Press, 1967), against impressionistic but intelligent content analysis by Nathan Leites, *On the Game of Politics in France* (Stanford University Press, 1959). MacRae's book is a more important contribution on methodology, particularly applied to legislative behavior, than to the understanding of French politics by the large community of political scientists; it is a highly sophisticated book meant for methodologists and for francophile political scientists. Leites's book can be read by everyone, but his conclusions have so far been accepted by few, at least in France.

For lawmaking in Germany, the most comprehensive study is Gerhard Loewenberg, *Parliament in the German Political System* (Ithaca: Cornell University Press, 1967).

On the role and functioning of the Italian parliament, there is no systematic book in English. The chapter by Samuel H. Barnes on Italy, in Robert A. Dahl, editor, *Political Oppositions in Western Democracies* (New Haven: Yale University Press, 1966), is a convenient introduction, as is J. C. Adams and P. Barile, *The Government of Republican Italy* (Boston: Houghton Mifflin, 1966).

The policy of planning is one of the newest and most important aspects of the political process, at least in France and Italy. See Pierre Bauchet, *Economic Planning: The French Experience* (New York: Praeger, 1964); M. Einaudi, M. Byé, and E. Rossi, *Nationalization in France and Italy* (Ithaca: Cornell University Press, 1955); W. Friedmann, editor, *The Public Corporation: A Comparative Symposium* (London: Stevens, 1954).

Surveys of particular relevance here include *Decisions and Decision-Makers in the Modern State* (Paris: UNESCO, 1967); Brian Chapman, *The Profession of Government* (London: Allen & Unwin, 1959); and Andrew Shonfield, *Modern Capitalism* (London: Oxford University Press, 1965). Detailed national bibliographies concerning government may be found in Richard Rose, editor, *Policy-Making in Britain* (New York: Free Press, 1969); and in William G. Andrews, editor, *European Political Institutions: A Comparative Government Reader* (Princeton: D. Van Nostrand, 1966), which contains a series of official documents, important speeches by political leaders, and articles by various scholars.

ALFRED GROSSER

The Evolution of European Parliaments

Institutionally, all democratic governments in Europe differ from the American form of government, for they are governed through parliamentary institutions. Except in the Fifth French Republic, the president or reigning monarch is a symbolic but politically unimportant chief of state. Within Europe there are different forms of parliamentary government, for institutions are not independent of party systems, federalist or revolutionary pressures, and cultural and social divisions. In a survey of European parliaments, Alfred Grosser indicates that the one thing common to all countries today is a decline in the significance of this classical instrument of representative and responsible government.

Within the constitutional systems the place of parliament depends on how popular sovereignty is exercised. All the constitutions affirm forcefully that sovereignty lies in the people, without giving this affirmation a really precise meaning. When we read in the fundamental law of Bonn (Article 20, Number 2), "All power comes from the people, who exercise it through election and through the intermediary organs of legislative power, executive power and judicial power," we see at once that the parliament in West Germany has a lesser place than under the Fourth Republic in France. Did not Article 3 of the Constitution of 1946 say, "National sovereignty belongs to the French people . . . the people exercise it in constitutional matters through the votes of their representatives and through referenda. In all other matters, they exercise it through their deputies in the National Assembly"?

The order of chapters or subdivisions in the various European con-

Abridged from Alfred Grosser, "The Evolution of European Parliaments," *Daedalus*, 93, 1, 1964, pp. 153–178. Reprinted by permission of *Daedalus*, Journal of the American Academy of Arts and Sciences.

stitutions is very significant in this respect. In Italy the order is as follows: I Parliament, II the President of the Republic, III the Cabinet, IV the Judiciary, V Regions, Provinces, Communes. In the Fourth Republic in France: I Sovereignty, II Parliament, III Economic Council, IV Diplomatic Treaties, V the President of the Republic, VI the Council of Ministers. In the Fifth Republic: I Sovereignty, II the President of the Republic, III the Cabinet, IV Parliament. The order of subdivisions in the West German Constitution is Bund and Länder, Bundestag, Bundesrat, the Federal President, the Federal Government. These comparative lists show us the relative importance of the different aspects of government as the framers of the constitutions conceived them. We shall have to consider whether they correspond to reality. In any case two observations should be made.

First, the nature of the national legislature is a function of the structure of the state, centralized or federal. The German bicameral system is justified in ways similar to bicameralism in the United States or Switzerland. The sovereignty of the people is supposed to express itself through two channels because the national collectivity rests on a double notion of equality and each must find its own means of expression. There is the equality between the citizens and there is the equality (or near equality) of the territorial collectivities. In the House of Representatives the idea of equality between American citizens is expressed, while the Senate expresses equality between states, even though they are very unequal in population. The composition of the Italian Senate reflects a much less clear-cut situation in this respect. In France, the way in which the Senate is chosen strengthens the small communes at the expense of the large ones. It does not appear to us certain that the utility of this double representation will in the long run be sufficient to justify the existence of a separate legislative chamber. . . .

The second necessary observation is that what is meant by parliamentary representation is not defined in the constitutions. . . . The notion of the parliament as the real center of political life, with citizen-spectators and power to govern delegated by the representative assembly, already disputable at the time, is today in the process of disappearing because of the changed relations between parliament and administration that we shall analyze subsequently — and because of recent social changes. As it is not possible here to present a kind of sociology of Europe serving as a basis for institutional change, I shall confine myself to one example, which, in my opinion, is particularly important because it relates to one of the most important functions of parliament — even if this function is not spelled out in the text of the constitution — to wit, parliament's role as a transmission-belt of political information.

How does an administration proceed when it wants to inform the citizens about policy or has important news to communicate? The tradition of the parliamentary regimes gives a clear answer: a representative of the cabinet makes a statement in parliament or answers questions from the members. Subsequently the information is promulgated in two ways: the press reports the parliamentary sessions and the members, returned to their constituencies, explain to important groups and individuals how the administration statements should be interpreted.

Today this model no longer holds. This is because, first, the powerful organization of the parties often leads the administration to use the channel of the majority party, and second, and above all, because the development of the mass media (everywhere to some extent) has brought about a diminution of the role of parliament both as the representative of public opinion and as the intermediary between administration and the citizens. Radio and television permit direct contact between the governing and the governed that calls into question the very essence of representative democracy. As in other matters, General de Gaulle has simply carried to extremes a tendency discernible almost everywhere. . . .

In the other direction, of the government informing itself on the state of opinion, the situation is slightly different. Here there are two rivals to the legislatures as intermediaries or representatives, the press and the public opinion polls. Government depends less and less on members of parliament for information about the state of public opinion. Instead, it increasingly depends on the press, and unfortunately, in my opinion, on polls, because passive citizens, who must be sought out and then interrogated, are thus equated with active citizens who show their positions. The government uses the opinion polls to know how to conduct itself, what to say and also how to act. At the same time, especially in countries with single-member constituencies, the deputy often succeeds in maintaining his own role because he is in a position to be in contact with a psychological reality that often is not accessible to the executive branch, the other source of official information.

THE PROBLEM OF THE TRIANGLE

In classic textbooks political regimes were largely defined in terms of relations between the executive and the legislative powers, between parliament and administration. This model almost completely neglected the existence and the role of parties. The first question to ask is, "Does a dominant party exist?" The second is, "If so, what is the relation between the three vertices of a triangle formed by administration — party — parliamentary group?" A few examples will show better than theoretical considerations why this triangular problem always underlies what we will have to say about the relations between parliament and administration, and between parliament and the parties.

Can one still speak of a separation of powers in Great Britain when the parliamentary majority and the cabinet — or Government, as the British call it — both arise from the same party? It is useful to make some distinctions: when the Conservatives are in power the cabinet dominates both the parliamentary group and the party; when the Labourites are in power the influence of the party on the Government is stronger, while the parliamentary group retains important prerogatives, not the least of which is the power to choose the head of the party, as in the recent election of Harold Wilson to succeed Hugh Gaitskell. The head of the party is at the same time prime minister or shadow-prime minister, which is not always the case with the Conservatives, where the prime minister is not formally designated by the party but by the Queen, as in the case of the choice of Macmillan over Butler. . . .

In the Fifth French Republic the dominant party has a feeble structure, but the parliamentary group lacks independence because the real head of the executive and the party are the opposite of what they are elsewhere: while Messrs. Kennedy, Adenauer, Macmillan and Khrushchev owe their positions respectively to the victory of the Democrats, Christian Democrats, Conservatives and Communists, whatever may be their personal merits or popularity, the Union pour la Nouvelle République and its leaders owe their political existence to General de Gaulle. Thus we see why we must keep the problem of the triangle in mind even when we are referring to the traditional functions of the various legislatures.

LEGISLATION AND THE BUDGET. The legislature makes laws; the executive carries out the laws. Reality does not any longer correspond at all to this official statement. Everywhere the legislative initiative has passed into the hands of the administrations. The legislatures sometimes amend, rarely reject, usually ratify. Their members continue, indeed, to call themselves collectively "the Legislative Power" in the law books, but in most cases they merely participate in a procedure of registration. Here, for example, is the summary of twelve years' legislation in Bonn:

	1949–1953 Bills submitted	1949–1953 Number enacted	1953–1957 Bills submitted	1953–1957 Number enacted	1957–1961 Bills submitted	1957–1961 Number enacted
By the Cabinet	472	392	446	368	401	348
By the Bundestag	301	141	414	132	207	74
By the Bundesrat	32	12	17	7	5	2

The reality is both a little less and much more serious, from the point of view of parliament, than the figures suggest. On the one hand, the federal organization of the German state does after all permit the Landtage to play a certain legislative role, although even at the level of the Land, the administration predominates. On the other hand, the administration can bypass the assemblies to a considerable extent by issuing directives. As in other spheres, the Fifth French Republic has pushed to extreme limits a tendency that is general but less pronounced elsewhere. While tradition reserves to parliament whatever is not specifically designated to the administration, the Constitution of 1958 describes the domain of the law in a limiting way, after having stipulated that "laws are voted by Parliament."

Why is the legislative function of the parliaments in decline? There seem to me three competing ways of explaining this phenomenon:

1. The nature of the law has changed. With rare exceptions, laws, which used to be few, formerly served to make more explicit the rights and duties of citizens or the organization of society, conceived as a stable whole. Civil law, criminal law and administrative law belonged in the legislative assemblies. The administration was there to direct, to administer. Except in the international sphere, did the administration even need to have a policy? It is not by chance that the constitutions framed since World War II no longer define the administration as an executive but as an initiator of policy. Administrative action is destined to transform society, and the law is the privileged instrument of this transformation, but if the legislative assembly expresses its adherence to a policy in instituting an administration, does not the administration have the right to claim the means to carry out the policy? Or in other words to demand that laws be passed to provide the means?

2. The epoch of the "representative of the people" is largely over. The existence of organized parties, whenever one of them is in a dominant situation, involves a relative dispossession of the members of the legislature. Should the members of a majority party in a parliament criticize an administration proposition — or should they, on the contrary, defend it against opposition attacks?

3. The technical complexity of economic and social legislation is such that the administration, using its bureaucracy and its experts, is able to impose it on the legislature. It is no longer enough, as in the nineteenth century, to be a good speaker and well versed in the law to be an impressive legislator. We shall see why this point is even less applicable to the United States than the previous points.

Even if parliamentary resistance were strong, the administrations often have effective means of constraint at their disposal. The vote of confidence is to parliamentary life what the referendum is to the political life of the French Fifth Republic. It might be phrased, "Even if you do not like this particular text, vote yes, or you will oblige me to resign, which you do not want either."

The Constitution of 1958 has brought to fruition an inheritance from its two predecessors. In France, as it does still in the other countries, it used to require a positive vote to enact a law. Today, all that is needed is for the prime minister to indicate that the administration is committed to a given text. "In such a case," says Article 49, "the text is considered as enacted unless a motion of censure . . . is passed." This is how, for example, the nuclear striking force, an essential element in French foreign policy, came into being without being approved by a parliamentary majority. At the end of the parliamentary session where the motion of censure was being voted upon, the chairman said:

> Here is the result of the vote on the motion of censure. Two hundred and seventy-seven votes are required for adoption.
>
> For adoption, 214 (applause on the Right and Extreme Left).

Since the necessary majority was not reached, the motion of censure is not adopted (applause on Left and Center).

As a result, the law establishing the program for certain military installations is considered to be adopted. . . .

The Magna Carta imposed on King John in 1215 said, "No scutage nor aid shall be established in our kingdom without the consent of the common council of our Kingdom." Since then the power of the purse, or exclusive right to tax, has constituted an essential prerogative of parliament. But is this not also more a matter of form than of substance? There are, in any case, several phenomena which suggest that this is so.

1. National budgets have become monstrously complex. What member of a legislature, in spite of simplified versions prepared to help him, can find his way in such a jungle of chapters and provisions? Furthermore, at a certain level of importance, figures lose their meaning. The famous meeting of an administrative council described by Parkinson could be reproduced in a parliamentary assembly. At this meeting it was decided to authorize fantastic expenditure for the construction of an atomic reactor, but the cost of installing a bicycle rack was considered too high. In the same way, the average deputy will dispute the subsidy accorded to a small private association but will allow tremendous military expenses to pass without much discussion.

2. The limitation of the budget to one year and the annual debates on the budget do not fit the conditions necessary for good policy or efficient administration. In practice, the basic funds are granted once and for all and are not later called into question. Other items, especially in countries which tend to long-range planning, cannot safely be changed in less than several years. What a relief it would be for the President of the United States — and for the countries receiving United States aid — if foreign aid could be granted clearly and with carefully worked out detail for a period of four or five years. Things are moving in this direction. In Europe, programs for disposition of land, industrial development and the transformation of agriculture make it increasingly necessary for budgetary commitments to be made for longer periods.

3. Pressures put on members of legislatures do not cause them to call into question the main lines of the budget, but they do cause them to quarrel among themselves over particular points. Pressure groups bring pressure either on the government or on party leaders rather than on individual deputies. The real struggle often takes place before the budget is presented to the parliament. In a hierarchy of western legislatures based on the criterion of budgetary control, the Congress of the United States would be at the top: Congress is almost as much of a force to be reckoned with by the administration after the budget has been voted as before. At the bottom of the ladder would be the House of Commons, whose lack of power is striking once the Chancellor of the Exchequer has revealed "his" budget to the public.

CONTROL. The third function of the parliaments, after legislation and consent to taxation, is the control of executive action. This is a less well defined area than the others. First, what *is* the legislature in relation to the administration? Or what is the cabinet's relation to the assembly? The physical arrangements are very revealing of the political or psychological situation. In Westminster, the Government, or cabinet, is not separated from the parliamentary group. The arrangements anticipate an exchange between a majority and a minority rather than a confrontation between the administration and Parliament. At the Palais-Bourbon, the cabinet sits in the front row of the members, facing the speaker and the chairman. Is the cabinet not an emanation of the assembly and do not persons speaking from the rostrum — even members of the ruling majority — address the cabinet at the same time (and even more) as the other members? At least this was the case under the Third and Fourth Republics. Since 1958 it would have been more appropriate to adopt the arrangements of the Bundeshaus in Bonn: the government bench, a long raised table, is placed beside the presidential armchair, slightly behind the rostrum, facing the deputies. This gives the government the air of attending as a spectator the parliamentary game it dominates.

In Europe, it is rare for a parliament to control the administration by acting as a whole. The hearings of ministers before committees cannot be compared to the hostile grilling to which administration leaders are subjected by congressional committees in the United States. The West German Federal Republic has developed an interesting technique as a result of a delicate and controversial problem. Article 45 b of the fundamental law, passed in March, 1956, anticipates the establishment of a *Wehrbeauftragter des Bundestages* "for protection of fundamental rights and as an auxiliary organ to the Bundestag in the exercise of parliamentary control." This permanent commissioner of the assembly, chosen jointly by the opposition and by the majority, received in the year 1961 alone 4380 complaints, of which 1330 were found to be entirely justified, and 296 partly justified. The annual reports of the commissioner to the assembly show the extent to which he has become a kind of parliamentary control on the military administration.

In a more general way, administrative action is controlled by means of questions posed by individual deputies. The two most usual methods at the present time are those of the written question and of the so-called oral question, which is submitted in writing but answered orally. Two points are important here:

1. In a highly centralized country like France, where, moreover, the deputy is traditionally considered to be the representative of his constituents in the sense that a traveling salesman represents his employer, a member of parliament does not ordinarily use the procedure of written or oral questions to control the administration, or more precisely to bring his weight to bear on its decisions. The French member of parliament spends a considerable part of his time writing directly to ministers

in various departments of the administration or in taking steps to hasten an administrative decision. We must remember that the financing of the construction of a village street by a savings bank in the neighboring town cannot be arranged in France until all the relevant documents have been to Paris and back.

2. In London, Bonn or Paris, if the oral question is usually a method of controlling executive management or efficiency, it can also be easily transformed — in the first two capitals — into a method of exerting political control. When M. Debré was drawing up the constitution of the Fifth Republic, he hoped to achieve the same sort of relation between the administration and parliament in France. The result has not fulfilled his intention. In vain would one search for examples of a real political dialogue arising from an administrative response to an oral question in French parliamentary life since 1959. It is true that the rules of the French parliament do not permit further debate by other members, while in Bonn the debate on the Spiegel affair in December, 1962, grew to great importance because the minister (administration spokesman) had to undergo a real crossfire of related questions and was forced to admit that he had lied in an earlier part of the discussion. From that moment his resignation seemed probable.

It is important to note that Mr. Franz-Josef Strauss had to resign because he agreed to submit himself to questions and also because the chairman of the Bundestag conducted the debate with total impartiality. The Spiegel affair proved the reality of parliamentary control in the Federal Republic, a control made possible because the minority can oblige the government to discuss a point seriously. We cannot overemphasize the point, because from the exchange or dialogue arises a political reality which is not defined in any constitutional text or regulation. At the end of a clash with the opposition the government can sometimes no longer maintain a certain decision, or it is compelled to modify a certain stand. No vote has forced the government into a change of position, however; it is a matter of purely moral constraint. For such a force to exist, the necessary and sufficient condition is that the cabinet and the majority party accept the fundamental idea of pluralist democracy: respect for the minority.

A supplementary condition should also be fulfilled. The minority must follow the rules of the game also. The French deputies in the Fifth Republic are not used to debates except those which threaten to bring down the government. Between 1875 and 1958 the principal means of political control of the executive by parliament consisted of attempts, often successful, to overthrow the government by the technique of what the Germans call *Grosse Anfragen*, although other means were also used.

In France there was and still is a long debate to determine how efficient executive control could be obtained by the legislature without constantly calling into question the existence of the administration. I cannot go into the details of this debate here, all the more because the remedies proposed were extremely varied — (the establishment of an American-style regime, for instance, with a president directly elected and not responsible to the assembly and without power of dissolution; automatic dissolution of the assembly when it voted against the administration, etc.) It must suffice to re-emphasize the extent to which the situation of the Fifth Republic is unique and does not allow one to make predictions: The government is stable and parliamentary control limited because General de Gaulle, the chief of state, is so popular. In other words, if he threatens to dissolve the Assembly it gives in because the voters would choose the general rather than the majority deputies. This is what happened in 1962. With another president one might find the reverse situation: The president would not dare to dissolve the Assembly because the nation would rally to the support of the anti-administration majority. Furthermore, as we shall see later, the system of parties is undermined by the fact that the present dominant party derives its strength from the personality of the chief of state. . . .

PARLIAMENT, PARTIES AND PRESSURE GROUPS

WHAT IS THE ADMINISTRATION? The European regimes are theoretically parliamentary, that is, the administrations are responsible to the parliaments; but what is the administration? It is possible to give a variety of very different answers.

In the France of the Fifth Republic the government, in contrast to what the constitution says, is in fact a group. The administration is a group of ministers, some of whom are direct collaborators of the president of the republic, an executive head who is not responsible to parliament, while others work under the prime minister, himself a sort of chief of staff of the president. In the Fourth French Republic, the administration was a kind of executive committee of the parliamentary majority, although the scattered nature of the groups permitted the president of the republic to exercise initiative in the choice of the président du conseil or premier, as in the case of Antoine Pinay in 1952. Although the framers of the constitution wanted to make the government a team of ministers under a head who was exclusively responsible for cabinet policy, in reality the ministers were transformed into delegates of their respective parties. In 1954 the Socialist party did not take part in the cabinet of Mendès-France, largely because its secretary-general, M. Guy Mollet, had refused to allow the premier to exercise his constitutional prerogative to choose his own ministers. Mollet took the position that the premier should take as ministers those whom the party considered worthy or there would be no Socialists in the administration.

In Italy, the power to make and unmake cabinets does not belong to parliament, but to the Christian Democratic party. Only De Gasperi's eighth cabinet (1953) and Fanfani's second cabinet (January, 1959) fell as a result of parliamentary action. The fate of the others was determined by the internal struggles of the Christian Democratic party.

Curiously, the much discussed Article 67 of the West German fundamental law arranges for administrative succession between two elections by means of a crisis within the coalition. Established in anticipation of preventing the negative majorities that had blocked the parliamentary system in the death-throes of the Weimar Republic, the mechanism of the constructive no-confidence motion can only function in the Federal Republic if there is a coalition government and if one of the member parties of the coalition changes sides. . . . How does one explain the fact that Adenauer's third cabinet (1957–1961) experienced no change in its entire period in office while his second cabinet (1953–1957) had internal difficulties in 1955 and 1956, and his fourth cabinet had great difficulty coming into existence in 1961 and underwent a serious crisis a year later? The answer is simply that the Christian Democrats having obtained an absolute majority in the election of 1957, the third cabinet did not depend on negotiations between parties. . . .

In most of the parliamentary regimes the cabinet is no longer an outgrowth of the legislative assembly. The citizens, in voting for this or that party, understand that they are taking a hand in the selection of the executive. In Great Britain, in Belgium and in Germany one votes for or against the outgoing administration. Under the Fourth French Republic — as in the Weimar Republic — the rise and fall of coalitions forced the citizen to give a blank check to his party without knowing what cabinet the party would accept or overthrow and without having the power to pass judgment on the administrative action of the past cabinet at the following elections, because his party was sometimes in power (and never alone) and sometimes in opposition. One of the major causes of the alienation of the French people from politics, one of the chief reasons they have several times given a plebiscite to de Gaulle and voted for the UNR in 1962, is that they had formerly disliked feeling themselves dispossessed by the parties and they are now pleased to be asked their opinion about the administration.

Parliamentary democracy thus seems to me to have changed. One of the chief functions of parliament used to be that it constituted the source of executive power. Today one might say, with hardly any exaggeration, that the freedom of the members of the legislature to choose the administration — in regimes which function well — is not much greater than that of the American electoral college in a presidential election.

THE LEGISLATOR AND HIS PARTY. In theory, a member of a legislature is responsible only to his conscience and his constituents. The reality is shown in the following figures. According to an analysis of the 288 roll-call votes taken in the Bundestag in the first two legislatures, between 1949 and 1957, deputies were overwhelmingly loyal to the decision of their parties: Social Democrats, 99.8 per cent; Christian Democrats, 94.5 per cent; Liberals, 90.5 per cent. The concept of the deputy as an individual has given way to the concept of the deputy as a member of a parliamentary group which itself depends on a political party.

The mechanisms of decision in parliamentary groups have not yet been sufficiently studied. We know only that sometimes the party dominates the group, sometimes the group enjoys great freedom, and sometimes the party ministers, arising from the group, dominate the party. In France the Socialist party, the Radical party, and the Mouvement Républicain Populaire represent these three possible models of the relations of power. In Italy, Article 84 of the statutes of the Christian Democratic party says: "In all questions of a political nature the Parliamentary groups should respect the general lines fixed by the Congress [of the party] and the directives of the National Council and the Governing Board which interpret and apply the said orientation." The domination of members of parliament by the party in Italy is so real that breaches of party discipline do not occur in votes of confidence (by roll-call) but in the ordinary votes, which are secret. Immediately following the elections of 1963 the political game depends even more on the relative strength of factions within the Christian-Democratic party. It is up to the dominant party to make the essential choice concerning the future orientation. But a second element has intervened: the struggle within the Socialist party in which Pietro Nenni was outvoted by the "leftists," who would have nothing to do with a pact with the Christian Democratic party. The Italian example clearly shows the transformation of the political system: the elections furnish the brute facts, that is, the numerical composition of the assembly, but this raw material is manipulated outside the assembly.

The dependence of members of parliament on the party can sometimes be explained in financial terms, especially in socialist parties, where a good many of those elected are officers of the party; but above all it stems from the simple fact that the party machinery fairly generally plays a decisive role in the designation of candidates in the elections. The voter votes for a party rather than for a man. The electoral system does not influence this phenomenon. If Macmillan were to leave the Conservative party tomorrow and present himself in his constituency against a Labour candidate, a Liberal and an unknown Smith or Jones chosen by the Conservative party, he would have only a feeble chance of retaining his seat. In France, the elections of 1962 as a whole confirmed the triumph of the label over the personality. Certain electoral systems can reinforce the deputy's dependence still further. In the West German Federal Republic, for example, half the members of the Bundestag are not really elected in the true sense of the word. In fact, the parties have a right, according to the number of votes received, to a certain number of "places on the list"; the voters do not know even the names that are on the lists.

PARLIAMENT AND PRESSURE GROUPS. Candidacies in single-member districts and the drawing up of slates in multimember districts must, of course, reckon with the interest groups the party wishes to reach. This phrase has two possible — and quite different — meanings. Interest groups may be defined as social groups, the voters of a given economic level or political orientation, considered as a group. The other meaning is, organizations whose members share the same status or political orientation. Interest groups in both senses intervene between parties and the members of parliament on the one hand and the electorate on the other. In the first and looser sense it is a question of the party or member of parliament mobilizing a sector of the electorate, of undertaking to represent its interests directly; in the second sense it is a matter of agreements negotiated between the party and the leaders of the associations or groups. These leaders wish to be the primary representatives of a given sector of the electorate; the party and the member of parliament are only its representatives at second hand.

The Conservative party in Great Britain obtains the vote of most of the middle class without having to go through a national association of "upper middle class" or "lower middle class." The MRP can address itself quite directly to practicing Roman Catholics in the eastern and western parts of France, but it has to negotiate far less with the hierarchy of the Roman Catholic Church than the Italian Christian Democratic party or the Belgian Christian Social party. The German Social Democratic party would get the majority of working class votes in Germany without the existence of a powerful unified union movement, but it is in continual contact with the German Labor Union (DGB), and the power relations between the two organizations may vary according to the circumstances. As for the British Labour party, it is closely tied to the trade unions by its very origins and by its constitution. Many other examples and variations could be added. Sometimes the organized groups bring pressure on the members of Parliament, sometimes the leaders of an organized group penetrate the hierarchy of a party; sometimes the party controls and dominates one or several of the organized groups; sometimes the leaders of such groups try to get commitments from several parties at the same time; sometimes there is competition between a party and an organized group to represent a given segment of society.

What is essential for our subject is to determine how members of the legislature enter into the representation of interests and to ascertain whether they actually do so. Here we might return to certain observations made earlier. It often happens that organized groups bring pressure on the government or on the parties without going through the parties' representatives in the legislature. New structures seem indeed to deprive the parliament of its classic prerogatives, as in the case of the committees of the Commissariat au Plan in France. Is it necessary, then, for the representation of interests by the organized groups to be channeled through parliament? In the West German Republic the important bill submitted in 1950 by the DGB to set up co-determination at the level of the national economy would have moved in this direction. It was never passed, however. In France, above and beyond the Social and Economic Council, the plan to replace the Senate by a second economic chamber reveals the same process. Everyone has in mind the Yugoslav example. Another solution would be to carry even further the direct action of the organized groups on the parties, as is done in the United States, where different groups confront each other within each of the two major parties, which thus become real centers of arbitration, preparing the way and making easier the task of final arbitration in Congress and in the administration.

The problem is all the more acute in Europe because the unification of Europe has already given rise to organized groups which cross national lines (in contrast to the embryonic public institutions, administrative or parliamentary, and to the feeble international organization of parties). These new supranational groups are likely to assume power themselves in the absence of a firmly established authority upon which they might act.

THE NATIONAL PARLIAMENTS AND THE MAKING OF EUROPE

The construction of a unified Europe from the beginning of the OEEC to the development of the EEC has posed many problems to the national parliaments of the European states and, furthermore, has called into question their structure, their nature, their very purpose. Limitations of space confine me to a few observations on this matter.

1. The very existence of the European treaties and institutions limits the parliaments' sphere of action. . . .

2. Deprivation of national powers by the European institutions began with the treaties themselves, that is, with texts that the parliaments could not amend. . . .

3. The existence of the European institutions obliges observers, if not men in public life, to re-examine both the nature of foreign policy and the nature of parliaments. . . .

One has the right to believe that except on rare occasions there is no such thing as the national interest, but different national interests, and that the highest function of the political game is precisely to arbitrate and settle these conflicting interests by majority decisions in which compromise certainly plays a considerable part. To paraphrase Raymond Aron, it is a question of taking into account the variety of objectives existing in every society operating as a political unit. There is not, then, especially on the European level, a basic difference between the essence of domestic policy and the essence of foreign policy. For General de Gaulle each Frenchman has, to some degree, two selves. He is a member of various groups, economic, social, ideological. As such he is represented by the parties and by the parliament. But whatever his socio-economic status, he is also a Frenchman, with the same dominant interest as all other Frenchmen, and as such he is represented by the state embodied in the president of the republic. The parliament is thus basically incompetent in matters of foreign policy.

More than any other institution the Common Market shows the difficulties involved in such a conception. Peasants, workers in the metallurgical industries, Protestants, academics, Sicilians: each social group within each nation-state has its own special interests. Should these interests be protected by the state — in relation to the outside world? Against the states themselves in cooperation with corresponding foreign groups? Arbitration and compromise are required, but by what means? Executive, parliamentary or others? At what level — regional? national? European? How can one say once and for all that the group known as the nation takes precedence over all others if not by an ideological choice which is always controversial? . . .

CONCLUSION

If one no longer defines as "parliamentary" a political system where the administration is responsible to the legislature, but a system where parliament as an institution exercises an important influence on political decisions, everything I have said leads me to conclude that the European governments are clearly less "parliamentary" than the government of the United States.

The indisputable decline of the European legislatures, their dispossession by the administrations on the one hand and by the parties on the other, should not be exaggerated. Their functions are still often important. To be a member of the legislature is not futile, even for the backbenchers. The dominant political ideology in western Europe has made the existence of a freely elected parliament so clearly the touchstone of democracy that the institution is in no danger of disappearing.

Nevertheless, the European parliaments are definitely in a state of crisis — precisely because the nature of the institution is at stake. Formerly, the institutionalized political power of a nation meant the legislative power and the executive power. Today, when one speaks of the government in Europe one means the administration, meaning only the former executive; whereas in the United States the word *government* continues to designate the political institutions as a group, Congress included. In Europe, the legislature has, to a great extent, become the intermediary body between the citizens and the administration, with greater legitimacy and tighter institutional structure than the pressure groups or the parties, but not necessarily more useful or more efficient in the eyes of the citizens. In Great Britain, Germany and Italy the parties have a tendency to displace the parliament as the intermediary between the citizens and the government, whereas in France it is the pressure groups that do this. Everywhere the original model of a parliamentary regime is to some extent in the process of disappearing.

A. H. BROWN

Prime Ministerial Power

The prominence of the prime minister in the parliamentary system of government has given the office the publicity that once surrounded the activities of monarchs. The comparison is double-edged, for it carries the implication that the actual power of a prime minister, like that of a king, may be greater in appearance than in reality. The debate about the power of the prime minister has been particularly heated in Britain in recent years. Looking across the Atlantic, some have seen a kind of "presidential" system of government emerge, for better or for worse. Analysis from analogy is often dangerous, especially when those drawing comparisons have little specific knowledge of at least one of the terms of the comparison. The following article by A. H. Brown not only examines theories explaining this change, but also questions the underlying assumption that prime ministerial power has been increasing.

Discussion of the Prime Minister's powers is not a new subject for academic writers on politics, but it has been taken up with a renewed gusto in recent years and has become a familiar theme of journalism. It would be going too far to say it has been a subject of debate, for whatever the reservations many academics may have had about the thesis propounded, for example, in R. H. S. Crossman's introduction to the 1963 edition of *Bagehot*, they have been in no hurry to commit them to print, other than implicitly. Prominent among those who have taken issue with the thesis are D. N. Chester[1] and G. W. Jones.[2] But

Abridged from A. H. Brown, "Prime Ministerial Power," *Public Law*, Spring and Summer, 1968, pp. 28–51 and 96–118. Reprinted by permission of the publishers, Stevens and Sons, Ltd.

[1] D. N. Chester, "Who Governs Britain?" *Parliamentary Affairs*, 1961–62, Vol. XV, p. 519–527. This is a review of John P. Mackintosh's important historical study, *The British Cabinet*, 1962.

[2] G. W. Jones, "The Prime Minister's Power," *Parliamentary Affairs*, Spring 1965, pp. 167–185.

the fashionable view would still appear to be that the Prime Minister's powers have greatly increased in recent years.[3] A number of writers have gone so far as to argue that the British system is now one of "prime ministerial government." . . .

Very few people, of course, would suggest that the Prime Minister is only *primus inter pares*, even in the sense in which John Morley originally used the term — still less with the emphasis on the *pares*. To attack this view of the Prime Minister's powers is to attack a virtually undefended position. As party leader, as head of the government (and thus appointing and dismissing ministers), as the ultimate co-ordinating minister, as chairman of the Cabinet, and as the member of the government who receives most publicity on radio and television and in the Press, the Prime Minister possesses a formidable set of advantages.

But if a Prime Minister has an influence and authority greater than that of any one of his colleagues (and few would argue with such a statement), it is by no means equally clear that this is a recent development. Whether there has been significant change in the importance of, and the powers attached to, the office of Prime Minister since the Second World War (perhaps even in the present century) is debatable. . . .

If a graph could be constructed to illustrate prime ministerial power from the time of the Second, or even of the First, Reform Act to the present day, it would show nothing as consistent as a steadily (far less rapidly) rising curve. It would be a picture of ups and downs, in which it would be possible to imagine a Prime Minister in the early 1840's appearing at a higher point than one in the mid-1930's and one in the early 1920's above one in the mid-1960's. Unfortunately, however, the question of prime ministerial power cannot be tackled in this way. By a selective use of evidence, as plausible a case could be made for the general proposition that the Prime Minister's power has declined as for the view that it has increased. It depends upon which of his "powers" one is talking about.[4] If progress is to be made, it becomes necessary to isolate the major variables and to attempt to distinguish the growth

---

[3] See, e.g., Mackintosh, *op.cit.*; R. H. S. Crossman, Introduction to *The English Constitution* by Walter Bagehot (Fontana edition, 1963); Sir George Mallaby, *From My Level: Unwritten Minutes*, 1965, p. 59; F. W. G. Benemy, *The Elected Monarch: the Development of the Powers of the Prime Minister*, 1965, especially p. 245; R. W. K. Hinton, "The Prime Minister as an Elected Monarch," in *Parliamentary Affairs*, Vol. 13, 1959–60, esp. p. 298; Bertrand de Jouvenel, "The Principate," in *The Political Quarterly*, January–March, 1965, esp. p. 21; and Humphrey Berkeley, *The Listener*, August 25, 1966.

[4] Or, as Robert A. Dahl puts it, "When one hears that X is highly influential, the proper question is: 'Influential with respect to what?'" (*Modern Political Analysis*, 1963, p. 45). Analytically, *power* and *influence* may be fairly clearly separated when the Prime Minister's formal institutional powers are being considered. Elsewhere the distinction becomes blurred. Thus, one tends to speak of *power* of *appointment*, but of *influence* over *policy*. For practical purposes, it is possible in the latter case to use *influence* and *power* almost interchangeably.

points in the Prime Minister's power from the aspects in which it has remained the same or has even declined.

THE POWER OF THE EXECUTIVE

There is no more important variable than that of the power of the Executive as a whole. A good deal of confusion arises through a failure to make a distinction between the position of the Prime Minister in relation to his government colleagues, on the one hand, and the increasing role of government in society (and its strengthened position in relation to Parliament) on the other. It is generally agreed that the powers and functions of the Executive in Britain have increased. There is a fairly general acceptance of the mixed economy, of governmental regulation of the economy, and of the "Welfare State" with the enormously expanded functions of government departments which it entails. Many who accept that this expansion has taken place argue that, as a consequence, individual ministers are less able to run their departments than they were in the past. Somewhat paradoxically, this point has been linked with the view that the Prime Minister's control has increased. As a matter of fact, it was precisely because the government as a whole did less over a century ago that Peel, for instance, was able to do more in the way of controlling policy within the various departments than a modern Prime Minister could hope to attempt.

As the scope of governmental activity has broadened, so the Prime Minister has come to *share* in an increased governmental power. But given the number of departments now in existence, and the nature and extent of their responsibilities, it is extremely difficult for the Prime Minister to get into the policy-making process at an early enough stage to exert influence. He does not have time to participate in policy-making within each department to anything like the extent either of the individual responsible minister or of the ablest Prime Minister of an earlier generation. There has been a slightly paradoxical trend towards greater governmental power, of which one major beneficiary is the Prime Minister, while, at the same time, an increasing number of decisions are being taken of which the Prime Minister knows nothing (or which are presented to him as a *fait accompli*) for the very simple reason that an increasing number of governmental decisions are being taken. . . .

APPOINTMENTS

There is a strong case for regarding the Prime Minister's right to appoint ministers, to dismiss them and to advise the monarch to dissolve Parliament as definite growth points in his power. But more far-reaching conclusions have frequently been reached about the power that the exercise of these functions has placed in the Prime Minister's hands than the evidence will support. So far as the actual appointing of ministers is concerned, this is a growth point in the Prime Minister's power only in the sense that there is a growing number of governmental posts to be filled. To that extent, his patronage has increased, but what the implications of this are for his control of personnel needs to be carefully argued, rather than merely asserted. In other respects the power is not a new one. The distinctions which Bagehot made in his discussion of Cabinet appointments still essentially hold good. That is to say, there is still a distinction between those ministers who, because of their party standing, the Prime Minister must include, and those whose presence in the Cabinet is not vital to the security and acceptability of the Prime Minister and in relation to whom he has a larger element of real discretionary power.[5] Similarly, Bagehot was perfectly correct in suggesting that the Prime Minister has a greater freedom in deciding to which office a minister will be sent than in deciding who will be left out of his Cabinet. . . .

But much more drastic implications are commonly drawn from the Prime Minister's power of appointment than a mere recognition that some ministers more than others owe their position to the Prime Minister, and that the Prime Minister has a certain amount of liberty to place them in the office of his choice. It is frequently asserted that unless an MP shows complete loyalty to the Prime Minister and toes the party line, he stands a poor chance of promotion. It is argued that an able man may be kept out of the government because he has been too much of a rebel or because of a personal quirk on the part of the Prime Minister. It is contended that a minister may be kept out of higher office because he has not been an ally of the Prime Minister in the past or has subsequently failed to cultivate his friendship. But there is little evidence to suggest that men of real ability, well qualified for office in every respect, are being kept out on account of the purely personal disfavour of the Prime Minister. . . . Even in the filling of junior posts, a Prime Minister, when forming a government, tries to achieve some kind of balance between different strands of party opinion. This has the effect of bringing in rebels and potential rebels from both right and left. In a reshuffle a Prime Minister will be governed by the overriding requirements of introducing men of promise and of consolidating the government's standing with those sections of the party and country with which it is in most need of improving its position. . . .

At the top there is also evidence which suggests a poor correlation between rebelliousness and an unsuccessful career. It is noteworthy that four of the last five British Prime Ministers (Churchill, Eden, Macmillan and Wilson) were, at different points of their careers, very prominent rebels within their party. Rebellious tendencies do not lead to the automatic rejection of able men. A Prime Minister will be judged, not only by the way in which he plays his personal part within the

[5] *Party* was a less solid part of the political scene that Bagehot was interpreting, and as he formulated this point, it is *"Parliament and the Nation"* who "have pretty well settled who shall have the first places; but they have not discriminated with the same degree of accuracy which man shall have which place" (*The English Constitution*, 1963 ed., p. 67).

government, but by how his government as a whole performs. This gives him a very strong incentive to disregard purely personal friendships or dislikes and to concentrate on ability and balance. The search for men of ability and the attempt to maintain harmony in the party will inevitably lead the Prime Minister into rebel territory.

DISMISSING MINISTERS

A Prime Minister's ability to dismiss colleagues as well as to promote them might be regarded as one of the growth points in his power. . . . The premierships of Attlee and Macmillan did much to underline this point. But the Macmillan purge of July 1962 proves less than is sometimes claimed for his action. Dismissing colleagues has its dangers for the Prime Minister. Those ministers who found themselves on the back-benches at very short notice were not all able to disguise their discontent, a discontent which was shared by a section of their parliamentary colleagues and by a considerable number of Conservative Party supporters.[6] One of the ministers who retained his place during those July Days, Reginald Bevins, expressed his puzzlement strongly: "This was making enemies on a grand scale, enemies of those dismissed, enemies of their friends in Parliament, and shattering confidence in the Party at large."[7] He even added: "Of one thing I was then convinced: no Conservative Prime Minister could behave like that and still survive. In July 1962 Harold Macmillan committed political suicide more certainly than if he had himself resigned."[8] Lord Butler, making the same point less dogmatically, agreed that an action such as this could help to stimulate countervailing forces within the government party "because all the people who go out have friends who mobilise round them." In Macmillan's case, the Prime Minister's reputation did suffer as a result of such large-scale dismissals, and there was particular back-bench resentment at the way he had rewarded the loyalty of Selwyn Lloyd.

A Prime Minister's constitutional right to dismiss ministers is not in dispute, but the idea that a Prime Minister can get rid of ministers more or less at will is an over-simplification. Everything depends upon the minister and upon the circumstances. If a minister is very inefficient, or if he is being run by his department, this will be known to other ministers. When the Prime Minister demotes or sacks the man who is not up to the job, he can rely upon the tacit approval of his colleagues and the cheerful acquiescence of those who hope to take the place of the departing minister. But to dismiss a man of high party standing, or one

---

[6] In the words of one of those dismissed, Dr. Charles Hill, the Minister of Housing and Local Government: "I find no pleasure in the reflection that, because of the way these changes were made, much of the advantage of bringing new blood into the Cabinet was thrown away, or that there was no marked improvement in the Government's image in the year which followed" (Lord Hill of Luton: *Both Sides of the Hill,* 1964, p. 248).

[7] Reginald Bevins, *The Greasy Pole,* 1965, p. 137.

[8] *Ibid.* p. 138.

held by a large section of the parliamentary party to be doing a good job, remains a procedure so dangerous that a Prime Minister can seldom contemplate it.

The corollary of the exaggerated idea of the Prime Minister's practical political freedom to *dismiss* a minister is the notion that a Prime Minister can now face the *resignation* of even important ministers without much need for worry. Macmillan's placid acceptance of the resignations from his Cabinet of Mr. Peter Thorneycroft and of Lord Salisbury is sometimes cited as evidence in support of such a view. It is true that these were senior ministers and that the Macmillan government survived their departure without much difficulty. But Thorneycroft had been Chancellor for less than a year and was not quite the major party figure which the office he held would suggest. Salisbury, who was important, made a deliberate decision to go quietly. He was out of sympathy with Cabinet policy over quite a wide area and deliberately withdrew on the relatively minor issue of the release of Archbishop Makarios from imprisonment. The effect of a resignation depends not only upon the importance of the person who resigns, but on the issue, the timing, and the state of party feeling.

Though it has sometimes been argued that the Prime Minister's power to force a minister to resign helps him to get his own way on matters of policy, it is an observable fact that Prime Ministers do not normally ask for a minister's resignation because they disagree with the minister's policy. It is more likely to be because of the minister's administrative failings or, in some cases, because of the department's bad image. In a resignation over policy, the initiative is much more likely to come from the minister himself, rather than from the Prime Minister. In these circumstances, it becomes a case of the minister having failed to get his way *in Cabinet* rather than one of divergence from the policies of the Prime Minister. In the case of the Thorneycroft resignation from the Treasury, all the spending ministers as well as Macmillan were firmly ranged against the Chancellor. . . .

DISSOLUTION

The right of the Prime Minister, rather than of the Cabinet as a whole, to advise the monarch to dissolve Parliament is, as Geoffrey Marshall has argued, largely a twentieth century development. This may reasonably be held to be a growth point in the Prime Minister's power — which is not the same thing as holding, with Marshall, the view that the Cabinet has the better constitutional entitlement to take this decision. Be that as it may, the more important point about dissolution as one of the Prime Minister's powers is that it is a power in relation to the Opposition — not power vis-à-vis his own colleagues. There is surely little life left in the idea that the Prime Minister's power to advise the Queen to dissolve Parliament is an important weapon which can be used against rebels in his own party. To fight an election when his party is openly disunited would be to do so at a most disadvantageous time for the Prime Minister, who, after all, has much to lose. A good time for the Prime Minister to call an election tends simply to mean a good time for his party. Their interests in this case are identical. Where dissolution *is* an important power is in relation to the other parties. If a Prime Minister is right in thinking that a particular time will suit the Government party, it follows that it will not be the best time for his opponents.

This tactical advantage in the hands of the Prime Minister has gained in importance with the development of techniques capable of ensuring at least short-term economic expansion (an important aid in creating a favourable electoral climate) and the advent of opinion polling, which enables a government to assess its current popularity. Indeed, towards the end of the thirteen years in which Conservative Governments held office, the argument was being put forward that this was too great an advantage for the Prime Minister and government to possess, and a system of fixed election dates was suggested. If the Conservatives had won again in 1964, pressure for this reform would undoubtedly have mounted. . . .

PERSONALITY IN POLICY-MAKING

A Prime Minister's power over the appointing and dismissing of ministers, though subject to limitations, and his modern right to choose the date of a general election, are relatively straightforward matters in comparison with the question of his power in policy-making and his role in the Cabinet. The variables, only some of which I can discuss, are almost infinite in number. So far as decision-making within formal Cabinet meetings is concerned, there are far more difficulties for the student of politics than those imposed by lack of access to recent Cabinet minutes. When there is a near consensus in the Cabinet (and it is by no means uncommon), the difficulties of isolating the inputs which contribute to that consensus are almost insuperable. There is also the problem of *apparent* agreement. As a rule, Prime Ministers do not like to appear in the minority in Cabinet and so there are occasions when a Prime Minister will keep his views to himself rather than indulgently identify himself with the losing side. No defeat for the Prime Minister will be registered — even in the Cabinet minutes. Only one or two of his colleagues who happen to know the Prime Minister's private views on the question will detect that he did not get his way.

If there is one element in the problem the importance of which cannot be overstressed, it is the extent to which "style" of government and the location of key decision-taking varies according to the personality of the Prime Minister and the experience and ability of the members of his Cabinet. The extent of the variation from one Prime Minister to another is remarkable and scarcely supports the notion that in the period since World War II, prime ministerial power has been greater than ever before. When Tom Jones spoke of the Prime Minister "who is a dexterous, perhaps brilliant, autocrat" who "feels intuitively the invisible and inaudible reasoning going on in the minds of his colleagues, knows when to insist, when to give way, and when to adjourn," who "will concede in matters of no consequence, develop a stiff resistance to compromise when big issues are at stake, postpone rather than be defeated and thus secure time for private persuasion,"[9] he was thinking primarily of Lloyd George, with whom he was most closely acquainted. The contemporary example of Neville Chamberlain may also have been in his mind. But no Prime Ministers in the twentieth century have exercised greater personal power than Lloyd George and Chamberlain. None have been more willing to interfere with, or completely by-pass, their Cabinet colleagues. Nor is it entirely coincidence that both came to a sticky end. Tom Jones (who knew Baldwin well) recognised that there were also Prime Ministers "who appeared, except on critical occasions, to allow matters to take their course and to be indifferent to the decision reached or evaded. They preside but they do not prescribe. If agreement is not forthcoming, there is always escape by means of a committee, the matter is shelved and the next item called."[10]

The Prime Minister's power in relation to government policy has not, in fact, followed a steady course. In the period since Lloyd George's premiership, it cannot be said to have increased either sharply or gradually. It has varied from time to time, according to the strength, style and aptitudes of the individual Prime Minister, and the ability, experience and determination of his colleagues. A closer look at the prime ministerial style of Lloyd George and of Neville Chamberlain is instructive, for it would be difficult to find any post-Second World War Prime Minister treating important colleagues with a comparable degree of disrespect. If the term "autocratic" can be applied to any British Prime Minister in modern times (and it can be applied only in a severely qualified sense), it should be reserved for these two men. . . .

Lloyd George's purely personal authority stands out among twentieth century Prime Ministers. World War I provided him with great opportunities and he attempted to continue his wartime style of government after the Armistice. He interfered with his ministers to the extent of taking policy decisions without their knowledge through the medium of his personal secretariat. This secretariat was unusually large for a British Prime Minister and, in addition to it, Lloyd George made some use of the Cabinet Office to promote his policies. His most extreme interference was in foreign affairs, for war and the post-war conferences had accustomed him to being the supreme authority in this field. It is remarkable that not only did the Prime Minister conduct departmental policy other than through the departments, but that he actively pursued policies with which his Cabinet disagreed — over Russia, for instance.

When Lloyd George wished to come to an economic and political

---

[9] Thomas Jones, *Of Prime Ministers and Cabinets*, B.B.C. Publication, 1938, pp. 26–27.
[10] *Ibid.*

settlement with the new Communist régime in Russia, he took with him Lord Swinton, then the Secretary for Overseas Trade, rather than Lord Curzon, who, as Foreign Secretary, might have been expected to conduct the negotiations and who was, at the very least, entitled to be present. Swinton recognised this, and once said to Lloyd George: " 'If you treated me as you do Curzon I would quit. I cannot understand why Curzon does not resign.' Lloyd George replied: 'Oh, but he does, constantly. But there are two messengers in the Foreign Office: one has a club foot, he comes with the resignation: the other is a champion runner, he always catches him up.' "[11] Curzon liked office too much to carry his numerous threats of resignation into action. He contented himself with letting off steam to his wife and close friends. "Girlie," he wrote to Lady Curzon, "I am getting very tired of trying to work with that man. He wants his Forn. Sec. to be a valet, almost a drudge. . . ."[12] But Lloyd George's by-passing of the Foreign Office served to weaken his own prospects of survival. Curzon, naturally, was not inclined to take a strong line for keeping the Lloyd George Coalition going. But, more important, the Prime Minister's treatment of Curzon and, to a lesser extent, of his predecessor, Balfour, was the decisive factor in keeping out of the Coalition the one man whose return might have saved it. Bonar Law was on three occasions — unknown to the Foreign Secretary — offered Curzon's job, once in 1921 and twice in 1922. But he refused, telling Birkenhead (who had conveyed the third offer) "that the Foreign Office was out of the question. His view was that if he undertook the task he would not be in the position to control foreign policy."[13] . . .

When Neville Chamberlain became Prime Minister, circumstances dictated that he devote a great deal of his time to foreign policy, but he was not content to run *only* foreign policy. He ensured his strong influence on major domestic policy by taking the chair at all the important domestic Cabinet Committees.[14] Chamberlain had strong views and he wanted his government and entire administration to reflect them. Accordingly, he showed little interest in bringing in able critics such as Churchill, Leo Amery or Macmillan. On Eden's resignation, the Earl of Swinton (who was himself sacked by Chamberlain from his office of Secretary of State for Air) has written: "Eden rightly resented the secrecy with which Chamberlain surrounded his personal contacts, his hush-hush messages from and meetings with mysterious go-betweens. It was an increasingly impossible position for a Foreign Secretary to be in, especially for one as sensitive about his importance and private feelings of pride as Eden was. . . . Neville was running a one-man band, and became angry if anyone appeared to question his judgment. All the negotiations and secret or official contacts with Mussolini were his own. Munich was his own. He was convinced that he, and he alone, could

---

[11] The Earl of Swinton, *Sixty Years of Power*, 1966, p. 49.
[12] Lord Beaverbrook, *The Decline and Fall of Lloyd George*, 1963, p. 40.
[13] Beaverbrook, *op. cit.* p. 172.
[14] Iain Macleod, *Neville Chamberlain*, 1961, pp. 200–201.

understand and get on with the dictators and secure a peaceful settlement with them."[15]

Chamberlain's successor was in some respects a special case. Many factors combined to give Churchill in wartime great power and authority. But his very preoccupation with the conduct of the war meant that he had to delegate authority on home affairs to Attlee and Sir John Anderson. In his second period of office as Prime Minister, Churchill still benefited from his wartime record and public prestige. Yet, partly no doubt because of his declining health, and partly because of his regard for constitutional propriety, his role in policy-making in the 1951–55 Government does not appear to have been extensive. He remained in full charge, however, at Cabinet meetings and took pleasure, for instance, in impressing his colleagues with analogies drawn from his experience as a minister in 1910! The fact that in the course of his long political career Churchill had held many offices was, arguably, one of his advantages, compensating in some measure for his failing physical and mental powers.

Attlee, as Prime Minister, interfered little with his ministers and this partly reflected his own inclinations, but it was also a reflection of the strength and experience of many of his Cabinet colleagues. When the supposed "prime ministerial government" of Wilson is contrasted with the Attlee administration, the outstanding difference is not an accretion of power to the office of Prime Minister. Nor are even the differences in the personality and ability of the men the most relevant factors. More important is the relative strength and experience of their Cabinet colleagues. Attlee was surrounded by men like Bevin, Cripps, Morrison, Bevan and Dalton, formidable personalities, who, with the notable exception of Aneurin Bevan, had already gained ministerial experience in the wartime coalition. In addition, these were men of great experience in the Labour Movement and people of unusual ability. Bevin, Cripps, Morrison and Bevan were also, in their different ways, politicians with strong support in different sections of the party and they could command a great deal of personal loyalty. The contrast between these men and Mr. Wilson's Cabinet is a notable one. . . . It would be scarcely surprising if Harold Wilson, though a comparatively young Prime Minister, found himself in a stronger-than-average position in relation to his colleagues. In experience as well as in political ability he has no party rival to compare with him. . . .

Among the other post-Second World War Prime Ministers, Eden's high party and national standing, and the great respect in which he had been held as Foreign Secretary, enabled him to become a domineering Prime Minister. But even before his Suez policy collapsed in ruins, this style of government had begun to irritate his colleagues and alienate support. Eden was also disadvantaged as Prime Minister by his unusually one-sided political background. He had spent his political life

[15] Swinton, *op. cit.* p. 116.

almost exclusively in foreign affairs. In valuable contrast, Macmillan had experience of the Treasury and the Ministry of Housing, as well as Foreign Affairs and Defence. Sir Alec Douglas-Home, however, suffered, like Eden, from relative lack of familiarity with the problems of home (and, in particular, economic) departments. Though there are ministers who served under Douglas-Home and Macmillan who regard the former as the better Cabinet chairman, his position vis-à-vis his colleagues was not as strong as was Macmillan's, following the election victory in 1959. Macmillan's assets, the electoral success apart, were his wide political experience, tactical acumen and sheer intellectual ability. Douglas-Home could not compete in these respects and could scarcely hope to dominate the policies of a Cabinet which included several men with political experience at least as great as his own (for example, Mr. Quintin Hogg and Mr. Selwyn Lloyd), one whose experience was considerably greater (Mr. R. A. Butler), and able, younger men who had already held important office, and whose further political ambitions had been given encouragement during the leadership crisis of 1963 (Mr. Maudling and Mr. Heath).

While the differences among twentieth century British Prime Ministers are necessarily a recurring point in this discussion, it is scarcely less important to take note of certain ministers who did not become Prime Minister but who carried great weight in the Cabinets in which they served. While there is no lack of evidence of the Prime Minister's importance (which no serious student of politics would wish to ignore), acceptance of the "prime ministerial government" notion may foster a tendency to overlook the role of other leading ministers, some of whom have had a more important influence on the course of British politics than a number of those who became Prime Minister. Ernest Bevin, Herbert Morrison, Aneurin Bevan and R. A. Butler are post-war names that spring to mind. Lord Butler's influence on policy-making within his party was a remarkable one for a single individual. Lloyd George, Neville Chamberlain and Harold Macmillan were prepared to argue in Cabinet and win many rounds *before* they became Prime Minister. A Prime Minister, as well as other ministers, may be bound by collective responsibility to support a policy he does not like. . . .

CABINET CHAIRMAN AND CABINET AGENDA

As Cabinet chairman, the Prime Minister undoubtedly enjoys an advantage in the discussion. He has more opportunities to express his views, for if any other minister ventured opinions on such a wide range of issues, he would be regarded as a dangerous bore. When a Prime Minister also possesses considerable intellectual and political ability (true, for example, of Macmillan and Wilson, among recent Prime Ministers), there will be no question as to who is the most powerful man in the Cabinet. Yet the power which the chairmanship bestows on the Prime Minister may too easily be exaggerated. Many of the decisions which are taken in Cabinet have effectively been taken elsewhere and it will be very difficult for the Prime Minister to change them at this late date. Though it is the Prime Minister's responsibility to sum up the sense of the meeting on each issue, his ability to affect the sense of the meeting is dependent upon a number of variables. These include his own personality and talents, the strength of feeling the issue arouses, and the standing of the ministers opposed to him. . . .

The Prime Minister's power to determine the Cabinet agenda has frequently been misinterpreted. Dr. Mackintosh is wrong in suggesting that "the Prime Minister . . . can keep any item off the agenda indefinitely."[16] This is greatly overstating the case. . . . There is a standard procedure for getting a matter discussed in Cabinet which is to submit the item in advance to the Cabinet Secretariat, who draw up the Cabinet agenda. This, in turn, requires the Prime Minister's final approval. But it is not in a Prime Minister's interest to keep matters off the agenda which his colleagues want to discuss. . . . If a minister feels particularly strongly about a matter which has been decided against him at Cabinet Committee or at inter-departmental level, he has the right to take the issue to a full meeting of the Cabinet. Enoch Powell is one former member of the Cabinet who has publicly asserted a minister's right "to bring a matter to his colleagues if he wants to."[17] Many past and present ministers who would agree with Powell on little else accept his view that "the very nature of collective responsibility implies that if a man wants his colleagues' assent or advice he can have it."[18]

Though the principal co-ordinating committee (and ultimate decision-taking body in the event of disagreement at lower levels) is still the Cabinet, the Prime Minister does have a special role in the co-ordination of policy. He is the ultimate co-ordinating minister. As Harold Wilson has put it: ". . . any decision which is not going through smoothly, possibly because two different departments do not see eye to eye, if it cannot be resolved by a Cabinet sub-committee, or an ad hoc get together — *which is what usually happens*[19] — comes to the Prime Minister." The Prime Minister must draw a careful line between observing a watchful general oversight and constantly interfering in his ministers' work. To know what is going on and to be able to intervene when things look as if they may soon go wrong is an attribute of a successful Prime Minister. Constant meddling with the business of his colleagues is not normally successful.

---

[16] John P. Mackintosh, *The British Cabinet*, 1962, p. 394.
[17] In a radio interview with Norman Hunt, *Whitehall and Beyond*, B.B.C., 1964, p. 59.
[18] Among ministers with whom I have spoken, the definite consensus of opinion is that a minister can get an item on the agenda if he wants to. A minister may occasionally be told that there is no room left on the Thursday agenda and that discussion of the question he wishes to raise will have to be held over until the following Tuesday, but there is no question of keeping an item off indefinitely.
[19] My italics.

THE MACHINERY OF GOVERNMENT

One of the most important developments in the machinery of government in the twentieth century has been the establishment of a system of Cabinet Committees — both permanent functional committees and ad hoc committees. It has sometimes been argued that these strengthen the position of the Prime Minister and give him a larger role in policy-making. But though this may from time to time happen, as it probably did in the case of Eden's Suez Committee, it does not necessarily follow. Cabinet Committees are a logical extension of the Cabinet rather than of prime ministerial power. The Prime Minister is not a member of all of these specialised committees, and where he is not, the members of the committee are likely to have a greater influence on the final shape of policy than he. . . .

The spread of Cabinet Committees is no argument for the passing of the Cabinet system. Though members of the Cabinet Committees are appointed by the Prime Minister, to a large extent the members (of, for example, the Overseas Policy Committee, Social Services Committee or Economic Affairs Committee) pick themselves in accordance with the departmental responsibilities of the ministers concerned. . . . Arguably, the extension of Cabinet Committees has strengthened all ministers. It keeps them informed of the sphere most relevant to their work, and gives them a greater opportunity to participate at the highest level of decision-making than they could hope to have in a meeting of the full Cabinet. There, with over twenty members present and time limited, each individual member must weigh carefully the likely effect of making too many contributions. It may also be argued that Cabinet Committees have, in particular, strengthened the party hierarchy — not only the Prime Minister, but his leading colleagues who now share the chairmanship of committees with him. The chairmanship of Cabinet Committees strengthened the power, for instance, of Sir John Anderson in Churchill's wartime coalition, of Herbert Morrison in the Attlee Government, and of R. A. Butler in more than one Conservative government. . . . Cabinet Committee chairmen are very important people and though a Prime Minister will keep in close touch with these half-dozen or so key men and doubtless exert some influence, this is not a fully effective substitute for chairing every meeting himself. Indeed, the latter course might appeal to a Prime Minister intent on short-term maximisation of his power, but it is no longer a practical possibility. In the long run it would be damaging to both the efficiency of, and contentment within, his government. . . .

The development of the Cabinet Office and of the Prime Minister's Private Office are also twentieth century developments, but the latter has not gone very far. Indeed, it is doubtful if the Prime Minister's private office has ever at any time reached the importance it had under Lloyd George. Though nowadays a highly efficient private office in terms of secretarial and personal services, it is absolutely minimal as an advisory body. Indeed, there are politicians with ministerial experience who regard it as quite inadequate if the Prime Minister is to comprehend departmental matters when they come to the Cabinet and when ministers go to him. Macmillan's advisers, it is said, were able to talk "globally," but did not have the skills required to sharpen the issues. The Prime Minister does not have in his Private Office anyone of the seniority, ability and experience of the abler Permanent Secretaries. . . .

On the other hand, the Secretary to the Cabinet (and to a lesser extent the Joint Permanent Secretary at the Treasury responsible for Civil Service establishment) normally enjoys a close relationship with the Prime Minister. It is through the Cabinet Office that the Prime Minister must largely work if he wishes to be well informed about the conduct of government departments. . . . The Cabinet Secretariat, however, through the circulation of agenda, minutes and background information, has enabled ministers to come to the Cabinet very much better informed about the business on hand than they could easily be before the creation of the Secretariat during the First World War. There is a myth of a golden age of Cabinet government which is just as misleading as the myth of the golden age of the House of Commons, when the House was allegedly the scene of free, vigorous and well-informed discussion. (In fact, one of the distinguishing marks of fairly recent recruits to the House of Commons is not only their greater professionalism and representativeness, as compared with their nineteenth-century predecessors, but their greater *awareness* of ignorance and the need for better sources of information.) Some Cabinets are greatly superior to others in talent, and Asquith's, for instance, may compare favourably with some more modern specimens. But most Cabinets include members who try to keep themselves informed over a wide range of policy, as well as those who leave themselves time for nothing but the problems of their own department. If the extension of governmental activity has made the individual minister's job a more exacting one, the development of the Cabinet Office has had a compensatory effect, enabling the abler and less myopic ministers to keep in touch with the work of their colleagues. In spite of the Prime Minister's continuous use of the Cabinet Office, it is incorrect to regard it as no more than a glorified Private Office of the Prime Minister. The Cabinet Office acts as guardian of correct Cabinet procedure, is professionally concerned with the distribution of information to ministers, and would be unwilling to go on record (especially now that the records are to be published after thirty years!) with a deliberate by-passing of Cabinet ministers. Even if the Secretary to the Cabinet works more closely with the Prime Minister than with any other politician (and is, indeed, the *only* high official in constant touch with the Prime Minister), men such as Lord Bridges, Lord Normanbrook and Sir Burke Trend have been conscious of their duty towards the Cabinet as a whole and could not readily be suspected of supporting an autocratic tendency on the part of the Prime Minister.

The fact that the Prime Minister is political head of the Civil Service is of some importance, in so far as it indicates his considerable role in the initiation of changes in the machinery of government, including substantial power in the creation and winding up of departments.[20] The Prime Minister has a special responsibility in these matters, though this does not mean that he is quite free to follow his vision of administrative rationality. There are generally political pressures to be absorbed, loyal colleagues to reward, and potentially disloyal colleagues to be accommodated.

R. H. S. Crossman has argued that "the centralisation of authority, both for appointments and for policy decisions, under a single head of the civil service (quite recently the task has been given to a committee of three[21]) responsible to Downing Street, has brought with it an immense accretion of power to the Prime Minister."[22] . . . It is true that high civil service appointments and, most notably, permanent secretaryships require the Prime Minister's consent. But Crossman's argument would carry more conviction if Prime Ministers had acquired the habit of pressing their own nominees for these posts. This has not in fact happened. The practice has been for Prime Ministers to give their official blessing to the choice made by the permanent heads of the civil service machine. . . .

As things stand, civil servants are in general appointed by civil servants and on the comparatively rare occasions when a Permanent Secretary is rejected by a politician (or transferred at his behest), the initiative comes from the departmental minister. Indeed, when a new Permanent Secretary is being appointed to a department, the minister has a de facto right of veto. It is not often exercised, for few ministers are equipped with knowledge which enables them to judge the relative merits of possible candidates for the job.

During the period of Mr. Wilson's prime ministership, there have, however, been several cases of ministers objecting to their Permanent Secretaries, though this has been done successfully only when an imminent retirement has brought about the need for a change. Somewhat ironically, the most notable ministerial victory was Mr. Richard Crossman's. When Dame Evelyn Sharp retired as Permanent Secretary to the Ministry of Housing, her job (to the consternation of Whitehall) remained vacant for seven months while the determined Mr. Crossman refused to accept the choice of successor that the "machine" had ordained for him. The Prime Minister, as usual, supported the Civil Service Establishment view and quite a tussle ensued. For Crossman not only named the civil servant he did not want, but said whom he did want. There was an eventual compromise in which a third person (neither the "machine's" original choice nor Crossman's) was appointed to the Permanent Secretaryship. The process confirmed the departmental minister's right of veto in the case of a new appointment, but failed to establish his right to choose his own chief adviser.

---

[20] The constraints upon this power are fewer at the time when a Prime Minister is first forming his government than they are later.
[21] Crossman's summary is slightly misleading. For a brief but more precise account of the present arrangements, see Lord Bridges: *The Treasury*, 2nd ed., 1966, pp. 161, 164–165, 176–177.
[22] Crossman, Introduction to Bagehot, *op. cit.*, p. 51.

AREA OF POLICY

A distinction of some importance may be made between the role and influence of the Prime Minister in certain areas of policy as compared with others. Prime Ministers, by convention, have special responsibilities in the field of foreign policy, defence and national security. Though it is true that they also have an overall responsibility for the conduct of the government, their special interest in foreign affairs, the demands made by the speed of modern communications and the tendency towards conduct of diplomacy at head of government level simply do not leave them with time to participate so knowledgeably or so frequently in the work of other departments.

The Prime Minister's role in foreign policy is subject, of course, to the same qualifying factors as affect his conduct of government generally. The personality and strength of the Foreign Secretary are highly relevant, as are the interests and aptitudes of the Prime Minister himself. The variations from one government to another over the past fifty years have been considerable. . . . MacDonald, reverting to a practice by no means unknown to earlier Prime Ministers, became his own Foreign Secretary. Baldwin's Foreign Secretaries, on the other hand, enjoyed as much independence as any other departmental minister (indeed, rather more[23]), while, in contrast, Neville Chamberlain reverted to a policy of by-passing the Foreign Office which was reminiscent of Lloyd George's tactics. Churchill during the war was a special case, but in the period from 1951 to 1955 Anthony Eden had a great deal of freedom as Foreign Secretary.[24] This may be attributed in part to Churchill's failing powers, of which Lord Moran has provided ample evidence.[25] It also reflects Churchill's "constitutionalism," his belief in the importance of the Cabinet[26] and the rights of individual ministers, as well as his respect for the judgment and experience of his particular Foreign Secretary.[27] The importance of the last point should not be underestimated. Eden's position as heir apparent, his seniority within the party and long experience in foreign affairs made him the major figure in foreign policy-making, just as Ernest Bevin had been before him. Somewhat similar factors were operating in the Attlee-Bevin re-

---

[23] See *The Life and Letters of Sir Austen Chamberlain*, ii, p. 246, quoted in Sir Ivor Jennings, *Cabinet Government*, 3rd ed., p. 189.

[24] See, e.g., *Political Adventure, The Memoirs of the Earl of Kilmuir*, 1964, p. 193.

[25] Moran, *Winston Churchill: the Struggle for Survival, 1940–65*, 1966.

[26] In April 1953, Churchill remarked: "We had 110 Cabinet meetings in the past year; while the Socialists had only 85 in a year—and that in a time of great political activity. I am a great believer in bringing things before the Cabinet. If a Minister has got anything on his mind and he has the sense to get it argued by the Cabinet he will have the machine behind him" (*ibid.* p. 404).

[27] Occasionally, however, Churchill felt he should be consulted more. "Anthony tells me nothing," he complained to Moran in June 1954. "He keeps me out of foreign affairs, treats them as a private preserve of his own" (*ibid.* p. 553).

lationship. Bevin was an experienced minister, one of the outstanding successes in Churchill's small War Cabinet, and a tremendous figure in the Labour and Trade Union Movement. Attlee had the greatest respect for him and, in turn, Attlee's safety when conspiracy threatened depended much upon Bevin's loyal support. Bevin and Eden, accordingly, had a position and power within their governments which Eden's successor, Selwyn Lloyd (a junior and inexperienced politician by comparison), could not be expected to command.

. . . Foreign affairs remains, however, one area of policy where it is almost impossible for a Prime Minister to keep out. If Baldwin dabbled no more in foreign policy than he had to, it is arguable that he did less than he ought. Certainly the pressures to participate are great. . . . The frequency and speed of modern international consultation, the fact that diplomacy at the highest level now means diplomacy carried out by heads of executive in many countries with which Britain has important dealings, brings the Prime Minister in, whether he likes it or not. In foreign affairs such quick action is frequently required that the Cabinet cannot be consulted until after the Foreign Office has made an important move. In these circumstances, a Foreign Secretary will often welcome the opportunity of consultation with the Prime Minister and the possibility of sharing the burden and responsibility.

Sometimes the Prime Minister will take important initiatives in foreign policy, though in the period since the Second World War these have always been taken in consultation with the Foreign Secretary (and often with a Cabinet Committee as well). There is, however, at least a case for arguing that the Cabinet as a whole have not always been adequately informed. The examples which are invariably used in support of such a contention (and, more generally, to promote the view that Prime Ministers have increased their power) are those of Attlee and the manufacture of the British atom bomb, and of Eden and Suez policy.

The use of these examples has not been entirely fortunate. In so far as they are pathological cases, they may be misleading, and the extent, furthermore, to which they demonstrate the Prime Minister's individual power has almost certainly been exaggerated. It seems fairly clear that Attlee was strongly in favour of the manufacture of the atom bomb and that he exerted a strong influence in this decision in his role as chairman of the Defence Committee of the Cabinet. The minutes of the committee were, however, circulated to Cabinet members and if none of them chose to raise the issue within the Cabinet, this may be interpreted either as acquiescence or negligence (a failure to read the minutes with due care), but it cannot convincingly be interpreted in terms of the by-passing of the Cabinet by the Prime Minister.[28] Nor has any evidence been produced to show that a majority of members of the Labour Cabinet at that time were opposed to the decision taken.

---

[28] *Cf.* R. H. S. Crossman, Introduction to Walter Bagehot's *The English Constitution,* Fontana paperback (1965 impression), p. 55.

A more thoroughly researched case is the Suez crisis of 1956. In this instance, a good deal of evidence is now available, though there is still ample room for difference of interpretation. . . . Both Hugh Thomas and Anthony Nutting[29] describe convincingly how Eden carried his Foreign Secretary, Selwyn Lloyd, along with him, even though Lloyd had doubts about the wisdom of hitting back at Nasser in the way Eden and the French intended. Suez was a pathological case, not only because Eden deliberately misled the House of Commons, the country, the United States and the United Nations, but because he by-passed the normal machinery of government. The Middle Eastern specialists in the Foreign Office were not fully aware of what was afoot. Anyone who might have been in a position to offer expert advice against the Suez adventure was deliberately not consulted. This was the Prime Minister's decision. Even the British Ambassador in Egypt was not told of the ultimatum to Egypt until it was delivered. He, like almost everyone else in the diplomatic service, including Sir William Hayter, the British Ambassador in Moscow, was strongly opposed to the venture. Eisenhower was just as opposed as was Dulles, and so the Americans were not told what was going on. For all this, Eden must bear a good deal of individual responsibility.

Yet it would be wrong to suppose that Eden by-passed his Cabinet in the way in which he largely ignored the Foreign Office specialists and his allies. The Cabinet Committee which considered the Suez policy included the major figures in the Cabinet who were departmentally involved — for example, Harold Macmillan as Chancellor, Selwyn Lloyd (the Foreign Secretary), Lord Home, Lennox-Boyd, and Anthony Head, as well as (for some of the time) R. A. Butler. In addition, the Cabinet as a whole took the vital decision on August 2, 1956, that "force would be used if negotiations failed within a measurable time."[30] Though Lord Butler has gone on record as suggesting that the Cabinet was not consulted as much as it might have been, he has also pointed out that "the Cabinet could have blown up if it had wanted to, but the Cabinet had confidence in Eden at the time and what doubts there were were not expressed until, I think, a later stage." Furthermore, "the party in the House at the time of Suez was on the whole behind the Prime Minister and very indignant with Nasser; so there wasn't the seed-bed for opposition to the policy in the Conservative Party in the House that you would expect if the Prime Minister was acting contrary to the general line of what the back-benchers thought." . . .

The case of the British attempt to join the Common Market . . . is a good example of the possibility of prime ministerial initiative in the field of foreign policy. It involved no deals behind the Cabinet's back. On the contrary, a decision to seek membership of the EEC required a major Cabinet decision, and though Macmillan devoted himself with some

---

[29] Hugh Thomas, *The Suez Affair*, 1967, and Anthony Nutting, *No End of a Lesson–The Story of Suez*, 1967.
[30] Hugh Thomas, *op. cit.* p. 55.

passion to the task of persuading his Cabinet colleagues, agreement was not immediately forthcoming. Only after many meetings held over several months was something like a consensus obtained. A long and tactful process of persuasion was necessary before influential doubters (who included R. A. Butler) could be won over. The final result of Macmillan's pressure and the Cabinet deliberations illustrates three points which may be offered as generalisations.

First, the Prime Minister has the power to give a lead to his colleagues on a major issue of policy — in particular, on overseas policy. This opportunity (perhaps duty) is most clearly the Prime Minister's when the issue affects almost every department and is the exclusive responsibility of none. Secondly, if the Prime Minister has (in the terms which Richard Neustadt applies to the President of the United States) "the power to persuade," the Cabinet remains the principal body which must be persuaded. This is no mere formality, as Macmillan found out. Thirdly, and this point is linked with the second, in the course of long deliberation on a policy in Cabinet and Cabinet committee, the policy becomes modified and hedged with qualifications as part of the process of obtaining consensus. . . .

HOME POLICY

Foreign affairs and defence have engaged the continuous interest of all post-Second World War British Prime Ministers. . . . This goes some way towards restricting the part they can play in domestic policy-making. There are . . . many Cabinet Committees in the home policy field which are not chaired by the Prime Minister, and where important decisions are being taken in the Prime Minister's absence. . . . There are whole areas of major domestic concern, such as health and education, in which the Prime Minister seldom attempts to be a policy-maker. There are many good reasons for this. One is that the policy-making process in departments such as these tends to be a long-drawn-out affair involving argument and consultation with interested parties and a fair measure of acquired expertise on the part of the minister. The Prime Minister is not in a strong position to sustain an argument on policy with, say, his Minister of Education.[31] No doubt, like everyone else, Prime Ministers reckon they know a good deal about education. But in fact none since Balfour has had real expertise on the subject or departmental experience of it. . . .

---

[31] As one fairly recent Minister of Education put it to me: "There is a tendency to forget the limits on a Prime Minister's activities. Macmillan knew a lot about Housing — he had been Minister of Housing. But he did not know much (and it is not surprising) about state education." Emphasising that this was not a criticism of Macmillan "who was better informed generally than many Prime Ministers," he added: "Not only does the Prime Minister not know, but he has his own interests. Every Prime Minister since Baldwin has taken a great interest in foreign affairs — though independent actions by the Prime Minister in foreign affairs usually do not work."

When a Prime Minister does take an interest in a matter within the province of a particular departmental minister, reaction will obviously depend very much on the personalities involved and the relationship between them. But it would be abnormal and unwise for a minister not to take an interest in a departmental matter which has attracted the attention of the Prime Minister. If the P.M. wishes to question what is being done, the departmental minister, if he is up to his job, should be able to supply the answer. So far as senior ministers, at least, are concerned, there is no question of prime ministerial dictation. The Prime Minister makes suggestions rather than issuing orders. A former Conservative Chancellor of the Exchequer told me that he received about a suggestion a week from the Prime Minister. He (and the Treasury) looked into them all, but found objections to most of them. Perhaps half a dozen in the course of a year were accepted. . . .

In a ministry as important as the Home Office, interference by the Prime Minister is not common, nor is his influence generally great. As ever, time and knowledge are necessary prerequisites of influence, and the Home Office is a demanding and complex department. It is, moreover, usually in the hands of a fairly important minister. The fluctuations in Home Office policy under, say, Mr. Henry Brooke, Mr. R. A. Butler, Sir Frank Soskice and Mr. Roy Jenkins reflect the differences of view and of ministerial style among these Home Secretaries rather than the attitudes of Prime Ministers. Indeed, under the same Prime Minister, Home Office policy changed quite radically when Soskice was succeeded by Jenkins. The reforming zeal of the Home Office under Jenkins and its support of causes which Jenkins has long espoused are a good illustration of the extent to which an able political head can still influence the work of his department.

The power of Prime Ministers over major economic decisions is difficult to determine, but this is one area of domestic policy in which Prime Ministers cannot avoid close involvement. The importance of economic strength for every other government policy, its electoral significance, and the fact that the Prime Minister will sometimes be forced to answer economic questions in the House of Commons and on television are among the main reasons for his continuous interest. Certain Prime Ministers are, of course, very much better equipped for this aspect of their role than others. . . . Harold Macmillan, in contrast with his predecessor (Eden) and his successor (Douglas-Home), had been Chancellor of the Exchequer and had long taken an interest in economic policy and organisation. Harold Wilson not only began with the advantage of being the first professional economist to become Prime Minister, but he had his years of experience as President of the Board of Trade and as Chairman of the Public Accounts Committee behind him.

Macmillan's memories of the inter-war years made him a steadfast and ardent economic expansionist. His Chancellors did not always feel able to share his expansionist views, and Macmillan's relationship with the four Chancellors of the Exchequer who served under him was not entirely easy. In particular, he had to put up with two credit squeezes (imposed by Thorneycroft and Selwyn Lloyd) which he heartily disliked. Though supporting them in public, he argued against them in Cabinet. Eventually defeat in the Cabinet led to Thorneycroft's resignation, but Selwyn Lloyd was able to win many Cabinet arguments when he made it clear that he regarded the issue as a resigning one. On the other hand, much as Macmillan detested Selwyn Lloyd's pay pause, Lloyd and the Prime Minister saw eye to eye on several of the important organisational developments which took place during Lloyd's period at the Treasury. They were in agreement, for instance, on the setting up of the National Economic Development Council, though Samuel Brittan has argued that the Chancellor, rather than the Prime Minister, should be regarded as the Founding Father.[32] The setting up of the National Incomes Commission was a clear case of the comparatively rare instance when a Prime Minister takes matters into his own hands and plays a basic part in sponsoring a new development and determining the ultimate decision. Brittan, in his careful study, writes: "In the end Macmillan lost his patience with the argument and delay and himself summoned a group of officials, including Sir Laurence Helsby, to Admiralty House in the spring of 1962 to hammer out the main lines of NIC — an extremely unconventional kind of initiative for a British Prime Minister to take.[33]..."

In the eyes of the spending minister power is seen to lie, first, with the Treasury and, secondly, with the Cabinet (or its appropriate committee). These are the bodies he must persuade, since they have the power to frustrate or facilitate his good intentions. The Prime Minister's importance to the spending minister lies in the fact that he is normally the most important single ally he can secure for a fight with the Treasury. If the Treasury has stood firm against a spending department at the inter-departmental official committee and Cabinet Committee level, a determined minister may want to carry the matter further and put it on the Cabinet agenda. His chances of winning his point in Cabinet are improved if the Prime Minister is on his side. Many — probably most — of the informal meetings between ministers and Prime Ministers take place on the initiative of a departmental minister seeking advice and influential support. It is virtually unknown, for example, for the Prime Minister to take the initiative in interfering with the Scottish

[32] Brittan, *The Treasury Under the Tories, 1951–1964*, 1964, p. 219. Brittan's view is that "there is no sign that Macmillan ever tried to initiate anything himself on these lines before his Chancellor took up the idea, and it is Lloyd who must be given the credit for it." Sir Edward Boyle has, however, pointed out the element of oversimplification involved in such personal attribution of credit. In his words: "NEDC was the fruit of a number of things, not least the growing interest of the National Institute of Economic and Social Research in the work of the Commissariat in France. I would say the biggest stimulus to NEDC was the conference on the work of the Commissariat organized in April 1960 by the National Institute." (Proceedings of an RIPA Conference on "Who are the Policy Makers?" Published in *Public Administration*, Autumn 1965.)

[33] Samuel Brittan, *op. cit.* p. 239.

Office. But it is not uncommon for a Secretary of State for Scotland to attempt to win the Prime Minister's support. Macmillan was an invaluable ally for the Scottish Office against the Treasury, not only because he was a thoroughgoing expansionist, but since he was strongly in favour of special treatment for the less developed areas of the country. . . .

But, helpful though he may be, the Prime Minister can only defy a Cabinet majority at his own peril and by putting the fate of his government in the balance. (It was this risk which Eden was not prepared to take at the time of the Suez cease-fire.) There is nothing unusual about a Prime Minister in the course of Cabinet discussions being forced to modify his views, compromise, or keep his mouth shut. It is when the Cabinet is fairly evenly divided on an issue that the Prime Minister's views gain in importance, for he would not be where he is if his opinions and judgment did not command a more than average respect. . . .

A variable factor in the Prime Minister's power which should be touched upon briefly is the exigency of the situation. . . . An emergency situation can lead to the Prime Minister exercising a more than normal personal power (with the tacit acquiescence of his colleagues). This was true of Baldwin, who was not given to asserting himself, during the General Strike and the Abdication crisis. It would apply to the present Prime Minister over the Rhodesia crisis, and the economic crisis of July 1966. . . . The corollary of such extraordinary activities on the part of a Prime Minister is his corresponding, temporary neglect of other areas of governmental activity. (Baldwin indeed implied in conversation with R. A. Butler that one reason why he did not devote more attention to the growing international crisis in his last year of office was the extent to which that period was occupied with the problems of the Abdication.) For while the Prime Minister is devoting most of his attention to one matter, other activities in Whitehall do not grind to a halt. Life — and the political process — goes on.

P.M.'S PARTY STANDING

. . . The roles of party leader and of Prime Minister (when the party is in office) are so interwoven that they are exceedingly difficult to disentangle. . . . Though no Prime Minister's power is ever negligible, the same Prime Minister may be stronger at some periods than others. The variation is largely due to his party standing. Macmillan's ministerial colleagues, back-bench MP's and constituency party supporters were inclined to give the Prime Minister a good deal of personal credit for the recovery of party morale after Suez and the subsequent sweeping victory in the 1959 general election. In the period immediately following the election, Macmillan's influence was at its height, and it may be surmised that the Conservative Party would have "put up" with more from him at that time than they were prepared to tolerate three years later. . . . It was on the high tide of his post-1959 popularity that Macmillan was able to float his most controversial policies and those most likely to alienate traditional Conservative support — for instance, the coming to terms with African nationalism which followed Lennox-Boyd's departure from the Colonial Office and his Common Market initiative. Douglas-Home, in contrast, at no time enjoyed such a position of strength vis-à-vis his party. There were always sceptics who had doubts about his ability or popular appeal, and eventually, of course, the rumblings of discontent were sufficiently loud to force his resignation from the party leadership. . . .

G. W. Jones has argued that dissension in the party makes for dissatisfaction in the leadership, for support tends to coalesce around the Prime Minister's principal colleagues. In Jones's view: "There is no loyalty at the top because the Prime Minister's colleagues are his rivals, eager to replace him, and he is engaged in a constant battle to fend them off."[34] But this is not acceptable as a generalisation. Much still depends upon the Prime Minister's party standing which is sometimes so high that there are no rivals in sight and at other times quite the reverse. Douglas-Home always had serious rivals, whereas Wilson faced no similar problems during his first two years of office. The Prime Minister's health and age are also relevant factors. Macmillan had no rivals in 1959, but plenty in 1962–63. Between 1951–55, there were attempts (eventually successful) to unseat Churchill, though in this case there was little rivalry, since the heirdom was not in dispute. The Prime Minister's leading colleagues tend to have temporary rather than permanent followings. They are not rivals in the sense that they are constantly engaged in conspiratorial activities. But alternative Prime Ministers are important in that they are there — even if they choose only to stand and wait.

A SUMMING UP

. . . "Prime ministerial government" is but the latest of many short-hand expressions which have been coined to convey the essence of the British system of government. "Parliamentary democracy" and "Cabinet government" were predecessors and remain rivals. Each phrase contains an element of truth, but none is an adequate brief description of the political system. There is much to be said for eschewing all three. In very general terms it may be said that a Prime Minister who is autocratic pays the penalty not only in terms of policy failures but party rebellion and, in all probability, ultimate dismissal. He stands where he is because his party put him there and he must continue to satisfy them broadly if he is to remain. Should he be deficient in important respects, there are good precedents (especially in the Conservative Party) for his replacement as party leader and, accordingly, as Prime Minister. . . . Even when a strong and able Prime Minister, and one popular with his party, is in office, effective policy-making power is much more widely diffused than the idea of prime ministerial government would suggest. The increase in powers and functions of the executive has done little

---

[34] G. W. Jones, *op. cit.* p. 176.

to simplify the Prime Minister's task. It has done much, in fact, to exacerbate the difficulties in the way of his effective supervision and intervention. As government becomes more complex and the range of governmental activity continues to expand, a Prime Minister has to run fairly hard simply to stay in the same place.

KENNETH N. WALTZ

Executive Government in Britain: A Structural Analysis

Control of the executive in Britain is formally concentrated in the Cabinet, all of whose members are expected to hold seats in Parliament too. The concentration of responsibility in a few dozen men, headed by a prime minister who is chief legislator as well as chief executive, has long been the subject of admiring comments by American authors. Kenneth Waltz differs: from his comparative analysis of foreign-policy making, he draws the conclusion that the concentration of authority in Britain gives less party control of government than the more disjointed system operating in Washington.

How executive offices are arranged and who fills them will determine much of the content of policy and the manner in which it is conducted. The administrative procedures and the appointment practices of Britain and America are affected by the presence of disciplined parties in Britain and by their absence in the United States. In Britain, the sharp distinction between governing and opposing denies to the

Abridged from Kenneth N. Waltz, *Foreign Policy and Democratic Parties*, pp. 133–140 (Boston: Little, Brown and Co., 1967), with a new introductory paragraph by the editors. Reprinted by permission.

party in power the opportunity to draw on the talents to be found in the opposition party. The filling of offices is a means of building political support and broadening the base upon which policy rests. The major offices of state must go to Members of Parliament who have served their apprenticeships in the party in the House of Commons over a period of years. For example, of twenty-three Cabinet Ministers in Harold Wilson's first Cabinet of 1964, all except two were established Members of Parliament. In this system, there is little opportunity to refresh the bureaucracy by bringing in people from outside of government, as is often done in Washington.

In Great Britain one can, with fair hope of success, play the game of guessing who the next Chancellor of the Exchequer, Foreign Secretary, or Defence Minister will be. In the United States, to bet on who will be appointed to comparable offices would usually be folly. President Kennedy chose as his Secretary of State and as his Director of the Bureau of the Budget men he had not met until he interviewed them for the jobs. Robert McNamara he scarcely knew before asking him to be Secretary of Defense. Britons, marveling at the procedure, expected incoherence or worse.[1] Their worry was intensified by the apparent contrast with British and Western European practices. As in the Third and Fourth French Republics, so in Britain there is a considerable group of *ministrables,* men who by political affiliation and length of service constitute the pool of Parliamentarians from which the large majority of Ministers will be drawn.

Though in Great Britain problems of turnover are markedly different from those that prevail in America, they are perhaps as important. Most politicians spend years climbing to Cabinet rank. Once having attained it, they do not long endure. By the Prime Minister's decision, offices in general are rapidly exchanged; and over a period of years the body of men who have served becomes surprisingly large. After his party's victory in October of 1959, Macmillan formed a government of 81 members. Upon the adjournment for the summer recess in July of 1964, not quite five years later, 41 no longer held any office at all, and only 7 still occupied their original posts. In ten years of Tory rule, beginning in October of 1951, a total of 230 persons held office in successive Conservative Governments. Of 16 members of Sir Winston Churchill's peacetime Cabinet, 4 had survived — Macmillan, Butler, Thorneycroft, and Viscount Kilmuir. Of 18 non-Cabinet Ministers, 5 were still in office ten years later. Of more than 30 Parliamentary and Under-Secretaries, only 3 had lasted upon receiving promotion — John Boyd-Carpenter, Ernest Marples, and Dr. Charles Hill.[2]

Few ministers serve long in any one position. There were 8 Secretaries of Defense in the United States from 1947 to the autumn of

---

[1] See M. J. C. Vile, "The Formation and Execution of Policy in the United States," *Political Quarterly,* XXXIII (April–June, 1962), 162–71.

[2] Gerald Kaufman, "Profile of a Parliament," *New Statesman,* LXVIII (July 31, 1964), 146; James Margach, "10-year Turnover at the Top," *Sunday Times* (London), October 29, 1961, p. 13.

1966; in Britain there were 12 during the same period or a total of 13 since the war. In the United States, years of stability have been interspersed with periods of rapid turnover. In Britain, only one Defence Minister has been in office for as much as three years, A. V. Alexander, from December of 1946 to February of 1950. Four have served for more than two years; five for less than one year. Three of the 13 moved up from the Admiralty or the War Office to become Ministers of Defence. Secretaries of State for War and for Air and First Lords of the Admiralty (to use their old and familiar titles) have been almost as numerous, with 12, 9, and 11 for those services, respectively, though a few individuals among them remained in their places for approximately five years. Defence Ministers have appeared and disappeared more frequently than most Ministers have, which, as with foreign-assistance agencies in the United States, is partly a reflection of British difficulties in defense policy. . . . Nevertheless, in other Ministerial offices, except for Foreign Affairs and the Home Department, tenure for as long as four years is unusual. Two years is nearer the norm.

The MP out of office lacks the incentive to engage himself deeply in legislative affairs, for he is scarcely able to affect the conduct of administration or the writing of legislation. The MP in office, though a political specialist, remains a policy and administrative amateur confronting an entrenched bureaucracy. Where the American Secretary of a department or Assistant Secretary within it is expected to administer and manage, to draw up programs and put them into effect, a British Minister is more nearly in the position of a gentleman who presides, who explains to the civil servants what is politically supportable and to his fellow Parliamentarians what is practically possible. Ministers, who are the instruments the Prime Minister uses in dealing with the departments of government, come and go with a frequency that impedes the exercise of political control and increases the difficulty of carrying through changes in policy. Such habits were sensible when the society and economy were left to manage themselves, with the government intervening seldom and then only to make marginal adjustments. They still coincide with the requirements of any Conservative Government that is not intent upon legislating great changes and is therefore content to preside over affairs while making occasional modifications. Supposedly Ministers, supported by Parliament, frame overall policies, while civil servants contrive the necessary adjustments. The familiarity of the Crown's permanent servants with the arts of adjustment, the paucity of information available to the public and to Parliament, the short term that Ministers typically serve in any one position, the smallness of their number as compared to the mass of the bureaucracy, the demands made on their time by duties in Parliament and in their constituencies: all of these factors working together make it difficult for Ministers to take hold of their departments' affairs.

One might think that in these circumstances the Prime Minister would gather still more power unto his office by actively concerning himself with the affairs of the separate departments. On occasion he may do so, though he is not well equipped for the task. Two handicaps are especially detrimental. The first, generally overlooked, is the Prime Minister's customarily short term of office. Though the Prime Minister's ascendancy is based in part upon his outlasting his party associates, the Prime Ministerial office itself is not often long held. Since the Second Reform Act, Asquith holds the record, of nearly nine years, followed by Salisbury with intermittent terms of six and seven years, and then by Macmillan, Attlee, and Lloyd George, each of whom lasted about six years. In addition to the handicap of short and uncertain tenure that Prime Ministers frequently bear, the Prime Minister's staff is too small to elicit quantities of information and to uncover alternative viewpoints. There is for the Prime Minister no equivalent of the Executive Office of the President with Special Assistants who can reach for him into the affairs of the various departments. Prime Ministers since World War II have been inclined to play a personal role in foreign policy. It is striking that only seldom or belatedly have they done so in order to force decisions or hasten changes of direction in policy. They have instead specialized — as have leaders of the opposition — in making trips to Moscow and Washington in order to be able upon their return to instruct the Commons and impress the electorate.

In England as in America, some department heads will be men of great energy. If supported by the Prime Minister or President, they will impress their personalities and their policies upon their staffs. Also in both countries, some Ministers will be mere passengers, rewarded for past service, recognized for their political standing, and expected to make little present contribution. The executive arrangements that prevail in Great Britain, and this is the key point, make it more difficult than it is in the United States for the Minister who would effect changes to impress his will upon the bureaucracy. It is less a question, one must carefully note, of civil servants resisting the wills of their political masters than it is of Ministers not being in a position to behave masterfully. The stability of personnel just below the top heightens the effect of the rapid turnover that prevails among the Ministers who guide the policies of departments, which is compounded by the smallness of the number of the Prime Minister's appointees. The political appointees of the President occupy positions that reach down into the hierarchy of departmental offices. The Prime Minister's political appointees are a thin layer spread over a large bureaucracy.

"When a government changes in Britain," Anthony Sampson points out, "only seventy people change their desks in Whitehall, while in America hundreds of officials migrate." One should, of course, add that those seventy people change places frequently, with many disappearing as they do so. "Most civil servants," to cite Sampson again, "spend their whole lives in the same department, and only the most senior are switched around."[3] Senior civil servants in the military departments,

[3] Sampson, *Anatomy of Britain* (New York: Harper & Row, 1962), pp. 218, 230.

for example, have spent on the average twenty-five years in government, with most of their time in a single department.[4] Permanent Secretaries in Britain have served on the average in 2.5 departments.[5] Other members of the administrative class who are of comparable age have ordinarily a still more limited experience.

Civil servants in Britain are divided into three classes, with movement between levels quite difficult.[6] Members of the top class especially are high in intelligence and competence and long on experience, but having their experience confined mostly to one realm of affairs, they may also be narrow in viewpoint. The American civil service, with its eighteen grades, permits a wider recruitment, a greater flexibility, and an easier movement both between grades and between departments. Government service in the United States has been a route to distinction easily open to those of middle-class origins. In England, men of high birth and expensive education have heavily populated the upper reaches of the bureaucracy, just as, outside of the trade unions and the Labour movement, they have occupied the "commanding heights" of the polity, economy, and society. A survey made several years ago by the Labour Party showed "that forty-four out of 148 directors of the joint stock banks, forty-six out of 149 directors of the large insurance companies and thirty-five out of 107 directors of big City firms were all Etonians." The Financial Secretary to the Treasury reported to the Commons in June, 1963, that in the open competitions for appointments at the Assistant Principal level in the past ten years, 194 places went to Oxford men, 149 to Cambridge, 35 to London University, and 15 to "redbrick" universities.[7] In the United States, it is necessary to lump twenty-seven universities together in order to account for half of the degrees held by officials in foreign-affairs agencies.[8] In Britain the Foreign Office, more than the other departments of state, is populated by elegantly educated gentlemen of little experience outside their profession. Over 94 percent of foreign-service personnel have graduated from Oxford or Cambridge, and 70 percent went to British public rather than state-operated schools before attending university.[9]

Brian Chapman has pointed out that "apart from the occasional architect or surveyor recruited by the Ministry of Works, there are

---

[4] William P. Snyder, *The Politics of British Defense Policy* (Columbus: Ohio State University Press, 1964), p. 119.

[5] Sampson, *Anatomy of Britain*, p. 238.

[6] R. K. Kelsall, *Higher Civil Servants in Britain: From 1870 to the Present Day* (London: Routledge & Kegan Paul, 1955), chap. 3.

[7] Cited by Nicholas Davenport, *The Split Society* (London: Gollancz, 1964), p. 174n.

[8] James L. McCamy, *Conduct of the New Diplomacy* (New York: Harper & Row, 1964), p. 211.

[9] Lord Plowden, *Report of the Committee on Representational Services Overseas*, Cmnd. 2276 (London: HMSO, 1964), Annexes J and L. For a critical essay on personnel practices by an ex-Foreign Officer, see Geoffrey McDermott, "Reforming the Foreign Service," *New Statesman*, LXVI (August 16, 1963), 189–91.

virtually no appointments made to senior posts from outside the ranks of the Civil Service itself."[10] Wider recruitment and provisions for bureaucracy's refreshment have long been called for. The Report of Lord Plowden's Committee, which gives some emphasis to these needs, finds its place in an honorable lineage. The government, reacting, now proposes to recruit yearly as many as three Assistant Secretaries (in the forty to forty-five age range) and as many as five Principals (from thirty to thirty-five years old), all of them to come from industry, commerce, and the universities.[11]

With departments displaying their competence in handling the affairs of each day, with most Ministers, including the Prime Minister, ill placed or badly equipped to wrench policy from its established direction, and with the legislature largely inactive, a situation has developed in which ad hoc bodies, committees or commissions, are appointed to study problems that cannot easily be ignored and to suggest courses of action. Educational problems at various age levels were in recent years examined by committees headed by John Newsom, Sir Geoffrey Crowther, and Lord Robbins. After Britain's economic growth had lagged badly behind that of her European competitors for more than a decade, the National Economic Development Committee was established, with "Neddy," as it is called, paired with "Nicky" (National Income Commission) to deal with the problem of keeping wages and prices in step with the economic growth rate. Between January of 1955 and March of 1961, social and economic problems in Britain were investigated by four Royal Commissions and seventy-six committees. As is the case with the top levels of the civil service, recruitment of members to serve on committees is narrow. Many of the same names reappear on their rosters.[12]

C. H. Sisson, who is well satisfied with Britain's political institutions, has beautifully captured their spirit:

> Whatever politicians may make out of the electoral procedures which may result in their losing their jobs, an electorate which votes in such a way that an existing cabinet is overthrown is not saying that it will not continue to be governed substantially according to the same laws as before. It is in effect not objecting to the things that in general are done but in a greater or less measure to the way in which some of them are done. The Crown in short remains; the Constitution remains; the officials, who are ultimately the Queen's servants and not the politicians', raise their eyebrows and continue as before, only noting that certain emphases must be changed.[13]

---

[10] Chapman, *British Government Observed: Some European Reflections* (London: Allen & Unwin, 1963), p. 23.
[11] "Swing Doors in Whitehall," *Economist*, CCXI (June 13, 1964), 1220.
[12] See Peter G. Richards, *Patronage in British Government* (London: Allen & Unwin, 1963), p. 112.
[13] Sisson, *The Spirit of British Administration and Some European Comparisons* (London: Faber & Faber, 1959), p. 158.

In America it is still cause for dismay when a committee report calls for policies that then fail to materialize.[14] In Britain, the failure to produce a result or the inclination to edge slowly and cautiously toward one is by now an old story. Civil servants may "raise their eyebrows," and the government may bring in a modest program; but the committee is most often a device for exposing the complexity of problems and the perplexities of choice, for demonstrating a good intention while delaying action or postponing it indefinitely.[15] In the United States, while the expectation that the reports of committees will stimulate new actions or policies would seem to be misplaced, the intended effect of appointing a committee is often to gain support for a policy for which the President is already fighting or to increase support for an existing program.

With the prestige of the House of Commons at a low ebb and its ability to control the government waning, the civil service is often said to be the last and best check upon the Prime Minister. Though such a statement is badly elliptic, the truth it contains is suggestive. In British government, there is an uneasy juxtaposition of career amateurs entrenched in the civil service and Ministers passing through at the top, an institutionalized habit of veiling information and playing down problems and of temporizing by adjustment rather than changing by decision. The arrangements that have evolved and now prevail are not bad in themselves. One must, however, ask whether they permit a reasonable combination of effective democratic control and administrative efficiency in an era of big government and during a period, which gives no promise of ending, of rapid change amidst the growing complexity of affairs. The circulation of officials becomes more important as governments come to impress themselves more widely and deeply upon the life of a nation. It was once the glory of Parliament and the pride of its Members that being an MP was but a part-time job, which, in permitting Members to remain gainfully employed, enabled them to bring to their legislative tasks the experience of their business or professional concerns. The broadening of governmental activity has long since created a situation in which political business, if it is to be done well, has to be done full time. Alternation of public with private engagements is more effective than the constant but part-time practice of politics. British governments shuffle their Ministers from one department to another in such a way as to lose the advantages of political control without gaining the benefits of different perspectives and varied individual experiences.

---

[14] See Morton H. Halperin, "The Gaither Committee and the Policy Process," World Politics, XIII (April, 1961), 360–84.

[15] A. P. Herbert, "Anything But Action? A Study of the Uses and Abuses of Committees of Inquiry," in Ralph Harris, ed., Radical Reaction: Essays in Competition and Influence (2d ed.; London: Hutchinson for the Institute of Economic Affairs, 1961), pp. 249–302.

MICHEL CROZIER

French Bureaucracy as a Cultural Phenomenon

Public administration is very strong in France for many reasons. First, ministerial instability must be balanced by the stability of the higher civil servants. "The government changes, but the administration remains," is a popular saying. Second, "macrocephalism," a very large head — Paris — on a relatively small body, centralizes all the essential activities of the country. And finally, a centralist cultural tradition, dating back in history to Louis XIV and Napoleon, prevails; it has been reinforced by the policy of the planification *of the economy. It is this last aspect that Michel Crozier analyzes here.*

Since this study was written, a referendum took place in April, 1969, on regional reform, involving the decentralization of public administration. Many agreed with the principle of bureaucratic decentralization — the object of the referendum — but the majority of Frenchmen voted "No" as a means of putting to an end the reign of Charles de Gaulle. Such a reaction is typically French.

One of the major characteristics of the French political system has always been the contrast between the permanent and efficient administrative bureaucracy, able to remain impervious to successive political crises, and the unstable governments unable to choose and to carry out consistent policy. This contrast has become a commonplace for the many who have written on France's political troubles. Yet few of them, we believe, have understood it correctly. It is no paradox. The institutional patterns are merely two sides of the same coin and tend

From Michel Crozier, *The Bureaucratic Phenomenon* (Chicago: The University of Chicago Press, 1965), pp. 251–263, with footnotes abridged. Reprinted by permission.

to reproduce, at the level of the whole society, the opposition we have noted at the organizational level between the power of the central authority as regards routine and its helplessness as regards change. This contradiction may have been expressed differently after 1958, but it has persisted nevertheless under the fiction of the *pouvoir fort*.[1]

Society, of course, does not function as a close-knit organizational system, but this is not simply an analogy. Patterns of action operating at the organizational level have lasting effects on the system of interrelations prevailing at the global societal level, which itself relies on the same cultural traits. These correspondences were already apparent in the educational system and in the industrial relations system. They may be even clearer, if somewhat more complex, in the case of the political system, if one considers its functioning around the central issue of decision-making.

In the French political and administrative system, we should like to submit, decisions are made through the working of three different subsystems, all of them simultaneously closely interdependent and very far apart operationally: the administrative subsystem, responsible for all decisions that can fit into the multiple routines and programs already well elaborated; the deliberative policy-making subsystem, which takes care of all problems that go beyond the accepted routines; and, finally, the revolutionary grievance-settling subsystem, which forces decisions outside the approved legal framework.[2]

THE ADMINISTRATIVE SUBSYSTEM

We consider the administrative subsystem as the basic one — not only because it is regarded more or less as common law and most decisions fall under its jurisdiction, but also because it corresponds to the ideal pattern of decision-making in France, since the decisions it produces present the qualities of rationality, impersonality, and absoluteness that fit the basic French cultural traits.[3]

---

[1] The constitutional amendment calling for the direct election of the president by universal suffrage and the subsequent parliamentary election giving a clear majority in the UNR may, however, lay foundations for a much deeper change.

[2] This hypothesis should be discussed at much greater length. But we would like to consider it, for the moment, as a convenient way to explore the interrelationships between different, and even opposite, patterns on action in France.

[3] The term "administrative system," as used here, covers all the public administrations and all the semipublic organizations which must use the same administrative procedures. It is surprising to see that, in spite of its central importance for the political and social life of the country, the French administrative system has very seldom been studied from a sociological point of view. De Tocqueville and Taine have made a magistral analysis (in, respectively, *L'ancien régime et la Révolution* [Paris, 1857] and *Les Origines de la France contemporaine* [Paris: Calman Levy, 1877]). Since that time, however, one can point to only a few English-language investigations, such as the excellent thesis of Walter Rice Sharp on the functioning of French public administration in the 1920's (*The French Civil Service: Bureaucracy in Transition* [New York:

The administrative system operates through a complex network of public agencies which are deeply influenced by the bureaucratic traits of the French model. As such, it suffers from the same basic dysfunctions that are inherent in the model. Three major difficulties are apparent. First, decisions can never be really adequate, because people who have the power to decide remain far above the pressures of those who are affected by their decisions.[4] Second, the rigidity of each organization's relations with the environment and the parallel rigidity found in the relations between different organizations raise difficult problems of co-ordination. Finally, the over-all and recurrent problem of adjusting to change that plagues bureaucratic organizations cannot be satisfactorily solved.

To meet these problems, the administrative subsystem has elaborated special institutions and special patterns of action which entail general consequences for the whole political and administrative system. Let us take, for example, the problem of co-ordination. It is extremely difficult to solve, because of the fears of conflict and of face-to-face relationships.... French administrative organizations attempt to solve it, on the one hand, by exerting a great deal of self-restraint in order not to risk a conflict with another organization — this is the generalized fear of overlapping which is a characteristic paralyzing feature of French administration[5] — and, on the other hand, by calling for an over-all supra-organizational centralization.

Macmillan, 1931]); Brian Chapman's very good book on the *prefects* (*The Prefects and Provincial France* [London: Allen & Unwin, 1955]); and a more general and ambitious analysis by Alfred Diamant ("The French Administrative System," in William J. Siffin, *Toward the Comparative Study of Public Administrations* [Bloomington: Indiana University Press, 1959], pp. 182–218), which is, however, much too simplified and relies too heavily on the image of a static France popularized by Herbert Luethy. Numerous valuable works have appeared in France, but they give only a technical and narrow view of the field, whether written by jurists like Duguit and Hauriou or by administrative experts (see, e.g., the book by Roger Grégoire *La fonction publique* [Paris: Armand Colin, 1954], which centers on the technical aspects of the problems of personnel; and the book by Gabriel Ardant, *Techniques de l'Etat* [Paris: Presses Universitaires, 1953] which deals only with problems of efficiency).

[4] In order for a reform to be successful, it must be elaborated by people who are in a position to keep aloof from all pressure groups and thus also from all experts.

[5] French higher civil servants have a sort of panicky fear of possible overlapping. While American administrators do not mind setting up two or three competitive agencies whose conflicts will certainly entail waste, but which will also bring new ideas and interesting change, French administrators spend much of their time trying to avoid possible overlapping. They are motivated, we suggest, by their conception of authority as an absolute that cannot be shared, discussed, or compromised. If they prefer restraint to imperialism, this is not for co-operative purposes, but for the preservation of the integrity of the organization's power; this attitude tends, therefore, to result mostly in caution and conservatism, and to reinforce the pattern of over-all centralization which curtails the possibilities of initiative and autonomous development of each organization.

This pattern of co-ordination reinforces the lack of communication between strata and increases the remoteness from the field of decision-making. To meet this problem, administrative authorities multiply consultative committees at the middle and higher levels. This makes it possible to avoid gross inadequacies, but it also has negative consequences. Conflict cannot be solved within these committees. It can only be brought before the representatives of the responsible agency, which will later make its decision unilaterally. This means that the affected interests represented in these committees will be defended in a rigid and uncompromising way; every one of the participants will insist on his rights and principles for fear of his voice being silenced by his antagonists.

All these pressures, finally, will tend to paralyze still further the responsible agency. We come to the following paradox: all these administrative practices have only entailed more detours, more delays, and more conservative pressures, so that reform-minded administrators tend to be contemptuous of the influence of the committees and to adopt a disrespectful attitude when they have to deal with them — which, of course, does not foster co-operation.

The more ancient institution of the *prefects* is more efficient in this respect. The *prefects* are the only strong link between the local and field problems and the different bureaucratic systems of organization. This explains their strength and the prestige and influence they wield. Basically, however, their situation vis-à-vis the public and the local interests is not very different. They are extremely powerful in keeping order and insuring the maintenance of equilibrium between the ranks and privileges of all participating groups, but they cannot play a long-range innovating role, since they are not in a position to help solve conflicts dynamically.[6]

The consequences of these patterns of co-ordination and of the decision-making together reinforce the extreme caution and routinism of the organization leaders, and the frustrations and lack of initiative of the lower echelons and the public that are characteristic of a bureaucratic system of organization. This indicates again that change is the basic problem of the whole administrative subsystem.

We have already discussed at length the pattern of routine and crisis that is the logical response of a bureaucratic organization to change. We have also noted that the French administrative establishment has developed, with the *Grands Corps,* certain tight groups of higher civil servants, remote from all kinds of pressures, who can act as agents of change capable of cushioning the difficulties of at least minor crises. This integration of change within the model and the existence of absorption-of-crises functions make for a much greater smoothness in the older administrative agencies, where the pattern has been better

---

[6] The constructive aspect of their role consists in helping to rationalize administrative methods and to extend, to all parts of the country, initiative and progress that has been halted for various reasons.

elaborated. But these rather esoteric interventions do not make for much participation on the part of the citizens. Administrative reforms develop only in the direction of more centralization, by extending the application of principles arrived at in earlier crises. Like the *prefects*, therefore, the *Grands Corps* cannot really play the role of prime mover. Their influence is exerted more in the interests of peace, order, and harmony than in the interests of experimentation and innovation. The administrative subsystem, therefore, must finally resort to the deliberate policy-making system. But it does so only at the highest level, and its preponderance at all other levels has direct consequences for the process of change, its timing, and its rhythm. Because of this arrangement, French policy-making authorities are too much estranged from the actual problems of the citizens and cannot play their role properly.

THE POLICY-MAKING SUBSYSTEM

There is nothing surprising, of course, in the fact that deliberative bodies and political figures are given the rights and duties of making decisions to promote new policies, i.e., to permit adjustment to change. This happens in all Western democracies. But until now there has been something peculiar in the French model. First, these functions were performed only at the very top level. Second, they were performed in an anarchistic and confused way without any kind of specialization. Parliamentary seeming omnipotence and simultaneous powerlessness reflected very well the central dilemma over authority which we have discussed and were, at the same time, consequences of the predominance of the administrative patterns of action.

Traditionally, the French policy-making system has been formed by the national parliament and the government. No other deliberative body of any importance has existed. They have all disappeared in the course of time during the long process of centralization, and the void was filled everywhere by administrative bodies. Having no rivals and no political authority with which to compete, parliament has had attention focused on it. However, its powers were not enhanced, because the predominance of Civil Service at the local and intermediate level has estranged it completely from actual conflicts.

The curious paradox, however, is that this very narrow and centralized policy-making system has also been very much divided and almost anarchist. The main trouble has resided in the relations between the government and parliament. These institutions have been strongly interdependent and there has been considerable overlapping and confusion of roles between them. Finally the great difference of status between presidents and ex-presidents, ministers and ex-ministers, and at the bottom simple deputies has had a much deeper influence on the strategy of mass participants than their role as members of the majority or of the opposition.

Both institutions have had the same competence, since conflicts that could not be solved within parliament — and these have been all the important ones — were solved by bargaining and compromises within the government or by a change of government. The recurrence of such cycles has meant, at the same time, the predominance of the government, since matters could be settled only at the government level, and its helplessness, since parliament has been the constant arbiter of the intragovernmental struggles and has yielded to the government only for as long as necessary to handle the crisis it has been unable to solve alone.

This system can be considered a perfect method for institutionalizing the crises necessary to an omnipotent and centralized administrative power. It embodies once again the paradox of the helplessness of absolute bureaucratic authority when facing compromise and change. It has not, however, provided a satisfactory solution, inasmuch as it has met only partially the needs of mediation between the social forces at work at the local level and the administrative system.

This is due to the fact that the political class has behaved according to the same cultural traits that are at the root of the development of the bureaucratic system of organization. The volatility and instability of the political game are, of course, far removed from the stability and strength of commitment necessary for the administrative game. Yet we can discover some exactly comparable traits. The "political class," just like the bureaucratic strata, has become an isolated group, extremely equalitarian, rebellious against any kind of authority, unable to build stable leadership and to engage in constructive collective action. Its main failure has been its inability to understand that it cannot deny the government the right to act independently, coupled with its refusal to assume its own share of responsibility.[7] The French political class has fought and debated endlessly — but on abstract principles and not bargaining realities. It has consented to compromise only at the last minute, when the force of circumstances could be invoked. Finally, the distance created by the complexity of the game has been equivalent to the distance created by impersonality and centralization. It has helped to preserve the isolation of the parliamentary stratum and of the possible ministers' stratum, preventing control by a higher authority, government, or electors, and insuring the fundamental autonomy and equality of each of its members.[8]

This isolation of the political class, its fear of face-to-face relationships, and its inability to solve conflicts have tended constantly to bring together the political and the administrative system, whose symbiosis has become nearly perfect. But the more the political system has become bureaucratic, the less has it been able to bring to the administrative

[7] Nathan Leites, *On the Game of Politics in France* (Stanford: Stanford University Press, 1962), pp. 6–53.

[8] The decisive steps taken in 1962 toward a presidential and a majority system, however, have profoundly altered the rules of the game of the policy-making system; but . . . as long as the predominance of the administrative system persists, the whole political system will remain unbalanced.

system the renewal needed. Thus the very kind of sophistication that enabled the parliamentary game to institutionalize and to smooth over crises finally prevented the political system from answering the deeper questions and solving the deeper conflicts constantly developing in society.

Like all other French institutions marked by the bureaucratic patterns of action, the political system has been conservative, more preoccupied with safeguarding the elaborate equilibrium of rank and privilege than with experimenting with new policies. Mediation has been possible only for the very local problems, for whose solution members of parliament have been able to bargain with the administration on a sufficiently distant and abstract level. It has not been able to develop for national and even regional problems, from which parliament, and administration as well, have not felt sufficiently remote.

Such a game should not, however, be too severely judged. It was well suited to the problems of the bourgeois society of the late nineteenth century, for which Stanley Hoffmann has coined the very adequate term of the *stalemate society*.[9] The combination of a strong administrative system with an unstable policy-making system insured, in the smoothest possible way, the introduction of the exact amount of change that was tolerable without endangering the bourgeois equilibrium. Even at this period, however, it had three far-reaching drawbacks: (1) it allowed citizens to participate only in a very remote and indirect way;[10] (2) it deliberately excluded whole groups from any actual possibility of participation; and (3) it slowed down considerably the rhythm of economic and social change.

THE REVOLUTIONARY GRIEVANCE-SETTLING SUBSYSTEM

These drawbacks have assumed greater importance with the acceleration of change and with the general social evolution, which make it more difficult to accept the exclusion of one or several groups and increase the frustration of all citizens, since the functions of the state affect the latter increasingly without a comparable improvement in the possibilities of their participation. The development of the revolutionary grievance-settling system has been the answer to this difficult situation. It is the direct consequence of the failure of the policy-making system to make decisions and to associate all groups constructively in problem-solving. And it is the indirect consequence of the predominance of the administrative system, which prevents joint problem-solving at all but the highest levels.

We have already glanced at this third method of decision-making

[9] Stanley Hoffmann, "Paradoxes of the French Political Community," in *In Search of France* (Cambridge, Mass.: Center for International Affairs, Harvard University, 1963), p. 3.

[10] Complaints on this account have come repeatedly from the right as well as from the left. See, e.g., André Tardieu, *Le Souverain captif* (Paris: Flammarion, 1937); and Maurice Duverger, *Demain la République* (Paris: Julliard, 1958).

when considering the industrial relations system. French working-class politics, which constitute the most elaborate part of this subsystem, derive directly from it. To start with, let us analyze the scheme we had elaborated in terms of a political game.

1. For the working class, the central state (administration and government) is the main decision-making center, even for problems of minor importance and of local scope. This does not mean that workers are actually prevented from reaching their goal. But it is easy to understand that they should feel frustrated by the cumbersomeness of the whole system and especially because it is impossible for them to participate in the discussion at the decisive level. Thus they naturally remain suspicious about the results they finally obtain, since they can never experiment themselves to find out to what extent these were the best possible.

2. Since the main decisions must be made at the political center, there is, even at the primary level, an overwhelming preoccupation with national politics and a sort of myth has developed around political power. Working-class militants are almost fascinated by political power as such. They do not care about the power for what it can achieve. They are not worried about what kind of use can be made of it. They feel that political power is a cure-all, that if only they could get power everything would be settled. As a consequence, with them tactics take precedence over long-range and even short-range goals.[11]

3. Frustration with present-day, possible accomplishments and fascination with power are in accord with a radical approach toward politics and a revolutionary philosophy. The myth of revolution has been the only way for the French working class to mobilize its members into some kind of participation.[12] Even now, whenever the hold of the myth declines, so does participation in political activities at all levels and also the pressures on the central state and consequently the possibility of progress.

4. This revolutionary philosophy conceals and helps a shrewd if limited game played against the state that can be characterized as a general blackmailing strategy.[13]

In a country where the central state is the only authority responsible for the maintenance of law and order, and where there is an equal and pathological fear of anarchy and disorder on the one side, and of violent repressive measures on the other, the working class is in a

---

[11] This may ostensibly be contradicted by the almost Byzantine disputes of working-class politicians over programs. But programs, in this as in many other contexts, are only tactical elements and cannot be considered as rational goals.

[12] This role of revolution as a mobilization myth for the working class had been understood long ago by Georges Sorel.

[13] The word "blackmail" can be used for the working-class strategy only if one accepts at the same time that power politics in any field always involves a good deal of blackmail.

good position to discredit the central governing authorities by making it impossible for them to preserve internal peace.[14]

Most observers of the French scene have explained some of these traits by the alienation of the French working class. This is partially true, but the expression may be misleading. The French working class is surely deeply alienated as regards participation in decision-making, but most French citizens are also somewhat alienated on this account. The difference is one of quantity and not of kind, and on most other counts it does not seem that the French working class is more alienated than the less revolutionary working classes of England, Germany, or Belgium.[15]

The behavior of the French working class can be analyzed much better in rational terms if one considers the conditions of the game it is playing with the higher-ups. French workers have learned, through long years of dealing with the national state, how to exploit their natural frustrations to obtain as many advantages as possible without endangering what they have already won. They try to make the higher authorities pay dearly for the tutelage which the latter are imposing on them, but they are not over-eager to change the rules of the game and consequently have many conservative reactions.

It is true in a sense that French workers' one-day general strikes and warning manifestations are part of the traditional international working-class upheaval. But they can and must be analyzed also as a very specific pattern of action often witnessed within French society whenever a deprived group has felt unable to make its voice heard

[14] Let us take, for example, the very significant case of the struggle between Clemenceau, the strong man of pre-World War I French politics, and the postal workers. This was one of the most famous episodes of the labor history of the time. Postal workers had been organizing for a few years, and they were making decisive headway. Clemenceau, then a very strong premier, saw the importance of their progress and decided to fight. His postmaster general, Simyan, was instructed to go ahead. He started a long-range reform of the promotion system which could be used to deny advancement to labor people. The union struck in March, 1909. The whole labor movement came to its help. Taken aback, Simyan and Clemenceau had to play for time, and they accepted a compromise favorable to the strikers. A few weeks later, however, it appeared that they had only intended to prepare for a more decisive battle. Reorganization went on and the union had no other course but to strike again, but this was too much and in May the second general strike was a complete failure. It was followed by mass firing of strikers as the prelude to complete elimination of the union. What is very often overlooked, however, is that less than two months later, Clemenceau and, of course, Simyan, had to go, and the union finally won, because no political figure, even one as powerful as Clemenceau, had enough leeway to run the risk of antagonizing as small a group as the postal workers. Such a pattern was at first characteristic only of the Civil Service, but Civil Service unions were the first to succeed; and little by little the whole labor movement was pervaded by this philosophy. For the details of the struggle see Edouard Dolléans, *Histoire du mouvement ouvrier* (Paris: Armand Colin, 1953), II, 157–63.

[15] It can even be argued that on some important counts it is less alienated than most other European working classes; that social distance, for example, is not so overbearing in France as in England or Germany.

through the legal system of action. It has always been implicitly accepted that such behavior should be tolerated.

Notwithstanding the bloody episodes of civil war of 1848 and 1871, the interplay between the state and the working class in France has not been primarily one of oppression and revolt. As soon as the workers began acting as a relatively autonomous group on the political scene, the state tried to act as a tolerant arbitrator between them and the other groups. The Second Empire did not oppose trade unions, and protected the labor leaders who founded the First International. The Third Republic, but a few years removed from the terrible shock of the Commune, made strenuous efforts to integrate the rebel working class in the republican order. Not only did it legalize the trade unions, but it subsidized them indirectly by providing them with housing in the *Bourse du Travail* buildings.[16] It is true that the French working class responded very negatively; yet the contact was never broken completely. The threat of anarcho-syndicalism, the myth of the general strike, and even the ominous souvenirs of the repression of the Commune were used as a sort of indirect moral pressure in a general game of power politics that paid off in the long run, whatever the short-run emotional reactions of the politicians in power.[17]

This kind of strategy is not specific to the working class. Other deprived groups in France have acted at times in the same way, threatening and finally provoking some spectacular uproar to force the state into action. Wine-growers, for example, made a perfect demonstration of this mode of conduct in 1907. Its development, however, has been much greater since the end of World War II. In the case of the working class, it has become more and more elaborated and even abstract and, at the same time, it has tended to spread to other groups. Civil servants, teachers, shopkeepers, and peasants — to mention only the leading groups — resort to it more and more. This was finally also the basic strategy of the white settlers in Algeria and even of the Army officers.[18] Groups and individuals who cannot resort to such

[16] These labor exchanges built by municipalities with state subsidies housed many local unions and most local labor councils. It is no small paradox that the French labor movement, so jealous of its independence, was in very large part housed in buildings paid for by the bourgeois state.

[17] In the same period the German working class, even after the disappearance of Bismarck's exceptional laws against the Socialists, had to face a national state siding completely with the employers, while the English trade unions progressed half by bargaining with the employers and half by playing politics at the national level. These were three different games. In Germany, the working class had to bargain with the closely allied state and employers. In England, it bargained with the employers for the material stakes and with the state for improving the rules of the game. In France, it pressured a more aloof state into forcing the employers to yield.

[18] President de Gaulle has called off such blackmail, which had begun some years before his coming to power, by forcing the Army to choose between rebellion and yielding, fully convinced that as rebels the Army officers were bound to lose. But twice their cause regained momentum as soon as they had yielded, since De Gaulle continued to play the French political game of putting harmony first, pretending to ignore the officers' attempts at disrupting it.

violent unrest because of their status have utilized it in a milder, attenuated form by staging spectacular, well-timed resignations supported by consistent group pressures and all sorts of irresponsible actions which can weaken a government whose main function is to maintain peace and order.[19]

THE INTERRELATIONS BETWEEN THE THREE SUBSYSTEMS

The third subsystem, however uncontrolled it may appear, should not be considered only as a succession of haphazard explosions. It is, in a sense, a rather elaborate functional pattern that provides satisfactory solutions for the maintenance of the over-all system. It is the necessary substitute for the inadequate policy-making subsystem that tends always to become so perfect in its procedures that it is no longer able to assume responsibility and to provide the administrative subsystem with the necessary innovations. But it is also a very rough and imperfect method of social control, since it does not allow either good communication between the partners of the game or serious study of the issues involved. It inevitably engenders a much greater number of errors to both sides and fosters uncompromising radical attitudes.

We have, therefore, a curious balance between an overly esoteric political game that is losing its grip on the problems and a primitive revolutionary game that is too rough and unelaborated to favor sensible discussions and progressive compromises. Viewed in this way both subsystems may be characterized by a pattern of avoidance of serious face-to-face contacts. Evasion occurs in two opposite directions: either through the complexities of a game functioning only for specialists who lose touch with the conflicts they should mediate, or through the outrageous simplification of irresponsible explosions. Both methods, whatever their opposition, have this in common: they rely on and reinforce the basic patterns of the bureaucratic system of organization embodied in the administrative system.

The three subsystems are interrelated not only through the basic cultural traits they have in common but also at the institutional level. They are directly and functionally interdependent, and it is this independence which is the basis of the equilibrium of the whole system. The pressure of the administrative system, through its patterns of coordination and centralization, tends to push decision-making to such a high level and to restrict its scope in such a way that policy-making becomes isolated from society's real problems. Thus government and parliament tend to be restricted to the role of an "omnipotent" yet helpless monarch which fits best a generalized bureaucratic society of the French type. But the more the policy-making subsystem comes close to the elaborate routine of the administrative system, the more

[19] Stanley Hoffmann has presented a very similar argument in a brilliant paper, "Protest in Modern France," in M. A. Kaplan (ed.), *The Revolution in World Politics* (New York: Wiley, 1962).

likely it is to omit problems that must be settled one way or another, thus making it necessary to resort to the explosions and extra-legal compromises of the revolutionary subsystem. The errors, frustrations, and fears generated by such a rough pattern of conflict-solving, however, strengthen the administrative subsystem and prevent progress in group participation and in more responsible policy-making methods.

The equilibrium between the three subsystems depends, of course, on a number of factors, and especially the rate of social and economic change, the stability of the social structure, and the problems which society must solve. The Third Republic before World War I was the chosen time of the preponderance of the deliberative methods. The Fifth Republic, with the decline of the parliament and the concomitant increase in extra-legal action, has offered us an extreme example of the predominance of blackmailing tactics. It seems reasonable to argue that periods of accelerated change will be marked by a greater development of extra-legal grievance-settling methods.

The traditional French deliberative system was too brittle and sophisticated to resist the tremendous pressure of a period of social upheaval. But a question immediately comes to mind. What will happen when the acceleration of change becomes the dominant trait of an industrial society whose rhythm of growth will be more and more qualitatively different? One may submit that then the equilibrium of the whole system will be called into question. The extra-legal system is efficient only when it is not used too frequently. It loses its innovating properties when it becomes one of the rules of the game, and the last resort of the system thus disappears. Finally, the administrative system, as the cornerstone of the whole political system, has become much more vulnerable now, just at the time when it seems to supersede the deliberative system that had been actually protecting it. The political system will not change deeply as long as the bureaucratic patterns of action remain preponderant, but they are now, notwithstanding appearances, more directly threatened than ever before.

BERNARD GOURNAY

Higher Civil Servants in France

The instability that characterized party politics and prime ministerships of the Fourth Republic in France did not affect greatly the personnel of the civil service. Regimes come and regimes go, but the higher civil service continues at its own tempo. In this, it is characteristic of all European administrative groups. The much vaunted success of the French economy in the late 1950's and early 1960's won these officials a high repute for contributing to positive government. In this article Bernard Gournay summarizes the main characteristics of this distinctive political group.

The group traditionally called the high civil servants *(hauts fonctionnaires)* in France, which comprises between three and ten thousand people, according to the criteria used, is too heterogeneous to form a category significant for a political scientist. Within this group, several hundred individuals should be distinguished, men who work in constant relationship with political personnel and who play an intimate part in the preparation and application of major decisions affecting the nation: they will be designated under the generic heading, the higher civil servants *(grands fonctionnaires)*.

It goes without saying that there is no clear separation between the higher and the high civil servants as they have just been defined. The former's opinions and attitudes are similar to those which prevail throughout the administrative corps in which they receive their original training, or in the executive offices and departments which they direct.

Abridged from Bernard Gournay, "Un groupe dirigeant de la société française: les grands fonctionnaires," *Revue française de science politique* XIV: 2 (1964), pp. 215–231. Translated by Allen Rozelle and Mattei Dogan.

However, their views are not identical. Filtering and selection mechanisms play a part; those individuals most representative of the average tendencies of the group are not necessarily those appointed to command positions by politicians. Besides, the accession of high civil servants to executive posts, which alters their situation, the network of their daily contacts, and the type of problems they must deal with modify their perspectives and thus their manner of thinking and behaving. In that way they draw apart from their group of origin, the general administrative corps. . . .

Observation of the behavior of the higher civil servants reveals that within the category are differentiated and sometimes conflicting subgroups. However, powerful cohesive factors compensate for that heterogeneity.

DIFFERENCES

The high administration is not a monolith. It reveals three major lines of cleavage: competition of an occupational nature, rivalries between different crops, and the political affiliations of certain administrators.

Those conflicts which can be termed "occupational" are common to all large organizations: industries, armies, churches, etc. Their amplitude depends on the size of the organizations, the heterogeneity of their tasks, and the complexity of their internal structure.

The French administration can be considered both as a single organization and as a group of organizations simultaneously autonomous and interdependent. The civil servants who direct these organizations (ministerial executive offices, police commissariats, semi-autonomous establishments, local administrations) have a natural tendency to identify the objectives they have been assigned with the groups they direct. Each of these objectives appears to them, if not an end in itself, then at least an activity which must be developed to its maximum in quantity as well as in quality. To use the jargon of economists, each administrator tends to maximize the activities of his service by increasing his turnover and by improving the quality of the service he renders.

To achieve this result, the higher civil servant uses his skill to increase the means available to him whether they are expressed in terms of decision-making power, personnel, or credits. However, credits and personnel are scarce resources; it is impossible to satisfy all the demands or, given the interdependence of state functions, to permit the director of each governmental organization to undertake any program which he thinks falls within his competence.

Moreover, since there is no pre-established harmony in the life of organizations, it is hardly realistic to expect each participant willingly to limit his own claims in order to permit at the same time the fulfillment of his associates' aspirations. From this situation ensue innumerable rivalries which permeate the higher civil servants' daily work. Certain of those conflicts are settled by the ministers or by the head of the government; others persist latently.

Conflicts between administrations can thus be explained in large measure by the fact that governmental action is a perpetual compromise between the diverse objectives of the various administrations. Of all these struggles the most intense are those which pit the service responsible for financial stability, the Office of the Budget, against those services seeking credits. In the economic realm sharp divergences of views separate "vertical" administrations charged with managing one sector of production or one socio-professional group (for example, the Office of Mechanical Industries or the General Secretariat of the Merchant Marine) from "horizontal" services whose task of coordination covers the entire economy (the Office of Prices, the Office of International Economic Relations, etc.). Finally, another type of conflict is that which opposes central bureaucracies, anxious to preserve coherence and uniformity, and their local services, which are more sensitive to the particular needs of the local population than concerned with conforming to abstract norms.

Internal divisions within the administration originate not only from conflicts over positions and functions; they also stem from the fact that higher civil servants act, whether consciously or unconsciously, as spokesmen for the groups of administrative agents situated in the organizations for which they as executives are responsible. Such an attitude is easily explained: having been trained in a corps of administrators, the higher civil servant is emotionally attached to the values and objectives of that group. Even if he did not come up through the ranks, he endeavors to gain the confidence and to boost the morale of his collaborators by acting as an advocate for at least part of their demands. Thus it is often in the persons of higher civil servants that the various administrative corps confront one another to defend the status quo and to seek further advantages.

Administrative quarrels and jealousies express in part the conflicts over functions. Among the goals pursued by groups of agents is the desire to accomplish to their fullest those missions officially assigned them. Their esprit de corps thus only exacerbates any conflict regardless of its source. However, struggles between groups of administrators go much further: the survival and growth of the group becomes an end in itself, and the accomplishment of goals theoretically assigned to the organization becomes secondary or no more than an official justification.

Within the civil service, rivalries do more than oppose administrators with different educational backgrounds; they also embroil agents with the same backgrounds or the same type of background.

Permanent opposition exists between the corps of "technicians" and those civil servants whose education was liberal or general, especially in the ministries where both types of administrators are in competition for executive positions. A few years ago, the *Revue administrative* published a series of articles in which a civil servant in the Ministry of Agriculture denounced the quasi-monopoly of agronomists in the key posts of that department. "Those distinguished agronomists," he concluded after having exalted the merits of those administrators trained in law, "bear a heavy responsibility for the backwardness of French agriculture." Angered by an attack on their competence, the agronomists retorted with a condescending and ironic reply.

Rivalries among civil servants with administrative backgrounds are no less intense. Without discussing either the quarrels about prestige carried on by the higher administrative corps or the irritation caused among older administrators who were recruited differently by the occasionally arrogant attitude of former ENA students, one can point to the strained relations in the Ministry of Finance between the corps of civil administrators and the corps of the Office of Inspection of Finances. Three years ago the review *Promotions* published an interesting article on this subject by G. Bonin and P. Lelong, who belonged to the two groups in question. They wrote that "the presence of the Office of Inspection within the ministerial executive offices was hardly favored by the civil administrators but even in the best instances, simply tolerated; it is occasionally fought openly and not without some success." They concluded that the creation of a uniform system of recruitment via the ENA, far from having lessened a long-standing opposition, had actually aggravated it.

Finally, the disputes between technical corps, and notably between groups of engineers, must be mentioned. The conflict between engineers of the Department of Bridges and Roads and those of the Department of Rural Engineering, whose activities are very similar, is nowhere near abating. However, it is not as violent as that within the American administration which involves the Army Corps of Engineers and the technicians of the Department of the Interior, both of which are responsible for hydraulic projects. In his study of "the climate of human relations in the French tobacco industry," M. Crozier analysed the tensions which exist between the engineers educated at the *École Polytechnique* and the mechanical engineers from less prestigious institutions. The former, while admitting their inferiority in practical engineering, vigorously demanded the right to supervise the latter. Crozier was able to bring out the "widespread exasperation" at the mechanical engineers, "people it's difficult to get along with." Several of the engineers interviewed considered that "the corps of mechanical engineers had to be eliminated." As for the mechanical engineers, they declared themselves hostile to what they called "the caste of polytechnicians" and demanded that they be integrated into the executive group on a par with the higher engineers.

These few examples reveal the emotional aspects which characterize intercorps rivalries. Certainly the higher civil servants do not always share the chauvinism of their colleagues. Their loyalty to the group which they direct and in which they trained is tempered by the loyalty they feel toward the whole organization and also by their tendency to identify with another group, that of the executive elite. However, they must at least bear in mind the morale of "their men" and defend certain of their demands lest they lose the respect of the group.

THE POLITICAL AFFILIATIONS OF CERTAIN ADMINISTRATORS

The French civil service is not entirely "apolitical." In whatever concerns nominations to certain posts, the formal norms which govern the course of careers in bureaucratic organizations (recruitment by national examination, evaluation of the applicants' aptitudes by immediate hierarchical superiors, examination of the decision of promotion by an unbiased, representative committee) are not always respected or are not always the only criteria. Instead of or along with the official norms, other factors enter into consideration — membership in a party or a political group or the fact of having collaborated personally with a minister. If this definition is permitted, the relative politization of the French administration seems to be linked to two series of practices.

The first of these is the nomination of men without administrative experience to technical posts. Under the Fourth Republic some deputies defeated for re-election to Parliament were nominated to head organizations in the quasi-public sector. The Fifth Republic has not renounced such practices. Cases where persons completely outside the administration have been appointed to executive posts are fairly rare in spite of everything.

What is more common is abnormal administrative careers ("abnormal" because they deviate from the pattern usually described as bureaucratic "channels," rather than because of their rarity). Two extreme cases can be cited in this respect. The first is the case in which, thanks to ministerial intervention, a member of the civil service is promoted to a post higher than he could ever have achieved through normal channels, by his expertise (an engineer from Forests named director at the Ministry of Health) or by his statutory rank (an inspector at the Treasury named director of the Public Accounting Office). The second case is that in which political favoritism or a position on a minister's staff permits a civil servant to occupy a post "normally" open to him but sooner than he would have without political intervention (for example, a young civil administrator named assistant director after serving on a minister's staff). Between those two extremes there is of course room for every possible intermediate situation, e.g., outside influence in nominations to the Council of State and to the Audit Office, nominations of members to the prefectoral or diplomatic corps, etc.

In the general sense given to the term "political," are such nominations frequent? According to a survey undertaken in 1960, 50 percent of the actual directors of the central administration had collaborated with a minister, and 31 percent of them were nominated after working on a minister's staff.[1] It should be added that in the majority of these

---

[1] Pouydesseau, *Les directeurs des administrations centrales*. Dissertation for a doctorate in Political Science, Paris, 1962.

cases, the nominations benefited polyvalent civil servants of superior rank or whose particular specialty corresponded to the available post.

This relative politization of the higher posts in the French administration has several consequences for the homogeneity of the group of higher civil servants. In a limited number of cases, relations between a bureaucrat and a politician are not confined to technical assistance furnished by the former while serving on the minister's staff; the bureaucrat is politically active and remains so after his nomination to a higher post. Such fidelity to a party or a political figure makes a bureaucrat an outside element within the corps of higher civil servants; it is quite probable that he will not subscribe to an apolitical conception of the general interest.

In other cases, which seem to represent the norm, a higher civil servant does not consider his service on a minister's staff to have had any political significance. As far as he is concerned, it simply made him more sensitive to political life, taught him to appreciate problems from the point of view of someone in the government, and unveiled horizons vaster than those to which routine, compartmentalized work commits a civil servant. This process can turn him against certain technocratic conceptions, but at the same time it can separate him from other higher civil servants who remain tied to a strictly apolitical concept of the state. . . .

THE COHESIVE FACTORS

The elements of division to be found within the category of the higher civil servants are largely compensated by factors of uniformity of opinions and behavior. The common denominators seem to be the similar educational backgrounds; the existence of "channels" which favor certain psychological types; urban, bourgeois origin; the unifying influence of the higher administrative corps; and a certain community of goals and values.

The higher civil servants have not all received an identical education, but the majority of them graduate either from the Faculty of Law, the Institute of Political Sciences, or ENA, whose homogeneity cannot be denied, or from the École Polytechnique. Those different university backgrounds represent from the outset an element of division and an obstacle to good communication within the group of higher civil servants.

At the same time, the different backgrounds also have the effect of creating partial solidarities within the corps, which reduces the intensity of occupational conflicts, of intercorps rivalries, and of generational divisions. A common language and a similar manner of thinking and working facilitate the flow of information. School friendships make possible the institution of informal networks of communication between the ministries, which attenuates, at least in part, the insufficiencies of official coordination.

The above analysis has shown that despite everything it is fairly rare for a higher civil servant to have risen to that status through purely political channels.

The most frequent situation is the nomination either of men who have followed strictly bureaucratic channels but who have passed through the various stages more rapidly than their peers or of men who have pursued a partially bureaucratic career, which has been interrupted by political phases, thus permitting them to skip certain steps or to speed them up. In both cases, the careers began with a national examination. The phenomenon of the national examination has considerable importance because it tends to select individuals as much on their psycho-social attitudes as on their knowledge per se.

Any national examination tends to classify individuals on the basis of knowledge and aptitude deemed indispensable first by the authorities who wrote the examination and then by the graders and examiners — the latter being free to interpret the former's decisions. As for those national examinations which lead to civil service careers, the ministerial committees which determine the material for the test and the juries which evaluate the candidates are composed of civil servants who have a very understandable tendency to think that the knowledge and aptitudes which the candidates must possess are the same that they themselves formerly displayed so brilliantly. The officers' schools have always awarded highest marks to those officers who show an aptitude for winning battles from the preceding war; likewise, administrative examinations are inclined to favor those candidates who carry the credentials of traditional knowledge. The national examination is selective in another way: if knowledge is equal, highest marks go to the sensible, well-balanced, skillful candidates. That leaves less chance for the inventive or heterodox mind.

The mechanism of selection which prevails at the beginning of a career continues to function throughout it at moments of advancement. If technical abilities are equal, the authorities responsible for promotion often prefer individuals who know how "to play the game" and to adapt themselves rather than the imprudent or intransigent candidates. This is even more true the closer one gets to the top of the hierarchy.

A system founded on a recruitment by national examination and on a notion of a career such as that which prevails in the French administration gives therefore the maximum advantage to individuals who have assimilated if not accepted the norms inherent in the system: the gamut of temperaments and types of minds is thereby reduced and the homogeneity of the group reinforced.

In the United States, where many of the higher administrative posts (under secretaries, assistant secretaries, assistants to the secretary, etc.) are filled from outside the normal channels, the high administration is much less homogeneous; professional politicians maintain close relations with university professors, attorneys, and industrialists, who bring to their administrative tasks knowledge and temperaments much more diversified than in Great Britain and France.

During the nineteenth and the beginning of the twentieth centuries, the corps of high civil servants was recruited almost exclusively from the upper levels of society: the Parisian and, to a lesser extent, the provincial aristocracy, the commercial bourgeoisie, and the liberal professions. In many patrician families, a son succeeded his father in service to the state; the tradition persists to this day. Evolution in the last fifty years has increased social mobility. This transformation has obviously not occurred without shocks. Bureaucrats from privileged social groups have more or less unconsciously tended to slow down the development, but little by little recruitment methods, which once openly permitted social favoritism, have been abolished or amended.

How can this relative democratization of the state elites be explained? The extension of the number of state functions and the growth in the volume of service furnished by the public services by multiplying the number of bureaucrats have increased the available executive posts; thus numerous internal promotions were facilitated. Wars, purges, the development of *pantouflage*,* and advancements due to service on ministers' staffs have contributed equally to the mobility of elites.

Democratization of the high administration is thus real, but limited in scope. The urban and landed aristocracies and the privileged upper bourgeoisie are no longer in the majority. If their absolute number remains constant, the percentage of them in the administration has decreased to the benefit of the middle bourgeoisie and to a certain extent of the lower bourgeoisie of merchants, artisans, employees, and lower industrial managerial personnel. On the other hand, the proportion of industrial and agricultural workers' sons and of small farmers (even those whose standard of living is fairly high) is extremely low.

Thus the higher civil servants have one trait in common: they all belong to the bourgeoisie or to those social groups which hope to enter the bourgeoisie, and as a result they all accept the same norms of behavior. Besides, they come almost exclusively from urban backgrounds; although the rural or agricultural sector of the French population is still appreciable, such origins are not represented in the high administration.

Numerous observers, French and foreign, reduce the French high administration to the traditional high administrative corps. Such a simplistic view may be explained by the fact that the institution has no equivalent in any other country in the world. Seen in correct proportion, the influence of the high corps is nonetheless real. Just as one can speak of *dominant economies,* so one can speak of *dominant administrations* with regard to the high corps.

The influence of the high corps manifests itself in the first place in that its members exercise their control within every sector of the administration. The jurisdictional control of the Council of State extends to all governmental decisions while the activities of its consulta-

---

* [*Pantouflage:* the practice of taking the former civil servant into private business at a high salary for the prestige of his association as well as his contacts.—Eds.]

tive sections concern most ministerial projects. The controls exercised by the Office of Inspection of Finances and by the Audit Office cover all or almost all central and local administrations.

The ubiquity of the high corps is also explained by the fact that its members are present in all or almost all ministries and major administrations. There are thirty to fifty permanent higher civil servants on ministerial staffs; by assignment administrators of the Office of Inspection of Finances and of the Council of State are appointed to head numerous ministerial executive offices. The Office of Inspection in particular controls most of the command posts of the financial and economic sector. Finally, members of the high corps, notably those of the Council of State and the Audit Office, are involved in numerous administrative decisions because of their participation in multiple consultative commissions where they serve as presidents, secretaries-general, or reporters.

By accomplishing the tasks officially assigned them and even more by their activity and ubiquity throughout the entire administration, the high corps contributes to the unification of French bureaucracy. The majority of higher civil servants belong to the corps; their presence in elite governing circles is without a doubt one of the factors which assists most forcefully to preserve a certain ideology exclusive to the French high administration.

COMMON OBJECTIVES AND THE DOCTRINE OF THE GENERAL INTEREST

Does the group of higher civil servants possess its own particular will? Are the members consciously or unconsciously guided by their desire to attain certain specific objectives or by a preoccupation to make certain values prevail?

1. The behavior of the higher civil servants is explained in the first place by an elementary concern for survival, without which the pursuit of other ends would not be conceivable. This will to survive includes both the personal security of the civil servants themselves, who attempt to hold on to a position whose precariousness they understand, and the will to preserve the institutional framework within which they are situated.

2. Is the conduct of the higher civil servants also explained by their concern with maintaining or increasing their personal incomes? Such an interpretation should not be excluded a priori. It is important to note, however, that the higher civil servants are generally found at the top of the hierarchy of public salaries — in the category called the *échelles-lettres*. It is not, therefore, within the public service as such that they could hope to augment their incomes. Usually they would have to leave the high administrative corps to achieve that.

It has often been said that the European sentiments among French higher civil servants stem from the golden prospects which the creation of supranational administrations hold out for them. It is possible that such a calculation played a part for certain individuals when the question of creating those institutions was before them. It is also true that the establishment of those organizations would scarcely have elicited any enthusiasm from the higher civil servants if they had thought their careers were threatened.

3. Are the higher civil servants animated by a concern for increasing their personal prestige as well as the glory of the group to which they belong? The concern for personal and collective honor holds an important place in the minds of the higher civil servants. As the reputation of the great engineering institutes and of the high administrative corps demonstrates (the constant use of the words "great," "high," and "superior" is significant), considerations of prestige seem to be one of the fundamental individual motivations, as much within the French administration system as in its relations with outside elements. The sense of prestige is even more savored since it offers at least partial compensation for the frustrations higher civil servants experience because of the differences between private and public remunerations. The prestige attached to certain functions or to certain corps is carefully preserved; it permits the corps to attract numerous qualified candidates and thus to maintain a high level of recruitment which in turn contributes to the permanence of the system.

The higher civil servants' consciousness of being at the top of the ladder of prestige and values recognized by the French society explains their psychology to a large extent, e.g., their concern with preserving their rank and keeping their distance and their attitude toward other executive groups, so willfully expressing superiority.

4. "This profession obtains power which has grown with the importance of the state in economic life, research into which is today the principal concern of the high civil servants. The director of the Treasury receives a much lower salary than the director of a private bank, but his power is greater. Moreover, he exercises that power over a much larger area, the nation as a whole. The higher civil servants like being part of the hundred or so persons who debate the affairs of the nation among themselves; they consider it more satisfying, to paraphrase Cicero, to command the rich than to be rich themselves."[2] This quotation from an article by C. Brindillac expresses in a felicitous manner the well-founded or illusory sentiment of the higher civil servants, who direct national affairs, and the satisfaction they derive from it.

A few years ago in certain business circles of economic liberalism, the high civil servants were frequently described as beings driven by a dark *libido dominandi* or as megalomaniacs who wanted to reduce the entire country to slavery. Such statements are patently extreme, but it is true that most higher civil servants identify in good faith with the state they desire, a centralized, conformist-minded state, which would not tolerate alongside it any force capable of holding its own. They feel that the authority of such a state is constantly being thwarted by centrifugal

---

[2] "Les hauts fonctionnaires et le capitalisme," *Esprit,* June, 1953.

forces and dismemberment.[3] Numerous administrators experience the anxiety over *public power,* which is found in the books of M. Debré: do not lawbooks on which they were nourished repeat continually that the essence of the relationship between the state and the citizens is their fundamental inequality?

The institutional reforms of the Fifth Republic have been greeted with favor by the young bureaucrats graduated from ENA, even if "their hearts are on the left," because they see such reforms as moving in the direction of a restoration of the state, which is one of the leitmotivs of education at that school.

5. Do the higher civil servants as a group profess a doctrine unique to them? Besides those doctrines proper to each service or each corps, does there exist a common understanding which gives a certain ideological unity to the group? If one questions the members of the civil service about the ideal which those who are responsible for the state endeavor to achieve or at least should try to attain, the response will almost always be the same: the satisfaction of the general interest. Such a formula is tautological according to all evidence: the general interest is a notion without objective meaning, which everyone applies to his own objectives or his own conception of power and society.

What does the general interest represent for the higher civil servants who claim it as their authority? Their private opinions can be organized around two basic themes. The first body of opinion believes that the search for the general interest is identical to the effort to transform society in terms of technical and economic progress. For these individuals the role of the administrative elite is to incite or at least to encourage the forces which are moving toward expansion and modernization. The society of tomorrow, for which these civil servants more or less confusingly long and whose advent they feel they hasten by their daily actions, is not an inhuman collectivity peopled by robots. It is a prosperous city free from misery, suffering, and ignorance. The state civil servants are humanists . . . , but the increase in the standard of living and the growth of population are inseparable from a certain rationalization of society. That implies the elimination of waste in any form and the organization of a cooperative life-style, where individuals and institutions would be united by clear, stable relationships.

It is precisely the high administration which must be the agent for these transformations — the enlightened minority which will reveal society to itself. By a prolonged effort of education, the state must teach the various economic and social groups to perceive their true interest. But even before this awareness comes about, the administration must act; it must not hesitate to compel the governed, for their own sake, to change their routines and to drop their quarrels.

The higher civil servants who share this viewpoint sometimes consider themselves revolutionaries. They are certainly not in the usual sense of the word: the overthrow of public institutions, the accession to power

---

[3] See the last report of the Audit Office (Cour des comptes), "Les démembrements de l'administration," public report 1960–61, pp. 42–51.

of new political groups, or changes in the laws of property seem to them false problems. Rather, they are profoundly reformist. The state with which they identify appears to them capable of conceiving and applying by persuasion or force structural changes which they deem necessary. The state can do anything it wants to do, they would say. If they have sufficient breadth of views and a capability confirmed by experience, men of character can surmount any obstacle and disprove any determinism.

Within the corps of higher civil servants, there is also a second school of thought, whose conception of the general interest and of the role of the administration is very different. These men are less concerned with making society progress by means of long-term plans than they are with maintaining stability and harmony. For them the general interest rests with the preservation of certain values (national unity, order, state sovereignty), which a victory of particular interests would threaten. The state must act as arbiter before everything else. According to this opinion, the higher civil servants have a mission to prevent the dynamism of technology and economics or the tests of strength between political and social groups from dislocating society. To eliminate the use of violence in relations between individuals and groups; to anticipate and reduce conflicts by getting adversaries to join and accept state arbitration; to prevent necessary economic and social mutations from occurring in a disorderly fashion; to maintain the state above the confusion in order to safeguard its prestige, without which it would not be able to exercise its regulatory functions: such are the principal concerns of the second body of higher civil servants.

The two visions of the general interest and of the elite role of the administration are not contradictory. In many respects they are complementary and often coexist in the same mind. The reformist optimism of the first school and the belief in the virtues of rational organization and long-term planning are widespread among the younger bureaucrats, particularly those educated at ENA, the agents of the economic and financial services, and the technicians (engineers, architects, city planners, etc.). Among the most striking expressions of this current of thought are the writings of the group, "Prospective," of which many either former or actual higher civil servants are members. The second body of opinion commands more attention among the older generations of civil servants — in the judicial corps such as the Council of State or the Audit Office, and among the higher polyvalent bureaucrats who exercise functions of authority or representation (the prefectoral and diplomatic corps).

Both conceptions have a common characteristic: they are apolitical (without a doubt it is truer of the first group than the second). That trait stems less from their hostility on principle to politicians and parties, their passions, and their games than it does from an unconscious or deliberate dismissal of them as negligible phenomena or problems about which a neutral expert does not have to make a decision. The state of the higher civil servants — avant-garde for some, impartial arbiter for others, authoritarian but paternal for both — is a state free of all political ferment.

JOSEPH LA PALOMBARA

Parentela *Relationships in Italian Government*

The phenomenon of favoritism for political clients and relatives is not specifically Italian; it is universal and old. For example, feudalism rested on "clientelism." Political clientela *are a general phenomenon in most of the countries of Latin America, and in a restrained form, political patronage is practiced in the United States, too. Political* parentela *are found in Communist countries as well as in Ireland. But in Italy, for reasons analyzed by Joseph LaPalombara, the* clientela *and* parentela *relationship take on a particular importance because of the conjunction of many factors: the hegemony of a political party without interruption for a quarter of a century; the fact that this party is in reality a federation of tendencies and factions; the existence of a public administration of the Napoleonic type; the feeling among part of the population that they are on the periphery, far from the capital; the preferential vote, which permits the voter to choose from among various candidates of the same party; and the existence of very well-organized, para-political groups.*

In its strict Italian sense, *parentela* means consanguinity, lineage, or kinship. A *parente* is a member of one's family and in Italian culture is entitled thereby to special consideration. In the traditional South, whence most of Italy's bureaucrats are recruited, ties of *parentela* are particularly strong, implying the kind of rights and obligations that are generally associated with pre-industrial societies.

As used here, *parentela* involves a relatively close and integral relationship between certain associational interest groups, on the one hand,

Abridged from Joseph LaPalombara, "Bureaucratic Intervention: Parentela," in *Interest Groups in Italian Politics*, pp. 306–348 (Copyright © 1964 by Princeton University Press). Reprinted by permission of Princeton University Press.

and the politically dominant Christian Democratic Party (DC), on the other. It is this relationship between group and party — and not strictly between group and bureaucracy — which is of interest to us. The generalized proposition we shall explore is that where *parentela* exists, and where certain other related conditions are met, interest groups that enjoy the relationship can exercise considerable influence over a bureaucracy quite apart from any consideration of *clientela*.

At first glance it may appear truistic to suggest that interest groups can have an impact on the bureaucratic process as a result of the intimate relationship the groups may enjoy with the party or parties in power. However, the phenomenon is much more complex than may appear at first. How pervasive and intensive may be the impact of any particular group on public administration will depend on a number of *parentela* conditions or variables that are discussed below. Moreover, it must be remembered that, according to the strictures of the classical democratic model, the administrative sector of government is supposed to represent an instrumental meritocracy, unblemished by patronage, and the party or parties in power presumably are there to guarantee that the access of organized groups to the points of decision and policy is not too badly unbalanced.

Obviously the groups that intervene in the bureaucracy do not do so exclusively on the basis of *clientela*, on the one hand, or *parentela*, on the other. Very frequently, aspects of both relationships are present. However, a central tendency can usually be isolated for any of the major groups and the nature of that central tendency, in the Italian setting, will tell us a great deal about group style as well as the relative influence — in both the short and the long run — that the group involved can expect to exercise over public administration. . . .

What are the conditions or variables on which successful *parentela* is based?

I. THE HEGEMONIC QUALITY OF THE PARTY

This is the key variable affecting *parentela*, and it has two dimensions — spatial and temporal. Spatially, the hegemonic party is overwhelmingly dominant; its bases of support outweigh by far those of all others; other parties with which it might collaborate in the business of governing do so not so much because of intrinsic power qualities but because they are essentially *guests in power*. In short, this dimension of hegemony is not present where there exists any uncertainty regarding which of the several parties that may be competing is the dominant one. Thus, despite the omnipresence of the French Radical Party in succeeding governments through the years of the Third and Fourth Republics, it did not possess this quality of hegemony. On the other hand, Adenauer's Christian Democratic Union has manifested this quality at the national level over most of the life of the Bonn Republic. Similarly, the Italian Christian Democrats . . . are clearly the hegemonic party as far as the spatial dimension is concerned.

Christian Democratic leaders frankly recognize that they enjoy this privileged status. They speak of the "governmental vocation" of the DC, of the fact that there would occur a very serious power void in Italy should the party step out of government. One of the leaders whom I interviewed candidly says: "Christian Democracy is the party of government, and as such it exercises a clear monopoly of power, of the opportunities for acquiring and exercising it, and, more important, of its distribution in Italian society."

This respondent goes on to point out that this favored position regarding political power is critical to an understanding of why and how the DC can bring together under one roof a number of contrasting groups and a number of political leaders whose views are far from compatible with each other. Concerning the attractive quality of political hegemony, he says: "It may well be that every group or individual within the party cannot enjoy the same opportunities for the control or·exercise of power. But at least they have no intention of cutting themselves out of the power game — that is, they would not cut themselves out of the major instrument through which power can be secured, exercised, and generally controlled."

The DC is then described as an organization with which two kinds of groups are associated. First, there are the *internal* groups (i.e. those that enjoy *parentela*), which seek to condition the Party from the inside. Although it is true that these groups are often in conflict, it is not accurate to conclude, as many in Italy do, that the issues that divide them are irreconcilable. For example, differences between Giulio Pastore, Paolo Bonomi, and Giuseppe Togni — all of whom lead different *parentela* groups — are not as acute as may appear in the national press or in the parliamentary debates. These men are all Christian Democrats — Catholics who share not merely an urge to exercise power but also the methodology of moderation and compromise that is implicit in Catholicism itself. Even when the internal groups genuinely differ, they do so within narrow parameters; revolution or radical, intemperate proposals are not likely to emerge from any of them.

The DC is also seen as having to cope with groups that are *external* to it. These groups do not share a *parentela* relationship but, to some extent, they seek to make their influence felt through the agency of the dominant party. Confindustria is seen in this light. . . .

The spatial quality of *parentela* we are discussing is not only understood by Christian Democratic leaders but also and necessarily by the bureaucrats as well. Thus, an official of the Ministry of Foreign Affairs states that while his ministry tends to ignore interventions of single deputies or senators on behalf of interest groups, there are important mitigating circumstances to this practice. According to this respondent, an MP who represents the party in power is always accorded more respectful attention than any other. If the MP is also the chairman of a parliamentary committee, he will receive still more attention. If, to add to his qualifications, the lawmaker is on the Cabinet or close to the Cabinet, or if he is viewed as a potential Cabinet member, even greater attention will be accorded his requests. In short, public adminstrators are capable of making careful and rational calculations regarding exactly how much influence on behalf of a group an individual legislator is potentially entitled to exert on the machinery of public administration. Reflecting exactly such a calculation, as well as the spatial dimension of party hegemony, the respondent observes: "As far as the political party affiliation of the deputy is concerned, the only party that counts at the moment in public administration is Christian Democracy. We find little need to pay attention to the demands or the threats of the other political parties, or their representatives, or their deputies, or their senators. The political parties are certainly aware of this game and they understand that things would change to some extent if the DC were no longer in power."

If the dominance of the DC were absolutely, unqualifiedly unchallenged, we might suppose that certain of Italy's interest groups would be totally excluded from the policy process. Such a consequence would logically follow from the extreme nature of intergroup antagonism and from the discernible widespread tendency of group leaders to assume that to share political power means to keep the "enemy" completely bereft of it. But the fondest hopes of many of the more ardent DC Catholics have been somewhat dashed by the electoral results of 1953, 1958 and 1963 which compel the dominant party to rely on the collaboration of the minor Center parties, and in 1964 of the PSI. A result of this is the according of some influence to groups that are not in a *parentela* relationship to the DC but that may have such a relationship with one of the minor parties in a governmental coalition. The Italian Union of Labor is one of these, and one of its leaders, in explaining why his organization is not completely impotent in administrative circles, says: "The reason for this is that the DC does not yet have an absolute majority in the parliament and therefore really has need of its allies, particularly among Social Democrats." The point is, however, that even when such a pattern exists, it is made possible not because of any intrinsic strength of the minor party involved but really because of its more or less temporary relationship to the dominant, hegemonic party. In short, minor parties and the groups they encompass may be guests in power and share in the feast of influence which is everyday fare for the *parentela* groups.

The temporal dimension of party hegemony involves the perception of the party's dominant position as being stable over time and not transitory. The interviews evince a great deal of attention to this particular dimension of hegemony, as they naturally would. An official in the Ministry of the Treasury stresses, when discussing the impact of groups on the administrative process, that "the situation for the Italian bureaucrat has become aggravated by the continuous presence over a period of a decade of a single party in power in Italy." A leader of the Italian Union of Labor, attempting to analyze the patterns of bureaucratic response to group demands, says, "Much depends on the kind of judgment that the bureaucrat can make regarding the permanency of the party involved in the government coalition." . . .

A member of the Senate whose perceptions regarding public administration are very acute treats the matter of permanency in office as a significant variable. He points out that, to some extent, the pressure that can be exerted on the bureaucracy is in part a function of the character of the bureaucracy itself. To put this matter simply, bureaucrats will differ in both their capacity and their willingness to resist attempts to dictate administrative decisions on the basis of *parentela* considerations. However, even when bureaucratic characteristics are held constant, it is apparent that a group's relationship to a party long in power will make a significant difference to its influence potential in bureaucratic circles. The increasing incidence of *parentela*-dictated administrative decisions, in the view of our respondent: ". . . is due primarily to the fact that the same party has been in power for ten years. If there had been more frequent changes in the Parliament, then this might very well have worked to the advantage of the bureaucracy itself. But when, year after year, the same men are in power, it is inevitable that the bureaucracy will begin to take on a political coloration that does not conflict with that of the majority party. This is instrumentalization of the bureaucracy with a vengeance. I feel that this tendency would be true of whichever dominant party were in a position to appoint the superior bureaucrats."

Regarding France, this matter has been explored by Henry Ehrmann, who points out that "in twentieth-century France the bureaucracy has enjoyed an unusual degree of autonomy because of the absence of a stable political leadership and the ineffectiveness of parliament and political parties as a voice and molder of public opinion."[1] At another place, the same author tells us that "many French functionaries maintain that, under the Fourth Republic, they were perfectly able to defend themselves against parliamentary pressures transmitting requests of interest groups."[2] This is precisely because there did not exist a strong party system capable of aggregating interests and exercising control over the bureaucratic apparatus. Under these conditions, the bureaucrats could comply with or ignore group requests almost at will.

Parentela would not be possible under the conditions that Ehrmann describes for France. In Italy, on the other hand, the postwar situation has been dramatically different. Beginning as early as 1946, the DC has been a major factor in politics; from 1948 to 1953 it enjoyed absolute majorities in both branches of the legislature; and from 1953 to the present it has been the unchallenged dominant political party. Its leaders have acquired considerable skill in dealing with power centers such as

---

[1] Henry W. Ehrmann, "French Bureaucracy and Organized Interests," *Administrative Science Quarterly*, 5 (March, 1961), p. 535. Cf. the important supporting evidence presented by Alfred Diamant, "The French Administrative System—The Republic Passes but the Administration Remains," in W. J. Siffin, ed., *Toward the Comparative Study of Public Administration* (Bloomington, Indiana, 1957), pp. 182–218.

[2] Henry W. Ehrmann, "Les Groupes d'intérêt et la bureaucratie dans les démocraties occidentales," *Revue Française de Science Politique*, 11 (September, 1961), pp. 555 [translated in this reader, pp. 333–353].

the bureaucracy, and, if our respondents are to be believed, they have not hesitated to use their considerable power to bring the bureaucracy into line when such a move was felt to be important. For these reasons it would indeed be very surprising if groups sharing a *parentela* relationship to the DC did not derive a certain advantage from the Party's hegemony.

II. WILLINGNESS OF PARTY TO INTERVENE

But hegemony is not alone sufficient to create the *parentela* pattern I am describing. A second condition requires that the bureaucrats perceive the dominant party as willing to intervene in the administrative process on behalf of its own narrow interests, or those of groups affiliated with the party. The DC's "will to power" is so often uttered by the Party's leaders and so widely understood in Italian society as to require little documentation here. Public administrators, interest-group leaders, and political officials are almost unanimous in viewing the dominant party as perfectly willing to go to considerable lengths to impose its will on the country. The increasing talk of the "under-government" (*sottogoverno*) that has characterized the country in recent years reflects not only this widely held perception but also the conviction that the Party will not be hobbled or restrained by genteel considerations of legality or democratic propriety.

It should be noted, however, that the perceived "will to power" does not necessarily imply massive intervention in favor of implementing a coherent and cohesive political program. The same party that is seen as having created a vast and complicated labyrinth of *sottogoverno* is generally criticized for offering the country little by way of an integrated program, for temporizing with many of the basic problems that cry out for attention, and for reflecting in its behavior the disparate groups, interests, and orientations that make up the Party itself. Thus, when speaking of the Party's willingness to intervene in the bureaucracy, UIL and CGIL leaders remark that it does so in favor of CISL; leaders of, say, the Italian General Association of Entertainment claim that intervention occurs on behalf of Catholic Action; Confindustria representatives see the intervention as designed to favor ENI and other state-owned economic enterprises; Confagricoltura officials worry that the Party may be favoring Paolo Bonomi's Coltivatori Diretti. . . .

Given the nature of the DC, it is probably reasonable to suppose that, depending on the issue and the occasion, intervention in the bureaucracy may occur for any one of the particular and sometimes antagonistic groups that make up the party. The DC is perhaps the only political party in Italy that substantially encompasses groups of somewhat varied ideological and programmatic persuasion, and it would therefore be surprising if the Party did not perform a relatively important role as both interest articulator and interest aggregator. If every issue that involved the bureaucracy succeeded in mobilizing at opposed points all of the major groups that enjoy a *parentela* relationship to the DC, the Party would very quickly break to pieces. Even under existing circumstances, where major groups might be defined as interested in particular policy spheres, there is overlapping of interests that causes considerable strain within the Party. . . .

But from the vantage point of the public administrators, the critical consideration is not so much the nature of the *parentela* groups on behalf of which the DC is willing to act as it is the knowledge that the Party is willing to intervene at all. To be sure, it may be that members of the Ministry of Industry and Commerce would prefer to have the Party approach the bureaucracy to further Confindustria's rather than organized labor's interests. Or, to put this obvious surmise differently, the bureaucrats would welcome political interference in favor of decisional directions in which the bureaucrats were moving in any case. When this is not the case, the demand of a *parentela* group, or of the party on behalf of such a group, clearly raises for the bureaucrat the question of how far the Party is willing to go in having a particular interest prevail.

Bureaucrats who respond to the stimulus of *parentela*, and few of them do not, even though they may claim immunity, are prone to take certain presumed rewards and punishments into consideration. The most apparent of these involves the Party's perceived willingness and ability to have an impact on bureaucratic careers. Bureaucrats who candidly speak of this matter insist that most sensible public administrators will not react to *parentela* group demands in a manner that will in some way jeopardize professional mobility. It may be, as some of our bureaucratic respondents suggest, that fewer of them will deliberately work out a pattern of behavior designed to encourage promotion on the basis of political considerations; but the absence of initiative to use the dominant party opportunistically does not imply that the bureaucrat who is under pressure will also be tenacious in resisting that pressure. . . . It is far from my intention, therefore, to suggest that the Italian bureaucracy is a limp instrument to be used by the DC and its *parentela* groups exactly as they desire. I do mean to say, however, that bureaucrats believe that the Party can and does interfere in the careers of public administrators and that the presence of this fear is an important reason why the *parentela* pattern is possible at all. . . .

III. GROUP CAPACITY TO CONDITION THE PARTY

Obviously not all interest groups in Italy are in a *parentela* relationship to the DC, and, among those that are, not all represent for the bureaucracy equally powerful aggregations. We can begin by observing that *parentela* requires that a group succeed in finding a place *inside* the Christian Democratic Party. For most of the groups that fall into this category, a basic commitment to Catholicism seems to be important, although not absolutely essential. For example, in the days when Angelo Costa was president of Confindustria, the Confederation was to some degree a *parentela* group — not as closely related, perhaps, as Catholic

Action or the Coltivatori Diretti, but a *parentela* group nevertheless. Whatever else might be said about Confindustria, it would certainly be far-fetched to maintain that, as an organization, it is committed to the goal of aggrandizing Catholic power in the society. Even though, in terms of reactions to such problems as economic planning and industrial nationalization, Confindustria and Catholic Action often appear on the same side, the leaders of both organizations agree that the industrial Confederation is strongly opposed to the integralistic tendencies that many Catholic groups manifest. Indeed, when speaking of their own political goals, Catholic Action leaders are almost certain to observe that they wish to reduce the degree of influence that the Freemasons and Liberals in Confindustria have long been able to exercise over the social, economic, and political systems. When leaders of left-wing or laical groups indiscriminately couple Confindustria and Catholic Action politically, they not only obscure the difference between *clientela* and *parentela* but slide over the very real points of conflict that exist in the interaction between these two associations.

It is also obvious that DC groups such as CISL, on the one hand, and ACLI, on the other, differ considerably in the extent of their commitment and devotion to the aims of organized Catholicism. For all of their having to adhere to the general policy orientations of the DC, it is obvious that CISL leaders are often restive in this role, that they are strongly cross-pressured by basic trade-union needs, on one side and the requirements and demands of Catholicism, on the other. The fact is that even if non-Christian Democrats constitute a very minute proportion of CISL's total membership, the Confederation does purport to recruit from various political groups and is also adamant in proclaiming its nonconfessional nature. No such considerations characterize or inhibit the ACLI. It is openly a Catholic organization, intervening in the labor sphere specifically for the purpose of counteracting among Italian workers what it (and organized Catholicism in general) considers the nefarious consequences of Marxist, materialist, and laical ideas.

Thus, in thinking of *parentela* groups within the DC, it is of importance not to assume that they are all equally confessional. While it may be true that a basic confessional thread is what holds the many varied DC units together in the Party, it is manifestly too simplistic to assume that what the group leaders share in common is a firm devotion to Catholic philosophy and a commitment to increasing Catholic power. To some extent — and it is now clear to me that Catholic Action leaders recognize this — Italians have joined Catholic groups for purely opportunistic reasons. In a country where the Catholic Party has enjoyed unchallenged political hegemony for fifteen years, those who experience strong drives toward the exercise of political power see the *parentela* groups as channels of political mobility. In any event, the fact that most such groups seem to have same fairly strong relationship to Catholicism should not lead to the conclusion that this commitment is the central condition on which *parentela* status can be achieved. To cite the one most dramatic exception, it is apparent that, at least in the years before the DC had established its own strong bases of patronage and financing,

Confindustria managed to develop reasonably strong *parentela* simply by providing the Party with badly needed campaign funds.

As far as the relative *parentela* strength that a group can achieve is concerned, the critical factor seems to be how many votes the group controls and can deliver to the party. One member of the Chamber of Deputies comments that an important reason why Catholic Action has strength in DC is that it is strongly and directly represented on party councils and in the legislature. Men who entered politics after long years of activity in Catholic Action or who, even after entering politics, retain positions of leadership in Catholic Action units can be counted on to articulate the interests of the latter organization. However, he goes on to stress that direct representation and the voicing of Catholic Action views is in turn related to a much more significant phenomenon. . . .

As far as the bureaucracy is concerned, it is fairly apparent that the *parentela* groups that loom as the most formidable are generally the ones with the greatest vote-getting strength. Catholic Action is seen as enormously powerful in this regard and quite able and willing to do whatever is necessary to have its views accorded a very respectful hearing in bureaucratic circles. Bureaucrats who mumble about priests and bishops who scurry about ministerial corridors in search of concessions tend to associate this activity with Catholic Action, even when the connection between the clergy's personal intervention and the massive Catholic holding company is anything but clear. Depending on the ministry involved, the other *parentela* groups of the DC are identified as deserving of special consideration because of the mass basis of their memberships and the presumed ability of group leaders to use them to elect Christian Democrats in general and group leaders in particular. The one important exception to this generalization is ENI, which does not have a mass membership base. In its case, however, bureaucrats, like Confindustria's and those of other groups, are convinced that ENI's advantaged position grows out of its unchallenged ability to use funds to aid in the election of some legislative candidates and the defeat of others. . . .

IV. CHARACTERISTICS OF THE BUREAUCRACY

As we noted briefly earlier, the ability of a *parentela* group to utilize the dominant party to make its influence felt in the bureaucracy will also depend on certain salient structural characteristics of the latter. When attempting to understand the impact of this variable, we are led to ask such questions as: How much centralization of decisional authority does the bureaucracy manifest? Regardless of the requirements of formal authority, how much decentralized decisional power exists in fact? Is there a merit system and, if so, how far up the public administrative hierarchy does it extend? What are the norms that are in fact applied in matters of personnel, such as recruitment, placement, transfer, and promotion? Are there particular types of agencies that seem to be more or less susceptible to the application of *parentela* pressure?

The Italian bureaucracy has been characterized by extreme centralization of authority, both geographical and functional. Internally, the directors-general are at the apex of the structure of authority. Presumably nothing of any consequence can occur within their directorates for which they fail to affix their formal approval. A complaint frequently voiced by those administrators lower in the hierarchy is that decisions are held in abeyance, pending the signatures of section and division chiefs, inspectors-general, directors-general, and frequently the ministers themselves. One result of this hierarchical review of decisions, it is claimed, is to inhibit initiative and to encourage administrative timidity. A bureaucrat who wants to be absolutely sure of himself — who wants to avoid trouble or embarrassment — will react to each situation according to the rule book, leaving it to the person immediately above him in the hierarchy to exercise creative departures from stultifying routine.

In the years since administrative reform has become the subject of attention, some efforts, most of them weak and ineffective, have been made to encourage decentralization of authority. . . . Directors-general and others who are defined as extremely jealous of their status and prerogatives are evidently unwilling to see formal authority slip out of their hands. The criticism that administrative reform, in almost all its facets, has thus far been either stillborn or a total fiasco is a widely held view in Italy.[3]

An official of the Ministry of the Treasury describes the 1957 Reform Statute as a "tragicomedy." He notes that there is widespread hostility to bureaucratic reform among many groups in the country. Included among the opposition "is the Bourbonic indifference of the higher bureaucrats, many of whom are actually hostile to scientific administration." Another official, in the Ministry of Finance, claims that the obstacles to change are to be traced to the unification of Italy and the superimposition on the Italian bureaucracy of a paternalistic administrative system with "the tendency toward the protection of the interests of privileged classes, the negation of private individual rights, and opportunism deprived of justice." He adds that notwithstanding the posture of the highest-level bureaucrats, there are many younger people in the bureaucracy who favor reform and who would like to see decisional authority more widely and substantially dispersed within the ministries. A third official, a section leader in the Ministry of the Treasury, laments that delegation of authority and other reforms will never take place as long as the political leadership is unwilling to compel directors-general to accept change. Regarding these latter officials, most of whom date from the Fascist era, he says: "These directors-general and inspectors-general are often opponents of reform for ideological reasons. That is, they have never actually been able to accept the democratic state. They are very

---

[3] For a criticism of the bureaucracy and its desperate need for reform, see Cesare Zappulli, "La Burocrazia vista da un giornalista," in *Problemi della pubblica amministrazione* (Bologna, 1960), pp. 203–10. Some of the examples of bureaucratic waste and irrationality cited by the author are not unlike those discovered in the U.S. federal bureaucracy by the Hoover Commission task forces.

frequently opponents of the Republic. They are, in any case, likely to resent any effort on the part of the new political regime to suggest that the usages of the past are inefficient or otherwise wanting. . . . In the last analysis, the most impressive willingness on the part of a minister or other political representatives in the ministry to effect change will surely run up against the enormous power of inertia and sabotage that resides in the hands of the directors-general and the inspectors-general."

I do not intend to challenge here either the assumption that Italian administration is highly centralized internally or that many top-level administrators — for ideological, psychological, or other reasons — are opposed to change. Directors-general who were interviewed in this study certainly agree that little actual delegation of authority has occurred, though they tend to ascribe this failure to the unwillingness of subordinates to accept greater responsibilities.

I do wish to suggest, however, that if the actual distribution of power in the bureaucracy mirrored the formal distribution of authority, interest-group leaders would be advised to limit their interaction to those occupying the very highest positions in the bureaucratic hierarchy. The fact is that no such restricted pattern prevails; any number of group leaders assure us that they effect contacts with officials at several bureaucratic levels. As a matter of fact, organizations such as Confindustria and the Italian Banking Association have developed an organizational pattern of status equals and counterparts who maintain close relations with bureaucrats at various levels.

The point is that, while authority is highly centralized in the bureaucracy, effective power is somewhat dispersed. It could not be otherwise. Thus the bureaucrats themselves recognize that a considerable amount of de facto decentralization exists and it is not alone those at the top who have the power to make important concessions to interest groups. It is this failure to recognize what exists in fact that results in a certain amount of disorientation, even chaos, in administrative behavior.

To paraphrase a number of bureaucrats who spoke to this point, it is of great utility for interest groups to seek the support of directors-general and inspectors-general. This is particularly the case where the group is attempting to prevent action — that is, to function as a veto group. One bureaucrat, summing up the importance of such a strategy, notes that "not very much that a director-general or inspector-general is opposed to can take place within a ministry." On the other hand, if it is positive action that a group seeks from the bureaucracy, all directive levels are of significance. To relate just one of many examples cited, a section director who is in charge of processing applications from private industrialists for financial credit to spur the industrial development of the South is in a key position either to facilitate or seriously to hamper the claims of any single group. Even when the actions of such an individual must be checked by twelve or more other officials, the cards can be stacked in favor of one line of action rather than another. Moreover, the mere ability of a bureaucrat to speed up or delay the ordinary administrative procedure is a power strongly respected by the groups themselves.

One perceptive bureaucrat suggests that it is the very extent of rigidity in the administrative hierarchy that increases the discretionary powers of the lower-level official who formally has none at all. If between such a bureaucrat and the minister there exist fifteen levels of formal approval, those near the bottom do not review decisions carefully because they assume that care will be taken at the top. Those at the top, on the other hand, also react in a completely formalistic way, either because they assume that underlings have done their work well or because they have too much to do to permit a substantive review. The upshot is that, at least for the great majority of decisions that do not raise serious controversy, lowly officials have enough power to make them attractive targets for interest-group representatives.

Perhaps the best way to summarize this discussion is by pointing out that interest groups thrive in administrative situations that are muddy and confused. If this obtains, the Italian administrative hierarchy in its unreformed state is a striking example of susceptibility to interest group incursions. . . .

Bureaucratic centralization has a geographic dimension too. Little has been done so far to encourage the development of the regional autonomy anticipated by the Constitution. Where certain functions have been delegated to the provinces or municipalities, these latter are hamstrung in their functioning because they do not possess adequate revenue-raising powers.[4] In this type of setting, the local prefect takes on the qualities of omnipotency over the political and administrative activity that occurs within his province. While the field representatives of other ministries do indeed exercise some discretion and operating freedom, the single most important official to seek out as a means of exercising local influence remains the prefect.

Because of this situation, a number of respondents insist that any complete understanding of the role of interest groups, particularly *parentela* groups, in directing administrative policies would have to take the prefects into account. An official of the Ministry of Agriculture, for example, comments that in the implementation of land reform programs priests and bishops seek to intervene through the prefects. He notes that when direct efforts of this nature fail to yield the desired results, the clergy will transfer their intervention to Rome, but that this is not necessary very often. Although the respondent, a Christian Democrat, notes that not all members of his Party approve of such clerical interference in strictly governmental affairs and that it is a grave error for the DC to permit it, the practice nevertheless persists.

A representative of IRI notes that the *Cassa per il Mezzogiorno* (Fund

---

[4] For a scathing criticism of geographic centralization of administrative power and an argument for greater regional autonomy, see Massimo S. Giannini, "Il Decentramento nel sistema amministrativo," in *Problemi della pubblica amministrazione* (Bologna, 1958), pp. 155–83.

for the Development of the South) has become a gigantic patronage organization which employs people and awards developmental contracts strictly on the basis of political considerations. While he is aware that this sort of behavior occurs in any society, he asserts that in Italy the Christian Democrats and Catholics have managed to raise it to a colossal scale. An Italian writer with a deep understanding of the South echoes the generalization that through the activities of bishops and prefects the programs of land reform have become essentially instruments of local patronage. Land is awarded, loans are made, credit is secured, fertilizer is distributed, and contracts are awarded on a fairly strict basis of loyalty to the Christian Democratic Party. He adds that this practice is certainly no secret. "The clergy and the party do not advertise this, but they have an interest in making the system known; that is, they wish to impress upon some of the recalcitrants the difficulty of making any economic progress if they persist in supporting political formations not approved by the Church. . . . This basic truth is so widely understood in the South today that families that wish to prosper will place family members in several of the political parties. Thus, one will go into Christian Democracy, another into the Communist Party, another to the Monarchist Party or Italian Social Movement as a means of hedging against all of the probable or possible political eventualities of the country."

Enough has been said here to demonstrate not so much that Italy is unique as that the patterns of public administration at the local as well as national level do not seriously inhibit the application of bureaucratic pressure based on *parentela*. As far as the use of political criteria to influence placement, transfer, and promotion is concerned, the interview evidence is somewhat mixed. We have already noted, for example, the view of the Christian Democratic leader who emphasizes that on these matters the bureaucracy is something more than a passive element. In a similar vein, we have the assertion of an official of the Ministry of the Interior who insists that merit is so important on matters of tenure and promotion as to quite definitely limit the importance of *parentela* factors. But statements from other bureaucrats we noted earlier contradict this position. Furthermore, it seems rather far-fetched to assume that Communists and Socialists, say, would have equal chances as Christian Democrats to enter the very sensitive Ministry of the Interior and to rise to important positions there. On the basis of what we can learn from the data at hand, it seems reasonably clear that *parentela* considerations are fully operative at the highest bureaucratic levels. Indeed, legislation permits the President of the Republic to appoint directors-general and other top-level administrative officers on the recommendation of the Council of Ministers and without regard to questions of seniority. Presumably such key appointments are understandably matters of political patronage, and *parentela* groups may be presumed to be very much involved in the process. This surmise is confirmed by an official of the Ministry of Foreign Affairs who states that no top-level position in his Ministry is likely to be awarded until the person involved has been accepted by the Italian clergy. He holds that while this does not mean that the clergy dominate public administration, it is evidence that they are able to have a considerable impact on it.

A further point concerning promotion, stressed by a number of bureaucrats, is that the criterion of comparative merit for promotion is a two-edged sword. On the one hand, it introduces a certain amount of needed flexibility into the system. Able young persons who might leave the public service for other employment may be kept in the system if their chances for professional mobility are not narrowly tied to considerations of seniority. On the other hand, comparative merit can be, and according to some has been, abused for political purposes. Thus, where merit is established not on the basis of examination but by standards that are much vaguer, individuals can move up to higher positions as a result of their strong connections with the dominant party or its *parentela* groups. It is doubtful that Catholic Action has made use of this weapon as strongly as interview responses suggest, but that it has been used to some extent in recent years is not in doubt. More important, perhaps, is the considerably widespread belief in the bureaucracy and interest-group circles that successful administrative careers are not as open to outsiders as they are to those who have found some sort of accommodation within the Christian Democratic Party.

A final point on the bureaucracy's susceptibility to *parentela* pressure involves the differences that one can detect within the bureaucracy itself. Even though our evidence on this point is somewhat limited, it seems apparent that highly technical agencies are often less open to *parentela* pressure than other kinds of units.[5] For example, an official in the Comptroller General's office holds that the highly technical nature of its work protects it somewhat against group incursions. Another bureaucrat in the Ministry of Foreign Affairs cites the strong mystique and prestige of the Ministry as providing some protection against *parentela* pressures. He adds that the absence of such factors at the provincial and local levels is what provides the clergy and other Catholic groups with considerable ability to affect bureaucratic policy there.

Perhaps a basic difference should be drawn here between *clientela* and *parentela* influence. Where the basis of the group's approach is essentially the former, it is likely to be much more successful in the vertical, technical, highly specialized administrative agencies. Where, on the other hand, the basis of the intervention is *parentela*, the highly politicized agencies, such as prefectures, reform and development units, and sensitive ministries like Foreign Affairs and Interior are likely to

[5] I am aware that this suggestion conflicts with the views of Jean Meynaud, who holds that the more functionally specialized agencies are open to greater interest-group influence in France. Here, however, I am thinking primarily of *parentela* pressure, although I would repeat my caveat that the age or function of an administrative agency is not necessarily protection against *clientela* pressure either. See his "Les Groupes d'intérêt et l'administration en France," *Revue Française de Science Politique*, 7 (July–September, 1957), pp. 573–93.

represent the major sectors of successful intervention. It seems reasonably clear that the two kinds of approach we have described exist in fact, and that whichever one of them represents a group's central tendency will tell us a great deal about the group's ability to influence bureaucratic policy.

ROBERT C. FRIED

The Italian Prefectoral System

While Italy, France, and Britain are not classified as federal states, as are America and West Germany, it does not follow that the government of each is equally unitary. The articulation of central, regional, and local government differs in each of these three countries. In none of them is it practical politics for everything to be directed from the capital city. France most closely approximates this ideal-type. Centralization has certain disadvantages, for it means that demonstrations or uprisings in one city, i.e., Paris, can paralyze the whole of a nation's government. Italy's unification into a single state was a relatively recent event of the nineteenth century. Robert Fried discusses some of the consequences of this phenomenon for the structure of Italian government in a careful analysis of prefectoral administration, a form of government little understood in the Anglo-American world.

A modern central government can implement policies throughout its territory by means of three basic types of administrative structure. It can, in the first place, establish specialized networks of field

Abridged from Robert C. Fried, *The Italian Prefects: A Study in Administrative Politics*, pp. xvii–xviii, 296–314 (New Haven: Yale University Press, 1963). Copyright © 1963 by Yale University. Reprinted by permission.

offices throughout its territory, each of which is responsible to a particular functionally specialized unit of the central government and each operating more or less autonomously from the others. This structural pattern, exemplified by the various field services of the American federal government, may be called the functional pattern of field administration because it projects throughout the country the functional division of labor of the central administration.

In the second place, a central government may choose instead to make its decisions effective through a network of general agents (prefects) in the major territorial subdivisions of the state, each of whom is responsible for the execution of all central government programs within his area. This second pattern may be called a prefectoral system of field administration and finds its *locus classicus* in France.

Finally, a central government may decide to utilize the services of legally distinct minor units of government, such as states, provinces, or municipalities, to carry out its policies in what we may call a pattern of decentralization. This pattern may be found in such countries as Great Britain and West Germany.

Of the three patterns, only the first and the last have been intensively studied. Prefectoral systems, with the exception of the French system, have not received much scholarly attention despite the fact that they are to be found in most countries of the world. . . .

I

A retrospective analysis of the history of the Italian prefectoral system reveals *inter alia* that that system, as it exists today, is the product of a long, basically uninterrupted evolution, rather than the deliberate creation of a particular time. It is the continuity of the system, rather than the changes within it, that is impressive. The system has been maintained essentially intact throughout modern Italian history, organized in much the same way to serve much the same purposes.

The over-all pattern of the system since unification has been marked by four major traits:

1. a high degree of centralization, of resistance to pressures for local autonomy and power;
2. a high degree of concentration, of resistance to pressures for greater local autonomy and power within the state bureaucracy;
3. a predominantly political, rather than administrative, Prefect;
4. the substantial administrative independence from the Prefect of a growing number of technical state field services.

These constants, in turn, are closely related to the basic continuity in the purposes and origins of the ruling groups in Italy since unification. The prefectoral system was designed for and has continued to serve the purposes of social conservatism and national unity in a society with perhaps no other nationally integrative institution apart from the state bureaucracy itself. The fragmentation of the Italian political culture underlies the continuing strength of the centralizing impulses of the ruling groups. For decentralization would imply the strengthening of dissident ideological or social groups — a result which is seen to be at once immoral and dangerous.

There have been, to be sure, other factors accounting for the persistently high level of centralization: the financial straits of the national government and its inability to devolve a greater share of national resources to minor units of government in order to support greater services; the widespread preference for state, rather than local, administration, as being less partial or "factious"; the differential socioeconomic development of the various regions of the country, with concomitant differences in social skills, standards of public behavior, and economic resources. Poverty of resources, differential social development, and local factiousness are, however, only different facets of the same problem: the lack of a national political community.

The second element in this enduring pattern — the high level of concentration within the state administration itself — rests upon the same oligarchical tendencies supporting centralization. It reflects a traditional lack of responsiveness to the public at large and to pressures upon the bureaucracy for impartial, swift decision-making at a publicly convenient level. Concentration is part of a general cultural pattern of authoritarian decision-making, as, for example, is to be found in the management of private organizations, such as political parties, religious organizations, business corporations, and trade unions.[1] It is also, perhaps, a reflection of a fear of anarchical elements in the national character and of the resulting general expectation that devolved or dispersed power will be abused.

The "political" Prefect has fitted neatly into this pattern of centralization and concentration. The Prefect has existed primarily as policeman and supervisor of local government, exercising and symbolizing central government control over local groups and institutions. Administrative power in the central government agencies has remained concentrated in the capital and this concentration has avoided the pivotal problem of *integrated* prefectoral systems: how to apportion deconcentrated authority between the Prefect and the functional services of the newer agencies in the field.[2] If the various technical ministries had wished or been forced to deconcentrate large amounts of authority to the field, this spiny question could scarcely have been avoided.

The substantial administrative independence of the various state field services from the Prefect was established in the early years of the unified nation under the influence of the liberal ideology of the founding

---

[1] See, e.g., F. H. Harbison and E. W. Burgess, "Modern Management in Europe," *American Journal of Sociology*, 55 (1954), 15–23.

[2] On this problem, see Alfred Diamant, "The Department, the Prefect, and Dual Supervision in French Administration: A Comparative Study," *Journal of Politics*, 16 (1954), 472–90.

fathers, hesitant to create what would have seemed an oriental or Napoleonic despot in each of the provinces of the new realm. The dispersion of ministerial power among the heads of the several central departments encouraged the drive of these departments toward self-sufficiency in the field as well as in the national capital. The Prefect's major responsibilities were essentially political and nontechnical, involving the mobilization of support for the new regime and the repression of dissent. These factors . . . continued to operate in the years following unification.

Under the liberal constitutional regime, the administrative independence of the technical services became firmly rooted in the customs and practices of Italian administration and in the formal laws and regulations that governed them. The few services that were placed under the directive authority of the Prefect succeeded in liberating themselves either through ministerial decree or parliamentary statute. Attempts in the 1890's to expand prefectoral control were bound to founder on the numerous shoals of vested ministerial interests; the drive for functional autonomy and freedom from political interference; ministerial resistance to deconcentration; prefectoral identification with one ministry, the Interior, and its electoral and police functions; and the political difficulties involved in redrawing the geographical areas of prefectoral jurisdiction so as to reduce the number of Prefects and to permit prefectoral coordination of regional services.

Fascism does not appear to have made any basic innovation in the prefectoral system, betraying thus its links to traditional statist conservatism. It is curious in an allegedly totalitarian dictatorship for members of the Party to deny that by permitting "political" coordination of the field services by the Prefect, they were transforming him into a Viceroy or Governor; and for a minister to deny that such coordination would in any way interfere with the "technical-administrative" decisions of the functional specialists: presumably in a totalitarian dictatorship, the ruling party would not bother to profess such scruples. In such statements and in the fact that the Prefect was never subordinated to the Party Secretary one might find grounds to doubt whether the Fascist regime merits entire inclusion in the category of *totalitarian* dictatorships.

However this may be, the reaction to the centralized dictatorship after 1943 found one of its chief targets in the Prefect, who had become a symbol of Fascist oppression, identified with the regime whose policies he had often so zealously promoted. The anti-Fascist coalition that emerged to govern the country was united on this point at least and, being hostile to the prefectoral institution in general, could hardly have been expected to favor a strengthening of prefectoral control over the rest of the state administration in the province. Given the general postwar antipathy toward the prefectoral institution, it is not surprising that the conservative governments since 1947 should have contented themselves with the mere maintenance of the institution about as it was before Fascism, rather than have attempted to strengthen the ties among the various field services in the province and thus enlarge the scope of prefectoral power.

II

[There are] also ... some propositions concerning prefectoral systems in general. Some of the major questions about prefectoral systems that remain to be investigated [are]:

A. What are the major traits of a prefectoral system?
B. What are the major differences between prefectoral and functional systems with regard to (1) structure, (2) origins, and (3) functions?
C. What are the major types of prefectoral systems and how do the types differ in origins, structure, and functions?
D. What are the major challenges to the stability and survival of prefectoral systems?
E. Is there any necessary relationship between prefectoral systems and stable democracy?

Naturally, this study does not permit us to answer these questions with any degree of completeness, but it does permit us to make more informed hypotheses to be tested in subsequent research.

THE MAJOR TRAITS OF PREFECTORAL SYSTEMS. Prefectoral systems have certain common characteristics.

1. The national territory is divided into areas variously called "provinces," "departments," "governments," "prefectures," etc.
2. In each of these areas there is appointed a high functionary representative of and responsible to the central government (and in particular to a Minister of the Interior, or Justice, or Government) to carry out the following kinds of functions:
   a. political and social representation of the central government;
   b. maintenance of law and order;
   c. supervision of central government officials operating in the area;
   d. supervision of minor units of government in the area.
3. This official is a civil functionary operating independently of the military and the judiciary.
4. He does not enjoy the security of tenure enjoyed by other officials and may be dismissed or transferred at the pleasure of the central government.
5. He is not a resident or native of the area which he governs.
6. He may be either a career functionary or a "political" appointee from outside of the career service.
7. And he is usually supervised by a specialized central department — a Ministry of the Interior — which is nationally responsible for such matters as public safety and local government.

THE DIFFERENCES BETWEEN PREFECTORAL AND FUNCTIONAL SYSTEMS.

Structure. The structural differences between prefectoral and functional systems may be summarized in the following chart.

1. PREFECTORAL. The national territory is divided into areas of general government and in each of these is placed a general representative of the central government (Prefect).
   FUNCTIONAL. There is no general representative of the central government in the various regions of the national territory.

2. PREFECTORAL. Each of the central ministries issues commands to its functional counterparts in the field via the Prefect.
   FUNCTIONAL. Lines of command run directly from the central ministries to their field units.

3. PREFECTORAL. Most state services use the areas of general government presided over by the Prefect.
   FUNCTIONAL. State services use varying sets of administrative areas in accordance with their particular requirements.

4. PREFECTORAL. The Prefect's area of general administration also constitutes an area of local self-government.
   FUNCTIONAL. There is no necessary identity between field administrative and local government areas.

5. PREFECTORAL. Central government control over minor units of government tends to be (a) more penetrating than in functional systems; (b) administrative rather than legislative; and (c) unified under the Prefect.
   FUNCTIONAL. Central government control tends to be (a) less penetrating; (b) legislative rather than administrative; (c) and dispersed among several central and field institutions.

Origins. It is much more difficult to ascertain and generalize about the factors that account for the establishment and maintenance of a prefectoral, rather than a functional, system of field administration. Such a broad question has yet to be studied and certainly cannot be answered on the basis of the foregoing historical study of a single prefectoral system.[3] The basic factors involved would seem to be the nature of the political system; its prevailing ideologies; its relative degree of consensus, internal security, and national cohesion. Functional systems, with their greater diffusion of administrative power, are more apt to develop within liberal political systems, in states with a high degree of consensus, security, and cohesion. The various areas of such states tend to be regarded as units deserving of some degree of autonomous decentralized power, rather than as dependencies and "wards" of the

---

[3] On this question, see James W. Fesler, "The Political Role of Field Administration," in Ferrel Heady and Sybil L. Stokes, eds., *Papers in Comparative Public Administration* (Ann Arbor, Institute of Public Administration, 1952), pp. 117–43.

central government. Prefectoral systems are rarely to be found where there are strong and *generally accepted* centrifugal or decentralizing tendencies.

Conversely, more authoritarian systems and those with greater political fragmentation, dissension, and insecurity tend to develop prefectoral systems — primarily as instruments of centralization. The dominant political groups tend in such systems to view decentralization as potentially destructive of the political unity of the state. They are not averse to the concentration of administrative power in a single official within each area. They consider regional interests as dependencies requiring on-the-spot tutelage by the central government. Prefectoral systems will rarely, if ever, be found within genuine federal unions or highly decentralized unitary states. It would seem (although this remains to be tested) that the choice of a prefectoral, rather than a functional, system depends less on considerations of how the central government bureaucracy is to be organized than on what is to be the distribution of power as between the central and minor units of government. In other words, the choice hinges less on the desired pattern of *deconcentration* within the state administration as between central and field officials than on the desired pattern of *decentralization* as between central government and local government officials.

Prefectoral systems seem to suit best the purposes of absolutist governments and the traditions of those emerging from a period of absolutist, especially colonial, government. In Western Europe, prefectoral systems evolved from the institutions devised by absolute monarchs in order to centralize power and control of economic resources within their kingdoms at the expense of the nobility and medieval communes. They constituted a basic arm of monarchy in conflict with domestic feudalities and foreign dynasts. They were the major element in the royal administrative machinery designed to deprive feudal lords and communes of their privileges and functions, to transform feudal serfs into royal subjects, and to elaborate and implement the economic policies of mercantilism. Mercantilist policies had, in turn, been devised to promote national unification and national power. They called for active state intervention in social and economic life: they required and made possible the development of the royal bureaucracy.

In an age of growing overarching allegiance to the Crown and of primitive bureaucratic specialization, the prefectoral system provided for the unified symbolic representation of the Crown in the provinces of the realm; for the reliable enforcement of royal commands; and for the reproduction in each province of the unified and theoretically absolute authority of the monarch. The same purposes were served in the Napoleonic model, which rationalized and modernized the prefectoral institutions of the old regimes, abolishing venality and inheritance of office. The Napoleonic system clarified the division of functions as between civil, military, and judicial officials. It strengthened prefectoral control over minor units of government, now uniform in structure and functions and subject to nationally uniform rules. It exalted the Prefect to clear supremacy over other government officials in his province. And it emphasized monocratic as opposed to collegial forms of administrative power and responsibility.

Prefectoral systems were part of the heritage of the old autocratic regimes, together with institutions such as the monarchy, which were accepted by and adapted to the purposes of the liberal constitutional regimes established in Scandinavia, the Low Countries, and Italy during the nineteenth century, withstanding the liberal attack upon both centralization and mercantilism. Retention of the prefectoral system — as of the monarchy — may indeed have been one of the prices paid by the liberal movement to secure the acceptance of the new regime by the older ruling elements.

TYPES OF PREFECTORAL SYSTEMS. One of the major conclusions of this study is that there are at least two polar types of prefectoral systems: the integrated, exemplified by the classical French system of the nineteenth and early twentieth centuries; and the unintegrated, exemplified by the contemporary Italian system. The difference between the two systems lies in their structure, origins, and functions.

Structure. Structural differences between the integrated and unintegrated systems can be seen in the following chart.

1. *Locus of authority*
    INTEGRATED. Authority is exclusively or largely deconcentrated from the central ministries to the Prefects, who become a link in all or most chains of command. The Prefect is the hierarchical superior of the technical field directors in his province.
    UNINTEGRATED. Authority is largely reserved to the specialist functional officials in several purely functional chains of command.

2. *Communications*
    INTEGRATED. The Prefect is the sole channel of communication between the functional departments in the capital and those in the field.
    UNINTEGRATED. The Prefect is neither the normal nor the exclusive channel of communication between central and field functional units.

3. *Auxiliary services*
    INTEGRATED. The prefecture houses all or most of the state field offices and provides them with the administrative services needed to accomplish their technical programs.
    UNINTEGRATED. The technical services in the province do not depend upon the prefecture for accounting, supplies, secretariat, or space, which are instead provided by the central ministries or by the technical field units themselves.

4. *Areas*
    INTEGRATED. Most state services use the prefecture's area of operations.
    UNINTEGRATED. The functional services, organized independently of the prefecture, use varying sets of areas.

5. *Echelons*
   INTEGRATED. Regional offices, standing between the prefecture and the central ministries and/or using interprovincial areas, are exceptional.
   UNINTEGRATED. Regional offices, with direct operational responsibilities and/or supervisory authority over provincial offices, are common.
6. *Local government*
   INTEGRATED. The Prefect is chief executive of the provincial self-government unit, the staff of which is organized within the prefecture.
   UNINTEGRATED. The provincial self-government unit includes a directly or indirectly elected executive authority, with control of separately organized provincial staff.

Origins. Given these types of prefectoral systems, why is one type adopted rather than another? . . . In the case of the best known *integrated* prefectoral system, that of the French, the reasons for making the Prefect the undisputed hierarchical superior of the various state services in the department probably include the clear supremacy of the chief of government, the King and later Napoleon, over his ministers; a desire by the ruler to reproduce this clear supremacy in his direct representative, the Intendant and the Prefect; the absolutist conceptions of the ruler which legitimized monocratic administrative forms; and Napoleon's military conception of responsibility, authority, and efficiency as requiring one-man direction.

Functions. One type of prefectoral system is maintained presumably because of its relative advantages over the other type, because of its functions or consequences, because of the costs of changing over to the other type. The Italian system remained unintegrated after unification for many reasons, including the continuance of several of the factors initially responsible for the adoption of such a system. Once going, the unintegrated system acquired the force of customary behavior. Ministries enjoyed and defended the almost complete control that the unintegrated system afforded them over their particular field services. Separate technical offices were established in a growing number of sectors and each of these offices was vested with an interest in self-preservation as an autonomous entity responsible only to its technical superiors in Rome.

The relative *advantages* of the unintegrated Italian prefectoral system, as opposed to the integrated system, seem to be the following:

1. Theoretically, at least, the authority of the Prefect can be adjusted to allow him to control or coordinate some programs or activities where the case for such coordination is particularly strong, rather than a general desideratum. It may, however, prove difficult to insert prefectoral control in the traditionally strong vertical hierarchies, given the absence of a countering tradition of prefectoral control such as has long existed in France.

2. The unintegrated system gives free rein to all the functional

services which may carry out their nationwide responsibilities in accordance with their particular, technically informed judgment, allowing for the necessary geographical adaptation within their respective services.

3. The system does provide for a natural coordinator within each of the major areas of the country, a natural chairman of interagency committees, a neutral arbiter for the adjustment of interservice difficulties. It may, however, be difficult for the Prefect to coordinate the activities of services using various areas, enjoying varying amounts of deconcentrated authority, such as the unintegrated system tends to produce. The Prefect's area, moreover, may not be the appropriate level for interagency coordination in some or most matters.

4. The unintegrated system avoids the serious problem of dual supervision, of defining satisfactorily the respective spheres of authority of the central ministries, Prefects, and technical specialists in the field — or it does so long as the Prefect's authority over the technical specialists is restricted to the submission of recommendations and excludes final decision-making. Thus avoidance of the problem of dual supervision hinges upon the maintenance of a high degree of concentration in matters to be coordinated by the Prefects. Actually, the problem is not avoided but merely shifted to each of the separate field services, in some of which it may become highly acute.

The relative *disadvantages* of the unintegrated system would seem to be the following:

1. It is relatively uneconomical since, unlike the integrated system, it does not provide for common housekeeping services. The administrative overhead expenses involved in running several distinct offices is greater presumably than in running joint services in the prefecture.

2. It tends to place administrative burdens on technical field directors which distract them from their specialized tasks. They are forced to be generalist office managers and to attend to matters for which they have little aptitude, liking, or training.

3. It requires a greater over-all number of talented administrators capable of directing independent offices.

4. It tends to de-emphasize the interrelations of various technical programs within particular areas and communities.

5. It fosters a tendency toward undue concentration of administrative authority, since there are no strong generalist Prefects pressing for and defending larger amounts of authority.

6. It requires constant negotiations among the services with no hierarchical arbitrator short of the Prime Minister or Council of Ministers.

CHALLENGES TO PREFECTORAL SYSTEMS. What are the major challenges to the survival or stability of prefectoral systems?

The Political Challenge. The prefectoral system may become identified with a regime or with the policies of a regime and accordingly share its fortunes. If the regime falls, as Fascism fell, there is apt to be a drive to abolish the prefectoral system as an accomplice in the regime's activities.

The prefectoral system may also become identified with some of the policies of a regime or rather, with one element of the system, such as centralization, and if a drive develops to change those policies or to change one element of the prefectoral system, the whole system may be placed in jeopardy. The prefectoral system in Italy has become identified with centralization. Hence, the drive for greater local self-government has brought in its train a demand for the abolition of the prefectoral system — despite the fact that a prefectoral system is not necessarily tied to any particular level of centralization.

A political challenge of another sort may develop in a revolutionary situation in which not so much the *legitimacy* as the *effectiveness* of the system is challenged. The loyalties of the Prefects may be subjected to severe strains in a situation, such as existed in 1919–22, where the Prefects are required to act against groups to which they are socially allied and politically sympathetic. Rapid renovation of the prefectoral cadres may not prevent the undermining of prefectoral discipline.

The Technical Challenge. Prefectoral systems may also be undermined by processes of social and technological change, leading to the expansion of state functions into new and highly technical fields of activity. Separate central units are established to take care of the expanding functions of central administration and each of these is apt to press for an autonomous field service under its complete control. The newer technical departments in the capital, based on changed social expectations and new technological possibilities, project their drive for autonomy in the central administration into field administration as well. They will also press for the organization of their field service along lines suited to their particular function.

The prefectures are apt to be bypassed in this process of administrative growth and ramification for three reasons: (1) they will tend to lack the necessary expertise or the appropriate geographical jurisdiction to perform the new functions; (2) they cannot be as uniformly responsive as can distinct field services to the needs and desires of the newer technical central agencies; and (3) they may be the victims of a long-standing process of institutional decline, involving the routinization of duties, the flagging of esprit de corps, the petrifaction of customary ways of thinking and acting.

PREFECTORAL SYSTEMS AND POLITICAL SYSTEMS. The question of the relationships, if any, between prefectoral systems and stable democracy is as interesting as it is difficult to answer. There appears to be no simple or necessary relationship between the two. Some stable democracies have no prefectoral systems; some stable democracies do.[4]

---

[4] Seymour M. Lipset in *Political Man* (New York, Doubleday, 1960) lists thirteen European and English-speaking countries as stable democracies (p. 49). Of these thirteen, six have prefectoral systems: Belgium, Denmark, the Netherlands, Norway, Sweden, and even Luxemburg.

Prefectoral systems, moreover, vary considerably among themselves in at least three ways: (1) the level of centralization they sustain, (2) the degree of integration in the state field administration they permit, and (3) the policies administered through them and with which they may become identified. Of these three variables, only the first (the level of centralization) and the last (the policies administered) seem relevant to the stability of the political system.

Yet just how relevant centralization is to the stability of democracy has still to be demonstrated. It is frequently asserted that stable democracy requires a considerable degree of decentralization, of local self-government. It may be, however, that there are stable democracies that are highly centralized. If there *are* no stable democracies that are highly centralized, if all stable democracies are highly decentralized, then it will follow that those stable democracies with prefectoral systems must all permit considerable local government power and autonomy. This has yet to be tested.

Possibly there is a necessary relationship between the level of centralization and stable democracy. It seems reasonable to expect that political cultures that tolerate the dispersion of power involved in decentralization may more readily support the other forms of dispersed social and constitutional power that constitute pluralistic democracy. It is often asserted, however, that centralization leads to *incivisme* and "widespread public disaffection from governmental authority."[5] One might, on the basis of this study, invert the terms and assert that it is *incivisme* and widespread disaffection that lead to centralization.

Does a prefectoral system facilitate the establishment of dictatorship, provoke the downfall of a democratic regime, or facilitate the conquest of power by undemocratic forces? It may just as easily be maintained that a prefectoral system may be used to defend a democratic regime, to bolster democratic forces, to provide a sense of security and order, and to dissolve or alleviate the tensions that might undermine a democracy. A prefectoral system is basically a neutral device which can be made to serve a wide range of purposes. Like other formal structures of government, its function in the political system may be derivative and of marginal importance.[6] It is rather the social and ideological forces that work through and upon political and administrative structures that are the autonomous and decisive factors in determining the fate of a democracy.

---

[5] Nicholas Wahl, "The French Political System," in Samuel Beer et al., *Patterns of Government: The Major Political Systems of Europe* (New York, Random House, 1958), p. 331.

[6] This institutional skepticism sems to be shared by Lipset in *Political Man*, pp. 90–92; see also Robert A. Dahl, *A Preface to Democratic Theory* (Chicago, University of Chicago Press, 1956), pp. 134–37.

KARL W. DEUTSCH
and LEWIS J. EDINGER

Who Prevailed in the German Foreign Policy Process?

The interplay of influences in making government policy is so complex that usually no one official can be said to be the key decision-maker. It does not follow from this that all who participate in policy deliberations are of equal influence. The following study of German foreign policy by Karl Deutsch and Lewis Edinger is noteworthy because they develop, from a series of cases, a clear set of distinctions between more and less influential groups within German government. It also provides a precise assessment of the extent to which basic foreign policy decisions were determined by pressures from foreign governments upon Bonn.

In politics, no one is likely to win all the time. In the give and take among many domestic and foreign influences over foreign policy, no single group, individual, or government can always be expected to prevail. In the case of Germany, no foreign power — not even the United States — could completely dictate domestic decisions or override the consensus of mass opinion and elites. The external and the internal influences may go some way to balance each other; elites may balance or overbalance mass opinion; some elite groups may be counterpoised to others; and key individuals, such as the Chancellor, may try to shift the balance by their

Abridged from Karl W. Deutsch and Lewis J. Edinger, *Germany Rejoins the Powers*, pp. 195–203, 214–216. © 1959 by the Board of Trustees of the Leland Stanford Junior University. Reprinted by permission of the publishers, Stanford University Press.

Further aspects of German politics are discussed in Karl W. Deutsch and Eric Nordlinger, "The German Federal Republic," in R. C. Macridis and R. E. Ward, editors, *Modern Political Systems: Europe* (Englewood Cliffs, N.J.: Prentice-Hall, 1968, 2nd edition), pp. 299–450; and in Lewis J. Edinger, *Politics in Germany* (Boston: Little, Brown, 1968).

actions. Nevertheless, some actors have tended to prevail far more often than others, or, at least, to find themselves more often on the winning side. Does this indicate that they had greater influence?

JUDGMENTS ABOUT INFLUENCE

On some particular issue, any group may embrace a distasteful policy in order to join the stronger battalions, or to rush to the assistance of the victors. But unless we assume a very unusual group indeed, we may expect that a group will tend to support in the long run such policies as appear rewarding to them. These policies might have prevailed, of course, without their help; but if their assistance were always useless, we might expect that in the long run such a group would cease to be taken seriously in politics. In short, if a group continues to be regarded as politically significant, and if the policies which it favors continue to prevail, then we may reasonably infer that it is more influential in politics than some other group for which these conditions do not hold, or hold only to a markedly lesser degree.

Influence is thus inferred provisionally from repeated association with prevailing policies, together with the continuing enjoyment of substantial status and prestige. It cannot well be inferred in this manner from any one decision, but only from several or many; and the inference should be tested and checked against other types of evidence.

In the end, the ascription of political influence to some person, group, or government is a matter of judgment. The use of operational definitions, quantitative codings, computations and the related apparatus of measurement at best can check and aid such judgments; it cannot replace them. Some charts and codings of this kind, concerning data about various policy decisions, will be presented later in this chapter. . . . None of these, however, are intended to represent anything more than aids to judgment. . . .

A GENERAL ESTIMATE OF INFLUENCE

With these qualifications in mind, what can we say about the actors in the German foreign policy process?

The record of actual decisions between 1952 and 1958 confirms the intent of the Basic Law. The most influential single actor appears to have been the Chancellor, followed at a small distance by the cabinet and by the leadership group of the CDU and at another distance by the diplomatic elite.

All these are domestic actors. No foreign government, not even that of the United States, has matched the influence of the first three. The evidence suggests clearly that this leading constellation did not act like puppets of the United States; in several decisions they supported and carried policies very different from, and indeed partly opposed to, the policies preferred by the United States.

The United States, for its part, did exercise considerable influence over

German foreign policy decisions — or, at least, such decisions more often than not had a way of yielding results closely in line with stated American policy preferences and objectives. No other foreign power approached this influence of the United States.

Of the other foreign powers, France had some influence on German policies; or, to put it differently, German policies were not infrequently so framed as to accord with the wishes and interests of France. The United Kingdom was markedly less often accommodated in this manner by German policy, and the Soviet Union had most of the time little or no direct influence, or a negative one, on the German policy decisions taken.

Associated with the leading domestic elite groups most influential in foreign policy — the cabinet, CDU leaders, and diplomats — are two other elites with a not dissimilar basic outlook. The Roman Catholic bishops and the high-level civil servants both appear to have some marked influence on, or reason for satisfaction with, the trend of foreign policy decisions. They are followed, at a distance, by the big business leaders — insofar as these cared to interest themselves in foreign policy matters — and by the press elite. The military had not yet appeared in sufficient strength to write a political record in the field of foreign policy for the Bonn Republic.

Finally, three elites — the Social Democratic leaders, the trade union leaders, and the bishops of the Evangelical Church — appeared to have had relatively the least influence over the making of foreign policy. These groups usually could expect to feel neutral or slightly negative about an "average" decision, or they might expect to have a policy decision favorable to their wishes balanced in short order by another decision carried despite their opposition. The Social Democrats and the trade union leaders showed interest in foreign policy issues, but had relatively few channels of access to the places where decisions were made. The Protestant bishops showed less interest in foreign policy, and their opportunities for access to decision making and decision makers were likewise limited. Both Labor and the Protestant Churches seemed unlikely to cooperate effectively in the near future, and they were handicapped by class and residential barriers to their political appeals. Social Democrats and trade unionists have persistently failed to win much middle-class support, or to make much headway among the rural population. The major Protestant churches, on the other hand, are predominantly middle-class and rural; the urban and industrial working class in considerable part has become estranged from them. The influence of these elites on foreign policy has been mainly indirect, and seems likely to remain so unless there should be some major change within one of them or in the general political situation.

The pattern of influence indicated thus an inside group of elites with marked influence: the politicians of the cabinet and CDU leadership; the administrative elite in diplomacy and the civil service, and the Roman Catholic bishops. In contrast to these, three elites seemed somewhat debarred from influence and access to policy decisions: the Socialist and trade union leaders and the Protestant bishops. Three intermediate elites showed a clear potential for increasing their influence; big business, the press leaders, and the military, and the influence of all three has been rising since 1955.

The distribution of influence has changed in time. Two stages or periods stand out in contrast. The first, preceding the granting of sovereignty to the Federal Republic, extends from 1949 to May 1955. The second, after sovereignty, extends from May 1955 to the time of writing, and quite possibly beyond. The two periods are distinct not only in legal form but in the substance of the policy decisions taken and in the considerable changes in regard to influence over the policy process.

INFLUENCE PATTERNS BEFORE SOVEREIGNTY: 1949 TO MAY 1955

The first stage in the political development of the Federal Republic was the period of occupation. It lasted from the formation of the Republic in September 1949 until its emancipation from the rule of the Allied High Commission in May 1955.

Throughout the period, German policy had to follow the lead of the allies, and in particular of the United States, in order to earn their confidence and win the next concessions from them on the road to sovereignty.

The five major German foreign policy decisions of the period, pertaining to the agreements on ECSC, EDC, Israeli reparations, the Saar, and NATO membership, respectively, were made in full accordance with known desires of the government of the United States. Britain and France, supporting the same policies, though not always with the same enthusiasm, shared this American success, and thus, presumably, had an only slightly lesser degree of influence. The Soviet Union was strongly opposed to the four policies which linked Germany more firmly to the Western bloc, and it was presumably at least mildly opposed to the fifth, the German-Israeli Reparations Agreement.[1] Soviet opposition, however, was ineffective in all cases; it produced no visible modifications in the outcome.

Within Germany, only Chancellor Adenauer had identified himself completely with policies that were adopted. German mass opinion was usually, on the average, lukewarm, divided, or indifferent. Among the German elites, the groups closest to the Chancellor — the cabinet, the leaders of his party, and the chief diplomats — gave substantial support to his foreign policy. Two other groups closely identified with his regime — the senior civil servants and the Roman Catholic hierarchy — supported the same policies but not always with equal consistency or vigor.

The main opposition to the four "Western bloc" policies came from

---

[1] It will be recalled that the German Communist party opposed the agreement, and that the Soviet-controlled German Democratic Republic accepted no reparations obligations of this kind.

the Social Democrats; but this produced no major changes in the decisions taken. It was the solid support of just this party, however, which enabled Adenauer to carry the fifth decision — the Israeli agreement — on which he was deserted by a substantial portion of his own party. Many of the Social Democratic views on these matters were shared, with a lesser degree of intensity, by the trade union leaders and possibly by the Protestant bishops. Though these groups were no more successful in modifying the policies of the government, they had been less strongly committed to any such endeavor.

The leaders of the business community were closely associated with many domestic policies of the government, but it seems that in this period they took far less interest in most foreign policy matters, or else they were divided, or even in some instances moderately opposed to the government's course.

The press elite was often noncommittal or divided, reflecting the coolness of mass opinion and the divisions among the political parties and major interest groups. Even the relatively most popular decisions of the government, those in favor of ECSC and of the Paris Agreements, were only mildly supported by the balance of the press. The military leaders, finally, were as yet not much in evidence. They seem to have made no concerted major effort to exert influence, nor are there any indications that they did so.

In sum, the main influence over German foreign policy between 1949 and May 1955 was exercised from abroad, by the United States and its main Western allies. There was relatively little spontaneous domestic support for the policies that emerged. For the most part they were accepted as means to an end — the removal of the occupation regime, the preservation of Western protection and support, and the restoration of Germany's national independence and international position. Chancellor Adenauer and his associates undertook to procure these ends by sponsoring the decisions required, but mass opinion and most of the elites remained more or less aloof from the highly circumscribed German foreign policies of the occupation era. With the coming of sovereignty, this situation was to change.

THE REALIGNMENT OF INFLUENCE: 1955 TO 1958

The most striking fact about the foreign policy decisions of the sovereign Republic since mid-1955 is the shift of influence from the external to the internal actors in the policy process. The period since 1955 has been rich in foreign policy decisions. These decisions . . . did not support consistently the interests of any power except Germany.

The United States government was not enthusiastic about Germany's opening of diplomatic relations with the Soviet Union. Nor was it pleased with the decision to shorten the length of military training for conscripts to twelve months as against the eighteen months planned within Germany's NATO program, or indeed with the decision to cut back the scale and tempo of the German military build-up.

France and England would have preferred more "European" or "NATO" solidarity from Germany in their dealings with the Arab world, but Germany decided on a policy of Arab friendship, loans and trade, neutrality in the Suez war of 1956, and the conspicuous early recognition of the Iraqi revolutionary government in 1958.

Russia finally must continue to oppose the basic pro-Western trend of German policy and the continued emphasis on American friendship, NATO alliance (including the acceptance of atomic weapons for the German army and the possibility of American missile bases on German soil), and efforts toward European integration in such decisions as the conclusion of the Euratom and Common Market Treaties.

Taken together, these policies were neither opportunistic nor chaotic. They were based on an estimate of self-interest, loyalty to explicit alliances and treaty obligations, and on a decent respect for the feelings of allies as well as for the feelings of Asian and African peoples. They involved an independent appraisal of German interests as well as of the interests of the non-Communist world. Vis-à-vis the West as a whole, Germany's policy was not that of a pupil or a puppet, but that of an ally.

It is not certain, however, whether this will make Germany more popular abroad. Foreign governments are not always more pleased with allies than with satellites. No foreign power has been able to dominate German foreign policy, and no foreign power has had cause to be more than mildly pleased — and sometimes even displeased — with the sum total of its course.

Compared to the pre-1955 period, United States influence has declined. Seen in international terms German foreign policy has become markedly more independent. It stands by its allies but it will now override their known wishes in regard to particular issues. As it pleases its allies somewhat less, it also is less consistent in displeasing their adversary. German policy is now less completely lined up with United States preferences, and less consistently resented by the Soviet Union.

The influence of France and the United Kingdom has fallen even more. Neither country can present any longer even the appearance of controlling, or substantially influencing the whole of German foreign policy, even though they may obtain accommodation on particular issues.

Of the two, France has been more successful in obtaining such concessions, particularly in regard to economic problems on the European continent, even if on other occasions German policy makers have preferred to cultivate Arab friendship, particularly in Egypt and Iraq, rather than defer to French wishes in those regions.

England, on the other hand, has found fewer accommodations from Germany, while feeling equally keenly German political and economic competition in the Arab world. On balance, England may well feel somewhat displeased with the trend of German policies since 1955, and embarrassingly unable to influence them with effect. The markedly cool attitude of a good deal of British opinion on the occasion of President Heuss's visit to England in the fall of 1958 — despite the President's consistent democratic record and splendid human qualities — may be understood more readily against this background.

The shifts from the pre-1955 period were particularly drastic during the first two years of readjustment, from the winning of sovereignty in May 1955 to the Soviet intervention in the Hungarian uprising in October 1956. The mood of relaxation of international tensions after the Geneva Conference of 1955 between Russia, the United States, France, and Britain may have contributed to the markedly greater independence of German foreign policy in this period. It is possible, however, that some form of psychological rebound after the occupation years would have occurred in German politics and foreign policy even if current East-West tensions had remained unchanged. In any case, the relatively greater independence of German foreign policy has persisted, to some degree at least, even in the tense years after 1956; the early German recognition of the Iraqi revolutionists in 1958 may serve as an instance. An even more striking illustration is the ignoring of United States objections to the cutting of United States coal exports to Germany by a new German coal tariff in early 1959. An American newspaper report reflects eloquently the changed atmosphere in Bonn:

> The Bonn Government brushed aside a last-minute request of the United States for a sixty-day delay and the Bundestag approved a 10 per cent tariff today on foreign coal imports.
> The tariff is aimed at curbing the import of United States coal. It was approved by the Bundestag, the lower house of Parliament, by a substantial majority. Party discipline was imposed on reluctant Government Deputies to carry the bill against Socialist and Free Democratic opposition.
> Twelve hours earlier the Foreign Ministry advised the United States Embassy that it was too late to hold up the tariff measure, designed to overcome the overproduction crisis in the Ruhr coal industry.
> The Embassy had requested the sixty-day delay in imposing the tariff after it had become clear that the United States protest, delivered Tuesday, would be ignored. . . .[2]

As the external influences on German foreign policy have declined, the internal ones have risen. Taking the average of eleven policy decisions in 1955–58, mass opinion has been moderately but markedly favorable to the general course adopted, even though particular decisions — such as the acceptance of atomic arms for German soldiers and the possible establishment of American missile bases on German soil — have remained unpopular.

With its greater freedom of maneuver, German foreign policy has increased its ability to accomodate domestic elite opinions and interest groups. All elites that were surveyed appear to have drawn more closely together, and they seem to have moved, on balance, toward a markedly greater support of, and satisfaction with, the foreign policies adopted.

[2] Arthur J. Olsen, "Bonn House Votes Coal Import Duty," *The New York Times,* January 31, 1959, p. 2:8.

Only the Chancellor's influence has declined somewhat. He could no longer point to the overwhelming need to adopt his policies in order to win critically needed concessions from the West. He had to modify his position on the issues of the length of military service for conscripts in late 1955, and on the manpower levels of the armed forces in October 1956. Though less towering than before 1955, his over-all influence nevertheless remained high, and so did that of his close associates, the cabinet, the CDU leaders, and the high-ranking diplomats.

Another group, however, has now joined the ranks of those visibly influential in foreign policy matters. Big business now appears far more clearly in favor of the particular policies pursued than was the case before 1955. The more independent German policy after 1955, opening up additional opportunities and markets in areas outside the main Western countries, and often in competition with them, has been more in line with business interests. In the Near and Middle East, in Latin America, and even in Communist bloc countries the current German policies have helped German exports to reach third rank in world trade, reaching 8 per cent of the total in 1957. In the same year, nearly 18 per cent of the German national product went into exports, compared with hardly 10 per cent in 1936. In the 1957 exports, capital goods predominated heavily, particularly in the trade with underdeveloped countries, in contrast to the consumer goods emphasis of the 1930's.[3] These trade patterns imply the need for more trade with neutralists, more competition with other Western countries, and a more skillful and independent foreign policy. Since 1955, trends in German foreign policy have often been responsive to these needs.

Though overtaken by big business, the senior civil service and the Roman Catholic hierarchy have retained their inside position; German foreign policy continues to be markedly compatible with their views. The military leaders have gained in importance. Though their views have not always been heeded, they seem to be moving toward the status of insiders in the foreign policy process.

Even the opposition has abated. While it has remained intense on some issues, its views have been accommodated on others. The press elite, reflecting in part mass opinion, may find recent foreign policy more to its liking. The Social Democrats and trade union leaders, too, may feel at least mildly pleased, on balance, with the trend of many of the foreign policy decisions since mid-1955. Reflecting the reduced cleavage between the other elites, the balance of press opinion is now more often in favor of official foreign policies. Only the Protestant bishops seem still to be much of the time outside the circle of those whose views are heeded. Whether by choice and lack of interest, or because of political ineffectiveness, they still rank at the bottom of the foreign policy elites.

It should be recalled at this point that all that has been said so far in this chapter has been based on impression. . . . (Cf. Table 1.) These

[3] Wolf Dieter Lindner, "The Balance Sheet of German Foreign Trade," in *Meet Germany* (5th rev. ed., Hamburg, Atlantik-Brücke, May 1958), pp. 45–47.

TABLE 1. AVERAGE SATISFACTION SCORES FOR THE CHANCELLOR, 11 DOMESTIC ELITES, AND 4 FOREIGN GOVERNMENTS

Score	5 Decisions 1952–May 1955 Internal	External	11 Decisions June 1955–1958 Internal	External
3.0	Chancellor 3.0	United States 3.0		
2.8		United Kingdom 2.8		
2.6		France 2.6		
2.4			Chancellor 2.3	
2.2	Cabinet 2.2		Cabinet 2.0	
2.0	Diplo., CDU 2.0		CDU 1.9	
1.8			Diplomats 1.6	
1.6	Civil serv. 1.6		Business 1.5	
1.4	Rom. Cath. 1.4		Mass opinion 1.2	
1.2			Rom. Cath., civil serv. 1.0	United States 1.0
1.0			Press 0.9	
0.8			Trade union, military 0.6	
0.6			SPD 0.5	
0.4				
0.2				France 0.2
0.0	Milit., press 0.0		Ev. Ch. −0.1	
−0.2				
−0.4				
−0.6	Mass op., bus. −0.6			United Kingdom −0.6
−0.8				USSR −0.8
−1.0				
−1.2	Trade union, Ev. Ch. −1.2			
−1.4				
−1.6				
−1.8	SPD −1.8			
−2.0				
−2.2				
−2.4		USSR −2.4		
−2.6				
−2.8				
−3.0				

estimates may prove fallible indeed. Is there any empirical evidence of elite attitudes than can be used to check them? A sample survey of elite members in 1956 revealed their attitudes toward a number of 1952–55 policy decisions in regard to European integration.[4] The results are shown in Table 2.

[4] This survey was carried out in 1956 by the University of Cologne for a research project under the direction of Professor Daniel Lerner at the Center for International Studies at the Massachusetts Institute of Technology. The data are given in Suzanne Keller, "Attitudes Toward European Integration of the German Elite" (Center for International Studies, Massachusetts Institute of Technology, October 1957, multigraphed), p. 26, Table 6.

TABLE 2. GERMAN ELITE ATTITUDES IN 1956 TO PAST POLICY DECISIONS CONCERNING EUROPEAN INTEGRATION[a]

	Politicians	Civil service	Big business	Journalists	Military	Ave. 5 elites (1956)	Mass opinion (1954-56)
Western Eur. Union (1955)							
For	94	96	90	85	81	89	68
No opinion or no info	0	0	5	3	0	2	25
Against	5	4	5	13	19	9	7[b]
Paris Agreements (1955)							
For	77	80	80	62	70	74	42
No opinion or no info	4	0	15	10	10	8	34
Against	18	20	7	28	20	19	24
NATO (1955)							
For	78	79	78	67	69	74	29
No opinion or no info	8	8	11	3	6	9	60
Against	13	13	9	31	25	18	11
ECSC (1952)							
For	81	79	68	74	50	70	10
No opinion or no info	6	0	10	13	6	7	85
Against	13	21	22	13	44	23	5
EDC (1952)							
For	69	63	63	64	56	63	37
No opinion or no info	5	8	13	0	6	6	34
Against	26	29	25	36	38	31	29
Average, 5 issues							
For	80	79	76	70	65	74	37
No opinion or no info	5	3	11	6	6	6	48
Against	15	17	14	24	29	20	15

[a] Sources: Suzanne Keller, "Attitudes Toward European Integration of the German Elite," M.I.T. Center for International Studies, multigraphed (October 1957), p. 26; Jahrbuch I, pp. 343, 362, 365; Jahrbuch II, pp. 340, 349.
[b] In the poll of mass opinion, respondents were asked in September 1955, without details, whether they would vote for or against forming of a United States of Europe. This question is not exactly comparable to the one about elite attitudes to the somewhat more specific Western European Union agreement of 1955.

While the selection of the surveyed does not make the results wholly comparable with other data, they reveal some interesting cleavages between elites and mass opinion and between different elites. All elites appeared more strongly in favor of European integration and of a military effort than was mass opinion, and they were far less indifferent. While the public was most strongly opposed to the military aspects of these pro-Western policies, the civil service, business, and military elites were relatively most opposed to any loss of sovereignty. All elites agreed with the public in giving most support and least opposition to relatively ambiguous and innocuous propositions, such as "Western European Union," with no clearcut implications of new military efforts or new restraints on sovereignty.

Of all elites surveyed, the military — who included key officers engaged in organizing the new German army in association with Theodor Blank, the first Federal Minister of Defense — showed on the average the relatively lowest levels of support, and the highest levels of resistance, to all schemes of supranational integration. Among all elites, support fell off and opposition increased with extent of interference with national sovereignty implied by each scheme. . . .

If foreign policy decisions were mechanically determined by the relative weight of pressure groups, then German foreign policy could be expected to show in the future an increase in nationalism and an eventual abandonment of serious attempts at European integration. Foreign policy, however, is not thus mechanically made. Rather, it is largely shaped by a process of individual and group learning, and it can be greatly influenced by the effects of personality and the impact of events.

News of events change attitudes, even though they are screened at first by most men in terms of the attitudes which they already hold; if the new experience is sufficiently impressive, a net change results. But governments and leaders can make news. They can provide experiences, vicarious or actual, for elite members and for the rank and file of voters — experiences strong enough to produce changed attitudes. The results of foreign policy decisions taken at any one time can thus change the elite preferences and mass opinion which will influence the next foreign policy decisions.

The content and the results of a foreign policy decision can make or break the political fortunes of its makers. The last, but major, influence on the foreign policy process is thus the substance of foreign policy itself.

GERHARD LEHMBRUCH

The Ambiguous Coalition in West Germany

The concept of constitutional opposition is subject to major reservations in France, Germany, and Italy because of persistence in these three countries of political groups that have sought, sometimes successfully, to overthrow the existing regime. In Germany, particularly, the concept of loyal opposition is inconsistent with traditional cultural values emphasizing the "right reason" of the state. The formation of a Grand Coalition between the German Christian Democrats and Social Democrats in 1966 is striking evidence of the weakness of conventional Anglo-American conceptions of opposition in Germany. It occurred notwithstanding the existence of a long tradition of distrust between the two main parties, traditionally more distant from each other than Democrats and Republicans in America. Gerhard Lehmbruch's article analyzes carefully the sources and operation of this coalition, and its implications for German politics.

On 1 December 1966 the *Bundestag* elected the christian democrat leader Kurt Georg Kiesinger as head of a government formed by christian democrats (CDU) and social democrats (SPD), by a majority of 340 (out of 496) members.[1] The liberals (FDP), with 49 members, were pushed aside into opposition. For the first time since 1930 the social democrats entered a German central government, not as the result of an electoral victory but at the conclusion of an inner crisis within the hitherto existing majority. The CDU whose prestige was badly damaged by this crisis continued to provide the chancellor. This helps to explain why some 60 members of the coalescing parties voted against the candidate. Public opinion oscillated between feelings of relief because of the end of a period of insecurity, and feelings of discomfort in view of an experiment which seemed unorthodox and hazardous. The disputes around the *grosse Koalition* (great coalition) thus revealed the ambiguity of conceptions of parliamentary government as they had developed since the establishment of the Federal Republic.

The constitution makers of Weimar, in 1919, thought it essential that a strong and stable executive should be vigilantly criticized by a parliament representing all shades of public opinion. Stability of the governing body was to be guaranteed by a popularly elected president (an *Ersatz-Kaiser*) on the one hand and a strong, politically moderate centre group in the assembly on the other. This pattern was, of course, quite inconsistent with the idea of alternative government represented by British traditions. In a country which had just experienced revolutionary class conflict and was marked by religious and regional heterogeneity, the system of alternative government was regarded as inappropriate. Moreover, this concept ran counter to German ideological traditions which regarded party conflict as prejudicial to consensus rather than as a prerequisite of liberal government.

Among the factors which contributed to modify this state of public

---

Abridged from Gerhard Lehmbruch, "The Ambiguous Coalition in West Germany," *Government and Opposition*, III, 2, 1968, pp. 181–204. Reprinted by permission.

[1] The members for West Berlin, where votes are counted separately, not included.

opinion one may point to changes in West Germany's party system after the second world war; to the fusion of political catholicism and protestant conservatives within a single political movement, the CDU, and to the subsequent decision of the SPD not to join a coalition with the christian democrats but to stay in opposition (at first in the bizonal Economic Council in 1947, and then in the newly elected federal parliament in 1949) — a decision which fitted Adenauer's strategic concept as well as that of Kurt Schumacher. The party system, which before then had formed a rather complicated pattern of overlapping affinities and shifting majorities, became strongly polarized, and federal elections took the form of a contest for power between two rival blocs, with a progressive concentration of votes on the two large parties. While at first the CDU advanced much more than did the SPD and obtained an absolute majority of seats in 1957, the steady increase of social democratic strength nevertheless maintained hope alive in the left that the opposition party might finally gain a decisive electoral victory.

It is true that, except for the third *Bundestag*, formation of a government always implied a coalition. But this was increasingly perceived to be a somewhat abnormal situation, a regrettable deviation from government based on "unequivocal majorities." Traditional admiration for the British pattern of parliamentary politics grew in intensity as the system of alternative government, once a rather academic idea, began to seem to offer a realistic chance of political and constitutional development.[2] This applied, of course, to the perceptions of the political system among the elite; but at the same time, mass opinion polls pointed to a growing understanding of the functions of party conflict and of parliamentary opposition. Correspondingly, the idea that large or all-party coalitions should be preferred as representing a higher form of consensus was abandoned in ever larger sectors of public opinion. This explains why the Austrian coalition of conservatives and socialists (knowledge of which was in general rather superficial) was generally regarded as highly objectionable; it was referred to slightingly as *Proporzdemokratie*.

These more recent constitutional conceptions were subject to a hard test by the decline of the fourth and fifth Adenauer cabinets and the Erhard cabinets. . . . The resulting *immobilisme* of the late Adenauer

[2] This was helped by the evolution of the party system in the *Laender*. The CDU-SPD coalitions, which (generally with the support of other, minor parties) existed in all the *Laender*, broke up successively, the last one (that of Baden-Wuerttemberg) in 1960. Since then some *Laender* have seen the hegemonic rule of one of the parties; others (such as Bavaria, Northrhine-Westphalia, Hamburg, Lower Saxony) an alteration of CDU-led and SPD-led governments. On the other hand, it was significant that the formation of a SPD-CDU cabinet in Lower Saxony, in May 1965, preceded the crisis of the Erhard government. Since then the great coalition has been re-established in Baden-Wuerttemberg, while in Northrhine-Westphalia the social democratic backbenchers thwarted the party leaders' project to form a government with the CDU and pushed the christian democrats into opposition with the aid of the liberals.

and Erhard governments created a situation which, in the logic of alternative government, could have been overcome only by a reversal of the parliamentary majority. However, this reversal of forces did not occur. Neither the presidential crisis of 1959, nor the *Spiegel* affair of 1962, nor the resignation of Adenauer led to a decisive breakthrough of the socialist opposition. In 1961, the CDU lost its absolute majority, but mainly to the benefit of the FDP. In 1965 it succeeded in improving its position again. . . .

Additional strategic considerations seemed to justify the great coalition as a transitory stage on the way to authentic two-party competition. For the CDU, it might mean the opportunity to recover from the inner crisis of the previous years and thus to face the ensuing elections in a better condition. For some SPD leaders, a coalition meant that the christian democrats had ceased to regard the advancement of social democrats to positions of governmental responsibility as (in Adenauer's words) the imminent "ruin of Germany." The party got the opportunity to prove its political maturity and governmental capacity, and this was considered to be an important condition in order to compete for power with equal chances of success. In short, for many in the CDU as well as for the SPD leadership a temporary alliance of both parties fitted well into their strategy which in both cases aims in the long run at achieving a monopoly of governmental power for the whole legislative period. Hence, the great coalition could be quite consistent with the idea of alternative government.

Yet there are other motivations which, without being given the same publicity, point rather in the opposite direction. This is most clearly the case of those socialists who, in view of the "waning of opposition in parliamentary regimes,"[3] see in the great coalition a pattern more adequate to the necessities of modern democracy than alternative government. An important SPD member of the *Bundestag*, for example, argued some years ago that — considering the concentration of political power in the hands of the administration — a parliamentary opposition no longer had the means to criticize the holders of power efficiently, and that a coalition might re-establish some sort of separation of powers in which parliamentary criticism of the executive might gain new vigor. "The existing power cartel of parliamentary majority, government and administration would thus be overcome." The same author then pointed to the fact that all-party government is an established rule in West German local government. This brings us to an important aspect of our problem: large sectors of the political system preserve traditions of proportional participation which date back to a situation when alternative government was a notion alien to German political thought. The law provides for proportional representation of political parties in local executive authorities, while in parliament not only presi-

---

[3] See the article by Otto Kirchheimer, in *Social Research,* vol. 24, 1957, pp. 127–156 [reprinted in this volume, pp. 280–296. — Editors' note].

dents and vice-presidents of the assembly, but also those of specialized committees are elected by *Proporz* in virtue of the standing orders or of convention. Judges of the Federal Constitutional Court are elected by a parliamentary majority of two-thirds. This rule guarantees a quasi-proportional share of "black" and "red" on the bench. Public institutions of political education (such as the *Bundeszentrale fuer politische Bildung,* an agency under the administrative jurisdiction of the Federal Minister of Interior) are placed under all-party supervisory boards, and the supervisory boards of radio and television are formed by representatives of the political parties, large interest groups and churches in order to establish the political neutrality of these media.[4] Of course such institutional arrangements need not be incompatible with a competitive party system, as is demonstrated by the fact that local executive authorities in Great Britain (but not in France or Italy) are likely to be composed of representatives of the rival parties according to their importance in local councils. But in Germany they can be regarded as an older stratum of political culture in which party co-operation is viewed as a condition of impartial, hence just and rational decision-making,[5] which has only recently been partially overlaid by a stratum constituted of the above mentioned trends towards alternative government. On the whole, the political system of West Germany may be characterized as a mixed system which combines elements of party competition and majority rule with elements of proportional division of influence and of bargaining, and its *Proporz* segments keep alive political attitudes which may regain preponderance on the level of national policy-making too.

The ambivalent motivation of the formation of the great coalition appears most clearly in another argument frequently put forward by its advocates: any government resting only upon a small majority in parliament and facing a strong opposition might be unable to carry out certain fundamental and drastic reforms which public opinion and political leaders tended to regard as urgent. These reforms presumably requiring a "broad majority" might be, according to these arguments, the restoration of public finances, including the adjustment of relevant constitutional rules; constitutional amendments concerning "common tasks" of Federation and *Laender* in areas until then under the exclusive jurisdiction of the latter (areas where the action of the *Laender*

---

[4] The Federal Constitutional Court, in its decision condemning chancellor Adenauer's attempt to establish a governmental television network, ruled that, as a consequence of the constitutional guarantee of liberty of the press, "all relevant forces should be represented in the bodies governing radio stations." (Judgement of 28 February 1961, in *Entscheidungen des Bundesverfassungsgerichts,* vol. 12, 1962, pp. 262 ff.)

[5] Similar traits of the political culture are dominant in Switzerland, and play an important role in Austria. Cf. Gerhard Lehmbruch, *Proporzdemokratie. Politisches System und politische Kultur in der Schweiz und in Oesterreich,* Tübingen, 1967.

is considered to be insufficient or lacks co-ordination, as, for example, in aid to scientific research, urbanism, etc.); constitutional amendments on the role of executive and parliament and on civic rights during an eventual state of emergency; perhaps (but this was true only for some of the supporters of a great coalition) even a cautious revision of foreign policy vis-à-vis the Soviet Union and its East European allies. That these tasks could only be performed by a "broad majority" is by no means self-evident. The political crisis was a crisis of the majority rather than of the state; there was no dramatic situation that called for some sort of "national government." In the past the socialist opposition had collaborated in such important reforms as the legislation on national defence. The aspirations for a government based on a broad majority may, however, be explained by the peculiar institutional and social conditions of West German politics.

First, as the projected reforms implied amending the constitution and hence necessitated a *Bundestag* majority of two-thirds, negotiation with the social democrats (who hold over 40 per cent of the seats) was inevitable and perhaps could be facilitated by giving them their share of governmental responsibility. However, such reasoning may be contested for it remains doubtful whether the SPD could use its key position to block constitutional reforms as long as it remained in opposition. Since the failure of Kurt Schumacher's intransigent opposition strategies most social democratic leaders were convinced that the electors expected them to conduct what has been called "constructive" opposition politics. Refusal to co-operate in important political reforms might easily be interpreted as "obstruction," an attitude unpopular with West German public opinion. Moreover, a strategy of co-operation and bargaining gave them the opportunity to exert strong influence on legislation. The turning point might be dated in 1956 when the SPD participated in the elaboration of legislation on national defence. In more recent times, the party has engaged in negotiations on constitutional emergency provisions. Indeed, in contrast with the increasing polarization of the West German party system, the *Bundestag* has developed a particular style of conflict management in which the distinction of governmental majority and opposition has largely been blurred and public contest of parties replaced by private bargaining among party leaders.[6] In historical perspective this trend towards increased interparty co-operation in parliament could be interpreted as the prelude to co-operation in coalition government. But it may equally be argued that a great coalition was not necessary as long as pending problems could be resolved by bargaining in parliament.

Things were complicated, however, by the distribution of power within the federal system. Although it lacks the support of public opinion, West German federalism, by the fact that it is a stronghold

---

[6] This point has been emphasized by G. Loewenberg, *Parliament in the German Political System*, Ithaca, N.Y., 1966, pp. 393–7.

of autonomous bureaucratic bodies, sets limits to the efficiency of majority rule and alternative government. Conflict management takes the form of tiresome bargaining among federal and *Laender* bureaucracies, party groups on the federal and on the regional level, and interest groups. Constitutional amendments concerning public finance proved difficult as long as a strong group of social democratic *Laender* governments acted in concert with stubborn christian democratic *Landesfuersten* to block the federal government's proposals.

Furthermore, the pluralism of interest groups seemed to raise serious problems for economic and financial policy decision-making. Neo-liberal ideology with its straightforward condemnation of "pressure group egoism" lost much of its persuasive power in the middle of the 1960's. But "organized pluralism"[7] and some sort of *économie concertée*, as they had developed in other European countries, might be difficult to establish under the existing party constellations. Stabilizing the economy and developing a long-run fiscal policy necessitated, on the one hand, that the public authorities should co-ordinate their financial policy (Federation, *Laender* and municipalities) and, on the other hand, coordination of the wage policies of management and labour was also required. Given the distribution of power existing in the West German political system, such action can be obstructed by coalitions formed by opposition parties, autonomous political entities such as *Laender,* and unions or other important interest groups. It was tempting to speculate that, lacking the support of a strong opposition in parliament, such obstructive coalitions might henceforth become impossible. One should therefore include the social democrats in the federal government in order to bring about the collaboration of all relevant holders of power. . . .

Coalition committees and formalized coalition agreements have been a rather familiar institution in German politics and have played an important role in some *Laender*.[8] But they were familiar to the initiated rather than to public opinion, for their existence was generally neglected by the press. Only in 1961 did a heated legal controversy arise on the constitutionality of the coalition agreement of the CDU and the FDP, especially on the role of the coalition committee which had been formed on the demand of the liberals. Critics argued, for example, that such an institution infringed upon the chancellor's right to determine the general direction of policy (according to article 65 of the Basic Law). However, the committee failed to fulfil the hopes which the FDP had entertained that it might serve as a counterweight to the cabinet dominated by Adenauer (a function, by the way, significantly different

[7] Cf. Robert Dahl, "Epilogue," in Robert Dahl (ed.), *Political Oppositions in Western Democracies,* New Haven, 1966, pp. 395 ff.

[8] For example in Bavaria, where the heterogeneous coalition of the Hoegner cabinet, consisting of socialists, liberals, Bavarian particularists and the refugee party, was held together during its existence (1954–1957) by a coalition committee in face of a strong christian democratic opposition. Formal written coalition agreements had already existed in the Weimar Republic.

from that of its Austrian counterpart). When the Kiesinger government was formed coalition spokesmen told the public that this time no formal coalition agreement had been concluded. Instead, the chancellor's governmental declaration to the *Bundestag* should serve as the fundamental document of the coalition. The practical difference seems to be negligible.[9] Of greater importance is the decision not to create a coalition committee. Of course this does not mean that Kiesinger can make use of his constitutional powers as Adenauer did. The determination of the general direction of policy, according to vice-chancellor Brandt's declarations to the SPD party conference of November 1967, could only take place by agreement between chancellor and vice-chancellor — a view which Kiesinger confirmed. The phrase of article 65 (*Richtlinien der Politik*) thus loses importance. When in January 1967 the chancellor blamed two cabinet members (a christian democrat and a social democrat) for having publicly disclosed legislative projects of their ministries, on which the cabinet had not yet come to a decision, he was in fact not determining policy but demanding observance of the rules of procedure concerning cabinet discipline.

Within the cabinet, guidance is in part exercised by small bodies in which both parties are represented. Chancellor and vice-chancellor may confer with each other, or together with two cabinet members who occupy important party functions, namely Wehner, vice-chairman of the SPD, and Heck, general secretary of the CDU. In matters of economy and finance, the collaboration of the social democratic Minister of Economy, Schiller, and the Christian Democratic Minister of Finance, Strauss, has been widely remarked; it played an important role in justifying unorthodox measures such as deficit spending and in restoring confidence within the business world and the general public. In some cases, compromises may be worked out at the level of *Staatssekretäre*: the project on constitutional amendments for the state of emergency for example was worked out by Benda, parliamentary secretary of Interior (CDU), and Ehmke, permanent secretary (but a social democratic party nominee) of Justice. In such cases, of course, the project is finally agreed by the cabinet. Generally speaking, the cabinet seems to play an important role because influential — and sometimes rival — party leaders belong to it, such as Schröder (CDU) or Leber (SPD), besides the personalities mentioned above. The chancellor thus cannot be much more than *primus inter pares*.

RELATIONS BETWEEN THE PARTIES

Chancellor and vice-chancellor, as leaders in the cabinet, are chairmen of their respective parties and thus continue a tradition estab-

---

[9] In November 1967 the SPD objected to the demands of certain CDU leaders that majority representation should be introduced for the elections of 1969, on the grounds that such an objective had been fixed for 1973 only, and that this agreement could only be changed by formal negotiations within the coalition.

lished by Adenauer.[10] But this does not mean that, if cabinet leaders agree on a matter of policy, their parliamentary parties (*Fraktionen*) feel automatically bound by these decisions. The parliamentary parties, on the contrary, constitute a rather autonomous locus of power. This is in part due to the personalities of their chairmen, Barzel (CDU) and Helmut Schmidt (SPD), who are often considered as potential candidates for the chancellorship.[11] About once a week, there is an informal reunion of the cabinet leaders (Kiesinger, Heck, Brandt and Wehner) with the two chairmen to discuss current affairs. This body, known as the *Kressbronner Kreis*,[12] resembles in its composition the controversial Austrian coalition committee. It cannot, however, take binding decisions because the party leaders do not feel free to commit their *Fraktionen*; it fulfils a communication, rather than a decision-making function. The decision to implement coalition compromises must in general be arrived at within parliament, by agreement among the *Fraktionen*. Their chairmen are in permanent and close contact with each other which greatly facilitates negotiations. More important problems are settled with the participation of some other party leaders and experts. Major budgetary decisions on social security and related matters, for example, were reached by an ad-hoc committee consisting of four leading CDU deputies (among them three former ministers) and four of the SPD *Fraktion,* which met on 24 October 1967. This agreement was then regarded as strictly binding upon members, in committee as well as in the plenum.[13]

Observers have sometimes deplored a decline of parliamentary influence which they attribute to the coalition. Indeed, at the end of 1967 the parliamentary parties of the CDU and the SPD accepted the governmental proposals for "middle-term budgetary planning" without major discussions or modifications. But the *Bundestag* has always been

[10] Kiesinger, as Erhard before him, at first showed a certain reluctance to accept this supplementary burden but soon had to acknowledge that the logic of party government, as it had developed since 1949, required him not to allow anyone to use the party machine as a rival source of leadership power. On the other hand, Brandt may have committed an error of judgement when he claimed for himself the important portfolio of foreign affairs; this task absorbs him more than his position as party chairman really allows.

[11] In 1966 Helmut Schmidt renounced entering the cabinet because he failed to obtain the portfolio of first order to which he felt entitled. Barzel was, with Schröder, one of Kiesinger's rivals for the chancellorship; today he seems to have recovered from the disgrace into which he had fallen as a consequence of his manoeuvres against chancellor Erhard.

[12] The first important reunion of these personalities took place in summer 1967 at Kressbronn, the chancellor's holiday resort on the Lake of Constance. It was then felt that closer contacts between party leaders would be necessary to improve the working of the coalition.

[13] This was drastically demonstrated when the *Bundestag* committee on finance had to revise its own amendment tending to limit a supplementary income tax to a period of four years. The CDU members of the committee, who had voted with the liberals, argued in vain that they had not been informed of the "coalition agreement" of 24 October, according to which the tax should be levied without any limitation in time.

badly equipped to develop initiatives of its own in budgetary matters, and it would perhaps be premature to generalize from the case. The obvious decline of parliamentary controversy and debate is largely due to the importance of the private negotiations of party leaders and specialists which, in itself, is not a new element in German parliamentary politics — the new element is rather the pooling of the already existing "oligarchies" within the *Bundestag* which has resulted from the coalition. This does not mean that the role of parliament itself within the political system is declining: while the parliamentary leaders endeavour to take a strong line with members, they have also not hesitated to demonstrate their independence in relation to the government.[14] And in this they take into consideration the mood of their rank and file. Sometimes a parliamentary party objects to a compromise worked out in the cabinet; then bargaining may begin again, this time *interfraktionell,* and eventually among parliamentary leaders and government.[15] Parliament thus serves as a locus of *Bereichsopposition,* with, for example, a centre left coalition of social democratic and left-wing CDU members opposing governmental attempts to check the expansion of expenditure on social security, a strong CDU group opposing a more flexible policy in the relations with East European countries, and socialists backing the FDP counter-project concerning the state of emergency.

It has even been argued by some that with the great coalition the political system has been regressing towards an older form of parliamentary government in which the government is no longer the leader of the parliamentary majority, according to the doctrine of party government, but confronts the parliament in its totality — a confrontation which would bring to mind the constitutional framework of Imperial Germany. But this argument is likewise misleading: on the one hand it oversimplifies the relationship between cabinet and parliamentary majority under the Adenauer governments, which cannot adequately be described as "cabinet leadership." On the other hand it overestimates very considerably the independence of the *Fraktionen* of the majority in relation to the cabinet. Unlike the Austrian parliament, the *Bundestag* has preserved a remarkable degree of autonomy under the "black-

---

[14] The chancellor himself manifested his irritation when Helmut Schmidt insisted in public declarations on the subordination of government to parliament.

[15] In February 1967 the SPD objected to the government's decision to raise unemployment compensation by ten per cent and demanded a rise of twenty per cent. In a new coalition bargain with Barzel and the cabinet a compromise resulted which raised the compensation by 15 per cent. At the end of 1967 it became evident that the compromise worked out in the cabinet on constitutional amendments for the state of emergency had no chance of passing in parliament without important modifications taking into account the strong objections of SPD members. In January 1968 the government's project to impose taxes and *dirigistische* restrictions on private long distance motor traffic (proposed by the SPD Minister of Traffic Leber) met with strong opposition within the CDU parliamentary party; a counter-project was proposed by christian democratic spokesmen.

red" coalition; but as the coalition feels "condemned to succeed" the solidarity of the coalition in parliament and government is in general rather high.

A second field in which the coalition diverges from its former Austrian counterpart is patronage. When the alliance was concluded in November 1966, its leaders denied any intention of establishing a *Proporz* with equal distribution of spoils. As, under the Adenauer and Erhard governments, many leading posts in the federal administration had been filled with sympathizers of the CDU and its minor allies, this meant in practice that the SPD gave up the demand for a major *revirement* in its favour. Seven out of eleven *beamtete Staatssekretäre* (permanent secretaries) in the ministries now headed by social democrats were replaced, but only some of the new nominees came from the party ranks. In the lower levels of the administration there were on the whole few changes (except, of course, in the personal staffs of ministers). The proportional staffing of a ministry by members of both parties was even more rejected, with the only exception of the Federal Press and Information Office.[16] Among the SPD rank and file this cautious policy has caused some discontent; but socialist party leaders have frequently avoided yielding to such pressures.[17] The nomination of parliamentary secretaries (*parlamentarische Staatsekretäre*) was a more controversial issue. Adversaries of such an institution (the most important among them was chancellor Adenauer) had been afraid that it might become a favourite object of coalition bargains and that parliamentary secretaries coming from the ranks of another party than the minister might undermine the authority of the latter. Again Austria, where some ministries under the jurisdiction of one of the parties had been controlled by a *Staatsekretär* belonging to the other party, provided a negative example. The Kiesinger government finally decided to conform to the British example in that parliamentary secretaries should serve as junior ministers to take some of the burden off the head of the department and at the same time to become acquainted with governmental affairs, and that they should belong to the same party as the minister and

---

[16] This agency is perhaps the most "politicized" administrative body within the federal government. Consequently, the SPD demanded the position of deputy speaker of the government; but it nominated Konrad Ahlers, once the principal defendant in the *Spiegel* affair, who was not a member of the party. In January 1968 the SPD demanded the post of deputy chief of the Federal Intelligence Service (*Bundesnachrichtendienst*), a post it has held for a long time in the *Bundesamt für Verfassungsschutz* (Federal Office for the Protection of the Constitution) which fulfils the functions of a "political police."

[17] It should be added that there are rather few candidates available in the ranks of the SPD who are qualified for top positions in the federal administration. Qualified younger party members have generally preferred to enter the civil service of the *Laender* or municipalities governed by SPD majorities to the rather modest chances of a career at Bonn. Thus, when Klaus Schütz left his post of permanent secretary of the Ministry of Foreign Affairs (which he had held since the forming of the coalition) in order to become mayor of West Berlin, his successor was a diplomat without party ties, Mr. Duckwitz, for no suitable SPD member could be found.

enjoy his confidence. Thus, in spite of some controversial aspects which still survive (especially in regard to the relationship between parliamentary and permanent secretaries), the coalition could not be blamed for practising *Proporz*.

THE PRICE OF COMMON RESPONSIBILITY

Some of the differences between the West German and the Austrian coalition systems are the result of deliberate political decisions. These decisions in turn arise from differences in the character of the respective party systems. While Austrian parties are still rather strongly antagonized by ideological conflict, the West German parties have advanced much further on the road to transforming themselves into "catch-all-parties" which have abandoned much of their original ideological motivations. In Austria party leaders and members perceived the system in such a manner that they felt the need for strong mutual guarantees against possible disloyal moves by the partner in the coalition. The rigid structure of the alliance, the centralization of decision-making within the coalition committee and the highly developed *Proporz* patronage may be understood as substitutes for a lack of confidence in the rules of the democratic and parliamentary game. The future evolution of the Austrian system may lead to the strengthening of such confidence, just as happened in West Germany in the course of the past two decades. In Germany the rules of the game have proved to be quite efficient, and thus the CDU-SPD coalition depends much less on a system of institutional, procedural and personal guarantees such as had developed in Austria. The resulting greater flexibility of the German great coalition signifies, however, that the co-ordination of political forces is more difficult. The strong segmentation on party lines so characteristic of Austrian social structure has no real equivalent in West Germany. This means that the vertical integration of interest groups into party "camps," which made it possible in Austria to control wage policies if the coalition parties agreed, is of less importance in Germany. Hence co-ordination is more difficult here, as is demonstrated by the example of what has been called (by a barbarism of language) *konzertierte Aktion*: spokesmen of the federal administration (of the Ministries of Economy, Labour and eventually Finance) meet at a round table with union and management representatives. This procedure, which resembles practices current in some Scandinavian countries, is much less formalized than that of the Austrian *Paritätische Kommission für Preis- und Lohnfragen* which controlled wage policies (and, with less success, price policies) by agreement between unions and employers with the assistance of the government.[18] In West Germany the system of labour relations is much more complex, and spontaneous co-

---

[18] On the Austrian case see: Herbert P. Secher " 'Representative Democracy or 'Chamber State': The Ambiguous Role of Interest Groups in Austrian Politics," in *Western Political Quarterly*, Vol. 13, 1960, pp. 890–909.

ordination of the *Sozialpartner* accordingly more difficult. These are much less subject to party leadership, and besides industrial unions enjoy a considerable measure of autonomy within the Trade Union Federation. Likewise the co-ordination of public authorities has not been as successful as some had expected. To be sure, the SPD no longer has an interest in encouraging social democratic minister presidents of *Laender* to resist the policies of the federal government; but, on the other hand CDU minister presidents no longer feel obliged to back the federal government for reasons of inner party solidarity. Thus constitutional reorganization of public finance and long-term financial policy have progressed no further with the great coalition than they would probably have done with a small coalition. . . .

The coalition faces an important handicap owing to the ambiguous, not to say paradoxical, character of its aims. Such an alliance, if it is to function without serious friction, must be conceived of as more or less permanent. If, on the contrary, the marriage has been contracted with the intention of divorcing as soon as possible, each partner will try to establish his innocence in the rupture. The efficiency of the work of government and coalition is thus hampered by strong rivalries and animosities within the CDU and SPD and between several of their leading figures. Under these conditions it was unrealistic to assume that the great coalition would noticeably facilitate structural reforms. This would have meant to break up the complex and balanced network of veto groups which form the potential allies of either CDU or SPD in coming electoral contests. In a more general manner, the advocates of drastic reforms failed to assess realistically the conditions of a strategy of political reform in democratic societies with an advanced socioeconomic system. Such reforms may become possible if a profound crisis leads to sudden shifts in the institutional and political setting and thus disorganizes (at least temporarily) the channels of access of veto groups — as happened in France during the summer of 1958, to take a more recent example. In Germany in 1966 this was not the case. There was, to be sure, a crisis of the majority; but since the CDU remained in office the existing political setting was only slightly transformed by the great coalition. . . .

A condition of political innovation is the articulation of alternative policies, which depends on the degree to which political conflict is managed by public controversy. The West German political system, already before the formation of the great coalition, was characterized by a reduction of public debate. Since then the importance of discreet management of party conflict by private bargaining has increased in spite of the efforts to preserve some autonomy of parliamentary life. There is of course a liberal opposition party which, by skilful parliamentary moves, has recently succeeded in enlarging somewhat the area of open discussion; but it continues to suffer from internal dissensions and is therefore strongly handicapped for the crystallization of deviating political attitudes. Trade union leadership too has preserved a certain autonomy in front of the CDU-SPD alliance and has forced the social democratic leadership to press for a public debate of controversial political issues.[19] Important independent newspapers, by maintaining a critical attitude to the "cartel" of the political parties, have preserved elements of public discussion although the vital importance of conflict over alternative policies for a liberal democracy is not always understood in German journalism. All this prevents the complete depoliticization of the public but it does not solve the problem of how the votes can articulate their discontent within the democratic system.

The revival of extremist movements on the right and on the left acquires a particular significance in this context. Leftist extremism, especially among students (where it takes the form of a neo-anarchist protest movement against industrial society in its "capitalist" or Soviet communist form[20]) is clearly a reaction to the closed character of the political system which has been accentuated by the formation of the great coalition. Whether it will be able to crystallize discontent outside the academic world remains to be seen. Yet rightist extremism, which had been assumed to be dead, undoubtedly again constitutes a factor which cannot be neglected within the political system. The "National Democratic Party" (NPD) is not, as its leaders would like to suggest, a mere conservative movement but clearly continues the specific German tradition of the extreme right. This does not mean that the proportion of voters with explicit and consistent rightist-extremist orientations has increased. Their numerical importance, which had continuously fallen since the beginning of the 1950s, is still less than it was a decade ago, and dictatorship in its national-socialist form as well as in principle is disapproved of by an overwhelming majority of the electorate.[21] But this is not the problem. The problem is rather that in Germany, as in other Western societies, important numbers of voters hold inconsistent orientations, partly liberal and democratic, partly — as a response to strains inherent in industrial societies — authoritarian, which, under specific circumstances, may be mobilized for anti-liberal, authoritarian movements and eventually may threaten the democratic system.[22] . . .

---

[19] One may doubt whether the discussion on constitutional emergency powers, which had hitherto taken place in the privacy of "expert talks," would have been given public hearings in committee of the *Bundestag* if the existence of a FDP counter-project and the tenacious opposition of trade union spokesmen had not put strong pressure on the social democratic leadership.

[20] The political ideas of the student protest movements are largely derived from the Marxist-Freudian social philosophy of Herbert Marcuse. Its "Maoist" aspects seem to be more a matter of "style" than of ideology or platform.

[21] This emerges from opinion polls and is acknowledged by the NPD leaders who insist on their respect for the rules of the democratic game — an attitude dictated not only by fear of a possible interdiction by the Federal Constitutional Court but obviously also by the fact that many electors with authoritarian opinions nevertheless continue to believe in these rules.

[22] This argument follows the hypotheses developed by Erwin K. Scheuch as a result of his research on extreme rightist movements and, in particular, the NPD. See: Erwin K. Scheuch, unter Mitarbeit von Hans D. Klingemann, "Theorie des Rechtsradikalismus in westlichen Industriegesellschaften" *Hamburger Jahrbuch für Wirtschafts- und Gesellschaftspolitik*, 12th Year, 1967, pp. 11–29.

Stability is by no means certain and if new strains were to appear the political opportunities for the expression of dissent within the framework of liberal institutions and of a democratic party system would be rather limited precisely because of the existence of the great coalition. This has repeatedly been acknowledged by CDU and SPD leaders: by forming their alliance, these parties have run the risk of excluding any alternative democratic solution. They are "condemned to succeed together."

EDGAR MORIN

The Faceless Revolution

The idea of order is intrinsic to the notion of government, whether the reference is to democratic or authoritarian politics, to a Western or to an Afro-Asian society. Without order, attending to the arrangements of a large society, let alone directing its activities, becomes a matter of happenstance. The French revolution of May, 1968 was striking in two respects. The upheaval occurred in a country that had come to show, outwardly at least, most of the attributes of a prosperous society. It was not a protest against a Gaullist regime in the name of another recognizable type of regime, but rather, it was a protest against the concept of modern government itself. Edgar Morin's article, written shortly after the most eventful days of the revolution, catches the sense of things falling apart and the center failing to hold. Incidentally, the paragraph that opens the article echoes in its prose style Charles Dickens's A Tale of Two Cities; *the two cities of that novel are London and Paris in the 1790's.*

France was at the peak of her powers, having triumphed internationally with the Paris opening of the Vietnamese Conference where East and West had come to render homage; confident that her franc was solid as gold at a time when the dollar was shaky; having surmounted a recession and about to enter a new period of economic growth as a modernizing, reformist nation, dominated by a liberal patriarch-leader. This France, where protests and convulsions seemed the ultimate manifestation of provinciality and economic backwardness; this France of the Fifth Republic, which had liquidated a long and violent crisis of decolonization where the opposition, capable neither of uniting nor of masking its divisions, could profit only extremely slowly from the mistakes of the government; this Gaullist France saw broken, in a few days, all the bonds of her social and economic life — her power gone, herself poised on the edge of the abyss.

The political crisis threatened not only the Establishment and its organizations, but also the powers and parties in opposition, including the Federation of the Left and the Communist Party. They were mute, impotent witnesses, ignored by the torrents of May which raged about them and also against them, powerless vessels at the mercy of the tide which might yet sweep them away. The old official Left could allow itself to be carried along by the movement only if it succeeded in controlling it, channeling it, and turning it to its own advantage.

The incredible fact is perhaps to be found elsewhere. The emptiness of the domestic policy of the Fifth Republic, whose government was nothing more than a vast administrative council where only God the Father enjoyed the luxury of making policy, and then only international policy, was already noticeable. The political emptiness of the old Left, simultaneously paralyzed and protected by its bureaucratic armor, was also clear to many. What is incredible is that the current crisis is more than a crisis of Gaullism and a crisis of the Left. It is the sudden crisis of a grand consumer society which revolved, moved, hummed, and purred, peaceful and active, a society which the most ferocious assaults of politics and the most perilous unrest of decolonization were never able to jeopardize, an ascendant society, where the per capita income, one of the highest in Europe, ought to have continued rising, where the islands of misery and backwardness so common fifteen years ago were disappearing. Then, in that society well on its way toward American happiness without cancers of race problems and Vietnam, in that society everything suddenly convulsed, cracked, collapsed, and stopped, and the prodigious cybernetic apparatus is turning out millions of malcontents who stop, protest, and challenge.

Something cracked that did not crack in May, 1958, that did not crack under the strain of the OAS,[1] something that cracked in 1940

From Edgar Morin, "Une révolution sans visage," *Le Monde,* June 5–6, 1968. Reprinted by permission. Translated by Allen Rozelle and Mattei Dogan.

[1] *Organisation de l'Armée Secrète* — paramilitary rightist opposition to Algerian independence during the Algerian War.

only under the relentless pressure of German tanks. This time something cracked in a machine which seemed to be working normally. After two weeks of furious but extremely limited, almost parochial assaults by students, the society came apart between the 18th and the 23rd of May with a strange gentleness. . . .

A gigantic, savage strike began throughout the society. It was savage in the sense of the 18th century Noble Savage. Everything moved as towards a state of nature, with everyone retreating to their work, occupational associations, and family. That it was a society losing for a time its capacity for organized work was made clear by the accumulation of overflowing garbage cans, by the plethora of refuse scattered about Les Halles, by the lines in front of banks before closing time, and by the timid panic of housewives scurrying to grocery stores to gather provisions as though for a long hibernation.

Then for several days, from May 14th to May 21st, before the first reaction from Parliament, everyone remained quiet — the state, the government, the opposition, the Communist Party. Only the CGT spoke up for the silent millions, but even then as though it were only a matter of ordinary labor demands. Even the strike itself was quiet. Everything happened as though the political process had been paralyzed, *as if the country had simultaneously become apolitical and entered a revolution.* It is truly a faceless, leaderless revolution that has suddenly broken out. While I write, I do not know whether it will metamorphose by drifting or by positive action, before taking its real shape. The striking workers claim no man as leader; whereas the student revolt, a revolt of the youthful masses, has found its symbolic face in Daniel Cohn-Bendit, the fiery redhead without a country, the street democrat who embodies anarchism and Marxism and marches under the two flags — the red and the black — whose unity is the symbol of the student revolt. Nowhere during May, 1968 have you heard a "Vive Waldeck Rochet" or a "Vive Mitterand" or a "Vive Mollet"; it is only now, at the end of May, that you hear here and there a "Vive Mendès-France." It is only now that political life has begun again.

What happened in May 1968? A sociological accident, something which had not been included in the normal processes of society, an internal injury caused by a ruptured vessel inside the body of society, very close to the head, paralyzing the entire central nervous system. It is this incredible, overwhelming accident that must be understood.

FROM THE STUDENT COMMUNE TO THE FACELESS REVOLUTION

Until May 1968, student revolts in liberal western societies had not infected in any way the societies they challenged. In Germany they did not alter the peaceful, social-democratic discipline of the workers; in Italy they did not affect the electoral game being played while the revolt raged most violently; in the United States, the Berkeley campus, like all the other campuses, remained an advanced island utopia, somewhere between heaven and the future.

Initially, there was nothing original about the character of the French revolt. It was not only in France that student protest cracked like lightning. On the one hand, there is university inadequacy in coping with both the demographic pressure from the student-age population and the shortage of professional opportunities — that is to say, too much selectivity in choosing university students and too high a production of graduates for the positions existing on the outside. On the other hand, there is too thorough an adaptation of the university curriculum to the techno-bureaucratic careers of the bourgeois society. The fear or the refusal to accept quietly the bleak existence of the "one-dimensional" man and the contradictory fear of not having an assured and rising career in the civilization of well-being, these two fears constituted the fermenting agents of the French student's dual consciousness. Doubly discontent and demanding were the Italian students, where the situation was as bad as, if not worse than, in France.

We must look for its explosive force in the phenomenon of progressive amplification and intensification between November, 1967 and the beginning of May, 1968. The phenomenon was made possible by two factors which coincided exactly: first, the audacious intelligence of a small group of students at the University of Nanterre who succeeded in uniting other students in support of its avant-grade, political ideas, first on March 22nd at Nanterre and then from May 3rd to May 13th in Paris; and second, the inept attitude of the university's high administration, of the Ministry of National Education, which was informed or influenced by the university administration, of the government, and finally of the state. One might say that the "Leninist" audacity of the March 22nd group was able to find on the other side of the barricades a "Kerenskyism" which gave it time to deploy its forces. (Kerenskyism means vain threats followed by niggardly concessions, and between the heated phases, periods of total immobilization during which no one in the government knew how to utilize the time for strategic reform.) This stupidity is certainly not a psychological trait proper to any particular figure in the upper reaches of the university. It is a sociological trait common to an anachronistic caste which has survived every historical earthquake since the Middle Ages; not a bourgeois caste but prebourgeois, feudal, a caste of high university administrative officials and professors by divine right, office-holders who no more understood what their students were thinking and feeling than the Algerian *pieds noirs* did when they saw their "faithful" Arab servants rebel against them. While the whole world watches the student revolt unfurl, no one at the summit of the university administration wants to see the first symptoms of the French experience as anything more than a classroom disorder; no one wants to see anything in the political agitation but pathological agitation. The only remedy proposed has been the elimination of the leaders. However, the rules of the liberal university prevent repression quickly and completely at that still propitious moment when the fire smolders only in very small groups. There were half-hearted attempts at repressions which served only to swing larger and larger cohorts of students toward the threatened students.

At the same time, the tension building up around the Vietnam war, the pro-Vietnamese pressure which grows stronger and stronger among young revolutionaries and which has already forced the French Communist Party to change its slogan from peace to victory for the Vietnamese people — this tension created by international demonstrations more and more synchronized and ardent — has been translated on the student front into the unleashing of pre-guerrilla terror raids between the commandos of the "Occident" and the groups of revolutionary students.

It was the simultaneous explosion on two fronts — the closing of Nanterre for fear of a student boycott and the closing of the Sorbonne for fear of a virtually armed battle between students — which provoked the first large spontaneous movement which spread through the ranks of youth, encompassing lycée students, some young workers, and some young "black shirts" — those three groups being the most combative during the days of insurrection. In fact it is the juvenile mass which constitutes the movement, but the latter will always have as its political leaders, steering it in the black and red direction, the small revolutionary elite who were joined on May 3rd and on the following days. The pleiades of experienced militants aged 20 to 30 are veterans of former student political struggles who have become the rebellious dependents of the bourgeois society and who have thrown themselves into the great political game. Thus in France, the student revolt is much more widespread among the nation's youth than in the other western countries, since it includes adolescents from 15 to 18 and young workers and it is much better organized and directed thanks to the revolutionary leaders who constitute a political general staff of extraordinary quality of action and thought.

Police repression has permitted this revolt to attract the sympathy or acquire the benevolent neutrality of its primary enemy, the professional corps of the university. Such repression and the revolt's own ragamuffin audacity often attract more sympathy than reprobation. It was this equivocal position that permitted the revolutionary movement to spread openly at the moment when, with established power withdrawing on all fronts, the students seized the Sorbonne and made it the soviet of the modern Petrograd. From that point the revolt became a veritable harvest of protest. Tens of thousands of youths moved from a visceral reaction to an active radical political consciousness.

The repression was brutal enough to stir opinion against it and to radicalize a large number of students and youth. Yet it has never dared go far enough to break up the movement. The state was threatened, but did not yet know with what and did not dare to crush the most pampered class of all, the young. Remember that the prime minister, a former student from the *École Normale Supérieure,* opposed the repression.

What has preceded may explain the breadth and intensity of the student revolt, but it does not explain why it resulted in such enormous disturbances.

THE ECHOES

The occupation, profanation, desecration, and violation of the sanctity of the Sorbonne, which was turned into a revolutionary club, released vibrations which spread to universities in the provinces, to entire sectors of the intelligentsia, scientific researchers, the ORTF,[2] the cinema, and writers. The same vibration stirred up the labor world, and everything started to tremble at the same time, like a bridge, the marvel of engineers, which not even the heaviest weights had shaken, but which collapsed under the synchronized vibrations caused by the rhythmic tread of a regiment of marching men.

If there was a vibration strong enough to cause collapse, it was because there was the Act and the Word at the same time. The act, that audacious occupation of the university by the students, reminded the worker of the typical act expected of him, "the factory to the workers," and linked itself with the great emancipating actions of June, 1936: the occupations of factories, offices, and large department stores. In fact, the occupation of the Sorbonne accomplished and mimed an action which was fundamentally that of workers, and this was brought home to the working class. The astonishing revival of the identity of the working class, accomplished by the students, succeeded only through the desecration of authority which the seizure of the Sorbonne constituted and which seemed to make the Latin Quarter of Paris an insurgent, radical, soviet island state.

The mass media contributed much to the vibrations. During the ascendant and combative period of the movement of the student revolt, it could be said — because of the news from peripheral stations and from the ORTF which had partly cut itself off from government tutelage — that every quantum of news became a quantum of action:

1. During the street fighting, news broadcast direct by radio-telephone gave the dispersed, decentralized camp — the rebels — an opportunity to know immediately what the general situation was and what was happening in particular at any point.
2. Broadcast appeals by organizations or individuals became immediate means by which to mobilize participants on a very large scale.
3. UNEF[3] and SNE-sup,[4] officially recognized union organizations benefiting from legal status and a sort of bourgeois approval, could express themselves directly at any moment, and thus profited from the gigantic scope of the mass-media.
4. The emotional simplification, the need for sensation, and extraordinarily among the large news services, the subterranean rela-

---

[2] The French National Radio and Television Network.
[3] *Union Nationale des Étudiants de France* — leftist student union.
[4] Radical French teachers' union.

tion between the juvenile mythology of mass culture and the real events helped to make a "star" of the student revolt.
5. The immediate coverage of acts of representative brutality attracted general sympathy to the "ragamuffins" faced by the CRS[5] Goliath.

All this mixed and mingled to give an extraordinary emotional amplification to the ascendant, combative period, which helped to create a contagious, victorious, and even epic dimension to what might have remained an enormous classroom outburst in the Latin Quarter.

Thus amplified and magnified, the resonance was felt throughout the country, sustained by the act of occupation, the desecration of authority, and by the Marxist working-class ideology. That dialectic, winning over first the young workers and then the factories, sparked the first occupation of a factory at Nantes, which in turn set off a chain of occupations with mimetic rapidity. Radio news, to which the country had been listening attentively for two weeks, spurred the movement, in spite of the CGT,[6] which tried to brake it originally, the Communist Party, and the other parties, all stunned into a silent stupor.

The phenomenon of the desecration of authority was enormous: the power of the state withered on the vine in the aftermath of what was originally a feverish push to take a small Bastille. The overturning of the university Bastille struck at the *paternalistic essence of social power*.

Thus, born unexpectedly and tumultuously of the blind, badly-organized resistance of the high university establishment, the student movement, from May 3rd to May 13th, had multiple functions for the young. All strata were reunited in a sort of 1789 spirit. One party brought together in solidarity students, young workers, and lycée students: intellectuals, leading and exalting an intelligentsia which up to that time had dreamed of revolution and signed verbally militant manifestos; a sort of avant-garde, pseudo-workers' party, calling for the proletarian revolution; a true populist party in its desire and attempt to fraternize with the working class. All were functions not fulfilled by the traditional leftist parties. They were performed simultaneously with an astonishing aggressiveness provoking the combustion of society.

DISINTEGRATION AND DYNAMISM

The combustion caused the general disintegration of the power of industry and the state, and in the resulting power vacuum a new revolutionary dynamism began so that a close collaboration between the government and the student political vanguard soon developed as they danced the political ballet of Kerenskyism-Leninism. For example, when the government banned Cohn-Bendit from French territory, the revolutionary dynamism regained a force at the very moment it was beginning

---

[5] A national paramilitary security force.
[6] *Confédération Générale du Travail* — Communist-dominated and largest labor union.

to wane. This led to the 22nd of May, the second and decisive cycle of student-worker cooperation. These two aspects, the temporary power vacuum in the society and the new dynamism which sought to create new structures, are at this point so confused that they cloud the face of a revolution *which knows neither what it is nor whether in fact it is a revolution*. At the same time, they do reveal two fundamental dimensions: on the one hand, a general demand for change; on the other hand, a narrowly confined revolutionary aspiration.

Between the pole of workers' demands and the pole of revolutionary aspiration, there is therefore a mist which envelops both; everything is present, but cannot take shape before the definitive cutting of a channel for the torrents. It has been noted that the breaching of the dike, caused by the student revolt, led to *a general crisis of authority*. As far as the intellectuals are concerned, France is experiencing a revolt against gerontocratic or paternalistic authority: the lycée students fight their principals, and the university students attack divine professorial right, and go so far as to demand that examinations be supervised by the students if not suppressed altogether; young hospital doctors attempt to break the executive power of the older doctors; the researchers at the CNRS[7] demand to participate in the administration of the gigantic organism in order to eliminate surveillance by appointing themselves to positions of power; writers seize the old Massa Palace and dream of imposing their control on the paternalistic editors; and Jewish Scouts occupy the old rabbinical consistory and involve themselves in facets of synagogue affairs almost as far as God the Father.

The revolt against the paternalistic state has spread wherever the intelligentsia, chained to techno-bureaucratic organizations of culture, suffers the snooping, niggling authority of the spy-state and sees itself in a position of dependent tutelage (the ORTF and its news section in particular). This revolt against the state has even broken out among the film directors whom the state was protecting from the producers and distributors. Thus the anti-gerontocratic revolt of the university has grown into an anti-paternalistic rebellion throughout large sectors of the population. In the labor world, it has become a revolt attacking managerial authority. The initial occupation of a factory is indeed an act of the half-symbolic, half-real overthrow of established power. However, only the extremist and often juvenile minority of the workers has dared dream of destroying the industrial class of managers; the majority has expressed its will either by the demand for co-management (CFDT)[8] or as is more often the case (CGT and other unions) by the demand that union power in the factory be officially recognized. In this respect, union authorities have already been able to manipulate the movement they ignored at the beginning.

---

[7] *Centre National de Recherche Scientifique* — National Center for Scientific Research.

[8] *Confédération Française Démocratique des Travailleurs* — Largest non-Communist labor union.

There is, therefore, in this faceless revolution a generalized challenge to power, including the most lowly and insignificant forms of demands, as well as those of the great national unions. Whatever the form, this challenge demands a modification of power relations at the expense of managerial authority.

This challenge to authority as such, permitted and released by the sudden disappearance of established power, has, because of that very fact, an archaic character, in the fundamental and principal meaning of the word, for a working class world which has been bent under oppressive discipline since the dawn of the industrial age. In one blow, May, 1968 reopened the great libertarian inspiration of the French labor movement and at the same time joined traditional struggles against the capitalistic factory-penitentiary. This archaic revolt also attacked the new techno-bureaucratic style of work, be it statist or capitalistic, where "humanization" envelops without destroying the hierarchic foundation of authority. However, the creative intelligentsia, whether tied to the culture industry or threatened and devalued by the new techno-bureaucratic order, has been most deeply affected by the events. It is not by chance that the term "self-management" blossomed more intensely and widely among the intelligentsia than within the working class. On the other hand, it is in the ranks of the youth that the truly modern character of the revolt — its anti-paternal aspect — has been most clearly expressed. That aspect is the advanced point of a movement which has radically questioned adult civilization and the idea that the parental adult is the highest achievement of homo sapiens. Against this, youth is formulating the idea of incomplete, permanent adolescence — an idea with an astonishing similarity to the Trotskyist concept of the permanent revolution.

The modernist, anti-paternal revolt is strong among the youth, and the old libertarian revolt has reappeared among the working class. These two characteristics, archaic and modern, mixed with one another in diverse ways and provided the force of May, 1968, for the force of a revolution is always the confluence of archaic and modern currents. Thus constituted, the waves of May struck the established powers a stunning blow. They struck not only the government administration, whose power has no more soul than that of private enterprise; they also struck the soul itself of that which dominates the administration, which is concentrated in the image of the guide-patriarch. By a strange reversal, the conspiratorial effectiveness of the powers and tempests which comprised the strength of the old Prospero for the last ten years has been his weakness for three weeks. Unlike the crisis of May, 1958, which appealed for the help of the father-leader, the eruption of May, 1968 has directed against de Gaulle the old parricidal hatreds graven in the French political unconscious since the death of Louis XVI. Only prolonged chaos can in the long run restore the desire for a paternal image.

This anti-paternalistic, anti-authoritarian, anti-gerontocratic wave struck France suddenly, and hesitates between two poles, those of specific demands and of general revolution.

THE MOVEMENT OF MARCH 22ND

At its core the movement of the 22nd of March is a fusion of Leninism and anarchism. In revolutionary action it is supple and passionate; it refuses to form a party organization, but it welcomes openly the active support of all revolutionary currents. The March 22nd movement is an original formula for an action front with a minimum of organization and at the same time a maximum of strategic and tactical intelligence. The 22nd of March group is revolutionary in its substance, and wherever it imposes itself, a new order is created — direct democracy, permanent assemblies, elective recall, a soviet order. With the creation of the 22nd of March movement the soviets, in their original and unadulterated sense, entered a land which is also the France of Guy Lux, the Renault 4, and the Citroen DS 19. The 22nd of March mimics all the revolutions of the past — the Spanish Civil War, the Cultural Revolution, October 17th, the Paris commune — in order to cultivate and to force itself to live a form of committee socialism. The 22nd of March is at the origin of everything; it has accomplished the most extraordinary subversion that France has ever experienced, with the collaboration of the University, the Pompidou government, General de Gaulle, and, thanks to the spontaneous movement among French youth, in the face of opposition by the Communist Party and the CGT. The student movement would have been capable of taking power from the 22nd of March, but the revolutionary elite was able to maintain its position at the crest of the wave. It succeeded in making the university a self-administered, soviet territory, and wishing to spread that model throughout society, it has launched constant appeals to the working class. It has declared war not only on the Gaullist regime, but also on the bourgeois state and the capitalist system and on the parties of the established Left, the Stalinist party and labor organizations. Initially, the fraternal student wave broke on the gates of the factory at Billancourt, which the CGT had rung down like an iron curtain to protect "its" working class. But the constant pressure of the student movement, especially after the Kerenskyist measure banning Cohn-Bendit from France, finally resulted in the creation, at the beginning of the week of May 27th, of novel soviets, "worker-student committees."

The revolution is thus committee socialism, which the revolutionary dynamism is multiplying in the form of action committees and which, if it continues, will be transformed into administrative committees. The eruption of administrative communism in France is indeed the most stupefying novelty of the events. The contemporary idea of self-management, neglected and disdained by French workers and the intelligentsia, has renewed interest here and there in the old forgotten idea of "the factory to the workers," and has reawakened also among the intelligentsia, wherever they find themselves bound to bureaucratic organizations, statist or capitalistic, the idea of co-management if not of self-management.

The phenomenon is very sharply defined at the ORTF, where the reporters are demanding self-administration of the news services. It is more complex and confused among the writers and film directors, who continue issuing proclamations rather than considering the means for revolutionizing conditions of production, which are extremely complex in the movie industry. The writers, for example, have not yet dreamed of demanding from the publishers the abrogation of draconian contracts, preferential rights, or the traditional reviewing of manuscripts at a reduced rate.

Thus the revolution has made unequal advances among the intelligentsia and the working class. It has been vehement in its egalitarian and libertarian demands which condemn *all undelegated, irrevocable* authority, and in its profound communist desire to overcome the division between manual and intellectual labor and to create a common front for the exploitation of life's riches. Whether the movement has a future or not, it remains true, nonetheless, that for the first time in an advanced western society, true communism surging forth, cleansed of all Stalinism, Marxist-Leninism and bolshevism, has become *a concrete utopia lived by thousands of young students and also by the astounded older generation in the most combative centers of the faceless revolution.*

THE DEMANDS

The breaking of the dike provoked general salary demands, demands which have for years occupied the most important place on the list of workers' wants, even today outstripping in importance any demands for the reorganization of work, including the co-management attempts timidly and paternally proposed here and there. Although the economic upswing had already begun, the demand for wage increases exploded violently in May, 1968. Wages had been compromised by deflationist policies and reduced even more by the attempt to change the social security system. Wage demands have grown constantly, being no more than a growing desire for well-being, security, and individual development of the private life in a bourgeois society based on consumer leisure. To these demands must be added those of their brothers in the country who have claimed the right of the disfavored classes and regions to participate in the advances of the consumer society.

Thus, the faceless revolution has stimulated a dual consciousness on the part of the workers. The first concerns the system of labor and demands the reorganization of work. The second concerns the private individual and the amelioration of the working-class' position in bourgeois civilization. Both wish to transform the worker's existence, the first by revolutionizing industry, the second by developing his private life along the lines of the petty bourgeois model. Until 1968 the latter concern held undeniable sway over the demand for a reorganization of work; any hopes of changing labor conditions were abandoned or invested in the vague hope of a "popular government" or even in the myth of the Soviet Union, which no one was examining too closely to make sure it was truly the country of the workers. It is on this duality — a revolutionary consciousness founded on the myth of the Communist Party and the USSR, and a consciousness revolving around the demands for wage increases — that the CGT has built its power. Its simultaneous mission is to nourish the myth and to defend effectively the demands of the workers.

The CGT had opposed the 22nd of March group on those grounds. Each occupies one of the two poles in the situation: the 22nd of March group, the revolutionary, soviet, pole; the CGT, the moderate functional pole. Each one occupies one of the two poles of the worker's double consciousness, one awakening among the young, unassimilated workers, the other springing from the limited hope of profiting from the power vacuum. The faceless revolution does not know how to combine the two. A satisfaction of salary demands seemed derisive on the morning of May 27th; something else, something more is needed. However, the demands for a role in industrial management seem impossible, dangerous and utopian. There is also a contradiction between the student intelligentsia who challenge the civilization of well-being, but who have lived in a part of it, and the mass of wage-earners who would like to get into that civilization before superseding it.

The CGT has disassociated itself from any recent event in order to match its realistic salary demands against the heady and provocative self-management aspirations of the 22nd of March group. (Remember that self-management is still condemned by all national Communist parties except that of Yugoslavia.) The 22nd of March group, on the other hand, wants to keep the pot boiling. It knows that revolutionary dynamism will persist only so long as wage demands and demands for self-management combine to form a global challenge, however confused and anarchistic, which contests *all* authority in a real struggle to modify the power relations in industry and society. Any halt to this dynamism would be to the sole advantage of moderate salary demands. Any reduction of the dynamic pace would open the way to reformist solutions. The astonishing thing is that everything had to wait until the 26th of May for the provisional reformer, Edgar Faure, to appear, not from within the movement, but from the political deep-freeze where both the Fourth and the Fifth Republics had locked him.

In any event, the students' need to stimulate the demands of the workers, by encouraging them, by reminding them of their Marxist vocation, shows that the workers also want to integrate themselves into a society of well-being. But the surge of revolutionary aspirations has also revealed that if the workers have accustomed themselves to industrial labor, and even more generally if all wage earners have become used to working in subordinate and fragmented positions, *these habits express the resignation of the vanquished and are not "natural" adaptations; they have repressed to a great depth all distress and anger, and they have neutralized but not eliminated the great problem of personal relations between men.*

THE WHIRLWIND

Later, the thousands of elements mixed in the May, 1968 revolution will be decanted. It has been a faceless revolution and a revolution with a thousand faces, with liberal bursts and libertarian eruptions, with a myriad of regional, provincial, peasant, worker, employee, student, and intellectual revolts against the authorities and against authority, with autonomous, decentralizing, revolutionary attempts at self-determination all indicative of a great demand for a better individual life and for a modification of the power relations of industry. What torrential, fabulous richness in one month, what an impetus for liberty-equality-fraternity, this modern rebirth of the French Revolution mixed with blood of the Russian and Spanish soviets, of surrealism, of Castroism, and of the spontaneous cultural revolution. It will take years and years to understand what has happened, but already at the heat of the moment, astonishing broad lines are materializing.

First, it is a whirlwind where a struggle along generational lines has raged (young against old, youth against the adult society), but which has unleashed class struggle at the same time — a revolt of the downtrodden, the workers. In fact, the struggle between youth and age set into motion the struggle between workers and authority (management and state) not only because it created mimetic, isomorphic situations (the occupation of the Sorbonne — the occupation of factories; the struggle against the university authorities — the struggle against management and the manager-state), but also because the youths were moved and marked by the revolutionary labor ideology with which the revolutionary minorities had inoculated it. *In short, the conflict between generational classes unleashed a struggle of social classes which has remained all the while a generational class struggle.* Equally important has been the new conflict between the rebellious and the assimilated. It is there that the problems of bourgeois society are fermenting. The rebels are going to refuse to pay for bourgeois well-being at the price of self-mutilation or assimilation into the demi-nirvana of the consumer society.

Here the traditional and avant-garde character of this revolution has been handicapped because it was the student avant-garde, already suffering from the "evils" of the affluent society, that revolted and incited the workers' rebellion by speaking the language of the Marxist, proletarian revolution. The students garbed themselves in labor traditions at the beginning to cover their nudity, and then utilized Trotskyism-Leninism as a dialectic for their permanent revolution. The liaison between workers and students has done nothing but re-establish the alliance of the days of 1830 and 1848; it has organized and powered the relationship between western revolutionary aspirations during the first half of the 20th century and those of the second half of the 20th century. All the extreme energy of May, 1968 is contained in this simultaneously real, effective, and mythological student-worker relationship.

Moreover, the double character, old and new, of May, 1968 has found its source in the archaic revolt that is ultimately unleashed by every profound breach in the dike which channels human energies in order to transform them into work and obedience. On these lines the rebels have been able to express themselves in unity against the capitalist society and against the techno-bureaucratic society; they voice the demand not only for well-being, but for something else beyond. Thus in May, 1968, those who are oppressed by the conditions in the new society have passed the word to those who were oppressed by the old, the old and the new still being profoundly mixed one with the other. Now, both speak the common, equivocal language of oppression. A premature revolution has joined a belated revolution. An equivocal attitude — productive or tragic, both fecund and tragic at the same time — links and strains at the part of the workers' consciousness which wants to destroy the world.

From this conjunction of turbulent events, can we try to disentangle the most modern characteristics?

1. It is the first time in an economically developed, politically liberal western society that a specifically student and youthful movement has sparked an even vaster movement throughout the entire society. That permits us to suggest the roles which the following may play in the future:
   a. youth as a force for disruption, rebellion, and renovation in modern society — which permits the inclusion of the hippie or beatnik phenomenon in the U.S.A.;
   b. the university, soon to contain half of the juvenile population, which will find itself at the heart of society's problems, as Alain Touraine has indicated;
   c. the intelligentsia, which reacts more and more violently against the techno-bureaucratic organization to which it finds itself partly chained and against the bourgeois life itself.

   The drive for future mutations thus seems to be the alliance between the intelligentsia and youth clustered around many universities.
2. This is the first act in the socio-political drama of the modern bourgeois or industrial society. The old traditional values according to which the bourgeois societies were formed until now have been progressively eroded by economic dynamism and by the infiltration of these values to the private individual; everything outside the private individual is nihilism. Effectively, nationalism has become extraordinarily insensitive. The gathering of thousands of demonstrators with black flags and red flags under the *Arc de Triomphe* — virtually on top of the grave of the unknown soldier — singing the *Internationale* without arousing the enormous horror usually provoked by sacrilege or violation of taboo, illustrates very clearly how dead nationalism has become in an atomized society with no fear of war. In the same respect the decadence of paternal values, the decline of family authority, and

the retreat of religious values toward the soul and conscience has created not only an extraordinarily soft and protoplasmic society, virtually unprotected against a sudden and severe blow, but also a society with a very weak sense of community, an almost inorganic quasi-mechanic aggregate which collapses at the first tremor. Despite the national proclamations from the summit, despite the fact that General de Gaulle has been playing the role of France on the world stage *con brio,* we now know that France has become a sort of large impersonal business corporation, a computerized accumulation of wheels and gears, a *Gesellschaft* bound together with very little *Gemeinschaft.*

In short, in such a society, subversive, revolutionary messianism on the part of the most militant students and intellectuals, playing the juvenile game of revolution in a terribly prosaic world, was able to provoke a sociological and political cataclysm. It was a moral not an economic crisis of the bourgeoisie, possible in the absence of any messianic doctrine justifying the dominant class.

All this foolishness will occur precisely because of the refusal to consider honestly, in its resistance and its slowness, the duration of historical time. It is from this perspective, however, that May, 1968 will shine as another 1789. At bottom, it is the same paradox as 1789. At a time when she was not at all the leader of socio-economic development, it has been France, not the United States or Germany, that has set the model not only for revolution, but also for the most advanced revolution — at least if one considers its level in May, 1968. This extreme advance may provoke an extreme reaction according to the dialectic so common in the history of France. In fact, the new discontents are weaker in France than elsewhere, and only partly disentangled from former discontents; the new have again inflamed the old discontents, which have leaped higher than ever before. The wild explosion of May has thus reintroduced traditional forms of challenge and protest into the modern world of prosperous nations. Modifying both the world and themselves, these forces will hasten the mutations of the 20th and 21st centuries and thus prepare a world beyond bourgeois civilization — if humanity ever reaches that point in a civilized form.

APPENDIX A

Bibliography

The compilation of a large-scale bibliography of European politics is a major, multi-national task outside the scope of this volume. For each country, there are already good working bibliographies in print, and academic journals provide a means of updating older lists. These bibliographies include:

BRITAIN: The best full-length bibliography of books can be found in R. M. Punnett, *British Government and Politics* (New York: Norton, 1968), pp. 423–65. This can be complemented by two bibliographies of journal articles contained in Richard Rose, editor, *Studies in British Politics* (New York: St. Martins, revised 1969 edition), pp. 410–28, and Richard Rose, editor, *Policy-Making in Britain* (New York: Free Press, 1969), pp. 369–75. These may be supplemented by references to articles and reviews in the following journals: *Political Studies, Parliamentary Affairs, Political Quarterly, Public Administration,* the *British Journal of Sociology,* and *Sociology.*

FRANCE: A convenient and lengthy bibliography of books in English and French can be found in the footnotes and appendix of Henry W. Ehrmann, *Politics in France* (Boston: Little, Brown, 1968). This can be supplemented by an older exhaustive bibliography by Alfred Grosser, published in Otto Stammer, editor, *Politische Forschung,* Vol. 17 (Cologne and Opladen, 1960). These may be brought up to date by reference to the *Revue française de science politique, Revue française de sociologie, Revue de droit public, Revue economique, and Cahiers internationaux de sociologie.*

GERMANY: A detailed bibliography of books in German and English is contained in Lewis J. Edinger, *Politics in Germany* (Boston: Little, Brown, 1968), especially at pp. 343–54. An older exhaustive bibliography by Otto Heinrich von der Gablentz can be found in Otto Stammer, *op. cit.* This may be supplemented by referring to such journals as

Politische Vierteljarhreschrift, Politische Studien, Zeitschrift für Politik, Der Monat, and the *Kolner Zeitschrift für Soziologie und Sozialpsychologie.*

ITALY: No bibliography exists for Italy as comprehensive as those referred to above. A short, current listing can be found in Dante Germino and Stefano Passigli, *The Government and Politics of Contemporary Italy* (New York: Harper, 1968), pp. 203–207, and an older list in Norberto Bobbio's chapter in the volume edited by Otto Stammer, *op. cit.* These listings may be supplemented by reference to *Rassegna Italiana de Sociologia, Nord e Sud, Tempi Moderni,* and *Occidente.*

EUROPE: Four European journals concentrate upon publishing articles drawn from multi-national contributors: the *International Social Science Journal,* the *European Journal of Sociology, Social Science Information,* and *Government and Opposition.* In addition, two American journals, *Comparative Political Studies* and *Comparative Politics,* make special efforts to include articles relevant to the focus of this reader.

APPENDIX B

Basic Statistics

The study of politics is both deductive and inductive. Generalizations formulated by political theorists must be tested against empirical evidence. Reciprocally, a fund of empirical data can provide the inspiration for generalizations, or at least avoid the formulation of general theories of politics derived only from knowledge of one country.

The following tables, summarizing a range of social, economic, and political data, are presented as a convenience to readers to ensure that they do not lack basic facts about the societies covered in this book. For example, the population of each of the four major European societies is about equal to the collective population of the smaller European democracies. In turn, the population of the United States is about equal in size to that of Britain, France, Germany, and Italy combined. The inclusion of data from smaller European democracies, non-democratic Mediterranean countries, and the major extra-European democracies of Japan, Canada, and the United States places the four European powers in perspective.

Readers interested in exploring statistical comparisons and relationships further will find two volumes of special relevance to politics: Bruce Russett et al., *World Handbook of Political and Social Indicators* (New Haven: Yale University Press, 1964); and A. S. Banks and Robert Textor, *The Cross-Polity Survey* (Cambridge, Mass.: MIT Press, 1963). The UNESCO *Statistical Yearbook* (Paris: annually) is a useful source of social data. Factual information of a non-numerical as well as numerical kind can be conveniently found in such reference volumes as *Whitakers Almanack* (London: Whitaker, annually), and the *Statesman's Yearbook* (London: Macmillan, annually).

582 APPENDIX B

FIGURE B.1. DECLINE OF THE AGRICULTURAL POPULATION.
STAGNATION OF THE INDUSTRIAL WORKING CLASS.
DEVELOPMENT OF THE WHITE-COLLAR STRATA.

Civilian employment by sector (percentages plotted on logarithmic scale)

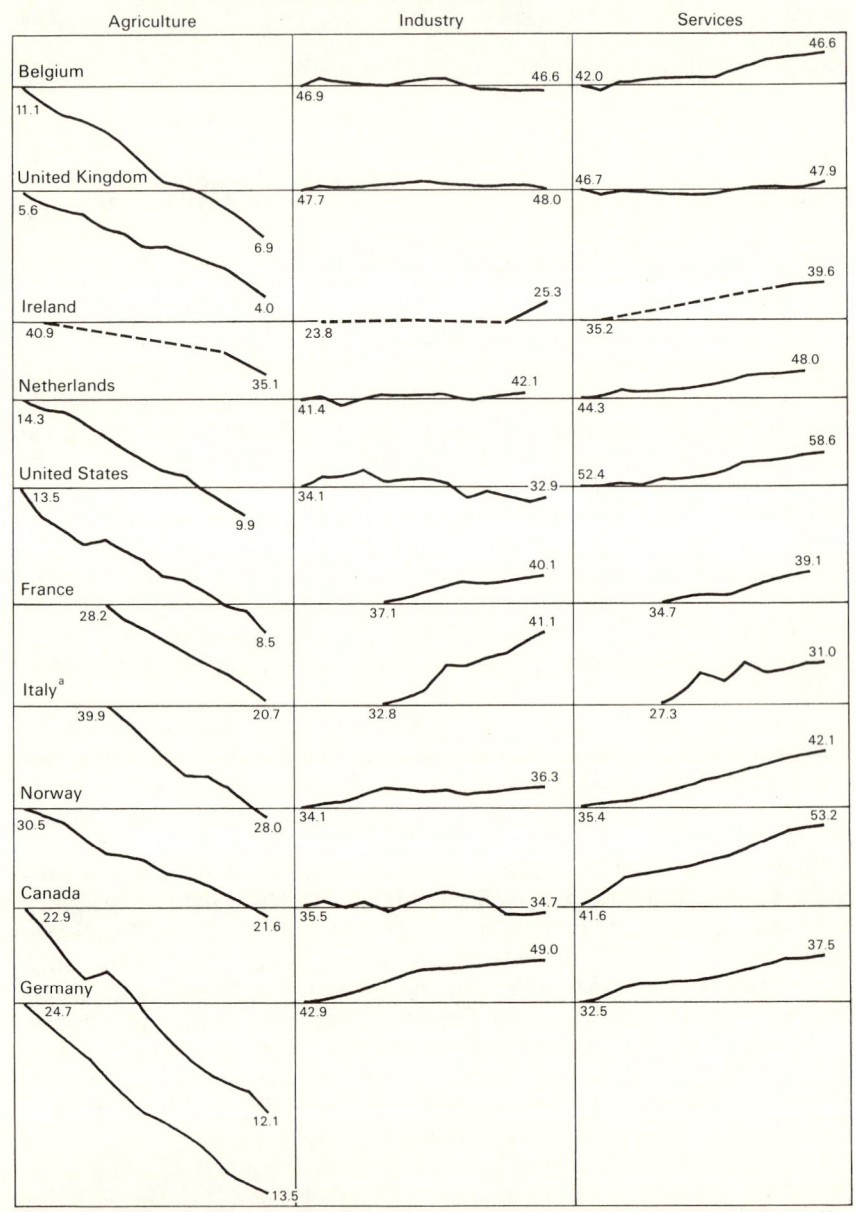

Source: OECD, Manpower Statistics, 1950–1962, Paris, 1963, p. 17.

[a] Figures for Italy are obtained on the basis of sample surveys. The sampling errors are responsible for the lack of regularity of the curve.

BASIC STATISTICS 583

FIGURE B.2. DEMOGRAPHIC STAGNATION OF THREE "OLD" EUROPEAN COUNTRIES; AND DEVELOPMENT OF THREE "NEW" AMERICAN COUNTRIES

From the conquest of the continent by Napoleon to the conquest of the moon by Americans.

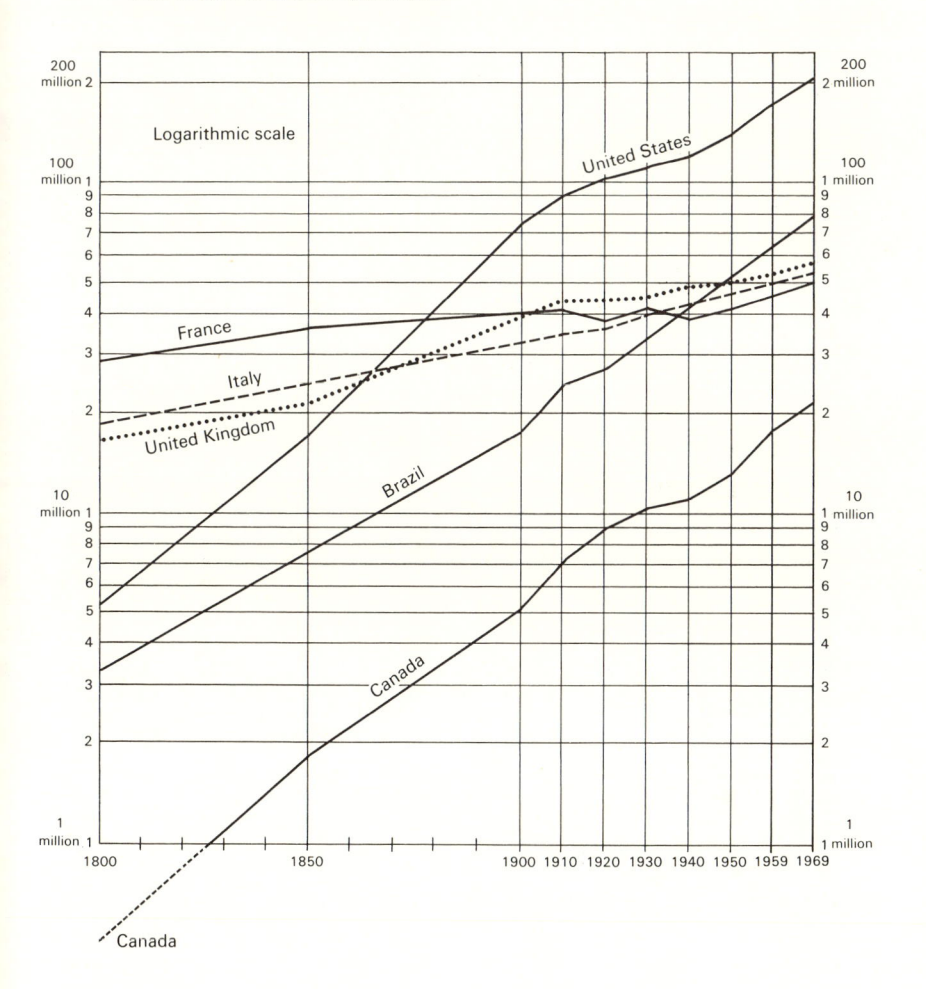

TABLE B.1. MAJOR EUROPEAN NATIONS IN COMPARATIVE PERSPECTIVE

	Population (in thousands)	Inhabitants per sq. km.	Area (1000 sq. km.)	Agricultural area (1000 sq. km.)	Total civilian employment (in thousands)	Of which Percentage agriculture, forestry, fishing	Percentage industry	Percentage other
France	49,866	90	551.2	335.5	19,588	16.6	40.6	42.8
Germany (F.R.)	59,879	241	248.5	140.0	25,802	10.6	48.0	41.4
Italy	52,334	174	301.2	203.8	18,920	24.1	41.1	34.8
United Kingdom	55,202	226	244.0	195.9	24,996	3.1	47.2	49.7
Belgium	9,581	314	30.5	16.3	3,616	5.8	45.5	48.7
Netherlands	12,597	375	33.6	22.4	4,407	8.3	41.9	41.5
Denmark	4,839	113	43.0	30.2	2,274	16.6	41.9	41.5
Norway	3,785	12	323.9	10.0	1,505	18.5	35.8	45.7
Sweden	7,869	17	449.8	36.8	3,734	10.1	41.1	48.8
Ireland	2,899	41	70.3	47.8	1,058	31.6	27.7	40.7
Austria	7,323	87	83.8	39.3	3,284	20.1[a]	40.3[a]	39.6[a]
Switzerland	7,071	147	41.3	21.8	2,740	8.8	51.8	39.4
Spain	32,140	64	504.7	407.2	11,837[a]	34.8	35.0	30.2
Portugal	9,415	103	91.5	49.4[a]	3,072	33.5	35.5	31.0
Greece	8,716	66	131.9	90.9	3,610	50.1	21.2	28.7
Turkey	32,978	42	780.6	543.8	13,194[a]	72.6[a]	11.1[a]	16.3[a]
Japan	99,970	270	369.7	70.0	49,940	20.6	34.3	45.1
Canada	20,441	2	9,976.2	643.6	7,379	9.0	32.9	58.1
United States	199,118	21	9,363.4	4,402.0	74,372	5.2	33.7[a]	61.1[a]

Source: OECD, The Statistics and National Accounts Branch, and The OECD Observer, February 1969.
Most of the figures are for 1967; the few exceptions refer to 1966.
[a]OECD Secretariat Estimate.

TABLE B.2. SOCIAL AND ECONOMIC INDICATORS

	Calories per person per day	Educational expenditure (percentage of GNP)	Cars per 1000 people	Televisions per 1000 people	Telephones per 1000 people	Electricity (KWH per person per year)
France	3,250	4.20	234	166	132	2,120
Germany	2,867	3.23	184	231	160	2,760
Italy	2,905	5.19	136	144	132	1,580
United Kingdom	3,250	5.04	180	254	206	3,178
Belgium	3,090	5.57	152	185	174	2,215
Netherlands	—	6.30	136	200	203	1,960
Denmark	3,370	5.76	169	70	287	1,850
Norway	—	5.31	150	174	260	11,520
Sweden	3,005	6.06	240	282	498	5,550
Ireland	3,460	4.16	104	129	80	1,166
Austria	2,950	3.63	120	117	149	2,610
Switzerland	3,154	3.83	179	143	417	3,420
Spain	3,121	2.20	41	86	99	976
Portugal	2,580	1.44	21	29	62	530
Greece	2,950	1.89	21	—	65	590
Turkey	3,060	3.84	3	—	8	187
Japan	2,206	4.64	27	234	130	1,930
Canada	3,130	6.32	274	284	394	7,104
United States	3,180	5.27	396	376	502	5,836

Source: The OECD Observer No. 38, February, 1969. The figures are for 1967 or 1966, with the exception of public educational expenditure, for which the figures refer to 1965 or 1964.

TABLE B.3. DISTRIBUTION OF ECONOMIC POWER

	Gross national product at the market prices		Structure of gross domestic product at current prices (percentage)			Private consumption expenses		Current government expenditure (% of GNP)
	At current prices (in millions of US $)	Per capita at current prices (in US $)	Agriculture	Mining, manufacturing, construction, etc.	Other activities	Percentage of GNP at current prices	Per capita at current prices (in US $)	
France	109,280	2,190	7.4	47.3	45.3	63.7	1,400	35.5
Germany (F.R.)	121,400	2,030	4.1	49.7	46.2	58.2	1,180	33.6
Italy	67,090	1,280	12.4	40.5	47.1	63.5	810	31.9
United Kingdom	109,250	1,980	3.3	45.7	51.0	63.8	1,260	32.9
Belgium	19,660	2,050	5.5	40.9	53.6	64.3	1,320	30.9
Netherlands	22,830	1,810	7.2	41.2	51.6	57.2	1,040	35.4
Denmark	11,130	2,320	10.2	40.0	49.8	63.0	1,460	30.6
Norway	8,320	2,200	7.5	38.2	54.3	54.4	1,200	33.9
Sweden	23,920	3,040	5.9	45.2	48.9	54.8	1,670	35.8
Ireland	3,120	1,080	19.5	33.1	47.4	68.8	740	27.7
Austria	10,680	1,460	8.6	51.6	39.8	59.7	870	30.6
Switzerland	15,930	2,620	—	—	—	58.9	1,550	22.7
Spain	26,620	830	16.4	34.7	48.9	70.7	590	20.8
Portugal	4,600	490	19.7	43.7	36.6	69.6	340	—
Greece	7,110	820	23.5	26.1	50.4	68.3	560	24.9
Turkey	10,600	320	35.8	25.6	38.6	—	—	—
Japan	114,990	1,150	11.6	36.7	51.7	52.5	600	14.8
Canada	53,500	2,670	5.9	38.5	55.6	60.5	1,610	27.4
United States	803,910	4,040	3.0	36.6	60.4	61.5	2,480	28.3

Source: OECD, The Statistics and National Accounts Branch. See also: OECD, Manpower Statistics, Main Economic Indicators, and Statistical Bulletins of Foreign Trade. Most of the figures are for 1967; some are for 1966.

TABLE B.4. RELATIVE ECONOMIC AUTONOMY OF THE EUROPEAN "BIG FOUR" AND RELATIVE ECONOMIC INTERDEPENDENCE OF THE "SMALL" EUROPEAN COUNTRIES

	Total (C.I.F.) (in millions of US $)	From other OECD countries (in millions of US $)	From rest of world (in millions of US $)	Total imports as percentage of GNP at current prices
France	12,377	8,412	3,964	11.3
Germany (F.R.)	17,351	12,572	4,757	14.3
Italy	9,697	6,007	3,665	14.5
United Kingdom	17,715	10,394	7,316	16.2
Belgium	7,176	5,699	1,470	35.2
Netherlands	8,337	6,645	1,692	36.5
Denmark	3,134	2,561	572	26.9
Norway	2,746	2,373	373	33.0
Sweden	4,703	3,784	919	19.7
Ireland	1,078	872	185	34.6
Austria	2,309	1,898	411	21.6
Switzerland	4,099	3,595	504	25.7
Spain	3,470	2,520	950	13.0
Portugal	1,059	744	315	23.0
Greece	1,186	892	294	16.7
Turkey	691	522	169	6.5
Japan	11,663	5,031	6,631	10.1
Canada	10,250	9,159	1,091	17.1
United States	26,816	17,982	8,825	3.3

Source: OECD, The Statistics and National Accounts Branch. See also: OECD, Manpower Statistics, Main Economic Indicators, and Statistical Bulletins of Foreign Trade. Most of the figures are for 1967; some are for 1966.

TABLE B.5. ONE HUNDRED AND THIRTY-THREE NATIONS AND ONLY TWENTY TRADITIONAL PARLIAMENTARY DEMOCRACIES (IN ITALICS)

Total Population 1961	Less than $100	$100–200	$200–500	More than $500	Total
More than 20 million inhabitants	China[a,b] India[a] Pakistan Nigeria Thailand Ethiopia Burma 43.9%	Indonesia Poland[a,b] Egypt[a] South Korea Iran 6.5%	Japan[a] Brazil[a] Mexico[a] Spain[a] Philippines[a] Turkey[a] Argentina[a] 10.2%	*U.S.S.R.*[a,b] *United States*[a] *West Germany*[a] *Italy*[a] *France*[a] 19.8%	25 countries 80.4%
Between 5 and 20 million inhabitants	North Vietnam[b] South Vietnam Congo (Leopoldville) Afghanistan Sudan Tanganyika Nepal North Korea[b] Kenya Mozambique Uganda Madagascar Yemen Cambodia 4.5%	Morocco Algeria[a] Taiwan Peru[a] Ceylon[a] Rhodesia & Nyasaland Iraq Ghana Saudi Arabia 2.8%	Rumania[a,b] Yugoslavia[a,b] South Africa Columbia[a] Hungary[a,b] Portugal[a] Greece[a] Bulgaria[a,b] Chile[a] Malaya Cuba[a,b] 4.1%	*Canada*[a] East Germany[a,b] Czechoslovakia[a,b] *Netherlands*[a] *Australia*[a] *Belgium*[a] *Sweden*[a] Venezuela[a] *Austria*[a] *Switzerland*[a] 3.5%	44 countries 14.9%
Between 2 and 5 million inhabitants	Angola Cameroun Upper Volta Mali Bolivia[a] Ivory Coast Senegal Guinea Rwanda Chad El Salvador[a] Niger Sierra Leone Burundi Dahomey Somalia 1.6%	Syria Ecuador[a] Tunisia Haiti Guatemala[a] 0.7%	Hong Kong Dominican Republic[a] Uruguay[a] 0.3%	*Denmark*[a] *Finland*[a] *Norway*[a] *Ireland*[a] *New Zealand*[a] Puerto Rico *Israel*[a] 0.8%	31 countries 3.4%
Less than 2 million inhabitants	Laos Togo Central African Republic Libya Mongolia[b] Congo (Brazzaville) Mauritania Gabon 0.4%	Honduras[a] Paraguay[a] Jordan Albania[b] Liberia Nicaragua[a] Aden Sarawak South West Africa Surinam Netherlands-Antilles 0.4%	Lebanon[a] Singapore Jamaica[a] Costa Rica[a] Panama[a] Trinidad and Tobago[a] Mauritius British Guinea Cyprus[a] Malta & Gozo Barbados 0.4%	Kuwait *Luxembourg*[a] *Iceland*[a] 0.1%	33 countries 1.3%
Total	45 countries 50.4%	30 countries 10.4%	32 countries 15.0%	26 countries 24.2%	133 countries 100.0%

[a]Western or Westernized countries (cf. Banks and Textor, A Cross-Polity Survey).
[b]Communist countries.

Contributors

EDWARD C. BANFIELD. Professor of Government, Harvard University.
REINHARD BENDIX. Professor of Sociology and Research Sociologist, University of California, Berkeley.
SAMUEL BRITTAN. Economics Editor, *The Financial Times,* London.
A. H. BROWN. Lecturer in Politics, University of Glasgow, Scotland.
PHILIP E. CONVERSE. Professor of Political Science and Sociology, and Program Director, Survey Research Center, University of Michigan.
MICHEL CROZIER. *Maître de Recherche, Centre National de la Recherche Scientifique,* Paris.
HANS DAALDER. Professor of Political Science, University of Leiden, the Netherlands.
RALF DAHRENDORF. Member of Parliament and Parliamentary Secretary of State, Federal West German Republic. Formerly Professor of Sociology, University of Constance, Germany.
KARL W. DEUTSCH. Professor of Government, Harvard University.
MATTEI DOGAN. *Directeur de Recherche, Centre National de la Recherche Scientifique,* Paris, and recurring visiting Professor, Institute of the Social Sciences, Trento, Italy.
GEORGES DUPEUX. Professor of History, University of Bordeaux, France.
MAURICE DUVERGER. Professor of Political Sociology, University of Paris.
HARRY ECKSTEIN. IBM Professor of Foreign and International Studies, and Director, Workshop in Comparative Politics of the Center of International Studies, Princeton University.
LEWIS J. EDINGER. Professor of Government, and Associate Director of The Bureau of Applied Social Research, Columbia University.
HENRY W. EHRMANN. Joel Parker Professor of Law and Political Science, Dartmouth College.
ROBERT C. FRIED. Associate Professor of Political Science, University of California, Los Angeles.
GIORGIO GALLI. Editor, *Il Mulino,* Bologna, Italy.
BERNARD GOURNAY. Director, graduate program, *Fondation Nationale des Sciences Politiques,* Paris.
ALFRED GROSSER. Director, graduate program, *Fondation Nationale des Sciences Politiques,* and Professor, *Institut d'Études Politiques,* Paris.
STANLEY HOFFMANN. Professor of Government, Harvard University.
RONALD INGLEHART. Assistant Professor of Political Science, University of Michigan.

CONTRIBUTORS

OTTO KIRCHHEIMER. Until his death in 1965, Professor of Government, Columbia University.
ROBERT E. LANE. Professor of Political Science, Yale University.
JOSEPH LA PALOMBARA. Arnold Wolfers Professor of Political Science, Yale University.
GEORGES LAVAU. Director of Research and Study, *Fondation Nationale des Sciences Politiques,* and Professor of Law, University of Paris.
GERHARD LEHMBRUCH. *Institut für Politische Wissenschaft,* University of Heidelberg, Germany.
KLAUS LIEPELT. Director, *Institut für Angewandte Sozialwissenschaft,* Bad Godesberg, Germany.
S. M. LIPSET. Professor of Government and Social Relations, Harvard University.
GERHARD LOEWENBERG. Professor of Political Science, University of Iowa.
JOSEPH LOPREATO. Professor of Sociology, University of Texas, Austin.
VAL R. LORWIN. Professor of History, University of Oregon.
ROBERT T. MC KENZIE. Professor of Sociology with special reference to Politics, London School of Economics and Political Science.
ROY MACRIDIS. Lawrence A. Wien Professor of International Cooperation, Brandeis University.
PETER MERKL. Professor of Political Science, University of California, Santa Barbara.
EDGAR MORIN. *Maître de Recherche, Central National de la Recherche Scientifique,* Paris, and Deputy Director, *Centre d'Études des Communications de Masse.*
ERIC A. NORDLINGER. Associate Professor of Politics, Brandeis University.
FRANK A. PINNER. Professor of Political Science, Michigan State University.
ALESSANDRO PIZZORNO. Professor of Sociology, University of Urbino, and Research Director, *Istituto Lombardo per gli Studi Economici e Sociali,* Milan, Italy.
ALFONSO PRANDI. Editor, *Il Mulino,* Bologna, Italy.
STEIN ROKKAN. Professor of Sociology, University of Bergen, Norway, and recurring visiting Professor of Political Science, Yale University.
RICHARD ROSE. Professor of Politics, University of Strathclyde, Glasgow, Scotland.
GIOVANNI SARTORI. Professor of Political Science, University of Florence, Italy.
ERWIN K. SCHEUCH. Professor of Sociology, University of Cologne, Germany, and Director, *Zentralarchiv für Empirische Sozialforschung* and *Institut für Vergleichende Sozialforschung,* Cologne.
DONALD D. SEARING. Assistant Professor of Political Science, University of North Carolina, Chapel Hill.
DEREK W. URWIN. Lecturer in Politics, University of Strathclyde, Glasgow, Scotland.
SIDNEY VERBA. Professor of Political Science, University of Chicago, and Senior Study Director, National Opinion Research Center, Chicago.
KENNETH N. WALTZ. Adlai E. Stevenson Professor of International Politics, Brandeis University.
RUDOLF WILDENMANN. Professor of Political Science, University of Mannheim, Germany, and State University of New York, Stony Brook.

74309

DATE DUE	
NOV 10 2003	

GAYLORD — PRINTED IN U.S.A.

St. Scholastica Library
Duluth, Minnesota 55811
WITHDRAWN